RASHBAM'S COMMENTARY ON EXODUS
An Annotated Translation

Program in Judaic Studies
Brown University
BROWN JUDAIC STUDIES

Edited by
Shaye J. D. Cohen and Calvin Goldscheider

Number 310

RASHBAM'S COMMENTARY ON EXODUS
An Annotated Translation

edited and translated by
Martin I. Lockshin

RASHBAM'S COMMENTARY ON EXODUS
An Annotated Translation

edited and translated by
Martin I. Lockshin

illustrations by
Channa Lockshin

Scholars Press
Atlanta, Georgia

RASHBAM'S COMMENTARY ON EXODUS
An Annotated Translation

edited and translated by
Martin I. Lockshin

Copyright © 1997 by Brown University

All rights reserved. No part of this work may be reproduced or transmitted in any form or by any means, electronic or mechanical, including photocopying and recording, or by means of any information storage or retrieval system, except as may be expressly permitted by the 1976 Copyright Act or in writing from Brown Judaic Studies, Brown University, Box 1826, Providence, RI 02912.

Library of Congress Cataloging-in-Publication Data
Samuel ben Meir, 11th/12th cent.
   [Perush ha-Torah. Shemot. English.]
   Rashbam's commentary on Exodus : an annotated translation / edited and translated by Martin I. Lockshin ; illustrations by Channa Lockshin.
   p. cm. — (Brown Judaic studies ; no. 310)
   Includes bibliographical references.
   ISBN 0-7885-0225-5 (cloth : alk. paper)—ISBN 1-930675-11-9 (paper : alk. paper)
   1. Bible. O.T. Exodus—Commentaries. I. Lockshin, Martin I. II. Title. III. Series.

BS1245.3.S26L6313 1997
222'.1207—dc21   96-52640

Printed in the United States of America
on acid-free paper

To Ruth

See Proverbs 19:14

TABLE OF CONTENTS

Table of Illustrations viii

Acknowledgements ix

Introduction 1

Table of Abbreviations 5

Rashbam's Commentary and Notes 9

Bibliography 439

TABLE OF ILLUSTRATIONS

Illustration A
  The Tabernacle in Enclosure 310

Illustration B
  The Cherubim 313

Illustration C
  The Table 316

Illustration D
  The Shape of the Planks 328

Illustration E
  The Planks (flat view) 334

Illustration F
  The Bars 336

Illustration G
  The Central Bar 339

Illustration H
  The Ephod 356

ACKNOWLEDGEMENTS

I have been a student of Jewish biblical exegesis, in general, and the works of Rabbi Samuel ben Meir, in particular, for many years. It would be impossible for me to acknowledge my debt to all the many teachers, colleagues and students who have inspired me, helped me or offered constructive criticism of my work. Still I will name a few whose help has been indispensable.

Among my many wonderful teachers over the years I would like to mention my graduate advisor, Professor Marvin Fox, who played a crucial role in my education, both while I was at graduate school and in more recent years. Professor Fox's recent death has saddened many in the world of Jewish scholarship. May his memory be a blessing.

For the last eighteen years, York University has been a most hospitable home to me. My position there has allowed me the opportunity to live a scholarly life, to read new books and discuss new ideas and get paid for it. York has had a direct role in the production of this book, as much of the research for the book was done during my recent sabbatical, granted by York University. (The sabbatical was spent at the Bible department of the Hebrew University of Jerusalem, where many colleagues shared with me their friendship and their knowledge.) I have also been the grateful beneficiary of a number of grants from York's Faculty of Arts that allowed me to finish the work on this book.

My colleagues in York's Division of Humanities and in its Department of Languages, Literatures and Linguistics have made my job an enjoyable one; it is easy and pleasant to work with them. I am particularly indebted to my colleagues at York's Centre for Jewish Studies for the way that they have enriched my life and have supported me in my work. The current director of the Centre, Professor Michael Brown, has always been a true friend. The founding director of the Centre, Professor Sydney Eisen, has been a source of sage counsel to my family and myself for many years now. I am pleased to have the opportunity to acknowledge my debt to them publicly.

Students, particularly those who have studied biblical exegesis with me at York University and in the "Brandes Study Group," have listened to my ideas and theories with respect, and have criticized them intelligently and politely. They have taught me much.

Two students in particular must be mentioned for their direct and invaluable help in producing this book. Janine Muller and Eric Grossman, at different stages in the project, read the entire manuscript and offered valuable suggestions for its improvement. They also checked numerous references, proofread, and did other scholarly tasks that can be assigned to bright, capable and enthusiastic young people like them. I thank both of them for all their help. I am also most grateful to Rabbi Eliot Feldman and the staff of LTB Solutions, Inc., for their expert help in preparing this manuscript for publication.

But as much as this book and I have benefitted from my teachers, my colleagues and my students, I feel that my greatest debt of gratitude is to my family. My mother, Sylvia Lockshin and my mother-in-law, Rita Mendelsohn, have supported me in many ways and have tolerated and even encouraged me to pursue the life of a *luftmensch*. The love shown to me and the wise advice proffered to me by both of them and by my mother-in-law's husband, Dr. Bernard Weisberger, an honorary member of the Lockshin family, are truly appreciated.

One of my greatest pleasures in my life is studying Torah with my children, Channa, Shoshanna, Noam and Reva. Each, on his or her own level, takes an interest in my work and in the works of Rashbam.

Channa undertook a difficult task for this book. She produced all the illustrations for the book, after studying all the relevant texts with me. She gave the work her special brand of painstaking attention and I think readers will agree with me that she produced excellent results. Thank you, Channa!

Aside from myself the person most responsible for this book is my wife, Ruth Lockshin. Ruth takes a keen interest in everything that I do, at work and in the non-academic world. She listens well and advises intelligently and, usually, persuasively. She is an excellent critic of my overly academic style of writing. Many of the more readable passages of this book are a result of her painstaking editorial work. She read (and studied!) every word of this manuscript and offered numerous suggestions for improvements for every page. For this, and for so much more, I am eternally grateful.

INTRODUCTION

Not much is known about the life of Rabbi Samuel ben Meir (Rashbam). Even the dates of his birth and death, generally cited as 1085-1174, are conjectural, and it is difficult to know precisely where in Northern France he lived at different stages of his life. Like many greats of the past, much more is known about his works than about the man himself.

Rashbam was primarily a halakhist, a student and scholar of Jewish law. The majority of his literary outpout was concerned with the Talmud and its proper interpretation and the ways in which talmudic law impacted on the lives of twelfth-century Jews. He is much more remembered, and revered, in the religious Jewish world for his contributions to the study of Talmud than for his contributions to the study of the Bible.

However, in modern times there has been increased interest in the type of biblical exegesis that was produced by Rashbam, and by contemporaneous Jewish commentators. Rashbam and his colleagues "discovered" *peshat* exegesis--the attempt to find the "plain" meaning of the text, the contextual meaning, the linguistically- and contextually-grounded meaning. These exegetes attempted to liberate themselves from the what was, until then, the standard rabbinic approach to the Bible, the approach of midrash, where commentators generally saw edification and "relevance" as much more important than contextual and grammatically-grounded explanations.

Rashbam, like a modern university reader of a text, searched out and found meanings in the Bible that were often prosaic and not particularly uplifting or relevant to the lives of his contemporaries. His primary purpose (unlike the purpose of most religious Jews and Christians who have written or who write today about the Bible) was *not* to make the Bible speak to his generation. Rather, his purpose was to let the Bible speak, as much as possible, with its own voice.

Interest today in the biblical works of Rashbam comes from two different sources. Scholars of the Bible in universities--who also try themselves to find the "original," plain meaning of the text, i.e. the

interpretations of biblical texts, and was able to identify numerous literary patterns in biblical texts. The notes in this book will often point out instances where twentieth-century university-based biblical scholars who did *not* consult Rashbam's commentary (which, until now, was available only to readers of medieval Hebrew) "rediscovered" interpretations that are actually over 800 years old.

The second group, scholars of Jewish intellectual history are very interested in understanding why medieval Jews decided to dedicate so much time and effort to the "plain" meaning of the text. To be sure, in medieval times there were Karaite Jews, who rejected centuries of midrashic exegesis, also rejecting rabbinic law. Karaites, not surprisingly, prided themselves on *peshat*, and delighted in pointing out the differences between *peshat* and traditional midrash. But Rashbam and his colleagues were not Karaites. They were pious, learned rabbinic scholars, who practiced and promoted the punctillious observance of Jewish law, even when such observance had, as its source, a midrashic reading of a biblical text.

It is not easy to understand what motivated Rashbam to search for *peshat*. It is somewhat easier to understand how and why, for example, Rashbam's Sephardic younger contemporary, Rabbi Abraham ibn Ezra, came to the pursuit of *peshat*. ibn Ezra was a product of the so-called "Golden Age of Spain," and came from a world where philosophy, logic and careful grammatical and linguistic analysis were valued highly. Rashbam did not. As far as we know, his only education was traditional Jewish learning. It is unlikely that he read any language other than Hebrew or Aramaic, or that he ever studied any works other than the Bible and rabbinic literature. And yet he came to value *peshat*.

In recent years, Eliezer Touitou has argued cogently that a strong motivating factor for Rashbam in his pursuit of *peshat* was the fact that he was an anti-Christian polemicist. Many of the notes in this book will show the ways in which comments of Rashbam should be interpreted as serving polemical purposes.

But not all of Rashbam's *peshat*, not even most of it, can be interpreted that way. To my mind, the strongest motivating factor for Rashbam's exegetical innovations is inextricably connected with the one incontrovertible biographical fact that we know about Rashbam, his lineage.

INTRODUCTION

Rashbam's maternal grandfather was Rashi (Rabbi Solomon ben Isaac), perhaps the most illustrious and most universally respected rabbi of post-talmudic Jewish history. Rashbam lived in his grandfather's shadow. Both in Rashbam's rabbinic writings and in his biblical commentaries it is clear that completing and improving his grandfather's *oeuvres* was a primary, if not the primary purpose.

Rashi had written a commentary on most of the Talmud but had not finished it. Rashbam tried to complete the unfinished sections, and wrote the odd "improved" version of his grandfather's commentary (e.g. the commentary on the tenth chapter of the talmudic tractate, Pesahim). A similar state of affairs obtains in the world of biblical commentaries. Rashi had proudly written in his works that he was writing a new type of biblical commentary, a commentary that would pay attention to *peshat*, and make only limited use of midrash. Much excellent recent scholarship, especially the works of the late Sarah Kamin, has attempted to explain just what Rashi meant when he used the word *peshat*. To be sure, his attempt to liberate himself from midrash was only partial. But he did flirt with what we today would call *peshat*, and he inspired the next generation to try to do it better. Rashbam rose to the challenge, first, in his youth, by arguing about *peshat* with his grandfather, and later, in his more mature years, by writing his own commenatary.

The translation section of the present volume will give the reader of English access to Rashbam's commentary. It will show what state-of-the-art *peshat* meant in the twelfth century. The notes will explain Rashbam's often terse style and they will also help the reader appreciate the ways in which Rashbam's commentary broke with the common Jewish exegetical tradition, the midrashic one. Much attention in the notes will be focused on the relationship of Rashbam's commentary to Rashi's, primarily because, to my mind, that issue was always paramount in Rashbam's mind.

The commentary to the book of Exodus is the best vehicle for demonstrating just how new and daring Rashbam's approach was. Exodus consists both of long sections of narrative and long sections of law. At times, traditional Jewish exegetes have allowed themselves more latitude when dealing with the interpretation of narrative than when dealing with the interpretation of legal texts. Rashbam, however, as the notes shall explain, offers innovative and at times radical interpretations of both.

One of the many things that Rashbam has taught us is that finding the "plain" meaning of the biblical text is not always simple and straightforward. Sometimes, as Rashbam says, there is a "deep *peshaṭ*" in the text, which one will presumably discover only if one spends much time and effort looking for it. (See e.g. his commentary to Exodus 13:9.) Furthermore, Rashbam teaches us that finding *peshaṭ* is not something that is done once and then never has to be done again. There are, according to Rashbam, *peshaṭ* interpretations of biblical texts "that are newly thought of day by day." (See commentary to Genesis 37:2.)

Rashbam attempted to identify the *peshaṭ* of the biblical text. Many of his conclusions would be accepted by scholars of today; many would not. I would like to believe that Rashbam would not be in the least troubled by the fact that "newly thought of" *peshaṭ* interpretations have displaced some of his suggestions in the world of biblical studies.

I, too, for my part, have attempted to identify the *peshaṭ* of Rashbam's work. It is often not a straightforward task. Rashbam's style is laconic and even the best printed editions of his commentary (there are no surviving manuscripts, other than tiny fragments) appear at times to be hopelessly garbled. There are times when I have vacillated between two (or more) very different ways of understanding a passage of Rashbam's. I am certain that I myself and others will come up with "newly thought of" ways of understanding Rashbam, that will displace some of things written in this volume.

Note: The text of Rashbam's commentary that underlies the translation is, except when otherwise noted, the best available printed edition, produced by David Rosin (Breslau, 1882). Translations of biblical verses into English follow the New Jewish Publication Society version, except when it is clear that Rashbam's understanding of the Bible differs from that version's.

TABLE OF ABBREVIATIONS

B.	Babylonian Talmud
BDB	*Hebrew and English Lexicon of the Old Testament*, edited by F. Brown, S. R. Driver and C.A. Briggs
Ben-Yehuda	*Thesaurus Totius Hebraitatis*, ed. by Eliezer ben Yehuda
BH	*Biblia Hebraica*
BR	*Bereshit Rabba'*
BT	Babylonian Talmud
Childs	*The Book of Exodus: A Critical, Theological Commentary*, by B.S. Childs
comm.	commentary
D. Berger	*The Jewish-Christian Debate in the High Middle Ages*, by David Berger
Ehrlich	*Mikra ki-pheshuto*, by A. Ehrlich
EJ	*Encyclopaedia Judaica*
Esh	S. Esh, "Variant Readings in Medieval Hebrew Commentaries: R. Samuel ben Meir (Rashbam)," *Textus* 5 (1966), 84-92

fn.	footnote
G.-K.	*Gesenius' Hebrew Grammar*, as edited by E. Kautzsch and revised by A.E. Cowley
Greenberg	*Understanding Exodus*, by M. Greenberg
Hizq.	*Ḥizquni*
HUCA	*Hebrew Union College Annual*
iE	Abraham ibn Ezra
Japhet-Salters	*The Commentary of Rabbi Samuel ben Meir (Rashbam) on Qoheleth*, ed. by S. Japhet and R. B. Salters
JBS	Joseph Bekhor Shor
Kasher	*Torah Shelemah*, by M. M. Kasher
LT	*Midrash Leqaḥ Ṭov*
LXX	Septuagint
Maim.	Moses Maimonides
Mish.	Mishnah
MT	Masoretic Text
Nahm.	Moses Nahmanides
NJPS	*The New Jewish Publication Society Translation of the Bible*
NJPSC	*The New Jewish Publication Society Torah Commentary*

TABLE OF ABBREVIATIONS

Noth	*Exodus: A Commentary*, by M. Noth
Onq.	Targum Onqelos
PAAJR	*Proceedings of the American Academy for Jewish Research*
PDRE	*Pirqe derabbi 'Eli'ezer*
PG	J. P. Migne, ed., *Patriologiae Cursus Completus . . . Series Graeca* (Paris, 1844-65)
PL	J. P. Migne, ed., *Patriologiae Cursus Completus . . . Series Latina* (Paris 1844-65)
Ps.-Jon.	The Targum attributed to Jonathan ben Uzziel
P.T.	Palestinian Talmud
Qara	Joseph Qara
Qimhi	David Qimhi
Rosin	Rashbam's Torah Commentary as edited by David Rosin (Breslau, 1881/2)
RSBM	David Rosin's *Rabbi Samuel ben Meir als Schrifterklärer*
RSV	Revised Standard Version
Samar.	Samaritan
SH	*Sefer ha-shorashim*
SR	*Shemot Rabba'*
Tanh.	*Midrash Tanḥuma*

Tanh. B.	*Midrash Tanḥuma ha-qadum veha-yashan*, ed. by S. Buber
VR	*Vayyiqra' Rabba'*

EXODUS I

1.1 ואלה THESE ARE THE NAMES: Since the text intends to explain that "The Israelites were fruitful and prolific . . ." (vs. 7), it had to reiterate[1] that when they came to Egypt they numbered only seventy. After the "death of that generation" (vs. 6), "they were fruitful and prolific" (vs. 7). Then "a new king arose" (vs. 8) who dealt shrewdly with them to lessen their numbers but he failed.[2]

1:6 וכל AND ALL THAT GENERATION: The "seventy souls" (mentioned in the previous verse).[3]

---

[1] The same information is first provided in Genesis 46:27.

[2] Rashbam, along with all of the classical commentators, tries to explain why the text lists the sons of Jacob at this point after the much more complete genealogical listing in Gen. 46:8-27.
    Rashi, following the midrash in Tanh. B., claims that the repetition serves the didactic purpose of teaching us that God, because of his love for the Jews, is always counting them. The *peshaṭ*-oriented commentators are not satisfied with that answer and all offer more literary reasons for the repetition. Consider Nahm.'s tongue-in-cheek comment that while Rashi is of course correct when he describes how much God loves the Jews, the midrash about that love does not explain the purpose of this verse.
    JBS, iE, Nahm. and Rashbam all see the abridged repetition of the genealogy as serving as a contrast to the description coming up (in vss. 7 and 12) of the rapidly growing Israelite nation. JBS and Nahm. both add the point that the repetition is appropriate at this point since a new book is beginning. iE sees the repetition as flowing naturally from one of the last verses in Genesis (50:23). Rashbam's unique angle is that the text should be seen as clarifying the precise order of events. The people were small but then rapid growth began "after the death of that generation." Rashbam is then telling his readers that concerns about the size of the Jewish people can be seen as the major theme of the next few chapters.

[3] In fact, the "seventy souls," as enumerated in Genesis 46, make up much more than one generation. Still Rashbam feels that the word דור applies to all the people mentioned in that list. Cf. LT who says that the phrase "all that generation" applies specifically to Joseph and his brothers, not their children.

1:7 פרו [implies success] in conception. וישרצו [implies success] in birth--that the womb did not abort. Small creatures are generally referred to [with this same root, ש-ר-צ] as [in the phrase] "שרץ על הארץ--creep on the earth" (Gen. 7:21). וירבו means that they grew. The small ones grew up; they did not die young. ויעצמו means that they did not die when they became adults. Rather they lived long[4] and became so VERY VERY strong that THE LAND WAS FILLED WITH THEM.[5]

[The phrase ותמלא הארץ is] like the phrase (Ez. 10:4), "The court was filled with (מלאה את) the radiance of the Presence of the LORD," as if מילאה had been written. Or like the phrase (Is. 6:1), "The skirts of His robe filled (מלאים את) the Temple," as if ממלאים had been written.[6]

---

[4]See a similar explanation in Rashbam's comm. ad Ex. 23:26.

[5]The large number of words of growth in this verse (six, according to most counts) served as fertile ground for midrashic explanations. Rashi and LT both quote the midrash (Mekhilta *Bo'* 12 and Tanh.) that Jewish women gave birth to sextuplets. Rashbam opposes this explanation and tries to find distinctions between the various terms for growth, thus "justifying" in a *peshaṭ*-like manner why the text had to use so many apparently synonymous terms. See similarly iE.

[6]Rashbam's comment on the root מ-ל-א is very difficult to understand. Rashbam cites two prooftexts that are different both from our verse and from each other. In our verse, the verb is in *nifal*. In the two prooftexts, the verb is in *qal*. In both prooftexts the phrase "א' מלא את ב'" appears. However, in the first one it means that 'ב fills 'א, while in the second it means the precise opposite, that 'א fills 'ב.

It would appear that Rashbam is trying to comment on the nature of the verb מ-ל-א when it appears in what he calls a רפי construction, i.e. in *qal* or *nifal*. In Rashbam's grammar book (e.g. p. 42), he argues that roots will often have an intransitive meaning in רפי constructions--*qal* and *nifal*--and a transitive meaning in דגש constructions like *piel*. Rashbam argues that this pattern is not hard and fast and, in fact, cites (there, on page 62) Gen. 1:22 where the verb מ-ל-א appears in the *qal* and says כמו משקל דגש, i.e. that the *qal* form is transitive there just like a *piel* form would be. So too here Rashbam appears to be making the same point, that there is no consistent difference between *piel* uses of the verb מ-ל-א and uses in the *qal* (and in *qal*'s partner, *nifal*). Melammed, p. 502, apparently understands Rashbam's comment here similarly.

EXODUS I

1:10 נתחכמה LET US DEAL SHREWDLY WITH THEM: so that they do not increase.[7] For if they increase, then, IN THE EVENT OF A WAR from our enemies, ...

[The singular noun מלחמה is used with the plural verb תקראנה] just like in the phrase (Jud. 5:26), "Her hand [ידה, singular noun] reached [תשלחנה, plural verb] for the tent pin." One can find the plural used with the singular.[8]

כי תקראנה: means "should it occur." [The root ק-ר-א can mean to occur] as in the phrase מקראי קדש (Lev. 23:2 and passim) [which Onqelos translates into Aramaic as] מערע קדשא, a holy occurrence, [which in turn is] like [the post-biblical Hebrew word] מאורע, an occurrence.[9]

---

[7]The phrase הבה נתחכמה לו has been interpreted as implying a plot against God, against Israel's savior, or a sneaky method of a generalized plot against the Israelites. (See Rashi, LT, and Nahm.) Rashbam, iE and JBS simply see the phrase as meaning that Pharaoh wished to take steps to control the size of the Israelite population. Rashbam seems untroubled by the fact that the Jewish people had, until this point, been referred to in the plural and now (beginning in vs. 9) the text refers to them in the singular--the problem that motivated Rashi to offer a midrashic explantion. See Greenberg's explanation for the singular form here in *Understanding Exodus*, p. 20.

[8]See similarly Rashbam's comm. to Gen. 1:14. This problem is also discussed by iE in his shorter commentary and by Qimhi in *Sefer ha-shorashim*, s.v. קרא and s.v. עוג.

[9]Rashbam notes well that the verb תקראנה in this verse means to happen and should be understood as if it were written without an *'alef*. So also JBS here. There are many examples of in the Bible of קרא meaning קרה; see e.g. Even Shoshan's list of seventeen occurrences in his Concordance, s.v. קרא-2.

Nevertheless, the prooftext that Rashbam does cite, the phrase מקראי קדש, is not the best available proof. It is true that Onq. uses a form of the Aramaic verb ע-ר-ע to translate the Hebrew word מקראי. However Onq. also uses the verb ע-ר-ע to translate the Hebrew word תקראו in Lev. 23:2, a verb that could hardly mean "to happen." The more reasonable conclusion is that Onq. sometimes uses the Aramaic verb ע-ר-ע in the meaning of "to call," and not that the Hebrew verb ק-ר-א in those phrases means "to happen." See e.g. Jastrow, s.v. ערע-II, p. 1121 and s.v. ארע-II, pp. 124-125. For further insight into Rashbam's understanding of the phrase מקראי קדש, see Rashbam's comm. to Lev. 23:2. Rashbam's interpretation of מקראי קדש is opposed to that of Rashi, ad Ex. 12:16.

ונלחם **AND THEY WILL FIGHT US AND LEAVE THE COUNTRY**: to return to their native land. It is not good for us to lose our slaves[10] and be called "a truncated kingdom."[11]

1:11 מסים (TASK): is from the geminate root, מ-ס-ס, just as פתים in the phrase (Lev. 2:6) פתות אותה פתים is from [the geminate root,] פ-ת-ת.[12]

מסכנות: means storehouses. [The root ס-כ-נ is connected to storage as we see that a steward is called a סוכן] as in the phrase (Is. 22:15), "Go in to see that steward (סוכן), that Shebna,[13] in charge of the palace."[14]

---

[10]The phrase ועלה מן הארץ troubles all the commentators, ancient and modern. Simply put, it is not clear what Pharaoh's concern was. Rashi offers two explanations. The second, taken from Sotah 11a, sees ועלה, "they will leave," as a euphemism for ועלינו, "we will leave." Pharaoh's fear then was that the Jews would expel the Egyptians from Egypt.

Rashbam prefers Rashi's first interpretation in which ועלה is understood in its standard sense. Rashbam expands on Rashi's terse two-word explanation--בעל כרחנו, "against our will"--and tries to explain why Pharaoh would want to stop the Israelites from emigrating. Rashbam's interpretation was criticized by Luzzatto who pointed out the obvious weakness: since the Israelites were not slaves at this point, why would Pharaoh say, "It is not good for us to lose our slaves"? Still, Rashbam's interpretation is defended logically by Greenberg, pp. 22-23. Pharaoh can be seen as concerned about his potential loss of face from losing authority over so many subjects who are ostensibly under his absolute control. See also JBS who seems to anticipate and todeal with Luzzatto's objection. (Luzzatto himself cites a possible defense of Rashbam's position, offered by Luzzatto's son.)

[11]The phrase מלכותא קטיעא is taken from a Talmudic story (Avodah Zarah 10b) where a Jew is quoted as telling the Romans that, if they annihilate all the Jews of their kingdom, people will call them "a truncated kingdom."

[12]Rashbam could be making a simple grammatical point about the word מסים. See similarly iE in both of his commentaries. Alternatively, he may be taking issue with Onq., who translated שרי מסים as שלטונין מבאישין (cruel officers), apparently connecting the word מסים to the root מ-א-ס or basing the translation on the interpretation offered in Sotah 11a that connected מסים to the rabbinic and late-biblical Hebrew verb, משים (the *hifil* form of the root ש-ו-מ).

[13]Rashbam's citation הסוכן הלז לשבנא differs somewhat from the MT in Isaiah. See the discussion in Esh, *Textus* 5 (1966), 89.

EXODUS I

1:12 כן ירבה: [The imperfect verb ירבה, is to be seen as connoting the past tense and] meaning, "So they increased as before."[15]

ויקוצו: AND THEY WERE DISGUSTED WITH their own lives,[16] as in the phrase (Gen. 27:46), "קצתי בחיי--I was disgusted with my life." Similarly (Is. 7:16), " . . . that you are disgusted (קץ) [with your own life] because of their two kings."[17]

---

[14]The same interpretation is offered by Rashi, JBS and iE. All of them reject the midrashic interpretations offered in Sotah 11a that connect מסכנות to מְסֻכָּנוֹת ("endangering") or to מְמַסְכְּנוֹת ("empoverishing"). That latter midrashic interpretation was known even by Rashbam's Christian contemporary, Hugo of Saint Victor. See PL 175:61.

[15]Rashbam sides with the first of the two interpretations offered by Rashi, according to which the imperfect form here can and does connote here an action in the past. Rashbam rejects the midrash (again in Sotah 11a) cited as Rashi's second interpretation, according to which the imperfect is seen as a future, and the text is recording God's promise that the Israelites *will* increase, despite Pharaoh's efforts. Cf. Cassuto's comm. where he argues that seeing the contrast between פן ירבה (vs. 10) and כן ירבה (here) as alluding to God's response to Pharaoh's plot is a *peshaṭ* interpretation, not "just" a midrash.

[16]See similarly Rashbam and Rashi to Num. 22:3.
   The phrase קץ מפני appears in the Bible four times. Once, the word בחיי appears in the phrase. Rashbam claims that the other three times the word בחיי should be understood. Presumably Rashbam wishes to emphasize that this phrase does not mean that the Egyptians were disgusted with the Israelites but rather that the Egyptians found their own lives to be intolerable *because* of the Israelites. See similarly Rashi's comm. to Sotah 11a, s.v. ויקוצו.

[17]Yet again Rashbam follows Rashi's first, *peshaṭ*-like explanation and rejects his second midrashic interpretation, taken from Sotah 11a, that connects ויקוצו to the Hebrew word for thorns.

1:13 בפרך RUTHLESSLY: בפרך has the meaning of breaking. In the Talmud,[18] [one finds the root פ-ר-כ in the meaning of breaking, as in the phrase] מפרכין באגוזים--one cracks nuts.[19]

1:14 ובכל AND ALL SORTS OF WORK IN THE FIELD: [Like] ploughing and harvesting. את כל עבודתם means *together with* ALL THE WORK THAT THEY RUTHLESSLY IMPOSED ON THEM in the city.[20]

1:15 למיילדות העבריות: means to the midwives who were Hebrews themselves [not to the Egyptian midwives who served the Hebrews].[21]

---

[18]This precise phrase, as cited by Rashbam, does not seem to appear in any of our texts of the Talmud and it is not clear what text Rashbam is alluding to here. It may be Shabbat 115a which, according to Maimonides' reading (in *Shevitat 'asor* 1:3), reads מפצעין באגוזים ומפרכין ברמונים (standard texts = ומפרסכין) or perhaps Betsah 12b, מוללין מלילות ומפרכין קטניות.

[19]Rashi and Rashbam both interpret בפרך in the same way. They both reject the midrashic interpretation of R. Elazar in Sotah 11b ("בפה רך") but follow the view of R. Samuel b. Nahmani there ("בפריכה"). Rashbam alone offers a prooftext from rabbinic literature. (See also Sekhel Tov who offers a prooftext from rabbinic literature for the same interpretation.) It is interesting to contrast his position here with his position in his comm. to Ex. 12:7 where he rejects the etymology that Rashi provided for the word משקוף on the grounds that it was not based on biblical Hebrew, but on rabbinic Hebrew. See the discussion of this issue in my Genesis volume, pp. 422-424.

[20]The syntax of the second half of the verse is problematic. It seems to constitute a sentence fragment ("All the tasks that they ruthlessly imposed on them . . ."), apparently unconnected to the first half of the verse and lacking a main verb. See NJPS which entirely restructures vss. 13-14.

iE solves the problem by suggesting that the second half of the verse is really a free-standing sentence. The words עבדו בהם serve double duty and must be read twice in order to give the verse meaning: "All the tasks that they imposed on them, they imposed on them ruthlessly."

Rashbam, however, sees the second half of the verse as constituting an adverbial phrase, introduced by the word את which would mean "with," as it does back in vs. 1 and many times in biblical Hebrew. See Mendelssohn who adopts this interpretation both in his comm. and in his translation.

[21]Rashbam follows the general position of most of the classical Jewish exegetes and midrashim that העבריות is to be seen as an adjective modifying מיילדות and that the midwives themselves were Hebrews. The phrase could also mean "the midwives to the

1:16 עַל הָאָבְנָיִם: means on the birthstool, [which is commonly called a מַשְׁבֵּר] as in the phrase (2K 19:3), "The babes have reached the birthstool (מַשְׁבֵּר) [but the strength to give birth is lacking]." The term אבניים also appears in the context of a potter's vessel, as Jeremiah wrote (18:3), "[So I went in to the house of a potter, and found him] doing work at the אבניים."[22]

וָחָיָה: The stress is on the penult. Just as from the root שב one says שָׁבָה [with the stress on the penult, in the perfect of the third-person singular feminine. The masculine perfect form חַי, as in the phrase] (Gen. 11:12) "Arpachshad lived (חַי)" becomes חָיָה [with penultimate stress] in the feminine. However, [the word חָיָה in the phrase] (Eccl. 6:6) "If he lived (חָיָה) a thousand years twice" has stress on the ultima and is a masculine form [of the perfect, from the root ח-י-ה] just like רָאָה, עָלָה or עָשָׂה.[23]

Hebrews" and was so understood by LXX, Josephus (*Antiquities* 2.206) and the occasional midrash. See Kasher, p. 38, note 166. See further discussion of the exegetical issues (both grammatical and ideological) involved in identifying these women as Jewish or non-Jewish in Luzzatto's comm. and in Nechama Leibowitz's *'Iyyunim*, pp. 29-33.

Aryeh Grabois ("The *Hebraica Veritas* and Jewish-Christian Intellectual Relations in the Twelfth Century," *Speculum* 50 (1975) 621, note 36) claims that Hugh of Saint Victor's commentary on this verse (PL 175:61) is clearly dependent on that of Rashbam. While Hugh does show in that passage that he knows that the Jews interpret the phrase as meaning that the midwives themselves were Jewish, there is no reason to assume that Rashbam was the only Jewish source from which Hugh could have learned of this interpretation.

[22]Rashbam's comment to this phrase is virtually identical to that of Rashi. They both are rejecting the midrashic explanation of Sotah 11b (cited approvingly by such exegetes as LT and Sekhel Tov) that the word אבניים constitutes some kind of hint about the art of midwifery--how to identify a woman just about to give birth or how to identify a woman giving birth to a male child. The midrashic explanation in the Talmud also makes use of the verse from Jeremiah in order to make its point.

[23]Rashbam suggests, as many modern grammarians do, that there are two separate roots that both mean "to live"--the root ח-י-י and the root ח-י-ה. See iE's longer comm. and his *Sefer ṣaḥot*, p. 26, where he attributes to Hayyuj and Dunash the position that Rashbam took here and still takes issue with that approach, based in part on his idea that no root in Hebrew should end with the letter *yod*. See Mendelssohn who argues at length for Rashbam's position.

1:17 ותיראנה: is from [the root י-ר-א, meaning] fear. However, ותראנה written without the letter *yod* is from the root ר-א-ה, to see, as the text will say (Ex. 2:6) "ותראהו--and she saw him" [written without the letter *yod*].[24]

ותחיין: There is no [orthographic] distinction between third- and second-person plural [feminine forms of the imperfect].[25]

1:19 כי חיות הנה: means that they are healthy and clever and give birth in a hurry.[26]

1:21-2 ויעש AND HE [Pharaoh!] MADE HOUSES FOR THEM: to keep an eye on them to make sure that they not go to the Israelite women who

---

[24] Rashbam provides useful information about how to tell the difference between the imperfect forms of the root י-ר-א on the one hand, and the root ר-א-ה, on the other hand. Rashbam may be taking issue with Sekhel Tov who claims that the reason that the *'alef* in the word (וַתִּירָאןָ) has no vowel is to distinguish between that form and the form that would mean "they (fem.) saw." (Similarly iE, in his longer comm.) Rashbam's explanation, to my mind, makes much more sense. The corresponding masculine forms ותראו and ותיראו, or ויראו and ויראו are always distinguished by the presence or absence of a *yod*. The first form of each pair, the one with the *yod*, is from the root י-ר-א; the second form is from the root ר-א-ה. (See Rashi ad Gen. 43:18, s.v. וייראו.)
   The more likely explanation for the fact that the *'alef* in the word ותיראנה in our verse has no vowel is that it elided, like the vowels following many other *'alefs* in the Bible, and that the letter was "only retained orthographically" (G.-K. 74i).

[25] So also Rashi at much greater length, in an attempt to explain why Onq. translates ותראנה in this verse differently from the way he translates the same word in vs. 18.

[26] Rashbam rejects both explanations offered by Rashi. Rashi's midrashic explanation (his second one), taken from Sotah 11b, interprets this phrase as an allusion to the fact that the Jewish people is often compared in the Bible to various (strong) animals (the most common meaning of the Hebrew word חיות). Rashbam also rejects Rashi's *peshaṭ* interpretation in which Rashi, following Onq., connects the word חיות in this verse to the post-biblical Hebrew word חיה, midwife. It is possible that Rashbam objects to the use of rabbinic Hebrew to explain a biblical Hebrew word. See my note above on 1:13, s.v. בפרך.
   LT, Sekhel Tov and iE also explain the phrase the way Rashbam did, as do NJPS and most moderns.

were giving birth.[27] And furthermore,[28] (1:22) PHARAOH CHARGED ALL HIS PEOPLE "לאמר"--and this is what he said to them.[29] For the word לאמר in the Torah is always a reiteration of the word ויצו--he commanded, or ויקרא--he called, or וידבר--he spoke, or ויאמר--he said, as I explained in the Torah portion, *Noah*.[30]

---

[27]This interpretation appears to be a novel reading offered by Rashbam. Most exegetes have assumed that the subject of the verb ויעש must be God and that the phrase ויעש להם בתים means that God gave some type of reward to the midwives (Sifre Numbers *Beha'alotekha* 78, Sotah 11b, Rashi, iE etc). Before Rashbam, LT and Sekhel Tov offer an interpretation according to which Pharaoh could be seen as the subject of the verb (ויעש) and the phrase means that Pharaoh planted Egyptian spies among the Israelites (להם) to try to find out when Jewish babies were being born. Also Rashbam's Christian contemporary Hugh of Saint Victor (PL 175:62) offers two possible readings of the text, one of which sees the subject of ויעש as being Pharaoh. Rashbam's unique suggestion is that the verse describes some form of house arrest imposed on the midwives by Pharaoh. While Rashbam's reading was roundly attacked by Mendelssohn and Luzzatto, NJPSC deems it "the most probable explanation."

[28]It seems that Rashbam's interpretation is based on the joining together of the end of vs. 21 and the beginning of vs. 22 and reading back the word פרעה from vs. 22 to be the subject of the verb ויעש in 21b.

[29]In general Rashbam objects to the common rabbinic explanation that the word לאמר means that the person being spoken to was asked to pass the message on to someone else. See the next note. He may also be taking issue with the specific interpretation of Sekhel Tov here who suggests that the phrase ויצו פרעה לכל עמו לאמר means that Pharaoh commanded all of his people *to snitch* on the Israelites.

[30]In the lost section of Rashbam's comm. to Genesis. See however his comm. to Gen. 32:5 and my notes there, p. 198.

EXODUS II

2:1 וילך A MAN OF THE HOUSE OF LEVI, i.e. Amram, WENT AND MARRIED Yocheved,[1] THE DAUGHTER OF LEVI, who was "born to Levi in Egypt" (Num. 26.59). He married her many years before Moses' birth, for Aaron [Moses' brother was three years older than Moses, as it is written (Ex. 7:7) that Aaron] was eighty-three years old while Moses was [only] eighty years old when they spoke to Pharaoh.[2]

2:2 ותהר THE WOMAN CONCEIVED at the time of Pharaoh's decree to cast the males into the river, AND SHE BORE A SON.[3]

---

[1]Touitou (*Tarbiz* 51 [1982] 232) argues that Rashbam's immediate emphasis here on the names of Moses' parents is to be seen in the context of a polemic against the Christian view of Moses as similar to Jesus in that, among other supposed similarities, both of their birth narratives do not make their parentage clear.
See further discussion in notes below ad 4:10.

[2]As Greenberg (pp. 37-38) notes, the first two verses of our chapter provide the distinct impression that Moses' parents married only *after* Pharaoh's decree and that Moses was the first born. Yet other passages suggest that Moses had both an older sister and an older brother, both born presumably before Pharaoh's decree. Rashbam attempts to harmonize this story with the other passages in the Torah regarding Moses' birth and parentage. He does so, however, without having recourse to the midrashic approach of Rashi (following Sotah 12a and other rabbinic sources) that Amram and Yocheved had been married for many years before Pharaoh's decree and had had two children, had separated when Pharaoh made his decree but had come back together at Miriam's urging despite the decree.
The approaches of JBS and Nahm. are very similar to Rashbam's.

[3]According to Rashbam, from a chronological perspective the next event after Pharaoh's decree to kill all male Israelite babies (at the end of chapter 1) is not the marriage of Moses' parents (2:1) but rather the conception of Moses (2:2).

ותרא SHE SAW THAT HE WAS GOOD AND SHE HID HIM: The explanation that she hid him because of [something special] that she saw in him is false.[4] All babies elicit the compassion of their mothers. Rather one must explain [the verb] SHE SAW (ותרא) like in the verse (Gen. 1:31), "God saw (וירא) all that he had made and found it very good."[5] There the phrase means that God] looked and examined all His works and His actions that He had done to see whether there was something to correct therein; everything was proper and correct. Here also, since Moses was born [prematurely] after [a pregnancy of only] six months--just as we find that Samuel was born [after a six-month pregnancy, as it is written (I Sam. 1:20)] לתקופות הימים, i.e. after two *tequfot*[6] and two [more] days.[7]

That is why she [=Moses' mother] was able to hide him for three months, for the Egyptians used to check the pregnant women [only at the anticipated end of a full term pregnancy] at the end of nine months.[8]

---

[4]Rashbam is taking issue with a number of midrashic explanations that impute some special significance to the phrase, "she saw that he was good." He is presumably most directly opposing the explanation offered by his grandfather Rashi (following Sotah 12a) that the phrase means that the entire house was filled with light when Moses was born. That midrashic explanation is based on seeing a similarity between our verse and Gen. 1:4. Curiously Rashbam too points out a similarity between those two verses (in his comm. to Gen. 1:4) but does not use that similarity to reach midrashic conclusions.

Touitou (*Tarbiz* 51 [1982] 232) again argues that the diminution of the miraculous aspects of Moses' birth should be seen in terms of Rashbam's anti-Christian polemic.

[5]In his comm. on Genesis 1:4, Rashbam compared our Exodus verse to that verse, not to Gen. 1:31. In fact the comparison to Gen. 1:4 makes more sense as that verse has a similar structure to the verse in Exodus: ר-א-ה את . . . כי טוב. The phrase כי טוב does not appear in Gen. 1:31, so Rashbam's argument here is not as clear as it is in his Genesis comm.

[6]In rabbinic Hebrew a tequfah is a ninety day period, from one solstice to the next equinox or from one equinox to the next solstice.

[7]The verse in Genesis, the verse in I Samuel and our verse are all discussed in a similar way in Rashbam's comm. to Gen. 1:4. See my notes, there, pp. 34-5.

[8]So also Rashi, s.v. ולא יכלה and JBS, in the name of "our rabbis."

EXODUS II

Accordingly, [since he was born so prematurely] she examined him when he was born to see whether he was a stillborn that need not be hidden. But she saw that he was fine and good-looking, for his signs of maturity, which are his hair and fingernails--as we learned in Yevamot (80b)--were completed. So she knew that he was capable of surviving[9] and therefore she hid him for three months--i.e. until the end of [what would have been a pregnancy of] nine months, which is the standard length of pregnancy for most women. When they came to check on her either she told them that the child had been a stillborn or that the Egyptians had already thrown him into the river.[10]

2:3 בחמר WITH BITUMEN: on the inside AND PITCH on the outside, so that the water would not penetrate.[11]

---

[9]See similarly JBS who interprets the phrase כי טוב as meaning viable (ראוי לחיות).

[10]It is interesting that Rashbam, the champion of *peshat*, accepts the midrashic tradition that Moses was born after a pregnancy of only six months. (On the sources of that tradition, see Berliner's notes to Rashi, here.) Still both Rashbam and Rashi can be seen as rejecting the more common rabbinic tradition that says that when Amram "remarried" his wife Yocheved, she was already three months pregnant (Sotah 12a, adopted by LT, Sekhel Tov and others). Perhaps Rashbam felt that the midrashic tradition of the premature birth was closer to the text's *peshat* than the explanation in Sotah. Furthermore, as noted above, Rashbam avoided any reference to the supposed "remarriage" of Yocheved and Amram.

Also, the way Rashbam presents the tradition of the premature birth differs from the way most other exegetes do. Other interpreters understand that the basis for the midrash about the premature birth is the fact that after three months she could no longer hide the child (vs. 3). For Rashbam it would seem that the basis of the midrash is found in vs. 2, in the fact that Moses' mother had to examine him to see if he was likely to live.

[11]Rashbam's comment can almost be seen as mocking the words of his grandfather, Rashi. The first five words of Rashbam's comment are virtually a verbatim citation of Rashi: "בחמר מבפנים ובזפת מבחוץ שלא --with bitumen on the inside and pitch on the outside so that . . . ." Rashi's explanation (following Sotah 12a)--that the specific choice of two different caulking materials for baby Moses' basket was designed to insure "that that righteous one would not have to smell the bad smell of pitch"--was too midrashic for Rashbam. His explanation, on the other hand is quite prosaic and simple. The suggestion that the choice of two caulking materials was in order to seal the basket well is also offered by Sekhel Tov, who offers both that explanation and the midrashic one.

ותשם SHE PLACED IT AMONG THE REEDS: that were close to the bank of the river. She hid it well so that people walking on the bank of the river could not see the basket, but those bathing in the river could see it. This was the case because Yocheved had not gone into the river to hide the basket well [so that it couldn't be seen] from all angles. That is why Pharaoh's daughter who was bathing in the river (vs. 5) saw it, while her maids who were walking along the river bank (vs. 5) could not see it.[12]

2:5 אמתה: means her maiden.[13]

2:6 ותפתח ותראהו את הילד: He who explains that [the verse means that] she saw the child[14] is mistaken. Does not everybody know that if she opened the basket she would see the child?! [Why bother writing

---

[12]Rashbam explains why it appears that Pharaoh's daughter alone, and not her maids, saw the basket in the water. (Sekhel Tov also notes that it was only Pharaoh's daughter who saw the basket, but he provides no explanation as to why that happened.)

Rashbam's detailed comment here on the logistics of the placing of the basket must be seen as directed against the comm. of Rashi to vs. 5, s.v. על יד היאר. There Rashi adopts the fanciful midrashic explantion of Sotah 12b that the phrase, "her maidens walked along the Nile," should be understood as a reference to the *death* of Pharaoh's daughter's maidens. Rashi argues that the midrash on the phrase, "her maidens walked," *is* textually grounded (והכתוב מסייען). Were it not for the midrash, the phrase would be seen as superfluous, as there is no reason for the text to provide us with information about where it was that the maidens were walking. That is why Rashbam goes to such great length to explain that the information about the place where Pharaoh's daughter and her maidens were standing is needed for the understanding of the details of the story and that, accordingly, the midrash about the death of the maidens is not necessary.

[13]The Talmud (Sotah 12b) provided two possible explanations for the word אמתה--either "her hand" or "her maiden." Rashi argues at great length that only the explanation, "her maiden," can be considered a reasonable reading of the text. So also Rashbam and iE. Cf. LT who offers both readings.

[14]Rashbam's comment is directed against the comment of his grandfather, Rashi. Rashi, reacting to the midrash (Sotah 12b) that claimed that "she saw *him*," should be seen as a reference to seeing God's presence, writes that the *peshat* actually is that she saw the child. Rashbam, who certainly rejects the midrashic reading, argues that even Rashi's reading is not really *peshat*.

EXODUS II

such an obvious detail?] Rather this is the explanation: she opened the basket and examined the child to see if it was male or female. And she saw that[15] it was a נער, i.e. that the child (הילד) was male, not female.[16] And she saw that his male organ was circumcised so [she was able to deduce] that he had been hidden, not abandoned.[17] Had it been a daughter, one could reasonably suppose that she had been abandoned.

We have found [a further example] that a newborn child can be called a נער, in the verse (Jud. 13:8), " . . . how to act with the child (הנער) who is to be born."[18]

---

[15]See Orlinsky, *Notes*, who cites Rashbam as the source for NJPS's non-literal translation here of ותראהו as "she saw *that*."

[16]The question of the text's alternation between calling Moses a ילד (generally rendered "child") and a נער (generally rendered "young man") is raised already by the Talmud (Sotah 12b). Rashi and iE follow the same principle as the Talmud's answer and assume that the word נער implies that in some (presumably miraculous) way he was like an older child, not like an infant. So also LT and Sekhel Tov. Rashbam sees the distinction between ילד and נער differently. ילד is the generic word, "child," and conveys no meaning about the baby's gender. נער, on the other hand is used only of male children. So she looked at the child (ילד) and discovered that he was male (נער). See Mendelssohn, at great length, who follows Rashbam's reading and cites the verse (Ex. 21:4), "וילדה לו בנים או בנות האשה וילדיה--she has borne him sons and daughters, the woman and her children (וילדיה). . .," as proof that the Bible sometimes uses the word ילד as a generic word for both boys and girls.

[17]The assumption that it was his circumcision that made Pharaoh's daughter assume that Moses was Jewish and had been hidden goes back to the Talmud (Sotah 12b) and is adopted by many other Jewish exegetes.

[18]See Nahm. who argues similarly and with the same prooftext that נער is not necessarily a term for an older child. Rashbam's phrase, "ביום היולדו נקרא נער--a newborn child is called a נער," is reminiscent of the Talmud's language (BQ 65b) about newborn animals (שור בן יומו קרוי שור or איל בן יומו קרוי איל).

והנה A BOY, CRYING. SHE TOOK PITY ON HIM: Because he was crying, she took pity on him. And since she saw that it was a boy, a circumcised male, she said, "THIS MUST BE A HEBREW CHILD."[19]

Another example [of chiastic structure within a verse] is (I Sam. 1:5), "To Hannah he would give [only] one portion, אפיים--[but] a choice one."[20] And why [did he give her the choice portion]? "Because Hannah was his favorite"; that is why he gave her the choice portion, the one from his own plate. In that case, why [is it that she received only] one portion? For "the LORD had closed her womb."[21]

---

[19]Rashbam explains the structure of our verse. He argues that following the word of discovery, והנה, there are two things that are listed that she discovered and then the two reactions that she had to the two discoveries are listed, but in opposite order (chiasm) to the way that the two discoveries are listed. The verse should be understood as saying that Pharaoh's daughter discovered:

A boy (A)
Crying (B)
She took pity on him (B¹)
And she said: This must be a Hebrew child. (A¹)

B¹ explains the reason for B. After that A¹ explains the reason for A.

[20]Rashbam cites the translation of Ps.-Jon., "חולק בחיר--a choice portion," to support his interpretation. So also Rashi, there. See also Rashbam's comm. below ad 25:30.

[21]Rashbam cites another example of a verse that, to his mind, had a chiastic structure (I Sam. 1:5):

To Hannah he would give [only] one portion (A)
[But] a choice one--אפיים (B)
Because Hannah was his favorite (B¹)
But the LORD had closed her womb. (A¹)

Again here, according to Rashbam's reading, A and B are followed first by B¹, the explanation of B, and then by A¹, the explanation of A.

The sensitivity to literary issues such as chiasm is central to much modern reading of the biblical text. See e.g. Michael Fishbane's *Text and Texture*, p. 46 and IDB, Supplemental volume, s.v. chiasmus. It is interesting to see that Rashbam was aware of such issues. Arguably such a way of understanding texts, at least rabbinic texts, can be found in the Talmud, for example in Berakhot 2a where the Talmud's comment, "עד דקאי בשחרית פריש מילי דשחרית והדר פריש מילי דערבית"--since the Mishnah was dealing with morning prayers it completed explaining matters relating to morning prayers, and only then it returned to deal with issues of evening prayers," can be seen as drawing attention to the chiastic structure of Mishnah Berakhot 1:1-4. See also the discussions about the structure of the Mishnah in Nedarim 2b and Nazir 2a. See

On the other hand, to Peninah and all her daughters and sons he gave many portions, since she had [many] children.

[This verse should be read as follows:] SHE LOOKED AT THE CHILD *and it was* A BOY CRYING.

2:7 וְתֵינִק is a *hifil* verb [used of the adult woman who suckles the baby]. וְתִינָק [is a *qal* form that] would be used to describe a young baby girl who herself sucks at the breast.[22]

2:9 וַתְּנִיקֵהוּ: It is not necessary to say that this verb form is from a two-letter [i.e. hollow] root, like ב-א, ש-ב or ק-מ, which in the *hifil* become וַתְּבִיאֵהוּ, וַתְּשִׁיבֵהוּ (e.g. in vs. 10) or וַתְּקִימֵהוּ.[23] Rather, the root is י-נ-ק. In order to shorten the word [and ease the pronunciation] it says וַתְּנִיקֵהוּ, instead of [the expected form] וַתֵּינִיקֵהוּ.[24]

2:10 מְשִׁיתִהוּ: means "I drew him out." This root is applied to drawing out of water, as it is written (Ps. 18:17), "He drew me out (יַמְשֵׁנִי) of the mighty waters." [The root is מ-ש-ה, and the verb declines like any final-*heh* verb,] just as from the root ק-נ-ה one would say "קָנִיתִהוּ:--I

---

also LT ad Ex. 9:31 who compares chiastic structure in the Mishnah and in the Bible.

[22]Rashbam's grammatical comment is solid and uncontroversial. Perhaps he is setting the ground here for his next comment on the anomalous form, וַתְּנִיקֵהוּ (vs. 9).

[23]The interpretation that Rashbam rejects here is precisely the one that he himself offered in his grammar book, p. 39. There he wrote that there are in fact two separate roots with the same meaning, י-נ-ק and נ-ו-ק (or נ-ק). Rashbam must have changed his mind between the writing of the two works. iE also argues (only in his longer comm.) that there are two distinct roots for nursing in Hebrew, both having the same meaning.

[24]See G.-K. 70c who describes the "irregular shortening" of this form.

purchased him" in the *qal* [like מְשִׁיתִיהוּ] and one would say in the *hifil* "יַקְנֵנִי--he will acquire me" [like יַמְשֵׁנִי].²⁵

2:11 מכה BEATING: Perhaps he beat him but did not kill him.²⁶

2:14 הלהרגני DO YOU MEAN TO KILL ME: for [the crime of] beating my friend, just AS YOU KILLED THE EGYPTIAN [simply] because he was beating a Hebrew man?²⁷

---

²⁵Again Rashbam offers a straightforward grammatical explanation. Rashi offered the same explanation, with the same prooftext from Psalms, at much greater length. Both of them oppose the opinion of Menahem who saw the root of משיתיהו as being the same as the root of ימיש (e.g. Ex. 13:22; i.e. the root מ-ו-ש, "to move").

One minor difference between Rashi and Rashbam is that Rashi explains that the root מ-ש-ה is a general term for taking something out. Rashbam, on the other hand, argues that it is a specific term for taking something out of water.

²⁶Rashbam opposes the opinion found in a minority of midrashim according to which the Egyptian had killed the Hebrew slave. See PDRE 48 and the discussion in Kasher, p. 77, note 94, and p. 78, note 97. Such a reading could draw support from the fact that the same verb is used to describe Moses' action in vs. 12, where there is no doubt that he killed the Egyptian, and the Egyptian's action here in vs. 11. Among moderns, Noth continues to argue (pp. 35-6) that the word מכה must be seen as meaning that the Egyptian had killed the Israelite.

It is possible that Rashbam's next section of commentary is meant to explain how he knows that the Egyptian had not killed the Hebrew slave.

²⁷See also Rashbam's comm. to vs. 11 and my notes there.

Rashbam's interpretation is opposed to the midrash quoted by Rashi (following PDRE 48 and Tanhuma) according to which this verse teaches us that Moses had killed the Egyptian by using the powers of pronouncing the divine name (based on the wording הלהרגני אתה אומר).

Rashbam's colleague, JBS, also offers an explanation that slightly resembles that of Rashbam. He says that the Hebrew man's comment means: "Do you mean to kill me without justification--for I am only guilty of the crime of assault--the same way that you killed the Egyptian without justification--for he was simply following the king's orders?"

EXODUS II

אכן: means אך כן--rather yes. It is not as I had previously thought, when I buried him in the sand, that the matter had not become known. Rather yes, it had become known.[28]

2:15 וישב HE SAT IN THE LAND OF MIDIAN [AND HE SAT DOWN BESIDE THE WELL]: The text first makes a general statement and then explains the details[29] of how it came about that he settled in Midian. First HE SAT DOWN BESIDE THE WELL to rest right away, like someone who wants to relax. [But then the story begins to unfold, as it continues:] NOW THE PRIEST OF MIDIAN HAD . . . .[30]

2:18 אל רעואל TO REUEL, [THEIR FATHER: i.e] their father's father. Accordingly their father's name was Jethro; and as for "Hobab the son of Reuel" mentioned below (Num. 10:29), Hobab and Jethro are one and the same person.[31]

---

[28]Rashbam's explanation opposes those of Onq. and of iE (long and short comm.) who see אכן as a word of conclusion without necessarily any contrastive meaning to it. Rashbam's explanation of אכן can be found in BDB, s.v. אכן-b: "emphasizing a contrast . . . expressing the reality in opposition to what had wrongly been imagined."
See similarly Rashbam's comm. to Gen. 28:16 and my notes there.

[29]Rashbam often uses this principle of exegesis, usually to attempt to deal with an apparent redundancy in the text. See e.g. his comm. to Gen. 1:27 s.v. זכר, Ex. 19:8 and Ex. 21:3.

[30]Here the perceived redundancy is the repetition of the verb וישב in the verse. The same explanation as Rashbam's can be found in iE, but only in his longer comm.

[31]The problem of the name of Moses' father-in-law troubled all the classical Jewish exegetes. Here his name appears to be Reuel. In Exodus 18 it appears to be Jethro. In Exodus 4:18 it appears to be Jether (presumably just an alternate form of Jethro?). In Jud. 4:11 it appears to be Hobab. In Num. 10:29 the phrase appears חבב בן רעואל המדיני חותן משה--Hobab the son of Reuel the Midianite, Moses' father-in-law. In that phrase it is not certain whether it is Hobab or Reuel who is being described as Moses' father-in-law.
Generally moderns are wont to solve the problem either by assuming that the confusion arises from a variety of traditions or by harmonizing the diversity by means of textual criticism (R. de Vaux and Albright, respectively, both cited by Childs, p. 332). On the other hand, the common midrashic approach, adopted by Rashi ad 4:18

[However,] if [one were to read the phrase in our verse "TO REUEL, THEIR FATHER" literally and then posit that] Reuel and Jethro are one and the same person, then [one would also have to posit that] Hobab is Jethro's son [i.e. Moses' brother-in-law].[32]

A passage in the prophets (Jud. 4:11), "descendants of Hobab, Moses' חותן" proves that Hobab [is Moses' *father*-in-law, not his brother-in-law, and that he] and Jethro are one and the same person.[33] The phrase, חותן משה, [which is applied to Hobab in the Judges passage] is [otherwise] invariably[34] applied to Jethro.

---

and ad 18:1, is that Moses' father-in-law had seven different names: Jethro, Jether, Hobab, Reuel and a few others (Mekhilta *'Amaleq* 3 and Tanh. B. *Shemot* 11).

Neither of those two solutions, the critical or the midrashic, would appeal to Rashbam. He attempts to harmonize by assuming that Reuel was the grandfather of Moses' wife and that Reuel's son, Moses' father-in-law, was named alternatively both Hobab and Jethro (and Jether). The assumption that Reuel was Moses' wife's grandfather can be found before Rashbam in a number of sources including Ps.-Jon. here and Sifre *Beha'alotekha* 78. It can also be found in iE, in his longer comm. to Exodus, and it is mentioned by Rashi as one possible interpretation ("ויש אומרים") in his comm. to 18:1 and then apparently adopted by Rashi in his comm. to Num. 10:29.

[32]Rashbam argues that the midrashic approach that Moses' father-in-law had seven names is not consistent with the texts. Even if Reuel and Jethro are the same person, we must say, on the basis of Num. 10:29, that Hobab was Reuel's son and that Hobab could not be a name of Moses' father-in-law, as Rashi and the midrash would have it.

His comment here may also be directed against the interpretation adopted by iE in his comm. to Num. 10:29 (and alluded to in his shorter comm. to Ex. 3:1), that argues that Reuel was Moses' father-in-law and that Reuel's son, Moses' brother-in-law, was alternatively known as Hobab or Jethro. This interpretation is based on the premise that the word חותן, as in the phrase חותן משה, could mean father-in-law in some biblical passages and brother-in-law in other biblical passages. Rashbam does not accept that assumption and assumes that חותן always means father-in-law, as the continuation of his remarks below proves.

[33]This same argument can be found in Rashi's comm. to Ex. 18:13. See similarly Sifre *Beha'alotekha* 78.

[34]Seven times, all in Exodus 18.

EXODUS II

2:22 בארץ IN A FOREIGN LAND: That is what the name גרשם implies: גֵר--a stranger, שָׁם--there, in a faraway land.³⁵

2:23 ויהי A LONG TIME AFTER THAT: after [all the above events occurred, that] Moses killed the Egyptian and Pharaoh, the king of Egypt, wanted to kill Moses so that Moses ran away from him, and so on, until Moses was now eighty years old (Ex. 7:7) when God spoke to him,³⁶ *then* THE KING OF EGYPT, the one who had wanted to kill Moses, DIED. THE ISRAELITES *had been* GROANING up to this point³⁷ and God marked well their plight³⁸ And when (3:1) MOSES

---

³⁵So also JBS and Driver.

³⁶Rashbam explains the reason why the text writes, "a long time (בימים הרבים) after that." He opposes the midrashic tradition (SR 1:34, VR 19:5), adopted here by LT and Sekhel Tov, according to which these days are referred to as רבים because they were days of sorrow. He also opposes the position of his colleague, Joseph Qara (cited by Gad, p. 19) who explains that the verse means that the amount of enslavement that God had promised Abraham (Gen. 15:13) had now been completed. Rashbam explains more simply that a significant number of years and events had passed.

³⁷As is often the case, the reason for Rashbam's long excursus here is to explain carefully how and why he disapproves of the midrashic approach of his grandfather Rashi.

The midrash on this verse (SR 1:34, Ps.-Jon.) reacts to the strange juxtaposition of the two phrases, "the King of Egypt died" and "the Israelites groaned under the bondage." As LT puts it, why would the death of the king be an occasion for *more* groaning? The midrash then says that the king did not really die but only contracted leprosy (a condition that the midrash saw as being tantamount to death, based on Num. 12:12). In an attempt to cure his leprosy he began to kill Israelite children and bathe in their blood. That is why the text can imply that the death (i.e. the leprosy) of the king was a cause for further Israelite groaning. This midrash is adopted by Rashi, LT and Sekhel Tov in their commentaries to this verse.

Rashbam explains that the statement, "the king of Egypt died," must be understood literally. While in the context of this verse it serves no immediate purpose, it does have an anticipatory purpose, preparing us, just before the encounter between Moses and God is about to begin (3:1), for God's words in the middle of their conversation, "all the men who sought to kill you are dead" (4:19). (See similarly Driver.) The groaning of the Israelites is in no way a result of that death. It had been going on beforehand also.

JBS offers three explanations of the phrase, "the king of Egypt died," the second of which ("ויש מפרשים--some interpret") is Rashbam's explanation.

WAS TENDING . . . and God appeared to him and charged him to return to Egypt, Moses, out of fear, did not want to return until God told him that "all the men who sought to kill you are dead" (4:19), referring to Pharaoh who had died.

That is why the text now says that "the king of Egypt died," [to anticipate and] to testify to the truth of what God will say (4:19), "all the men who sought to kill you are dead." [The verse is anticipatory,] like (Gen. 9:18) "Ham being the father of Canaan."[39]

2:24 ויזכר GOD REMEMBERED HIS COVENANT: that he had sworn to the three forefathers to give them the land of Canaan.[40] And now the four hundred years that were mentioned to Abraham[41] were about to elapse.

---

[38] An allusion to Ex. 3:7.

[39] On Rashbam's concept of anticipation, see my Genesis volume, pp. 400-421.

[40] Perhaps Rashbam is opposing here the midrashic tradition that sees in the word covenant (ברית) in this verse a reference to circumcision and argues that the Israelites were redeemed from Egypt primarily because they observed the covenant of circumcision. See Kasher, here, p. 108, note 199.

[41] Genesis 15:13.

EXODUS III

3:2 איננו WAS NOT CONSUMED: Even at the point of contact between the bush and the flame there was not any ember glowing at all.[1]

3:4 וירא THE LORD SAW: The text uses God's name when it is [actually] referring to the angel[, not to God].[2]

3:5 שַׁל: means "cast off!" It is from the [root נ-ש-ל, the] same root as ונשל in the phrase (Deut. 7:1), "He dislodges (ונשל) many nations." Just as from the root נ-ס-ע one says [in the imperative plural] (e.g. Deut. 2:24) סְעוּ and one would say [in the imperative singular] סַע, so also [the imperative singular of נ-ש-ל is] שַׁל.[3]

---

[1] Rashbam may be opposing the reading of LT and Sekhel Tov who see איננו אכל as meaning that the bush was not totally destroyed. Rashbam argues that no part of it even became a glowing ember.

[2] One finds in the text both the claim that an angel appeared to Moses and the claim that God Himself appeared to Moses. Rashbam and iE harmonize by explaining that God appeared to Moses in the form of an angel. Cf. Nahm. who, basing himself on a passage in BR, takes issue with this interpretation and argues that first an angel and then God Himself appeared to Moses.

It is not so rare for a Jewish exegete to interpret the word 'elohim as a reference to an angel. What is unusual is Rashbam's willingness to see even the tetragrammaton in this verse as referring to the angel. Cf. iE who, in his shorter comm. writes that the tetragrammaton here refers to God, not to the angel, while in his longer comm. iE vacillates between the two readings of the tetragrammaton. See also Rosin, RSBM, p.87, note 2, Rashbam's comm. to Gen. 18:1 and my notes, there, pp. 58-9 and Rashbam's comm. to 13:21, 19:11 and 24:1 below.

[3] My translation is based on the second of the two possible emendations suggested by Rosin here, fn. 1.

Rashbam's explanation is generally like Rashi's but written with more grammatical detail. See similarly iE (longer comm. only).

3:7 ואת THEIR OUTCRY I HAVE HEEDED BECAUSE OF THEIR OPPRESSORS: I.e. the outcry, that they cry out because they are being oppressed, I have heeded.[4]

3:8 וארד I HAVE COME DOWN: here, to speak to you, in order TO RESCUE THEM FROM THE EGYPTIANS.[5]

3:10 והוצא AND YOU SHALL FREE MY PEOPLE THE ISRAELITES FROM EGYPT: by means of the speeches that you shall deliver to Pharaoh from me.[6]

3:11-12 ויאמר BUT MOSES SAID TO GOD, "WHO AM I?": He who wishes to understand the true plain meaning of these verses should seek

---

Rashbam's explanation can be seen as opposing that of Onq. who saw של נעליך as meaning "*untie* your shoes (שרי סינך)."

[4] Rashbam reorganizes the word order of the verse in a way that is reflected in most modern translations. Cf. Sekhel Tov who sees the phrase, "their outcry I have heeded," as referring to one complaint of the Israelites and the phrase, "because of their oppressors," as referring to another entirely different complaint.

[5] The perceived difficulty is that the verse might make more sense with a verb in the future tense, i.e. with God promising that he *will* come down soon to save the Jews from Egypt. The verse as it stands implies that God had already, before this point in time, come down to save the Jews from Egypt and that does not appear to be the case. Rashbam explains that speaking to Moses constitutes the beginning of that process of redemption so then it is accurate to say that God had already come down to save the Jews. See similarly Sekhel Tov.

[6] Rashbam here is setting the ground for his next, long comment on vss. 11-12. There he attempts to explain that Moses' first question in vs. 11 means "How could I possibly go call on Pharaoh?" and his second question in that verse really means "What persuasive ruse could I possibly use when talking to Pharaoh?" Rashbam explains that in verse 10 God asks Moses to do those two things that Moses asks questions about in the next verse. He asks him to go to Pharaoh (לכה ואשלחך אל פרעה), and to *speak* to Pharaoh about letting the Jews out (Rashbam's understanding of "והוצא את עמי בני ישראל ממצרים--free my people the Israelites from Egypt").

wisdom in this, my commentary, for those who preceded me did not understand them at all.[7] Moses reacted to two things that God said to him: (1) to go to Pharaoh and (2) to take the Jews out [of Egypt] at Pharaoh's command.[8] Moses reacted to those two requests in order:

> (1) WHO AM I THAT I SHOULD GO TO PHARAOH, even to bring him a gift or a present? Is a foreigner like me worthy to enter the king's court?
> (2) AND THAT I SHOULD FREE THE ISRAELITES FROM EGYPT? In other words, even if I were worthy to enter Pharaoh's court for some other purpose, what could I say to Pharaoh that would be acceptable? Is Pharaoh such a fool that he would listen to me to send such a large nation of his slaves free from his country? What acceptable thing could I say to him to lead to my taking them out of Egypt with his permission?[9]

Then God reacted [to Moses' two points also] in order[10] and said:

> (1) FOR I WILL BE WITH YOU and I will dispose the king favorably towards you; you will go to Pharaoh and not be afraid. As for your fear [about appearing] before Pharaoh, THIS [i.e.

---

[7]The precise meaning of Moses' two questions and the answer(s) that he received from God were interpreted in many different ways by different exegetes. Still it is fairly certain that the main target of Rashbam's criticism here is the comm. of his grandfather, Rashi.

See E. Touitou, HUCA LXI (1990), p. 162, who cites this statement of Rashbam as proof that the attitude of intellectual self-confidence characteristic of the twelfth-century renaissance had permeated into the circles of French rabbis.

[8]See Rashbam's comm. to vs. 10 and my note, there.

[9]Rashbam objects to Rashi's explanation of the second question asked by Moses. Rashi interpreted that second question as meaning that Moses was questioning whether the Jewish people deserved to be redeemed from Egypt.

[10]Rashbam and Rashi agree that God answered Moses' two points even though they disagree about what the second point was.

the bush]¹¹ IS YOUR SIGN THAT IT IS I WHO SENDS YOU--surely you see through the burning of the bush that I¹² am God's messenger. This sign is for you¹³ so that you will be certain that I will be with you. Similarly one finds concerning Gideon (Jud. 6:14ff.) that the angel said to him, "I herewith send you."¹⁴

(2) As for that which you said," [who am I] THAT I SHOULD FREE THE ISRAELITES FROM EGYPT?"--i.e. "through what claim that I say to Pharaoh will he listen to me and free them?"--WHEN YOU FREE THE PEOPLE FROM EGYPT I command you now that you should WORSHIP GOD AT THIS MOUNTAIN and offer sacrifices. This is the claim that you should make, for he will let them go to sacrifice to God.

---

¹¹Rashi also writes in his first interpretation of his phrase that the word, "this (זה)," refers to the bush. Both Rashi and Rashbam are opposing the alternative explanation according to which the phrase, "this is your sign," should be seen as introducing the next phrase, "when you take the people out of Egypt." See e.g. iE's shorter comm., LT and JBS. See similarly Rashi in his second interpretation of this phrase, beginning with the words דבר אחר. Moderns using that interpretation include Greenberg, p. 76, and Cassuto.

See the long "Form-critical study of Ex. 3:12" in Childs, pp. 56-60, where all the syntactical and interpretive possibilities for this phrase are considered. Childs eventually concludes, like Rashbam, that the אות referred to here must be the burning bush. It is worth noting that the cantillation signs also support Rashbam's reading of the phrase.

¹²Following Rashbam's comm. to vs. 4, it was an angel who was speaking to him all this time.

¹³Rashbam is again opposing the idea that the Jewish people will receive the אות that this verse refers to when they come to the theophany at Sinai. See also LT who expresses an idea very similar to Rashbam's about the word אות ("למי אלא אינו [אות] שמדבר אליו ולא לאדם אחר--a 'sign' is meant only for the person who is being addressed, not for someone else") although his interpretation of the phrase in its context is very different from Rashbam's.

¹⁴שלחתיך, language very similar to "ואשלחך--I will send you" here in vs. 10. And following the commission of Gideon, the same sequence as here--an expression of fear and inadequacy, followed by the angel's promise to be with him, followed by a sign that validates the angel--occurs. Rashbam again compares the story of the commission of the Moses and the story of the commission of Gideon in his comm. below, ad 4:25 s.v. ותכרות.

Even though it[15] is not spelled out clearly here, below (vs. 18) the text clarifies, "They will listen to you; and you will go with the elders of Israel to the king of Egypt [and say] . . . 'Now therefore let us go a distance of three days into the wilderness to sacrifice'." Each and every time that is what Moses said to Pharaoh.[16]

Similarly one finds concerning Samuel that when God commanded him to anoint David, Samuel said to God (I Sam. 16:2), "If Saul hears of it he will kill me." Then God answered him, "Take a heifer with you and say, 'I have come to sacrifice to the LORD'." So here also God wisely charged Moses, "WHEN YOU FREE THE PEOPLE, this is what you could say to him."[17]

---

[15]I.e. what Moses is supposed to say to Pharaoh.

[16]This interpretation--that God's second answer to Moses provided him with the wording that he should use when speaking to Pharaoh--appears to be unique to Rashbam. See NJPSC which sees here " a subtle hint to Moses on how to handle the negotiations with the Egyptian authorities." See Rashbam's comm. to 19:2 where it appears that Rashbam is saying that the Israelites really did come and worship God at this same mountain when they came to the theophany at Mount Sinai.

[17]Here Rashbam addresses the question of the deception involved in the claim to Pharaoh that the Jews were not requesting the right to emigrate but simply wanted to go sacrifice to God in the desert and then come back. Rashbam cites the comparable example of the deceptive wording that God tells Samuel to use when dealing with another unreasonable monarch, King Saul. The deception involved in I Sam. 16 is cited already in the Yevamot 65b as proof that it is permissible and even desirable to lie for a good purpose. Kasher (p. 161, note 235) cites a midrash which derives the principle that one may lie for a good purpose (שמשנין בדברי שלום) from God's instruction here to Moses to deceive Pharaoh.

Rashbam may be interested in this issue because of his contact with Christian exegetes who were often very troubled by passages in the Bible that suggest that lying is ever justified. See e.g. the discusssion in Childs, pp. 23-24, of the way that Christian exegetes over the centuries were troubled by the question of how the midwives could have been rewarded for lying (1:19-21). Rashbam's contemporary, JBS, is sufficiently troubled by the question of the morality of the claim that the Israelites were simply going on a three-day journey into the desert and would return that he writes (ad 14:2 and 14:5) that that is just what they did. (Cf. Rashbam's comm. to 14:3 and my notes there.) See also N. Leibowitz, 'Iyyunim, pp. 73-5, for a discussion of the approaches of various other Jewish exegetes to the question of the morality of the deception involved in this claim.

Those who interpret these verses as referring to other matters are totally wrong.[18]

3:13 מה WHAT SHALL I SAY TO THEM?: Since I do not know and am not acquainted with your proper name.[19]

3:14-15 ויאמר GOD SAID TO MOSES: "If you do not know my name, I will tell you that my name[20] is אהיה לעולם--I [am the one who] will always be--and I can fulfil my promises.[21] Now that I have told you

---

[18]This is not the only passage where Rashbam expresses himself very strongly against his grandfather, Rashi's, commentary. See e.g. his comm. to Gen. 37:2 (p. 243, in my Genesis volume).

Rashbam's interpretation of this verse is forcefully attacked by N. Leibowitz (in her 'Iyyunim, pp. 54-56) who offers an impassioned defense of Rashi's reading. Leibowitz argues that Rashbam's interpretation of this verse illustrates well how a rationalist like Rashbam who has no use for midrash often misses the profound plain meaning of the verse (עומק פשוטו--attacking Rashbam with his own phrase; see e.g. his comm. to vs. 14).

[19]Rashi does not offer an interpretation of the phrase, "[when] they ask me 'what is His name?' what shall I say to them?" Still one can infer from Rashi's explanation of God's answer in vs. 14 that Rashi did *not* see the question in vs. 13 simply as an enquiry about God's proper name but as an enquiry about God's attributes. See also similarly Rashi's comm. to 6:3, where the phrase, "I did not make myself known to them by my name," is again explained as a reference to God's attributes, not as a simple reference to God's name. See also Sanhedrin 111a where to ask about God's name is seen as a sign of lack of faith.

Rashbam, on the other hand, says simply that Moses wanted to know what God's name was.

[20]Rashbam opposes the midrashic reading of Berakhot 9b, adopted by Rashi, LT and Sekhel Tov, according to which the phrase אהיה אשר אהיה represents a statement by God about his relationship with the Jews: God promises to be with the Jews in this and other difficult times. Rashbam sees אהיה simply as God's name, the one by which He refers to Himself.

[21]While Rashbam disputes with Rashi about the basic meaning of the question and answer here, it is interesting to note that, like Rashi, Rashbam sees in the tetragrammaton (and its variant אהיה) some reference to God's ability to fulfil the promises that he has made. See Rashi's comm. to 6:3 and see also Rashbam's comm.

EXODUS III

that my name is Ehyeh, THUS YOU SHALL SAY TO THE ISRAELITES, 'EHYEH SENT ME TO YOU'."[22]

AND GOD SAID FURTHER TO MOSES: "It is not proper that they should refer to Me by My [real] name in all their discourse, just as one does not refer to kings by their [proper] names, but rather [you should refer to Me as] 'THE LORD (YHWH) THE GOD OF YOUR FATHERS'," which is a[n appropriate] term of lordship and kingship. One refers to kings similarly [without using their proper names]: "Long live the king" (I Sam. 10:24) or "The king has ordered me on a mission" (I Sam. 21:3).[23] "THIS, the name Ehyeh, written in the first verse (14), SHALL BE MY NAME FOREVER; WHILE THE OTHER ONE, the one written in the second verse (15), the tetragrammaton, the royal name, SHALL BE MY APPELLATION FOR ALL ETERNITY."[24] This is how kings are referred to, not by their own names.

That which is written about י-ה [God's name], I shall explain in *'Atbash*:[25]

---

to 6:2, s.v. אני, and my notes there.

[22]Rashbam here opposes the second half of Rashi's interpretation of this verse, again adopted from Berakhot 9b, according to which God changed the meaning of his message to Moses between the time that he said the phrase, "*'ehyeh 'asher 'ehyeh*," and the end of the verse when He said, "*'ehyeh* sent me to you." According to Rashbam, though, the second phrase simply recapitulates the first one.

[23]Rashbam makes the same point in his comm. to Gen. 41:10 (p. 282 in my edition).

[24]While Rashbam is an exegete who often shows great sensitivity to the phenomenon of parallelism (see Kugel, *The Idea of Biblical Poetry*, pp. 176-177), here he does not interpret the two parallel stichs--"this (זה) shall be My name forever," and "this (וזה) shall be my appellation for all eternity"--as referring to the same basic idea in different language. Rather he sees them as meaning: "This one (זה)--the name אהיה-- is my real name forever, but that one (וזה)--the name י-ה-ו-ה--is the name by which people of all generations should call me." Rashbam's interpretation--that the phrase " זה . . . וזה -- this. . . and this" here refers to two separate items--appears to be unique. See also his comm. to 6:3, s.v. ושמי.

[25]*'Atbash* is a code in which one exchanges the first letter of the alphabet with the last, the second letter of the alphabet with the second last, etc . . . . So every time one wishes to write א one writes ת, and every time one wishes to write ת, one writes א; every time one wishes to write ב one writes ש, and every time one wishes to write ש one writes ב etc. The following paragraph of Rashbam's comm. is written entirely in

He calls Himself אהיה ('I am'), while we call Him יהיה ('He is'). As for the name י-ה-ו-ה, the letter *vav* substitutes for the letter *yod* [and the tetragrammaton is simply a variant of the common Hebrew word יהיה ("He is" or "He will be")], as in the phrase (Eccl. 2:22) "For what comes (הֹוֶה) to a man."[26] This is the true profound plain meaning of these verses; it should be revealed only to a select few.[27]

'Atbash. Here follows a "translation" of Rashbam's *'Atbash* into standard Hebrew orthography:
הוא קורא עצמו אהיה ואנו קורים אותו יהיה י-ה-ו-ה ויו במקום יוד כמו כי מה הוה לאדם.

[26]Where one sees that הוה is a legitimate variant of היה. So also י-ה-ו-ה should be seen as a legitimate variant of "יהיה--he will be."

Again Rashbam's interpretation, that the tetragrammaton is simply a variant of the common verb "יהיה--he will be," which in turn is simply a variant of the common verb "אהיה--I will be," appears to be unique among medievals. A somewhat convoluted variant of this reading can be found in JBS. That same interpretation can be found verbatim in the name of Joseph Qara in Gad's collection, p. 20. JBS refers to Rashbam's interpretation and rejects it based on the common practice of religious Jews, who refrain from pronouncing God's name, י-ה-ו-ה, but *do* pronounce the name/word אהיה. Following Rashbam's line of thinking, says JBS, there would be more reason to refrain from pronouncing the name אהיה, which Rashbam thinks is God's real name, the one that He calls Himself.

A similar objection to Rashbam's interpretation is raised in a strident manner (והאומר כן לא יחוה דעת"--he who says such things does not speak words of wisdom") by Y. L. Shapira in his comm., *Ha-rekhasim leviq'ah*. Shapira accuses Rashbam of hiding his face behind a mask of *'Atbash*, which any fool could figure out (וילט פניו בא"ת ב"ש שגם אוילים לא יטעו בו).

Still, Rashbam's interpretation is adopted by such moderns as Greenberg (p. 81, note 2: "This explanation of Rashbam's represents correctly the view of the biblical author") and Cassuto.

[27]Rashbam shows deference to the tradition that knowledge about the tetragrammaton should not be passed on to everyone. See Qiddushin 71a and other sources cited by Kasher, p. 155, note 200.

EXODUS III

3:18 אלהי THE GOD OF THE HEBREWS (העברים): Since they came from the other side (מעברי) of the river,[28] they have to worship the god of their own realm.[29]

3:19 ואני YET I KNOW: Do not lose courage over the fact that he will not, initially, listen to My words and let them go. It is not because of *his* strong arm;[30] he has no power against Me. Rather it is I who will harden his heart in order to stretch out My hand[31] against him first, so that all will know that I have the upper hand and they will know through My wonders that I am the LORD and that I have the power.[32]

3:22 ושאלה EACH WOMAN SHALL REQUEST FROM HER NEIGHBOR: [שאל here means to request] as an outright and absolute gift. That is why it says (vs. 21), "I shall dispose the Egyptians

---

[28]Rashbam explains the word העברים similarly in his comm. to Gen. 43:32. See my notes there, p. 305.

[29]Rashbam here shows sensitivity to the fact that this divine epithet, "The LORD, the God of the Hebrews," appears "exclusively in the Exodus stories, invariably in connection with addressing the pharaoh and always coupled with a demand for permission to worship in the wilderness." (NJPSC) He explains that the epithet is particularly fitting in that context: the request to leave the country in order to worship God is more easily understood if the Jews and their God are portrayed as exotic Hebrews with customs different from those of Egypt.
See also Rashbam's comm. to 5:2 and 5:3 and my notes there.

[30]Explaining the phrase ולא ביד חזקה in this verse.

[31]ידי (vs. 20). See also iE, longer comm., who also points out the literary play here between the description of Pharaoh's hand and of God's hand.

[32]The phrase ולא ביד חזקה at the end of vs. 19 is a difficult one. Rashi interprets it as meaning that Pharaoh will not let you go "unless (ולא) God uses His strong arm (ביד חזקה)." At the end of Rashi's comment on the verse he mentions the interpretation that Rashbam offers here (introduced by Rashi by the phrase ויש מפרשים) and Rashi writes that he heard this interpretation in the name of Rabbi Jacob ben Rabbi Menahem. So also iE, longer comm. This interpretation may also have been offered already by Onq., although there are questions about what the proper reading of Onq. on this verse is. See Luzzatto's comm., here.

favorably to the people."[33] Similarly [שאל means to request as an outright gift, not to borrow, in the verse] (Ps. 2:8) "Request (שאל) it of me and I shall make the nations your domain."

This interpretation is the true plain meaning of the verse and an appropriate rebuttal[34] for the heretics.[35]

---

[33] Rashbam argues that in order to get the Egyptians to *lend* items to the Israelites, divine aid would not have been required; God had to intervene and dispose the Egyptians favorably to the Israelites' request because the Israelites were asking for outright gifts.

[34] E. Touitou argues ("The Meaning of *teshuvat ha-minim* in the Writings of our French Masters," *Sinai* 99 [1986], pp. 144-148) that the word תשובה in the phrase תשובת המינים need not always mean "rebuttal." He shows well that it can also be used to describe a polemical argument that was not offered to rebut an opponent's position. Here, though, it seems clear to me that a rebuttal is what Rashbam is offering.

[35] Rashbam's primary purpose in this comment is to defend the Jews who left Egypt against the charge of immoral conduct for deceiving the Egyptians by claiming to "borrow" items which they never intended to return. Christian anti-Jewish polemicists often raised the issue of the supposed traditional immorality of Jewish behavior. iE, in his longer comm. here also mentions the fact that medieval Jews were attacked for the supposed immoral behavior of their forefathers reflected in this verse. In fact, an echo of criticism of the Jews for stealing the wealth of the Egyptians can be found in a Talmudic story about Alexander the Great (Sanhedrin 91a) and it would seem clear that Philo and Josephus also tried to defend the Jews against such an accusation. (See N. Leibowitz, *'Iyyunim*, pp. 130-131.)

While iE attempts to solve the moral dilemma simply by saying that no action may be deemed immoral if God commanded it, Rashbam, following in the footsteps of Saadiah and ibn Janah (*Sefer ha-shorashim*, s.v. ש-א-ל), attempts a linguistic solution. (See also Rashbam ad 12:36, s.v. וישאילום, and my notes there, and Rashbam ad 11:2.) His claim that the verb ש-א-ל should be seen as meaning "to request," not "to borrow," has been dismissed as apologetics by such later Jewish scholars as Mendelssohn (ad 11:2) and Luzzatto. In fact, Avraham Grossman ("The Jewish Christian Polemic and Jewish Biblical Exegesis in Twelfth Century France," *Zion* 51 [1986] 53-4) cites this comment of Rashbam as proof that even an exegete as dedicated to *peshat* as Rashbam would be willing to offer an obviously far-fetched interpretation when he needed to do so for polemical reasons. Still this interpretation has been accepted as a reasonable reading by such moderns as BDB, NJPSC and Greenberg.

EXODUS III

כלי OBJECTS OF SILVER AND GOLD: Ornaments in honor of the festival that you will celebrate in the wilderness.[36]

ושמתם AND YOU SHALL PUT: them[37] ON YOUR SONS.

---

[36]See JBS who also connects the ornaments of this verse with the festival mentioned in vs. 18.

[37]Rashbam supplies the missing word אותם, which seems to be demanded by the syntax. See similarly Mendelssohn.

EXODUS IV

4:9 והיו המים: The repetition in this verse[1] is similar to the repetition in (Ps. 93:3) "The ocean *sounds*, O LORD, the ocean *sounds* its thunder," or (Ps. 94:3) "*How long* shall the wicked, O LORD, *how long* shall the wicked exult."[2]

4:10 כי כבד פה וכבד לשון אנכי: "I am not an expert in speaking the Egyptian language fluently, for I ran away from there when I was young and now I am eighty years old."[3]

---

[1]The fact that the word והיו is repeated in the phrase והיו המים אשר תקח מן היאר (literally "and *they shall be*, the waters that you take from the Nile, *they shall be* blood").

[2]Rashbam identifies these verses in Psalms and a number of other biblical verses of poetry as being examples of what modern scholars call "ladder parallelism" or "repetitive parallelism." See Kugel, *The Idea of Biblical Poetry*, pp. 35 and 173-177 and Rashbam's comm. to Gen. 49:22 and my notes, there, p. 376. The fact that Rashbam also sees the doubling of the word "והיו--they shall be" in this verse, a prose verse, as being an example of the same phenomenon seems somewhat forced. The simpler explanation is that the verb is repeated here for clarity after the somewhat long subject, המים אשר תקח מן היאר--"the waters that you take from the Nile." See the comm. of Nahm. here, who, basing himself on "בעלי הלשון--the linguists," (presumably a reference to ibn Janah, *Sefer ha-riqmah*, p. 296) classifies our verse together with a number of other prose biblical passages where the subject is repeated for various reasons including because of some long interruption (בעבור מיצוע ארוך שבא ביניהם). See also Jouon 176b, note 2.

In any case, Rashbam is opposing the interpretation offered by Rashi who argues that some change in meaning results from the repetition of the word והיו. Rashbam argues that the repetition is simply part of the common literary style used in the Bible.

[3]See also iE in his shorter comm., who explains the phrase כבד לשון in a similar manner. However, in his longer comm., iE argues against the interpretation offered here by Rashbam. See the discussion by E. Margaliot, in *Sefer 'Asaf*, p. 361 and p. 367, where he cites this text as proof that iE read Rashbam's comm. after he had written his

So we find also in Ezekiel that such a phrase [as כבד לשון] is used to describe someone who does not speak the language of the realm well. It is written there (3:4-6): "Then He said to me, 'Mortal, go to the house of Israel and repeat My very words to them. For you are sent not to a people of unintelligible speech and difficult language (כבדי לשון) . . . . Not to many peoples of unintelligible speech and difficult language (כבדי לשון), whose talk you cannot understand . . .'."

Could one imagine that a prophet whom God singled out, face to face[4] and who received the Torah in his hands directly from God's hand used to stutter?![5] This [legend, about Moses stuttering,] is not to be found in the words of the *tanna'im* or the *'amora'im* and no attention should be paid to apocryphal works.[6]

---

shorter comm. on Exodus but before he wrote his longer comm. See also Simon's arguments against Margaliot in *Bar Ilan Annual*, 3, p. 133.

Most exegetes, including Rashi, explain the phrase as a statement about Moses' lack of ability as a speaker, either as a result of some speech impediment or because of a lack of rhetorical polish.

[4]See Dt. 34:10.

[5]The major target of Rashbam's criticism here is the legend that Moses stuttered as a result of an event that occurred in his childhood when an angel, in an attempt to save Moses' life, caused Moses to put a burning coal into his mouth. Rashbam may be perturbed that LT, in his comm. to this verse, cites that legend, which Rashbam sees as apocryphal.

Y.L. Shapira, in his comm. *Ha-rekhasim leviq'ah* attacks many aspects of Rashbam's interpretation of this verse, including Rashbam's assertion that there would be something amiss in God asking a person with a handicap to lead the Jews.

[6]The primary source of this legend is in the midrash entitled *Divre ha-yamim de-moshe rabbenu*. Rosin notes (in RSBM, p. 63 and in the introduction to his edition of Rashbam's comm., pp. xxv-xxvi) the inconsistency in Rashbam's approach. Ad Num. 12:1, when Rashbam liked the interpretation offered by that midrashic work, he quoted it and adopted it. Here, on the other hand, he dismisses the work as unreliable and unauthoritative.

Talmage has argued (in *Parshanut ha-miqra' ha-yehudit: pirqe mavo'*, edited by M. Greenberg, pp. 108-109) that a passage such as this proves that Rashbam was influenced by Christian Bible exegesis and its tendency to canonize great biblical figures such as Moses. That, according to Talmage, explains the inconsistency here. In his comm. to Numbers, Rashbam cites a story that redounds to Moses' greater glory from *Divre ha-yamim de-moshe rabbenu*. Here Rashbam pretends to reject any midrash from *Divre ha-yamim de-moshe rabbenu*, when really his objection is to this particular

EXODUS IV

4:13 ביד תשלח: [Send] through the hand of whomever you would like, but not through me.[7]

4:14 ויחר אף THE LORD BECAME ANGRY: According to the plain meaning of Scripture, here also a perceivable effect ensued from God's anger, as it says below (vs. 24), "The LORD encountered him and sought to kill him," as I explained concerning the text when Jacob was limping on his hip.[8]

---

midrash, which diminishes from Moses' honor.

Rashbam's exegetical approach to Moses is then understood in two very different ways by Talmage and Touitou. As cited above a number of times (e.g. in notes above ad 2:1), Touitou argues that Rashbam's approach to the Moses story must be seen as a reaction *against* the tendencies of Christian exegesis. Talmage says that Rashbam is *positively* influenced by contemporaneous Christian exegesis about Moses.

For more information on the sources of the legend alluded to by Rashbam here, see Buber's notes to LT, here.

[7]Rashbam's comment opposes both interpretations offered by Rashi. Rashi's first interpretation (following Tanh. B. *Shemot* 24; so also LT, Sekhel Tov and both comms. of iE) is that the phrase ביד תשלח means "through the hands of the person that you *usually* send," and refers to Moses' brother, Aaron. Rashi's second interpretation is closer to that of Rashbam. Both explain that ביד תשלח means "through the hands of whoever you wish to send," but Rashi (following PDRE 40) adds a midrashic element to his comment, saying that Moses was expressing dissatisfaction with the fact that the redemption that he was to accomplish would be an incomplete one. Rashbam interprets the phrase simply as another statement of Moses' desire that somebody else, or perhaps anybody else (see JBS and Nahm.), be given the assignment. So also NJPS; see Orlinsky, *Notes*.

[8]In his comm. to Gen. 32:29. There Rashbam explains explicitly that he is opposing the Talmudic discussion of this verse (Zev. 102a), cited by Rashi, here in Exodus. The Talmud suggests that at first blush it appears that God's anger (חרון אף) has no perceivable effect (עושה רושם) in this verse. Then it suggests that the real effect was that, as a punishment to Moses, Aaron received a greater role in the leadership of the Jews than what had originally been planned. Rashbam says that the perceivable effect that resulted from God's anger is described below in vs. 24: "God encountered him and sought to kill him." Rashbam both here and in Genesis uses the Talmud's own language, חרון אף עושה רושם--"a perceivable effect ensued from God's anger," to oppose the Talmudic explanation.

כי דבר ידבר הוא HE, I KNOW, SPEAKS READILY: He grew up there and he has good fluency in the Egyptian language.[9]

4:16 ודבר הוא לך AND HE SHALL SPEAK לך: On your behalf.[10]

תהיה YOU WILL PLAY THE ROLE OF אלוהים FOR HIM: The role of a chief and ruler;[11] whatever you command him, he will do.[12]

See at greater length Rashbam's comm. to Gen. 32:29 and my notes, there (pp. 209-210). See also iE's strident criticism, in his longer comm. to this verse, of the explanation that Rashbam offers here. iE's comment that this verse is *not* similar either to the Jacob story or the Balaam story is a clear reference to Rashbam's explanation in his comm. to Genesis where the three passages are compared. See E. Margaliot's discussion of this dispute in *Sefer 'Asaf*, p. 361

At the same time as opposing the common rabbinic understanding of God's anger, this interpretation of Rashbam also opposes the accepted rabbinic interpretation of why it was that God (or the angel) wanted to kill Moses. See Rashbam's comm. and notes below ad vs. 24.

[9]The phrase could mean either that "he will become the official speaker" or that "he is a good orator." Rashbam opts for the second alternative and connects this verse to Moses' concerns about his inability to speak Egyptian properly. See comm. above ad vs. 10.

[10]I.e. the words דבר . . . לך do not mean "speak *to* you" in this verse, as they usually do.
So also Rashi, at greater length.

[11]שר ושופט. Rashbam uses in a positive context the sarcastic language of the "offender" in 2:14.

[12]Again Rashbam's explanation is basically the same as that of Rashi for this difficult passage where the word אלוהים is used to describe Moses' role vis-à-vis Aaron. Cf. iE (longer comm. only) who suggests that Moses is being compared to an angel in this passage.

4:18 וישב MOSES WENT BACK: from the wilderness TO HIS FATHER-IN-LAW JETHER.[13]

4:19 ויאמר THE LORD SAID TO MOSES IN MIDIAN: He had settled there in Midian after he ran away from Pharaoh, as it is written (Ex. 2:15), "Moses fled from Pharaoh and settled in Midian." Now, in Midian, God said to him, "Return, for that Pharaoh who sought your life and the other slanderers have died." That is why it says above, after Moses ran away, that "the king of Egypt died" (2:23).[14]

---

[13]Rashbam may be opposing the midrash in SR 4:4 according to which Moses, after speaking to God, first went to Egypt ("וילך משה--Moses went") and then later returned to Midian to his father-in-law ("וישב אל יתר חותנו--[Moses] returned to his father-in-law Jether"). Rashbam explains more simply that Moses "returned" to Midian not from Egypt but from the wilderness, where he had been speaking with God.

[14]Rashbam's interpretation opposes that of Rashi (following Nedarim 64b) that the reference here to the death of Moses' pursuers is actually a reference to Dathan and Abiram, who, according to this midrash, had not really died but had become very poor. Rashbam's simpler explanation here reiterates in shorter format his long comment to Ex. 2:23.

4:24 ויפגשהו THE LORD: I.e. the angel, ENCOUNTERED HIM [AND SOUGHT TO KILL HIM].[15] For he was dawdling on the way and taking his wife and children along.[16]

4:25 צר: [means something sharp,] as in the phrase (Josh. 5:2), "sharp knives (חרבות צורים)." [It means] a sharpened blade or a sharp knife. Similarly [that is the meaning of the word צור] in the phrase (Ps. 89:44), "You have turned back the blade (צור) of his sword," i.e. the sharp part of his blade became crooked and bent, and that is how (*ibid.*) "you have not sustained him in battle."[17]

ותכרת AND CUT OFF HER SON'S FORESKIN: This good deed (מצוה) was efficacious to save Moses' life. [It can be understood

---

[15] Back in his comm. to 3:4, Rashbam explains that the tetragrammaton (YHWH) was being used to describe an angel, not God, who was conversing with Moses. That conversation continued through chapter three and most of chapter four. Rashbam also explains (ad 4:14) that the anger (חרון אף) of YHWH (i.e. the angel) was aroused against Moses when he refused to follow the road set out for him. Now Rashbam explains that it is that same angel who seeks to take Moses' life here.

Onq. and LXX also write here that it was an angel, not the LORD Himself, who sought to take Moses' life. (There is no reason to think that Rashbam was aware of LXX's reading.) From the continuation of Rashi's commentary to this pericope it would appear that he also saw the threat to Moses' life as coming from an angel. See e.g. Rashi's comm. to vs. 26, s.v. וירף.

[16] As stated above ad 4:14, Rashbam saw the main reason that the angel was attacking Moses as being that Moses did not fulfil God's requests in a timely manner. Rashbam is reworking a Talmudic idea (Nedarim 32a), adapting it to his own theory. The Talmud argues that Moses was punished for dawdling in the performance of the commandment of circumcision. Rashbam says that he was dawdling in his performance of the commandment of returning to Egypt to set the Jews free.

[17] Rashbam, living so many years after the Iron Age began, is probably uncomfortable with the explanation that Zipporah used a rock to preform a circumcision. He explains that צר need not mean rock or stone, but may simply be a reference to anything sharp. So similarly JBS and also iE, in both his comms., with the exact same two prooftexts.

Even many of those commentators who see here a reference to circumcision with a rock still write that, in other biblical pasages, צר can mean "a sharp item." See e.g. Qimhi, *Sefer Ha-shorashim*, s.v. צור and BDB, s.v. צ-ר-ר V.

EXODUS IV 49

somewhat] like the sacrifices offered by Gideon[18] and Manoah[19] after an angel appeared to them.[20]

וַתַּגַּע: is a *hifil* form, but וַיִּגַּע, in the phrase (Job 1:19), "it struck (ויגע) the four corners of the house," is a *qal* form of the root נ-ג-ע.[21]

---

[18]Judges 6.

[19]Judges 13.

[20]Rashbam explains that the idea of this passage is that Moses was saved through the merit of the performance of a good deed and/or the expiating power of the spilling of some blood. Rashbam compares our passage to two others where an angel appears, some concern about the impending death of the person who saw the angel is raised (Jud. 6:23 and 13:22), a sacrifice is offered (i.e. a good deed is performed) and no one dies.
Rashbam may see a further connection between our passage and the two stories in Judges. In all three stories there is initial hesitation or at least doubt about accepting a task from God. Perhaps Rashbam then feels that in all three stories the concerns about dying are because of not having accepted God's task immediately. Then the sacrifice (or circumcision) expiates for the sin of hesitation and as a result no one dies. See also the way Rashbam compares the story of the commission of Moses with the story of the commission of Gideon in his comm. above ad 3:11-12. See also my notes there.
In general, Rashbam's comment here should be seen as opposed to the midrashic tradition (e.g. Nedarim 31b-32a) adopted by Rashi (s.v. ויבקש) and most other Jewish exegetes according to which Moses was being punished for not circumcising his son in a timely manner.

[21]Rashbam's grammatical explanation is clear and not controversial. He often gives his readers instructions about how to tell the difference between *qal* and *hifil* forms. See e.g. his comm. to Gen. 26:26 and Ex. 2:7, 2:10 and 15:22 and his grammar book, p. 36.

לרגליו [TOUCHED HIS]: i.e. Moses'[22] LEGS, to appease the angel in that way. For I do not want to interpret that she touched the angel's legs, for who knows whether she saw the angel's legs?[23]

כי YOU ARE TRULY A BRIDEGROOM OF BLOOD: He will remain my bridegroom (חתני) because of the blood.[24] חתני means my husband.[25]

---

[22]PT Nedarim (3:9) offers three interpretations for the ambiguous phrase, "touched his legs": either that she touched Moses' legs or that she touched the angel's legs or that she touched her son's legs. Rashi, LT, Rashbam and iE all opt for the interpretation that it was Moses' legs. Ps.-Jon. and Targum Yerushalmi interpret that it was the angel's feet and Samuel ben Hofni, quoted in iE's longer comm., says that it was her son's legs.

[23]Rashbam is not arguing that angels never have legs that can be seen, for very often Rashbam interprets passages in such a way that an angel is appearing in the form of a man. See e.g. his comm. to Gen. 18. He is simply saying that angels do not always appear in human form and that there is no reason to assume that the angel here did. On the level of sophistication of Rashbam's theory of angels, see Rosin, RSBM, p. 116.

[24]The phrase, "you are a חתן of blood," is an extremely difficult one. It is not clear what it means or even whether Zipporah said it to her son or to her husband. (Both possiblities are discussed in PT Nedarim 3:9). See e.g. JBS who sees the חתן of the verse as Moses and interprets the word "דמים--blood" as meaning "someone who is liable for the death penalty."

The more common position of the Jewish exegetes (Rashi, iE, Samuel ben Hofni cited by iE) is that the phrase is addressed by Zipporah to her son and the sentence is to be understood in the subjunctive mood: "you are a חתן who would have caused the death (דמים) of your father because you were not circumcised" or "you, my son, would have caused the death of my husband (חתן) because you were not circumcised."

This interpretation cannot be offered by Rashbam for he does not accept the idea that the lack of circumcision is what brought on the problem in this scene. He therefore explains the verse in a manner quite similar to Onq., that Zipporah is addressing Moses and telling him that he will remain her husband (חתן) because of the expiating blood (דמים) that was just now touched to his feet. Among moderns, Cassuto interprets the verse that way.

[25]Rashbam is opposing the reading of חתני as meaning "my son" that one finds in Nedarim 32a and in PT Nedarim 3:9 and in a number of medieval exegetes. NJPSC labels that interpretation conceivable but considers the evidence for it "meager."

EXODUS IV

4:26 וירף AND HE: the angel,[26] LET HIM ALONE. From [the root ר-פ-ה, the same root as in the phrase] "the day is waning (רָפָה) toward evening" (Jud. 19:9), one says וַיִּרֶף, just as from [the root] ק-נ-ה, one says וַיִּקֶן.[27]

אז SHE ADDED, "A BRIDEGROOM OF BLOOD BECAUSE OF THE CIRCUMCISION." It was because of the delay in circumcision that my husband was deemed worthy to die, for [one can see] now [that] it was the circumcision that saved him.[28]

4:27 לך GO TO MEET MOSES IN THE WILDERNESS: [God told Aaron to go meet Moses] in order to fulfil what God had told him [Moses], "He is setting out to meet you and he will be happy to see you" (4:14).

---

[26] So also Rashi.

[27] E.g. Gen. 33:19. Rashbam often comments on the fact that a *segol* vowel appears in the final syllable of the *vav*-consecutive imperfect of some final-*heh* verbs. See his comm. to Gen 1:22, s.v. ירב, and other sources cited in my notes there, p. 50.
  Both in his remarks about the root of the verb וירף and in his remark about its subject Rashbam may be arguing with the reading of LT who seems to have understood the word וירף as meaning that Moses was healed, as if the verb were from the root ר-פ-א, "to heal."

[28] So also Rashi.
  It is difficult to understand why Rashbam seems here to be abandoning the way that he has interpreted this pericope until now and adopting the more traditional reading. Until now (ad Gen. 32:29 and Ex. 4:14 and 4:24) Rashbam explained that Moses was being attacked for hesitating and dawdling when God asked him to go to Egypt and free the Israelites. Now he seems to say that Zipporah discovered at this point that the real reason that Moses was attacked was that he had failed to perform the circumcision in a timely manner. One wonders if the last few words of Rashbam's interpretation of this verse may be an addition from some later hand.

EXODUS V

5:2 מי WHO IS THE LORD THAT I SHOULD HEED HIM AND LET ISRAEL: who are my servants, **GO** from my country to serve Him? What claim does He have on this people that they should serve Him?[1]

5:3 ויאמרו THEY ANSWERED, "THE GOD OF THE HEBREWS . . .": In other words, the Israelites came here to live from the other side of the river[2] and this [God] is the God of the people from the other side of the river. They are His people and they have to worship Him, **LEST HE STRIKE US . . . .**[3]

5:4 תפריעו: means to interrupt or to separate and move apart, as in the phrase (Num. 5:18), "he shall loosen the braids (ופרע) of the woman's hair."[4]

---

[1] Rashbam may be opposing the midrashic tradition (e.g. Tanh. B. *Va'era'* 2) cited by LT and Sekhel Tov on this verse that Pharaoh searched through all his books about religion before declaring that he did not know who God was. Rashbam explains the verse not as a theological statement but as a question about property rights. The slaves, Pharaoh asserts, belong to me. Why does the LORD think that he has some claim on them?

Through this explanation of Pharaoh's question, Moses and Aaron's non-theological answer in vs. 3 becomes more understandable. Pharaoh asks what claim the LORD has on the Israelites and he receives the answer that they originate from His territory, the other side of the river, and that they owe Him allegiance.

[2] See Rashbam's comm. to 3:18 and my notes there.

[3] See Rashbam's comm. to 3:18 and to 5:2 and my notes there.

[4] Rashbam has a different explanation of the root פ-ר-ע than the one offered by Rashi in this verse. They both see פ-ר-ע as being connected to the idea of separation but Rashi sees the root as often having a nuance of separating something that is disgusting and worthy of being held apart. Rashbam's explanation, on the other hand, imputes no

לסבלותיכם: to your work. [The verse as a whole means:] "Do not be idle from your own business and do not cause other people to be idle from performing my work."[5]

5:6 הנגשים THE TASKMASTERS: are in charge of the overseers (שוטרים) [who are directly in charge of the workers]. Similarly in the phrase (Deut. 16:18) "magistrates and overseers," the magistrates (שופטים) are appointed to give orders to the overseers (שוטרים) whose job it is to enforce among the people[6] the magistrates' orders.[7]

---

negative nuances to the root פ-ר-ע. The difference between their positions becomes clearest when they interpret the phrase כי פרוע הוא, below ad 32:25. See Rashi, Rashbam and notes there.

Rashbam's understanding of the verb ופרע in Numbers is the same as that of Sotah 8a, cited also by Rashi ad Num. 5:18. See however Rashi there and ad Ex. 32:25 where Rashi emphasizes that the untieing of the braids is a form of uncovering and a sign of degradation; accordingly the root פ-ר-ע, with its negative connotations, is appropriately used in Numbers 5. For Rashbam, though, the untieing of the braids is described by the root פ-ר-ע only because it is a type of separating.

[5]Rashbam appears to be opposing the common midrashic tradition (e.g. Tanh. B. Va'era' 4) cited by Rashi and LT in their commentaries to this verse, according to which the tribe of Levi, including Moses and Aaron, did not have to participate in the slave labor of the Israelites in Egypt. Rashbam, on the other hand, emphasizes that Pharaoh in this verse is concerned both about the work that Moses and Aaron are not performing themselves and about the possible effect that Moses and Aaron might have on other Israelites to keep them from their work. See also iE's longer comm. to this verse where he too opposes that tradition of exegesis.

[6]רודים בעם, using the same language that Rashi used in his definition of a שוטר, in his comm. to Deut. 16:18.

[7]The idea that the שוטרים should be seen as lower ranking officials whose job it is to enforce the decisions of the higher ranking officials is a common interpretation among Jewish exegetes (e.g. Rashi here and in Deut.16, LT and iE here) and among moderns (e.g. BDB s.v. שטר: "appar. subordinate officer"). Rashbam seems to have been the first exegete to draw attention to the similarity between the status of the שוטרים in this passage and in the passage in Deut. Rashbam also differs from the other medieval Jewish exegetes who almost all write that the שוטרים were Jews but the נוגשים were Egyptians. (See e.g. Rashi, iE and LT; so also NJPSC and Greenberg.) There is no hint in Rashbam's comm. about the nationality of those two groups.

EXODUS V

5:7 לתת תבן PROVIDE STRAW: They would mix straw with mortar and make bricks that way.[8]

5:8 מתכונת: means "total."[9]

כי נרפים הם FOR THEY ARE SHIRKERS: and they are capable of doing more.[10]

5:9 ישעו: *Attendent* in Old French.[11] Just like (Gen. 4:4), "paid heed (שעה) to Cain," or (Is. 17:8) "they shall not turn (ישעו) to the altars."[12]

5:11 כי אין נגרע THERE IS NO DECREASE: נגרָע is written with a *qames* because it is present tense. (It is a passive form and means the

---

[8]Rashbam's comment is, from a content point of view, identical to Rashi's. The major difference is that Rashbam uses the Hebrew word--חומר, perhaps because it is the more common biblical word for mortar. Rashi uses the more common later Hebrew word--טיט. טיט in the Bible generally means mud or something filthy; only twice in the Bible, in poetic passages, does it appear to mean "mortar." See BDB, s.v. טיט.

[9]Or "amount." So also Rashi, at much greater length, and most other exegetes. See also Rashi and Rashbam ad Ex. 30:32.

[10]NJPS's translation, "shirkers," follows Rashbam; see Orlinsky, *Notes*.

[11]איטנדאנט. "Let them not hope" or "let them not depend." Cf. JBS who offers the translation אנטרנטא, which appears to be a form of the French verb, *tourner*, "to turn." It is possible, though, that Rashbam and JBS both said the same thing (they did both cite Gen. 4:4 as a prooftext) and that one of the two texts that reached us is corrupt.

[12]Rashi explains at great length why he refuses to interpret the verb ישעו here as connected to the standard meaning of turning towards or depending upon. Nevertheless Rashbam, without any explanation, adopts the reading that his grandfather found unacceptable.
  Rashbam's interpretation is not his innovation; it can be found in ibn Janah's *Sefer ha-shorashim*, s.v. שעה, and is quoted, unapprovingly, by iE in his shorter comm. in the name of "יש אומרים--some say." It is also the way that most moderns understand the verb. See e.g. the long discussion by Mendelssohn.

same as גָּרוּעַ.) If נגרע were written with a *pataḥ*[13] it would be a past tense form.[14] Similarly נִשְׁגָּב[15] with a *qameṣ* [is a present tense form] while נשׁגב[16] with a *pataḥ* is a past tense verb. If נגרע in this verse were a past tense form, the verse would have to read כי לא נגרע.[17]

5:13 אצים: means pressing and hurrying [them along].[18] Similarly (Gen. 19:15), "the angels urged (ויאיצו)."[19]

---

[13]As in Lev. 27:18.

[14]The grammatical point made by Rashbam is not controversial. He makes the same point again concerning the verb נָתַן) in his comm. to vs. 16. Before Rashbam, the point was made concerning the verb form in our verse by ibn Janah, SH, s.v. גרע. Rashbam's explanation appears to be drawn out. Perhaps that is what prompted iE to write tersely in his longer comm. that the *qameṣ* here is simply what one would expect.

[15]E.g. in Is. 12:4.

[16]E.g. Is. 2:11.

[17]Rashbam is saying that this verse proves that a form like נגרָע must be considered a present tense form. We know that, in biblical Hebrew, noun clauses (i.e. "the present tense") are negated by the word אין, while the past tense is negated by the word לא. (See G.-K. 152.) The fact that the word אין is used in this verse may be seen as proof that the form נגרָע must be a present tense form.

[18]So also Rashi, here and ad Gen. 19:15.

[19]It is possible that Rashbam compares the two verses because of the anomalous use of the *qal* here in a transitive context. All other uses of the *qal* of the root א-ו-צ in the Bible have an intransitive meaning; they mean to hurry up, not to hurry someone else along. Rashbam may be saying that the *qal* form here has to be understood like the *hifil* form in Genesis 19. See similarly iE's longer commentary. Cf. Sekhel Tov who compares the verb form in this verse to three other uses of the root א-ו-צ in the *qal* in the Bible, none of which has the same nuance of meaning that אצים in our verse has.

5:16 תבן NO STRAW IS ISSUED: נִתָּן is written with a *qames*; it means that it *is* not given to us. But נֻתַּן with a *patah* is a past tense form, as in (Eccl. 10:6), "Folly *was* placed (נִתַּן)."[20]

וחטאת עמך: If the form is to be read[21] וְחָטָאת, with a *dagesh* and a *qames*, then one should explain it as follows: "we are being beaten and an injustice (חטאת) is being done [to us] by your people." However, if the text had read וְחַטָּאת, with a *patah*, then one could explain it as being [two nouns in the construct state]: "the sin of (חַטָּאת) your people."[22]

---

[20]See similarly Rashbam's comm. to vs. 11 above and my note, there.

[21]Rashbam discusses two possible ways of reading the word: וְחָטָאת or וְחַטָּאת, and seems to express a preference for the first reading. Neither of these readings is the one found in our MT. It would appear also that Rashi had the same textual variant as Rashbam in his Bible. See the discussion in RSBM, p. 59, note 2 and in Esh, *Textus 5* (1966), 86. See also BH, who offers Rashbam's vocalization as one of his proposed emendations to the verse.

[22]There is much similarity between Rashi's comment and Rashbam's comment on this form. Both of them consider but dismiss the reading וְחַטָּאת, and do so using the same language, "אילו היה--if [the text] had." They both read the text וְחָטָאת, and they both add a few words to the text in order to make the phrase וְחָטָאת עמך meaningful. There is a slight difference between them in the meaning that they apply to the phrase. Rashi sees חָטָאת as meaning "guilt" and would render the phrase: "[this action brings] guilt [to] your people." Rashbam, on the other hand, sees חָטָאת as meaning "injustice" and would render the phrase: "your people [are doing] an injustice."

In the commentary to Eccl. (ad 7:7) attributed to Rashbam, there is a different understanding of our phrase in Exodus ("the people are called 'sin'"; trans. of Japhet-Salters) than the one recorded here. There has been much discussion of whether the "contradiction" between these two explanations constitutes evidence that the Eccl. comm. was not penned by Rashbam. See Japhet-Salters' Hebrew introduction to their edition of the Eccl. comm., p. 20, and the literature cited there. Z. Ben-Chaim (*Tarbiz* 47, 247-248) emends the text of Rashbam's comment here and concludes that there is no difference between what Rashbam wrote here and in the Eccl. comm.

Most other Jewish exegetes offer different interpretations of this text, based on seeing MT's text, וְחַטָּאת as a verb form. See e.g. ibn Janah, SH, s.v. ח-ט-א, and iE. In his longer commentary, iE makes what may be a veiled reference to Rashbam's comm. when he writes "ואין צורך לשום דגש בטי"ת--there is no reason for there to be a *dagesh* in the letter *tet.*"

5:22 וישב MOSES RETURNED: to the place where God had been speaking to him.[23]

לָמָה: [has stress on the last syllable and has no *dagesh* in the *mem*] because it precedes [a word that begins with] the letter *heh*.[24]

למה הריעותה לעם הזה WHY DID YOU BRING HARM UPON THIS PEOPLE: And if You would answer that [You brought harm upon them because] they are deserving of punishment because of their many sins and they do not deserve to be redeemed, in that case WHY DID YOU SEND ME, if they are not worthy to be redeemed and saved?[25]

---

[23] Rashbam is offering a more *peshaṭ*-like version of the standard midrashic approach (e.g. LT here and Rashi ad 9:29) that Moses had to leave the city any time he wanted to talk to God because there was too much idolatry going on in the city itself. Rashbam says more simply that Moses returned to the spot where he had just been speaking with God. See also Rashbam's comm. below to 6:2, s.v. וידבר.
   Mendelssohn adopts Rashbam's explanation of this verse verbatim.

[24] Rashbam refers correctly to the rule that למה has the stress moved to the final syllable and the dagesh dropped from the *mem* when the next word begins with the letter *heh* (or *'alef* or *'ayin*). See G.-K. 102l. Rosin (RSBM, p. 131, note 5) notes also that knowledge of this rule can be seen also in a ms. of Qara's comm. to I Sam. 19:17 (not in our standard editions of Qara's comm.).

[25] Rashi also attempts to provide the link between Moses' first and second questions in this verse. According to Rashi the connection is: "Why did you bring harm to this people? And if you ask what business it is of mine, then I retort 'why did you send me?'." (So also LT and see similarly JBS.) Rashbam opposes Rashi's attempted link and offers one of his own. Again Mendelssohn adopts Rashbam's explanation of this phrase.
   Rashbam also opposes Sekhel Tov's attempt to see the second question, "Why did you send me?" as a criticism of the Jewish people. In other words, Sekhel Tov interprets the question as being, "Why did you send me to such a difficult and obstinate people?"

EXODUS VI

6:1 כי ביד חזקה ישלחם WITH A STRONG ARM HE WILL SEND THEM OUT: Pharaoh will eventually chase the Jews away from his country whether they want to leave or not, as it is written (Ex. 12:33), "The Egyptians pressed the people strongly to hurry and leave the land."[1]

6:2 וידבר GOD SPOKE TO MOSES: in the land of Egypt.[2]

אני I AM THE LORD: And the meaning of My name is that I am able to fulfil what I promise.[3]

---

[1] Rashbam, Rashi (in one explanation) and JBS offer the novel interpretation that the strong arm (יד חזקה) of this verse is Pharaoh's. Pharaoh will force the Israelites to leave, whether they want to or not, with his strong arm. Generally other exegetes see this "strong arm," like all other instances of the phrase here in Exodus, as a reference to God's strong arm.

Rosin suggests (footnote 5) that Rashbam's comment is actually about the second phrase, "with a strong arm he will drive them from his land," not about the first phrase, "with a strong arm he will send them out." Rosin writes that even Rashbam sees the first "strong arm" of this verse as a reference to God's power. See Rashi's commentary where that distinction is made explicitly.

Alternatively it might be the case that Rashbam's comment should be read as our manuscripts have it, as an explanation of the first phrase, "with a strong arm he will send them out." If that is the case then Rashbam should be seen as going one step further than Rashi. Rashi saw only the second יד חזקה of this verse as a reference to Pharaoh's power while Rashbam saw them both that way. The verse does have a poetic nature and Rashbam, who is more sensitive to the phenomenon of parallelism, may be more willing than Rashi to see the two stichs of the line as repeating the same idea. On the other hand, see Luzzatto's defense of the poetic sensitivity of Rashi's reading.

[2] Rashbam apparently continues to make the same point that he made above ad 5:22, s.v. וישב, that it is not necessary to say that Moses left any specific Egyptian territory when he communicated with God.

[3] As noted above (ad 3:14), Rashbam accepts Rashi's interpretation that the primary meaning of the tetragrammaton is that God is able to fulfil his promises. The meaning of verse three, then, is that God has not yet showed Himself as being YHWH because

6:3 באל [I APPEARED . . .] AS EL SHADDAI: I made promises about the future and I did not keep them yet.[4]

ושמי MY NAME YHWH: This is how the verse should be interpreted:[5] "I appeared to them with My Name El Shaddai, although My true name is YHWH." Then the verse repeats that same idea with the words לא נודעתי להם, i.e. "I did not appear to them with My true name, only with the name El Shaddai. But to you I revealed My true name, אהיה,

---

he hasn't yet fulfilled the promises that he made to the forefathers. Rashi (in his comm. to vs. 9) attributes this interpretation of the tetragrammaton to Rabbi Baruch b. Eliezer who cited Jer. 16:21 as proof. See similarly Noth's comm., here, "The new thing which the new divine name signifies is this, that God now means to fulfil the promises which are still outstanding . . . ." (See Nahm.'s criticism of this understanding of the tetragrammaton in his comm. here.)

[4]As pointed out in the previous note, Rashbam is following Rashi's interpretation of this verse. God is seen as saying that, when He appeared to the forefathers using the name El Shaddai, He made many promises but He has not yet demonstrated the quality that is connected to His name YHWH, the quality of keeping His promises.

A reason that the name El Shaddai is connected by Rashi and Rashbam with the making of promises to the forefathers may be that the three times that the name appears connected with a theophany in Genesis, the theophany involves promises by God about a glorious future that has not yet been achieved.

[5]The exegetical problem of the verse is that the phrase ושמי ה' לא נודעתי להם seems to imply that God never appeared to the forefathers using His official name, the tetragrammaton, but a number of verses in Genesis (e.g. 15:7 and 28:13) have God speaking to one of the forefathers and calling Himself by the tetragrammaton. Rashi's solution is to say that the phrase ושמי ה' לא נודעתי להם actually does not refer to the name that God used when speaking to the forefathers but rather to the qualities that He showed to them when He appeared to them. See NJPSC which continues to offer this suggestion and offers the same prooftext (Jer. 16:21) which Rashi cites. (See previous note.) For other modern scholars who see here a reference to God's qualities, not His name, see N. Leibovitz, 'Iyyunim, p. 98, note 1.

Rashi explains in his comm. to vs. 9 that his explanation of the opening verses of this chapter should be seen as opposed to the midrashic understanding of these verses in Sanhedrin 111a. Rashbam's comm. here, which is simply a version of Rashi's, should also then be seen as opposed to that understanding.

and my appellation, YHWH,[6] and in your days I will fulfil My promise to give them the land of Canaan.[7]

---

[6]See Rashbam's comm. to 3:14-15 where he explains that the two stichs of the poetic line, "This shall be My name forever/This shall be My appellation for all eternity," refer respectively to the two names of God, אהיה and YHWH.

[7]Rashbam is now interpreting the opening words of vs. 4 as meaning that God is promising that He *will now fulfil* (והקימותי) the words of the covenant that He already made with the forefathers (בריתי אתם).

Rashbam's interpretation of this phrase appears to be unique. Almost all other exegetes see הקימותי as meaning that God *established* (in the past) a covenant with Abraham, Isaac and Jacob. Rashbam surprisingly interprets this perfect form as a reference to an action in the future.

There may be a number of reasons for this unusual interpretation. First, the previous verses imply that something special is happening now that never happened in the past. The subsequent verses imply that something special is going to begin to happen now. In the middle of these references to current and future events a reference to an event in the distant past (making the covenant with the forefathers) seems misplaced.

Secondly, it may be that Rashbam, like Cassuto (here and ad Gen. 6:18; see also his *The "Quaestio" of the Book of Genesis*, [Heb.], p. 99), was not happy with seeing the phrase להקים ברית as being synonymous with the phrase לכרות ברית (to *make* a covenant). Cassuto argues that the phrase להקים ברית must be seen as meaning to fulfil or to ratify a covenant that already exists. He does not follow Rashbam's reading entirely here as he prefers the suggestion that God is here ratifying (in the present or perhaps in the not too distant past; see 2:24) the covenant that he had made long ago with Abraham, Isaac and Jacob. But Cassuto does support a different syntactical reading of the verse. He writes that the word אתם should *not* be read as connected to הקימותי ("I established My covenant *with them*") but rather as connected to בריתי, yielding the phrase בריתי אתם ("I now ratify בריתי אתם--my [old] covenant made with them [the forefathers]"). This syntactical understanding also presumably underlies Rashbam's reading. (Cf. Sekhel Tov who also sees here a distinction between הקימותי and כרתי, and writes that God fulfils or ratifies אתם--with the Jews of Moses' days--that covenant that he had made before with the forefathers.)

Cassuto also argues (here and ad Gen. 6:18) that the word ברית can be seen as a synonym for הבטחה, a promise. That is precisely the word that Rashbam uses in his paraphrase of the verse ("I will fulfil my promise--אקיים הבטחתי").

The words ושמי ה' must be read together with the first part of the verse, as I explained. If the verse read לא הודעתי להם,[8] then the words ושמי ה' would be read forward as connected to לא הודעתי.[9]

6:9 ולא שמעו THEY WOULD NOT LISTEN TO MOSES: now, even though they had believed in the beginning, as it says (4:31), "The people believed." They had expected that they would have respite from their cruel bondage but now their load had become even greater.[10]

---

[8] Instead of לא נודעתי להם.

[9] In essence Rashbam's explanation of vs. 3 is an "improved" version of Rashi's commentary. Both say that the true meaning of the verse is that God never appeared to the forefathers as one who fulfils His promises, the quality that is inherent in His name, the tetragrammaton. Both draw attention to the fact that the verse reads לא נודעתי, not לא הודעתי. Rashi derives from that fact the claim that the verse is not referring to God revealing (הודעתי) a new name but making a new quality known (נודעתי). Rashbam accepts all that, but is still not pleased with the syntax of the verse as explained by Rashi. As Nahm. later noted, Rashi's explanation does not fit well into the words of the verse, for it looks as if Rashi is seeing the words ושמי ה' as a direct object of the *nifal* verb נודעתי.

Rashbam tries to reach the same conclusion as Rashi by a very different syntactical understanding of the verse. The verse has two parts: (1) וארא אל . . . ושמי ה' which means "I appeared to the forefathers using the name El Shaddai, even though My name is YHWH." Then the verse reiterates the same idea with the words (2) לא נודעתי להם which means "I did not really make myself fully known to them." See Nahm.'s comm. where he hesitatingly suggests that maybe even Rashi was reading the verse using that syntactical division.

JBS offers a similar syntactical reading of the verse. He suggests that the words וארא אל . . . ושמי ה' mean that God appeared to the forefathers using both the name El Shaddai *and* the tetragrammaton. Then the words לא נודעתי להם express an entirely new idea.

The suggestion of Rashbam and JBS that the major pause in the verse should be seen as coming after the word ה' seems to ignore the cantillation signs. (The *'etnahta'* can be found before the phrase ושמי ה'.) Cf. however JBS who suggests that the cantillation can support such a division and so also Sekhel Tov.

[10] A number of exegetes attempt to deal with the apparent contradiction between our verse and 4:31. (See e.g. iE's longer comm. and Nahm.) Rashbam suggests that the problem was not a lack of belief. His remarks may be directed against the midrash (Mekhilta *Pisha'* 5) that, when explaining this verse, says that the Jews were so addicted to idolatry that they did not wish to listen to Moses. See also Sekhel Tov's comm. to this verse where he refers to the Israelites as people of little faith (קטני אמנה).

EXODUS VI

6:14 אלה **THE FOLLOWING ARE THE HEADS OF THEIR RESPECTIVE CLANS:** The Mekhilta[11] explains that the text now provides the genealogies of [only] those three tribes that Jacob had censured just before he died[12] in order to teach us that those tribes are still important. According to the plain meaning of Scripture, [this genealogy is provided in a partial manner because] the text had to get as far as Moses and Aaron and as far as Korah and the sons of Uzziel and Phinehas in order that the reader should know who they all are when they are mentioned below in the Torah.[13]

6:16 ושני חיי לוי **AND THE SPAN OF LEVI'S LIFE:** [The information about the lifespans of the various people listed here is provided] according to the plain explanation that I gave in [my commentary to]

---

[11]The explanation that Rashbam cites here is a common midrashic tradition but it is not found in our texts of the Mekhilta. For sources of this midrash and for a discussion of the possibility that Rashbam was alluding to the *Mekhilta derabbi Shimon bar Yoḥai*, see Kasher, p.19, note 82.

[12]Jacob's "blessings" of his sons from his deathbed (Genesis 49) are not all positive. Reuben, Simeon and Levi received more censure than blessing from their father (vss. 3-7).

[13]Rashbam explains the problem of the partial genealogy here by referring to his exegetical principle of anticipation. The reader needs to know the identity of the various characters who will appear in later stories in the Torah and so is provided with a limited genealogy which gives information about the descent of only those characters who will later play a role. Exodus 6:14-25 should be seen as akin to being the *dramatis personae* of the Torah. See Rashbam's comm. to vs. 18 below where he expands on this explanation.

On anticipation in general in Rashbam's comm., see Genesis volume, pp. 400-421.

JBS (in his comm. to vs. 13, s.v. ויצום) quotes Rashbam's explanation in his name. A similar explanation to Rashbam's can also be found in iE, but only in his longer comm., the commentary that he apparently wrote after reading or at least hearing about Rashbam's comm. (See Margaliot, "*Ha-yaḥas* . . .," and Simon, "*Ledarko ha-parshanit* . . . .") Among moderns, Cassuto and Greenberg cite Rashbam's solution approvingly.

Genesis:[14] the text lists the years of all the generations until Noah[15] and then the years from Noah until Abraham;[16] after Abraham,[17] Isaac's years[18] and then Jacob's years[19] and then his son, Levi,[20] and then Kohath[21] and then Amram[22] and then Moses[23] and then Joshua[24] and the Judges[25] and the kings[26] and the seventy years of the

---

[14] Presumably in his comm. to Gen. 5. While Rashbam's comm. to the opening chapters of Genesis is lost, Rosin reconstructs in his edition of Rashbam's comm. (pp. 10-11) what Rashbam probably wrote in his comm. to Gen. 5:31, based on a number of medieval sources that quote or paraphrase Rashbam's views about why so many genealogies--and particularly the genealogies of evildoers--are provided in Genesis. The principle enunciated there is that enough information is provided to enable the reader to calculate the age of the world. If we know the lifespan of one person who lived in each generation and we know how old he was when his son was born then it will be possible to figure out the chronolgy of the world. See similarly Driver, *Genesis*, p. 75: "The aim of the writer is . . . to give a picture . . . also of the duration of the first period of the history."

[15] Gen. 5.

[16] Gen. 11:10-26.

[17] Gen. 21:5 and 25:7.

[18] Gen. 25:26 and 35:28.

[19] Gen. 47:28.

[20] Ex. 6:16.

[21] Ex. 6:18.

[22] Ex. 6:20.

[23] Deut. 34:7.

[24] Josh. 24:29.

[25] E.g. Judges 3:11.

[26] E.g. I Kings 11:42.

EXODUS VI

Babylonian exile[27] and then the years of the second temple[28] in the book of Daniel.[29]

6:18 ובני THE SONS OF KOHATH: AMRAM, IZHAR, HEBRON AND UZZIEL: The text lists the descendants for three children of Kohath--Amram, Izhar and Uzziel--but nor for the fourth one, Hebron. Should you attempt to explain that [no sons are listed here for Hebron because] he had no sons, [one cannot make that claim because] in Numbers (26:58) there is a reference to "the clan of the Hebronites." So

---

[27] Jer. 25:11 and passim.

[28] See Rosin's reconstruction of Rashbam's comm. to Gen. 5:31 where Rashbam interprets the phrase שָׁבֻעִים שִׁבְעִים in Dan. 9:24 as meaning 490 years--seventy years of exile and 420 years that the second temple ostensibly stood. See Nazir 32b and Rashi there, s.v. והא כתיב.

[29] Rashbam's approach appears to be that it is common biblical style to list the lifespans of some person from each generation. Presumably this is done in order to help the reader calculate precisely how long various events took. His approach differs from that of JBS and that of Rashi. JBS writes that the lifespans of Levi, Kohath and Amram are listed in honor of their descendants, Moses and Aaron. (So also iE, longer comm. only.) Rashi writes (ad vs. 18) that all that one can learn from the lifespans listed here is that the "four hundred years" of enslavement (predicted in Gen. 15:13) must refer to some period (including but) greater than the Israelite sojourn in Egypt. The combined lifespans of Kohath (who was born in Canaan; see Gen. 46:11), Amram and Moses total less than four hundred years and, as Rashi points out, Kohath and Amram's lives, it can reasonably be assumed, must overlap somewhat, and so also must Amram's and Moses'. Rashi also claims (in his comm. to vs. 16) that the information about the lifespan of Levi is significant because it tells us when the enslavement began, because as long as any one descendant of Jacob was alive the enslavement, according to the midrash (Seder Olam 3), had not yet begun.

It is hard to understand what Rashbam means by his comm. to this verse. Since we do not know how old Levi was when Kohath was born nor how old Kohath was when Amram was born nor how old Amram was when Moses was born it is difficult to see how the information contained here in chapter 6 helps the reader figure out a precise chronology of the events. Rashi's approach (ad vs. 18) appears to make more sense here: that all that one can deduce from the chronological information provided here is what "four hundred years" does *not* mean. It does *not* mean that the sojourn in Egypt lasted that long. Any precise information about how long the Jews *did* spend in Egypt will have to come from a source other than Exodus 6.

why are the sons of Hebron not listed here? [It must be] because they are never mentioned below in the Torah by name.

But the sons of the other three--Amram, Izhar and Uzziel--*are* mentioned. The sons of Amram [have to be listed here (vs. 20) because of] Moses, Aaron and Miriam. The sons of Izhar [have to be listed here (vs. 21) because of] Korah [who is mentioned below in the Torah,] as it is written (Num. 16:1) "Korah the son of Izhar . . . betook himself." The sons of Uzziel [have to be listed here (vs. 22) because of] Mishael and Elzaphan [who are mentioned below in the Torah,] as it is written (Lev. 10:4), "Moses called Mishael and Elzapahan, sons of Uzziel the uncle of Aaron."

"The sons of Korah: Assir and Elkanah" (vs. 24) [are listed here] because [they are alluded to later in the Torah, as] it is written (Num. 26:11) "The sons of Korah, however, did not die."

The sons of Aaron [have to be listed here (vs. 23)] because it is written below (24:1), "Come up to the LORD, with Aaron, Nadab and Abihu."

And [the sons of] Eleazar, the son of Aaron, [had to be listed here (vs. 25) because of Phineas the son of Eleazar.[30]

But the children of Itamar are not listed here since there will be no reason to mention them later in the Torah.[31]

6:26-27 הוא IT IS THE SAME AARON AND MOSES: This Aaron, about whom it was just written that he was born before Moses, and this Moses are the ones TO WHOM THE LORD SAID . . . . IT WAS THEY WHO SPOKE TO PHARAOH . . . THESE ARE THE SAME

---

[30]Who is mentioned a number of times in the Torah; see e.g. Num. 25:11.

[31]Rashbam continues the theme that he first began in his comm. to vs. 14. He explains in detail why each of the elements of the partial genealogy of the Levites provided in this chapter is necessary in order to introduce a character who will later play a role in the Torah.

The final point that Rashbam makes, that the text does *not* list any descendants of Itamar, is illustrative of this principle. It can be seen from other biblical books that Itamar *did* have children. (See e.g. I Chron. 24:3.) Hizkuni, following Rashbam's line of thought, explains that there was also no reason for the text to provide a list of descendants for Moses or Hebron since their children played no further roles in the Torah narratives.

MOSES (who, when it comes to questions of communication,[32] is listed first) AND AARON.

When reference is being made to their birth order, Aaron is listed first. When reference is made to their communicative roles, the text puts Moses before Aaron.[33]

6:30 ואיך HOW THEN SHOULD PHARAOH HEED ME: This section (vss. 28-30) is simply a repetition of the previous section (vss. 10-12), [where Moses' answer begins with the words] "The Israelites would not listen to me . . .." [It was necessary for the text to describe the same conversation between God and Moses a second time because] above the text wrote [about that conversation between God and Moses] in a condensed form until it could explain who were the "heads of the respective clans" (vs. 14f.), so that we would know who Moses and Aaron, who spoke to Pharaoh, were.[34]

---

[32] הדיבור. It is not clear to me whether Rashbam is referring to the role of Moses and Aaron in *receiving* communication from God (a common use of the word דיבור) or to their role in *passing on* the messages from God to Pharaoh (an explanation that would fit in better with the context of vs. 27). Perhaps the reference is to both.

[33] Almost all the classical commentators address the question of why the text, in vs. 26, lists Aaron before Moses but in vs. 27 it uses the opposite order. Rashbam opposes the midrashic answer (e.g. Mekhilta *Pisḥa'* 1 [Lauterbach ed., p. 2] and Tosefta Keritot 4) adopted by Rashi, LT, Sekhel Tov and others, according to which the purpose of that alternation is to teach the reader that Moses and Aaron are of equal merit. Rashbam's explanation is that the text chose the appropriate order for the context of each verse. See similarly iE, in both his longer and shorter commentaries.

[34] Almost all exegetes, ancient and modern, deal with the question of the apparent repetition of the same material in vss. 10-12 and then again in vss. 28-30. While some exegetes (like LT and the יש אומרים quoted by iE in his shorter commentary) see here another discrete speech of Moses attempting to avoid the task placed upon him, almost all classical Jewish commentators see vss. 28-30 as repeating material from vss.10-12 because of the principle of repetitive resumption. See similarly to Rashbam, Rashi, iE, and JBS. See also Childs, p. 117: "The genealogy had interrupted the narrative in vs. 12. In order to pick up the broken thread the author, following a common Old Testament practice, recapitulates a bit of his story (28ff.) before continuing with his narrative."

See Touitou (*Tarbiz* 56 [1987], 225) who argues that the comment of Rashi to vs. 30 in most printed editions of Rashi's comm. did not come from Rashi's pen but was added from Rashbam's commentary into Rashi's commentary by a copyist.

EXODUS VII

7:1 נביאך: means a speaker (דברן) instead of you.[1]

7:2 ושלח TO LET THE ISRAELITES DEPART: I.e. Aaron will tell him to let the Israelites leave his country.[2]

---

[1] The references in this verse, both to Moses as an אלוהים and to Aaron as his נביא (generally rendered "prophet"), trouble the classical Jewish interpreters. Rashbam has already dealt with the question of the reference to Moses as an אלוהים in his comm. to 4:16. Unlike Rashi, Rashbam does not repeat that interpretation here.

But the reference to Aaron serving as Moses' נביא remains troubling, for it again seems to impute some divine status to Moses. Rashbam, JBS and Rashi basically all follow the same line of interpretation when they suggest that נביא means "spokesman" here. (So also NJPSC.) This interpretation is based in part on seeing 7:1 as parallel in meaning to 4:16: "He shall serve as your spokesman (לפה), with you playing the role of אלהים to him."

iE, only in his longer comm., argues at length against the interpretation offered here by Rashbam. See Margaliot, p. 362, who notes that iE appears to be quoting Rashbam's comm.: מה טעם . . . אם פירושו דברן --what would be the meaning . . . if it [נביא] is interpreted as spokesman (דברן)." But see Simon's reservations in his "Ledarko ha-parshanit," p. 131f.

See also Rashbam's comm. to Gen. 20:7, s.v. כי, and notes there, pp. 81-2, and see comm. and notes below ad Ex. 15:20, s.v הנביאה.

[2] Rashbam's problem is a syntactical one. The phrase, ידבר אל פרעה ושלח את בני ישראל מארצו, can be understood to mean: "Aaron will speak to Pharaoh and Pharaoh will then let the Israelites go." From the immediate context here and from the continuation of the narrative, that is not what the verse means. Rashbam therefore explains that ושלח should be seen as having the force of an infinitive form: "Aaron will tell Pharaoh *to let* the Israelites go."

Rashbam's interpretation may be meant to oppose that of Sekhel Tov who implies that ושלח is to be understood as an indicative verb. According to Sekhel Tov the last phrase of this verse is a promise from God that Pharaoh will eventually let the Israelites go, willy-nilly. It is noteworthy that both Rashbam and Sekhel Tov misquote the verse the same way: וישלח (instead of MT's ושלח), a reading that is, as far as my research has gone, otherwise unattested.

7:5 וידעו מצרים THE EGYPTIANS SHALL KNOW THAT I AM THE LORD: I.e. that I am the master and the ruler.[3] For until now they have been saying (5:2), "I do not know the LORD."[4]

7:13 ויחזק PHARAOH'S HEART STIFFENED: He believed that even what Aaron had done[5] was done through sorcery.[6]

7:14 כבד: "Pharaoh is stiffening his heart," as I explained above. Intransitive verbs have [in the imperfect] forms like וַיִּשְׁמַן (e.g. Deut. 32:15), וַיִּכְבַּד (e.g. Ex. 9:7), וַיִּשְׁפַּל, (e.g. Is. 2:9), וַיִּזְקַן (e.g. II Chr. 24:15) and וַיֵּחָכַם (e.g. IK 5:11).[7] And in the past tense [i.e. in the perfect] one says זָקֵן (e.g. Gen. 18:12), כָּבֵד (e.g. here), שָׁמֵן (e.g. Hab. 1:16), and שָׁפֵל as in the phrase (Is. 2:17) "And the pride of man brought low (שָׁפֵל)"; they are all on the פָּעֵל paradigm.[8]

---

[3]Rashbam offers, presumably based on context, an interpretation of the tetragrammaton that is different from the interpretation that he offered in his comm. to 3:14, s.v. ויאמר, and in his comm. to 6:2, s.v. אני.

[4]See also Rashbam's comm. to vs. 17 below and ad 9:15-16 and ad 12:12. Rashbam repeats this idea more than once as he realizes the significance of the question of "knowledge" here in the opening chapters of Exodus. See NJPSC here and ad 1:8 and see N. Leibowitz, 'Iyyunim, pp. 124-125.

The connection between this verse and 5:2 is also made by LT and Sekhel Tov, who also continue throughout their commentaries to emphasize the importance of the "knowledge of God" theme in the story of the plagues.

[5]Just like what Pharaoh's magicians did (vs .11).

[6]See similarly iE, in his longer comm. only.

[7]I.e. intransitive verbs generally have a *patah* in the last syllable of the *qal* imperfect, not a *holam*. See G.-K. 47h.

[8]Rashbam is opposing Rashi's comm. on this verse. Rashi, following Onq., sees כבד here as an adjective. Rashbam insists that it is a verb form, the standard perfect *qal* form for an intransitive verb. (See G.-K. 43a.) So also iE, only in his longer comm. That part of Rashbam's explanation is reasonable and logical.

However, the opening line of Rashbam's comm. here is difficult for two reasons. First, in his comm. to vs. 23 Rashbam distinguishes between Pharaoh's heart

EXODUS VII

7:15 הנה HE IS COMING OUT TO THE WATER: The way that noblemen go strolling in the morning and go riding here and there.⁹

7:17 בזאת BY THIS YOU SHALL KNOW THAT I AM THE LORD: For you previously said (5:2), "I do not know the LORD."¹⁰

7:18 ונלאו THE EGYPTIANS WILL FIND IT IMPOSSIBLE: I already explained in the story of Lot that the verb ונלאו is always synonymous with לא יוכלו--they will not be able to.¹¹ *Enoy* in the vernacular.¹²

---

stiffening on its own and Pharaoh actively stiffening his own heart. There it is clear that he feels that in our verse Pharaoh's heart stiffened on its own. So as Rosin points out (note 5) it does not make sense for Rashbam to write here that Pharaoh actively stiffened his own heart. Secondly, it is difficult to know what Rashbam meant by the statement, "as I explained above." If the reference is to his grammatical explanation here, it cannot be found in his comm. above (although it can be found below in his comm. to 12:39 and in his grammar book, p. 43). Rosin's explanation that the reference is to Rashbam's comm. to 1:7 does not seem to be to the point.

⁹Rashbam opposes the midrashic explanation quoted by Rashi (from Tanh. *Va'era'* 14) according to which Pharaoh would sneak out to the river in the morning to relieve himself when no one was looking so that he could claim that he was a god who never had to relieve himself. (So also LT and Sekhel Tov.) Rashbam explains more simply that people of the leisure class often stroll by the river in the morning and that is why God suggested to Moses that that would be the best place to find Pharaoh. See similarly JBS who provides a more colorful description of what aristocrats do when strolling along the riverside.

¹⁰So also LT and the gloss in JBS. See similarly Rashbam's comm. to vs. 5.

¹¹Rashbam opposes Rashi's reading (so also Sekhel Tov, here and ad vs. 24) which would see ונלאו as meaning "to become tired," i.e. that the Egyptians would become tired out from all their efforts to find good drinking water. Most moderns follow Rashbam's understanding; see NJPS; "will find it impossible," and see Orlinsky, *Notes*.

In his comm. to Gen. 19:11 Rashbam draws his primary proof for his interpretation of the meaning of the root ל-א-ה from the verse here in Exodus. Rashbam there notes that this phrase--ונלאו מצרים--must be seen as equivalent to the phrase in vs. 21, "ולא יכלו מצרים"--the Egyptians will be unable." Accordingly ונלאו must mean "to be unable." See Rashbam's arguments and proofs at greater length in his comm. to Gen. 19:11 and see notes there, pp. 74-5.

7:20 לעיני פרעה [AARON . . . LIFTED UP HIS ARM AND STRUCK THE WATER IN THE NILE] IN THE SIGHT OF PHARAOH: This was to Moses' honor, that Aaron, Moses' emissary, was the one who always lifted the rod and used it for striking.[13]

7:21 מתה DIED: The word מתה has penultimate stress here as it is in the past tense.[14] But מתה in the phrase (Gen. 30:1), "I shall die (מתה)," has stress on the ultima because it refers to the future.[15] מתה

---

[12]A form of the modern French word, *ennui*. "Difficulty" in English.

[13]Rashbam opposes the midrash cited by Rashi (from Tanh. *Va'era'* 14) in his comm. to vs. 19 and then again in Rashi's comm. to 8:12 that claims that it would not have been appropriate for Moses to strike the Nile or the dust of Egypt himself and that that is why such actions had to be done by Aaron. According to the midrash and Rashi, it would have been inappropriate for Moses to strike the Nile because the Nile had protected him when he was hidden in it as a baby (2:3) and it would have been inappropriate for him to strike the dust of Egypt because the dust had protected him when he killed the Egyptian and buried his body (2:12). Rashbam, on the other hand, explains more simply that the physical tasks were not assigned to the leader, Moses, but rather to his underling, Aaron.

The midrash is apparently reacting to the fact that Aaron's role of striking something with a rod is mentioned only in the first three plagues, the ones that involved striking the Nile or the earth of Egypt. In order to dissociate himself from that approach Rashbam emphasizes that it was *generally* (תדיר) Aaron who did such things. Presumably Rashbam feels that after the text explicitly described Aaron's role in the first three plagues the reader is to infer that Aaron had such a role also in later plagues.

For other approaches to the question of why Aaron has a clearly defined role only in the first three plagues, see iE, longer comm. to 8:12 and see Philo, *Life of Moses* I, 97 (Loeb edition: volume 6, 324-326).

[14]I.e. the perfect.

[15]I.e. because it is a present participle that in that verse has the nuance of a future verb.

EXODUS VII

in the phrase (Gen. 48:7), "Rachel died (מתה) to my sorrow," has penultimate stress because it is in the past tense.[16]

7:23 גם לזאת [PAYING NO REGARD] EVEN TO THIS: [The reason the phrase "*even* to this" is written is because this is the second time that Pharaoh's heart stiffened on its own,] for already it occurred once (vs. 13) that "Pharaoh's heart stiffened" [on its own] and here also (in vs. 22) his heart stiffened on its own. But concerning the plague of frogs it is written (8:11) "stiffening (וְהַכְבֵּד) his heart" because he himself consciously decided to stiffen his own heart. And that is why it says concerning the plague of wolves[17] (8:28), "Pharaoh stiffened (וַיַּכְבֵּד) his heart this time *also*," for he had already stiffened his heart one time before that.[18]

---

[16] I.e. in the perfect. Rashbam made this same point in his comm. to Gen. 30:1. Both here and there Rashbam's comment can be seen as opposed to Sekhel Tov's who, both here and in Genesis 30, attempts to offer a different and quite dubious distinction between the meanings of מתה with ultimate and penultimate stress. According to Sekhel Tov, מתה with ultimate stress means that someone really did die ("מתה ממש") but with penultimate stress it means that someone was close to death ("קרובה למות") or ("אכתי לא מתה לגמרי"). On מתה as meaning "in the process of dying," see also Mekhilta *Beshallaḥ* 7 (Laut. ed. p. 250) and Midrash Shemuel 11. However, only Sekhel Tov distinguishes between the meanings of מתה with ultimate and with penultimate stress.

[17] See Rashbam's interpretation of the word ערוב in his comm. to 8:17 below.

[18] A common tradition of interpretation, first found in Tanh. *Va'era'* 3, notes that there is a progression: in the first five plagues Pharaoh stiffens his own heart but then in the last five plagues God stiffens Pharaoh's heart. Rashbam, though, offers his own explanation of the progression involved. In the events of chapter 7, Pharaoh's heart naturally stiffened itself; he was simply not moved by the miraculous events that he witnessed. In chapter 8 he *is* moved by the miracles but he forces himself to stiffen his heart. Rashbam bases this explanation on the fact that *qal* verbs (כבד and שת, וַיֶּחֱזַק) are used to describe Pharaoh's intransigence in chapter 7 but afterwards *hifil* verbs (like והכבד) are used. (See also Driver who notes the same distinction in his comm. to 7:13.) He may be opposing the opinion of LT (ad 8:6) and Sekhel Tov (ad 8:11) who claim that the *hifil* form in 8:11 implies that God was the one who stiffened Pharaoh's heart already then, after the second plague.

See also Rashbam's interpretation below ad 8:11 and ad 8:28 and see also notes above ad 7:14. Rashbam's distinction between the natural stiffening of Pharaoh's heart

RASHBAM

7:25 שבעת ימים WHEN SEVEN DAYS HAD PASSED: That was the length of the plague of the Nile.[19]

7:26 ויאמר THE LORD SAID TO MOSES, "GO TO PHARAOH": Moses would warn Pharaoh for two plagues and then for the third one he would not warn him. That order continues throughout the plagues. Each third plague has no warning. For the plagues of "blood" and "frogs" Moses provided warnings;[20] for "lice" he did not. For the plagues of "wolves" and "pestilence" Moses provided warnings;[21] for "boils" he did not. For the plagues of "hail" and "locust" Moses provided warnings;[22] for "darkness" he did not.[23]

---

and a conscious decision by Pharaoh to stiffen his own heart appears to be unique.

[19] Rashbam apparently opposes the opinion of a number of midrashim (e.g. Tanh. Va'era' 13) adopted by LT (ad 8:10) and Sekhel Tov (and later by Bahya and Gersonides) according to which one can learn from this verse that *all* of the plagues lasted one week. Presumably Rashi also feels that way, and when he writes in his comm. to this verse שהיתה המכה משמשת רביע חודש he means that *all* of the plagues lasted for "a quarter of a month," i.e. for a week. Gur 'Aryeh also explains Rashi's position that way.

Rashbam also opposes the alternate midrashic explanation (also found in Tanh. and in other midrashim) according to which the reference to seven days here is to a week's respite that occurred after the first plague and after all subsequent plagues.

Rashbam on the other hand says that one week is a reference to the length of the plague but only to the length of this first plague, the plague of the Nile. See similarly iE, in his longer comm. only, here and ad 9:10.

[20] Ex. 7:17 and 7:27 respectively.

[21] Ex. 8:17 and 9:3 respectively.

[22] Ex. 9:18 and 10:4 respectively.

[23] It would appear that this pattern was first discovered by LT; see his comm. to 8:15 (חשבתי בלבי לומר על אלו השלושה למה הן בלא התראה--"I thought to myself, 'why did these three plagues have no warnings attached to them?'"). In fact the language of Rashbam's comment follows that of LT almost verbatim. However LT adds a "halakhic" explanation to the pattern, arguing that our text follows the principle enunciated in Sanhedrin 9:5 that after two crimes are committed for which the perpetrator received

EXODUS VII

7:27 נֹגֵף PLAGUE: נֹגֵף means the same as מַכָּה.[24]

---

warnings, extraordinary measures are then allowed. Rashbam notes the pattern but does not provide a rationale. Apparently he feels that identifying a literary pattern provides enough of an explanation.

See also similarly JBS in his comm. to 8:12. Both JBS and LT argue further that the midrashic tradition (e.g. SR 5:6) that divides the plagues into three groups--plagues 1-3, plagues 4-6, and plagues 7-10 (דצ"ך עד"ש באח"ב)--is in fact an allusion to the pattern described here. (For other medieval sources that mention this pattern, see Kasher, p. 65.) See JBS's comm. to 9:8 where he notes other characteristics of the plagues that are best understood if they are seen as being in three groups of three.

Among moderns it has become common to see the plagues as presented in three groups of three and to expand upon the characteristics of these groups as first noted by LT, JBS and Rashbam. See e.g. NJPSC, p. 38. Moderns who wish to argue for the literary integrity of the plague cycle, as opposed to the documentary reading, often make much of the threefold pattern. See e.g. Cassuto's introduction to the plagues (pp. 92-23). Cf. Childs' criticism of this approach, p. 150.

[24]"To strike," as in 7:17. So also Rashi, at greater length. See similarly Sekhel Tov and iE, longer comm.

EXODUS VIII

8:5 התפאר עלי: means "you assume the honor over me" by asking whatever you want and I will do it. Just like [the meaning of the word יתפאר in the verse] (Jud. 7:2) "Israel might assume the honor over Me (יתפאר עלי), thinking, 'our hand has brought us victory'."[1]

למתי אעתיר לך FOR WHAT TIME SHALL I PLEAD IN BEHALF OF YOU: On what day and at what time do you want the frogs to retreat. I will pray immediately[2] that they die by that time that you request of me, for it would not be normal for them all to die at one moment.[3]

---

[1]Rashbam opposes the interpretation offered by LT, Sekhel Tov and iE (both comms.) that sees התפאר as meaning that Pharaoh will be able to get glory (תפארת) by having the frogs disappear at the precise time that he himself would choose.

The interpretation offered by Rashbam is close but not identical to that offered by Rashi. Rashi sees more of a nuance of boasting in this verse and cites Is. 10:15 as his prooftext. For Rashi, Moses is challenging Pharaoh, somewhat sarcastically, to make Moses' job as difficult as possible. Rashbam, on the other hand seems to see the phrase as "a polite address to a king" (BDB). See also NJPSC: "I defer to you."

On the difficulty of this phrase, see Childs' note, p. 128.

[2]So also Rashi and ibn Janah, *Sefer ha-riqmah*, p. 55. Both Rashi and Rashbam emphasize that למתי does not mean מתי. Moses was not asking when he should pray. It was clear that he would pray immediately. The question was only when the frogs would disappear. Cf. however Nahm. who claims that when Moses would pray, the frogs would immediately die so if the time that Pharaoh set was "tomorrow," then Moses did not pray until then. (So also iE, shorter comm., ad vs. 8.) Presumably there was some other exegete who preceded Rashbam who offered that same interpretation that Nahm. offered later. In order to argue against that reading Rashbam adds that it makes sense to assume that the frogs would not die all at one moment and that there would be some period of time between the prayer ("immediately") and the deadline (tomorrow).

[3]See also Rashbam's comm. to vs. 6 and the note there.

8:6 למחר FOR TOMORROW: Pray now that they should die by tomorrow.[4]

8:10 חמרים: means "heaps."[5]

8:11 והכבד AND HE [HIMSELF] STIFFENED HIS HEART: Since this plague was a difficult one, Pharaoh's heart did not become stiff of its own; in an evil manner he himself stiffened his heart.[6]

8:12 לכינים TO LICE: [The plural form כינים means] different kinds of lice and fleas.[7]

8:13 הכנם LICE: [The letter *mem* in הכנם is an "extra" *mem*] like the *mem* in ריקם ("emptyhanded"; Gen. 31:42).[8]

---

[4] Rashbam continues to explain the verses the way he did in the previous verse. His language is similar to Rashi's with one significant difference. While Rashi writes שיכרתו למחר ("that they should die *tomorrow*"), Rashbam writes שימותו עד מחר ("that they should die *by tomorrow*"). While his grandfather writes that the frogs will all disappear on the same day, Rashbam again emphasizes that the frogs will die over a period of time.

[5] So also Rashi, at greater length.

[6] See Rashbam's comm. to 7:23 and my notes there.

[7] Rashbam attempts to distinguish between the plural form כינים and the collective form כנם, found in the next verse. The plural form, he argues, is used to describe a number of types of lice together.

[8] Rashbam is saying that the letter *mem* should not be seen as a plural ending or as part of the root; it is simply a suffix. So also iE in both his commentaries. iE clarifies that part of the problem here is the apparent lack of agreement between the feminine verb ותהי and the noun הכנם.

Rashbam often refers to "extra" letters that are attached to words but do not serve an obvious grammatical role. See e.g his comm. to Gen. 1:24 (and notes there, p. 50), his comm. to Gen. 49:24 (and notes there, p. 381), and his comm. to Ex. 36:7. (In the last two examples, Rashbam makes reference to our verse.) See also Rosin's list

EXODUS VIII 79

8:15 אצבע אלהים היא "THIS IS THE FINGER OF GOD": I.e. [the magicians said] "this is a natural disaster and was not caused by those [i.e. by Moses and Aaron]; for if these lice came through sorcery [of Moses and Aaron], then we would be able to replicate that sorcery."[9]

8:17 הערוב: I say that ערוב means various kinds of wolves that are called ערוב because they generally go to look for prey at night,[10] as it

---

(RSBM, p. 141) of places where Rashbam considers some letters to be "extra." Rosin (footnote 9, there) traces this idea back to Menahem.

[9]The exegetes generally agree that the phrase that Rashbam is commenting on here means: "This plague is not from Moses and Aaron, but it is rather אצבע אלהים." However, there are two different ways of understanding the idea of what Pharaoh is saying in those words. The phrase could be saying: "Moses and Aaron did not do this through sorcery. God is behind it. The problem is *more* serious than we thought." Following this reading, the end of the verse, where Pharaoh's heart stiffens must be understood to say: "*Despite* what his magicians said, Pharaoh's heart stiffened." That is the way that Rashi, LT, SR, Sekhel Tov and others read the verse.

Rashbam offers a different reading. He suggests that the text means: "This plague is not from Moses and Aaron. It is a natural disaster. The problem is *less* serious than we thought." Following this reading, at the end of the verse Pharaoh logically stiffens his heart since he now believes that Moses and Aaron had nothing to do with this plague. Rashbam had written ad 7:26 that there had been no warning for the plague of lice; that would make it easier for Pharaoh to claim now that Moses and Aaron and their God had had nothing to do with this plague. Rashbam continues to deal with this theme of the connection between warnings and the interpretation of the plagues as natural disasters in his comm. below ad 8:19, s.v. למחר, and ad 9:5.

iE (in his longer comm. only) offers an interpretation very similar to Rashbam's.

Although Rashbam offers a rather different interpretation than Sekhel Tov, the language that the two writers use is strikingly similar. Sekhel Tov attributes to the magicians the words: שאילמלי ממשה ואהרן היא גם אנו היינו יכולים לעשות. Rashbam quotes the magicians as saying: שאילו באו על ידי מכשפות אף אנו היינו עושים כן.

Among moderns, Rashbam's reading is not generally favored, though it is the one used by Dillman (cited by Greenberg, p. 156).

[10]And the root of ערוב should then be seen as connected to the Hebrew word for evening, עֶרֶב.

is written (Jer. 5:6), "The wolf ravages them in the evenings (ערבות),"[11] and it is written (Zeph. 3:3) "Wolves of the evening (ערב), they leave no bone until morning."

Just as from [the noun] אודם (redness) one says אָדוֹם (red),[12] and from [the noun] עמק (valley) one says [the adjectival form] עָמוֹק (deep), so also from [the noun] ערב (evening) one says [the adjectival form] עָרוֹב, which means *nuytrener* in the vernacular.[13] Wolves are called ערוב because they are nocturnal.

עמק (valley) is a noun; the corresponding adjective[14] is עָמוֹק (deep). So also [the adjectives] אָדוֹם (red) and שָׁחוֹר (black).[15]

---

[11]While most exegetes understand ערבות in the verse in Jeremiah as a reference to "deserts," Rashbam and some other exegetes see a reference to "evening." Rashbam makes the same claim in his comm. to Gen. 49:27. See my notes there, p. 385.

[12]I.e. the adjectival form of אודם is אדום.

[13]"Nocturnal."

[14]Rashbam makes an unusual terminological choice when he uses the word המעשה here in a context where it is clear that he means "adjective." (So also Rosin, note 5.)

[15]I.e. the vowel pattern, *qames-ḥolam*, is a vowel pattern that one standardly finds for adjectival forms. (So also Jouon 87c.)

Rashbam's interpretation could be summarized as follows: When looking at a difficult word like עָרוֹב, it is reasonable to note that it has the standard vowel pattern of an adjective. Since we know that the root ע-ר-ב is connected to the meaning "evening," Rashbam argues that ערוב was originally an adjective that meant "nocturnal." Then the adjective took on the meaning of "wolf," since the wolf is a nocturnal animal. (It is not unusual for an adjective in Hebrew to be used as a noun; cf. words such as חָכָם or גָדוֹל.)

Rashbam's conclusion as to what ערוב means is not that different from most standard Jewish exegesis, which would see ערוב as meaning "wild animals" in general. His etymology though is different and apparently unique. (Cassuto in fact labels it as "unacceptable.") Almost all Jewish exegetes (Rashi, iE, Sekhel Tov and a number of midrashim) connect the word to the idea of "mixing," another one of the standard meanings of the root ע-ר-ב. Rashbam alone sees a connection to the word עֶרֶב (evening). Many moderns prefer to understand ערוב as a reference to some insect. See e.g. Luzzatto and NJPSC.

EXODUS VIII

8:18 והפליתי BUT ON THAT DAY I WILL SET APART [THE REGION OF GOSHEN]: Since, once the plague is unleashed, ferocious animals can easily go to all parts of the kingdom, it was particularly necessary in this plague, more than in other plagues, to describe the separation and distinction [between the Israelites and the Egyptians]. So also in the plague of the pestilence of the animals.[16]

8:19 ושמתי פדות AND I WILL MAKE A DISTINCTION: [פדות means "distinction."] Similarly [forms of the words] ישועה (salvation) and הצלה (saving) and חלצה (rescuing) and פרקן (deliverance)--all are related to the idea of distinguishing and separating one thing from another.[17]

למחר TOMORROW THIS SIGN SHALL COME TO PASS: [Moses said, "I am telling you in advance when the plague will occur,] so that you will not claim that it happened by accident."[18]

---

[16]Ex. 9:4. In other words, according to Rashbam in all the plagues a distinction was made between Israelites and non-Israelites even though the text does not make that distinction clear for each of the plagues. See similarly Nahm., both here and ad 9:3-4. See also Rashbam's comm. and notes ad 10:23, s.v. היה.
  Cf. iE, longer comm., here and ad 7:24 and 9:8. iE says that this is the first plague in which a distinction was made between Israelites and non-Israelites.

[17]The word פדות generally means a "ransom" or "redemption." It is clear though from the context that the meaning "distinction" is called for here. As NJPSC writes, it is not clear how פדות came to mean "distinction" here. Rashbam's comment here extends the list of verbs of "saving" that he mentioned in his comm. to Gen. 31:9, where he also argued that they all have something to do with separating. See also Rashi ad Gen. 31:16.
  Rashbam is opposing the readings of such midrashim as SR or Sekhel Tov and such exegetes as JBS who try to connect the word פדות even here to the idea of ransom and redemption.

[18]Rashbam is saying that Moses here is relating to the way that Pharaoh and his magicians had reacted to the last plague, lice. Rashbam explained above ad vs. 15 that Pharaoh and his magicians were unmoved by the plague of lice for they thought that it was just a natural disaster to which Moses and Aaron had no connection. (Also above ad 7:26 Rashbam noted that there was no warning before the plague of lice, the plague that Pharaoh decided was not from the hands of Moses and Aaron.) That then is why this time Moses tells Pharaoh ahead of time this time precisely when the plague will

8:22 כי תועבת FOR [WHAT WE SACRIFICE] IS ABHORRENT TO THE EGYPTIANS: Sheep were seen as repugnant by the Egyptians.[19]

ולא יסקלונו "WILL THEY NOT STONE US?": is to be read as [a rhetorical question] expressing incredulity.[20] [The stoning being referred to here is] in a derisive manner.[21] As it is written (II Sam. 16:13), "Shimei walked alongside[22] on the slope of the hill, insulting him as he walked and throwing stones at him and flinging dirt."[23]

---

start. See similarly Rashbam's comm to 9:5 below.

[19]Rashbam opposes the common interpretation (see e.g. Rashi, iE, JBS, Sekhel Tov) that the Egyptians worshipped sheep and that that was why it would have been unthinkable for the Israelites to sacrifice them. According to that interpretation, the word, "תועבה--abomination," in our verse is to be understood as a euphemism. What the text really means is "an Egyptian divinity," but the text calls that divinity, an abomination.

See e.g. iE: "משה כתב כן לגנות עבודה זרה"--Moses wrote [the word 'abomination'] as an insult to idolatry." In other words, when Moses was speaking to Pharaoh, he certainly did not use the word "abomination" to describe an Egyptian deity. But when Moses later recorded that speech in the Torah he insultingly labelled sheep "Egypt's abomination," instead of "Egypt's god." Rashbam, on the other hand, interprets תועבה literally, as an abomination. Rashbam makes the same point in his comm. to Gen. 43:32 and Gen. 46:34. See my notes there, pp. 305-6.

[20]בתמיה. See also the same term in Rashbam's comm. to Gen. 27:36.

[21]The stoning referred to in this verse is more readily understood according to the interpretation that Rashbam rejects, that the Egyptians venerated sheep. Then it would make sense for them to stone anyone who dared kill their deities. Rashbam then has to explain that the stoning in this verse should be seen as derisive stoning, not as a punishment for cultic impropriety.

[22]Rashbam quotes the verse as reading לעמתם instead of MT's לעמתו. See Esh, p. 88.

[23]Again Rashbam makes this same point in his comm. to Gen. 43:32.
Rashbam cites the story of Shimei which constitutes good proof that stoning can have derisive intent. However, as I noted in my Genesis volume (p. 306), the proof is weakened by the fact that the verb ס-ק-ל appears in the Shimei story in the *piel*. Here it appears in *qal*, which is used in the Bible invariably for punitive stonings.

EXODUS VIII

וְהִעְתַּרְתִּי 8:25 I WILL PLEAD: וְהַעְתַּרְתִּי is like (Num. 21:2) וְהַחֲרַמְתִּי
וְהֶחֱזַקְתָּ (Lev. 25:35) and "אֶת עָרֵיהֶם--we will proscribe their towns,"
"בּוֹ--you should hold him" and (Ob. 8) "וְהַאֲבַדְתִּי חֲכָמִים מֵאֱדוֹם--I
will make the wise vanish from Edom" and (Ezek. 26:3) וְהַעֲלֵיתִי--I
will hurl." All of these [verbs] are in the future tense[25] and [that is
why] they have *pataḥ* vowels. So also (Jer. 17:4) "וְהַעֲבַדְתִּיךָ--I will
make you a slave." This happens as a result of the [guttural] letters.[26]
But in the past tense,[27] one says (Zach. 3:4) "הֶעֱבַרְתִּי מֵעָלֶיךָ חַטָּאתֶךָ--I
have removed your guilt from you," and (Mi. 6:4) "הֶעֱלִיתִיךָ--I brought
you up," and "הֶאֱבַדְתִּי--I destroyed".[28] All of those forms have *pataḥ
qaṭan*[29] vowels.[30] However, [when the root begins] with any other

---

[24]From the context it is clear beyond doubt that Rashbam is quoting this word as if it were vocalized וְהַחֲזַקְתָּ. MT reads וְהֶחֱזַקְתָּ. Esh, p. 87, writes that no support can be found for Rashbam's reading anywhere. Esh feels confident though that "for his own textual tradition this vocalization is confirmed by the fact that he quotes it in a list of words in the MT that are vocalized with patah." Esh also includes this example in his list (p. 85, note 10) of cases where Rashbam's evidence about the existence of another manuscript reading "cannot be disputed."

See on the other hand, Urbach (*Sefer 'arugat ha-bosem*, IV, 150, cited by Esh, pp. 84-85) who argues that most medieval authors quoted verses by heart and as a result, there are numerous errors.

[25]I.e. the *vav*-consecutive of the perfect.

[26]The roots of all the above verbs begin with gutturals and that accounts for the vowel changes.

Rashbam's language here, אותיות גורמים, is somewhat clumsy and perhaps the ms. is corrupt. One should note though that Rashbam uses a form of the verb ג-ר-מ in his comm. to Gen. 34:10 and to Ex. 14:16 to describe the way that a guttural changes the expected vocalization of a verb. So also in a citation from Rashbam in *Sefer 'arugat ha-bosem* I, 44.

[27]I.e. the perfect, but not in a *vav*-consecutive construction.

[28]The form האבדתי does not appear in the Bible. Perhaps Rashbam is quoting a theoretical form; the vocalization הֶאֱבַדְתִּי would certainly be expected if the form were in the Bible. Or perhaps a small error (one extra *yod*) entered the ms. of the comm. and the text should really read "הֶאֱבַדְתָּ" ("you destroyed"), a reference to Job. 14:19.

[29]I.e. *segol*.

[non-guttural] letter, the forms always have a *ḥiriq* vowel, whether in past or in future, e.g. (Mi. 5:12) "וְהִכְרַתִּי פְסִילֶיךָ--I will destroy your idols," and (Mi. 5:13) "וְהִשְׁמַדְתִּי--I will destroy."[31]

8:28 גם בפעם הזאת [BUT PHARAOH STIFFENED HIS HEART] THIS TIME ALSO: Just as he did after the plague of frogs.[32]

---

[30] The distinction that Rashbam makes here is accepted by modern grammarians. See e.g. G.-K. 63f and 63o and Jouon 68f. Both G.-K. and Jouon note that this shift of *segol-ḥataf-segol* to *pataḥ-ḥataf-pataḥ* in a *vav*-consecutive construction is connected to the fact that the stress is generally thrown forward to the final syllable of the verb in the *vav*-consecutive forms of the perfect. In the one erroneous example that Rashbam cites, והחזקת בו, the stress is *not* thrown forward to the last syllable, because the word is followed by a tone syllable. As G.-K. notes (49m), when a tone syllable follows a perfect *vav*-consecutive form there is no consistent pattern of whether the tone will shift to the last syllable or not. This fact can help to explain why Rashbam might have not remembered the correct vocalization of והחזקת. The vocalization the way that he cites it (with *pataḥ-ḥataf-pataḥ* vowels and with stress on the final syllable of והחזקת) is distinctly within the range of possible forms.

See also Rashbam's grammar book, pp. 50-52, where he discusses many ways in which gutturals affect the vocalization. On p. 51 there he makes the same point about perfect *vav*-consecutive forms. It is noteworthy that there he does not cite the non-existent form והחזקת בו, but rather the form וְהַחֲזַקְתִּי ("I will make firm"), a form found in Ezek. 30:25. Perhaps here also in his Exodus comm., Rashbam originally wrote והחזקתי, and some copyist "improved" his text by changing it to the better known phrase in Leviticus, והחזקת בו.

[31] On the tendency of *ḥiriq* vowels to change to some other vowel before a guttural, see G.-K. 22.

[32] In other words, Pharaoh had to stiffen his own heart again after this plague because this plague was sufficiently difficult that he would naturally have been moved by it. See Rashbam's comm. to 7:23 and 8:11 above, and my notes to 7:23.

EXODUS IX

9:5 מועד לאמר [THE LORD HAS FIXED] A TIME: So that they will not say that it was a natural disaster.[1]

9:8 פיח SOOT: Thin ashes that blow (שמתנפח) in the wind.[2]

9:9 פורח BREAKING OUT: Developing BOILS filled with pus and moisture.[3]

---

[1] See Rashbam's comm. to 8:15 where he explains that Pharaoh and his magicians were unmoved by the plague of lice, about which they had received no earlier warning. Accordingly Moses now gives an explicit warning about when the plague of pestilence will begin. See similarly the comm. to 8:19, s.v. למחר.
  Cf. the complex explanation of Sekhel Tov who sees in this verse a reference to standard court procedure, where the court gives the accused a certain amount of time to arrange payment. And see LT's explanation ad 9:18 that the warnings that something would happen "tomorrow" were done to toy with Pharaoh and make him suffer more psychologically.

[2] So also Rashi, with the same etymological connection to the verb נ-פ-ח. Cf. JBS who interprets פיח as רמץ, i.e. hot cinders or embers, and claims that miraculously Moses and Aaron were able to pick up such hot objects in their hands.

[3] So also Sekhel Tov, at much greater length, based on his reading of BQ 80b: שחין יבש מבחוץ ולח מבפנים . . . . --boils . . . dry on the outside and moist on the inside," as opposed to the reading of our texts in BQ: "לח מבחוץ ויבש מבפנים--moist on the outside and dry on the inside."
  Rashbam and Sekhel Tov both use the unusual Hebrew word לחלוח (moisture) in their commentaries as a description of the contents of these boils. Rashbam also uses that same word in his comm. to Num. 11:7-8.

9:14 מגפותי [FOR THIS TIME I WILL SEND ALL] MY PLAGUES: The different types of destruction and attacking that come from fire and hail and hailstones[4] and sulphur and snow and smoke.[5]

9:15-16 כי עתה FOR JUST NOW: When the plague of the pestilence of the animals was taking place I had it in mind[6] to stretch forth My hand[7] likewise against you and your people so that you would all die in that pestilence and you would have been effaced from the earth.[8] However,[9] I HAVE SPARED YOU FOR THIS PURPOSE: IN

---

[4]אבני אלגביש. See Ezek. 13:11.

[5]An allusion to the phrase "fire and hail, snow and smoke" (אש וברד שלג וקיטור) in Ps. 148:8.

The exegetical problem is why the text uses the phrase "all my plagues" in reference to the plague of hail. Midrash Hagadol (and perhaps Rashi, depending on what the correct reading of Rashi's text is; see the discussion in Kasher, pp. 132-134) says that this teaches us that the plague of hail was equal in severity to all the other plagues together. Sekhel Tov (perhaps based on Ps.-Jon.) interprets God as saying that during the plague of hail all the memories of all the other plagues would also come and haunt Pharaoh. Rashbam offers his own approach. The phrase, "all my plagues," is used because the plague of hail had various aspects to it (see 9:23-24) and it could attack the Egyptians in a number of different ways. See similarly JBS and iE, in his longer comm. only.

[6]Rashbam, like Rashi, LT, Sekhel Tov and others, explains all the verbs of this verse as subjunctives--"I *could have* stretched forth My hand and stricken you," as the context would seem to demand. See similarly Driver who corrects the indicative forms of the RV to subjunctive forms. See also Heidenheim, *Havanat ha-miqra'*, who points out that verbs in clauses that begin with the words כי עתה tend to be subjunctives.

[7]Rashbam's explanation of the words שלחתי את ידי.

[8]Rashbam's explanation of the phrase ותכחד מן הארץ.

[9]Rashbam paraphrases the text's ואולם as אלא. See similarly his comm. to Gen. 28:19, Gen. 48:19 and Num. 14:21, the four occurrences of the word ואולם in the Torah. See similarly Sekhel Tov who, in the first occurrence of the word, Gen. 28:19, quotes LT's explanation, and then says that his own opinion is that the word אולם is synonymous with the word אלא.

EXODUS IX

ORDER TO SHOW YOU MY POWER . . . and to show you how foolish you were when you said (5:2) "I do not know the LORD."[10]

9:17 הסתולל THWART: מסתולל is a *hitpael* form from [the root ס-ל-ל,] the same root as in (Is. 62:10) "סולו סולו המסילה"--build up, build up the highway." It means כובש אותם לעבדים--enslaving them, as in the phrase (Jer. 34:11) "and forced them to be your slaves (ויכבשום) again."[11]

Now I will tell you the pattern of *hitpael* forms: In all *hitpael* forms the letter *tav* appears before the letters of the root (aside from those exceptional cases that I shall list below).

From the root א-מ-ר one says [in the *hitpael* יתאמרו, as in the phrase] (Ps. 94:4) "all evildoers vaunt (יתאמרו) themselves."

[From the root ב-ר-כ, the *hitpael* form is] יתברך.[12]

[From the root ג-ד-ל, the *hitpael* form is] יתגדל[13] and (Ezek. 38:23) "והתגדלתי והתקדשתי--I will manifest My greatness and My holiness."

[From the root ה-ל-ל, the *hitpael* form is] (Jer. 9:23) "יתהלל המתהלל--should one glory."

---

[10]Again Rashbam emphasizes the importance of the theme of "knowledge of God" in the plague story. See e.g. his comm. to 7:5 above and my notes there.

[11]The phrase from Jeremiah that Rashbam cites here proves his explanation of the meaning of the verb כ-ב-ש, not the meaning of the verb ס-ל-ל. It would appear to me that Rashbam is taking issue with Rashi. Rashi cited approvingly Onq.'s Aramaic, כבישת ביה בעמי, and seems to understand it as meaning "to trample." Rashbam is writing here that that is not what the verb כ-ב-ש means.

[12]Not found in the Bible, but a word that comes easily enough to Rashbam's mind from the liturgy (e.g. the *qaddish* prayer). See also the example, ישתבח, that he cites below and in his comm. to Gen. 24:21, the other excursus on *hitpael* forms in Rashbam's Torah comm. See also Rosin, RSBM, p. 57.

[13]Another example from the liturgy.

[From the root ו-כ-ח,[14] the *hitpael* form is] (Mi. 6:2) "יתוכח--has a case."

[From the root ח-ב-א, the *hitpael* form is] (Gen. 3:8) "ויתחבא--he hid."

[From the root י-פ-ה, the *hitpael* form is] (Jer. 4:30) "לשוא תתיפי--you beautify yourself in vain."

[From the root כ-נ-ס, the *hitpael* form is] (Is. 28:20) "והמסכה צרה כהתכנס--the cover is too narrow for curling up."

[From the root ל-כ-ד, the *hitpael* form is] (Job 38:30) "יתלכדו--compacts."

[From the root מ-ד-ד, the *hitpael* form is] (IK 17:21) "ויתמודד--he stretched out."

[From the root נ-ש-א, the *hitpael* form is] (IK 1:5) "מתנשא--presumed."[15]

[From the root ע-ל-ל, the *hitpael* form is] (Ex. 10:2) "התעללתי--I made a mockery."

[From the root פ-ל-ל, the *hitpael* form is] (IK 8:28) "מתפלל--prays."

[From the root ר-ו-ש, the *hitpael* form is] (Prov. 13:7) "מתרושש והון רב--professes to be poor and has much wealth."

---

[14]From Rashbam's alphabetical list of roots one sees that he considers ו-כ-ח to be the root of יתוכח. Most grammarians, ancient and modern, would claim that the root is י-כ-ח. See iE's claim in his *Sefer ṣaḥot*, p. 21, that no root in Hebrew begins with the letter *vav*.

[15]At this point in the manuscript a further example, ויתלקטו, appears. (The form can be found in Jud. 11:3.) As Rosin notes reasonably, it is to be assumed that this example, which does not fit into the alphabetical listing that Rashbam provides, was a later insertion into the commentary. Perhaps it originated with a copyist who did not recognize the form יתלכדו and therefore added in the margin a more well-known example of a *hitpael* form beginning with the letter *lamed*, ויתלקטו. Later another copyist moved the form ויתלקטו from the margin into the text itself and at the wrong spot.

EXODUS IX

Now you see that the *hitpael* is formed by adding the letter *tav* before the first letter of the root for roots from the entire alphabet[16] with the exception of seven letters: דז"ט ס"ץ ש"ת .

For [roots that begin with] the letters *shin* and *samekh*, the *tav* follows the first letter of the root in their *hitpael* forms. For example, from [the root] ס-ל-ל,[17] the *hitpael* form is [here in our verse] מסתולל--"thwart." From [the root] ש-ר-ר,[18] the *hitpael* form is (Num. 16:13) "תשתרר עלינו--lord it over us." From [the root] ש-ב-ח, the *hitpael* form is ישתבח.[19] From [the root] ש-מ-ר, the *hitpael* form is (Mi. 6:16) "וישתמר חוקות עמרי--you have kept the laws of Omri." From [the root] ש-כ-ר, the *hitpael* form is (Hag. 1:6) "משתכר--earns."

For roots that begin with the letters *sade* or *zayyin*, no *tav* appears in their *hitpael* forms at all. Instead, after the letter *sade* [when it is the first letter of the root], the letter *tet* will appear in place of a *tav*, [the standard sign] of *hitpael*. From [the root] צ-ד-ק, the *hitpael* form is (Gen. 44:16) "נצטדק--prove our innocence." From [the root] צ-ב-ע, the *hitpael* form in Daniel (4:12) is "יצטבע--be drenched." From [the root] צ-י-ד,[20] the *hitpael* form in Joshua (9:12) is "הצטידנו--took as provision." From [the root] צ-ר-פ, the *hitpael* form is "מצטרף--join."[21]

[In a root whose first letter is a *zayyin*,] a *dalet* will follow the *zayyin*, instead of a *tav* [the standard sign] of *hitpael*. From [the root]

---

[16]Rosin notes (RSBM, p. 65, note 5) that the listing here of verb forms in alphabetical order may be following the pattern of Menahem, who provided in his *Maḥberet* (p. 1f.) a number of such alphabetical lists.

[17]I.e. the root ס-ל-ל. Rashbam had difficulties with identifying *hitpael* forms of geminate roots. See Rosin RSBM, p. 137, note 9, and see Rashbam's comm. to Gen. 25:22 and my notes there, pp. 131-2. See also Rashbam below ad 12:4, concerning the noun מִכְסַת and my notes there.

[18]I.e. the root ש-ר-ר.

[19]See note 12 above.

[20]Or perhaps the root צ-ו-ד.

[21]The *hitpael* of the verb צ-ר-פ does not appear anywhere in the Bible but such forms are very common in rabbinic literature. See e.g. "מצטרפים" (Ber. 7:5).

ז-מ-נ, the *hitpael* form in Daniel (2:9) is "הזדמנתון--you have conspired."[22]

The letter *tet* in נצטדק and the letter *dalet* in הזדמנתון and the letter *tav* in יתאמרו are all letters that are inserted in order to make the forms *hitpael*, and so also with all the examples above.

When one of those same three letters [*tet*, *tav* and *dalet*] is the first letter of the root, then no letter is added to the root in order to make a *hitpael* form. For example [from the root ד-ב-ר, the *hitpael* form is] (Num. 7:89) "וישמע את הקול מִדַּבֵּר אליו"--he would hear the voice addressing him"; one does not say מתדבר. [From the root ט-מ-א the *hitpael* form is] (Lev. 21:4) "לא יִטַּמָּא בעל"--a husband shall not defile himself"; one does not say יתטמא. [From the root ת-פ-ל, the *hitpael* form is] (II Sam. 22:27) "ועם עקש תִּתַּפָּל"--with the preverse You are wily"; one does not say תתתפל. [From the root ת-מ-מ the *hitpael* form is] (II Sam. 22:26) "תִּתַּמָּם"--You deal blamelessly"; one does not say תתתמם.[23]

---

[22]The one example that Rashbam cites, הזדמנתון, is from biblical Aramaic and the letter *dalet*, the crux of the proof, appears only in the Qeri. This is, however, the only example that he *can* cite from the Bible of a *hitpael* form of a root that begins with the letter *zayyin*. (See however IE, *Sefer ṣaḥot*, p. 17 and *Safah berurah*, p. 25, where he suggests that הִזַּכּוּ (Is. 1:16) is a *hitpael* form; so also G.-K. 54d.) In rabbinic and later Hebrew many examples can be cited to show that the *hitpael* form of a root that begins with a *zayyin* is formed by inserting the letter *dalet* after the *zayyin*. See e.g. "שנזדמנו" (Shev. 7:4) or "מזדוגין" (Sanh. 5:5).

[23]Rashbam provides here a detailed grammatical lesson about the formation of *hitpael* forms in Hebrew. See a shorter grammar lesson on the same subject in his comm. to Gen. 24:21 and my notes there. In Genesis it is understandable why at that particular verse he chose to explain how *hitpael* works. He explicitly tells us there that he is opposing those exegetes who interpret משתאה in that verse as related to the root ש-ת-ה. Here also it is possible that Rashbam goes into such detail on the rules of *hitpael* in order to oppose such a reading as that of LT who suggests (along with many other possible readings of this verse) that מסתולל might be read as two words, מס תולל, which, through some creative exegesis, he interprets as meaning "raising taxes."

Rashbam's excursus is clear and accurate. For possible sources that Rashbam may have used, see Rosin RSBM, p. 137, note 1. Short excurses on *hitpael* forms can be found in Rashi's comm. here and ad Gen. 44:16.

EXODUS IX

9:19 העז: means "gather," as in the phrase (Jer. 6:1) "Gather (העיזו), O people of Benjamin," or the phrase (Is. 10:31) "The dwellers of Gebim gathered (העיזו)."[24]

9:27 חטאתי הפעם I STAND GUILTY THIS TIME: I.e. this time I admit that I have sinned.[25]

9:30 כי טרם תיראון DO NOT YET FEAR: [The phrase should be understood] as the Targum renders it.[26] It means "you do not yet fear."[27]

9:32 לא נוכו [THE WHEAT AND THE EMMER] WERE NOT HURT: This is written so that the reader will know that that which was not

---

[24]So also Rashi and Sekhel Tov (both with the same two prooftexts), iE, JBS and LT. Most moderns render "bring into safety" (e.g. BDB and NJPS).

[25]In other words, it is not the case that Pharaoh is claiming that he now for the first time has sinned. Rather for the first time he admits that all along he was sinning against the Israelites. See similarly Mendelssohn and Luzzatto.
   Cf. SR 12:5 which interprets that Pharaoh's admission of guilt relates specifically to what he did in this plague: he sinned against his own servants by ignoring God's warning (vs. 19) and leaving his servants out in the field where they were killed (vs. 25).

[26]כען לא אתכנעתון.

[27]So also Rashi at greater length.
   Rashbam may be opposing the interpretation of LT and Sekhel Tov who claim that טרם means "before" and that the phrase must be seen as elliptical: "you fear God only before the plague finishes." JBS also insists on understanding טרם here as the conjunction "before" and he reads the phrase as meaning "before you let us go, you will come to fear God more." See also the criticism of Rashi and Rashbam's interpretation in iE's longer comm. (citing the interpretation as Rashi's) and in Nahm. In any case most modern translations agree with Rashi and Rashbam.

destroyed by the hail was eaten by the locust.[28] The hail destroyed crops that were brittle; the locust ate the soft crops.[29]

9:33 נתך: The word is connected with the idea of "pouring." Similarly (Ezek. 22:22) "as silver is melted (כהתוך) into a crucible so shall you be melted (תותכו) in it." [The verse means:] "the rain did not pour down upon the earth."[30]

9:34 ויוסף לחטוא HE [PHARAOH] COMPOUNDED HIS SIN: Until now he did not intend to sin. But since he just admitted about the hail (9:27), "I and my people are in the wrong," that is why the text now refers to him as a deliberate sinner.[31]

---

[28] Rashbam explains the idea based on his general principle of anticipation. The text said previously (9:25) that the hail had destroyed all the vegetation. Further on (10:5) Moses will warn Pharaoh that the locusts will devour whatever vegetation was left from the plague of hail. The text must therefore insert this explanatory note that tells the reader how it happened that some crops survived the plague of hail. See Hizquni, who makes this argument at greater length, and NJPSC.

[29] So also Rashi, in his first interpretation of the phrase. Cf. iE who claims that the text means that the wheat and the emmer were not damaged because they had not grown out of the ground at all yet, and see also the midrash quoted by Rashi and LT that says that the wheat and emmer were saved from the hail through a miracle, connecting the word אפילות in this verse with the word פלאות (miracles).

[30] So also Rashi, in his second interpretation, citing Menahem (s.v. תך), as opposed to Rashi's first interpretation that would see ניתך as synonymous with הגיע ("arrived"). Similarly to Rashbam see also Sekhel Tov and iE, longer comm. only.

[31] The verb י-ס-פ in the hifil can mean either "to do something again" or "to do something going further than before." The more common reading here would presumably be the first one: Pharaoh sinned before and now he continued (ויוסף) to sin. See e.g. SR 12:7 ("חוזרין לקלקולן"--return to guilty ways"), Cassuto ("ויוסף לחטוא: אותו חטא --'he continued to sin': at the same sin") and NJPS ("reverted to his guilty ways"). On the other hand Rashbam sees the verse as saying that Pharaoh added (ויוסף) a new dimension to his guilt and made it worse than before.

The connection to 9:27 (but not the intepretation of ויוסף) can be found also in LT, Sekhel Tov and in iE, in his longer comm. only.

EXODUS X

10:1 כי FOR I HAVE HARDENED HIS HEART: In none of the [other] plagues do we find that God told Moses that it was He who had hardened Pharaoh's heart. But in this plague it says that Pharaoh admitted (9:27) that God was in the right and that he and his people were in the wrong, and [on the other hand] it says (9:34) that "Pharaoh compounded his sin." That is why God had to explain to Moses "It was *I* who hardened his heart and the hearts of his courtiers" in order to explain how it happened that "ויכבד לבו--he stiffened his heart" (9:34).[1]

שיתי: means "that I might put."[2]

10:2 התעללתי: is a verb form connected with [the noun] עלילות.[3]

---

[1] Rashbam appears to be the first exegete to address the question of why it is specifically at this point that God tells Moses that God was the one who hardened Pharaoh's heart. See a similar explanation in Nahm.

[2] So also Rashi and iE. JBS writes that some claim that the *yod* of שיתי is "added" (יתירה), i.e. that it serves no grammatical role here. Perhaps it is against that interpretation that Rashi and Rashbam are arguing here. Alternatively Rashbam may be making the same point as Sekhel Tov here who writes that שיתי here, with stress on the ultima, means "that I might put," but with penultimate stress, as in Is. 16:3, the form is a feminine singular imperative.

[3] One of the more common meanings of the word עלילות in the Bible is "actions" or deeds." See e.g. (Is. 12:4), "Praise the LORD . . . make his deeds (עלילתיו) known." So if, as Rashbam would have it, התעללתי here is connected with the noun עלילות, the phrase simply means "that you may recount . . . what I did to the Egyptians."
   This interpretation is the one that Rashi explicitly rejects. Rashi distinguishes between *qal* forms from the root ע-ל-ל, which can mean "to do," and *hitpael* forms. (So also Qara, in Gad p. 21.) Rashi prefers the interpretation that התעללתי במצרים, the *hitpael* form in this verse, means "I made a mockery of the Egyptians." NJPS and most modern translators and commentators follow Rashi. LT offers a number of interpretations, including the one that Rashbam offers, and it appears that that is the way

10:3 לֵעָנֹת TO HUMBLE YOURSELF: From the root ע-נ-ה one says [in the *nifal* infinitive] לֵעָנוֹת, just as from the root ר-א-ה one says [in the *nifal* infinitive] לֵרָאוֹת.[4] It is connected with the words for poverty (עוֹנִי) and for affliction (עִינוּי). It means "to give in and to be humble before me."[5]

10:5 ולא יוכל AND HE WILL NOT BE ABLE: i.e. no one will be able TO SEE THE LAND.[6]

העץ הצומח THE TREES THAT ARE GROWING: [The reason that the text writes "the trees *that are growing*" is] because the hail had destroyed all the trees [that existed at that point in time]. The locust would eat [only] those trees that had grown since.[7]

---

that Onq. (עבדית) understands the text. It is possible that Rashbam avoids the interpretation that התעללתי means "to make a mockery" for apologetic reasons, i.e. so as not to see the text as portraying God as one who toys with his enemies. That may also be the reason why Mendelssohn adopts Rashbam's reading.

[4]See e.g. Ex. 34:24.

[5]So similarly Rashi, LT, Sekhel Tov and iE, longer interpretation, all without the grammatical explanation.

[6]Rashbam explains that the Hebrew phrase ולא יוכל לראות must be understood with the implicit subject הרואה. So also Rashi, virtually verbatim. Rashbam often helps the reader by providing the understood subject. See e.g. his comm. to Gen. 48:1 and his comm. below, vs. 11, s.v. ויגרש.

[7]Rashbam explains the apparent redundancy of the phrase, "the trees *that are growing for you in the fields*." See also Nahm.'s comment, at much greater length. Nahm. feels the need to explain how the trees could have grown in the three weeks that he presumes elapsed (based on a common midrashic tradition) between the plague of hail and the locusts. Rashbam does not feel bound by that timetable. See comm. to 7:25 and my notes there.

10:7 הטרם תדע: means "do you not yet[8] understand that Egypt has been destroyed (אבדה) through the pestilence and the hail and the other plagues?"[9]

10:10 כי רעה EVIL IS BEFORE YOUR FACES: You are contemplating evil in your hearts.[10] This [i.e. the fact that the phrase נגד פניכם means "in your hearts"] is proven by [the parallelism[11] in] the verse (Is. 5:21) "Ah, those who are so wise--in their own opinion (בעיניהם); so clever--in their own judgment (נגד פניהם)."[12]

---

[8]See Rashbam ad 9:30 and notes there. Again Rashi and Rashbam interpret טרם as meaning "not yet," while iE and LT interpret it as meaning "before" and see the verse as elliptical: "[Will you not let them go,] before you find out that Egypt has been totally destroyed?"

[9]See previous note. Rashbam emphasizes that the destruction spoken of here is not the expected total destruction of Egypt in the future (as LT would have it) but rather the partial destruction that they have already experienced.

[10]The phrase נגד פניכם was interpreted in many different ways by Jewish exegetes. Rashi offers two interpretations. The first is from Onq., who understands Pharaoh to be saying that the evil that the Jews are planning to do will come back "into their faces." Rashi's second interpretation is that Pharaoh is saying that an unlucky star or constellation (רעה; see Ex. 32:12) is "opposite your faces." JBS says that Pharaoh is telling Moses that the Jews' evil intentions can be plainly seen "on their faces." iE says that the phrase means that evil, from Pharaoh, is very close to falling upon you; "just in front of your noses," as we might say in English.
Rashbam appears to be alone among the classical exegetes in interpreting נגד פניכם as meaning "in your hearts" or "in your minds." Many modern translators and exegetes follow Rashbam.

[11]On Rashbam's sensitivity to parallelism and his use of the phenomenon to interpret difficult words, see Rosin RSBM, pp. 143-145 and Kugel, *The Idea of Biblical Poetry*, pp. 176-177.

[12]JBS cites this same verse to prove his own different understanding of the phrase נגד פניכם. The different understandings that Rashbam and JBS have for the verse in Isaiah affect the way that they interpret the verse here. According to JBS, the verse in Isaiah is mocking those who put on airs of being wise, who try to make themselves look wise outwardly (נגד פניהם). Accordingly the phrase נגד פניכם here would mean that the supposed evil intentions of the Jews can be plainly seen on their faces.

10:11 ועבדו GO AND WORSHIP THE LORD, SINCE THAT IS WHAT YOU ARE ASKING FOR: You have been beseeching me (אתם מבקשים פני)[13] to go worship God; in that case, why do you need the children and the women?[14] And that is [the purpose of this clause, כי אותה אתם מבקשים, to explain] why Pharaoh [refused their request and] said (vs. 10), "The LORD be with you the same [as I mean to let your children go with you . . .]."[15]

ויגרש AND HE: i.e. someone, EXPELLED THEM FROM PHARAOH'S PRESENCE.[16]

Rashbam, on the other hand, sees the verse in Isaiah as belittling those who, in their hearts (נגד פניהם), think of themselves as wise. Accordingly, he interprets our verse as meaning that Pharaoh is accusing the Jews of planning evil in their hearts.
Rashbam's reading of the verse in Isaiah is the more common one.

[13]Rashbam paraphrases מבקשים פני as מבקשים; he apparently feels that that means "to entreat." See e.g. Prov. 29:26, רבים מבקשים פני מושל, where the phrase ב-ק-ש פנים could be seen as having that meaning--"Many entreat the ruler."

[14]Rashbam's intepretation is basically the same as Rashi's. Rashbam emphasizes that the word, "אותה--that," is a reference to "the request to serve God." The word מבקשים then is seen as referring to an action that was going on in the past--i.e. this is what Moses had been asking for all along.
 It is possible that Rashbam is trying to oppose an interpretation of the phrase אותה אתם מבקשים as meaning "you are asking for trouble." Such an interpretation may be found in iE. According to that interpretation, אותה should be seen as a reference to the רעה of the previous verse and מבקשים refers to the action going on in the present. The phrase then would be a sarcastic comment of Pharaoh ("that's what you're looking for"), not a reference to the specific request of the Israelites.

[15]These last words of Rashbam on this verse are somewhat difficult to understand. It appears to me that Rashbam is explaining that, according to his interpretation, the clause, כי אותה אתם מבקשים, provides the reason why the request was turned down. He may still be explaining his opposition to the interpretation found in iE that I described in the previous note. According to that interpretation כי אותה אתם מבקשים is a sarcastic rhetorical statement, not an explanation of why the request was turned down.

[16]See Rashbam's comm. to vs. 5 above and my notes there. Again Rashbam explains here that an implicit subject, "המגרש--the one who expelled," must be understood for the verb, "expelled (ויגרש)." So also Rashi and see Menahem, *Mahberet*, p. 81, s.v. ג-ר, who cites this as an example of a verse where the subject must be provided.

EXODUS X

10:19 ויהפוך THE LORD CAUSED A SHIFT TO A WEST WIND: An east wind had brought them [the locust][17] from the sea and now a west wind returned them to the sea.[18]

10:21 וימש LET DARKNESS FALL: וימש should be understood as if ויאמש were written. Similarly in the verse (Is. 13:20) "No Arab shall pitch his tent (יהל) there," [יהל should be understood] as if יאהל were written.[19]

The meaning of the phrase is that the darkness of the night will continue (יאמש)[20] and it will remain dark for a long time. [This was the case] for the darkness did not turn into light for three days.

---

[17] See vs. 13.

[18] I.e to the Sea of Reeds. On the geography, see iE's shorter comm.

[19] So also Rashi at much greater length and Rashbam ad Gen. 22:2. See also his grammar book, p. 51. On the elision of the letter 'alef in the Bible, see G.-K. 35d and passim.

Rashi, in his first explanation of this word, explicitly writes that his comment is directed against those (e.g. Onq.) who connect וימש to the root מ-ו-ש. Rashbam would clearly agree with Rashi about that, too. The midrash (cited by Rashi and by LT and adopted by NJPS) connects the word to the root מ-ש-ש and claims that the text means that the darkness was palpable. Rashbam presumably opposes that reading. See JBS like Rashbam and see iE who opposes the reading of Rashi and Rashbam, in his longer comm. only.

[20] It is not certain what Rashi (in his first explanation) and Rashbam precisely thought that the meaning of the supposed verb form ויאמש would be. (See iE's criticism: "והנה אין טעם לפירושם--their interpretation is not meaningful.") No other verb from the root א-מ-ש appears anywhere in the Bible. The connection to the noun אֶמֶשׁ ("last night") would seem to suggest the idea that the darkness of last night will continue.

10:22 חשך אפילה: should be understood as if חשך ואפילה were written. It means a great darkness.[21]

10:23 מתחתיו NO ONE COULD GET UP FROM WHERE HE WAS (מתחתיו): According to the plain meaning, מתחתיו means "from their houses"; [they did not leave their houses] because they did not know where to go.[22]

היה אור במושבותם [BUT ALL THE ISRAELITES] ENJOYED LIGHT IN THEIR DWELLINGS: Even if they lived close to Egyptian houses.[23]

---

[21] Rashbam opposes the midrashic explanation found in Rashi that claims that there were a number of different kinds of darkness; only one of them was called חושך אפילה and it lasted for three days. In total, the plague lasted more than three days. Rashbam may also be opposing the reading of Sekhel Tov who saw אפילה here as an adjective and who explained the phrase חושך אפילה as meaning "darkness that knocks over (שמפילות) wayfarers."

[22] Rashbam opposes the midrashic intepretation (see e.g. Tanh. *Bo'* 3) offered by Rashi that explains the phrase, "no one could get up," as meaning that whoever was sitting was unable to stand up and whoever was standing was unable to sit. See iE (both commentaries) and Sekhel Tov who offer an explanation similar to Rashbam's.

[23] The midrashic explanation of this phrase (e.g. Mishnat R. Eliezer 19 and LT) claims that the Jews had light even when they were in the dwellings of the Egyptians. ("*Their* dwellings" was construed as meaning "the *Egyptians'* dwellings.") Rashbam rejects that midrash. Still, Rashbam does not explain the text in the simplest sense as saying that in the place where Jews lived (במושבותם), there was light. See e.g. Sekhel Tov, who is usually quite amenable to midrashic explanations, but who writes here that "their dwellings" simply means Goshen. Rashbam says that the text emphasizes that wherever Jews had their dwellings there was light.

Such an interpretation seems to me rather uncharacteristic for Rashbam. To be sure, as previously noted (ad 8:18) Rashbam did believe that all of the ten plagues affected only the Egyptians, not the Israelites. Perhaps, then, he is taking note of the fact that twice previously (8:18 and 9:26), when the text wished to describe that a plague did not affect the Jews, a specific reference was made by the text to the land of Goshen. (Thus Hizkuni: " בארץ גושן אין כתוב כאן כמו בשאר מכות, הוא שאמרו רבותינו וכו'--it does not say 'in the land of Goshen,' as it does in the other plagues; that is why the rabbis said . . . .") Here when the text refers to the Jews' dwellings, and not to a specific geographical area, Rashbam claims it means all dwellings of the Jews.

It appears that JBS is directly attacking Rashbam's interpretation when he writes that Jews who were in Egyptian territory had no light during this plague.

EXODUS XI

11:1 ויאמר AND THE LORD SAID TO MOSES: while he was still standing before Pharaoh, "I WILL BRING BUT ONE MORE PLAGUE . . . ." Then Moses answered Pharaoh (vs. 4), "THUS SAYS THE LORD, 'WHEN THE NIGHT SPLITS I WILL GO FORTH . . . .'."[1]

כלה ONE AND ALL: כלה means "all," men, women, children and livestock.[2]

11:2 וישאלו AND THEY SHALL REQUEST [OBJECTS OF SILVER AND GOLD]: As an outright gift. [The root ש-א-ל means here to request as an outright gift,] as in the phrase (Ps. 2:8), "Request (שאל) it of me and I shall make the nations your domain."[3]

---

[1] In the last verse of chapter 10 Moses tells Pharaoh that he will never again see Pharaoh's face. Then, in vs. 4 of this chapter one finds Moses speaking to Pharaoh. The solution proposed here by Rashbam is that after the angry exchange of words between Moses and Pharaoh at the end of chapter 10, while Moses was still standing before Pharaoh, God spoke to Moses (11:1-2) and then Moses spoke to Pharaoh (11:4-8a) and only then did Moses leave Pharaoh's presence.

This same solution can be found in SR 18:1, in Rashi LT and Sekhel Tov (all ad vs. 4) and in JBS (ad vs. 1). See similarly NJPSC.

[2] So also Rashi. Cf. Sekhel Tov and iE (shorter comm. only; see also his comm. to Is. 10:23) who connect כלה here to the phrase כלה ונחרצה (Is. 10:23) and who understand the phrase here as either a reference to destruction or as expressing certainty that the Jews will be driven out.

[3] Rashbam reiterates his solution to the problem of the alleged duplicity of the Israelites in "borrowing" items from the Egyptians and never returning them. See at greater length his comm. to 3:22 and my notes there.

11:4 ויאמר MOSES SAID: to Pharaoh,[4] "THUS SAYS THE LORD, 'WHEN THE NIGHT SPLITS (כחצות)'": כחצות is [an infinitive construct] from the root ח-צ-ה, just like כעשות from the root ע-ש-ה or "כעלות המנחה"--to present the meal offering" (II Kings 3:20) from the root ע-ל-ה. In other words, [God said] "when the time comes to leave Egypt, when the night splits (כשיחצה הלילה) I WILL GO FORTH AMONG THE EGYPTIANS." When the event itself takes place then it is reasonable for the text to write (Ex. 12:29) "ויהי בחצי הלילה"--in the middle of the night" [writing the word בחצי] with the letter *bet*. This is the plain meaning of the text. Before the time of the plague of the first-born it is reasonable for Moses to say כחצות, i.e. "when that time comes when the night splits."[5]

11:5 אשר אחר הרחיים [TO THE FIRST-BORN OF THE SLAVE GIRL] WHO IS BEHIND THE MILLSTONES: Below the text says (12:29), "to the first-born of the captive who was in the dungeon." The two verses say the same thing. The "first-born of the captive" could be found "behind the millstone" as captives were often put to work grinding

---

[4] According to Rashbam above ad vs. 1, Moses was still standing before Pharaoh while God spoke to him in vss. 1-2. Now in verse four when the text says that "Moses said," and the intended audience is not identified, Rashbam supplies the implied indirect object, "to Pharaoh."

[5] Primarily Rashbam opposes the midrashic explanation (e.g. Tanh. B. *Bo'* 17) quoted by Rashi that tries to explain why Moses said כחצות הלילה which was taken to mean "around midnight" while the event itself ostensibly really took place precisely at midnight (בחצי הלילה; Ex. 12:24). (So also LT and Sekhel Tov.) Rashi himself offers the same *peshat* interpretation as that offered by Rashbam here. Both argue that כחצות does not mean "around midnight (חצות)" and that חצות is not a noun here but an infinitve construct form. So also JBS. See iE (longer comm. only) who dismisses the entire issue. See also Rashbam ad 12:29, s.v. ויהי, and my notes there.

Rashbam's further assertion (so also Hizquni) here that there is reason to use the form כחצות when talking of the event beforehand and to use the form בחצי הלילה when describing an event that already took place is very difficult to understand and is apparently baseless. Cf. however Mendelssohn (both here and ad vs. 1, s.v. כשלחו) who cites Rashbam approvingly.

at the millstone, as it is written, "he [Samson] became a mill slave in the prison" (Jud. 16:21).[6]

11:6 אשר כמוהו לא נהיתה SUCH AS HAS NEVER BEEN: We find many examples [like this phrase] where a masculine form [כמוהו] and a feminine form [נהיתה] appear in the same phrase. See similarly (Gen. 32:9) "to the one [האחת; fem.] camp and attacks it [והכהו; masc.]."[7]

11:7 לא יחרץ כלב NOT A DOG SHALL SNARL AT ANY OF THE ISRAELITES: The angel will harm and destroy the first-born Egyptians but the first-born Israelites will not experience harm [from any source, not] even from the noise of barking from dangerous animals.[8]

---

[6]Rashbam opposes the reading of the Mekhilta (Pisḥa' 13; Lauterbach ed. p. 99) adopted by Rashi and Sekhel Tov (both ad 12:29) that distinguishes between the terms "first-born of the slave girl" and "first-born of the captive." Like Rashbam, see LT and Qara (in Berliner's Peletat Soferim, p. 17). See also iE's longer comm. here and ad 20:1 (Weiser ed., p. 127) where he sees this alternation as an example of what he considers the biblical phenomenon of insignificant stylistic alternations.

[7]Rashbam rejects the attempts of LT and Sekhel Tov to explain that the alternation between masculine and feminine forms is because there are two antecedents, צעקה (fem.) and לילה (masc.). iE (both commentaries) also attempts to identify two antecedents in order to deal with the grammatical anomaly. Rashbam says simply that such an alternation is not atypical and may be found in a number of biblical passages. See his comm. to Gen. 32:9 and my notes there.

[8]See similarly Driver, "Not only should they suffer no actual harm, but no unfriendly sound should even be heard against them . . .."
 Rashbam opposes Rashi's interpretation that sees יחרץ as meaning "to sharpen." (See Rashi ad Josh. 10:21 and ad II Sam. 5:24 where he interprets ח-ר-צ as meaning "to raise a war cry" and applies that meaning to our verse in Exodus.) He also opposes the reading of Sekhel Tov that sees the verse as meaning that the Jews' dogs will not be disturbed and will continue barking as before. Similarly to Rashbam, see LT, JBS and iE.

11:8 וירדו **THEN ALL OF THESE COURTIERS OF YOURS SHALL COME DOWN**: Moses spoke to Pharaoh in a deferential way,[9] for when the events actually took place (12:30-31) "Pharaoh [himself] arose at night . . . and called out to Moses and Aaron in the night . . . ."

The reason why Moses told him all this at this point was to reinforce what he had said (10:29) "I shall not see your face again." [He, Moses, said to Pharaoh, "I will never again go to you] but you and your courtiers will come to me."[10]

11:9 לא ישמע **PHARAOH WILL NOT HEED YOU**: I.e. after each of the plagues God would tell Moses and Aaron that Pharaoh would not listen to them until the end. [Similarly the phrase in vs. 10] **THE LORD HAD STIFFENED** [refers back to previous events and] means that after each one of the [previous] plagues God had stiffened Pharaoh's heart.[11]

---

[9] Moses really knew that Pharaoh himself would come and ask the Jews to leave Egypt (12:30-31) but he did not say that directly to the king. Instead he expressed himself in language that preserved the king's dignity. So also Rashi (= Zev. 102a).

[10] Rashbam's interpretation here is based on his comment above ad vs. 1 where he says that the events of 11:1-8 took place immediately after 10:29, while Moses was still standing before Pharaoh.

[11] Verse 9 appears to be out of place at this point in the narrative. Moses hardly needs a reassurance from God at this point that he should not be perturbed by the fact that Pharaoh will not listen. (Cf. however Nahm. who argues the opposite.) The reference to further "marvels" to come (in the plural) seems inappropriate when all but one of the plagues has already taken place. Rashi still attempts to argue that God did, even at this point, speak of marvels in the plural as both the plague of the first-born and the wonders at the sea were yet to come. On the other hand some moderns, like Bäntsch (cited by Childs, p. 139), dismiss this section as a "late redactional addition."

LT, Sekhel Tov, iE and JBS all argue that vss. 9-10 are chronologically out of of place. The verses mean that God before this point *had* told Moses that Pharaoh would not listen. The verbs should be understood as having the force of the pluperfect.

Rashbam's approach is very similar but not identical. He sees these verses as a summary of the plagues. After each of the plagues that had occurred until now God *had been telling* Moses each time that Pharaoh would not listen. In other words, while LT and Sekhel Tov see our verse as a reiteration of 3:19 ("I [God] know that the king of Egypt will not let you go"), Rashbam sees our verse as a summary statement that tells us that the promise of 3:19 (or perhaps 7:3) had been fulfilled throughout the plague narrative. Many moderns view the verse similarly. See e.g. Childs (p. 139): "11.9-10 conclude the plague account by confirming the prediction that Pharaoh would not listen."

EXODUS XII

12:1-2 בארץ מצרים [THE LORD SAID . . .] IN THE LAND OF EGYPT, "THIS MONTH . . .": Since this is a legal section the text had to specify that these commandments [as opposed to all the others] were given in Egypt. The rest of the commandments were given either at Mount Sinai[1] or at the Tent of Meeting[2] or in the plains of Moab.[3]

12:2 ראש חדשים [THIS MONTH SHALL MARK FOR YOU] THE BEGINNING OF THE MONTHS: If one follows the opinion of R.

---

[1] E.g. Ex. 20.

[2] E.g. Num. 1:1.

[3] E.g. Num. 33:50.
    Rashbam opposes the interpretation of the Mekhilta (Laut. ed., pp. 3-4), adopted by Rashi, LT and Sekhel Tov, according to which this phrase, "in the land of Egypt," teaches us that God spoke to Moses outside of the Egyptian cities, in the countryside (with emphasis on the word "land--ארץ"). According to Rashbam the text has a simpler purpose--to teach us that only the laws of Ex. 12 (and 13; see comm. ad 12:51) were given in Egypt.
    It is noteworthy also that Rashbam writes that the commandments of the rest of the Torah were given in a number of locations; Mount Sinai was just one of many places. See also Rashbam ad Lev. 25:1 and ad Num 1:1. He may be opposing the opinion of Rashi ad Lev. 25:1 that all the commandments originated at Sinai (and that some of them were re-taught to the Israelites at other locations). The dispute about how much of the Torah was given at Sinai is an ancient one. See the discussion in A. Heschel, *Torah min ha-shamayim*, vol. 2, pp. 88-90, 402-406 and passim.
    For another understanding of the purpose of this comment, see Touitou, *Tarbiz* 51, 234-235, who argues that Rashbam emphasizes for purposes of anti-Christian polemic that virtually all the commandments originate in the desert and it is for that reason that he must explain how it happened that some commandments were given in Egypt.

Joshua[4] that the world was created in the Hebrew month of Nissan then [one would explain that "this month marks the beginning of] the months of the year" means that whenever a month is labelled [for example] the "eighth month"[5] or "the ninth month,"[6] one counts from Nissan.[7] Or, following the opinion of R. Eliezer that the world was created in the Hebrew month of Tishre, one would explain the true plain meaning of the text as follows:

> "This month shall mark *for you* [the beginning of months]." Even though this month [Nissan] is not the first month for the other nations, *for you* it will be the beginning of the months,[8] for you to enumerate [for example] "the sixth month"[9] or "the seventh month"[10] or "the eighth month" or "the ninth month" or "the twelfth month, that is the month of Adar" (Est. 3:7). You should count from Nissan to remember that in Nissan you left Egypt.[11] And when it says in the Torah "in the seventh

---

[4] The dispute between R. Joshua and R. Eliezer about when the world was created can be found in RH 11a.

[5] E.g. I Kings 6:38.

[6] E.g. Jer. 36:9.

[7] Rashbam follows the second interpretation found in Rashi, the one that Rashi labels *peshaṭ*, and not the first interpretation of Rashi (based on the Mekhilta, Laut. ed. pp. 15-16) that sees in this phrase a reference to the laws of how to identify the new moon each month.

[8] This explanation that the phrase "for you" means only for the Jews can be found in the Mekhilta *Pisḥa'* 2 (Laut. ed. p. 18) and is cited also by LT. In the Mekhilta the phrase implies that for the Jews the calendar will be lunar but it will be solar for the non-Jews. LT reworks the Mekhilta's explanation and says that "for you" means that for the Jews Nissan is the first month, but for the non-Jews Tishre is first. Rashbam follows LT's understanding, although Rashbam adds the further refinement that only R. Eliezer would interpret the verse that way.

[9] E.g. Ezek. 8:1.

[10] E.g. Gen. 8:4.

[11] "כי בו יצאתם ממצרים"; echoing the language of Ex. 23:15.

month," it means if one counts months from the month of the exodus.
It is common for the text to count time from the exodus. For example (Ex. 19:1) "On the third month after the Israelites had gone forth from the land of Egypt." Similarly concerning the building of the Temple it says (I Kings 6:1) "In the four hundred and eightieth year after the Israelites left the land of Egypt."[12]

12:3 לבית אבות [SHALL TAKE A LAMB] TO A FAMILY [A LAMB TO A HOUSEHOLD]: [The phrases "to a family" (לבית אבות) and "to a household" (לבית) are synonymous] for generally the family[13] that lives in one house eats in that one house.[14] [The reason that this verse mentions only one family taking the paschal lamb is] because it is forbidden to eat the pachal sacrifice in more than one house, as it is written (here), "a lamb to a household" and (Ex. 12:46) "It shall be eaten in one house."[15]

---

[12]It is difficult to understand what motivates Rashbam to provide such a long excursus on this phrase. Presumably his goal is not really to explain a difficult text from the Bible but to explain a problem in the Talmud: how is it possible that the rabbis disagree about when it was that the world was created when we have such a clear indication in this verse that Nissan is the first month? Rashbam then explains that both rabbis could offer reasonable readings of the verse.

[13]I have translated the text the way it appears in the ms., משפחת. Rosin's emendation to משפחות is to my mind gratuitous.

[14]See similarly JBS.

[15]Rashbam agrees with Rashi that בית אבות means "family" and that בית here means "house." But they disagree about how to interpret the two phrases, שה לבית אבות שה לבית. According to Rashi (following the Mekhilta Pisha'3 [Laut. ed. p. 26]) the phrase שה לבית is there to limit and modify what was previously said, שה לבית אבות. Generally, says Rashi, paschal lambs are taken one per בית אבות--i.e. one per family, but if that family is too large to make do with one lamb (or perhaps too large to fit into one house) then the Torah says שה לבית, i.e. take one paschal lamb per house. (So also iE.)

According to Rashbam, though, the phrase שה לבית does not modify or limit what was previously written. It simply provides the *reason* why the lamb is to be taken one per family: since the idea is that the paschal lamb should be eaten in one house that is why the command was to take one per family as generally a family eats in one house.

12:4 ואם ימעט BUT IF THE HOUSEHOLD IS TOO SMALL FOR A LAMB: i.e. that they will not be able to eat all of it.[16]

במכסת: מכסת means count.[17] as it is written (Num. 31:37), "the count (המכס) of sheep for the LORD."[18] The letter *mem* [in מכסת and in מכס] is part of the root; [the noun מְכָס is] on the same paradigm as מֶלֶךְ--king, or מֶתֶג in the phrase (Ps. 32:9) "by bit and bridle" (במתג).[19] The form מִכְסַת is on the same paradigm as שִׁכְבַת in the phrase (Ex. 16:14) "the fall (שכבת) of dew." However the form תָּכֻסּוּ [in this verse] is from the root כ-ס-ס, just as תָּסֹבּוּ[20] is from the root ס-ב-ב. תכוסו then is entirely unrelated to the form מכס לה׳.[21]

Even if one were to argue that the letter *mem* in מִכְסַת is a prefix and not part of the root--as [in the nouns] מִצְוָה,[22] מִקְנֶה,[23] מַרְאֶה[24] and מַעֲשֶׂה[25]--still מכסת would not be from the same root as

---

[16]So also Rashi and Sekhel Tov.

[17]מנין. So also Mekhilta *Pisḥa'* 3 (Laut. ed. p. 27) and Onq. See similarly Rashi (חשבון).

[18]The more common understanding of מכס in Numbers 31 (the only place it appears in the Bible) is "tax" or "levy."

[19]See also BDB who sees מֶתֶג as being derived from the root מ-ת-ג.

[20]In Josh. 6:4, e.g.

[21]Despite the apparent similarity, the former is from a geminate root and the latter is from a regular, strong root.
Cf. iE, Hayyuj and Qimhi who all claim that both מכסת and תכוסו are from the geminate root כ-ס-ס. So also BDB. ibn Janah also says the same thing but he describes the explanation later offered by Rashbam as possible ("אינו נמנע").

[22]E.g. Prov. 6:23, from the root צ-ו-ה.

[23]E.g. Gen. 23:18, from the root ק-נ-ה.

[24]E.g. Gen. 12:11, from the root ר-א-ה.

EXODUS XII 107

תכוסו but from the root כ-ס-ה, like [the nouns formed from the roots] ר-א-ה and ע-ש-ה. In all these weak final-*heh* verbs, the letter following the [prefixed] *mem* [or any other prefixed letter used to form a noun] has a *hataf*,[26] e.g. תְּגְרָה,[27] תִּקְוָה,[28] as in the phrase (Ps. 39:11), "your blows--תגרת ידך," or מִצְוָה. But from the [hollow] roots ש-ב or ק-מ or [ג-ר,[29] the root of the phrase] (Num. 22:3) "וַיָּגָר מוֹאָב--Moab was alarmed," when forming nouns the prefixed letter is vocalized with a *hataf*--תְּשׁוּבָה,[30] תְּקוּמָה[31] and [מְגוֹרָה, as in the phrase] (Is. 66:4) מְגוּרֹתָם אָבִיא לָהֶם--to bring on them the very thing they dread."[32]

---

[25]E.g. Num. 31:51, from the root ע-ש-ה.

[26]I.e. a *sheva* or a *hataf-patah*.

[27]E.g. Jer. 31:16, from the root ק-ו-ה.

[28]From the root ג-ר-ה.

[29]I.e. the roots that we would generally refer to today as ש-ו-ב, ק-ו-ם and ג-ו-ר.

[30]E.g. II Sam. 11:1.

[31]Lev. 26:37.

[32]This same distinction between nouns formed from hollow verbs and nouns formed from final-*heh* verbs can be found in Rashbam's *Sefer dayqut*, p. 37.

The logic of this final section of Rashbam's comment is difficult to follow. Rashbam has been arguing that the root of מכסת is either מ-כ-ס or כ-ס-ה; but, he insists, it could not be the geminate verb, כ-ס-ס. He argues that the "*miqtal*" paradigm of מִכְסַת is appropriate for either a strong root or for a final-*heh* verb, but not for a geminate verb. Then instead of bringing proof by citing examples of what a noun formed from a *geminate* root would look like, he brings examples of what a noun formed from a *hollow* root would look like. As noted above (ad 9:17, concerning the form מסתולל), Rashbam often has difficulties distinguishing between hollow and geminate verbs.

The very same point that Rashbam makes here about the pattern to be expected for the noun had the root been hollow could have been made about the pattern to be expected if the root had been geminate. In fact NJPSC (p. 244, note 12) makes that very point: "... we would expect the geminate verb to yield a noun form *mekhissah*; cf. *megillah, mesibbah, meshissah*."

iE, in his longer comm. only, cites the example of מְמַר ("heartache"; Prov. 17:25) as another noun formed from a geminate root (מ-ר-ר), presumably in order to refute the point made by Rashbam that one would expect such a noun to have a *sheva*

12:7 המשקוף THE LINTEL: The משקוף is the upper [equivalent of the] threshold.³³ [It is called the משקוף, from the root ש-ק-פ, to see] because it can be seen by everyone at the entrance to the house, as in the phrase (Gen. 26:8), "וישקף אבימלך--Abimelech looked out."³⁴

He who wishes to explain the word as meaning "the place that the door hits (שקיפת) and strikes against"³⁵ [connected to the rabbinic Hebrew root ש-ק-פ, meaning to hit or knock] would have to find some other example [of the root ש-ק-פ meaning to hit or strike] in the Hebrew text³⁶ of the Torah or the Prophets.³⁷

12:8 ואכלו THEY SHALL EAT THE FLESH THAT SAME NIGHT, ROASTED OVER THE FIRE . . . : All these details about the eating are

---

after the prefixed letter. See however Heidenheim who feels that מָמֵר is from the root מ-ר-ה, "to rebel," and who praises Rashbam's grammatical comments to this verse.

³³Referring to the lintel as the "upper threshold (מפתן עליון) is somewhat unusual. Sekhel Tov, however, uses this same unusual locution and says that מפתן means איסקופה העליונה. Note that while Sekhel Tov uses the rabbinic Hebrew word for threshold, Rashbam uses the biblical Hebrew word.

³⁴See also Rashbam's comm. ad 28:36 s.v. ועשית ציץ.

³⁵Rashbam opposes directly the interpretation of his grandfather, Rashi. (See also Rashi ad Gen. 41:6, s.v. ושדופות and ad Ex. 21:25, s.v. חבורה, and JBS, here; see the discussion of Touitou in *Tarbiz* 52, 365-6.) iE in both his commentaries agrees with Rashbam's etymology. Qimhi mentions both opinions. BDB follows Rashi and cites proof from the Arabic.

³⁶Rashbam is criticizing Rashi's citations here of two Aramaic passages from Onq. as proof of what the root ש-ק-פ means in biblical Hebrew.

³⁷On Rashbam's attitude to the use of post-biblical Hebrew as a tool to understand biblical Hebrew see my notes above to 1:13 and the discussion in my Genesis volume, pp. 422-24.

connected to the idea of hurry and haste, like a person who is rushing to leave.[38]

12:9 נא: apparently means "roasted in a pot," (צלי קדר)[39] i.e. that it was cooked without water but also not in the manner of "roasted by fire" that is written here.[40]

---

[38]See also Rashbam below ad vs. 46 and notes there.
   Some of the details of how to eat the paschal sacrifice are specifically connected by the text to the idea of haste. (See e.g. vs. 11.) Rashbam adds, reasonably enough, that the commandment to eat the meat roasted also helps speed up the process for "it is the quickest means of preparation when time is short" (NJPSC). So also JBS ad vs. 9 and Qara, concerning the phrase in vs. 46, "בבית אחד יאכל--it should be eaten in one house" (cited by Gad, p. 21). This reason is also cited in Sefer ha-ḥinnukh, commandment 7. Cf. Hizkuni (ad vs. 8) who argues that the meat was roasted in order to further harass the Egyptians who would smell the odor of their deities being cooked all over Egypt.

[39]For no apparent reason, Rosin emends קדר to read קדרה. The expression צלי קדר occurs a number of times in rabbinic literature. See e.g. Pes. 41a.

[40]Rashbam rejects the common rabbinic interpretation (e.g. Pes. 41a) cited by Rashi that נא means half cooked. He also does not follow the common *peshaṭ* interpretation that נא means "raw." (See e.g. iE; see also BDB and virtually all moderns.) Presumably Rashbam considers it so unlikely that someone would consider eating the sacrificial meat raw that he rejects the understanding that the Torah here specifically forbids such an act. Instead he suggests that from the context it would seem that meat that was cooked in a pot without additional liquid is called נא.
   In the Talmudic discussion of the issue it would seem that צלי קדר--i.e. cooking the meat in a pot without liquid--is forbidden for the paschal sacrifice, either because the words בשל מבושל are interpreted to include all types of cooking in a pot, or because the words צלי אש are seen to exclude, by implication, צלי קדר. (See Pes. 41a and Tosafot there, s.v. איכא.) Rashbam attempts to reach the same halakhic conclusion as the Talmud--that the paschal sacrifice cannot be cooked in a pot even without additional liquid--but he sees that conclusion not as the result of a *derashah*, but as the simple meaning of the word נא in the text. Rashbam's interpretation appears to be unique.

ראשו על כרעיו [BUT ROASTED--]HEAD LEG [AND ENTRAILS--OVER THE FIRE]: All this was [also] done for the sake of haste.[41]

12:11 פסח הוא לה' IT IS A PASSOVER OFFERING TO THE LORD: [It is called Passover (פסח)] because the angel[42] will skip over the Israelite homes and leave them alone when he goes to strike down the first-borns in the gentiles' homes.[43]

12:12 אעשה שפטים I WILL METE OUT PUNISHMENT [TO ALL THE GODS OF EGYPT]: Because he [i.e. Pharaoh] depended on the gods of Egypt and he said (5:2) "Who is the LORD?"[44]

---

[41]See Rashbam above ad vs. 8. Cf. JBS who says that the entire animal had to be prepared in the same manner for the purpose of unity or uniformity.

[42]It is noteworthy that Rashbam refers to the striking down of the first-born Egyptians as something that was done by an angel, despite the forceful statement in the Passover hagaddah (based perhaps on Mekhilta *Pisha'* 13 (Laut. ed. p. 97); see also Rashi ad vs. 12, s.v. אעשה) that interprets vs. 12 as emphasizing that God alone, and not an angel, was responsible for killing the Egyptian first-borns. Rashbam's mention of an angel follows the simpler reading of the text; see e.g. 12:23, "the LORD will . . . not let the Destroyer (המשחית) enter and smite your home."

[43]Rashbam explains that the meaning of the end of verse 11--it is פסח for the LORD--is explained in verses 12 and 13: that God will strike down the Egyptians' first-borns while "passing over" (ופסחתי) the Israelites' homes. So also Rashi at greater length. Cf. Ps.-Jon. here and Onq. ad vs. 13 and Mekhilta *Pisha'* 7 (Laut. ed. pp. 57-58) who connnect the root פ-ס-ח to the idea of "mercy." And see Rashi ad vs. 13 who quotes that interpretation but rejects it. See NJPSC who sees that interpretation ("to have compassion") as "the most reliable."

[44]Again Rashbam emphasizes that a major theme of the text is refuting what Pharaoh had said in 5:2. See comm. ad 7:5 and my notes there.
  Rashbam may be opposing the interpretation of JBS who says that אלהי מצרים in this verse is a reference to the important people in Egypt, not to their deities.

EXODUS XII

12:14 תחגוהו YOU SHALL CELEBRATE IT: In texts of the Bible from outside of this kingdom there is a *ḥataf qameṣ* vowel[45] [following the letter *ḥet* in תחגוהו]. This is the correct reading. For from the root ח-ג-ג, one says [in the *qal*] תָּחָגֻּהוּ, just as from the root ס-ב-ב, one says (Job 40:22) "יְסֻבּוּהוּ עַרְבֵי נָחַל"[46]--the willows of the brook surround him." But the form תְּחַגֶּהוּ[47] would have to be [a *piel* form] from a [final-]*heh* verb, just as the form תְּכַלּוּהוּ[48] is from the root כ-ל-ה and the form תְּצַוּוּהוּ[49] is from the root צ-ו-ה.

12:16 אך ONLY WHAT EVERY PERSON IS TO EAT [THAT ALONE MAY BE PREPARED FOR YOU]: For that reason, [only] the phrase [כל] מלאכת עבודה [לא תעשו] ("[you shall do no] work at your occupations"; e.g. Lev. 23:7) is written concerning the holidays, so as to teach by inference that preparation of food is permitted. But on the Sabbath and the Day of Atonement [when even the preparation of food

---

[45]I.e. a *qameṣ qaṭan* vowel.

[46]The prooftext that Rashbam cites seems not to prove his point very precisely. Rashbam argues that the vowel following the first letter of the radical in תחגוהו must be a *qameṣ*, not a *pataḥ*. In the prooftext that he brings of another geminate verb, the vowel following the first letter of the radical is neither *qameṣ* nor *pataḥ*, but rather *qibbuṣ*. Essentially, though, those vowels (the *qameṣ qaṭan* and the *qibbuṣ*) are equivalent to one another in this context. See G.-K. 67.

[47]Rashbam informs us that the reading that could be found in the French mss. of his days was תְּחַגֻּהוּ, not MT's תְּחָגֻּהוּ. It is noteworthy that Rashbam investigated and compared the mss. of various countries and used his knowledge of grammar to determine which ms. should be seen as most trustworthy, rejecting the reading current in the "kingdom" where he lived.

See further discussion of this comment see RSBM. p. 59, note 2, and Esh, p. 86. For a list of other passages where Rashbam writes that he compared the readings in various mss., see Melammed, p. 501.

[48]That precise form does not appear in the Bible. See however וִיכַלֻּהוּ (Jer. 10:25).

[49]This precise form is also not in the Bible. See however תְּצַוֶּם (Dt. 32:46).

is forbidden][50] the text writes [לא תעשו] כל מלאכה ("you shall do no manner of work"; e.g. Lev. 16:29).[51]

12:17 ושמרתם YOU SHALL OBSERVE [THE COMMANDMENT OF] THE MATZOT: To eat them [each year] on this day as a commemoration.[52]

כי FOR ON THIS VERY DAY I BROUGHT YOUR RANKS OUT OF THE LAND OF EGYPT: and their dough did not have time to leaven,[53] as it is written (12:39) "And they baked unleavened cakes

---

[50] See also comm. ad 35:3 below.

[51] And since the text in this verse outlawed "כל מלאכה--all manner of work," the more restrictive phrase generally reserved for the sabbath and the day of atonement, it had to write specifically here that the preparation of food is permitted on Passover. Generally, though, in other passages concerning the holidays the text will not have to write explicitly that the preparation of food is permitted since the text will use the language "מלאכת עבודה–work at your occupations."

As noted by Rosin, this same distinction can be found in the later commentaries of iE here (longer comm. only) and of Nahm. ad Lev. 23:7. As far as I can determine no one before Rashbam made this reasonable distinction. On the problem posed by Deut. 16:8, see Nahm. ad Lev. 23:7.

[52] Rashbam breaks with the common rabbinic tradition that interprets this phrase as meaning that the matzot require some special supervision during their processing. See e.g. Mekhilta *Pisha'* 9 (Laut. ed. pp. 73-4) and Rashi here. Even a *peshat*-oriented exegete like iE interprets the verse that way. Rashbam also does not accept the midrashic reading that repoints the word המצות as המצוות, and interprets the phrase as a general encouragement to observe God's commandments. (Mekhilta, *ibid*.)

Rashbam's interpretation is a more simple reading, but curiously it also combines elements of both the interpretations that he rejects. It is not the matzot that are to be observed, and it is not the commandments in general that are to be observed. It is, according to Rashbam, the one specific commandment concerning matzot that one must keep. As far as I can tell he was the first to offer this interpretation, (although a similar interpretation may be reflected in the LXX) which was later adopted by many others (e.g. Hizquni and Mendelssohn).

[53] Rashbam's language, לא הספיק בצק להחמיץ, is taken from the Haggadah. In the Haggadah those words are also followed by the same prooftext, Ex. 12:39.

EXODUS XII

(*maṣṣot*) of the dough that they had taken out of Egypt, since they had been driven out [of Egypt and could not delay]."[54]

12:20 בכל מושבותיכם YOU SHALL EAT UNLEAVENED BREAD IN ALL YOUR SETTLEMENTS: Even in the areas outside of Jerusalem[55] where the paschal sacrifice is not offered.[56]

---

[54]Rashbam explains how the second half of the verse, "*for* on this very day . . .," provides the reason for the first half of the verse, "you shall observe [the commandment of] the matzot." Rashbam has to say that within the words, "I brought your ranks out . . .," the idea is implicitly included that the exodus took place quickly and there was not enough time for the dough to rise and that is why one eats matzot on Passover. While Rashbam's reading may be forced (the text will not mention the lack of time for the dough rising until vs. 39), he is the only classical exegete that I have found who attempts to explain how the second clause provides the rationale for the first clause.

[55]בגבולין, the common word in rabbinic Hebrew for all areas outside of Jerusalem. See e.g. Sheq. 7:3.

Rashbam appears to be playing with the language of Rashi, ad vs. 19. Rashi (following Mekhilta *Pisḥa'* 10 [Laut. ed. p. 77]) points out there that the phrase לא ימצא בבתיכם outlaws owning leaven only in one's house. Rashi then asks how we know that it is forbidden to own leaven בגבולין--i.e. outside of one's house--and he answers that we learn about the גבולין from Ex. 13:7. Rashbam, playing on the word גבולין which could mean either "outside Jerusalem" or "outside one's home," then writes that we learn about eating matzot in the גבולין--i.e. the area outside of Jerusalem--from 12:20 ("in all your settlements").

[56]Rashbam explains that while the commandment of eating the paschal sacrifice limits that eating to the central shrine (see Deut. 16:5-7), the text emphasizes that the commandment of matzot applies wherever Jews live. Rashbam's explanation opposes the midrashic reading of Rashi, LT and Sekhel Tov (following Mekhilta *Pisḥa'* 10 [Laut. ed. p. 80]) that "in all your settlements" means that only matzah that one would be allowed to eat in any city (as opposed to matzah made from, for example, *ma'aser sheni* wheat, which should be consumed only in Jerusalem; see Deut. 12:17-18) can be used for making the matzot that one eats at the seder.

12:21 למשפחותיכם [PICK OUT LAMBS] FOR YOUR FAMILIES: [The text is to be understood] as it is written above (vs. 3), "[shall take] a lamb to a family."[57]

12:22 בסף: means "in a vessel,"[58] as it is written "שומרי הסף--guardians of the vessels" (2 Kings 12:10)[59] or "ספות כסף--silver bowls" (ibid., vs. 14).[60]

לא תצאו NONE OF YOU SHALL GO OUTSIDE [THE DOOR OF HIS HOUSE UNTIL MORNING]: Because my sign, the blood on the doorposts, will protect you.[61]

---

[57] I.e. Moses is now fulfilling the mission that he was given in the beginning of chapter 12. So also Rashi.

[58] Two opinions are expressed in the Mekhilta (Pisḥa' 6 and 11 [Laut. ed. pp. 44 and 84]) about the meaning of the word סף here. R. Ishmael interprets it as "threshold" while R. Akiva sees it as meaning a "vessel." (In other biblical passages both uses of the word סף can be found; see BDB p. 706.) Both Rashi and Rashbam follow R. Akiva's opinion. So also Onq.

[59] One might imagine that this phrase, שומרי הסף, which appears a number of times in the Bible, would not be the best prooftext for Rashbam's claim, that סף here in Exodus means a vessel. In fact one might argue that it would be a good prooftext for the other position, that of R. Ishmael, that סף here in Exodus means a threshold. (See previous note.) Generally most exegetes have interpeted שומרי הסף as meaning "guardians of the threshold" or "door-keepers," particularly where the phrase appears in Est. 2:21. (See e.g. NJPS in Est. and BDB.) Still many Jewish exegetes, like Rashbam here, interpreted the phrase שומרי הסף as meaning "the guardians of the vessels," particularly in the verses that refer to officials of the Temple. See e.g. Qimhi and Gersonides to 2 Kings 12:10 and the opinion attributed to Qara in Jellinek's collection of French exegesis on Esther, ad Est. 2:21 ("שומרי הסף: שומרי הכלים"; however ad II Kings 23:4 Qara interprets שומרי הסף differently).

[60] This second prooftext is the same one used by Rashi, here. Rashi would not agree to Rashbam's first prooftext, as Rashi feels that שומרי הסף means "guardians of the threshold." See Rashi ad 2 Kings 12:10.

[61] As long as you stay indoors.

EXODUS XII

12:26 מה WHAT DO YOU MEAN BY THIS RITE?: which differs from [the rites of] the other holidays in a number of ways?[62]

12:27 אשר פסח BECAUSE HE PASSED OVER: פסח means that he skipped and passed over.[63]

12:29 בחצי הלילה IN THE MIDDLE OF THE NIGHT: When the Jews were eating their Passover sacrifices.[64]

---

[62] Rashbam explains why both here and in other biblical passages children's questions are often connected to the Passover. (See also Ex. 13:14 and Deut.6:20.) Rashbam's explanation--that questions are the natural result of the unusual observances of this holiday--is a common rabbinic idea. See e.g. Pes. 115b: "כדי שיכירו תינוקות וישאלו--so that the children will notice [the differences] and will ask." iE ad vs. 24 (in his longer comm. only) follows Rashbam in connecting the question of vs. 26 to the unusual rites of passover.

Rashbam opposes the midrashic explanation of the Mekhilta *Pisḥa'* 12 (Laut. ed. p. 94) that sees the hypothetical questioner here in this verse as posing an inappropriate question, one that would be asked only if the Torah would be forgotten. See LT and Sekhel Tov who cite that midrash and who point out (most clearly in Sekhel Tov) that the question in this verse is the one that the Passover Haggadah assigns to the wicked son. Rashbam explains that questions about the Passover are natural (and probably desirable).

[63] Rashbam again emphasizes that the verb פ-ס-ח in this story means to pass over, not to have mercy. See Rashbam's comment to vs. 11 and my notes there.

[64] Rashbam may be opposing the interpretation of the Mekhlita (*Pisḥa'* 13 [Laut. ed. p. 96]), cited by LT and Sekhel Tov, that the reason that the text says בחצי הלילה is to emphasize God's power and ability to make sure that the event would occur precisely at one moment, at the precise time of astronomical midnight. Rashbam says more simply that the phrase teaches that at the time that the Egyptians were being killed the Jews were eating their Passover sacrifices. (See vs. 8 above.) Cf. Tanh. B. *Bo'* 16 which suggests that this verse portrays the Egyptians dying while the Jews were safely in their beds.

I have found no other exegete who offers the interpretation that Rashbam offers and that fact is not surprising. A well known mishnah (Zev. 5:8) teaches that one must finish eating the paschal sacrifice *before* midnight. Why then does Rashbam go out of his way to say that the Jews were eating their paschal sacrifices בחצי הלילה, which one would think means "at midnight"?

Presumably Rashbam does not accept the interpretation that בחצי הלילה means "midnight," but like NJPS and iE (longer comm. ad 11:4) sees it as meaning less

היושב על כסאו [FROM THE FIRST-BORN OF PHARAOH] WHO SITS ON THE THRONE: means who, had he lived,[65] was destined to sit on the throne.[66]

12:32 וגם תברכו גם אותי: should be understood as if וברכתם גם אותי were written.[67]

12:34 בצקו ITS DOUGH: From בָּצֵק [one says] בְּצֵקוֹ, just as [one says] כְּתֵפוֹ[68] from כָּתֵף.[69]

---

specifically "in the middle of the night." There is then no halakhic problem in saying that the Jews were eating their paschal sacrifices "in the middle of the night." Still Rashbam's seemingly impish reading, for which there is no textual compulsion, will presumably disturb halakhists who are certain that בחצי הלילה means "at midnight."

[65]אילו חייה, an allusion to the language of Eccl. 6:6.

[66]So also Onq. here and ad 11:5, and also LT, Sekhel Tov and iE (longer comm. only) all ad 11:5. Cf. NJPS: "from the first-born of Pharaoh who sat on the throne," seeing היושב על כסאו as modifying "Pharaoh," not as modifying "first-born," as Rashbam would have it.

[67]Rashbam argues on a number of occasions (a list can be found in RSBM, p. 143, note 2) that the word גם is not always placed in the Torah precisely at the contextually desirable spot. A phrase like (Num. 22:33) "גם אותך הרגתי"--lit. "I will kill you also," should best be understood to mean "I will also kill you," as if גם הרגתי אותך were written.

However, as I wrote in my Genesis volume (p. 175, ad 29:30) it is hard to understand why Rashbam is troubled about the word order here in Exodus. The phrase וברכתם גם אותי seems perfectly reasonable the way it is written; see e.g. NJPS: "may you bring a blessing upon me also." Rashbam's proposed syntactical understanding, "take your flocks . . . go . . . and also bring a blessing on me," seems clumsy and unnecessary.

[68]This precise form does not appear in the Bible. See however כְּתֵפִי (Job 31:22).

[69]Rashbam's grammatical point seems simple and essentially superfluous. It is however possible that he is reacting to the interpretation found in Sekhel Tov's comm. where בצקו is seen as having the root צ-ק and as being related to the word בְּצֶקֶת in the phrase (Job 38:38), "בצקת עפר למוצק"--the earth melts into a mass."

משארותם THEIR KNEADING BOWLS: [A משארת is] a receptacle into which one puts dough. Proof of this interpretation can be adduced from the verse (Deut. 28:5) "Blessed shall be your basket (טנאך) and your kneading bowl (ומשארתך)." Just as the טנא is the basket into which one puts fruit, so the משארת is the receptacle into which one puts dough. That verse [in Deuteronomy] is a blessing for receptacles--that they should be filled with fruit and with dough.[70]

12:36 נתן THE LORD HAD DISPOSED THE EGYPTIANS FAVORABLY TOWARD THE PEOPLE: so that they gave them items as outright gifts.[71] This verse fulfills what is written in [the Torah portion] *'Elleh shemot* (3:21), "I will dispose the Egyptians favorably toward this people."

וישאילום: means that the Egyptians [gave presents] to the Israelites.[72]

Sekhel Tov attributes this interpretation to "מסלסלי התורה," (an unusual phrase that appears three times in that work [here and ad Ex. 9:25 and 18:8] and a few times in the work *'Even boḥan* by the same author) and it would seem that the reference is to Dunash. In our texts of Dunash's *Teshuvot*, number 150 (Filipowski edition), the issue of the roots ב-צ-ק and צ-ק is discussed, but no specific reference is made to the verse in Job. However, as Filipowski notes on p. 93, it is clear that our texts of Dunash's *teshuvah* 150 are missing some of the original text. Rabbenu Tam in his defense of Menahem, (Filipowski's edition, pp. 92-93) quotes Dunash as follows: גם כי אמר דונש למנחח עם בצק ועריסה חברת למה שכחת בצקת עפר. In other words Rabbenu Tam had a version of Dunash's *teshuvah* 150 in which Dunash connected the noun בצק to the word בצקת in Job 38 and Sekhel Tov may have had that same version too. It is possible then that Rashbam is reacting here either to the position of Dunash (Rashbam probably had the same version of Dunash's *Teshuvot* that his brother Rabbenu Tam had) or to the citation of that position in Sekhel Tov.

[70]Rashbam opposes the interpretation offered by Rashi (following Mekhilta *Pisha'* 13 [Laut. ed. p. 104]) that משארותם means "their leftovers (of matzot and bitter herbs)." Like Rashi, see LT; like Rashbam, see Sekhel Tov and iE (longer comm. only, with the same prooftext from Deut. 28). Moderns universally follow Rashbam's reading.

[71]See Rashbam's comm. to 3:22, s.v. ושאלה, and ad 11:2, and notes ad 3:22.

[72]"וישאילום: מצרים לישראל." These opening words of Rashbam here are, verbatim, the opening words of Sekhel Tov's comment to this verse. Rashbam's continuing explanation, though, is opposed to that of Sekhel Tov who, following the

The Israelites were the ones who requested (השואלים) and the Egyptians were the ones who fulfilled the request (המשאילים). [וישאילום means] "they fulfilled the requests and gave them gifts." The person who asks for something is described with a *qal* verb,[73] while the person who gives what was requested is described with a *hifil* verb.[74] "משאיל" means "to give that which was requested."[75]

וינצלו THEY STRIPPED THE EGYPTIANS: They requested the [Egyptians'] fine jewelry (עדיי) and[76] clothing. [After they received

---

Mekhilta *Pisḥa'* 13 (Laut. ed. p. 105), says that וישאילום means that the Egyptians hurried to lend things to the Israelites even before the Israelites finished asking for the items.

Rashbam also opposes the similar interpretation found in Rashi (also from the Mekhilta, *ibid.*, p. 106)) who says that וישאילום implies that the Egyptians gave the Israelites more than they asked for.

[73]קרוי פועל.

[74]קרוי מפעיל.

[75]Rashbam's long explanation here is prompted by the fact that he knows that the *hifil* form here, וישאילום, does not fit in well with his assertion that what the Egyptians did was give outright gifts to the Israelites. To support his interpretation, he has to posit that the *hifil* of the verb ש-א-ל in biblical Hebrew means "to grant a request."

Rashbam already argued reasonably back ad 3:21 that *qal* forms of the verb ש-א-ל need not mean "to borrow"; they can mean "to request [a gift]." However *hifil* forms of ש-א-ל consistently mean "to lend" in rabbinic Hebrew. (There is only one other example of a *hifil* form of ש-א-ל in the Bible, השאילתיהו in I Sam. 1:28. The passage there is difficult but most exegetes see it as meaning "to lend.") Accordingly Rashbam goes to great lengths here to argue that ש-א-ל in the *qal* can mean "to make a request," it makes sense that ש-א-ל in the *hifil* can mean "to grant a request."

Rashbam here follows the interpretation that can be found in ibn Janah, *Sefer ha-shorashim*, s.v. ש-א-ל. ibn Janah argues further that השאילתיהו in I Sam. supports his understanding that וישאילום means "to grant outright," not "to lend."

Like Rashbam, see NJPS here: "they let them have their request."

[76]The ms. reads עדיי טוב מלבושיהן שאלו, a syntactical construction that I cannot understand. I have translated as if ומלבושיהן were written. See 3:22: "shall request . . . objects of silver and gold, and clothing."

EXODUS XII

these items] they put them on their sons and daughters.[77] [The verb נ-צ-ל is standardly used for jewelry] as it is written (Ex. 33:6), "The Israelites remained stripped (ויתנצלו) of their jewelry from Mount Horeb onward."[78]

12:38 ערב A MIXED MULTITUDE: [ערב is] connected to the word תערובת--mixture. [In other words, the Israelites mixed with other nations,] as it is written (Ps. 106:35) "they mingled with the nations."[79]

12:39 עוגות CAKES [OF DOUGH]: [They are called "עוגות--cakes"] because the word "לחם--bread" can only be used about something that was baked in an oven.[80]

כי לא חמץ FOR IT WAS NOT LEAVENED: [חָמֵץ is not a noun, but a past-tense verb; the phrase means,] "because it had not leavened." So

---

[77] An allusion to 3:22: "Each woman shall request . . . and you shall put these on your sons and daughters."

[78] Rashbam apparently follows Sekhel Tov in saying that the verb וינצלו refers to jewelry. Sekhel Tov also cites the same verse, Ex. 33:6, to prove that point.

[79] Ps. 106 deals with the story of the exodus from Egypt, although from the context of vs. 35 it seems that that verse is describing the assimilation of the Israelites in Canaan, after the conquest.

Rashbam's interpretation of ערב רב is basically the same as that of Rashi and iE, although Rashi uses the term גרים (presumably "converts") to describe this multitude, while iE and Rashbam do not.

[80] Rashbam tries to distinguish between the phrase עוגות מצות here and the phrase לחם מצות in Ex. 29:2. (See also his comm. there.) He says that a regular matzah baked in an oven would be called לחם, while any matzah baked outside of an oven would be called an עוגה. His interpretation is then, practically speaking, similar to that of Rashi, Saadyah, LT, and Sekhel Tov who all say (following the Mekhilta *Pisha'* 14 [Laut. ed. p. 110]) that an עוגה here means a חררה, i.e. a cake baked over coals.

But Rashbam's language אין לחם אלא האפוי בתנור is noteworthy. It is a verbatim citation of the words of Rabbi Yehudah in Pes. 37b (said in an entirely different context). Rashbam presumably preferred this formulation over the words of Sekhel Tov (and the Mekhilta) אין עוגה אלא חררה words that have the precise same syntax as those of Rashbam.

also [כָּבֵד is neither an adjective nor a noun in the phrase] (Ex. 7:14), "כבד לב פרעה--Pharaoh's heart has stiffened"; it is a past-tense verb.[81] So also (Gen. 27:14) "אָהֵב אביו--as his father liked," and (I Kings 1:1) "והמלך דוד זָקֵן--King David grew old."[82]

וגם צידה NOR HAD THEY PREPARED ANY PROVISIONS for the journey[83] FOR THEMSELVES: And that is why they had to complain in order to receive bread and water.[84]

12:40 ומושב THE LENGTH OF TIME THAT THE ISRAELITES LIVED IN EGYPT WAS until FOUR HUNDRED AND THIRTY

---

[81]לשון פעל. Rosin (in RSBM, p. 134) suggests that לשון פעל in Rashbam's language means "a verb." I think that it means "a verb in the past tense." All the examples cited by Rosin there are of past-tense verbs.

[82]So also iE, shorter comm. (re חָמֵץ).
On the meaning of Rashbam's comment, see my notes above ad 7:14.

[83]Rashbam adds the word לדרך after the word צידה in his paraphrase of the verse. The phrase "צידה לדרך--provisions for the journey" occurs a number of times in the Bible; see e.g. Gen. 42:25. The Mekhilta, *ibid.*, also uses the same phrase, as does Rashi in his comm. to the verse.

[84]Rashbam explains this phrase as serving a literary purpose, using his standard principle of anticipation. The purpose of the phrase, "nor had they prepared any provisions for themselves," is to anticipate, preparing the reader for the fact that the Israelites will be complaining about the lack of bread and water very soon, right after the exodus itself. (See e.g. 15:24 and 16:2-3.) The text has to tell us that they had no provisions with them so that we will not be shocked by those complaints. (On anticipation in Rashbam, see my Genesis volume, pp. 400-421.)

Rashbam's interpretation is opposed to that of Rashi, LT and Sekhel Tov who (following Mekhilta, *ibid.*) say that the purpose of this phrase is to praise the Israelites for being willing to leave Egypt without any provisions for the road. Cf. JBS who suggests that the text is critical of the Israelites. They left Egypt without having prepared any provisions even though they had been told that they were leaving. They hadn't believed that they would be asked to leave so quickly.

EXODUS XII

YEARS had passed[85] from the time that God spoke to Abraham "between the pieces":[86] For Abraham was seventy years old when God spoke to him "between the pieces"[87] [and from that point until the exodus four hundred and thirty years elapsed. The four hundred years, spoken of in the verse that begins "Your offspring shall be strangers,"

---

[85]This verse was extremely problematic for classical Jewish exegetes. First of all, this text, on the literal level, says that the Israelites were in Egypt for 430 years; Gen. 15:13 says that it would be only 400 years. Furthermore, simple arithmetic based on the ages of Levi, Kohath, Amram and Moses (Ex. 6:16-20 and 7:7) shows that it is not possible that the Jews lived in Egypt for anywhere near 400 years, let alone 430 years. (See the calculations here in the commentaries of Rashi and iE and see my last note on Ex. 6:16.) Rashbam accordingly interprets this verse as meaning that "the length of time that the Jews lived in Egypt" finished at the same time that the "four hundred and thirty years [from the time of the 'covenant between the pieces']" also elapsed. Rashbam's approach to the problem is essentially the same as that of Rashi, Mekhilta (*ibid.*, p. 111), Seder Olam 1, LT, and Sekhel Tov, and, with minor variations, iE, JBS and Nahm.

[86]I.e. in the ברית בין הבתרים (Gen. 15:13-16).

[87]So also Rashi, Mekhilta (*ibid.*), Seder Olam 1, LT and Sekhel Tov.
   While the arithmetic does work out according to this approach, the problem with claiming that Abraham was 70 years old when God spoke to him "between the pieces" is that the text tells us (Gen. 12:4) that he was already 75 years old when he set out for Canaan from Haran. It is not easy to claim that the "covenant between the pieces" took place before Abraham moved to Canaan. The references to Canaan in God's speech of the covenant seem indisputable (e.g. "they shall return *here* in the fourth generation"). Rashbam presumably would have to claim, as Seder Olam does, that Abraham moved to Canaan twice. He came to Canaan before his seventieth birthday, heard the "covenant between the pieces," returned to Haran and then set off for the promised land a second time when he was 75 years old. Cf. the simpler approach of JBS and iE who claim that the *terminus a quo* for counting the 430 years should be Abraham's departure from his native Ur (which arguably might have been five years before he left Haran to go to Canaan; see Gen. 11:31: "they set out together from Ur of the Chaldeans for the land of Canaan; but when they came as far as Haran they settled there"), and not the "covenant between the pieces."
   It is surprising to find Rashbam offering an interpretation that is so heavily dependent on midrashim that are far from the plain meaning of the biblical text. Apparently the problems of the contradictions between Gen. 14, Exodus 6 and Exodus 12 are simply not solvable on the *peshaṭ* level and Rashbam had to have recourse to a non-*peshaṭ* approach.

(Gen. 15:13) began only with the birth of Isaac,[88] as I explained above in [my commentary on the covenant] "between the pieces."[89]

12:41 ויהי AT THE END OF THIRTY YEARS--since the "covenant between the pieces"--AND FOUR HUNDRED YEARS--since the birth of Isaac[90]--ON THAT VERY DAY [ALL THE RANKS OF THE LORD DEPARTED]: Still they lived in Egypt only for the last two hundred and ten years of the [total of] four hundred and thirty years.[91]

12:42 ליל IT WAS A NIGHT OF EXPECTATION (שמורים) FOR THE LORD: Since the days of their forefather [Abraham], God had been waiting for this night in order to rescue the Jews as He had promised.[92]

---

[88]Isaac was born when Abraham was one hundred years old (Gen. 21:5). So if four hundred and thirty years elapsed from "the covenant between the pieces" until the exodus, then there must have been four hundred years from the birth of Isaac until the exodus.

[89]Presumably in his comm. ad Gen. 15:13, in the lost section of his commentary on Genesis.

[90]See Rashbam's comm. on the previous verse.
    Instead of seeing the phrase שלושים שנה וארבע מאות שנה as referring simply to one time span of 430 years, Rashbam divides up the phrase into its two separate units: thirty years and four hundred years. Perhaps this is because he would like to see this verse as saying that the promise of Gen. 15:13, "for four hundred years," was in fact fulfilled.

[91]Based on two verses in Genesis (25:26 and 47:9) it is clear that 190 years (60+130) elapsed from Isaac's birth until Jacob went down to Egypt. If then one assumes that a total of 400 years elapsed from Isaac's birth to the exodus, then one has to say that the Jews spent 210 years in Egypt. The calculation that the Jews spent 210 years in Egypt is quite common in rabbinic literature; see e.g. PDRE 48, Seder Olam 3. See also Rashi ad Gen. 42:2.

[92]In the Mekhilta (*ibid.*, p. 116) and in Tanh. *Bo'* 9 one can find the interpretation that connects this verse to the fulfillment of those promises made to Abraham in Gen. 15. However, in those two sources that idea is connected to the phrase "הוא הלילה הזה לה'--that same night is the LORD's." (See similarly Rashi here, s.v. הוא הלילה). Rashi (s.v. ליל שמורים הוא) took that idea and connected it to the phrase "ליל שמורים"

EXODUS XII

And for the Israelites, it will be A NIGHT OF EXPECTATION THROUGHOUT THE AGES: In all their generations they will look forward to this night[93] to observe the Pasover holiday in accordance with all its rules.[94] שמורים means to await, as in the verse (Gen. 37:11), "His father waited for the matter to come true (שמר את הדבר)."[95]

הוא לה'--it was a night of expectation for the LORD." שמורים, according to Rashi, means that God had been looking forward to the opportunity to fulfil that promise. Rashbam's interpretation of the first half of this verse follows Rashi.

[93]Rashbam parts company with Rashi as to how to explain the second שמורים that appears in this verse. Rashi, following Pes. 109b, inteprets this second "שמורים" in a manner that is entirely unconnected with his understanding of the first "שמורים" in the verse. He says that this second one means that the Jewish people are especially protected from demons on the eve of passover. Rashbam, it would seem, is taking Rashi's interpretation for the first שמורים and saying that it must be applied, for consistency's sake, also to the second שמורים in the verse. The first one (שמורים הוא לה') means that God, for many generations, awaited this night; the second one (שמורים לכל בני ישראל לדורותם) means that Jews throughout the generations await the holiday of Passover.

Most exegetes, classical and modern, interpreted שמורים in a manner different from Rashbam, although there is no clear consensus about what the word really means. Like Rashbam, see also JBS and NJPSC to this verse.

[94]Rashbam's languge alludes to Numbers 9:3.

[95]Sekhel Tov in his comm. also cites this same verse from Gen. to prove the meaning of שמורים here, although his interpretation of the verse is not the same as Rashbam's.

Rashbam's interpretation here of Gen. 37:11 is the same as that of Rashi, there. (See also Rashbam ad Gen. 45:27 and Rashi ad Berakhot 3a, s.v. ושמר. See also Touitou, *Tarbiz* 52, 365.) Rashi's interpretation of the first שמורים in this verse (שומר ומצפה לו) is very similar to his interpretation of the phrase שמר את הדבר in Gen. 37 (ממתין ומצפה מתי יבא). Yet it is only Rashbam (and Sekhel Tov), not Rashi, who specifically points out the parallel between the two passages.

12:46 ועצם לא תשברו בו NOR SHALL YOU BREAK A BONE OF IT: [I.e. one should eat the paschal sacrifice] the way one eats when one is in a hurry.[96]

12:48 וכל ערל NO UNCIRCUMCISED MAN [MAY EAT OF IT]: [This refers to] an Israelite who [legitimately] was not circumcised because his brothers had died as a result of the circumcision procedure.[97]

---

[96]See Rashbam's comm. and notes to vs. 8, above. For another explanation of the purpose of this law, see *Sefer ha-ḥinnukh*, commandment 16.

It is definitely possible that there are polemical reasons why Rashbam keeps explaining that the laws of eating the paschal sacrifice are understandable according to the principle of "haste." Christians often cited the details of the paschal sacrifice in polemics with Jews, arguing that they were allusions to what happened to Jesus, "the lamb of God," during the crucifixion. In John 19:36, Exodus 12:46 is specifically applied to Jesus, who was ostensibly crucified without any of his bones breaking.

See for example the arguments of "the heretics" [i.e. the Christians] cited by the author of *Niṣṣaḥon Vetus* (Berger's edition, pp. 52, 54 and 64), concerning the meaning of all the details of the paschal sacrifice. There (p. 52) the Christians are quoted as saying that there could not be reasons for all these details about the paschal sacrifice and that accordingly these passages demand a symbolic interpretation concerning Jesus. ("Why do you not consider the apparently peculiar nature of the laws . . .? . . . There are many peculiarities in that passage and what could be the reason for them? Are you truly animals that you do not perceive what these things symbolize?") It is not difficult to imagine that Rashbam heard arguments of this nature about the paschal sacrifice and tried to demonstrate that on the *peshaṭ* level the details of that sacrifice were easily understandable and that there was no need for viewing these verses as symbolizing Jesus' crucifixion.

For many more references to arguments concerning the paschal sacrifice in Jewish-Christian polemics, see Berger, pp. 243-4.

[97]Rashbam adopts the intepretation of Rashi, LT and Sekhel Tov. See similarly Mekhilta (*ibid.*, pp. 127-128) and Pes. 96a (and Rashi there, s.v. ערל).

It is surprising to find Rashbam offering such a non-*peshaṭ*-oriented explanation. Sekhel Tov, in standard halakhic style, argues that something new must be learned from this phrase, something that was not included in the previous verses. ("למה נאמר והלא כבר נאמר כל בן נכר לא יאכל בו אלא כל ערל לא יאכל בו זה ישראל שלא מל מפני שמתו אחיו מחמת מילה--Why is this written? Does the verse not already say 'No foreigner shall eat of it'? Rather [one must say that the phrase] 'No uncircumcised man may eat of it' refers to an Israelite whose brothers died as a result of the circumcision procedure [and accordingly legitimately he was not circumcised]."

12:51 ויהי [On] THAT VERY DAY [that THE LORD FREED THE ISRAELITES]: Even though this was already written above (vs. 41) it is again repeated here to teach you that on that same day that they left, (13:1-2) God said to Moses, "CONSECRATE TO ME EVERY FIRST-BORN."[98]

It is possible that Sekhel Tov is quoting from the text of the Mekhilta that he had, although this precise language is not found in our texts of the Mekhilta. See the discussion in Kasher, p. 82, note 701.). Yet Rashbam with his orientation to *peshaṭ* is well aware of the tendency of biblical verses to write general statements such as "No uncircumcised man may eat of it" after listing a number of such uncircumcised people (the foreigner, the slave, the bound or hired laborer, the stranger [vss. 43-48]). And he is even willing occasionally to read a legal text from the Torah in such a manner. See his comm. ad Ex. 21:3, s.v. אם, and ad Lev. 12:2 for example. The same could easily have been said of this verse in Exodus. (See e.g. the comm. of Amos Hakham, *Da'at Miqra'* series, here ["לחזוק ולהטעמה כפל כאן הכתוב--the text repeats the idea here to reinforce it and explain it"]).

But Rashbam, the halakhist, feels that this all-inclusive language, "*No uncircumcised person,*" includes, even on the *peshaṭ* level, any man with a foreskin. This would naturally include all uncircumcised men, even Jews who legitimately refrained from circumcision because of a family record of fatalities from the procedure. This time, as Rashbam feels that he can, on some level, connect the halakhah to the *peshaṭ*, he does so.

See iE (longer comm. only) who also feels that something new must be learned from the phrase, "No uncircumcised person."

[98]In other words this verse is an example of repetitive resumption. The same idea is repeated here in order to inform the reader when it was that the events of chapter 13 occurred. They took place "On that very day that the LORD freed the Israelites." (As Cassuto notes, the connection of our verse to chapter 13 is reinforced by vs. 3, there, "Remember *this day* (היום הזה; the same phrase as in our verse) on which you went free."

Like Rashbam, see iE, both commentaries, and NJPSC. See the criticism of this interpretation by Luzzatto.

EXODUS XIII

13:2 פטר THE FIRST ISSUE: [The word פטר] is connected to the idea of "opening," as in the phrase, (Prov. 17:14) "To start a quarrel is to open (פוטר) a sluice."[1]

באדם [EVERY FIRST-BORN] MAN: In the beginning the service [of God] was entrusted to the first-borns.[2]

13:4 האביב ABIB: [The word אביב refers to] the early growth[3] and ripening of the crops, as in the phrases (Job 8:12) "While still tender

---

[1] Rashbam follows Rashi's interpretation of the verse, with one of the same prooftexts that Rashi used. See also Mekhilta *Pisha'* 16 (Laut. ed. p. 129), iE and Sekhel Tov.

[2] In other words, the roles that were later served by the *kohanim* were at first the responsibility of the first-borns. (See Zev. 115b.) "Consecrating the first-born men" then means assigning to them the job of the service of God. See also Rashbam's comm. ad 19:22 and ad 24:5.
   Verse 2 here makes a general statement about consecrating first-borns, human and animal. In verses 11-13 further details are provided about the treatment of first-borns. Rashbam distinguishes between this verse and those later verses. (Cf. his comm. here and ad vs. 13.) Our verse describes the consecration of the first-borns to conduct God's service. The details about redeeming the first-born males in the later verses begin with the words "When the LORD has brought you into the land of the Canaanites." The instruction to redeem one's first-born males was *not*, according to Rashbam, in force when the Jews left Egypt. It came into force only after the events of Num. 3:40-51, "in the second year [following the exodus] after the Tabernacle was set up" (Rashbam ad Ex. 13:13), after the decision was made to reassign the duties of conducting God's service to the Levites instead of the first-borns.
   Accordingly Rashbam cannot interpret that the consecration referred to in this verse means "redeeming" the first-borns. Cf. e.g. iE, shorter comm., and Seforno who interpret the "consecration" of vs. 2 as a reference to redemption. See like Rashbam NJPSC here: "It may . . . be safely inferred that Moses is here instructed to install the first-born to fulfill priestly duties." The simple meaning of vs. 15 would seem to go against Rashbam's interpretation, but see his comm. and my notes there.

[3] ביכור. Rashbam uses this word perhaps in an attempt to connect this verse with the previous section that dealt with the first-born (בכור).

(בָּאֻבּוֹ), not yet plucked" and (Song 6:11) "the budding (בְּאִבֵּי) of the vale."[4] [In those two words] the *dagesh* [in the letter *bet*] compensates for the missing second *bet* of the root.[5]

13:8 בעבור זה BECAUSE OF THAT REASON, that[6] THE LORD DID miracles FOR ME: in Egypt, that is why I am observing this practice.[7] So also [one should see the conjunction אשר as self-understood in the verse] (Ps. 118:24) "On that day *that* the LORD has made"--that I have become the chief cornerstone[8]--"let us exult and rejoice on it."[9]

---

[4]In other words אביב, באבו and באבי are all from the root א-ב-ב, which means "to provide early fruits." See also Rashbam's comm. to 23:16, s.v. וחג האסיף. Rashbam's etymological explanation was adopted also by iE, longer commentary only (iE also uses the same word, ביכור, in his comm.), and by Qimhi in *Sefer ha-shorashim*, s.v. א-ב. iE and Qimhi further attempt to connect these words to "אב--father." See the criticism of that approach in Luzzatto on this verse.

[5]See Qimhi, *ibid.*, who mentions that some argue that the *dagesh* compensates for a missing *nun*, and connect באבו and באבי to the Aramaic "אנבא--fruit." (Menahem, s.v. א-ב, also alludes to a similar explanation.) See BDB, s.v. א-ב-ב, which cites both explanations and prefers the one offered by Rashbam.

[6]Rashbam suggests that the verse is best understood if one reads it as if the word אשר were written before the words עשה ה'.

[7]עובד עבודה הזאת; using the language of vs. 5.

[8]An allusion to verse 22, there.

[9]As Rosin notes here, Rashbam wrote in his comm. to Gen. 18:5 that the word אשר is often omitted by the text and must be seen as self-understood.

The verse here in Exodus is problematic for at the simplest level it seems to say that God took the Israelites out of Egypt "בעבור זה--for the sake of *this*," presumably so that the Israelites would observe Passover. As noted already by ibn Janah (cited by iE here) the causation makes more sense in the opposite direction: it is not that God took the Israelites out of Egypt because he wanted them to observe Passover; rather they observe Passover because God took them out of Egypt. iE (in both his commentaries) takes issue with what he sees as ibn Janah's cavalier attempt to reverse the meaning of a biblical verse.

Rashbam arrives at the same conclusion as ibn Janah but does so by positing that the word אשר should be seen as understood here (and in other biblical verses). Nahm. independently comes up with the same interpretation as Rashbam. Modern

EXODUS XIII

13:9 לאות על ידך A SIGN ON YOUR HAND: According to the profound plain meaning of Scripture, it will always be a reminder for you as if it were written on your hand. Like the verse (Song 8:6), "Let me be a seal on your heart."[10]

בין עיניך ON YOUR FOREHEAD[11]: Like an ornament or a gold chain[12] that is customarily put on the forehead for decoration.[13]

---

translations generally follow Rashbam's approach.

[10]Rashbam does not feel that the *peshat* level of intepretation of this verse refers to *tefillin*. It goes without saying that a pious Jew like Rashbam feels bound by the commandment of *tefillin*. He may in fact feel that in Dt. 6:8, which speaks in terms of *binding* something to one's arm, even the *peshat* level of interpretation would refer to *tefillin*. (So argues Touitou, *Milet* 2, pp. 287-288.) He however feels that here in Ex. 13 the context demands another reading.

Unlike Deut. 6, which refers explicitly to God's "instructions" in general and what steps a Jew should take to remember them, Ex. 13 refers specifically to the observance of Passover. As NJPSC put it, Rashbam explains that the idea of verse 9 "is that observance of the foregoing precepts possesses the same commemorative function in relation to the Exodus as do physical memory-aiding devices placed on the hand and head." In other words, verses 5-8 mean that for the Jew who "observes the practices" of Passover--spelled out in verses six and seven--those ceremonies will become as real and concrete as reminders on one's hand and head. As noted by Rosin, Rashbam follows here in a line of interpretation found in Menahem, *Mahberet*, s.v. טס.

The intepretation of this verse as metaphorical aroused much opposition among a number of medieval exegetes. iE in his shorter commentary rejects the metaphorical reading in moderate language. However in his longer comm. (written apparently after reading or hearing about Rashbam's comm.) he castigates such a reading on both religious and methodological grounds. See also the strident criticism of this position in JBS ad Num. 12:7 and ad Dt. 6:8. Still it is not clear that either JBS or iE is referring in his criticism to Rashbam. It is at least equally likely that they are opposing Karaite exegetes who drew halakhic conclusions from that interpretation and did not observe the law of *tefillin*. See the discussion of the issue as it relates to JBS in Kamin, *Jews and Christians Interpret the Bible*, Heb. section, p. 95, note 61. See iE ad Dt. 6:8 where he explicitly refers to this intepretation as that of the מכחישים, i.e. the Karaites.

[11]Lit. "between your eyes." See NJPSC who argues for the traditional Jewish understanding that בין עיניך, even on the *peshat* level, means "on your forehead."

[12]רביד זהב. See Gen. 41:42 (although there the gold chain is put around the neck).

13:10 החוקה THIS LAW: The law of Passover.[14]

13:12 והעברת YOU SHALL SET APART: Separate it from your animals[15] and give it to the priest and he will sacrifice it.[16]

שגר: [is connected to the root ש-ג-ר, "to send" and refers to offspring, i.e.] that which is "sent forth" from the womb.[17]

---

[13]Even here Rashbam's interpretation of בין עיניך is somewhat at odds with rabbinic tradition. The rabbis interpret בין עיניך as meaning על גובה של ראש (Mekhilta *Pisḥa'* 17; Laut. ed. p. 152), i.e. above the hairline. Rashbam sees a reference here to an ornament that is worn on the forehead, not in one's hair.

[14]חוקת הפסח. Rashbam connects the word, חוקה--law, in this verse to the words, חוקת הפסח--the law of the Pasover offering," back in 12:43. Rashbam directly opposes the reading of LT and Sekhel Tov (following Mekhilta, *ibid.*, pp. 154-5) that say that the law referred to in this verse is the law of *tefillin*.

In Men. 36b two opinions are presented as to the meaning of חוקה in this verse. Rashbam may be seen as following the opinion of Rabbi Akiva that the reference is to the law of Passover. See also Tos. there, s.v. ושמרת, who conclude that the halakha follows Rabbi Akiva's position . See however iE's shorter comm. where he, like Rashbam, seems attracted to the interpretation that the reference is to Passover and yet he defers to what he thinks is the traditional rabbinic interpretation, that the reference is to *tefillin*.

[15]So also Rashi, Lt and Sekhel Tov, following Mekhilta *Pisḥa'* 18 (Laut. ed., p. 159).

[16]Rashbam's comm. may be taking issue with that of two of his contemporaries. Sekhel Tov emphasizes in his comm. that the first half of this verse refers specifically to human first-borns ("דהיינו בכורי אדם"; see also the end of Rashi's comment on this verse.). Rashbam's explanation disagrees ("give it to the priest and he will sacrifice it"). Furthermore Rashbam's interpretation opposes the explanation of JBS who understands the verb והעברת figuratively ("separate the first-born from his previous status"); Rashbam understands it literally ("separate it and give it").

[17]The etymology provided by Rashbam (based on the use of the root in Aramaic and rabbinic Hebrew) is the same as that of Rashi, from the Mekhilta (*ibid.*, p. 160). However, Rashi and the Mekhilta see the word שגר as implying that which was sent out of the womb *not* in a timely manner, i.e. a stillborn. Rashbam, following the lead of LT and Sekhel Tov, sees no such implication to the word. For him the word simply means offspring. See similarly ibn Janah, *Sefer ha-shorashim*, s.v. ש-ג-ר.

EXODUS XIII 131

13:13 תפדה YOU MUST REDEEM [EVERY FIRST-BORN MALE AMONG YOUR CHILDREN]: After the Levites were consecrated in place of all the first-born[18] in the second year [following the Exodus],[19] after the Tabernacle was set up, [the first "excess" first-borns were redeemed when God commanded that they] "take five shekels per head" (Num. 3:47). [Then the text commands that, from then on,] "Take as their redemption price, from the age of one month up, the money equivalent [of five shekels]" (Num. 18:16).[20]

Proof can be adduced for Rashbam's reading from the phrase (Dt. 7:13) "שגר אלפיך--the calving of your herd," where שגר clearly does not mean stillborn.

[18] תחת כל בכור, a quotation from Num. 3:12.

[19] See Num 1:1.

[20] The main thrust of Rashbam's comment follows the position of Rashi who points out simply that the amount required for the redemption mentioned in this verse is defined in another passage in the Torah. (So also JBS.) Beyond that Rashbam points out once again that the commandment to redeem first-borns, though mentioned here right after the exodus, did not become operative until after the Tabernacle was erected in the second year following the Exodus. See Rashbam's comm. to vs. 2 above, s.v. באדם, and notes there.

Cf. iE (shorter comm.) who, as mentioned above, writes (ad 12:51) that there was a commandment to redeem first-borns immediately after the exodus. It is perhaps for that reason that iE writes (again in his shorter comm.) here, ad vs. 12, that it is not possible to know the correct amount of the redemption "מהכתוב כי אם מדברי הקבלה--from the Torah, only from the words of the rabbis." The comment appears to be quite strange, for the book of Numbers *does* legislate a redemption amount quite explicitly. However it is possible that iE is forced to offer such an interpretation because of his assertion that there was a commandment to redeem first-borns before and independent of the events of the book of Numbers when the Levites take the place of the first-borns. Then iE argues that the five shekels mentioned in Numbers logically apply only to that second kind of redemption and that tradition is needed to tell us what redemption amount is alluded to here. (See other attempted explanations of iE's position in Fleischer's edition, p. 80, note 1.)

13:15 ויהי WHEN PHARAOH STUBBORNLY REFUSED TO LET US GO: All these words are part of what you shall say to your son.[21] One can adduce proof from the words (vs. 16) "the LORD freed us from Egypt."[22] For the one who relates this entire section to Moses is God;[23] and it is the Israelite who is saying to his son "the LORD freed us."

It cannot be that Moses is reciting this verse (16) on his own for what reason would Moses have to tell the Israelites that (vs. 16) "It shall be a sign on your hand . . . that with a mighty hand the LORD freed us;"[24] rather it is the father who says these words to his son.[25]

---

[21] In other words, the quotation that was introduced with the words (vs. 14) "you shall say to him," includes the end of vs. 14 and all of verses 15 and 16. None of these verses is to be seen as the narrator's words.

[22] In other words, one could not attribute the words "the LORD freed us" to the narrator, as the narrator is God himself, as it says in verse 1. So then we must assume that the quotation that begins in 14b continues to the end of verse 16.

[23] I.e. God is the narrator of these verses, not Moses. If Moses were the narrator of these verses then it would be possible to see verse 16, and, if one desires, verse 15, as the words of the narrator, Moses. But since, according to Rashbam, God is the narrator, it is not possible for Him to say "the LORD freed us." So the words must be part of the father's speech.

[24] In other words, it is not only the language, "freed *us*," that Rashbam cites as proof. The meaning, according to Rashbam, also makes more sense if one sees these verses as part of the father's speech to his son. It makes more sense for a father in Canaan years later to tell his child that they are doing something to commemorate the exodus than to posit that Moses is telling the very Israelites who experienced the exodus that they have to commemorate it.

[25] Presumably one further reason that Rashbam insists on seeing at least verse 15 as part of the father's speech to his son is that it includes the phrase, "therefore I . . . redeem every first-born among my sons." As discussed above ad verses 2 and 13 Rashbam says that there was no commandment to redeem first-borns at the time of the exodus. Therefore the reference to redeeming first-borns in verse 15 must be part of the father's speech to his son "in time to come." Furthermore, Rashbam is arguing against an interpretation that would see verse 16 (and perhaps verse 15) as part of Moses' comments to the Israelites. While I have not found that interpretation written explicitly in any of the commentaries that preceeded Rashbam, that reading has much to recommend it and is adopted by numerous moderns (NJPS, RSV, Luzzatto, Childs, Noth). As to Rashbam's claim that the narrator of these verses is God, not Moses, it

EXODUS XIII

13:17-18 ויהי NOW WHEN PHARAOH LET THE PEOPLE GO: And God wanted to bring them to the land of Canaan[26] but He was unwilling to direct them BY WAY OF THE LAND OF THE PHILISTINES BECAUSE IT WAS NEARER.[27] [In other words,] that would have been the way to take to enter Canaan immediately. [Had they taken that route, then,] when they would have encountered the trouble of the wars of Canaan, they would have "headed back for Egypt." On a number of occasions that is what happened as it is written (Num. 14:3-4) "It would be better for us to go back to Egypt . . . Let us head back to Egypt," or

---

would seem that the simple sense of verse 3 ("And Moses said to the people . . .") contradicts that assertion. Presumably Rashbam would defend his reading and argue that the laws found in, for example, verses 6 and 7 could not reasonably be assumed to have been invented by Moses. So the speech of Moses that begins in verse three must simply represent Moses' conveying the words of God to the people. If the speech is made up of the words of God, then the phrase "the LORD freed us" must be assigned to the father, not to the narrator.

[26]Rashbam clarifies the implicit connection between the clauses of the verse: "when God took them out *the goal was to reach Canaan*; yet God did not take them the direct way.

[27]The major exegetical problem in the verse involves the literal sense of the phrase כי קרוב הוא. What does it mean that God did not take them via Philistia *because* it was the close route? Rashi's solution is to attach the phrase to the second part of the verse: he explains that because it was so close and it would be so easy to return to Egypt, that is why God did not take them that way. iE quotes another solution, in the name of R. Moses Jiqatilia, that כי here means "although"; God did not take them via Philistia *although* it was the close route.

Some (e.g. Krinski, in his notes to iE's comm.) have argued that Rashbam agrees with Rashi here. While the text is not clear, I think that Rashbam's explanation is that the phrase כי קרוב הוא does not explain the reason for the course of action that God *did* adopt, but rather the reason for the course of action that he *did not* adopt. God refrained from a certain course of action. And what was that course of action from which He refrained? It was "taking-them-via-Philistia-because-it-is-the-closer-route."

In other words, for Rashi the sentence could be paraphrased: "Because it was closer, that is why God did not take the Israelites via Philistia." For Rashbam the thoughts of the sentence could be paraphrased: "God could very well have taken the people via Philistia because Philistia is closer. But he did not do so. I.e. God did not adopt the course of action of 'taking-the-people-via-Philistia-because-it-is-closer'." A similar explanation can be found in Nahm.

(Num. 11:5) "We remember the fish that we used to eat free in Egypt."[28]   So that is why (18) GOD LED THE PEOPLE ROUNDABOUT BY WAY OF THE WILDERNESS, the long way. So it is written (Deut. 1:2) "It is eleven days from Horeb to Kadesh Barnea."[29]   However, only the Philistines stood between Egypt and Canaan, as is proven in the story of Isaac who was leaving Canaan to descend to Egypt by way of Philistia until God told him (Gen. 26:2-3) "[Do not go down to Egypt . . . .] Reside in this land," and (*ibid.*, 26:6) "So Isaac stayed in Gerar."[30]

13:18 וחמושים [THE ISRAELITES WENT UP] ARMED: With weapons.[31]   For they were[32] on the way to capture Canaan,[33] as it

---

[28]A similar argument can be found at greater length in Rashi, s.v. בראותם, following the Mekhilta *Beshallaḥ* 1 (Laut. ed. p. 173).

[29]The precise function of this prooftext at this point in the commentary is hard to understand. Since the next line in the commentary says, "*However*, (אבל) only the Philistines stood between Egypt and Canaan," it would seem that this current line of commentary is meant to show just how *long* a route the Israelites actually did take. However, in his comm. to Deut. 1:2, Rashbam understands that verse as pointing out just how *short* a distance Canaan was from Egypt, had the Israelites taken the direct route. While the precise function of the prooftext may be unclear, the general direction of Rashbam's understanding is easy enough to follow. (And if one erases the word "אבל--however," then the text reads smoothly.)

[30]Concerning the Isaac story, see similarly Rashbam's comm. to Gen. 26:1 and JBS here.

[31]Rashbam apparently opposes both the interpretations offered by Rashi, both of which are reworkings of the Mekhilta, (*ibid.*, pp. 174-175). He clearly opposes Rashi's second, midrashic reading, that sees in the word חמושים a reference to the alleged death of four fifths of all the Israelites back in Egypt during the plague of darkness.

Rashbam, to my mind, also opposes Rashi's first *peshaṭ*-oriented explanation. It appears to me that when Rashi says that חמושים means מזויינים, he means "well provided for," having everything that they need (including, but not limited to arms). See Sekhel Tov who writes specifically that חמושים can mean supplied with arms or supplied with other items. See also JBS who says that חמושים means "provided with sufficient amounts of food." Rashbam says that the word has a specific meaning of "armed with weapons." So also NJPSC; see the sources cited there, p. 246, note 39.

is written above (3:17), "I will take you out from the misery of Egypt to the land of the Canaanites." ["Armed with weapons" is] also [the meaning of the word חמושים] in the phrase "shall go across armed (חמושים)" in Joshua (1:14).³⁴

13:21 וה' THE LORD [WENT BEFORE THEM]: ["The LORD" here means] the angel who was moving the pillar of fire and the pillar of cloud.³⁵

יומם [THAT THEY MIGHT TRAVEL] DAY AND NIGHT: So that when Pharaoh would hear he would say that they were trying to run away³⁶ and then the Egyptians would chase after them.³⁷

---

³²According to the original plan, before the sin of the spies; see Dt. 1:19f., esp. vs. 21.

³³Rashbam's comment can be seen as opposing the explanation of Qara, whose words were inserted into most editions of Rashi's comm. to this verse without attribution. (See Gad, p. 21, and Berliner, *Peleṭat soferim*, p. 17.) According to Qara, the reason the Israelites had to be "חמושים--well provided for" was that they were wandering through the desert and they would not have many opportunities to purchase supplies. Rashbam says that they were "armed" for the battles that they were to encounter in Canaan ostensibly right away.

³⁴Both Rashi and Rashbam cite this prooftext for their different interpretations of what חמושים means. See NJPS in Josh. which notes that the meaning of the word חמושים in that verse is uncertain.

³⁵Presumably the major reason why Rashbam says that "the LORD" in this verse is a reference to an angel is, as Rosin notes, out of a desire to harmonize between this verse and 14:19 which states explicitly that an angel was in charge of the workings of the pillar of cloud. See Rashbam there. Rashbam directly opposes the numerous talmudic and midrashic passages that point out how it was God Himself who provided this service for the Israelites. See Qid. 32a, BQ 92b, A.Z. 11a and Mekhilta, *ibid.*, pp. 184-186. He may also be opposing the opinion that the angel and the cloud are one and the same. See notes below ad 14:19.

On Rashbam's willingness to identify the tetragrammaton with an angel, see my notes to 3:4 above. Here iE, in both of his commentaries, agrees with Rashbam. So also JBS ad 14:19.

³⁶See 14:5.

13:22 לא ימיש: ["God will not move (לא ימיש) the pillar of cloud. The subject of the verb ימיש is] God and the verb is causative,[38] to make something else move. The intransitive form[39] is ימוש, as in the phrase (Josh. 1:8), "Let not this Book of the Teaching cease (ימוש)."[40]

---

[37]Rashbam explains why the Israelites had to travel both by day and by night: it was part of the divine plan to get Pharaoh to chase after them by purposely trying to look *as if* they were trying to run away. All the Israelites' behavior was intentional and was (as Rashbam explains in his comm. to vs. 21) part of God's plan. Rashbam's comm. may be a reworking of what Sekhel Tov writes that the Israelites were travelling both by day and by night because they *were* running away from Pharaoh.

See Rashbam below ad 14:5 where he gives a slightly different explanation of why it was that Pharaoh reached the conclusion that the Israelites were trying to run away.

[38]Or perhaps, "the verb is *hifil*."

[39]Or perhaps, "the *qal* form."

[40]So also Rashi, JBS and iE, in both his commentaries.
This is not the only grammatical explanation for this verb. As Sekhel Tov notes, קא סלקא דעתין דלא ימיש על אחרים קא משתעי . . . אלא על כרחך לא ימיש דומיא דלא ימוש --i.e. that while one might be tempted to think that ימיש here is a *hifil* form, one ought rather to conclude that ימוש and ימיש are simply variant forms of the *qal*. Verb forms of מ-י-ש often appear in the *qal* with an intransitive meaning; see e.g. Ex. 33:11, Is. 46:7 and Ps. 55:12 (all cited by Sekhel Tov). Like Sekhel Tov, see Hizquni, Luzzatto, Jouon 113f and most modern translations. Like Rashi and Rashbam, see BDB. Melammed, p. 506, lists this comment of Rashbam as a פליטת קולמוס--a slip of the pen.

EXODUS XIV

14:3 נבוכים הם: means that "the depths of the sea (נבכי ים)"[1] are in front of them. That is why they turned back, because they did not know where to go.[2] For behind them THE WILDERNESS HAS CLOSED IN their path, for it was a place of "seraph serpents and scorpions,"[3] dangerous wild animals[4] and many worries.[5] That is why they left the place that they had been encamped at Etham at the edge of the wilderness (13:20) and now they came "between Migdol and the sea" (14:2) and they were encamped at the sea and the נבוכים, "the depths of the sea" were in front of them. They had no place to escape, neither forward nor backward.

נבוכים[6] means closed off[7] by the depths of the sea, as in the

---

[1] See Job 38:16 and see the comm. of Rashi there and here where he also connects the phrase in Job with our verse.

[2] Two different reasons appear to be given, here and in vs. 5, as to why Pharaoh would chase or did chase after the Israelites. Critical scholars often argue that the inconsistency here is a function of the different sources. See e.g. Noth, p. 111.

JBS argues that the Israelites turned around in order to fulfil what they had promised (e.g. 5:3), that they would go for three days and then come back. JBS then says that in verse 5 when the text says that Pharaoh was told that the people had fled, it means that slanderers circulated that false accusation against the Israelites. Rashbam in his comment here clearly opposes such a reading. For Rashbam's attempt to reconcile verse 3 and vs. 5, see comm. and notes below ad vs. 5.

[3] Deut. 8:15.

[4] The connection between wild animals and the wilderness is also made here in the Mekhilta *Beshallaḥ* 2 (Laut. ed. p. 191) and is picked up also by LT and Sekhel Tov.

[5] ודואגים שם. A difficult phrase, probably a textual corruption.

[6] Note Rashbam's style of first discussing the meaning of the verse as a whole and then returning to a discussion of an individual difficult word. See e.g. his comm. to Gen. 39:6 and see my notes there, p. 271.

phrase (Job 38:16), "Have you penetrated to the depths of the sea (נבכי ים)?" or the phrase (Job 28: 11) "the sources of the streams (מבכי נהרות)."

14:5 כי [THE KING OF EGYPT WAS TOLD] THAT THE PEOPLE HAD FLED: [One could tell that they were running away from the fact] that they had turned around.[8]

---

[7]So also Rashi. Both of them reject the understanding that is common today and that can be found already in the Mekhilta (ibid., pp. 190-191) that נבוכים means "confused" or "perplexed." Connecting this root to the idea of being closed in can be found already in Menahem, s.v. ב-כ. Cf. iE, longer comm. only, who disagrees with the explanation that Rashbam offers here.

[8]As noted above ad vs. 3, Rashbam is attempting to establish a connection between the different descriptions of the travels of the Israelites and the reasons given here and in vss. 2-3 to explain why Pharaoh chased after them. The meanderings of the Israelites, described in vs. 2, are, according to Rashbam, what led Pharaoh to conclude that the Israelites were running away. Rashbam's logic appears to be as follows: Pharaoh saw that the Israelites were not headed straight for some specific destination where they would sacrifice and then come back. They were wandering through the desert and doubling back, presumably in an attempt to find a reasonable way to escape. (The logic of this reading is made explicit in the later commentaries of Nahm. and Seforno.)

Rashbam's reading, as I noted above ad vs. 3, is also virtually the opposite of JBS's. According to JBS, the Israelites turned back *because* they were trying to fulfil their promise of coming back after three days. Rashbam writes that from the fact that the Israelites turned back Pharaoh was able to deduce that the Israelites were *not* fulfilling their promise.

Rashbam at the same time opposes the midrashic reading found in Mekhilta (ibid., p. 194) that the way that Pharaoh knew that the Israelites were running away was because the Israelites had beaten up the guards that Pharaoh sent along to accompany them. Then the guards came back and reported that the people were trying to escape. So also LT and Sekhel Tov. Rashbam also rejects the *peshaṭ*-like reworking of that midrash found in Rashi: the guards came back and reported that the Israelites had not turned around at the end of three days as they had promised (e.g. 5:3); hence Pharaoh knew that they were trying to escape.

מֵעֲבְדֵנוּ: has a *ḥaṭaf-qameṣ*;⁹ it means "מֵעֲבוֹד אוֹתָנוּ--from serving us."¹⁰ So also [one finds a *qameṣ qaṭan* in the forms] (Deut. 7:8) בָּאֱכֹל"--מִשְׁמְרוֹ אֶת הַשְּׁבוּעָה--keeping the oath," (Num. 26:10) בָּאֱכֹל הָאֵשׁ--when the fire consumed"¹¹ and (Ex. 16:3) "בְּאָכְלֵנוּ לֶחֶם לָשֹׂבַע --when we ate our fill of bread."

14:7 רכב בחור: Means "important, choice chariots."¹²

ושלישים WITH OFFICERS [IN ALL OF THEM]: שלישים means "officers."¹³ [The officers had to be mentioned here] because of [i.e.

---

⁹I.e. a *qameṣ qaṭan*.

¹⁰So also Rashi, but without any further examples. When Rashi writes "מעבוד אותנו," he is presumably saying that one should understand the suffix on מעבדנו as an accusitive suffix ("serving us") and not a genitive suffix ("our serving"). So most super-commentaries of Rashi explain his comment. (See e.g. Mizrahi and Gur Aryeh.) Clearly that cannot be what Rashbam is trying to say since the other examples that Rashbam cites are not examples of accusative suffixes attached to the infinitive.

Perhaps Rashbam's comment might be better translated as "מעבדנו has a *qameṣ qaṭan*, as it is a *contraction* of מעבוד אותנו, [and the *qameṣ qaṭan* preserves the 'o' sound found in the form עֲבוֹד]." See also the next note.

¹¹The example of the phrase באכל האש appears not to be well chosen, as it does not have a *qameṣ* vowel in it. However it is possible to say, as I wrote in the previous note, that Rashbam is explaining that while the infinitive construct and infinitive absolute of *qal* generally have an 'o' vowel in their *second* syllable (e.g. עֲבוֹד), the suffixed forms of those infinitives have an 'o' vowel, in the form of a *qameṣ qaṭan*, in the *first* syllable (e.g. עָבְדֵנוּ). Here Rashbam gives the example of בָּאֱכֹל, an infinite construct with an 'o' vowel in the last syllable, followed by the example of בְּאָכְלֵנוּ, a suffixed infinitive with a *qameṣ qaṭan* in the first syllable.

For a similar point about elongated imperative forms (e.g. שָׁמְרָה-שְׁמֹר), see Rashbam's grammar book, p. 49. Concerning suffixed forms of the infinitive, see G.-K. 61a.

¹²So also Rashi.

¹³So also Rashi.

in order to anticipate] what is written below (15:4), "the pick of his officers (שלישיו) are drowned in the Sea of Reeds."[14]

14:8-10 יוצאים ביד רמה WERE DEPARTING FEARLESSLY: They were not afraid at all until (vss. 9-10) they saw Pharaoh and his men chasing after them; only then (vs. 10) THEY WERE GREATLY FRIGHTENED.[15]

14:11 המבלי אין WAS IT FOR A WANT OF GRAVES: [The two negatives, המבלי and אין, are an example of] linguistic doubling.[16]

---

[14]Perhaps Rashbam is opposing the series of midrashic interpretations of שלישים found in Mekhilta (ibid., pp. 202-203), e.g. "that they were triply armed" or "that there were three of them against each Israelite." Rashbam is then saying that there is no need to see the word שלישים as requiring a midrashic explanation; it serves a simple literary task, of anticipation.

On anticipation in Rashbam, see my Genesis volume, pp. 400-421.

[15]The phrase, "the Israelites were departing fearlessly," seems out of place here. As LT and Sekhel Tov ask, "וכי עכשיו יוצאים--was it now that they were leaving Egypt?" Furthermore, in verse 5-9 the subject of discussion is consistently the Egyptians, except for the one phrase "the Israelites were departing fearlessly." Rashbam explains how the phrase fits well into the story at this point: just before describing those actions of the Egyptians that caused the Israelites to be afraid it is necessary to emphasize that, up to that point, they had been fearless. Rashbam's explanation differs somewhat from that of the Mekhilta (ibid., pp. 203-204) and LT who see in the phrase ביד רמה an element of Israelite defiance of the Egyptians, not just fearlessness (continuing the midrashic theme of the Israelites beating up the Egyptian guards; see notes above ad 14:5).

Like Rashbam, see JBS and Luzzatto. Luzzatto suggests also that when the Mekhilta (in one of a number of explanations) and Onq. translate ביד רמה as "בריש גלי--with uncovered heads," they are offering the same reading as Rashbam, for an uncovered head was, for those writers, a sign of fearlessness.

[16]כפל לשון. In other words the double negative, when one would clearly suffice, is acceptable biblical style.

So also iE and JBS. On the phrase כפל לשון in Rashbam, see Rosin, RSBM, p. 143.

EXODUS XIV 141

למות במדבר [YOU BROUGHT US OUT [TO DIE IN THE WILDERNESS]: where "there is no bread and no water,"[17] and even if no one were chasing after us we would die of starvation.[18]

14:16 וּבְקָעֵהוּ AND SPLIT IT: The letter *'ayin* causes this pattern [*sheva* after the first letter of the root and *qameṣ* after the second letter]. Similarly, שְׁמָעֵנוּ in the phrase (Gen. 23:6) "Hear us (שמענו), my lord." However, from the root ז-כ-ר one would say זָכְרֵנִי [with a *qameṣ* after the first letter of the root and a *sheva* after the second letter].[19]

14:19-20 ויסע THE ANGEL OF THE LORD: the one who had been been moving the pillar of cloud[20] AHEAD OF THE ISRAELITE CAMP. NOW HE, i.e. that angel, MOVED BEHIND THEM. As a result, THE PILLAR OF CLOUD SHIFTED FROM IN FRONT OF THEM AND TOOK A PLACE BEHIND THEM. For the angel moved the cloud around (vs. 20) to separate the Egyptian camp from the Israelite and "to put darkness between them," as it says in Joshua (24:7),

---

[17]A quotation from Num. 21:5, another complaint of the Israelites about desert conditions.

[18]As Rashbam writes above ad 14:8, the Israelites in the desert had no fears at all until the Egyptians appeared. But after that, Rashbam says that the Israelites started complaining about other things, too, such as the desert conditions, problems unrelated to the military concerns. Perhaps that is also the meaning of the phrase here in the Mekhilta (*ibid.*, 3, p. 209) that these complaints about the desert conditions began, מאחר שנתנו שאור בעיסה--"once the leaven was put into the dough," i.e. after excitement was stirred up.

[19]In other words, suffixed forms of the imperative of third guttural verbs follow a different vowel pattern than that of strong verbs. See also Rashbam's comm. and the notes to Gen. 34:10 and to Ex. 8:25.

[20]See Rashbam's comm. to 13:21 and notes, there.

so that the one camp would not be able TO COME NEAR THE OTHER ALL THROUGH THE NIGHT.[21]

14:20 ויהי הענן והחושך THUS THERE WAS THE CLOUD WITH THE DARKNESS: for the Egyptians, BUT the pillar of fire,[22] ויאר את הלילה[23]--LIT UP THE NIGHT for the Israelites. ולא קרב זה אל זה, THEY DID NOT COME NEAR ONE ANOTHER, means that the

---

[21] Rashbam describes at great length how there are two separate "movements" in verse 19--the angel in charge of the pillar of cloud moved, and then, as a result, the cloud itself moved. It seems as if he is trying to be sure that we do not say that the angel and the cloud are one and the same. The latter interpretation was probably current in Jewish circles, for iE, in his longer comm., directly refers to it and argues against it at length. I have been unable to find a source against which Rashbam and iE could be arguing. Krinski correctly notes (in *Yahel 'or*, here and ad 13:21) that such an interpretation can be found in Philo's *Life of Moses* (I, 166: "Perhaps indeed there was enclosed within the cloud one of the lieutenants of the Great King, an unseen angel . . ." [Loeb edition: vol. 6, 361]) but there is no reason to think that Rashbam or iE knew of Philo's works. The reference might be to BR 35:3 where the two halves of our verse are seen as being synonymous ("כבר כתיב ויסע מלאך . . . מה תלמוד לומר ויסע עמוד הענן--after the verse says that 'the angel moved . . . ,' why does the verse have to say further that 'the pillar of cloud moved'?"). Such an identification of the angel and the cloud could also be reflected in Rashi here where, in explaining the phrase, "took a place behind them," which the verse applies only to the angel, Rashi writes that the angel would "intercept the arrows and the stones from their catapults," a function that Rashi's source (Mekhilta, *ibid.*, 4, p. 227) attributes to the angel *and* the cloud.

[22] So also Rashi.
The verse is very difficult. (See Childs, p. 218, note 20.) The subject appears to be "cloud and darkness," and as NJPSC puts it, "the usual meaning of *vayya'er*, 'it lit up,' would not seem to be consistent with 'the cloud and the darkness'." Rashi and Rashbam both solve the problem by saying that the "pillar of fire" is the implicit subject of the verb ויאר. See somewhat similarly iE and Mekhilta ("הענן על ישראל והחשך על מצרים--'the cloud' on the Israelites and 'the darkness' on the Egyptians"; *ibid.*, 5, p. 226).

[23] The ms. that Rosin used reads ויאר כל הלילה, instead of MT's את הלילה. See Esh, p. 86, who feels that the reading found in Rashbam may underlie Onq. and Ps.-Jon. Of course the simplest explanation is that the end of the verse ולא קרב זה אל זה כל הלילה, influenced either Rashbam or the copyist of the ms. to write כל הלילה in the first half of the verse too.

Egyptians were not able to come near the Israelites[24] ALL THROUGH THE NIGHT.

14:21 ברוח קדים [THE LORD DROVE BACK THE SEA] WITH A STRONG EAST WIND: God did this in a manner conforming with scientific principles,[25] for winds can dry up and freeze[26] rivers.[27]

---

[24]The simplest explanation of the phrase זה אל זה is the one found in the Mekhilta (*ibid.*, p. 227) which understands the phrase as reciprocal--neither the Israelites approached the Egyptians nor the Egyptians the Israelites. So also Sekhel Tov. Rashbam does not see the phrase as reciprocal (a legitimate grammatical possibility; see G.-K. 139e, note 3, and BDB), presumably because it does not seem that the Israelites would have any reason to be trying to approach the Egyptians. So also LT (although Buber attempts to add to the text of LT to get it to conform with the text of the Mekhilta). The strangest interpretation is that of JBS who does not see the phrase as reciprocal and says that it means only that the Israelites did not attempt to get close to the Egyptians all through the night.

[25]כדרך ארץ; concerning Rashbam's use of the phrase see Touitou, "*Shiṭato ha-parshanit* . . .," p. 65 and M. Berger, pp. 99-113.

[26]מקריח. Using a *hifil* form of the root ק-ר-ח to mean "to cause to freeze" is rather unusual in Hebrew. (Cf. Seforno who expresses the same idea as Rashbam's but uses more conventional language: רוח הקדים הקפיא.) Rashbam though was neither the only medieval Jew nor the first to use the root ק-ר-ח in such a way. See e.g. Shabbetai Donnolo, cited in Ben Yehuda's dictionary, s.v. ק-ר-ח.

[27]The tendency to explain that the miracles performed by God in Egypt conformed to some degree with the laws of nature can be found also in the comm. of Rashbam's colleague, JBS, ad Ex. 9:8 where JBS writes that God "אינו רוצה לשנות מנהג העולם ועשה מקצת לפי מנהג העולם--does not wish to change the 'way of the world' and performs [his miracles] in a way that conforms somewhat with 'the way of the world'." See also JBS ad Ex. 8:12 and 15:25. See similarly iE's long excursus in his longer comm. ad Ex. 20:1 (Krinski ed., p. 295) and see M. Friedlander *Essays on the Writings of Abraham ibn Ezra*, vol. 4, p. 76f.) See Nahm.'s explanation here of why it is appropriate that specifically this miracle was done in a manner that made it look like a natural occurrence.

Rashbam's interpretation of this particular verse may be directed against Rashi (following the Mekhilta [*ibid.*, 5, pp. 229-230]) who saw the east wind as God's standard vehicle for bringing punishment to wicked people. So also JBS. Rashbam writes more simply that the wind is a natural choice when one is trying to dry up bodies of water.

14:24 בעמוד אש ובענן [THE LORD LOOKED DOWN ON THE EGYPTIANS] WITH A PILLAR OF FIRE AND WITH CLOUD: With the noise of hail and fire flashing[28] and clouds, as it is written (I Sam. 7:10), "The LORD thundered mightily [. . .] and threw them into confusion (ויהומם)." [Similarly] ויהם [in this verse] refers to confusion caused by noise.[29]

14:25 ויסר THEY TURNED THE WHEELS OF THEIR CHARIOTS: When the Egyptians saw that they were confounded they worked hard to turn[30] the wheels of their chariots around so that they would be able to

---

[28] An allusion to Ex. 9:23-24. For some reason that is not clear to me Rashbam does not interpret the phrase, "with a pillar of fire and with cloud," here in its simple meaning of the pillars of cloud and fire (mentioned first in 13:21) but rather sees here a reference to hail accompanied by fire flashing.

[29] This last point, including the prooftext from I Sam., is made by Rashi. Rashi here and in his comm. to I Sam. 5:11 attributes this point to two different sources in midrashic literature but neither of those attributions are borne out by our texts of those midrashim. See the notes of Berliner and Kasher, here. See also Rashbam's comm. ad Ex. 23:27, s.v. והמותי.

Rashbam differs from Rashi in that Rashbam also sees the phrase, "with a pillar of fire and with cloud," as a reference to confusion caused by noise; according to Rashbam the phrase, "He threw the Egyptian army into panic," is a summary or a result of what was previously written in the verse. Rashi, though, sees the verse as making two different points. The first half of the verse describes how the pillars of fire and cloud were used to confound the Egyptians (following the reading of the Mekhilta [ibid., 6, p. 240]; so also LT and Sekhel Tov) while the second half describes the confusion of the Egyptians through noise.

Rashbam also connects noise to hail in his comm. to 20:15.

[30] Rashbam's understanding of this verse differs from earlier explanations in many ways. First Rashbam feels that the subject of the verb ויסר is the Egyptians (referred to in the singular throughout this verse: e.g. ויאמר מצרים or מרכבותיו.) Rashi following the Mekhilta (ibid., p. 241) sees God (or perhaps the pillar of fire; see Sekhel Tov) as the subject of the verb. Rashbam also interprets the verb ויסר here as meaning "to turn," not "to remove." As iE notes, if one wishes to interpret the verb as referring to removal, then one must posit that the form is hifil, and relate to it as if ויסר or ויסר were written. iE, in his longer comm. only, mentions Rashbam's understanding of ויסר, in the name of "others." Many moderns emend and assume that the root is א-ס-ר; see e.g. Childs, "he clogged the wheels of their chariots," and his comment on p. 218, fn. 25.

EXODUS XIV

run away and flee to the rear but they were not able to. They turned and steered the wheels to go backwards בכבדות, WITH DIFFICULTY, and with much travail, for the carts and the chariots were striving one in front of the other.[31]

And why were they doing that?[32] Because[33] the Egyptians said, "LET US FLEE FROM THE ISRAELITES, BECAUSE THE LORD IS now FIGHTING FOR THEM במצרים--i.e. against us [Egyptians]."[34]

14:26 נטה את ידך [THE LORD SAID TO MOSES:] HOLD OUT YOUR ARM [OVER THE SEA, THAT THE WATERS MAY COME BACK UPON THE EGYPTIANS]: This was after Israel had crossed to the shore on the other side of the sea.[35]

Concerning Rashbam and the verb ס-ו-ר, see also his comm ad Gen. 48:17, s.v. להסיר, and notes there, p. 344.

[31]As Rosin explains, since the Egytian chariots were moving forward one in front of the other, attempts to turn around led to collisions, not to an orderly retreat.

[32]I.e. why were they attempting to retreat?

[33]Rashbam understands the causation in this verse in a manner different from most other exegetes. Most feel that after the disasters described in the first half of the verse the second half describes the *result*, that the Egyptians decided to flee. Rashbam explains differently. The second half of the verse provides the *reason* for the first half. *Because* the Egyptians wanted to flee, they tried to turn around the wheels of their chariots.

[34]The Mekhilta (*ibid.*, p. 242) would see the phrase נלחם להם במצרים as implying that God had fought on the Israelite side back in Egypt, as if the past tense, נלחם, were written. Rashbam disagrees with that reading in two ways. First he emphasizes that נלחָם means that God *now* was fighting for the Israelites. Secondly he understands that במצרָיִם here does not mean "in Egypt," but rather "against us Egyptians." The Mekhilta's reading can be found in LT and Sekhel Tov. Rashi offers two alternate explanations--the Mekhilta's and the one found in Rashbam.

[35]Verse 29 may give the impression that the Israelites were still crossing the Sea of Reeds even after Moses held out his arm over the sea to get the waters to return. In fact, that is the way that iE interprets these verses: miraculously ("פלא בתוך פלא--miracle upon miracle") the Israelites were still crossing safely while Pharaoh and his men were drowning. So also Hizquni. Rashbam says simply that the Jews had

14:27 ומצרים נסים לקראתו [THE SEA RETURNED TO ITS NORMAL STATE] AND THE EGYPTIANS WERE FLEEING INTO IT: When they were turning the wheels of their chariots to flee, the sea came upon the. Before they could turn around entirely, the sea came into their faces.[36]

14:29 ובני ישראל THE ISRAELITES: had already MARCHED THROUGH THE SEA ON DRY GROUND.[37]

14:30 וירא ישראל THE ISRAELITES: who were ON THE SHORE OF THE SEA, SAW THE EGYPTIANS in the sea drowned and dead.[38]

---

already safely reached the opposite shore before Moses gave the signal for the sea to return to its normal state. (See also Mekhilta [ibid., 7, p. 245], LT and Sekhel Tov.) In order to support such a reading Rashbam writes below ad vs. 29 that הלכו in that verse must be understood as a pluperfect. So also NJPS there: "The Israelites *had* marched . . .." See also Rashbam's comm. ad 15:19-20 where he again must interpret הלכו as meaning "had marched," and see notes there.

[36]Rashbam opposes Rashi's interpretation that the Egytians were so crazed by this point that they were running straight into the water. He also opposes the explanation of the Mekhilta (ibid.) that "whatever direction an Egyptian fled, the sea would be rushing against him."

Rashbam explains that the Egyptians were walking safely through the sea, with walls of water on their right and on their left, when they decided to turn around and flee. (See comm. above ad vs. 25.) Before they could turn around a full 180 degrees, when they had turned only 90 degrees and were facing the walls of water, that water at their sides began to rush at them. Presumably this explanation is also meant to oppose the interpretation of JBS who says that the water had become piled up at the shore, and that when the Egyptians were facing the shore in their attempt to get out, the water from the shore started pouring out on them.

[37]In contrast to the Egyptians; see comm. and notes to vs. 26.

[38]Again Rashbam's explanation differs from the standard understanding of the verse. Rashi, like most exegetes, understands that the phrase "on the shore of the sea" modifies "the Egyptians": the Israelites saw the dead bodies of the Egyptians which had been spewed out "on the shore of the sea." Rashi also cites midrashic traditions that say that the Israelites did not see the dead Egyptians right away. Only after the Israelites

EXODUS XIV

The phrase "על שפת הים--ON THE SHORE OF THE SEA" [modifies "the Israelites."] When the Israelites arrived on the sea shore,[39] they immediately[40] saw the waters of the sea turning back on the Egyptians and the Egyptians drowning there. This is the true plain meaning of the text. Similarly, in my commentary to Genesis (3:8) I explained the verse, "Moving about the garden, they heard the sound of the LORD God at the breezy time of the day."[41]

---

expressed doubts about whether the Egyptians had really died did God provide the proof by spewing out the corpses onto the beach. (See e.g. Mekhilta [ibid., p. 250] and Arakhin 15a.) JBS offers a less miraculous version of the same explanation. The sea normally spews out dead things onto the shore and that is how the Israelites ended up seeing the Egyptians dead "on the shore of the sea."

Rashbam explains though that the phrase "on the shore of the sea" modifies the subject, "the Israelites." When they were standing on the shore of the sea they saw the Egyptians dead. So also iE, longer comm. only. (In the shorter comm. it appears that iE follows the more standard line of interpretation.) Rashbam's interpretation was criticized by Mendelssohn, among others, for not conforming with the cantillation signs.

[39]See comm. ad vs. 26.

[40]Rashbam emphasizes that they saw the dead bodies immediately, presumably to distance himself from the midrashim cited in the last note that claimed that the bodies were thrown onto the shore only after the Israelites expressed doubts about the demise of their pursuers.

[41]Since Rashbam's comm. on Genesis 3 is lost, one can only speculate as to how Rashbam interpreted that verse. The common syntactical understanding of that verse sees the phrase "מתהלך בגן--moving about the garden" as modifying "the LORD God." Naturally the anthropomorphism of that reading troubled many exegetes. Rosin feels that Rashbam is saying here that "מתהלך בגן--moving about the garden" should be seen as modifying the word "קול--voice" or "noise." (So also BR 19:12, iE in Genesis, Guide 1:24 and others.)

To my mind that is not what Rashbam is suggesting here. Rashbam compares the two verses because in each one of them there is a phrase--"on the shore of the sea" or "moving about the garden"--that appears to be part of the predicate but actually, to Rashbam's mind, should be seen as modifying the subject. "Moving about the garden" modifies neither "the LORD God" nor His "voice." Rather Adam (and Eve?), while moving about the garden, heard the voice of the LORD God. This interpretation was apparently first offered by ibn Janah (cited by iE in Genesis; see ibn Janah's *Sefer ha-riqmah*, p 49.) So later Abravanel.

While that reading has a certain attraction, there is one serious grammatical problem with it. Adam and Eve are the understood plural subject of that verse (hence "וישמעו--they heard" in the plural); accordingly, to see the singular form

14:31 ויאמינו THEY BELIEVED IN GOD: [They believed] that even in the desert they would not die of starvation.[42]

"מתהלך--moving" as part of the subject is difficult. Still it is possible that in the same way that ibn Janah was not troubled by that difficulty, Rashbam also was not. Curiously, in his comm. to our verse in Exodus, Rashbam (I presume unconsciously) misquotes the verse in Genesis in a manner that "solves" the grammatical problem, citing the verb as וישמע, instead of MT's וישמעו.

[42]See comm. and notes above ad vs. 11, s.v. למות. Rashbam writes that just as the military crisis stirred up fears that were unrelated to military concerns, so too when the immediate crisis was solved all the ancillary problems also no longer mattered.

Rashbam may be opposing the approach of the Mekhilta here (*ibid.*, pp. 252-255) that praises, in a long excursus, the power of "faith" and claims that as a result of the great faith of the Israelites described in this verse they were rewarded by the Holy Spirit descending upon them, leading to the Song of the Sea in chapter 15. (So also LT and Sekhel Tov.) Rashbam interprets more prosaically that the Israelites' above-mentioned (vs. 11) concerns about starvation disappeared. It is possible that Rashbam, concerned as he is with anti-Christian polemics, is particularly eager to avoid readings like that of the Mekhilta that might play into the hands of Christian polemicists who, following Paul, prefer "faith" over "works." See also Rashbam's comm. below ad 17:12 where he rids the word אמונה there of any theological significance.

EXODUS XV

15:1 גאה גאה HE HAS TRIUMPHED: The root ג-א-ה often refers to a military victory.[1] For example, (Ps. 94:2) "Give the victors (גאים) their deserts";[2] (Prov. 15:25) "The LORD will tear down the house of the גאים," i.e. the ones who steal and cheat; (Ps. 10:2) "The wicked with his upper hand (בגאות) hounds the lowly."[3]

רמה בים HE THREW INTO THE SEA: The root ר-מ-ה means "to throw," in Aramaic.[4] Also [it can be found in biblical Hebrew, as in the phrase] (Ps. 78:9), "רומי קשת--bow-shooters."[5]

15:2 ה׳ עזי וזמרת THE LORD: is the strength (עוז) and זמרת--the praise of Israel, and he became MY DELIVERANCE. עָזִּי is written

---

[1] Presumably Rashbam's problem is that the root ג-א-ה is often seen as having negative connotations, meaning "to be arrogant" or "to be overpowering." (See e.g. the comment of Mendelssohn: "והנה בבני אדם הלשון הזה יבוא על הרוב לגנאי--Generally this locution is a negative one when it is applied to humans.") Rashbam's solution differs somewhat from that of Rashi who proposes seeing the root as meaning "to be exalted." Like Rashbam, see NJPS, "triumphed."

[2] The context of that verse lends support to Rashbam's interpretation. God's vengeance is being solicited (vs. 1) against גאים who apparently have defeated the Israelites militarily (vs. 5).

[3] The last two examples cited by Rashbam do not seem to support his explanation to the same extent. But they do show that ג-א-ה may be seen as meaning "to have the upper hand," a meaning that could easily be applied to our verse too.

[4] השליך בים ולשון תרגום תרגום של השליך. See Sekhel Tov, almost verbatim (היא). So also Rashi, but not with the same phraseology.

[5] Rashbam adds an example from biblical Hebrew to support his reading. See his general statement above ad 12:7 that proof of interpretations ought to be adduced from biblical *Hebrew* ("the Hebrew text of the Torah or the Prophets"), and see notes there. See also my Genesis volume, p. 423, and footnote 2 there.

with a *ḥaṭaf qameṣ*[6] and has an "extra" *yod*.[7] So also [one may find an "extra" *yod* in the words] רבתי in the phrase (Lam. 1:1) "Great with (רבתי) people"; היושבי in the phrase (Ps. 123:1) "enthroned (היושבי) in heaven"; שכני in the phrase (Obad. 3) "you who dwell (שכני) in clefts of the rock."

However, the form עְזִי in the phrase (Ps. 59:10) "O my strength, (עזי)[8] I wait for You," means "*my* strength" [for the *yod* there is a sign of the first person possessive].

וזמרת: [is a construct form where the *nomen rectum* is missing[9] and must be understood as implicit] just like [ושכורת in the phrase] (Is. 51:21) "Who are drunk (ושכורת) but not with wine," or [שערת in the phrase] (Job 4:15) "The storm (שערת) made my flesh bristle." Because of parallelism with the first stich of the verse, "ורוח על פני יחלוף--A wind passed over my face," [one should interpret the second stich to mean] "תסמר שערת הרוח בשרי--the storm *of wind*[10] made my flesh bristle."[11]

---

[6] I.e. with a *qameṣ qaṭan*.

[7] I.e. the *yod* at the end of עזי is not a sign of the first person possessive. Accordingly Rashbam explains that עזי, just like זמרת, is really a construct form. Both are to be seen as connected to the understood noun, "Israel."

On Rashbam's attitude to "extra" or "epenthetic" letters, see comm. and notes above to Ex. 8:13.

[8] Esh (p. 91) notes that both Rashi and Rashbam here quote Ps. 59:10 in the same way, but in a manner that differs from MT's reading, עֻזִּי. As Esh notes, the reading found here in Rashbam, עְזִי, is attested in many mss. and is also attested to in the Massora. In fact, NJPS in Psalms has even chosen to translate that reading, not MT.

[9] As Rashbam explained above, עזי and זמרת are both to be seen as being in the construct state with the implicit noun, "Israel." Rashbam accordingly now presents further examples of nouns in the construct state where the *nomen rectum* is apparently missing and must be seen as implied in the text.

[10] Adding the noun הרוח to the second stich as the implicit *nomen rectum* of שערת.

[11] Rashbam's interpretation of Job 4:15 is different than the standard understanding. Generally שערה is seen as meaning "hair" in this passage and as being part of the predicate, not the subject. שערת בשרי is then "the hair of my flesh." בשרי is then the explicit *nomen rectum* of the construct form שערת. Thus e.g. Rashi, Qara, RSV and

EXODUS XV   151

So also one may find in R. Yosef's[12] Targum: תצלהב שלהוביתא
בישרי.[13] זמרת then should be seen as [a construct form,] missing [the *nomen rectum*], just like שכורת or ושערת.[14]

NJPS.
    Rashbam on the other hand sees שערת [רוח] as meaning "storm" and as the subject of the verb תסמר. Following that reading, and only that reading, שערת can constitute proof for his point here that the *nomen rectum* is often implicit. Rashbam correctly finds in the Targum support for his interpretation of the verse in Job. (See below.) He also argues from the parallelism in that verse.
    M. Ahrend has gathered together in an article a number of exegetical comments about the text of Job attributed to Rashbam. Two such comments offer the same interpretation of Job 4:15 that one finds here. Also, in those fragments from Rashbam there are two further justifications offered for this interpretation (aside from the argument from parallelism and the proof from the Targum mentioned here). There Rashbam argues that the verb ס-מ-ר in the Bible never refers to "hair" but does refer to "flesh" (e.g. Ps. 119:120). Furthermore, Rashbam cites the singular form שערת as proof of his reading, arguing that the plural שערות would logically be required by the standard understanding. See *'Ale sefer* 5 (1978), pp. 29-30.

[12]The standard way in which the Talmud cites a Targum to the Prophets is כדמתרגם רב יוסף. See Melammed, *Mefarshe ha-miqra'*, vol. 1, pp. 142-143.

[13]"The flame will consume my flesh." While the precise wording of that Targum may differ from Rashbam's understanding of the verse, the syntactical understanding is the same as his.
    The wording quoted by Rashbam is somewhat different from the reading of the Targum in our printed texts. Our texts generally read: מצלהבא עלעולא בסרי--"The storm consumed my flesh." Our text then provides even more support for Rashbam's reading as it understands שערת as meaning עלעולא, i.e. "a storm." It is the same word that the Targum uses to translate the word סערה ("storm" or "whirlwind") in Job 38:1.
    See Mandelkern's note in his Concordance, s.v. שערה, where he writes that the Targum (like Rashbam) understands שערה as storm (or perhaps, the Targum reads in our verse שערה, storm, instead of MT's שערת) based on the parallelism in the verse (יונתן קורא תסמר שערה [=סערה, עלעולא] בשרי, ומקביל אל ורוח על פני יחלף).

[14]See Rashi's very long excursus on this verse.
    Rashbam's understanding of this verse follows Rashi's on many points. Both agree that עזי does not mean the same as עָז. Both agree that the *yod* at the end of עזי is epenthetic or "extra." Both agree that both עזי and זמרת should be seen as construct forms.
    Yet Rashbam branches off in a somewhat new exegetical direction. According to Rashi, the *nomen rectum* of עזי וזמרת is explicit in the text; it is the Hebrew word י-ה. And according to Rashi, זמרת is related to a different meaning of the root

ואנוהו:[15] means "I will declare Him lovely [i.e. glorify Him]," as in the phrase (Jer. 6:2) "I described Zion as lovely (הנוה) and delicate." [The root נ-ו-ה here] is not connected to the meaning "home,"[16] as it is in the phrase (Is. 27:10) "homesteads (נוה) deserted."[17] One can prove [that it is related to the meaning "lovely" and not the meaning "home"]

ז-מ-ר--"to prune." In other words, Rashi reads the verse as meaning "The LORD's strength and vengeance have become my salvation"; Rashbam reads it as meaning "The LORD is the strength and praise of Israel and He has become my salvation."

To be sure, Rashbam's interpretation seems at first glance strained as it requires the addition of the implicit word "Israel" to the text. However Rashbam's explanation does help solve one of the problems involved with Rashi's interpretation. Rashi sees the words עזי וזמרת י-ה ויהי לי לישועה as constituting just one clause with one verb, ויהי. He explains the verb ויהי as being equivalent to the verb היה in this place. However, as iE points out in his longer comm., the use of a *vav*-consecutive form like ויהי in this place, following the subject, is not standard biblical syntax and, as iE suggests, no one who "knows any Arabic" would ever offer such an interpretation. (See also Jouon 155n.) However, according to Rashbam's interpretation the syntax is perfectly normal here. We have a noun clause, "עזי וזמרת י-ה--The LORD *is* the strength and praise . . .," followed by a second clause, a verbal clause introduced by ויהי: "and He has become my salvation (ויהי לי לישועה)."

[15]The interested reader may refer to Rosin's text in which at this point he introduces a pericope that is not found in any of the mss. or printed editions but simply represents a quotation from the book *Pa'aneaḥ raza'* (of Rabbi Isaac the son of Judah ha-levi, end of the thirteenth century) in which the author attributes to Rashbam an interpretation of the phrase זה א-לי.

[16]Rashbam opposes the understanding of Onq. and the first opinion cited in Rashi that the phrase means "I will build a נוה--a home or a Temple--for God." So also the opinion of R. Jose the son of the Damascene in Mekhilta *Shirata'* 3, [Laut. ed. pp. 25-26], iE and NJPS ("I will enshrine him").

[17]The specific connection between our verse and the verse in Is. 27 is made by ibn Janah in his *Sefer ha-shorashim*, s.v. נ-ו-ה.

EXODUS XV

because of the parallelism[18] with the end of the verse; both ואנוהו and "וארוממנהו--I will exalt Him" refer to giving honor to God.[19]

15:3 ה' שמו LORD IS HIS NAME: "The LORD has made Himself known: He works judgment" (Ps. 9:17).[20]

15:4 ירה בים HE CAST INTO THE SEA: [ירה is to be understood] as in the phrase (II Sam. 11:24), "ויורו המורים[21]--the archers shot"; it means to throw or cast.[22]

15:5 יכסיומו COVERED THEM: The form יכסיומו [with a *holam* as the final vowel] should actually have been written here [according to the rules of grammar],[23] but because of the first "u" vowel, [i.e. the vowel

---

[18]On Rashbam's use of parallelism as an exegetical tool, see notes above ad Ex. 10:10.

[19]Rashbam's opinion is the same as the second interpretation offered by Rashi to this word (beginning with the words דבר אחר). So also the opinion of R. Jose in the Mekhilta, *ibid.*, p. 25.

[20]I.e. God's name has become known through the miracles that he performs. See similarly iE, longer comm. only.
Rashbam opposes both of the interpretations of this phrase found in Rashi--that God does His miracles through the power of His Name or that God is the LORD, i.e. merciful, even though He executes punishments. (Both those interpretations can be found in the Mekhilta, *ibid.*, 4, pp. 31-35.)

[21]MT there = ויראו.

[22]Rashbam opposes the midrashic attempt of Rashi ad vs. 1 (= Mekhilta, *ibid.*, 4, p. 35) to distinguish between רמה בים in vs. 1 and ירה בים in vs. 4. According to Rashbam the verbs are synonymous; both mean "השליך--he cast." So also iE, shorter comm.

[23]See e.g. G.-K. 58g and 91l, concerning מו as a third person plural suffix in biblical poetry.

following the letter *yod*,] the next vowel also became "u."²⁴ Also [i.e. another example of such attraction] (Ezek. 43:11) "מוֹצָאָיו וּמוֹבָאָיו"--its exits and entrances." The [grammatically] expected form would be מְבוֹאָיו, as from the root ב-א²⁵ one says מָבוֹא (entrance), just as from the root ק-מ²⁶ one says מָקוֹם (place) and from the root ל-נ²⁷ one says מָלוֹן (lodging). However due to²⁸ [attraction with] the form מוֹצָאָיו, the form מוֹבָאָיו appears [instead of מְבוֹאָיו].²⁹

15:6 יְמִינְךָ YOUR RIGHT HAND, O LORD--You, who are³⁰--GLORIOUS IN POWER. That right hand SHATTERS THE FOE: "יָמִין--right hand" is feminine,³¹ as it says (Ps. 118:16) "The right hand of the LORD is exalted (רוֹמֵמָה)."³²

---

²⁴Rashbam is answering the question that Rashi left unanswered. Rashi points out the anomaly of the last vowel of יכסיומו but attempts no explanation. Rashbam's answer can be found in ibn Janah's *Sefer ha-riqmah*, p. 322.

²⁵I.e. what we would call the root ב-ו-א.

²⁶I.e. ק-ו-ם.

²⁷I.e. ל-ו-נ.

²⁸The word Rashbam uses here, "בעלילת--due to," is unusual. It is interesting that a similar phrase ("עלול העין--due to the *'ayin*") appears also ibn Janah's discussion of the issue (in Judah ibn Tibbon's translation), in the source cited in the next note.

²⁹See similarly ibn Janah, *ibid.*, p. 23 and Qimhi ad II Sam. 3:25. See the criticism of ibn Janah in iE's comm. ad Est. 8:17, but see iE's own comm. to Dt. 4:1 where he explains the form ויירשתם in a similar way. See Mendelssohn here, following Rashbam, and the long excursus in Luzzatto criticizing Rashbam's position. For another example of Rashbam's sensitivity to the phenomenon of attraction, see his comm. to Gen. 30:8.

³⁰Rashbam emphasizes that the words "glorious in power" modify "LORD," not "right hand."

³¹Accordingly the adjective "נאדרי--glorious" could not be modifying "right hand" and it must be modifying "LORD." So also Sekhel Tov. Rashbam opposes Rashi's understanding that נאדרי modifies יְמִינְךָ. iE offers both possible readings.

³²רוממה is clearly a feminine form.

EXODUS XV

This verse is like (Ps. 93:3) "The ocean sounds, O LORD, the ocean sounds its thunder" or (Psalms 94:3) "How long shall the wicked, O LORD, how long shall the wicked exult" or (Ps. 92:10) "Surely your enemies, O LORD, surely your enemies perish." [In all of these verses] the first phrase makes an incomplete statement; then the second phrase comes and repeats and then finishes the statement. The first phrase simply identifies the subject.[33]

15:7 תהרס YOU REMOVE YOUR ENEMIES: תהרס is connected to the idea of removal (הסרה). It means lowering or moving an object from its upright position. So also (Ex. 19:21) "Lest they move (יהרסו) towards the LORD,"[34] and "pluck you from your tent and remove you (ויהרסך) from your stand."[35]

---

[33]Rashbam correctly describes again the phenomenon of "ladder" or "elongated" or "incremental" parallelism. See comm. and notes to Gen. 49:22. (See also comm. and notes ad 4:9.) Some mss. of Rashi have him making the same point here. So also JBS and iE, longer comm. only.

Rashbam's reading should be seen as opposing the midrashic understanding of the Mekhilta, *ibid.*, 5, p. 41, that sees significance in the fact that ימינך is repeated in the verse. Rashi, LT and Sekhel Tov follow the Mekhilta in attributing referential (not just rhetorical) meaning to the doubling of the word ימינך.

[34]See also Rashbam's comm. and notes, there, and see RSBM, p. 147, footnote 9.

It seems unnecesssary for Rashbam to offer this interpretation of the verb ה-ר-ס here when the simple, accepted meaning of the verb, "to destroy," makes perfect sense in the context of our verse. Presumably Rashbam is more concerned about the more difficult verse, 19:21, which he cites here. There, in the only example of the verb ה-ר-ס being used intransitively in the Bible, Rashbam's explanation makes more sense. Presumably Rashbam offers this explanation here, at the first appearance of the root ה-ר-ס in the Bible, in order to lay the ground for his interpretation of Ex. 19:21.

[35]Apparently an inaccurate quotation conflating Ps. 52:7 and Is. 22:19. Even the two words from Isaiah ויהרסך ממצבך are cited inaccurately, mixing together the verb from one stich of the verse and the object from the other stich. (Rosin loyally assumes that some later copyist, and not Rashbam, must have been responsible for this misquotation.) Still the verse in MT's version in Isaiah constitutes some proof for Rashbam as there the verb יהרסך parallels the verb "והדפתיך--I will topple you."

15:8 ובדוח אפיך [THE WATER PILED UP] AT THE BLAST OF YOUR NOSTRILS: I.e. (Ex. 14:21) "with a strong east wind all that night."[36]

נערמו PILED UP: נערמו means "they were piled up high," as in the phrase (Song 7:3) "a heap (ערימת) of wheat."[37]

נד: is connected to height. So also concerning the Jordan River it is written (Josh 3:16) "piled up in a single heap (נד)."[38]

קפאו CONGEALED: Just like the phrase (Job 10:10), "Congealed (תקפיאני) like cheese."[39]

15:9 אמר אויב THE FOE SAID: When he saw the sea turn into dry ground.[40]

---

[36]Rashi gives a long explanation of the anthropomorphic reference here to God's nostrils, explaining that the phrase refers to God's anger. Rashbam explains that the reference here is to the same wind described in 14:21.

[37]So also Rashi and iE, all with the same prooftext. See Menahem, *Maḥberet*, s.v. ע-ר-מ III. This interpretation is opposed to that of Onq. who connected נערמו to the root ע-ר-מ, meaning "to be wise." Both interpretations can be found in Mekhilta, *ibid.*, 6, pp. 50-51.

[38]The Mekhilta, *ibid.*, interprets נד as meaning the same as "נאד--water bottle." Onq., Rashi and iE all disagree and interpret it as meaning "wall." Rashbam's interpretation is similar, though not identical to theirs. See also NJPS which translates נד here in Exodus as "wall" but in Joshua as "heap."

[39]So also Rashi. The interpretation opposes that of the Mekhilta, *ibid.*, p. 52, that connects קפאו to the word "קופה--vault."

[40]An allusion to the last phrase of Ex. 14:21, just as Rashbam explained the previous verse, 14:8 (s.v. וברוח), as an allusion to the first part of 14:21. (See also comm. below ad 15:12.)

Rashbam's explanation--that these words were spoken by the Egyptians at the Red Sea--opposes that of Rashi, according to whom the words "the foe said" introduce the arguments used by Pharaoh back in Egypt when he convinced his troops to follow and attack the Israelites.

EXODUS XV

אריק חרבי I WILL EMPTY OUT MY SWORD: means "I will empty out my sheath," by removing the sword from the sheath.[41] Similarly one should understand the phrase (Ps. 38:3) "For Your arrows were stretched (נחתו) at me"; [it is actually not the arrows that were stretched but the bow,] for He shot the arrows through the stretching or bending of the bow, as it says at the end of that same verse, "it is Your hand that stretched (ותנחת) it against me."[42] Furthermore [one sees that נ-ח-ת means "to stretch" a bow in] (Ps. 18:35) "my arms can bend (ונחתה) a bow of bronze."[43] That is why the word "נחיתה--stretching" can [also] be applied to the shooting of arrows.

---

[41]Rashbam points out that this phrase should be seen as an example of metonymy. In other words, although the verb, "אריק--I will empty out," seems improperly attached to the object "sword," actually the implicit object is the word "תער--sheath." So also Rashi at greater length, here and ad Ps. 38:3. Rashi writes explicitly here that he is opposing the interpretation that would connect the verb אריק here to the phrase (Gen. 14:14) "וירק את חניכיו." However in his comm. to Genesis it is Rashi himself who offers that interpretation, claiming that both here and there the verb means "to arm" or "to arm oneself." See the weak attempts to solve the discrepancy in Mizrahi and Gur Aryeh in Genesis.

The interpretation of אריק חרבי here can also be seen as opposing the midrashic interpretation of the Mekhilta here, *ibid.*, p. 56, that comments on the unusual phrase ("אתן חרבי אינו אומר אלא אריק חרבי--the verse does not say 'I will place my sword' but rather 'I will empty my sword'") and sees it as a reference to homosexual rape.

[42]See Rashi's comm. to Ps. 38:3 where this line of interpretation can be found at greater length. Rashi and Rashbam assume that the verbs נחתו and ותנחת there mean "to stretch" or "to bend" a bow, like the verb ד-ר-כ. Hence they are dealing with the difficulty that in Ps. 38:3 it appears illogically that the arrows are being bent, not the bow. So they explain that in the same way that in this verse the image of "emptying" was moved poetically from the sheath to the sword, so the image of bending was moved from the bow to the arrows.

Most moderns would not accept this assumption--that forms of the verb נ-ח-ת are all related to the idea of bending or stretching. Although there is general agreement that that is the meaning in the next example cited by Rashbam, Ps. 18:35 (=2 Sam. 22:35), generally it is felt that most forms of the verb נ-ח-ת mean "to fall upon" or "to strike." For example, concerning the verse in Psalm 38, see NJPS ("Your arrows have struck me, Your blows have fallen upon me") and see also Qimhi in *Sefer ha-shorashim*, s.v. נ-ח-ת.

[43]See also Rashi there.

15:10 צללו כעופרת במים אדירים THEY SANK LIKE LEAD IN THE MAJESTIC WATERS: In the waters that are majestic.[44] I.e. in the waters of the sea. [They sank in those waters] even though the waters were "as majestic as the breakers of the sea."[45]

15:11 מי כמוך WHO IS LIKE YOU, O LORD, AMONG THE CELESTIALS, WHO IS LIKE YOU, MAJESTIC IN HOLINESS: This verse also is one of the "doubled" verses that I described above in my comm. to (15:6) "Your right hand, O LORD, glorious in power."[46] The verse means "Who among the celestials is like You, as majestic in holiness as You are?"

נורא תהילות FEARED BECAUSE OF HIS PRAISEWORTHY DEEDS: I.e. because of the praises (תהילות) that are said about You, You are

---

[44]Rashbam emphasizes that אדירים is an adjective that modifies the noun מים, and that it is not a noun, "the majestic ones." His interpretation is opposed to that found in Men. 53a, according to which the verse says "the majestic ones sank like lead in the waters." Contrast the language of Rashbam here, "במימות שהן אדירים"--the waters that are majestic," with the language of Rashi in his comm. to Men., "מצרים שהם אדירים--the Egyptians that are majestic." JBS offers both interpretations.

[45]An allusion to Ps. 93:4.
   Presumably Rashbam is saying that although one would have expected the Egyptians to be tossed about in the majestic waves of the sea, still they sank straight down like lead. (That idea is expressed clearly by Qara [cited by Berliner in *Peletat Soferim*, p. 18].) At the same time Rashbam is also proving from the verse in Ps. that the adjective אדירים can be applied to water. The talmudic passage in Men. (mentioned in the previous note) makes a similar point--that the adjective אדירים can apply to water--and cites that same verse in Ps. as proof.

[46]See comm. and notes there.
   Rashbam's interpretation opposes those midrashim that would see some significance in the doubling of the phrase "Who is like you." See e.g. PDRE 42 who says that the Israelites chanted "Who is like You, O LORD, among the celestials" and then Pharaoh answered with his own chant, "Who is like You, majestic in holiness."

EXODUS XV

feared (יראוי)⁴⁷ and dreaded (ומאויים),⁴⁸ as it is written (14:31) "The people feared (ויראו) the LORD."⁴⁹

15:12 נטית ימינך YOU PUT OUT YOUR RIGHT HAND: refers to the verse (14:26) "The LORD said to Moses, 'Hold out your arm over the sea that the waters may come back [upon the Egyptians]'."⁵⁰

15:13 נהלת בעזך IN YOUR STRENGTH YOU GUIDE THEM: [Although נהלת appears to be the past tense, it should be understood as referring to an action in the present:] you are now guiding Israel⁵¹ to

---

⁴⁷As Rashbam does on more than one occasion (see e.g. comm. and notes ad Gen. 44:19), he uses here the same unusual Hebrew word, יראוי, as Rashi uses in his comm. to this same verse, even though he and Rashi interpret the verse differently.

⁴⁸Another unusual Hebrew word, probably coined by Rashi, and used by him on more than one occasion. In fact this identical pair of rare words, יראוי ומאויים, can be found in Rashi's comm. to Ex. 20:17, s.v. ובעבור.

⁴⁹Rashbam opposes the interpretation of Rashi (which iE also offers) that נורא תהילות means that one is afraid to offer praises to God because one will never succeed in praising Him as much as He deserves. (See Tanh. B Shemot 1, and see also Rashi's comm. to vs. 1, s.v. כי גאה גאה.) Rashbam explains instead that the phrase means that God's תהילות, his praiseworthy deeds, are the reason why He is feared. See somewhat similarly Nahm.

⁵⁰Rashbam opposes the explanations found in Rashi, taken from the Mekhilta (ibid., 9, pp. 67-68) that see in this verse a reference to some other miracle, either that the Egyptians were eventually buried or that their bodies were tossed around between the ocean and the dry land. Rashbam again interprets a phrase in chapter 15 in such a way that it is simply a reiteration of the events of chapter 14 in poetic form. See comm. and notes above ad 15:8, s.v. וברוח, and ad 15:9, s.v. אמר.

Rashbam's interpretation here is somewhat unusual in that he sees the reference here to ימינך, presumably God's right arm, as describing Moses stretching out his own arm.

⁵¹Rashbam explains that the reference here to bringing the Israelites to God's holy abode must be seen as something that will happen in the future, as the song is being recited at the Reed Sea, well before arrival at God's abode. So also iE, who, in his shorter comm., says that that is the interpretation of "all the commentators."

bring them into the land of Canaan, the land which is YOUR HOLY ABODE,⁵² and to make them capture it.

15:14-15 יושבי פלשת, אלופי אדום, אילי מואב THE DWELLERS IN PHILISTIA, THE CLANS OF EDOM, THE TRIBES OF MOAB: All these are neighbors of the land of Israel.⁵³

15:16 עד יעבר TILL YOUR PEOPLE CROSS OVER, O LORD, TILL YOUR PEOPLE CROSS: Both [of the phrases "until Your people cross"] are references to the crossing of the Jordan River to get to the land of Israel. According to the plain meaning of Scripture, the reference to crossing the Jordan is written twice [for poetic purposes,]

Among moderns there is a wide diversity of opinion about the dating of the Song of the Sea, with a few scholars arguing for a very early date. Some scholars argue that phrases like נהלת בעזך אל נוה קדשך prove that the Song must come after the conquest. Still a number of critical scholars assign a thirteenth century B.C.E. date to the Song, despite such phrases. See the discussion in Childs, pp. 245-247.

⁵²Rashbam opposes the explanation of the Mekhilta, *ibid.*, p. 70, that "Your holy abode" is a reference to the Temple in Jerusalem. (So also in some texts of Zev. 54b; see the discussion in Kasher, here, note 178.) iE mentions that explanation but prefers his own --that the phrase refers to Mount Sinai. Rashbam sees the phrase as a general reference to the Land of Canaan. See Childs: "scholars continue to debate" whether phrases like נוה קדשך "refer to the whole land or specifically to Zion" although Noth, like Rashbam, is certain that the phrase is "a general reference to the land promised to Israel."

⁵³Rashbam opposes the explanation found in the Mekhilta, *ibid.*, pp. 71-73, that sees these three groups as having specific reason to be afraid of the arrival of the Israelites--the Philistines because of their previous (midrashic) encounter with the sons of Ephraim, the Edomites because of the old enmity between Jacob and Esau, and the Moabites because of the old tensions between Lot and Abraham. This midrash is adopted by LT and Sekhel Tov, here and also, partially, by Rashi. Rashbam explains more simply that the fear of the Israelites fell upon the Canaanites and upon their neighbors. See somewhat similarly iE, shorter comm., and JBS who write that these three nations are ones that the Israelites are likely to encounter on their way from Egypt to Canaan.

EXODUS XV

on the same paradigm as (vs. 6) "Your right hand [O LORD, glorious in power, Your right hand . . .]."[54]

בגדול זרועך: should be understood as if "בזרוע גדלך--because of Your mighty arm" were written.[55] So also the phrase קדוש היכליך in Psalms (65:5) should be understood as if "היכל קודשיך--Your holy temple" were written.[56]

15:17 מִקְּדָשׁ THE SANCTUARY: מִקְּדָשׁ is written here with a *dagesh* in the letter *qof* and without a *dagesh* in the letter *dalet*.[57] So also (Ex. 2:3) "הַצְּפִינוֹ"[58] and מִשְּׁתֵי[59] in the phrase (Jud. 16:28) "of my two (מִשְּׁתֵי) eyes, from the Philistines." In the form מִקְּדָשׁ, the *dagesh* in

---

[54]I.e. this is yet another example of "ladder" parallelism. See comm. and notes ad vs. 6. See Luzzatto here who argues that the poetic pattern here in our verse is not the same as in the previous verses.
  Again Rashbam uses his understanding of the poetic nature of this chapter to oppose the midrashic reading that sees the doubled reference here to "crossing over" as references both to crossing the Jordan River and to crossing the Arnon River. See Onq. and Mekhilta, *ibid.*, p. 75. Rashi and Sekhel Tov follow Onq.; LT offers a version of that same interpretation.

[55]See G.-K. 132c: "In a few expressions (mostly poetic) the adjective appears not as an attribute *after* the substantive, but in the construct state governing it; so . . . Ex. 15:16."

[56]Mendelssohn adopts Rashbam's explanation of both these verses. Cf., however, Shapira (in *Ha-rekhasim leviq'ah*) who criticizes this understanding.

[57]The standard spelling is the opposite, a *dagesh* in the *dalet*, but not in the *qof*. See similarly iE.

[58]Where there is a *dagesh* in the letter *ṣade* when the rules of grammar would suggest that the *dagesh* should be in the letter *peh*. So also iE there.

[59]Where there is a *dagesh* in the letter *shin* although the rules of grammar would suggest that the *dagesh* should be in the letter *tav*. Cf. Qimhi, there, who argues that that one form is not anomalous.

the letter *qof* makes the *sheva* that follows a mobile *sheva*,[60] and that is why there is no *dagesh* in the *dalet* that follows that *sheva*.[61] The same thing happens in the form הַצְפִינוֹ and in the form מִשְׁתֵּי.[62]

---

[60]The ms. reads עושה את החטף שבא מניע. The normal word that Rashbam uses for a *sheva* in his Torah comm. is חטף. Accordingly Rosin at first made the suggestion (RSBM, p. 130, notes 11 and 14) that the ms. reading was not to be accepted. He felt that some copyist had written the word שבא (=שוא) as a (marginal) gloss on the word החטף and then a later copyist wrote the word in the text of the comm. itself. This emendation seems quite reasonable, for if the word שבא is really part of Rashbam's comment here, then (1) the text (החטף שוא) appears to be redundant and (2) this is the only time that Rashbam uses the word שוא in his entire Torah comm. Melammed, *Mefarshe ha-miqra'*, p. 501, note 109, continued to support the emendation.

However, later Rosin had second thoughts about this emendation. (See his notes here, p. 103, note 8). Now that Rashbam's grammar book, *Sefer dayqut*, has been discovered, it is clear that the text as it stands *is* accurate. First of all, one sees there that Rashbam often uses the term שבא. Secondly, one sees that a phrase like את עושה החטף שבא מניע is perfectly acceptable in Rashbam's Hebrew. See the very similar phrase there (p. 44): ונעשה החטף שבא שוכן. It seems that Rashbam generally uses the term חטף as a term for an undifferentiated *sheva*. However, when trying to distinguish a mobile *sheva* from an immobile *sheva* the terms that he uses are שבא מניע and שבא שוכן respectively.

[61]So also iE here and in Ex. 2:3.

[62]The Massora in fact was the first to point out the similarity between the three words that Rashbam compares here. See Minhat Shai ad Ex. 2:3. In his grammar book (p. 44) Rashbam also compares these same three forms.

Rashbam correctly notes that in all three of these words one would expect a *dagesh* in the third letter, following the immobile *sheva* under the second letter. However, because of the unexpected *dagesh* in the second letter, the *sheva* becomes mobile and the *dagesh* must drop out of the third letter. What Rashbam does not try to explain is why there is an unexpected *dagesh* in the second letter of each of those words. For an interesting explanation based on the cantillation signs, see Luzzatto ad 2:3. See also the explanation in G.-K. 20h.

Rashbam opposes the midrashic attempt of LT to justify the anomalous vocalization by saying that the *dalet* is written רפי, i.e. "weakly" (i.e. without a *dagesh*), because the temple was destined to be weak and to be destroyed. Accordingly Rashbam explains that the lack of a *dagesh* in the *dalet* is grammatically clear; it is a result of the mobile *sheva* that precedes that *dalet*. Rashbam also opposes the explanation of Sekhel Tov who sees מקדש ה' as meaning that the temple on earth is a replica of the heavenly temple (מעין קודש ה').

15:18 ימלך ה' THE LORD WILL REIGN: After you settle in the land of Israel, then God's kingship will become known in all kingdoms.[63]

15:19-20 כי בא WHEN THE HORSES OF PHARAOH ... [WENT INTO THE SEA]: and God hurled them[64] into the sea, and the Israelites had already[65] MARCHED ON DRY GROUND IN THE MIDST OF THE SEA, then MIRIAM THE PROPHETESS TOOK ....[66] Similarly (Ex. 16:34) "When the LORD commanded Moses, *then* Aaron placed it before the Ark of the Pact, to be kept." Also similarly (Jer. 37:16-17) "When Jeremiah came (כי בא) to the pit

---

[63]So also iE. This interpretation implies (as Luzzatto writes explicitly) that "the LORD will reign forever" is neither a prayer (as Nahm. and Hizquni would have it) nor a prophecy. It is simply a statement that, as a result of God doing all the things described in the previous verses, his status as king will become known throughout the world. See similarly iE.

[64]ויערו, using the language of 14:27. See notes above ad 15:12.

[65]As noted above ad 14:26, Rashbam opposes the reading that claims that the Egyptians were drowning in the ocean at the same time that the Israelites were crossing safely. Accordingly he must again interpret here (as he did ad 14:29) that הלכו means "had already marched." So also LT here. The interpretation is somewhat forced in this verse as Rashbam sees all of verse 19 as one relative clause with a number of verbs, most of them to be understood as past tense verbs but one of them to be understood as a pluperfect: "when the horses of Pharaoh *went* ... and when God *turned* back on them the waters and when the Israelites *had marched* ..., then Miriam the prophetess *took* ...." Cf. the commentaries of iE and Nahm. that again note that our verse implies simultaneity of the Egyptians drowning and the Israelites crossing safely.

[66]Rashbam opposes the interpretation that would see verse 19 as being part of the Song of the Sea. (See e.g. iE.) As Nahm. says, the style of this verse is certainly not poetic. It makes sense to see it as a comment of the narrator. Even if it is from the pen of the narrator, there are two ways of understanding the verse. One can say that it is connected to the previous 18 verses ("[1] Moses sang this song ... [19] when [or 'for'] the horses of Pharaoh ..."). See e.g. Nahm., Cassuto and NJPS. On the other hand, Rashbam argues that it should be seen as connected to vs. 20. So also JBS. See similarly Childs, p. 248.

and the cells and Jeremiah remained there a long time, *then* King Zedekiah sent for him."[67]

15:20 הנביאה [MIRIAM] THE PROPHETESS: The text uses the word "נביא--prophet" to describe a person who is the author of words of praise [about God] or who rebukes people.[68]

אחות אהרן AARON'S SISTER: She is referred to as Aaron's sister[69] because Aaron was the first-born, as I explained concerning the phrases (Gen. 28:9) "sister of Nebaioth" and (Gen. 36:22) "Lotan's sister."[70]

---

[67]Rashbam cites two more examples of verses that he sees as having the structure, "When . . ., then . . . ." The second of those two verses begins, as our verse does, with the words כי בא. Rashbam sees this as an introduction to a relative clause that will be followed by the main clause. Cf. NJPS in Jeremiah which again sees the verse beginning with the phrase כי בא as a summary statement to the previous verses ("Thus Jeremiah came to the pit . . ."), not connected to the following verse.

[68]In other words, in it not necessary to predict the future in order to be considered a prophet. Thus Rashbam disputes with Rashi and LT and Sekhel Tov who all cite the midrash (found in Sotah 12b-13a and other sources) that Miriam was a prophetess in that she had correctly predicted that her parents would give birth to the savior of the Jews.
    Rashbam offers a number of other definitions for the word נביא, not all of them consistent. See comm. and notes to Gen. 20:7, s.v. כי and to Ex. 7:1.

[69]And not as "Moses' sister" or "Moses' and Aaron's sister."

[70]See Rashbam's comm to both those passages in Genesis and see notes there, p. 162.
    The phrase, "Miriam, Aaron's sister," is troubling. (As Sekhel Tov phrased the question: "ולא אחות משה אתמהה--I am amazed [at this phraseology]; was she not also 'the sister of Moses'?") Many critical scholars argue on the basis of this phrase that the earliest traditions about the Exodus did not consider Moses to have been a brother of Aaron and Miriam for "Moses would have surely been named there instead of Aaron or at least alongside him" (Noth, p. 122). Naturally Rashbam rejects such a solution.
    But Rashbam also disputes with the midrashic solutions offered by Rashi (found in Sotah, *ibid.*, and in other sources) according to which Miriam is called "Aaron's sister" either because she began to be a prophetess when she was the sister only of Aaron, i.e. before Moses was born, or because of the special relationship between Aaron and Miriam as seen by his prayer on her behalf in Num. 12:11-12. So also LT and Sekhel Tov. Rashbam argues more simply that there is a biblical pattern that a woman is standardly referred to as the sister of her eldest brother. iE, in his shorter comm., offers a number of other solutions. Modern traditional commentators generally follow

15:22 וַיַּסַּע [MOSES] CAUSED ISRAEL TO SET OUT: וַיַּסַּע) is a *hifil* form, while וַיִּסַּע) [71](https://) [is a *qal* form, which] means "he himself set out." Similarly וַיַּפֵּל) in the phrase (Ps. 78:28) "making them come down (וַיַּפֵּל)) inside His camp," and וַיַּגֵּשׁ) in the phrase (Lev. 8:14) "He led forward (וַיַּגֵּשׁ)) the bull," are *hifil* forms. However וַיִּפֹּל)[72](https://) and וַיִּגַּשׁ)[73](https://) are *qal* forms.[74](https://)

15:25 וַיּוֹרֵהוּ [THE LORD] SHOWED HIM: The word ויורהו is like [the word יורו in the phrase] (Dt. 33:10) "They shall teach (יורו) Your laws."[75](https://)

Rashbam's approach here. See e.g. Mendelssohn, Luzzatto, and Hakham here. See also Cassuto here and ad Gen. 10:21..

[71]E.g. Gen. 12:9.

[72]E.g. Gen. 17:3.

[73]E.g. Gen. 18:23.

[74]Again Rashbam provides a clear explanation of how to tell the difference between *qal* and *hifil* forms, this time of prima-*nun* verbs. See comm. and notes above ad 4:25, s.v. וַתַּגַּע.
    There are a number of the midrashic attempts to explain why וַיַּסַּע משה, this "rather unusual formulation" (NJPSC), is used here. The most common explanation is the one found in Rashi, LT and Sekhel Tov (from Tanh. B. *Beshallah* 16) that the Jews were so involved in collecting the booty from the dead Egyptians that Moses had to use force to get them to move on. It is possible that Rashbam's grammatical comment here is meant to oppose that midrash by pointing out that there is nothing anomalous about the form.

[75]It is difficult to know precisely what Rashbam means by this comment as we do not have his comm. on Dt. 33:10. (See Rosin, *Commentary*, p. 231, note 11.) A number of both early and late midrashic sources (e.g. Mekhilta *Vayyassa'* 1 [Laut. ed. p. 92], Tanh. *Beshallah* 24 and LT) all note that the form to be expected here would be ויראהו, not ויורהו. They all then provide midrashic explanations of how the word ויורהו implies that God taught Moses something (so also Nahm. here: "שלא מצאתי לשון מורה אלא בענין למוד--I have always found the verb מורה related to the idea of teaching"), or that Torah (from the same root as ויורהו) was somehow involved in the miraculous sweetening of the waters here. Presumably Rashbam does not interpret the phrase here midrashically but it is not clear what he understands as the meaning of a form from the

15:25-6 שם **THERE HE MADE FOR THEM LAWS AND RULES AND THERE HE PUT THEM TO THE TEST:** There in Marah--as a result of the test[76] that He put to them, by making them thirst for water and then making the waters sweet--in that way He began to educate them that they should be willing to accept the laws and rules that He was going to give them[77] and as a result He would take care of their needs.

---

root י-ר-ה in this verse.
  While many moderns emend to ויראהו, see Childs' defense of MT (p. 266, note 25).

[76]Or perhaps "as a result of the teaching" or "the lesson." Rashbam does not comment here on the word נסהו, and simply uses another form from the same root, הנסיון, in his paraphrase of the verse. Yet from the continuation of Rashbam's comment here to this verse--combined with his comment on the word אנסנו in 16:4--it is possible to conclude that Rashbam feels that נסהו here refers to God's attempt to educate the Israelites about His providence and/or about the principles of reward and punishment, so that they will be willing in the future to accept the commandments. Rashbam then is opposing Rashi's interpretation here that the "test" was God's attempt to see how the Israelites would react to the lack of water. See comm. and notes ad 16:4 and ad 20:17 and ad Gen. 22:1.
  While Rashbam's explanation of the "test" in Gen. 22:1 is somewhat different from the explanation he uses here in Exodus, one common element in all these passages is that Rashbam appears to be carefully avoiding interpreting these "tests" as an attempt by God to find out information that He did not know before. See Rosin, RSBM, p. 109, who argues that Rashbam does that for theological reasons. Cf., however, Sara Japhet, "Rashbam's Commentary on Genesis 22: 'Peshat' or 'Derash'," [Heb.] in the *Sarah Kamin Memorial Volume*, pp. 349-366. Japhet correctly notes that in his comm. to Deut. 13:4 Rashbam *does* interpret the verb נ-ס-ה, applied there to God, as referring to a test. So Rashbam is not in principle averse to the idea of God testing humans. See Japhet's lengthy discussion of the issue there.

[77]The phrase, "there he made for them laws and rules," is a difficult one. Aside from this one phrase, the Torah provides no further details about anything that was taught at Marah. Midrashim try to provide extra-biblical details about a revelation of some laws at Marah, before the theophany at Sinai. See e.g. Mekhilta, *ibid.*, p. 94, Sanhedrin 56b, Rashi, LT and Sekhel Tov.
  Rashbam, true to form, attempts to explain the verse without recourse to extra-biblical information. The verse means, according to Rashbam, that God prepared the ground here for teaching the Jews "rules and laws" at some future date. See also JBS who suggests that שם לו חק ומשפט means that God gave them food to eat. חק is to be understood here in the same way as it is used in Gen. 47:22. JBS, like Rashbam is attempting to interpret the verse without assuming that in order to understand the verse

EXODUS XV

And in what way did HE MAKE FOR THEM LAWS AND RULES? By saying to them,[78] "IF YOU WILL HEED THE LORD YOUR GOD DILIGENTLY . . . AND KEEP ALL HIS LAWS that he will teach you, THEN ANY OF THE DISEASES THAT I BROUGHT UPON THE EGYPTIANS, when I turned their water into blood[79] and they had no water to drink,[80] I WILL NOT BRING UPON YOU FOR I AM THE LORD YOUR HEALER (רפאך). [God is called "healer"] because he "healed" the water.[81] [The root ר-פ-א can refer to making water drinkable;] a similar phrase is used about Elisha "healing" the water.[82] Thus the phrase "[I WILL NOT BRING UPON YOU] ANY OF THE DISEASES (מחלה)" also refers to diseases of water, as it is written (Ex. 23:25) "He will bless your bread and your water. And I will remove sickness (מחלה) from your midst."[83]

---

one must have recourse to an extra-biblical source. See also Nahm., beginning with the words ועל דרך הפשט. See also Rashbam's comm. ad 18:13 where he makes reference to the standard rabbinic interpretation of this phrase.

Touitou (*Tarbiz* 51, p. 235) argues that Rashbam, for the purposes of anti-Christian polemic, is interested in saying that no revelation of laws took place before Sinai and that that motivates his comment here.

[78] In other words, verse 26 does not contain a further new idea but rather is an elaboration of the last phrases of vs. 25, "He made for them laws and rules . . . ." So also Luzzatto.

[79] See iE, longer comm. only, who also sees here a reference to the first plague. Rashbam's language here, מימיהם דם, alludes to Ps. 105:29.

[80] An allusion to the language of Num. 33:14.

[81] Again Rashbam takes great pains to interpret the "healing" of this verse contextually as a reference to the sweetening of the water supply and not to something more general unrelated to the immediate text. Cf. e.g. the midrashic explanations of the Mekhilta, *ibid.*, pp. 96-97.

Touitou, (*ibid.*, p. 232) contends that Rashbam's explanation of these verses as a simple reference to sweetening the water should be seen as a polemic against the Christian exegetes who see here in the piece of wood of vs. 25 a pre-figuration of the cross.

[82] II Kings 2:21, "Thus says the LORD: I heal (רפאתי) this water."

[83] See also Rashbam's comm. and notes there and Tos. ad Eruv. 65a, s.v. וקרי.

EXODUS XVI

16:1 בחמשה ON THE FIFTEENTH DAY OF THE SECOND MONTH: That is when the cakes[1] that they took out of Egypt ran out.[2]

16:3 ביד [IF ONLY WE HAD DIED] BY THE HAND OF THE LORD: The death of "those who come to the grave in ripe old age,"[3] and not die of starvation.[4]

על [WHEN WE SAT] NEXT TO THE FLESHPOTS: [על in this verse means "next to," as in the phrase (Num. 2:20) "Next to it (עליו) the tribe of Manasseh."[5]

16:4 ויצא THE PEOPLE SHALL GO OUT AND GATHER EACH DAY THAT DAY'S PORTION: Even if they attempt to gather more, once they arrive home they will find that they have only THAT DAY'S PORTION, as it is written (vs. 18) "When they measured it by the

---

[1] See 12:39.

[2] A number of opinions can be found in the Mekhilta, *Vayyassa'* 2, pp. 98-100, about the significance of the date mentioned here. Both Rashi and Rashbam adopt the same one of the explanations offered there, that on that date the provisions from Egypt ran out.

[3] Using the language of Job 5:26.

[4] Rashbam opposes the explanation of the Mekhilta (*ibid.*, p. 100) that dying "at the hand of the LORD" alludes to the death of many Israelites during the plague of darkness. That explanation is also offered by LT and Sekhel Tov. Rashbam explains more simply that it means to die of natural causes.

[5] See Rashbam ad Dt. 4:11. See also similarly Rashi ad Neh. 3:2 and see Rosin's discussion (RSBM, pp. 21-22) of the authorship of the comm. on Nehemiah attributed to Rashi.
On על as referring to proximity, see BDB s.v. על, 6.

'omer, [he who had gathered much had no excess . . .] they had gathered as much as they needed to eat."[6]

למען אנסנו THAT I MAY TEST THEM:[7] "Since every day their eyes are turned[8] to Me for their sustenance, as a result they will believe in Me and follow My laws." This idea is explained explicitly in the Torah portion Vehayah 'eqev, on the verse (Deut. 8:3) "He subjected you to the hardship of hunger . . . ."[9]

---

[6] See comm. there. Vss. 17-18 can be understood to mean either that the Jews were obedient and gathered only the precise amount allotted (so Mekhilta, ibid. 5, p. 116) or that a miracle happened and that whatever amount they really gathered turned into the proper amount. See iE, longer comm. ad vs. 17, who mentions both possibilities. Like Rashbam, see also Rashi ad vss. 17-18 and see Rashi ad Yoma 75a, s.v. אם בן.

Rashbam, however, appears to be the only exegete who suggests that the phrase דבר יום ביומו here is an allusion to the miracle that will be described in vss. 17-18. Rashbam then opposes the understanding of Rashi (following the opinion of R. Eleazar of Modi'im in Mekhilta, ibid. 3, p. 103) who sees this phrase as part of the instructions to the Israelites, not as part of the description of a miraculous outcome. Perhaps Rashbam is interested in saying that Moses did not pass on to the Israelites any instructions from what God said to him in vss. 4-5 because, according to his interpretation of vs. 22, God's speech in this section is a description of what will happen, and not instruction about what the Israelites should do. See comm. and notes below ad vs. 22. Most commentators and translators follow Rashi's approach.

[7] Or perhaps "that I might teach them." See notes above ad 15:25.

[8] עיניהם תלויות, a common rabbinic phrase meaning "to look towards" and also "to hope" or "to depend upon." See e.g. SR 21:5: "תלו עיניהם למרום ועשו תשובה--they turned their eyes towards heaven and repented."

[9] There also (in vs. 2) the word "לנסתך--that He might test you" is used to describe the manna experience, and the purpose of the test there is to lead to the fulfillment of God's laws. (See vs. 6 and the end of vs. 2 there.) Rashbam's explanation of the manna can also be seen as following the opinion of R. Simeon b. Yohai in Yoma 76a. So also Sekhel Tov ad vs. 19.

Rashbam opposes the interpretation of Rashi who says that the test here is to see whether the Israelites will be willing to observe the specific ordinances concerning the manna. Rashbam says that the manna is to be seen as a learning experience that will teach the people to believe in God's providence and, as a result, they will learn to observe God's commandments in general. See above comm. and notes to 15:25 where again Rashbam and Rashi disagree about whether to see the "test" as a reference to some one specific event or law (Rashi) or whether to interpret it as God's general attempt to

EXODUS XVI

16:5 והכינו THEY SHALL PREPARE [WHAT THEY HAVE BROUGHT IN]: "Bake what you would bake and boil what you would boil."[10]

והיה משנה IT SHALL PROVE TO BE DOUBLE: Even though every day they found only one *'omer* per person,[11] on Friday they would find double, two *'omer*s for each.[12]

16:6 כי IT WAS THE LORD WHO BROUGHT YOU OUT [FROM THE LAND OF EGYPT]: Not as you said (vs. 3), "For you (viz. Moses and Aaron) have brought us out."[13]

---

turn the Israelites into observers of Torah (Rashbam). See JBS and Nahm., similarly to Rashbam.

[10] Rashbam's comment is a direct citation of vs. 23.
Rashbam's interpretation opposes the various talmudic explanations of what laws one learns from this phrase: either that one may not prepare on the sabbath for a weekday (Betsah 2b) or that sabbath preparations should be done first thing on Friday morning (Shabbat 117b) or that the laws of *muqṣeh* are derived from the Torah (Pes. 47b). Rashbam explains more simply that the reference here is specific to the immediate context and means that the Israelites should cook the manna before the sabbath begins. See comm. below ad vss. 22 and 23. Like Rashbam, see JBS. Cf. NJPS: "apportion," and Orlinsky, *Notes*, and the criticism of Childs, p. 273, note 5.

[11] Using the language of vs. 16: עמר לגלגלת.

[12] Using the language of vs. 22: שני העמר לאחד.
Rashbam's interpretation opposes that of the Mekhilta, *ibid.*, p. 104, that interprets משנה as related to the word "משונה--different or unusual." The Mekhilta specifically mentions and rejects the *peshaṭ* interpretation. Sekhel Tov follows Mekhilta. LT, here, and Rashi ad vs. 22 offer both the *peshaṭ* and the midrashic interpretations.

[13] So also Rashi, iE and Sekhel Tov. For another example of Rashbam's sensitivity to the issue of who is being described as taking the Jews out of Egypt, see his comm. to 32:11.

16:7 ובקר IN THE MORNING YOU SHALL BEHOLD THE PRESENCE OF THE LORD: When He makes bread rain down on you[14] in the morning.[15]

16:12 וידעתם YOU SHALL KNOW THAT I AM THE LORD YOUR GOD: who took you out of the land of Egypt.[16]

---

[14]ימטיר לכם לחם; a play on the language of vs. 4.

[15]Verse 7 predicts that the Israelites "will behold the Presence of the LORD" and verse 10 writes that the Israelites in fact did see "the Presence of the LORD." Yet Rashbam and most Jewish exegetes do not connect those two passages. Our verse is understood as meaning that the next day, the Presence of the LORD would be perceived through the falling of the manna, while verse 10 is understood to mean that before the manna came, the LORD appeared in a cloud. So also Rashi and see similarly Qara, cited in *Peleṭat Soferim*, p. 18 ("ואל יעלה על לב איש שיאמר בקר וראיתם זה גילוי שכינה--let no person imagine that 'in the morning you shall behold . . . ' refers to seeing the *Shekhinah*"). See also the continuation of the quote from Qara as cited by Gad, p. 23: "וראיתם את כבוד ה' על כרחך קאי על ירידת המן שהוא כבוד ה'--'you shall see the Presence of the LORD' must refer to the falling of the manna; that is [what is meant by the phrase] 'the Presence of the LORD'." (So also NJPSC.) Presumably the reason for that intepretation is that verse 7 appears to describe a solution to the crisis of the grumbling community but verse 10 in its context appears to describe a theophany that took place before the crisis was solved. See, on the other hand, iE, who sees the two references to the Presence of the LORD as referring to the same appearance of God and see what creative exegesis he must do (longer comm. to vs. 6) to support that reading.

Rashi, following the Mekhilta (*ibid.*, p. 105), argues that the reference to "the presence of the LORD" teaches us that the manna, as opposed to the quail, was given by God "בפנים מאירות--with a bright countenance." So also LT and Sekhel Tov. Rashbam opposes that understanding and writes that it is simply a reference to the manifestation of God's miracle when the manna falls in the morning. So also JBS.

[16]Rashbam completes this phrase, "I am the LORD your God," using the same words that the Torah uses to complete it a number of times, e.g. Lev.19:36.

Rashbam opposes the midrashic readings of this phrase--either that there is a threatening tone to the phrase implying that God will yet punish the Israelites for this grumbling (Mekhilta *ibid.* 4, p. 108, LT and Sekhel Tov) or that this verse is a source for the obligation to praise God after eating bread ("you shall have your fill of bread and you shall know that I am the LORD": see sources cited by Kasher, note 80.) Rashbam explains more simply that this verse is a continuation of the theme that he described above (in his comm. to vs. 6) of Moses trying to prove that it was not he, but rather God, who took the Jews out of Egypt.

EXODUS XVI

16:14 ותעל WHEN THE FALL OF DEW: that was overlaying the manna and covering it, LIFTED. Dew generally rises.[17]

מחספס: appears nowhere else [in the Bible];[18] from context it means[19] "scattered[20]."

ככפור AS HAIL: כפור is *gresle* in the vernacular.[21]

16:15 ויאמרו THEY SAID ONE TO ANOTHER מן הוא--[which means "WHAT IS IT?"]: because they did not know what it was. Dunash also explains the phrase that way.[22] The continuation of the verse, FOR

---

[17]In other words, the dew that had already "fallen" on top of the manna, now "lifted" or "evaporated." Rashbam follows the opinion of Rashi, who also provides a simple scientific experiment to prove that dew rises. So also Sekhel Tov and see also Rashi to Yoma 75b, s.v. כתיב ותעל. Both Rashi and Rashbam oppose the midrashim that claim that the "lifting" of the dew in this verse is a reference to the dew appearing by miraculously rising out of the ground, the opposite of what it usually does when it "comes down" from heaven, paralleling the fact that the bread this time miraculously came from the heavens instead of from the earth. See Tanh. *Beshallaḥ* 20 and Tanh. B. *Beshallaḥ* 20; see also Mekhilta *ibid.*, p. 110.

[18]I.e. it is a hapax legomenon. This fact is noted also by Rashi.

[19]פתרונו לפי ענינו. This phrase is commonly used by Qara but can also be found in the works of Rashi and Rashbam. See Rosin, p. 15, note 4.

[20]Rashbam opposes both interpretations offered by Rashi, that the word means "uncovered" or "enveloped." There are a variety of other explanations of the phrase in midrashim and other commentators. Rashbam's explanation appears to be unique.

[21]I.e. hail (*grêle* in modern French). So also JBS. Generally Rashbam provides translations into the vernacular only when Rashi does not. Here they both offer old French equivalents but those translations are not in total agreement. Rashi writes here that כפור is *gelede*, or "(hoar-)frost."

[22]In his *Teshuvot*, Filipowski's edition, p.20 (ופתרון מן הוא מה הוא). Rashbam's brother, R. Jacob Tam, also agrees with Dunash. See his comment there (מן הוא, דונש יפה פתרוהו).
  Rashbam's interpretation is opposed to that of Rashi who connects מן to the word מזון (food). Neither Rashbam nor Dunash was the first to offer the explanation that מן means what; see e.g. Mekhilta, *ibid.*, p. 114.

THEY DID NOT KNOW WHAT IT WAS, proves [that that is the correct interpretation of the phrase מן הוא].[23] However I say that מן actually means "*who*" [not "*what*"] in Aramaic.[24] But since this phrase is written in the *Egyptian* language[25] and in that language the common meaning of מן is "what,"[26] Moses wrote the phrase in the precise language that the people said it.[27] He did that in order to inform us that that is why (vs. 31) "The house of Israel called it מן (manna)," because they were wondering [what it was,] and they said "מן הוא--what is it?" Similarly[28] [one should understand the phrase] יגר שהדותא (Gen.

---

[23]So also Dunash, there.

[24]Again Dunash, there, suggests that the word מן here could be related to the similar Aramaic word. Dunash realizes that מן in Aramaic means "who," not "what," but he dismisses that problem since, he argues, the words for "who" and "what" are often interchanged in the Bible. Rashbam takes a different approach.

[25]In other words, if this were Aramaic then Dunash's explanation would not work. But the proper explanation is that the phrase is written in Egyptian.

[26]The idea that מן is the Egyptian word for "what" can be first found in LT. Presumably that is Rashbam's source for this interpretation. So also JBS. There is no reason to think that Rashbam (or LT or JBS or, for that matter, any members of their intended audiences) had any knowledge of the Egyptian language. Presumably the explanation here is speculative.

[27]The scholarly and historical sense of LT, Rashbam and JBS--that comparisons to Aramaic (or Arabic; see iE) are irrelevant to the proper understanding of this passage and that solutions should be found by recourse to Egyptian--is impressive. Rashbam is also, by the by, disputing the well known midrash (e.g. Mekhilta *Pisha'* 5, pp. 34-6) that the Jews continued to speak Hebrew, not Egyptian, during their sojourn in Egypt and that that is one of the reasons that they were worthy of redemption. On the other hand, there are midrashim that claim that the Israelites who left Egypt spoke only Egyptian. See e.g. Tanh. B. *Yitro* 16.

[28]The two following examples of the use of foreign words in the Bible are not found in LT or in JBS. They are presumably Rashbam's independent addition to the interpretation that he took from LT. Cf. Rashbam's comm. to Gen. 36:12 where he cites a long interpretation from LT and then adds one further example of his own to illustrate the point ("I, Samuel, have found a third such verse . . .").

EXODUS XVI

31:47).[29] Similarly [one should understand the phrase] (Est. 3:7) "הפיל" "פור הוא הגורל" ("*pur*--which means 'the lot'--was cast"). Bearing in mind that the *megillah* was written in Hebrew,[30] the biblical text need read only הפיל הגורל ("the lot was cast"). But [the Persian word, *pur*, was included] in order to inform us that (*ibid.* 9:26) "For that reason these days were named Purim, after *pur*." Had the word not been written beforehand in the local language we would not have understood why the holiday was called Purim.[31]

16:17-18 וילקטו THEY GATHERED: without estimation and without measurement[32] and then, when they got home, ויימודו--THEY MEASURED IT.[33]

---

[29]In other words, this Aramaic phrase is put into the Hebrew text in order to explain why the place is referred to as יגר שהדותא. Since the place name is based on the Aramaic, that is why the Hebrew text had to use Laban's precise wording in Aramaic, not just a Hebrew equivalent.

[30]Not in Persian. So there is ostensibly no reason to include Persian words in the text.

[31]In other words, the text in Est. 3 anticipates the needs of the reader of Est. 9 and provides ahead of time the information that that reader needs. On anticipation in Rashbam, see Genesis volume, pp. 400-421.

[32]בלא אומד ובלא מדה. At first, it is hard to understand why Rashbam would write that they did *not* estimate. But Rashbam's comment makes sense if it is seen as disgreeing with Sekhel Tov who writes לא שלקטו באומד הדעת והניחו אלא לקטו במידת העומר ("they didn't gather by estimation . . . but rather they measured"). Rashbam then says that they neither estimated nor measured, but took as much as they wanted.

[33]See notes above, ad vs. 4. As noted there, Rashbam, like Rashi, explains that it happened miraculously that no matter what they gathered, it ended up being the right amount. The other possible understanding is that the Jews were obedient, and the reference in vs. 17 to the different amounts gathered by "he who had gathered much" and by "he who had gathered little" mean that people with larger families gathered more than people with smaller families. See iE and LT and Sekhel Tov. See also Luzzatto's exasperated comment: "למה נהפוך מה שהוא צווי ונעשה ממנו נס"--why should we take words that refer to an instruction and turn them into the description of a miracle?"

The form וַיָּמֻדּוּ is [a *vav*-consecutive imperfect form,] from the root מ-ד-ד, just as וַיָּסֹבּוּ[34] is from the root ס-ב-ב.[35]

16:22 ויגידו AND THEY TOLD MOSES: that they had found double the regular amount and they asked if they should save some for the next day. [They had to ask Moses these questions because] up till now Moses had not told them what God had said to him on the first day [of the episode] (vs. 5) "On the sixth day they shall prepare what they brought home and it shall be double [the amount they gather each day]."[36]

16:23 ויאמר HE SAID TO THEM, "THIS IS WHAT GOD SAID: [to me] already on the first day [of the episode, in vs. 5], but I did not tell you."[37] [The reason that Moses had not told them yet what God had

---

[34]E.g. Josh. 6:14.

[35]Rashbam often discusses the grammar of geminate verbs (see the list of passages in RSBM, p. 137) and often uses the paradigm of the root ס-ב-ב to illustrate his point. See e.g. comm. ad Gen. 21:20 and 49:23.

[36]It is hard to understand why the chieftains of the community would have to come and tell Moses what had happened if they had heard already that this was going to happen. So, as noted above ad vs. 4, Rashbam argues that Moses never passed on those instructions to the Israelites. See Tanh. B. *Beshallah* 24 who argues that Moses forgot to tell them and see Rashi on vs. 22 who says that Moses was punished for not telling them. As I suggested above, it appears to me that Rashbam is saying that in vss. 4-5 there were no instructions that Moses was supposed to pass along and thus there is no difficulty in understanding why the chieftains have to come consult with Moses here. See also comm. to the next verse. Cf. Sekhel Tov who says that the chieftains came and reported that they had followed orders and collected double but they came to ask why those orders had been given since they didn't know what the sabbath was. So also iE and NJPSC.

[37]In other words, Moses told them now that they should not be surprised, as this course of events--finding on Friday double the amount of what they found on previous days--was predicted to him by God already from the beginning.

EXODUS XVI 177

said to him back in vs. 5[38] was because] Moses wanted them to ask[39] when they found double, so that he could now teach them about the honor of the sabbath day.[40]

אֵפוּ BAKE: [אֵפוּ is an anomalous form.] The expected form would be אֱפוּ, with a *hataf pataḥ qaṭan*,[41] just as from the root א-כ-ל one says אֱכֹל[42] [in the imperative] and from the root א-מ-ר one says אֱמֹר,[43] so also the imperative of the root א-פ-ה should be אֱפֵה [in the singular, and אֱפוּ[44] in the plural]. However, since the form is not connected to

---

[38]See note on the previous verse. Even if what God said to Moses in vss. 4-5 was not instructions to pass on to the Israelites but predictions about the future, one would reasonably think that Moses would pass on those predictions, so that the people would understand what was happening. Accordingly Rashbam explains what Moses' motives were for keeping those predictions to himself.

[39]Or perhaps "wanted them to wonder."

[40]In other words, it was not that Moses forgot or that he sinned by not telling them what God had said. (See notes on vs. 22.) It was part of his educational strategy--to shock the people and let them experience on their own how the sabbath differs from other days; only then would he teach them about the sabbath.

Rashbam uses in this passage some of the standard language that he uses to describe the phenomenon of anticipation ("להודיע להם", "תמיהים"; see Genesis volume, pp. 414 and 417). Essentially Rashbam is explaining why Moses did not "anticipate" here, why he did not let them know ahead of time what would happen. He explains that at times there are valid educational reasons to surprise one's audience and *not* to anticipate.

[41]I.e. what we would call a *hataf segol*. See Rashbam's *Dayqut*, pp. 50-51, where he explains that in prima-*'aleph* verbs, the way to tell the difference between the imperative masc. sing. and the infinitive is that the first begins with a "*hataf pataḥ qaṭan*" (e.g. אֱכֹל) while the second begins with a "*hataf pataḥ gadol*" (e.g. אֲכֹל).

[42]E.g. I Sam. 9:24.

[43]E.g. Gen. 45:17.

[44]Cf. iE, longer comm., who suggests that the expected form here would be אֲפוּ .

the following words[45] but rather its cantillation sign is a *revia'*, which is a disjunctive accent,[46] that is why it is vocalized with a *ṣere*. I have found no other forms like this except הָבוּ, in the phrase in The Twelve Prophets (Hos. 4:18), "Their kings disgracefully love to say 'give' (הָבוּ)."[47]

16:24 ולא IT DID NOT TURN FOUL: and even MAGGOTS, which generally come [more] quickly, DID NOT APPEAR IN IT.[48]

---

[45]מחובר לאחוריו. I.e it is not a context form but a pausal form. On the phrase מחובר לאחוריו in Rashbam, see RSBM, p. 157. Rashbam is generally interested in the issue of pausal forms. See e.g. his *Dayqut*, pp. 50 and 57.

[46]Or "distinctive accent"; "מנגוני המלכים." The phrase is a common Massoretic term but as far as I can tell this is the only time that Rashbam uses it.

Rashbam is saying that a pausal form is found here since the cantillation sign is disjunctive. Perhaps Rashbam feels the need to emphasize that *revia'* is a disjunctive accent because *revia'* generally does not cause pausal forms; sometimes though it does. See G.-K. 29i.

[47]I have translated that difficult phrase in Hosea the way iE and Qimḥi understand it, as they too, like Rashbam, understand הָבוּ as an imperative. (Cf. ibn Janaḥ, *Sefer ha-riqmah*, p. 277, who sees הבו as a perfect form from the root א-ה-ב.) In fact, iE there, like Rashbam here, says that הָבוּ and אָפוּ are on the same paradigm.

Rashbam's grammatical explanation here of the form אָפוּ is by no means certain. For another explanation see Luzzatto. iE just labels the form anomalous (זרה בדקדוק). See also G.-K. 76d who simply calls אָפוּ a "difficult form" from a doubly-weak verb.

[48]Rashi ad vs. 20, following a number of midrashim (e.g. Mekhilta *Vayyassa'* 5, p. 116), comments on the "difficulty" of the phrase there "it became infested with maggots and it turned foul." According to Rashi, the order in *that* verse, vs. 20, makes no sense: things first turn foul and then become infested with maggots. Rashi there says that, on the other hand, the order in *this* verse, verse 24, describes the process in a reasonable, step-by-step manner, with the phrases "it did not turn foul and maggots did not appear in it."

Rashbam seems to disagree with Rashi's basic assumption. According to Rashbam, items first become infested with maggots and then turn foul. (For long discussions of this issue, see Naḥm. ad vs. 20 and Kasher, note 109.) Accordingly, in the verse that describes the way the process *did* take place (vs. 20), the order is the natural, chronological one--maggots and then turning foul. In our verse where the description is of how the putrification process did *not* happen on the sabbath, it makes sense (particularly to someone with talmudic training) for the text to write first that the food did not go foul and then to write that even the first step of the putrification process--maggots--did not appear.

Rashbam would presumably argue against Rashi's interpretation of our verse as follows. "If you feel that the process is 'turning foul' followed by maggots, then, in our verse, after the text writes that the manna 'did *not* turn foul,' why would it have to tell us that there were no maggots? How could one imagine that there were maggots if it never even 'turned foul'?"

Rashi then sees the natural order to be expected (in both verses) to be the chronological one. Rashbam says that in our verse a different principle obtains, the principle of progressing from the minor to the major. This dispute of Rashbam and Rashi can be found also concerning other biblical passages, for example concerning the phrase "ברכות שדים ורחם--blessings of the breast and womb" in Gen. 49:25. (See comm. and notes there.) There Rashi offers the unusual interpretation that שדים does not mean "breasts," but rather "semen." Presumably he does that because he thinks that the list of blessings should go in the order that the blessings are required, so it does not make sense to bless the breasts *before* the blessing of the womb. Rashbam there explains explicitly that the principle of order used there is not chronological but is based on the לא זו אף זו principle ("not only this but also that"; a common talmudic principle for explaining the order of material in the Mishnah. See e.g. Yevamot 19a).

Yet another example of this same methodolgical dispute concerns the verse in Genesis (39:10) that records that when Potiphar's wife attempted to seduce Joseph, "ולא שמע אליה לשכב אצלה להיות עמה--he did not yield to her request to lie beside her, to be together with her." Rashi there explains that להיות עמה means to be with her in the World to Come: if he sleeps with her in this world then he will suffer the same fate as her in the next world. Again Rashi explains the two elements לשכב אצלה and להיות עמה as being written in the order that they would occur. On the other hand, Rashbam there again implicitly uses the לא זו אף זו principle to explain the verse. Not only did Joseph refuse to lie beside her (לשכב אצלה), he even made it his business to be sure never to be together with her alone in one place. Gur Aryeh, in his defense of Rashi there, writes that Rashi refuses to interpret להיות עמה in the way that Rashbam does, for if the text tells us that Joseph refused even to be alone with her, why should the text have to tell us that he also did not sleep beside her? Is it not obvious? However, the לא זו אף זו principle used by Rashbam deals with that problem. That principle says that texts may progress from the minor to the major and that, in truth, it would have sufficed for the second element alone to have been written. Yet it is acceptable style to write the first element and then to say "לא זו אף זו--not only is the first element true even the second element coming up is also true."

So also in our verse Rashbam argues that the progression is of the לא זו אף זו type. Not only did the manna not "go foul" on the sabbath (a sign of advanced putrification), even the first step of the process, maggots, did not occur.

See also Rashbam's comm. and notes to 21:33 and to 22:5.

16:26 לא THERE SHALL NOT BE ANY: manna.[49]

16:30 וישבתו SO THE PEOPLE OBSERVED THE SABBATH: from then on, ON THE SEVENTH DAY.[50]

16:31 וטעמו IT TASTED LIKE WAFERS IN HONEY: Below (Num. 11:8) it says that "It tasted like moist oil."[51] The Sages explained that [the manna tasted] "like honey to children but like oil to grown-ups" (Yoma 75b).

However, I say, according to the plain meaning of Scripture that [in our verse, the word] וטעמו means that when it is eaten as is, without grinding, then it tastes like wafers in honey, just like nuts[52] that taste sweet before they are ground or crushed. But when it is written below (Num. 11:8) "They ground it between millstones or pounded it into a mortar," that it why its taste became (והיה טעמו) oily,[53] just like nuts that turn into oil when ground up, or like olives. That is why in our verse it says "וטעמו--it tasted like," while there (in Numbers) the verse

---

[49]Rashbam provides the subject of the verb יהיה. So also Rashi and iE.

[50]So also iE. Rashbam's interpretation may be directed against the midrash (Sifre Zuta Numbers 9:4, cited by Kasher, number 179) that claims, on the basis of this verse, that during their forty years of wandering in the wilderness the Israelites observed properly only one sabbath, the first one.

[51]לשד השמן. My translation of that phrase is based on Rashbam's comm., there.

[52]אגוזים. Perhaps "walnuts."

[53]As Rashbam himself writes, his explanation of the apparent contradiction between Exodus and Numbers about what the manna really tasted like is opposed to that of the Talmud, an explanation that is cited, with variations, in numerous collections of midrashim. (See Kasher, note 190.) Interpretations similar to that of Rashbam can be found in JBS and in iE (longer comm.) here.

EXODUS XVI

says "והיה טעמו--its taste *became*";⁵⁴ i.e. its taste stopped being sweet and started to be oily.

כצפיחת LIKE WAFERS: The word צפיחת appears nowhere else in the Bible.⁵⁵ The word צפחת in the phrase (I Sam. 26:11) צפחת המים--the water jar," [is unrelated to the word צפיחת here and] is the name of a utensil.⁵⁶

גד CORIANDER: גד is a type of legume.⁵⁷ [The phrase כזרע גד means] "round, like the גד seed."⁵⁸

---

⁵⁴See Rashbam's comm. to Numbers where he reiterates this same explanation.
  Although as noted above, iE and JBS attempt to reconcile Exodus and Numbers in basically the same way as Rashbam, Rashbam is the only one who attempts to support this reconciliation by pointing to the alternation between וטעמו (here) and והיה טעמו (there). Rashbam is correct that והיה can and does often mean "to become" in biblical Hebrew. See e.g. the word's first appearance in the Bible (Gen. 2:10) "והיה לארבעה ראשים--it becomes four branches." While most often והיה (or other forms from the same root) will mean "to become" when the subjective completion begins with the letter *lamed*, it can and does sometimes mean "to become" even when not followed by a *lamed*. See BDB, s.v. ה-י-ה, II, 2.

⁵⁵אין לו חבר. The same phrase that Rashbam uses above ad vs. 14 to describe a hapax legomenon. So also iE.

⁵⁶Rashbam is arguing against an interpretation that would see צפיחת here as related to צפחת in I Sam. (see e.g. the [later] comm. of ibn Kaspi), but it is not known who before Rashbam interpreted the words that way. Qimhi in *Sefer ha-shorashim*, s.v. צ-פ-ח, quotes such an interpretation in the name of "the Gaon," but as noted there by Biesenthal and Lebrecht, the reference is not to Saadiah. In any case it appears that such an interpretation circulated, either orally or in writing, in the twelfth century and reached the ears or eyes of both Rashbam and Qimhi.
  Note that Rashbam does not explain the word צפיחת. He simply records that it is a hapax legomenon and argues against those who connect it to the word צפחת.

⁵⁷Cf. Rashi and Sekhel Tov who identify גד as "coriander." iE, on the other hand, claims that there is insufficient information in the Bible in order to identify which plant is referred to.

⁵⁸See Rashbam's next comment and note there.

לבן WHITE: Like the color of bdellium, as it says below (Num. 11:7), "in color it was like bdellium." But גד seeds are not white.[59]

16:33 ויאמר MOSES SAID TO AARON: after the Tabernacle was set up, in the second year [after the exodus], once the Ark of the Pact was there, "TAKE A JAR . . . ."[60]

16:34 לפני העדות BEFORE THE PACT: Before the Ark [of the Pact].[61]

16:35 אל קצה [THEY ATE THE MANNA] UNTIL THEY CAME TO THE BORDER OF THE LAND OF CANAAN: As it says in Joshua (5:12), "On that same day . . . the manna ceased."[62]

---

[59]Rashbam explains that the Torah compares the manna to the גד seed only as to shape, not as to color. The phrase כזרע גד לבן should not be understood as meaning "like a white גד seed." (See e.g. the second explanation offered by JBS.) The Torah makes two separate points about the manna, that it was round like a גד seed and that it was white. So also Rashi, following the opinion of R. Assi in Yoma 75a, and NJPSC.

While in Yoma, R. Assi's language is עגול כגידא ולבן כמרגלית, Rashbam attempts to make the interpretation closer to the words of the Torah by comparing the whiteness of the manna not to a מרגלית but to "bdellium." The precise meaning of "bdellium" in Numbers 11 is unclear. See NJPSC, here.

[60]Rashbam is troubled by the reference in vs. 34 to "the Pact" before the Tabernacle was built. He appears to suggest that while the events of verses 33-34 took place quite a bit of time after the other events in this chapter, they were attached to this chapter for literary reasons, not because of chronology. His solution can be found also in Rashi, iE and others. See also comm. and notes ad 13:13.

[61]This interpretation is generally agreed upon by all the classical commentators. Also NJPSC: "The Pact: elipsis for 'the Ark of the Pact'."

[62]See also LT who cites the same prooftext.

EXODUS XVII

17:7 היש IS THE LORD PRESENT AMONG US: to give us water [OR NOT]?[1]

17:11 כאשר WHENEVER MOSES HELD UP HIS HAND: with the rod,[2] THEN ISRAEL PREVAILED: For that is what happens at the battle lines:[3] as long as they can see their banner--*confanon*[4] in the vernacular--being raised, they prevail. But when their banner is lowered, they generally flee and are defeated.[5]

---

[1] Rashbam explains that the question is not really a theological one but a practical one--will God provide our needs. So also the opinion of Rabbi Eliezer in Mekhilta *Vayyassa'* 7, p. 134, and so also iE.

[2] See vs. 9 and see also JBS who emphasizes the role of the rod.

[3] ערכי המלחמה. An unusual phrase that does appear in rabbinic Hebrew; see e.g. the words of R. Pappa in Sotah 43b.

[4] The old French word for banner.

[5] Rashi and in fact most of the Jewish commentators explain these verses on the basis of Mishnah RH 3:8. That mishnah claims that the Israelites prevailed when Moses lifted up his hands, since the Israelites looked and "set their sights on High and subjected themselves to their Father in Heaven." However, the three famous Northern French *peshat*-oriented exegetes--Qara, Rashbam and JBS--all offer this explanation describing Moses' actions in terms of standard military strategy. (For Qara, see *Peletat soferim*, p. 18.)

See iE who argues against this interpretation in his longer comm. only. Margaliot (p. 362) cites this as proof that between writing his shorter and longer commentaries, iE read Rashbam's comm. However, as just noted, Rashbam's interpretation was common in Northern France. (See also Simon's general reservations about Margaliot's thesis [*Bar Ilan Annual* 3, p. 131f.].)

17:12 אמונה STEADY: אמונה means with lasting strength.[6] So also (Is. 22:23), "I will fix him as a peg במקום נאמן," i.e. in a strong place. So also (Ps. 100:5) "אמונתו is for all generations" means that He will endure forever.[7] So also (Deut. 28:59), "diseases that are malignant and נאמנים," i.e. long-lasting and virulent illnesses.

17:13 ויחלש: means that he was victorious over them.[8] So also in the verse (Ex. 32:18), "[It is not the sound of the tune of triumph or] the sound of the tune of victory (חלושה)."[9]

---

[6]Rashi and most Jewish exegetes see in the word אמונה here a reference to "faith." But Rashbam points out that the word has a physical, not a theological purpose in this passage. See similarly Menahem, ibn Janah (*Sefer ha-shorashim*, s.v. א-מ-נ), JBS and iE. Most modern translators follow Rashbam and translate אמונה as "steady."

For many Christians beginning with Origen (cited by Childs, p. 316) this passage was an important one in that the image of Moses with raised hands was seen as a prefiguration of the crucified Jesus. It may be then that Rashbam's comm. here, where he detheologizes the passage, is to some degree an anti-Christian polemic. See also similarly comm. and notes above ad 14:31. Still to my mind Rashbam's primary purpose here is to explain the word אמונה according to the *peshat*.

[7]This passage is particularly well chosen to illustrate Rashbam's point since, if אמונה is seen as meaning "faith" or "belief," the reference to God's אמונה is hard to understand.

Rashbam's citation of the text in Psalms (בכל דור ודור) differs slightly from that of MT (ועד דר ודר).

[8]Rashbam's interpretation opposes Rashi's midrashic understanding (following Mekhilta, '*Amaleq* 1, p. 146) of ויחלש as meaning that he killed all but the weak ones (חלשים). It also opposes the understanding of LT and Sekhel Tov that ויחלש means that he toyed with them or the understanding of JBS that it means that he killed them all. Rashbam says more simply that it means "to be victorious."

[9]Rashbam offers the same prooftext that Sekhel Tov used to prove a different understanding of the verse. Generally the word חלושה in that verse is seen as an antonym of the word גבורה there, and is interpreted as meaning "defeat." See Rashbam's comm. there where he says that the word means "victory," i.e. that it is synonymous with גבורה. See also notes there.

Among moderns there is still no unanimity about the meaning of the word ויחלש here. See e.g. NJPSC and Childs.

EXODUS XVII 185

17:14 באזני READ IT ALOUD TO JOSHUA: Since he will rule over them,[10] [instruct him] to fulfil my commandment[11] and blot out the name of Amalek.[12]

כי I WILL UTTERLY BLOT OUT THE MEMORY: I want his memory to be blotted out.[13]

17:15-16 ה' נסי THE LORD IS MY BANNER: I.e. God's rod[14] was our banner[15] on the hill. In the future, too, God will raise it as a banner on the mountains[16] to fight against Amalek, for He has just now

---

[10]As noted already by Mekhilta (*ibid.* 2, p. 149), a "hint" is provided here in the text for the first time that Joshua will take over Moses' position. So also Rashi.

[11]See next comment of Rashbam, s.v. כי.

[12]Rashi's interpretation differs only slightly from that of Rashbam. According to Rashi, Joshua was instructed to teach the Israelites that Amalek is to be destroyed. Rashbam says that Joshua was instructed to destroy the Amalekites. While Rashbam's interpretation appears to be the simpler one, it would appear that Rashi avoids it because he knows that Joshua in fact took no steps in his lifetime to defeat the Amalekites. (See Hizquni who makes this argument explicitly.) See however the end of Rashbam's comm. to vss. 15-16 where he rejects the idea that commandment to obliterate the Amalekites came into force only in the days of Saul.

[13]As noted by NJPSC, here the text says that *God* will blot out the memory of Amalek, while in Deut. 25:19 the *Israelites* are commanded to do so. Rashbam, like NJPSC, sees the texts as complementary and explains that here too the call to Joshua implies a command.

[14]See comm above ad vs. 11.

[15]Rashbam opposes the interpretation of Rashi who (following Mekhilta, *ibid.*, p. 159) sees נסי as related to the word for miracle. Like Rashbam, see JBS. See also Sekhel Tov who, after offering the explanation of the Mekhilta, writes: "פשטיה דקרא כך נראה לי ה' דגל שלי--To me, the *peshat* of the verse appears to be 'God is my banner'."

[16]An allusion to a number of prophetic passages, e.g. Is. 18:3, "When a banner is raised on the mountains," or Is. 49:22 "I will lift up my banner to the nations," or Is. 13:2 "Raise a banner over a bare mountain." (Sekhel Tov directly cites those last two passages in his comm., here.) Like here, in all of those passages God is promising to

said, "I will utterly blot out the memory of Amalek." And that is the meaning of the continuation of the passage, HE SAID "HAND UPON THE THRONE OF THE LORD [to swear that THE LORD WILL BE AT WAR WITH AMALEK THROUGHOUT THE AGES]."[17] [In other words, Moses in verse 16 is explaining that] "that is why I am naming[18] this altar 'the LORD is my banner', ([An altar may be given a name that constitutes a sentence about God,[19] like "the LORD is my banner,"] just as a person may be called "God is my helper," [אליעזר][20] or "God is with us" [עמנואל].)[21] because God raised up His hand onto His throne and swore that THE LORD WILL BE AT WAR WITH AMALEK THROUGHOUT THE GENERATIONS."

---

exert his authority over some nation(s) other than the Israelites.

[17]Rashbam is attempting to explain the connection between verses 15 and 16. When Moses proclaims in verse 15 that "the Lord is my banner," he means that God not only *was* the Israelite's banner in their past battle with the Amalekites, but also that he will *continue* to be their banner in future encounters with Amalek. Verse 16 then explains that God has committed himself to keep up the conflict with Amalek.

[18]Rashbam emphasizes that the subject of the verb ויקרא is Moses (following the opinion of R. Joshua in Mekhilta, *ibid*.) not God (the opinion of R. Eleazar of Modi'im there). See also iE's polemic against that last explanation in his shorter comm. here.

[19]Rashbam follows the interpretation of Rashi here that a sentence about God is a legitimate type of name in the Bible. So also iE. See also Rashi and Rashbam ad Gen. 33:20.

[20]See e.g. Ex. 18:4.

[21]Is. 7:14. This example is probably an important one for Rashbam. Ever since the first century (see e.g. Mt. 1:22-23) Christians have argued that the name Emanuel in Is. 7:14 is proof of the doctrine of incarnation as it is applied to a person who is called "God." Rashbam alludes here to the standard Jewish argument that the name Emanuel no more bespeaks the divinity of its bearer than the name Eliezer or dozens of other names of people, places or altars in the Hebrew Bible. See the argument provided explicitly in *Niṣṣaḥon Yashan*, Berger's edition pages 103 and 152, and see further sources in Berger's notes, p. 274f.

[God's raising His hand should be seen as implying an oath,][22] as in the verse (Dt. 32:40) "Lo, I raise My hand to heaven."[23] This is the true plain meaning of Scripture.

There are those who interpret the verse as follows: When my hand will be placed firmly on God's throne, i.e. when the kings of Israel will sit on their thrones, then that will be the proper time for war against the Amalekites.[24] But this interpretation does not make sense to me. If this were the meaning, the text would have to read "כי תהיה יד"--when the hand *will be* [on God's throne]." Rather the phrase HAND ON GOD'S THRONE should be seen as connected to the previous verse and as meaning that [Moses said (15) that God's banner will continue to be raised against the Amalekites in the future] *because* (16) "HAND ON GOD'S THRONE . . . ."[25]

---

[22]So also Onq. and Rashi. Cf. however the end of Rashbam's comment to this verse where he explains that he is rejecting another reading of the image of the hand raised onto God's throne.

[23]See Rashbam there, interpreting the phrase as a reference to an oath. So also Rashi and iE there.

See Sekhel Tov here who cites this same prooftext to show that raising one's hand is a reference to an oath.

[24]Thus JBS, following Sanhedrin 20b, Tanh. *Ki teṣe'* 11 and other sources. (According to Gad, p. 23, this explanation is also offered by Qara.) This reading is defended by Nahm. as the true *peshaṭ* reading. So also iE.

[25]I.e. because God has sworn to keep up the battle forever. The phrase should not then be seen, according to Rashbam, as a new idea defining the point at which the battle against the Amalekites will be joined, but rather as a continuation of the idea begun in the previous verse.

EXODUS XVIII

18:1 אשר ALL THAT GOD HAD DONE FOR MOSES: [The things that God did specifically for Moses[1] were] that Pharaoh did not harm him,[2] and that God caused him to be esteemed among Pharaoh and his courtiers,[3] and that it was through the hands of Moses that God performed miracles for the Israelites.[4]

18:2 אחר שלוחיה AFTER SHE HAD BEEN SENT HOME: [Usually this phrase is interpreted to mean] "after Moses sent her back from Egypt and returned her (to her father's home)." [This interpretation is offered even though] we have not been told until now that Moses ever sent them[5] back to his father-in-law's home.[6]

Others interpret the phrase to mean "afterwards he sent her her dowry." [שלוחים can mean "dowry,"] as in the phrase (I Kings 9:16), "gave it as a dowry (שלוחים) to his (Pharaoh's) daughter." This second

---

[1]The verse implies that God did things (a) for Moses and (b) for the Israelites. JBS for one suggests that the verse means "the things that God had done for the Israelites through the efforts of Moses." Rashbam disagrees and says that Jethro heard not only about what God did for the Israelites in general but also about the specific things that God had done for the benefit of Jethro's own son-in-law. See also Sekhel Tov who tries to find examples of things done by God specifically for Moses.

[2]See Ex. 2:15 and below vs. 4.

[3]See Ex. 11:3.

[4]See e.g. Ex. 4:21.

[5]Viz. his wife and sons.

[6]Zipporah's presence at this point in Midian after the events of 4:20 is difficult. The explanation cited here by Rashbam says that the phrase אחר שלוחיה is the text's way of telling us, after the fact, that Moses had, previously, sent her back to Midian. This interpretation may be found in Rashi, following Mekhilta 'Amaleq 3, pp. 167-168. Most moderns follow this understanding.

interpretation appears to be the plain meaning of Scripture.[7] [The problem with interpreting that Moses had previously sent Zipporah back to Midian is] that there are no verses to that effect. Before the text says that Jethro sent her and her sons to the desert it should have written above, after the section[8] describing the (4:26) "bridegroom of blood because of the circumcision"[9] that "Moses then sent her back again to her father's home with her sons." [If the first interpretation were correct, the text should have anticipated and warned the readers ahead of time that they had been sent back to Midian,] as in the verse (Gen. 9:18) "Ham being the father of Canaan."[10]

The word אחר in the phrase אחר שלוחיה [means "afterwards,"][11] just like in the phrase (Lev. 15:28), "afterwards (אחר)

---

[7]It is difficult to understand just how Rashbam interpreted this verse, despite his lengthy excursus here. (Most of his energy is expended on explaining why he rejects Rashi's reading, not on explaining the verse itself.) No matter how he understands the phrase אחר שלוחיה, presumably Rashbam would have to admit from the flow of verses 2-4 that Zipporah and her sons were with Jethro in Midian and only now were being reunited with Moses. So Zipporah's return trip to Midian after the events of 4:20 would in any case have to be postulated and assumed by the reader, despite the fact that the text did not mention it.

Furthermore it is still unclear how Rashbam understands what Jethro is doing now. The basic interpretation appears to be: "Jethro took Zipporah, then (אחר--afterwards; see comm. below) he sent her dowry to Moses, and then he came along with her to Moses in the desert." The function of the dowry at this point is not made clear by Rashbam. See also JBS, Sekhel Tov and R. Yeshua (cited approvingly by iE, shorter comm.) who all offer interpretations that differ from Rashbam's (and from each other's) but are based on seeing שלוחיה as meaning "her dowry."

[8]פרשה. The word can refer in Rashbam's comm. either to one part of the weekly cycle of Torah reading, or simply to a "section" of the Torah. See RSBM, p. 58.

[9]In fact, that is the spot at which the Mekhilta and Rashi and others who follow that interpretation assume that Zipporah and her sons were sent back to Midian.

[10]Rashbam's classic example of the phenomenon of anticipation.
Rashbam's argument here is that anticipation is so much a part of biblical style that the text *has to* anticipate and may not introduce new information after the fact without warning the reader ahead of time. See my discussion of this assertion in my Genesis volume p. 418f.

[11]I.e. Jethro took Zipporah and then he sent her dowry.

she shall be clean," as I explained[12] concerning the phrase (Gen. 22:13) "afterwards (אחר) getting caught in the thickets by its horns," and the phrase (Ps. 68:26) "Let the singers come first; afterwards (אחר) the musicians."[13]

18:6 ויאמר JETHRO's messenger HAD SAID TO MOSES, "I, YOUR FATHER-IN-LAW JETHRO [AM COMING TO YOU].[14]

18:8 התלאה ALL THE HARDSHIPS THAT HAD BEFALLEN THEM ON THE WAY [AND HOW THE LORD HAD DELIVERED THEM]:[15]   That Pharaoh chased after them and that [the people complained about thirst and hunger until] God provided them with water and manna and meat.[16]

18:9 ויחד JETHRO REJOICED: וַיִּחַדְּ is from the root ח-ד-ה, like in the phrase (I Chr. 16:27), "strength and joy (חדוה)." [The *dagesh* in the *dalet* is a *dagesh qal*,] just as any final-*heh* word that has a *begad kefat* letter [for the second letter of the root] has a *dagesh* [*qal*] in the final

---

[12] In his comm. to Gen. 22:13.

[13] See Genesis volume, p. 99, note 2, for a discussion of Rashbam's understanding of this verse in Psalms.

[14] Verse 7 creates the impression that Jethro had not yet arrived. Accordingly the phrase, "ויאמר אל משה--he [Jethro] said to Moses," in vs. 6 cannot easily be interpreted as meaning that Jethro spoke to Moses face to face. Rashbam's solution--that Jethro sent word ahead via a messenger--is the same as that of Rashi and most other Jewish exegetes, following the opinion of R. Eleazar of Modi'im in Mekhilta, *ibid.*, p. 172.

[15] Clearly from the continuation one sees that Rashbam's comment is not just about "the hardships" but also about the deliverance.

[16] The commentators attempt to identify the unspecified "hardships" listed here. Rashi, following Mekhilta, *ibid.*, p. 174, says that the reference is to the events at the Sea of Reeds and to the war with Amalek. Rashbam provides a list of "hardships" that goes through the major events of chapters 14-16 basically in order. His list is fairly similar to that of Sekhel Tov. See also iE, longer comm. only.

letter.[17]

For example, from the root ב-כ-ה one says וַיֵּבְךְּ,[18] from the root פ-ת-ה one says וַיִּפְתְּ, as in the phrase (Job 31:27) "I secretly succumbed" (וַיִּפְתְּ); and יַפְתְּ as in the phrase (Gen. 9:27) "May God enlarge (יַפְתְּ) Japheth," where the final letter has a *dagesh*, like [תּוֹסְףְּ[19] in the phrase] (Prov. 30:6) "Do not add (תּוֹסְףְּ) to His words, and like וַיִּשְׁבְּ[20] from the root ש-ב-ה.

---

[17]I.e. in the final letter of forms of the imperfect where the final *heh* drops off, e.g. the *vav*-consecutive form or the jussive or the imperative. See similarly ibn Janah, *Sefer ha-riqmah*, p. 205, and iE.

Rashbam often comments on the patterns of final-*heh* verbs ("more than about any other paradigm," according to Melammed, p. 504). See comm. and notes above ad 4:26 s.v. וירד, and see the list of twenty such passages in Melammed, pp. 504-505. This is the only passage, though, where Rashbam discusses the tendency of the second letter of the root to take a *dagesh qal* in various grammatical forms derived from the imperfect.

It is not difficult to understand why Rashbam chooses to comment on that grammatical phenomenon specifically here. As is often the case, his attention is directed to Rashi, who provides two interpretations for the word ויחד: the first is the same as Rashbam's, but the second is based on a midrash (Sanh. 94a). According to that midrash, Jethro's emotions were not pure happiness; ויחד means that his flesh became חדודין חדודין--i.e. prickly, for he felt the pain of the Egyptians. Presumably one of the "justifications" for Rashi citing this midrash which connects the word ויחד with חדודין is the *dagesh* in the *dalet*. Rashbam accordingly explains at some length that the *dagesh* is a *dagesh qal* (not the *dagesh ḥazaq* that would be required if the root were ח-ד-ד).

Significantly, LT and Sekhel Tov, who almost always cite the classical midrashim in their works, do not cite this midrash about Jethro's flesh. In fact, Sekhel Tov gives a lengthy grammatical explanation of the reason why there is a *dagesh* in the *dalet*.

There is some similarity between Rashbam's comm. here and that of Sekhel Tov. However there is striking similarity between Rashbam's comm. here and Joseph Qara's comm. on Job 3:6, s.v. אל יחד. See M. Ahrend, *'Ale sefer* 5 (1978), pp. 45-46.) The illustrative examples that both cite are almost identical. Rashbam here, like Qara there, refers to the "*begad kefat* letters," and as far as I can tell this is the only instance of that term in Rashbam's Torah comm. (However, he does use it in his grammar book, e.g. p. 44.)

[18]E.g. Gen. 27:38.

[19]The root of this word is more likely י-ס-פ, not ס-פ-ה as Rashbam seems to be implying. In any case the form is difficult and "anomalous" (G.-K. 69v).

[20]E.g. Num. 21:1.

EXODUS XVIII

18:10 אשר WHO DELIVERED YOU: i.e. Moses and Aaron, FROM THE EGYPTIANS AND FROM PHARAOH, AND [WHO DELIVERED] THE PEOPLE from the bondage[21] of Egypt.[22]

18:11 מכל [NOW I KNOW THAT THE LORD IS GREATER] THAN ALL THE GODS: Because they [viz. the other gods] do not have the power to take vengeance on those who cause distress to their worshippers.

כי בדבר FOR THE VERY SCHEMES [THAT THEY PLOTTED AGAINST THEM]: I.e. God repaid the Egytians FOR every SCHEME that the Egyptians PLOTTED AGAINST THEM. This is the true plain meaning of Scripture.[23]

---

[21]שעבוד. Rashbam paraphrases the phrase יד מצרים the same way that the Mekhilta (ibid., p. 176) and LT do. Cf. Rashi.

[22]The apparent redundancy between the first and second halves of this verse troubled many of the classical exegetes. (Many moderns simply emend; see e.g. Childs and Noth.) Sekhel Tov phrases the problem as follows: אשר הציל את העם... מה תלמוד לומר והלא כבר נאמר אשר הציל אתכם מתחת יד מצרים"--"why is the phrase 'who delivered the people . . .' written, when the text already said 'who delivered you from the Egyptians'?" iE in his shorter comm. suggests that the first half of the verse refers to the deliverance from Egypt while the second part refers to the miracles at the Sea of Reeds. Rashbam suggests that the phrase "delivered you" in the first half of the verse refers to Moses and Aaron, not the Israelite people. (So also Mekhilta de-rashbi, cited by Kasher, note 68.) The first half of the verse then describes the deliverance of Moses and Aaron, while the second half describes the deliverance of the people. iE in his longer comm. adopts this explanation. See also NJPSC, which interprets like Rashbam and cites 10:28 to explain why Moses and Aaron might have felt that their lives were threatened.

[23]The verse is a difficult one. The thought expressed in the second half of the verse appears to be incomplete. (The verse is an "anacoluthon," according to Childs.) The exegetical question is how to complete the thought that begins with the words כי בדבר אשר זדו עליהם.

Rashbam rejects the two interpretations offered by Rashi (following Onq. and Sotah 11b, respectively), both of which amount to the same explanation, that the verse means that the Egyptians were punished measure for measure. The thought, according to this explanation, should be completed as follows: "FOR THE VERY SCHEMES THAT THE EGYPTIANS PLOTTED, those same schemes came back to haunt them." Rashbam's explanation involves seeing a closer, causal connection between 11a and 11b. The verse is saying that "I now know that the LORD is greater than all the gods" by the

194 RASHBAM

18:12 ויבא AARON CAME WITH ALL THE ELDERS OF ISRAEL TO PARTAKE OF THE MEAL WITH MOSES' FATHER-IN-LAW: They all came in honor of Jethro.[24] The text did not have to mention that Moses was there,[25] as the gathering took place in *his* tent.[26]

18:13 לשפוט [MOSES SAT] TO JUDGE THE PEOPLE: [The fact that Moses was judging the people is not proof that the events of this chapter took place after the Torah was given to the Israelites.] Even if Jethro came [to the Israelites in the wilderness] before the giving of the Torah,[27] [Moses could still reasonably be functioning as a judge, for

---

way that God treated "the schemes that the Egyptians plotted against the Israelites." A similar explanation can be found in LXX and also in Nahm. (all presumably arriving at the same conclusion independently). While the explanation has the virtue of adding less to the text than Rashi's reading, its weakness, as Childs notes, is that it seems to disregard the word כי.

[24]Many midrashim and commentators (e.g. Mekhilta, *ibid.*, p. 177) portray Jethro as an expert in all forms of idolatry, based in part on vs. 11 where Jethro claims that he knows that the Lord is greater than all the other gods. Sekhel Tov attempts to apply that same midrash to this verse too. The reason, he says, that all the elders of Israel came, was to see this surprising spectacle of a former idolator worshipping God. Rashbam says more simply that the elders all came to honor Jethro.

[25]Rashbam is opposing the question of the midrash (Mekhilta, *ibid.*) adopted by Rashi, LT and Sekhel Tov: " ומשה להיכן הלך--where did Moses go?", and the midrashic attempts to see some significance in the fact that Moses' name is not listed among all the other characters in this verse. The question is not legitimate, says Rashbam, as one needs to list the guests only; the host's presence is assumed. See similarly JBS and iE, longer comm. only.

[26]Verse 7 says that they came "into the tent," without specifying which tent. Mekhilta (*ibid.*, p. 174) says that the reference is to the study hall. So also similarly the targumim. Sekhel Tov (here), iE (ad verse 7) and Rashbam say more simply that it is Moses' tent.

[27]Already in early rabbinic times there was a dispute about whether Jethro came to the Israelites in the wilderness before or after the giving of the Torah, i.e. about whether the events of chapter 18 took place before or after the events of chapters 19 and 20. See e.g. AZ 24a. Most midrashim and commentators discuss the issue of the chronology at the *beginning* of chapter 18. (See e.g. Mekhilta, *ibid.*, p. 162, iE and Nahm.) Rashi discusses the issue only in his comm. here to vs. 13. Rashbam also addresses the question here ad vs. 13 for his comment is, as we shall see below, more of a gloss on

EXODUS XVIII

one may logically *assume* that] they already had civil laws,[28] especially since the rabbis say[29] that they were given [civil] laws at Marah, for it is written (Ex. 15:25), "there He made for them laws and rules."[30]

Yet it makes sense to say that Jethro *did* come after the giving of the Torah.[31] Here it is written [that the events of chapter 18 took place] (vs. 5) "where he [i.e. Moses] was encamped at the mountain of God." But below it is written (19:1-2) "On the third new moon after the Israelites had gone forth from the land of Egypt, on that very day they entered the wilderness of Sinai. Having journeyed from Rephidim, they entered the wilderness of Sinai . . . Israel encamped there in front of the mountain [of God]." So one sees that the entire story of [leaving] Rephidim and encamping at the mountain preceded this chapter.[32] The

---

Rashi than an independent comment on the verse.

[28]See Rashbam's comm. to Gen. 26:5.
   Rashbam (see below) and Rashi both agree that Jethro came to the wilderness only after the Torah was given. Yet Rashbam opens his discusssion of the issue by arguing against Rashi's grounds. Rashi claims that the existence of laws in this chapter proves that the Torah had already been given. Such an argument can also be found in Tos. AZ 24b, s.v. יתרו.

[29]Sanh. 56b.

[30]In Rashbam's comm. to Ex. 15:25 he does *not* interpret that verse in the way that the Talmud in Sanhedrin does. Still the fact that he cites that interpretation here can be understood, for he is, at this point in his comm., merely arguing against Rashi. From the perspective of Rashi who *does* interpret 15:25 the way the rabbis do (in his comm. there, s.v. שם שם), there is, according to Rashbam, no reason for him to argue that the existence of laws in this chapter proves that the Torah had already been given. See also Hizq. ad vs. 16 who cites 15:25 to explain what laws existed before the events of this chapter.

[31]In other words, Rashbam reaches the same conclusion as Rashi about the chronology, but on different grounds.

[32]In other words, chapter 18 assumes that the Israelites are already encamped at the mountain of God. However at the beginning of chapter 19 the Israelites are *not* yet at the mountain of God. So the events of chapter 19 (and chapter 20, its obvious continuation), must have taken place before the events of chapter 18.
   Just like Rashbam, iE (ad vs. 1, in his longer comm. only) argues that verse 5 of our chapter, when compared with chapter 19, constitutes the clinching proof (העד הנאמן) that Jethro came to the wilderness only after the giving of the Torah. See also

story of Jethro [i.e. chapter 18] was written [out of chronological order] before [the story of the giving of the Torah] so as not to interrupt the continuity of the chapters that [follow, that all] deal with commandments.³³

מן [MOSES SAT TO JUDGE THE PEOPLE] FROM THE MORNING TO THE EVENING: [He sat judging all day long] because he alone had to judge the entire people; he had no helpers.³⁴

18:14 מדוע WHY DO YOU SIT ALONE: and, as a result, ALL THE PEOPLE STAND ABOUT YOU FROM MORNING UNTIL EVENING.³⁵

18:15 כי IT IS BECAUSE THE PEOPLE COME TO ME TO INQUIRE OF GOD: In other words "I alone have to make inquiries of God. They have no one else other than me who regularly speaks to God."

18:18 נבל תבל: [means "you will become confused,"] as in the phrase

---

Nahm. ad vs. 1.

³³Rashbam often argues that chronological order is sacrificed in the Bible for the sake of keeping some congruent unit of text together. See e.g. comm. and notes to Gen. 24:22, s.v. ויקח.

³⁴So also JBS.
Perhaps Rashbam and JBS emphasize the obvious as they wish to oppose other possible understandings of why Moses had to judge all day long. Rashi, following Mekhilta, *ibid.*, p. 179, says that this was the first possible day Moses could be judging the people (and presumably there would have been a backlog of cases). See also Hizq. who says that Moses had not done any judging on the previous day as he was taking care of his father-in-law and perhaps that too is meant to explain why Moses had to work such long hours on this day.

³⁵Rashbam opposes the explanation offered by Rashi (in his comm. to vs. 13, following Mekhilta, *ibid.*, p. 179) that Jethro's question was actually an accusation that Moses lorded it over the people too much, sitting like a king while everybody else stood. Rashbam explains, both here and ad vs. 15, that Jethro's question and Moses' answer have nothing to do with sitting and standing but only with the fact that Moses was working by himself. See the same argument at much greater length in iE, longer comm. only, and in Hizq.

(Gen. 11:7) "[Let us go down] and confuse (ונבלה) their speech there, so that they shall not understand one another's speech." [נבל תבל means that] "your speech will be confused from answering so many people at the same time and they will also become confused[36] in their speaking--one person yelling and then another one. You will not be able to answer everyone in order, one after the other."[37]

18:19 ויהי AND GOD WILL BE WITH YOU:[38] I.e. (verse 23) "you will be able to bear up."[39]

היה YOU REPRESENT THE PEOPLE BEFORE GOD: For those legal

---

[36] Explaining the words of the verse, "גם אתה גם העם הזה"--both you and this people."

[37] Rashbam opposes the fairly universal understanding (e.g. Mekhilta, Rashi, iE and LT) of נבל תבל as meaning "you will wither" or "you will wear yourself out." The explanation that Rashbam offers is not standardly accepted, for the root of תבל here is generally understood to be נ-ב-ל, while the root of ונבלה in Gen. (as noted already by Rosin, here) is ב-ל-ל. Like Rashbam, see JBS and Hizq.

[38] Or perhaps "and you will have the strength." See the next note.

[39] Rashbam opposes the interpretation of Rashi who says (following Mekhilta, *ibid.*, p. 182) that the words ויהי א-להים עמך constitute an *instruction* from Jethro to Moses to consult God; they should be rendered in English "*allow* God to be with you." For Rashbam they constitute Jethro's *prediction* that if Moses follows Jethro's advice ("Listen to me, I will give you counsel"), then God will give him sufficient strength to bear up.

In verse 23 below two phrases appear one after the other: first "וצוך א-להים--(if) God so commands you" and then "ויכלת עמד--you will be able to bear up." It is interesting to note that Rashi (here and ad vs. 23) says that the phrase in our verse, ויהי א-להים עמך, is synonymous with "וצוך א-להים--(if) God so commands you" of vs. 23. Rashbam then counters and claims that our phrase is actually synonymous with the immediately following phrase in vs. 23, "ויכלת עמד--you will be able to bear up." See also comm. and notes below, vs. 22, s.v. וצוך.

It is possible that Rashbam understands the word א-להים in this verse as meaning "strength," and not as God's name. (In that case, ויהי אלהים עמך would mean that "sufficient strength will be with you.") However, Rashbam's interpretation also works if one sees in the word א-להים here a reference to God. See JBS who interprets similarly to Rashbam and sees the word as God's name.

issues that require consulting God,[40] you will hear what God says to you and (vs. 20) YOU WILL ENJOIN UPON THEM [the legal decisions you receive from God].[41] (This phrase is synonymous with what is written in vs. 22, "Have them bring every major dispute to you.")[42] But (vs. 22) LET THEM DECIDE all other legal issues that can easily by adjudicated by the sages of Israel that you will appoint, and thus YOU WILL MAKE IT EASIER FOR YOURSELF.[43]

18:21 אנשי חיל: means men of wealth and bravery,[44] who will "fear no man."[45]

שנאי בצע WHO SPURN ILL-GOTTEN GAIN: בצע always refers to

---

[40]לדרוש א-להים; using the language of Moses from vs. 15. See also comm. and notes below ad vs. 22, s.v. כל הדבר.

[41]Rashbam opposes the midrashic reading of verse 20 (Mekhilta, *ibid.*, p. 182, LT and Sekhel Tov) as an instruction to Moses to teach all the different categories of Torah law to the Israelites. Rashbam explains more simply that verse 20 continues the idea of verse 19.

[42]So also iE, longer comm. only. iE's comment may well be dependent on Rashbam: they both misquote verse 22 the same way writing הדבר הקשה instead of MT's הדבר הגדול. (On the other hand, that error could easily have occurred because the phrase הדבר הקשה appears below in vs. 26.)

[43]Rashbam understands the phrase והקל מעליך in vs. 22 the same way that Rashi does there--as a description of what the result will be of following Jethro's plan. He disagrees with JBS who interprets הקל as an imperative.

[44]Rashbam's explanation agrees in part with Rashi who (following Mekhilta, *ibid.*, p. 183) sees אנשי חיל as meaning wealthy people (who will not be susceptible to illicit economic incentives). For that nuance of חיל, see e.g. Dt. 8:17-18. Rashbam adds that the phrase here also has the more common nuance of bravery. Cf. the allegorizing interpretation of Tanh. (*Yitro* 2) who interprets אנשי חיל as "גבורים בתורה--valiant in Torah study." See also Rashbam ad Gen. 47:6 where he offers a somewhat different interpretation of the phrase אנשי חיל.

[45]Using the language of the parallel passage in Deuteronomy (1:17) where Moses' appointing of judges is discussed.

EXODUS XVIII

bribery and theft.[46] For example (Hab. 2:9) "Ah, you have acquired gains (בצע) to the detriment of your own house," and (Gen. 37:26) "What is our בצע for killing our brother," which means "what do we earn,"[47] and (Job 27:8) "[What hope has the impious man] when he steals (יבצע),[48] when God takes away his life?"

18:22 כל הדבר הגדול [HAVE THEM BRING] EVERY MAJOR DISPUTE [TO YOU]: "to inquire of God."[49]

18:23 וצוך א-להים: means "*when* GOD WILL ASK YOU TO JUDGE THEM,[50] then YOU WILL BE ABLE TO BEAR UP, because of your

---

[46] Rashbam opposes one of two interpretations offered in the Mekhilta (*ibid.*) according to which בצע simply means money; hence שנאי בצע means people who do not care about money. So also Sekhel Tov, and see Nahm. at length. Rashbam, on the other hand, argues that בצע is a specific term for ill-gotten gain. So also JBS.

[47] And clearly money which is earned through murder constitutes ill-gotten gain.

[48] For Rashbam's understanding of יבצע in that verse, see Rashi and Targum, there.

[49] Again Rashbam uses the language of vs. 15. (See also comm. above ad vs. 19, s.v. והיה.)

Rashbam keeps emphasizing that the phrase לדרוש א-להים in vs. 15 simply means "to submit difficult legal issues to God for his adjudication." Verse 16, then, ("When they have a dispute, it comes to me . . .") is simply an expansion of the last phrase of verse 15. Rashbam opposes the reading of לדרוש א-להים offered by Rashi there which sees the phrase as meaning "to learn God's Torah." See also iE and Nahm. who interpret the end of verse 15 as meaning something distinct from verse 16.

[50] Rashbam opposes Rashi's interpretation of this phrase. Rashi (following Mekhilta, *ibid.*, pp. 184-185) sees the phrase as implying that Jethro told Moses to get God's approval for this plan. This is the second phrase in the story that Rashi has interpreted this way. See also Rashi ad vs. 19, s.v. איעצך, and Rashbam's comm. and notes, there, s.v. ויהי. See iE, longer comm. to vs. 19, who says that "And God will be with you" in vs. 19 does not mean to ask for God's approval but that the phrase in this verse does. (So also JBS and Nahm.) It seems that iE cannot imagine Moses undertaking a plan like this without God's approval ("ואין ספק כי כן עשה--without any doubt, he did that [=consulted God]"). Rashbam, however, interprets the text as having no reference to God's approval of the judicial process proposed here.

helpers.[51] AND ALL THESE PEOPLE TOO, who stand about you from morning to evening,[52] WILL all GO to their homes quickly IN PEACE.[53]

18:26 ישפוטו הם THEY WOULD DECIDE THEMSELVES: [The unusual form ישפוטו, with a *shuruq*, instead of a *ḥolam*, in the second syllable, is] just like the form תעבורי in the phrase (Ruth 2:8) "Don't go (תעבורי) elsewhere." A number of times an "u" vowel comes in place of an "o" vowel.[54]

---

[51]Rashbam's opposition to Rashi's interpretation (following the Mekhilta) continues. According to Rashi, the reason that Moses will be "able to bear up" is because of God's approval. According to Rashbam, Moses will have enough strength because of his human helpers.

[52]Using the language of vs. 14.

[53]Some midrashim see here a reference to the ability of justice to bring peace to the world. See e.g. Mekhilta *Neziqin* 1 (Lauterbach edition, volume 3, p. 2). Rashbam explains more simply that, as opposed to the confusion described above in vs. 14, now litigants will get home quickly. See similarly Sekhel Tov.

[54]So also Rashi. (iE understands Rashi as saying something else here, but Luzzatto's strident claim ["וזה שקר שאין לו רגליים--this is a baseless lie"] that iE does not understand Rashi appears more reasonable.) Cf. Sekhel Tov, ad vs. 22, who attempts to distinguish between the meanings of ישפטו and ישפוטו.

See Rashbam's discussion of the phenomenon of what modern grammarians call "attraction" in his comm. ad 15:5 and see notes there. Rashbam could have explained the anomalous *shuruq* here in ישפוטו (but not in תעבורי) as a result of attraction. Perhaps he does not do so because he feels that attraction can work forwards--from one syllable or word to the next one, as in the examples of יכסיומו and ומובאי that Rashbam discusses ad Ex. 15:5--but not backwards.

EXODUS XIX

19:2 נגד ההר [ISRAEL ENCAMPED THERE] IN FRONT OF THE MOUNTAIN: The mountain that was mentioned above (3:12) "You shall worship God at this mountain."[1]

19:4 על כנפי נשרים [I BORE YOU] ON EAGLES' WINGS: means that "I took you across the sea on dry land, like an eagle that can cross the seas flying." [The image of the eagle] also [means] that you were not injured, [for an eagle is a symbol of protection,] as it is written (Dt. 32:11), "Like an eagle who moves[2] his nest and hovers over his young."[3]

---

[1] Rashbam explains that the reference to "*the* mountain" in this verse is an allusion to the mountain mentioned above when God first commissioned Moses. See also the end of iE's comment to vs. 4, longer comm.

Rashbam's interpretation here does not appear to be consistent with his previously expressed opinions. It is Rashi who writes ad 3:12 that the phrase, "You shall worship God at this mountain," is a promise that the Israelites would receive the Torah at the mountain where God first appeared to Moses.

But Rashbam there dismisses Rashi's interpretation; "Those who preceded me did not understand [these verses] at all". There Rashbam explains that the line, "You shall worship God at this mountain," was simply a ruse, a claim that Moses could make to Pharaoh that that is what the Israelites had been commanded to do. From the context there it seems that Rashbam feels that there never was a plan that the Israelites would come to "worship God at this mountain." Hence for Rashbam to claim here that our verse alludes back to that verse is puzzling.

[2] That is how Rashbam understands the verb יעיר in Deut.; see his comm. there.

[3] The image of the eagle can conjure up different associations. It is used by biblical authors for a number of purposes. (See NJPSC's list here.) Rashi argues (following Mekhilta *Ba-ḥodesh* 2, pp. 202-203) that the image here refers to the protection that an eagle gives to its children when carrying them on his back, an allusion to the way that the pillar of cloud protected the Israelites before the crossing of the Sea of Reeds. Rashbam sees rather an allusion to the crossing of the Sea. So also Mendelssohn.

ואביא **AND I BROUGHT YOU TO ME:** so that I might be your God.[4]

19:5 כי **FOR ALL THE EARTH IS MINE:** All the nations are Mine, yet I chose only you.[5]

19:6 ממלכת כהנים **A KINGDOM OF PRIESTS:** ["Priests" here means] "nobles," as in the phrase (II Sam. 8:18), "David's sons were nobles (כהנים)."[6]

---

[4] Alluding to the common biblical phrase "להיות לכם לא-להים"--to be your God." See e.g. Lev. 11:45.
   Rashi explains (following the Targum) that this phrase means that God has now brought the Jews to a proper site at which they can worship Him. That interpretation is basically the same as that of LT (following Mekhilta, *ibid.*). Rashbam explains that there is no reference here either to the Israelites' location or to their duty to worship God, but rather to their election. In other words, vs. 4 leads into vs. 5: God brought the Jews to Him (vs. 4) to make them His treasured possession (vs. 5). So also Mendelssohn.

[5] Virtually all the exegetes try to explain the connection between the idea of Israel's election expressed in this verse and the assertion that all the earth is God's. ibn Janah (cited by iE) understands כי as meaning "although": i.e. although all the nations are God's, He chose only the Jews. The solutions of iE, Rashi and Rashbam follow similar lines without interpreting כי as "although." Rashbam basically interprets the verse the same way as Rashi does, although Rashbam does not make the same dismissive claim as Rashi that while all of the other nations are God's, He considers them "worth nothing in My eyes" (הם בעיני ולפני לכלום). Cf. Seforno, Mendelssohn and Luzzatto for an early modern liberal understanding of the verse.

[6] The problem in this verse is the assertion that *all* the Israelites will be priests when other Torah texts make it clear that the Jewish people is composed of priests and laymen. Rashbam's solution is the same as that of Rashi and JBS, who cite another (perhaps more) troubling passage in which כהנים could not be seen as meaning "priests" in the halakhic sense, namely descendants of Aaron. So just as כהנים in II Sam. does not mean priests, literally, so also in our verse. (The original comparison between our verse and the verse in II. Sam. was actually made by Mekhilta, [*ibid.*, p. 205] where a *distinction* is made between the use of the term כהנים in the two passages.)

EXODUS XIX

19:8 וישב MOSES BROUGHT BACK THE PEOPLE'S WORDS TO THE LORD: on the next day,[7] as the text continues to explain. First (vs. 9) "The LORD said to Moses, 'I will come to you in a thick cloud ...'," and then (*ibid.*) "Moses reported (ויגד) the people's words to the LORD." [That latter phrase refers to] the same event as the phrase (in vs. 8), "Moses brought back (וישב) the people's words to the LORD." The text first makes a general statement and then provides the details.[8] Moses said to God [after 9a], "Already yesterday they agreed to do whatever You command them."

One should understand similarly the verses (Lev. 9:24-10:2) "(9:24) Fire came forth from before the LORD and consumed the burnt offering." Then it says "(10:1) Aaron's sons, Nadab and Abihu took ... (10:2) and fire came forth from the LORD [and consumed them]." [It is the same fire being referred to in 9:24 and in 10:2.] The [divine]

---

[7]Rashbam begins his comment here the same way that Rashi does, but he soon diverges from Rashi's approach. See next note.

[8]כולל ואחר כך מפרש. See comm. and notes to Ex. 2:15.
 Rashbam explains that the end of vs. 8 tells us that Moses reported to God the people's words about their willingness to obey God but the text does not tell us how and when that reporting occurred. Then in vs. 9 the text explains: God, on the next day, told Moses what God would do to make the people be willing to listen to Moses. That is the point at which Moses reported to God what they had already said, on the day before, that they were willing to listen to everything that God commanded. Accordingly there are not two separate messages from the people brought to God by Moses in vss. 8 and 9. Both times the reference is to the same one reporting of the same one message.
 Rashbam opposes here the interpretation of Rashi that Moses brought two separate messages from the people to God and that the reporting of vs. 8 took place on the third of Sivan while the reporting of vs. 9 took place on the fourth. Rashi's interpretation follows Shabbat 87a, and see Rashi's comm. there, s.v. וישב ויגד. Rashbam also opposes the approach of JBS (later adopted by Nahm.) that in vs. 8 Moses only returned (וישב) to God bearing the people's answer but it wasn't until vs. 9 that he actually delivered (ויגד) that answer to God.
 As noted in the previous note, both Rashbam and Rashi begin their comments to this verse the same way, by writing that these events occurred "on the next day." For Rashi that comment is part of a general pattern of interpretation in this chapter as he, following the Talmud in Shabbat, attempts to map out precisely which events in this chapter occurred on which of the first six days of Sivan. That concern is not part of Rashbam's approach to this chapter. See Hizq. (ad vs. 11) who dismisses Rashbam's interpretation of this verse because he feels that if one follows Rashbam's approach, one will not succeeed in explaining the course of events in chapter 19 in a manner that is consonant with the Talmudic chronology.

fire found Nadab and Abihu at the golden altar, within the sanctuary, offering alien fire and [that divine fire] consumed them. Then that fire went out of the sanctuary and consumed the burnt offering that was on the copper altar, in the courtyard outside of the sanctuary.[9]

So also in the book of Judges in the story of Micah (chapter 17), it is written:

> (3) He returned the eleven hundred shekels of silver to his mother, and his mother said to him,[10] "I herewith consecrate the silver to the LORD" . . . (4) He returned the silver to his mother.

First the text writes [a general statement]--that (vs. 3) he returned the silver to his mother--and then the text provides the details of how that happened. When "his mother (vs. 4) said to him . . .," that is when "he returned the silver to his mother."[11]

---

[9] In other words, just as here Moses really reported to God only one answer from the people (despite the duplication in vss. 8b and 9b), so also while Lev. 9:24 and 10:2 both describe how a divine fire came forth from God, there was really only one, not two such divine fires. 9:24 describes how a divine fire came forth and consumed the sacrifices described previously in chapter 9. Then the next two verses explain how it happened that "a divine fire came forth" at all. ("The text first makes a general staement and then provides details": i.e. the text first tells us generally about the divine fire and then provides the details as to why there was a divine fire.) It was after the improper behavior of Nadab and Abihu (10:1) that that fire came forth and consumed them (10:2). And that is the reason that there was a divine fire available to consume the sacrifices in 9:24.

See in greater detail Rashbam's comm. to Lev. 9:24 and 10:2.

[10] Rashbam quotes the verse as ותאמר אליו instead of MT's ותאמר. Esh, p. 88, argues (unconvincingly to my mind) that this misquotation may represent another manuscript tradition.

[11] In other words, there also even though the verses report twice that Micah returned the silver to his mother, the two verses should be seen as referring to the same action. Cf. Rashi, Qimhi and Gersonides in Judges who all try to explain that the two phrases reflect two separate actions of Micah with the silver.

Rashbam was not the first to compare our verses in Exodus with the Micah passage in Judges. In a partial manuscript that A. Grossman has identified as a fragment of Joseph Qara's comm. on the Torah (*Pe'amim* 52 [1992], pp. 16-36), Qara also compares the duplication here and the duplication in Judges (*ibid.*, pp. 22-3). There are some similarities between the ways that Qara and Rashbam understand these verses. Both of them explain (in a manner that differs from most Jewish exegesis) that, despite

19:9 בעב הענן IN A THICK CLOUD: [God appeared in] cloud (עב)[12] and darkness[13] so that [Moses][14] would not look upon the Divine Presence.[15]

---

the duplicated phrases, Micah did only one action with the silver and Moses made only one report to God. The repetitions serve, according to both Qara and Rashbam, only literary purposes.

However, Qara and Rashbam provide two different explanations of what the literary purpose is that the repetition serves. According to Qara, the second time that each phrase is written, it is done in order to establish simultaneity between the action described and the next item written in the text. For example, here the phrase "Moses reported the people's words to the LORD," is repeated at the end of verse 9 in order to teach us that it was immediately after Moses reported to God, that (vs. 10) "the LORD said to Moses, 'Go to the people'." In Judges, the NJPS translation follows Qara's approach:

> (3) He returned . . . the shekels to his mother . . . his mother said, 'I herewith consecrate . . .'." (4) So when he gave the silver back to his mother, his mother took two hundred shekels of silver . . . .

Rashbam, on the other hand, provides a different literary explanation for the repetition, based on his principle that the text first makes a general statement and then provides the details. For Rashbam there is no new information about simultaneity or about anything else that the repetition provides to the reader. The repetition is simply a result of common biblical style.

[12]It appears that Rashbam opposes the explanation of Rashi (following Mekhilta, *ibid.*, p. 207) who explained the word עב as referring to "thickness," not to a cloud.

[13]See the description of the Sinai theophany in Dt. 4:11: "חשך ענן וערפל--darkness and cloud and heavy cloud."

[14]Or perhaps "so that the Israelites."

[15]Rashbam's comment appears to be directly opposed to Sekhel Tov who writes concerning this phrase that God now made His Divine Presence "truly visible to the eyes of all" the Israelites (עכשיו אני מראה מקום מחיצת שכינתי לכולם בעין ממש).

On the implication of Rashbam's comment here that God would be visible were He not obscured by darkness and cloud, see Rashbam's comm. ad Gen. 48:8 and notes there, pp. 338-339.

19:10 וקדשתם **LET THEM PREPARE THEMSELVES:** [The root ק-ד-ש at times should be seen as] referring to "preparation,"[16] as in the phrase (Num. 11:18) "Prepare yourselves (התקדשו) for tomorrow when you will eat meat."[17]

19:11 ירד ה' **THE LORD WILL COME DOWN IN THE SIGHT OF ALL THE PEOPLE:** One should understand that the phrase ויאמר ה' at the beginning of the verse[18] means that an angel, not God Himself, said these words to Moses. One can deduce that because the text reads here "THE LORD WILL COME DOWN" [in third person], not "I will come down."

I interpreted similarly [the double reference to the LORD in] the verse (Gen. 19:24) "The LORD rained down on Sodom . . . from the LORD out of heaven." In works of *'aggadah* one also finds [concerning the Genesis passage] that the first "the LORD" refers to the angel Gabriel and the second refers to God.[19]

19:12 והגבלת: Show them and make for them signs of boundaries (סימני גבול) [so that they will know] how close they may come.[20]

---

[16] Rashbam's explanation is the same as that of Rashi and Onq. None of them wants to see וקדשתם as referring to "purification" here. Perhaps their reasoning is the same as that of Nahm. who asks why (from a halakhic perspective) would two days of purification be necessary.

[17] See also similarly Rashi ad Num. 11:18 and see Rashi and Rashbam ad Gen. 38:21.

[18] Actually at the beginning of the previous verse.

[19] See comm. and notes there and ad Ex. 3:4 and 24:1.

While other Jewish exegetes, like Rashbam, often comment on the syntactical problem of verses like this where there appears to be an extra, unnecessary reference to God, it appears to me that Rashbam was the only classical exegete to note that problem here. See Noth (p. 158): "the occurrence of Yahweh in the third person in the middle of a speech of Yahweh is striking; perhaps it is an explanatory gloss."

[20] So also Rashi and iE.

19:13 לא תגע בו יד NO HAND SHALL TOUCH HIM: [The word "בו--him" refers to] the person who touched the mountain,[21] about whom I said above (vs. 12) that he shall be put to death. He should be killed from a distance; they should not go near the mountain to kill him lest they also be liable for the death penalty. Accordingly NO HAND SHALL TOUCH HIM to put him to death, but rather they should shoot him with arrows from a distance[22] or throw stones at him.[23]

במשוך היובל WHEN THE RAM'S HORN STOPS: When the Divine Presence departs[24] and the lightning and the blare of the ram's horns[25] cease.[26]

---

[21]From a grammatical point of view, the word בו could, theoretically, refer either to the person who touched the mountain ("no hand shall touch him") or to the mountain itself ("no hand shall touch it"). Mekhilta, (ibid. 3, p. 214) understands that בו refers to the mountain. Rashbam and other exegetes (e.g. JBS and iE) emphasize that the reference is to the person who touches the mountain, not to the mountain itself. See also LT who considers and explicitly dismisses the possibility that בו here refers to the mountain.

[22]Rashbam's explanation of the words ירה יירה. He opposes Rashi who (following Sanh. 45a) sees that Hebrew phrase as meaning to be thrown down from the heights. Like Rashbam, see iE and JBS.

[23]Rashbam's explanation of the phrase סקל יסקל.

[24]The same phrase is used by Mekhilta, (ibid., p. 215) and by Rashi.

[25]ואת הלפידם ואת קול; an allusion to Ex. 20:15: "קול השופרות והלפידים; השופר--the lightning and the blare of the ram's horn."

[26]Rashbam's comm. opposes the standard understanding of the word במשך. Most commentators, ancient and modern, understand that that verb describes blowing or sounding the ram's horn. In other words, the signal that it is safe to go close to the mountain would be a sounding (or perhaps a prolonged sounding; so Rashi) of the ram's horn. Rashbam and JBS however suggest that במשך means "when the ram's horn ceases." In other words the ram's horn would sound throughout the theophany at Mount Sinai; when it stopped sounding, that would be the signal that the theophany was over and that it was safe to go close to the mountain.

The verb מ-ש-כ can mean to cease or withdraw in rabbinic Hebrew, at least in the phrase מ-ש-כ יד. See e.g. Mekhilta Pisḥa' 11, p. 82. However such usage is not found in biblical Hebrew. Furthermore, usages of the verb מ-ש-כ in relation to a ram's horn (e.g. Josh. 6:5) all seem to refer to sounding the ram's horn, not to stopping it.

19:18 עשן כלו [MOUNT SINAI] WAS ALL SMOKING: עָשַׁן is written with a *qames* in the first syllable and a *patah* in the second syllable, because it is a past-tense verb;[27] it means "[Mount Sinai] smoked."[28] If עשן were a noun, it would be written with two *qames* vowels.[29]

כְּעֶשֶׁן: [is a participle that] means "like the smoking"; *fumée* in the vernacular. If כְּעֶשֶׁן were a noun here [in the construct case], it would be vocalized כַּעֲשַׁן. Just as the construct form of דָּבָר is דְּבַר, as in the phrase (Deut. 15:2) "the nature (דְּבַר) of the remission," and the construct form of בָּקָר is בְּקַר, as in the phrase (Num. 7:88) "herd animals (בְּקַר) for sacrifices of well-being," so also the noun עָשָׁן--which appears in the phrase (Is. 6:4) "the House kept filling with smoke (עָשָׁן)"--becomes עֶשֶׁן in the construct case.[30]

Presumably the reason that Rashbam and JBS were attracted to their unusual interpretation was that the simple reading of the text implies that ram's horns were sounding throughout the theophany. (See e.g. 19:19 and 20:15.) Accordingly they might argue that the signal that the theophany was over must have been that the ram's horns *stopped* sounding.

[27]לשון פעל. See notes ad 12:39, s.v. כי לא חמץ.

[28]העשין. Rashbam paraphrases the *qal* form using a *hifil* form (and a *hifil* form that does not exist in biblical Hebrew) not in order to make a statement about the meaning of the verb עָשַׁן, but simply because there can be no confusion that העשין is a verb form. (The form עשן could be a noun, at least when it is unvocalized.) See similarly Rashbam's comm. to 12:39 where he paraphrases the verb חמץ as being equivalent to החמיץ.

[29]So also Rashi, iE and JBS.

[30]Rashbam could in fact cite Josh. 8:20 and 8:21 (the only other passages in the Bible where עשן appears in the construct case) to prove his point, for there the vocalization is עֶשֶׁן, not עֲשַׁן. Still, almost all other exegetes, ancient and modern, see עֶשֶׁן here as a construct form. To be sure, exegetes other than Rashbam were also troubled by this unusual form. (See e.g.G.-K. 93dd.) See ibn Janah, *Sefer ha-riqmah*, p. 226, who suggests that there are two nouns in biblical Hebrew with the same meaning--the noun עָשָׁן (which becomes עֶשֶׁן in the construct) and the noun עָשֵׁן (which does not change in the construct).

EXODUS XIX

19:19 משה ידבר MOSES SPOKE: to God[31] and his voice could not be heard by any human, only by God. But GOD ANSWERED MOSES IN A loud VOICE because of the SOUND OF THE SHOFAR which WAS GETTING MUCH LOUDER; God had to make His voice louder than the sound of the shofar so that Moses would be able to hear it.[32]

19:21 פן יהרסו LEST THEY BREAK DOWN: their station to come close and see.[33]

---

[31]Rashbam opposes the interpretation of Rashi (following the opinion of Rabbi Akiva in Mekhilta Ba-ḥodesh 4, p. 223) that the reference here is to Moses speaking to the people, not to his addressing God.

[32]Again Rashbam opposes the interpretation offered by Rashi (s.v. משה ידבר) who suggests (still following Mekhilta, ibid.) that יעננו בקול means that God will help Moses project his own voice. (See also NJPS which sees the word קול as referring to the thunder and see Orlinsky, Notes.)
    JBS's interpretation is much closer to that of Rashbam. They both argue that יעננו בקול means that God made His voice louder. JBS says that God made His voice louder so that all of the Israelites would be able to hear what God was saying to Moses. Rashbam says that the purpose was only that Moses would be able to hear God's voice above the sound of the shofar. See also iE who interprets similarly (but not identically) to Rashbam the relationship between the two halves of the verse. According to iE, Moses, because of his special relationship with God, was able to hear God's voice above the sound of the shofar (not because of God raising the volume of His voice).

[33]Rashbam's comment is basically the same as that of Rashi. Rashi explains in detail at the end of his comm. to this verse that just as the verb ה-ר-ס generally means to knock down something built up, so too here in reference to people it means that they break away from their formation and position. While it appears that Rashbam is simply rephrasing the words of his grandfather, it is noteworthy that in R. Abraham b. Azriel's 'Arugat ha-bosem (I, 20) this interpretation is attributed to Rashbam, not Rashi. There Rashbam's comm. is quoted as יהרסו את מצבם not יהרסו ממצבם, a small but significant change, since, according to Abraham b. Azriel, Rashbam is arguing that ה-ר-ס is always a transitive verb. If that is the case, then Rashbam's comm. here is not just explaining the meaning of the verb, but also providing the implicit direct object, מצבם. (See similarly iE.) See also Rashbam's comm. and notes to Ex. 15:7.

19:22 הכהנים THE PRIESTS: I.e. the first-born males.[34]

יתקדשו SHOULD READY THEMSELVES: In their position.[35]

19:23 ויאמר MOSES SAID TO THE LORD, "THE PEOPLE CANNOT COME UP TO MOUNT SINAI . . .": Concerning the interpretation that Moses in this verse is saying to God, "You already told us three days ago (verse 12), 'You shall set bounds for the people[36] . . . beware of going up the mountain.' Why then do you have to tell me the same thing a second time?" He who interprets the verse that way[37] is

---

[34] So also Rashi, iE and JBS, following the opinion of R. Joshua b. Qorhah in Zev. 115a. As NJPSC explains, the problem of the classical commentators is that according to Exodus 28 and 29 there were no priests in Israel until after the revelation at Sinai. (So also Rashbam in his comm. to Ex. 13:2, s.v. באדם.) Accordingly the reference here to כהנים appears to be an anachronism, unless it is seen as a reference to the first-born males.

[35] The precise meaning of Rashbam's comm. is unclear. It would appear, though, that he is agreeing with Rashi who explains that the first-borns ("כהנים") are being asked to prepare themselves to stay in their own position.
   The difficulty that Rashi and Rashbam are dealing with is that since the first-borns do not appear to have any specific role in this theophany, why are they being asked "to ready themselves"? The explanation appears to be that it is not that the first-borns have some particular instruction that applies to them alone. This phrase means only that they are to follow the same instructions that everyone else does, and that they should not think that they are special. Such an understanding is made explicit in JBS's comm. Cf. iE who suggests that the first-borns stood closest to the mountain and as such they required some special preparation.

[36] Instead of MT's והגבלת את העם, Rashbam quotes the verse here as והגבלת את ההר. This latter reading is a common emendation, probably dating back as far as ibn Janah. (See iE's comm. to 19:12 and see Krinski's note 25 in Qarne 'or ad Ex. 21. See recently, Uriel Simon in *The Frank Talmage Memorial Volume*, volume 1, pp. 217-232.)
   Clearly, though, Rashbam is neither proposing an emendation here, nor citing a variant text. Either Rashbam or, more likely, some copyist is quoting the phrase in the manner that "sounds" best, not in the manner that it appears in MT.

[37] The reference is clearly to Rashi, who is reworking the interpretation of the Mekhilta, *ibid.*, p. 226. See Mendelssohn who, after citing Rashbam's criticism of Rashi, writes that Rashbam must have forgotten that much of Rashi's explanation comes from the Mekhilta. (Mendelssohn piously, and to my mind incorrectly, assumes that

mistaken. For as we have learned,[38] "You should warn people when the time for action comes even if you warned them previously, before the time for action," which means that you warn people a second time when the time for action comes by telling them that now is the time to do what you had told them before.[39] Furthermore,[40] what new information is conveyed[41] in the entire next verse (24) with its lengthy repetition, "Go down and . . . "?

Rather [the correct interpretation of this verse is that] Moses addressed a question to God.[42] Moses asked Him: "Three days ago You told me--when You warned the people through me about staying away from the mountain and You said to me (vs. 12) 'Beware of *going up* the mountain'--that the people should not *go up* Mount Sinai. Now You say to me (vs. 21), 'Lest they break through . . . [*to see*].' Are You perhaps adding that it is forbidden even to come a little closer [to the mountain] *to look and see* even from some distance away from the mountain?" God then answered him (vs. 24), "Go down and come back together with Aaron, but let not the priests or the people break through to *go up* to the LORD." [In other words, God was saying,] "I am not

---

Rashbam would not criticize that interpretation if he had remembered that it originated in a work like the Mekhilta.)

[38]See Mekhilta, *ibid.*, where this line appears in somewhat different wording, and see also Rashi ad vs. 24.

[39]Rashi argues that the meaning of God's answer to Moses in vs. 24 is that God taught Moses the principle that one warns people more than once about their duties. Rashbam's objection is that Moses would obviously know something like that and there would be no reason for him to challenge God for suggesting a repetition of the warning.

[40]I.e. another objection to Rashi's interpretation.

[41]Note that even when dealing on the *peshaṭ* level with a narrative text, Rashbam wishes to see some new information conveyed in each verse. See similarly comm. below ad 33:14, s.v. והניחותי.

[42]Touitou (*Tarbiẓ* 51, p. 233) argues that Rashbam is uncomfortable with an interpretation that would see Moses as questioning or expressing doubts about the need for God's orders. Rashbam, according to Touitou, prefers to portray Moses as more obedient and as simply asking of God an information-seeking question, a clarification of instructions. See also Rashbam's comm. to Num. 11:21.

talking about *seeing*; [when I said (in vs. 21) that the people should not *see*,] I was not referring[43] to the seeing that one can do without *going up*.[44]

19:25 ויאמר [MOSES WENT DOWN TO THE PEOPLE] AND TOLD THEM: about the commandment to stay away from the mountain beginning from now.[45]

---

[43]Perhaps the text of Rashbam should be emended from אמרתי to אסרתי. I.e. "I did not *forbid* seeing without going up."

[44]Like Rashbam, see iE (longer comm. only).

[45]So also Rashi and iE. Cf. Mekhilta, *ibid.*, p. 227 where a number of midrashic intepretations are offered about what it was that Moses told the Israelites (e.g. "He said to them: 'Be ready to accept the reign of heaven joyfully'.")

EXODUS XX

20:3 לא YOU SHALL HAVE NO [OTHER GODS BESIDES ME]: For I took you out of Egypt by Myself.[1]

20:5 לשנאי [VISITING GUILT UPON THE CHILDREN . . .] OF THOSE WHO HATE ME: If the children [continue to] hate me.[2]

20:6 ועושה SHOWING KINDNESS TO THOUSANDS: To the children of the third generation (שלישים), the fourth generation (רבעים), the fifth, the tenth, the hundredth [all the way to] the thousandth generation. The word לאלפים, TO THOUSANDS of children, means "to the thousandth generation."[3] Accordingly, following the plain meaning of

---

[1] Rashbam's interpretation explains how the verses of the Decalogue flow into one another. (See similarly his comm. to vs. 7.) The mention of the exodus from Egypt in verse 2 justifies God's demand in verse 3 that He alone be worshipped.

Cf. the midrashic attempts to connect betwen vss. 2 and 3, e.g. in Mekhilta *Ba-ḥodesh* 6, p. 237f.

[2] This is the common rabbinic answer to explain how God visits guilt of parents upon children, especially when Deut. 24:16 says that He will *not* do such a thing. See similarly Rashi, here, following Onq., Berakhot 7a and Mekhilta, *ibid.*, p. 246.

[3] Using the language of Deut. 7:9.

Rashbam is saying that אלפים should not be understood in its standard sense of meaning "thousands," but as a technical word for "the thousandth generation"--just like the words שלשים ("the third generation") and רבעים ("the fourth generation") in this verse.

Scripture, there is no contradiction between the verses.[4] Here [in Exodus] the text specifically mentions the children, grandchildren and great-grandchildren.[5] The reference to "בנים--children" is to one generation; the reference to their children is to a second generation, etc. And then the children of the one thousandth generation would be called בנים אלפים.

On the other hand, in Deuteronomy (7:9) there is no [previous] reference [in the verse] to children (בנים) or to the third generation (שלשים) or to the fourth generation (רבעים).[6] The verse there then says, "Know, therefore, that the LORD your God [keeps His covenant faithfully] for those who love Him and keep His commandments to the thousandth generation (לאלף דור)." The phrase אלף דור there is equivalent [in meaning] to בנים אלפים here.

20:7 לא תשא YOU SHALL NOT SWEAR FALSELY: This too is part of the theme of honoring God, as is the commandment of observing the sabbath below.[7] Also the commandment of honoring one's parents is connected to the theme, as the honoring of parents is compared to the honoring of God, as it is written (Prov. 3:9), "Honor (כבד) the LORD with your wealth."[8]

---

[4]I.e. between this verse and Deut. 7:9. Rashbam is opposing Rashi's comment to Deut. 7:9, s.v. לאלף, where Rashi (following Sotah 31a) comments on the supposed contradiction between God's promise (here and in Deut. 5:10) to show kindness לאלפים--"to thousands," in the plural--and God's promise in Deut. 7:9 to keep his covenant faithfully לאלף דור--"for *one* thousand generations," in the singular.

[5]In the phrase at the end of the last verse, "visiting the guilt of the parents upon the children, upon the third and upon the fourth generations."

[6]Accordingly if the word אלפים were written there, it would have to mean "thousands," in the standard plural sense. In that context the only way to convey the idea of "one thousand generations" is through the words לאלף דור.

[7]Rashbam continues the explanation (that he began in his comm. to vs. 3 above) of how the different commandments of the Decalogue flow together.

[8]I.e. the honoring of God and the honoring of parents are comparable as the Bible uses the same verb (כָּבֵד) to describe them both. This comparison of the honoring of parents and of God can be found in a number of rabbinic sources, e.g. Mekhilta *ibid.* 8,

EXODUS XX

20:8 זכור REMEMBER THE SABBATH DAY: The verb, "to remember," (ז-כ-ר) always refers to something from the past.⁹ For example (Deut. 32:7-8) "Remember (זכור) the days of old ... When the Most High gave nations their homes." Also (Ex. 13:3) "Remember (זכור)--in the future--this day, on which you--in the past--shall have gone free from Egypt."¹⁰

Also (Deut. 9:7-8) "Remember (זכור), never forget, how you provoked the LORD your God ... and in Horeb." Also (Ps. 25:6) "O LORD, be mindful of your compassion and Your faithfulness; they are as old as time." Here also the verse means "Remember that sabbath day that followed the six days of creation." The text then continues and explains [how one should remember that sabbath], as it is written below (vs. 11) "For in six days the LORD made heaven and earth ...." That

---

p. 258. It is rare to find Rashbam making use of the rabbinic exegetical tool of *gezerah shavah*--i.e. comparing to each other two verses in very different contexts, simply on the basis of a (not very remarkable) linguistic similarity--to prove his point.

⁹Rashbam's explanation is opposed to that of Rashi. Rashi argues that זכור in this verse means "to bear in mind"; i.e. think about the Sabbath that will soon be coming up. So Rashi sees the verb ז-כ-ר as referring to thinking about the *future*. Accordingly Rashbam, who opposes such a reading, writes that that verb always refers to remembering the *past*.

The verb, ז-כ-ר, just like the English verb "to remember," almost always refers to past events, as Rashbam claims. Yet, as Luzzatto argues, one can find a few examples such as "לא זכרה אחריתה--She gave no thought to her future" (Lam. 1:9) to support Rashi's reading.

¹⁰Rashbam explains that Ex. 13:3 does not contradict his explanation. To be sure, in Ex. 13 the Israelites, who have not yet left Egypt, are told to "remember" the day of the exodus, a day that has not yet come. But Rashbam explains reasonably that the verse should be understood as a future perfect construction: the Israelites are being told that in the future they should remember the day on which they *shall have* left Egypt.

is why the text says here: "Remember the sabbath day" *in order*[11] "to keep it holy," by refraining from work.[12]

20:10 על כן BECAUSE[13] THE LORD BLESSED THE SABBATH DAY AND HALLOWED IT: [The phrase should be understood] as I explained above in Genesis.[14] [Honor the sabbath,] because God blessed the sabbath day. [And how did God bless the sabbath?] By the

---

[11]Rashbam's explanation of the syntax of the verse differs from that of Saadiah and NJPS who suggest that לקדשו is best understood as meaning "*and* keep it holy." Like Rashbam, see Seforno: "וזה תעשה כדי שתוכל לקדשו--do this (i.e. remember it), so that you will be able to make it holy."

[12]Rashbam explains that "keeping the sabbath holy" does not mean doing anything positive; it just means refraining from work. So also iE, as opposed to the traditional explanation (e.g. Mekhilta, *ibid.*, p. 253) where לקדשו is explained as a commandment to recite the *qiddush* prayer in order to make the sabbath holy. See Nahm. who argues passionately for that reading ("וזהו קידוש היום וזה מן התורה אינו אסמכתא--this refers to reciting *qiddush* on the sabbath day. That obligation is derived from the Torah; it is not [merely artificially connected to this verse as] a mnemonic device"). See also Mendelssohn who explains the basis for the traditional explanation but ultimately supports Rashbam's reading as the true plain meaning of Scripture ("ואולם פשטות הכתוב כאשר פירש הרשב"ם ז"ל--however the plain meaning of Scripture is what Rashbam explained").

Rashbam then sees verse 7 as a general statement requiring two explanations. Verses 8-9 are an elaboration of what keeping the sabbath holy means (i.e. not working), and then verse 10 is an elaboration of what remembering the sabbath means (i.e. remembering the story of creation).

[13]Rashbam explains the causality in this verse in a new and unique manner. The verse is not to be understood in the traditional manner as meaning "that is why the LORD blessed the sabbath," but rather "Hallow the sabbath . . . *because* the LORD blessed the sabbath day." In other words, the traditional understanding of the causality here is that the previous verses give the cause for verse 10, while Rashbam says that verse 10 gives the cause for something written in a previous verse.

See comm. and notes to Gen. 18:5. There Rashbam, like many Jewish exegetes, explains that he understands the causality involved in the expression כי על כן in a manner that differs from the standard understanding. Rashbam now expands that claim and asserts that the causality implied in the phrase על כן here is also to be understood in that way. He appears to be alone in that understanding.

[14]Presumably in the lost section of his comm., ad Gen. 2:3.

time the sabbath arrived, God had already created food and everything else that humans need. So the sabbath was blessed with all good things.[15] That is why a person should "make the sabbath holy,"[16] by refraining from work on the sabbath as a testimony to God's rest, just as God first created everything and then rested.[17]

20:13 לא תרצח YOU SHALL NOT MURDER: The verb ר-צ-ח always--wherever it appears[18]--refers to unjustified homicide. For example, (Num. 35:16) "the murderer (הרוצח) must be put to death," or (I Kings 21:19) "Would you murder (הרצחת) and also take possession," or (Is. 1:21) "Where righteousness dwelt--but now murderers (מרצחים)." But the verbs ה-ר-ג and מ-ו-ת sometimes refer to unjustified homicide--e.g. (Gen. 4:8) "and he," Cain, "killed him (ויהרגהו)"--and sometimes to justifiable homicide--e.g. (Lev. 20:16) "you shall kill (והרגת) the woman."

When the verse says (Deut. 4:42) "one who unwittingly slew (ירצח)[19] a fellow man," since the greater context there deals with

---

[15]In other words, the claim both here and in Genesis 2 that God blessed the sabbath day does *not* mean that God did something additional and special to make the sabbath "blessed." Rashbam then opposes the explanation of Rashi (from Mekhilta, *ibid.*, p. 256) that God blessed the sabbath through the miracle of the manna. See also iE who understands that the verb "blessed" implies that God did something additional to make the sabbath an appropriate day for spiritual enterprises. Rashbam alone suggests that the claim that God "blessed" the sabbath is simply a summary statement--that by creating all things before the sabbath, the sabbath is found to be blessed.

[16]I suggest that the text of Rashbam's comm. would be easier to understand if one reads here ולכן יקדשהו, instead of ולכן ויקדשהו that appears in Rosin's text.

[17]On Rashbam's explanation of the reason for sabbath observance, see also comm. and notes to Ex. 31:13, s.v. כי.

[18]Rashbam's strident repetitive language here (בכל מקום ... כל רציחה) is probably a result of the polemical nature of his comments. See below.

[19]Rashbam cites this verse as a possible counter-example to his distinction between ר-צ-ח and ה-ר-ג. In that verse in Deut., the verb ר-צ-ח is used to describe a homicide that is not punishable. See next note.

premeditated murder, the text says that if such "murdering" (רציחה) takes place unwittingly, then there is no penalty.[20]

I offered this explanation as an argument against the heretics[21] and they admitted that I was right. Even though in their Latin books the same verb is used to translate the verb מ-ו-ת in the phrase (Dt. 32:39) "I deal death (אמית) and I give life,"[22] and the verb ר-צ-ח in this verse,[23] their translations are inaccurate.[24]

---

[20] Rashbam's comment as it stands is hard to understand. The context in Deuteronomy 4 does *not* deal with premeditated murder. Perhaps Rashbam intended to cite a verse from Num. 35 here. There the verb ר-צ-ח is used more than once to describe an accidental homicide (e.g. [vs. 11], "cities of refuge to which a murderer [רוצח] who has killed a person unintentionally may flee"), and there Rashbam may legitimately answer that the verb ר-צ-ח is used because the context there deals at length with premeditated homicide (vss. 16-21). Or perhaps Rashbam meant to cite Deut. 19:4, a verse that is very similar in wording to Deut. 4:42 ("the murderer [הרוצח] . . . who has killed another unwittingly"). There too the greater context deals with premeditated homicide (in. vss. 11-13). But that example does not really support the point that Rashbam is trying to make, for in Deut. 19 the verb ר-צ-ח, curiously, is used *only* when describing the accidental killer and not in the verses that discuss premeditated homicide.

Rashbam's answer here--that one may use the verb ר-צ-ח to describe accidental homicide in passages where it is being contrasted with premeditated homicide--seems reasonable enough. Yet the question that Rashbam poses about his own theory is not the strongest question that he could pose. The verb ר-צ-ח is used in Num. 35 not only to describe premeditated homicide and accidental homicide. It is also used to describe permissable and even required killing ([vs. 27] "if the blood-avenger murders [ורצח] the murderer there is no bloodguilt" or [vs. 30] "the manslayer [הָרֹצֵחַ] may be murdered [יִרְצַח] only on the evidence of witnesses"). Rashbam's claim, then, that the verb ר-צ-ח in the Torah describes only unjustified homicide seems difficult to sustain. See criticism of Rashbam's position and a detailed discussion of the issue in Gerald Blidstein's "Capital Punishment: The Classic Jewish Discussion," *Judaism* 14 (1965), 159-171.

[21] In other words, Rashbam made such an argument in his discussions of the Bible with Christians. As Touitou has shown in "The Meaning of *teshuvat ha-minim* in the Writings of our French Masters," *Sinai* 99 (1986), pp. 144-148, the word תשובה in the phrase תשובה למינים need not mean "rebuttal."

[22] Translated in the Vulgate as "*Ego* occidam *et Ego vivere faciam*."

[23] Translated in the Vulgate as "*non occides*."

20:15 רואים את הקולות ALL THE PEOPLE SAW THE VOICES (קולות): I.e. the hail and the stones, as it is writen (9:28) "voices (קולות) and hail from God."[25]

20:16 ויאמרו THEY SAID TO MOSES; after they heard the Decalogue,[26] "YOU SPEAK TO US [. . . LET NOT GOD SPEAK TO US]". Had they not said this, it appears that they would have heard all the commandments directly from God's mouth.[27]

---

[24]Klausner (*Leshonenu* 21 [1957], p. 201) concludes from this passage that Rashbam knew Latin. As far as I know there is no evidence to prove such an assertion other than this passage. Arguably Rashbam may not have really known Latin but may have discussed this exegetical issue sufficiently with his Christian interlocutors to know that the Vulgate does not distinguish between ר-צ-ח and ה-ר-ג. On the issue of the knowledge of Latin by medieval Jews, see the many sources cited by Ephraim Kanarfogel in *Jewish Education and Society in the High Middle Ages*, footnote 37, pp. 169-170.

In any case one does see clearly from this passage that Rashbam discussed issues of biblical exegesis with Christians, even a passage such as this that is not a central one in the history of Jewish-Christian polemics.

[25]Rashbam is dealing with the difficulty of how it is that one "sees" a voice. This difficulty was addressed by almost all Jewish exegetes, beginning with the Mekhilta (*ibid.*, 9, p. 266). Rashi does not follow the *peshaṭ*-like explanation of R. Ishmael there ("they saw what was visible and they heard what was audible") but prefers to explain the verse as referring to some miraculous type of seeing. Rashbam, on the other hand, says that the word קול is a reference to hail, something that can be seen. On the connection between the word קול and hail, see also Rashbam's comm. and notes to 14:24.

[26]So also iE (longer comm.), as opposed to the explanation that this passage was really said *before* the Decalogue (see Nahm.) or in the *middle* of the Decalogue, after the second commandment (LT ad 20:2, at the end of his comment).

[27]Two opinions can be found in midrashim (cited by Kasher, pp. 142-144) about whether it was a positive or a negative development that the Israelites asked that Moses serve as an intermediary between them and God. I would speculate that Rashbam sees it negatively. Presumably in Rashbam's view the original plan of unmediated contact with God would be the preferred option.

See Touitou, *Tarbiz* 51, p. 234, who cites this comment as part of his discussion of Rashbam's view on the relative importance of the roles of Moses and God in the giving of the Torah to Israel.

20:17 נסות אתכם: means "to educate you."[28]

20:20 אלהי כסף GODS OF SILVER AND GODS OF GOLD: even if they are only meant to remind one about [the true God of] heaven,[29] YOU SHALL NOT MAKE, for there are those who err[30] and feel that they [i.e. those represenations] are real [divinities].[31] Even though God commanded us to make cherubs on the ark, those cherubs are meant for God to sit on[32]—just like the cherubs in the heavenly throne[33]—and are not to be worshipped.[34]

---

[28]See comm. and notes above ad 15:25 and 16:4. Rashbam opposes the explanation of Rashi who asserts (following Mekhilta *ibid.*, p. 272) that נ-ס-ה here means "to make the Israelites great." Furthermore, while Rashi explains נ-ס-ה here in a manner different from his explanation in 15:25, Rashbam attempts to offer one consistent explanation.

[29]Like Rashi (following Mekhilta, *ibid.*, p. 276f.), Rashbam says that the reference here is not to the prohibition against worship of *other* gods, but rather to the prohibition against representing the true God. So also iE and JBS.

[30]טועים. As Touitou notes (*Milet* 2, p. 279), it would be theoretically possible to identify "those who err" as either Jews or Christians. Touitou points out, however, that the same point as Rashbam's is made by his younger colleague, JBS, in almost the identical language (in JBS's commentary ad 20:4) and JBS explicitly writes that this explanation is directed against the theology of the Christians ("כמו שאמרו המינים"). It is most likely that Rashbam is the source for JBS's comment and that both their comments should be read as anti-Christian polemic, against the iconography practiced in the churches that Rashbam and JBS knew. On Jewish criticism of Christian worship of images as a form of idolatry, see D. Berger, pp. 331-2.

[31]See similarly Maimonides' theory about the origins of idolatry in the beginning of his *Hilkhot 'avodah zarah*.

[32]See the common biblical description of God as יושב הכרובים—the one who is "enthroned on the cherubim" (e.g. I Sam. 4:4).

[33]The connection between cherubs and the celestial throne of God can be found in Ezekiel 10:1f.

[34]Rashbam's discussion of the cherubs in the context of this verse may simply reflect a common Jewish concern of explaining the tension between the laws against idolatry and the law about cherubs. Many Jewish exegetes deal with this issue, even as early as the Mekhilta (*ibid.*, pp. 276 and 282-3).

EXODUS XX 221

20:21-22 מזבח אדמה MAKE FOR ME AN ALTAR OF EARTH: Since the [idolatrous] nations place their *'asherot* on[35] their altars--as it says concerning Gideon (Jud. 6:25) "Cut down the *'asherah* which is on it,"[36] and it is written (Jer. 17:2) "While their children remember their altars and their *'asherot*, and it is written (Deut. 16:21) "You shall not plant an *'asherah*, any kind of tree, near the altar of the LORD."[37] That is why God said, "Even[38] if you make an altar for Me, make it only out of earth, a material which is usually kept smooth and on which drawings and images are not usually made.[39] And even IF you

---

Additionally, Rashbam's discussion of cherubs here may be seen as a continuation of his anti-Christian polemic. Christian polemicists often cited the cherubs as proof that icons are not outlawed quite as clearly as the Jews would maintain. For further Jewish and Christian sources that discuss the cherubs as part of polemics about idolatry, see D. Berger, pp. 260-1.

[35]על. Perhaps "beside."

[36]עליו. Perhaps "beside it."

[37]See Rashbam's comm. there where he explains that planting any tree near an altar is outlawed so as not to be like the idolators, and he cites the same two prooftexts, from Judges and Jeremiah.

[38]In other words, the verse continues the restrictions against idolatry in verse 20. That verse says, according to Rashbam, that one should not use gold or silver images in the worship of God. This next verse then adds that there are even restrictions about the use of altars in the worship of God.

[39]Rashbam opposes the two standard halakhic understandings of this verse found in Rashi here, based on Mekhilta *ibid.* 11, p. 284. (See also Zev. 61b.). One of the explanations offered by Rashi is that the verse here is a reference to the "outer altar" of the Tabernacle that was hollow and was filled with dirt whenever the Israelites set up camp. Rashbam himself in his comm. ad 27:8 says that that was how the "outer altar" worked. However, while agreeing with Rashi about the structure and use of that altar, Rashbam does not agree that that is what our verse means. See similarly iE's longer comm. here: "וקדמונינו אמרו כי הטעם לשום אדמה במזבח הנחושת ואמת אמרו כי כן עשו רק זה הפסוק לזכר ולאסמכתא ואין זה פשוטו--the Rabbis said that the meaning is that one should fill the 'bronze altar' with earth. This is true; that is what they did. But this is not the *peshat* meaning of the verse. The rabbis used this verse only as a mnemonic device to help us remember that law."

desire[40] to make AN ALTAR OF STONES, you must, as it says in Deuteronomy, (27:6) 'build the altar of the LORD your God of unhewn stones,' [and it should be] (*ibid.*, vs. 5) 'an altar of stones; do not wield an iron tool over them',[41] [and that is the meaning here in Exodus of the phrase,] DO NOT BUILD IT גזית."

For when altars are built גזית, i.e. with iron tools, the engravers often make drawings and images in them, as it says concerning images in Isaiah (44:12-13) "The craftsman in iron (ברזל) with his tools works it over charcoal and fashions it by hammering . . . marks out a shape with a stylus, forms it with scraping tools, marking it out with a compass."[42]

---

[40]Rashbam's language here (ואף אם תרצה לעשות מזבח אבנים) appears to be directed against Rashi who (following the opinion of R. Ishmael in Mekhilta, *ibid.*, pp. 287-288) writes that despite the word "ואם--if," at the beginning of verse 22, it is obligatory and not optional to build such a stone altar. Rashbam seems to be emphasizing that, at least on the *peshaṭ* level, the verse means, "If you *desire* to make such an altar."

[41]Presumably Rashbam feels that the parallel verse in Deuteronomy helps us understand better the passage here in Exodus since there, there is a specific reference to an iron tool, which, as Rashbam argues below on the basis of the passage in Isaiah, should be understood as a reference to engraved drawings.

[42]There is a weakness in Rashbam's prooftext in that the last phrases (which refer to the graven image) are describing a craftsman working with wood, not a craftsman working in iron.

Rashbam's interpretation of our passage in Exodus differs from the standard understanding--that whole, unhewn stones should be used to build an altar. The Mishnah (Middot 3:4) and the Mekhilta (*ibid.*, p. 290) explain that it is inappropriate that a tool of violence be used for a purpose like building an altar, which is meant to prolong a person's life. (See Rashi here, s.v. ותחללה.) Rashbam's explanation, that the Torah's purpose is to combat idolatry by ensuring that the stones not be engraved in any manner, appears to be unique. See Maimonides, *Guide* 3:45, who also explains this commandment as combatting idolatry.

iE, only in his longer comm. to Exodus, mentions that some people interpret the verse in the way that Rashbam does here, and he argues against such an explanation. Margaliot (*Sefer 'asaf*, p. 362) cites this verse to prove that between writing his shorter and longer commentaries on Exodus, iE read Rashbam's commentary. See also Simon's arguments against Margaliot's thesis (in Simon's article cited above in notes to 4:10).

ולא תעלה במעלות 20:23 DO NOT ASCEND MY ALTAR BY STEPS: That is why the ramp [in the temple] is made of stones on an incline.[43] The ramp is ten cubits high and thirty cubits wide.[44] They also used to throw salt on the ramp so that the priests who were ascending would not slip on the ramp.[45]

---

[43]So also Mekhilta (*ibid.*, p. 290) and Rashi. Rashbam in fact uses the same terminology here (משופע) as his grandfather.

[44]See Rosin's discussion here (footnote 9) of the difficulties involved in Rashbam's computation.

[45]See Eruvin 10:14.

EXODUS XXI

RASHBAM'S INTRODUCTION

Let those who love wisdom know and understand that my purpose, as I explained in Genesis,[1] is not to offer halakhic interpretations, wherein *haggadot* and *halakhot* are derived from superfluities in Scriptural language, even though such interpretations are the most essential ones. Some of those explanations can be found in the works of my mother's father, Rashi. But my purpose is to explain the plain meaning of Scripture.[2] I will explain the laws and rules [of the Torah] in a manner that conforms to the [natural] way of the world.[3] Nevertheless, it is the halakhic level of interpretation that is the most essential one, as the

---

[1] In his comm. to Gen. 1:1 and 37:2; see also notes there.
   Rashbam now reiterates, in an abridged manner, his position on the relative importance of the "plain" level of meaning--the *peshat*--and the level of meaning added by the rabbinic tradition--the *derash*. Since he is now beginning his commentary on the first lengthy "legal" section of the Torah, it is possible that he feels obliged at this point to reassert his orthodoxy before he begins to offer some essentially heterodox, non-halakhic readings of these texts.

[2] Rashbam's phraseology here, "לא באתי לפרש ההלכות--my purpose is not offer halakhic interpretations," and "ואני לפרש פשוטן של מקראות באתי--my purpose is to explain the plain meaning of Scripture," seems to be based on the language of Rashi in Rashi's most famous programmatic statement, in his comm. to Gen. 3:8 ("ואני לא באתי אלא לפשוטו של מקרא--my purpose is only to explain the plain meaning of Scripture"). Rashi there claimed that *his* purpose was to explain the *peshat* level of meaning of the text. Rashbam here claims that it is the halakhic level of textual interpretation that can be found in Rashi's works. Then Rashbam uses Rashi's own language to say that it is really he, Rashbam, who provides the *peshat* level of interpretation.

[3] לפי דרך ארץ; concerning Rashbam's use of the phrase see the variety of explanations suggested by Touitou ("*Shitato ha-parshanit* . . .," p. 65) and M. Berger (pp. 99-113).

rabbis said (Sotah 16a) "Halakhah uproots [the plain meaning of] the biblical text."[4]

COMMENTARY

21:2 כי תקנה WHEN YOU PURCHASE A HEBREW SLAVE: The verse here refers to a slave who was sold by the court [because of his inability to repay property that he stole], as it says below (22:2), "if he lacks the means he shall be sold for his theft." But the case of a slave who sells himself due to impoverished circumstances is described in the portion *Behar sinai* where the verse says (Lev. 25:39) "If your kinsman

---

[4]Rashbam understands this rabbinic saying as meaning that halakhah can and, on occasion, does cancel out the plain meaning of the biblical text. See Halivni, *Peshat and Derash*, pp. 198-9, note 63, who argues that this quotation in its original context has nothing to do with *peshat*.

This quotation may have come to Rashbam's mind here because it appears in rabbinic exegesis of the beginning of Exodus 21; see Yalqut Shimoni 317 and LT ad 21:6, s.v. במרצע.

Rashbam's argument here--that the more halakhically-oriented comm. of his grandfather "uproots" the *peshat* level of reading the text--seems different from what he writes in his concluding comment to the book of Exodus. There Rashbam says of Rashi's comm. that "most of the laws and midrashic interpretations there *are close* to the plain meaning of Scripture." Rashbam's attitude to his grandfather's comm. is certainly nuanced, and perhaps inconsistent. See also Rashbam's introduction to his comm. ad Gen. 37 and notes there.

The way Rashbam quotes this talmudic passage, הלכה עוקרת משנה, differs from the way that the quotation appears in our texts of the Talmud in two ways: in our talmudic texts the verb is עוקבת, not עוקרת, and the object is מקרא, not משנה. See Rosin's discussion here, note 3.

I assume that the word משנה in the text of Rashbam is a copyist's error; the passage makes no sense unless one reads here מקרא, as in the talmudic text. But Rashbam's reading of עוקרת, instead of עוקבת, is attested in other sources. *The Babylonian Talmud with Variant Readings*, ed. A. Liss, Sotah vol. I (Jerusalem, 1977), p. 238, note 23, lists a number of medieval sources where the talmudic statement is quoted as הלכה עוקרת מקרא. For example, on two occasions Rashbam's colleagues, the Tosafists, quote that talmudic passage (in Tosafot Qid. 16b, s.v. והא, and Tosafot Hul. 88b, s.v. שוחק) using the verb עוקרת, as Rashbam does here.

under you continues in straits and must sell himself."⁵ There the rule is (*ibid.*, vs. 40) "he shall serve you until the jubilee year." Here, where the slave was sold by a court, the rule is HE SHALL SERVE SIX YEARS.⁶

Some of our sages say, on the basis of a *gezerah shavah*, that the same rules apply in both cases and that if the jubilee year comes before the seventh year [of service] then the slave would go free in the jubilee year.⁷ Some sages, however, distinguish between [the rules that apply to] the two [kinds of slaves].⁸

ובשביעית IN THE SEVENTH YEAR: The seventh year from the time that he was sold as a slave, not the seventh year of the sabbatical cycle.⁹

---

⁵The same exegetical distinction between our passage and the passage in Leviticus can be found in Rashi, here (following Mekhilta, *Neziqin* 1, [Lauterbach ed., vol. 3, p. 3]).

⁶Rosin's edition here reads ששת ימים יעבוד. Obviously the text should read שש שנים יעבוד.

⁷In other words, one passage says that the slave goes free in the seventh year and the second passage says that he goes free in the jubilee year. Both passages are to be applied to both kinds of slaves. Any Hebrew slave is to be freed either at the seventh year or at the jubilee year, whichever comes first.

⁸See both opinions in Qid. 14b-15b.
Rashbam argues here, correctly, that his exegetical position concerning these verses has support in rabbinic sources. In fact, Maimonides in MT *'Avadim* 2:2-3 rules along the same lines as Rashbam's interpretation of the biblical text--that different periods of servitude apply to the two kinds of slaves and that it is possible for a man to sell *himself* as a slave for a period of more than six years.
It is possible that Rashbam's comments here--preferring the interpretation that says that different periods of servitude are applied to different categories of slaves--are meant to oppose those of Rashi who seems to be saying (both here and in his comm. to Lev. 25:40, s.v. עד) that *all* slaves--even those who sell themselves into servitude--are freed after six years of service.

⁹So also Mekhilta (*ibid.*) p. 7 and virtually all other Jewish interpreters. Cf. however Rashbam's colleague, JBS, who sees here a reference to the sabbatical year and says that slaves are logically set free in the sabbatical year since one does not need their labors then for agricultural purposes. See Kasher, note 70, who is amazed at JBS's exegetical audacity. ("It is amazing to me [that JBS inteprets that way]; not even one of the radically *peshaṭ*-oriented exegetes [הפשטנים הקיצוניים] interprets the text that way."

יצא לחפשי **HE SHALL GO OUT TO FREEDOM**: חפשי is a noun[10] [meaning "freedom"];[11] if it were [an adjective,] a reference to "a person who is חפשי, free,"[12] then it would have to be vocalized with a *ḥaṭaf*[13] [under the *lamed*]: לְחָפְשִׁי.[14]

21:3-4 אם בגפו IF HE CAME SINGLE HE SHALL LEAVE SINGLE: The text first makes a general statement and then explains the details.[15] In other words, "IF HE CAME, i.e. entered his master's home, בגפו,

---

Presumably the words, "the radically *peshaṭ*-oriented exegetes," refer to, or at least include, Rashbam.)

[10]פעולה, perhaps "an abstract noun"; see Rosin, RSBM, p. 140, note 1.

[11]So also Rashi (לחירות), as opposed to Onq. who sees חפשי as an adjective (לבר חורין). iE mentions both possible interpretations.

[12]As in, for example, Job 3:19, "the slave is free (חפשי) of his master."

[13]Rashbam's standard word for a *sheva* is *ḥaṭaf*. See Rosin RSBM, p. 130, and see chapter 15, note 60, above.

[14]See Mendelssohn who feels that Rashbam's argument from the vocalization clinches the debate about the meaning of חפשי here.

[15]See comm. and notes above ad 2:15.

Using a halakhic approach to this verse, the perceived difficulty is that the phrase, "If he came by himself, he would leave by himself," appears to serve no purpose. The end of this verse and the next verse sufficiently cover all the relevant possibilities ("If he had a wife" and "If his master gave him a wife"). Surely there is no need to tell the readers that he will leave single in a case where he came single and his master did *not* give him a wife! What then is learned from the phrase, "If he came by himself, he would leave by himself"?

This question is first posed in the Mekhilta (*ibid.*, p. 7: למה נאמר) and the common halakhic answer is that this phrase teaches us that it is not obligatory for the master to provide his slave with a wife. Rashbam explains that the phrase need not be seen a serving a specific halakhic purpose; at least on the *peshaṭ* level it should be seen as serving the literary purpose of making a general statement which will then be elaborated in the next verse and a half. In other words, for Rashbam sees no need to attribute referential meaning to this phrase; rhetorical meaning suffices for his purposes.

See similarly JBS.

i.e. BY HIMSELF,[16] because he did not yet have a wife, then even if his master gave him a wife,[17] HE WOULD, nevertheless, LEAVE BY HIMSELF. Because the wife that his master would give to him actually belongs to the master."

[After this opening statement] the text then explains in detail how this occurs: that IF HE HAD A WIFE, then he would not leave by himself, but rather HIS WIFE SHALL LEAVE WITH HIM. However, (vs. 4) IF HIS MASTER GAVE HIM A WIFE . . ., then just as he came single, he shall leave single.

The wife referred to [in vs. 4] is a non-Jewish slave given to him as a wife by his master.[18]

21:6 אל האלהים: means "to the judges."[19]

אל הדלת TO THE DOOR OR THE DOORPOST: His ear is pierced in full view of the public as a sign of slavery.[20] [The reason why the door and the doorpost were specifically chosen for this ceremony is because] even in a stone house, the door and the doorpost are made of wood, so it is possible to pierce through his ear and through the door.[21]

---

[16]So also Onq.

[17]Rashi (s.v. בגפו יצא, following the opinion of R. Eliezer b. Jacob in Qid. 20a) writes that a master is allowed to give a wife only to a slave who *is* already married, not to a slave who is single. (For a list of seven possible reasons for such a law, see Kasher, note 73.) Rashbam is, *en passant*, expressing his disagreement with that explanation.

[18]So also Mekhilta (*ibid.*, pp. 10-11) and Rashi.

[19]So also Onq., Mekhilta (*ibid.* 2, p. 14), Rashi, and almost all other Jewish exegetes.

[20]I.e. the location was chosen for the purpose of publicizing the ceremony. So also JBS and iE.

[21]Rashbam's prosaic explanation of why specifically the door or the doorpost is used is meant to oppose (and perhaps to poke gentle fun at) the midrashic explanation cited by Rashi (from Qid. 22b). According to that midrash, the door and the doorpost were chosen to teach an important moral lesson--that people should not give up their freedom.

לעולם: According to the plain meaning of Scripture, לעולם means all the days of his life,[22] as it says concerning Samuel (I Sam. 1:22), "he must remain there for good (לעולם)."[23]

The door and the doorpost had been smeared with blood on the first Passover eve (12:7 and 12:22); hence they had served as instruments of providing freedom to the Israelites when they left Egypt. They were then chosen, for didactic purposes, as the place where this slave would give up his freedom.

Rashbam, as he often does, suggests that the reason may be practical and prosaic, not symbolic or didactic. (See similarly comm. and notes to Ex. 2:3.) See also JBS who offers the same explanation as Rashbam for the choice of the door and the doorpost.

[22]Rashbam offers an explanation here that is opposed to the universal halakhic understanding of this verse. Based on the passage about slaves in Leviticus (25:40), the rabbis say that even a slave whose ear has been pierced serves only until the jubilee year. (See e.g. Rashi here, Mekhilta [ibid., p. 17] and Mishnah Qid. 1:2.) Even such peshaṭ-oriented exegetes as iE, in the Middle Ages, and Mendelssohn, in early modern times, feel obliged to interpret our verse in such a way that the peshaṭ will not directly contradict the halakhah. Accordingly they do everything possible to argue that לעולם does not necessarily mean "forever."

Rashbam, as far as I can tell, is the only rabbanite exegete who simply writes that, following the peshaṭ, לעולם really does mean "forever," and does not attempt to explain how and why the peshaṭ says something that simply does not conform to halakhah. See somewhat similarly the Responsa of Solomon ibn Adret (Rashba'), part 1, number 9 (cited by Kasher, note 140), who, after discussing the implications of לעולם meaning "forever," writes: ואל תשיבני מן הקבלה שאמרו לעולם לעולמו של יובל כי" זה אמת מצד הקבלה אבל איני אומר אלא לפשט הכתוב--Do not argue against my position by citing the rabbinic tradition that לעולם means until the jubilee year; that is certainly true from the perspective of the tradition, but I am discussing only the peshaṭ level of meaning."

For further discussion, see my "Truth or Peshaṭ," esp. pp. 276-278.

[23]Many of those exegetes who wish to interpret לעולם here as meaning "until the jubilee year"--i.e. the fiftieth year--offer the creative midrashic suggestion that there, in I Samuel, לעולם also means "for fifty years," for Samuel was brought to the House of the LORD when he was weaned (I Sam. 1:24), presumably when he was two years old, and he remained there until he died fifty years later, at age 52. Such an interpretation may be found in a number of sources, including Midrash Samuel 3, Taanit 5b, Rashi and Qimhi in I Sam. and Hizq. here. iE here also offers the curious explanation that לעולם in I Sam. simply means "until he grows up"; presumably the only grounds for such a reading is so that there will be no contradiction between his interpretations of לעולם here and there.

21:7-8 לא תצא [WHEN A MAN SELLS HIS DAUGHTER AS A SLAVE] SHE SHALL NOT BE FREED AS MALE SLAVES ARE: when the six years are over.[24] Rather he [the purchaser] should take her as a wife,[25] as the text continues to explain. (8) IF SHE PROVES TO BE DISPLEASING TO HER MASTER i.e. that he does not wish to fulfil the duty placed upon him through the words, "SHE SHALL NOT BE FREED AS MALE SLAVES ARE," which mean that he should marry her.[26]

Rashbam again opposes those readings and suggests here that the *peshaṭ* interpretation of לעולם as "forever" is appropriate in I Samuel too.

[24] Again Rashbam offers an interpretation that differs from standard rabbinic exegesis. Rashi (following the Mekhilta, *ibid.* 3, p. 23) entertains and dismisses the possibility that "she shall not be freed as male slaves are" means that she shall not go free after six years of service. But Rashbam offers the interpretation expressly rejected by his predecessors. See also the next note.

[25] Rashbam's innovative understanding of "She shall not be freed as male slaves are" need not be seen as halakhically troubling, (the way his interpretation of לעולם in the previous verse is). He may feel that female slaves, even according to the *peshaṭ*, *do* go free after six years of service. (See also comm. to vs. 8, s.v. והפדה, which gives the impression that Rashbam does accept the idea that the female slaves serve only six years.) And yet he interprets the verses as saying that female slaves *generally* do not remain slaves for six years but rather, in the optimal case, wed their purchasers. See e.g. Mendelssohn who interprets the verse that way ("תמתין עד כלות ששת השנים"--she should not [have to] wait for the six years to elapse."). Rashbam then would disagree with the traditional exegesis of the phrase, "She shall not be freed as male slaves are," but would still, arguably, interpret the verse in a manner that is consonant with halakhah.

See Luzzatto who interprets "She shall not be freed as male slaves are" as Rashbam does, but writes explicitly that it is self-evident that if six years of servitude pass, the female slave is to be freed ("הדבר מובן מאליו שלא בא הכתוב להחמיר על הבת אלא להקל--it is self-evident that the verse intends to make the rules more lenient for the daughter [who is sold as a slave], not more stringent").

[26] The general rabbinic understanding is that the real reason that the institution of the אמה עברייה--the Hebrew woman slave--existed was as a form of arranged marriage for young girls. Rashbam also accepts that assumption. The question is, though, where does it really say in the text that the purpose was that the purchaser marry the young girl that he purchased?

Rashi (following Mekhilta *ibid.*, p. 24) says that the words אשר לא יעדה are the ones that teach us that the preferred solution is marriage. (So also Mishnah Bekhorot

אם רעה IF SHE PROVES TO BE DISPLEASING: and unattractive,[27] TO HER MASTER, such that he does not want to take her (לייעדה) for his wife.[28]

בבגדו בה SINCE HE BROKE FAITH WITH HER: In other words since he broke faith with her by not taking her for his wife. ["Breaking faith (בגידה)" means failing to fulfil one's responsibility towards a (potential) wife,] as it says in Malachi (2:14), "the wife of your youth with whom you have broken faith (בגדת), though she is your partner and covenanted spouse."[29]

1:7.) Rashbam reaches that same conclusion on the basis of the contrast between the phrase "she shall not be freed as male slaves are" and the phrase "if she proves to be displeasing to her master."

[27]Rashi (following the Mekhilta, *ibid.*) also explains that רעה means that she did not find favor in his eyes. Rashbam explains that it refers specifically to being physically unattractive (מכוערת); see similarly Mekhilta de-rabbi Yishmael (cited by Kasher, here, note 169): "כעורה--unattractive." Hizq. follows Rashbam and explains that רעה is appropriately connected with being physically unattractive on the basis of Gen. 40:7, "Why does your face appear רעים today?"

[28]The Ketiv of the word לא in the phrase אשר לא יעדה is לא; the Qeri is לו. Rashi and iE attempt to explain the verse in a way that conforms to the Qeri; so also NJPS, "displeasing to her master, who designated her for himself." Saadiah (cited by iE) attempts to find meaning in both the Ketiv and the Qeri. Rashbam explains the verse on the basis of the Ketiv, only, not the standard approach of rabbinic exegetes (not even the *peshaṭ*-oriented ones) when dealing with Qeri and Ketiv. See e.g. iE here who says that the Qeri is the "true" meaning, both here and in general, and Melammed, p. 890, who writes that Qimhi generally explains the verse following the Qeri, not the Ketiv.

Like Rashbam, see here Luzzatto, who does nevertheless find some meaning in the Qeri, too.

[29]The Mekhilta (*ibid.*, pp. 25-26) presents two alternatives about how to understand the words "since he broke faith with her." R. Jonathan b. Abtulemos says that they apply to the father, who broke faith with his daughter by selling her as a slave, while Rabbi Ishmael says that they apply to the purchaser, who declined to marry her. Rashi offers both explanations. He says that both the father and the purchaser should be seen as having broken faith with her. Rashbam prefers R. Ishmael's understanding, that "breaking faith" applies to a (potential) husband, and brings a prooftext from Malachi. So also JBS.

EXODUS XXI 233

והפדה HE MUST LET HER BE REDEEMED: He [the purchaser] reduces her redemption price and then she goes free through payment of a redemption price that is based on the number of years [of servitude] remaining.[30]

21:10 HE SHALL NOT WITHHOLD FROM HER שארה: her food,[31] as in the verse (Mi. 3:3), "You have devoured my people's flesh (שאר),"[32] OR כסותה, her clothing, OR עונתה, which, following the plain meaning of Scripture, means "her lodging."[33] For the letter *mem*

---

[30] In other words, once the purchaser decides not to marry her, her father should buy her back. However, he should not have to repay the entire purchase price, only a percentage based on the amount of time that she already served her master and the amount of time remaining in her servitude. (Presumably Rashbam understands "the number of years remaining" as a reference to the six years of servitude, but perhaps he is thinking of the jubilee year or the age when the slave reaches the age of majority; see comm. ad vs. 11, s.v. ויצאה.)

Rashbam's comment here is an abridged version of that of Rashi, following Qid. 11b. Rashbam's opening three words here, מגרע מפדיונה ויוצאה, are a precise quotation of the talmudic formulation.

[31] So also Rashi and almost all Jewish exegetes.

See Rashbam's comm. to BB 109b, s.v. שארו זו אשתו, where he offers a midrashic reading of the word שאר. Rashbam in his talmudic commentaries did not confine himself to the *peshaṭ* level of meaning of the biblical text.

[32] See NJPSC: "*She'er* is an ancient word for 'meat,' perhaps, like *leḥem*, extended to cover food in general." Cf. Nahm.'s objections to this understanding.

This same verse is cited to prove that שארה means "food" by the Mekhilta (*ibid.*, p. 27) and by the Talmud (Ket. 47b).

[33] The common Jewish interpretation is to see עונתה as meaning "conjugal rights." In rabbinic Hebrew that is a common usage of the word עונה. Thus e.g. Rashi here, following Mekhilta and the Talmud (as cited in the previous note).

The common rabbinic explanation--that the purchaser must fulfil her sexual needs--is somewhat difficult in the context of this verse. The verse says that if the purchaser takes a different woman as his wife, he still should not forget about the שאר, the כסות and the עונה of the first woman. Rashi then must explain that "if he marries another" means if he marries another woman *in addition to* the first one; otherwise how could he be required to fulfil the sexual needs of the first woman if he did not marry her but married someone else? Rashbam's explanation of עונה would not require such an understanding of what "marrying another" means. The verse simply describes the

in מעון, "lodging," is [a prefix, and is] not part of the root, just like the *mem* at the beginning of the words מקום and מלון.[34] The verse then requires [the purchaser to provide] food, clothing and shelter.[35]

21:11 ואם שלש אלה IF HE FAILS HER IN THESE THREE WAYS: If he does not wed her, and he does not marry her to his son, and he does not allow her[36] to be redeemed,[37] then SHE SHALL GO FREE, i.e. the court will set her free. However, the rabbis explained that [SHE SHALL GO FREE means that] she is freed when she shows signs of

---

requirements of the purchaser towards the female slave that he purchased and says that those requirements do not stop even if he chooses to marry someone else instead of her.

Rashbam is not the first to suggest that עונתה refers to housing. The interpretation is mentioned by Menahem, s.v. ע, and by JBS, who both say that there are some exegetes who connect עונתה to "housing." See iE who argues against this interpretation. Among moderns, see Cassuto who follows Rashbam.

[34]The thrust of Rashbam's argument is that the word עונתה means "lodging," as it comes from the same root as the word מעון, which is known to mean "lodging." The root of a form like מעון or מקום is a hollow root. (Rashbam recognizes that; see his discussion of the form מקום [in Gen. 1:9] in his *Sefer dayqut*, p. 60.) If Rashbam is then assuming that the form עונתה also comes from a hollow root (ע-ו-נ), his assumption would be disputed by most grammarians who would see ע-נ-ה as the root of עונתה. See however BDB, s.v. ע-נ-ה, who suggests a possible connection between the two roots.

[35]On these being the three basic requirements, see also Maimonides, *'Ishshut* 11:11.

[36]Kasher, note 221, suggests that Rashbam's language here, ולא יניח לפדותה, is carefully chosen. He is trying, according to Kasher, to address the question of how the Torah can say that the owner failed to redeem her when the redemption is not up to him.

[37]So also Rashi and virtually all other Jewish exegetes, following Mekhilta (*ibid.*, p. 29).

Rashbam goes along with rabbinic tradition here and does not adopt the interpretation that the שלש אלה--the three items or ways--mentioned in this verse are the "food, clothing and shelter" (שאר כסות ועונה) of the previous verse, although that interpretation appears to be much closer to the *peshaṭ*. iE also argues at length against that interpretation. See Hizq. who does offer that reading.

EXODUS XXI

puberty, even if six years have not elapsed and the jubilee year has not come.[38]

21:13 ואשר לא צדה IF HE DID NOT DO IT BY DESIGN: [צדה is to be understood] like [צודה in the phrase] (I Sam. 24:11), "You are bent on (צודה) taking my life." [Accordingly אשר לא צדה means] that he did not kill him in a premeditated manner.[39]

אנה לידו BUT IT CAME ABOUT BY AN ACT OF GOD: Because[40] he [i.e. the one who was killed accidentally] deserved to die according to divine law.[41]

ושמתי לך מקום I WILL: once you have towns to dwell in,[42] ASSIGN TO YOU A PLACE TO WHICH HE CAN FLEE.[43]

---

[38]The rabbinic explanation can be found in Rashi, following Mekhilta (ibid., pp. 30-31) and Qid. 4a.
Like Rashbam, see Hizq.

[39]So also Rashi, with the same prooftext but at greater length. Rashi writes explicitly that his interpretation is directed against Menahem who connects צדה to the root צ-ו-ד, "to hunt." Like Menahem, see Sekhel Tov ad Gen. 25:27.

[40]The implicit question that Rashbam is answering here is "why would God have caused such a person to die?" The question is asked explicitly by Rashi here. See also Rashi Makkot 10b, s.v. והא-להים אנה לידו.

[41]The same answer is provided by Rashi, at much greater length, following Makkot 10b.

[42]ערים לשבת; an allusion to Num. 35:2 where the context is also about cities of refuge.

[43]Rashbam is explaining that the future form, ושמתי, is used here because the cities of refuge were not then functional and would not be functional until the Israelites had "cities to dwell in," i.e. until they captured and settled some territory. He is opposing the interpretation of Rashi who (following Makkot 12b and Mekhilta [ibid. 4, p. 36]) says that this verse means that even in the wilderness the levitical camp would function as an area of refuge for accidental murderers. Like Rashbam, see iE, shorter comm., and Luzzatto.

21:12-17   Since they were already told (Ex. 20:13) "You shall not murder," and also (*ibid.*, vs. 12) "Honor your father and your mother," now [in vss. 12-15 and 17] the text explains the penalty involved [if one breaks those laws].[44] Similarly [one should explain that the verse here] (vs. 16) "He who kidnaps a man and sells him," [is written as an elaboration of the penalty for a law written in Ex. 20,] for it is written (Ex. 20:13) "You shall not steal," and the rabbis explained[45] that that verse refers to kidnapping, for one sees from the context[46] that that text [Ex. 20:13] is referring to capital crimes.

21:15 ומכה אביו HE WHO STRIKES HIS FATHER: The rabbis explained that the text is speaking only of a blow that results in a wound.[47]

21:18 או באגרוף [ONE STRIKES THE OTHER WITH A STONE] OR WITH AN אגרוף: According to the plain meaning of Scripture, אגרוף is to be understood--as the Targum understands it (כורמיזא)--as meaning some type of stone or brick. The context of the verse [also proves this interpretation as it] deals with throwing a stone. [I know that the Aramaic word כורמיזא means a type of stone or brick for] I found a similar usage concerning the verse (Lev. 14:40) "they will pull out the

---

[44] Rashbam attempts to explain a number of the laws of chapter 21 as elaborations of the laws of the Decalogue. See also his comm. ad 23:1 below. This exegetical direction can be traced back at least as far as Saadiah. See the Arabic fragment of Saadiah's comm. published in JQR (N.S.) 6 (1915-1916), p. 369 (English translation on p. 379), where the suggestion is made that the laws concerning slaves may also be seen as expansions of the first verse of the Decalogue. (So also JBS ad vs. 2.) This approach was later expanded by Abarbanel who argued that all the laws of chapters 21 and 22 are simply elaborations of the last five commandments of the Decalogue.

[45] Sanh. 86a. See also Mekhilta (*Ba-ḥodesh* 8, pp. 260-261) and Rashi ad Ex. 20:13, s.v. לא תגנב.

[46] דבר הלמד מעניינו, the twelfth of Rabbi Ishmael's thirteen exegetical principles. Rashbam uses the same language as that of his source in Sanh., *ibid*.

[47] So also Rashi, following Sanh. 11:1 and Mekhilta (*Neziqin* 5, pp. 42-43). See also comm. and notes below, ad 21:25.

stones האבנים," where the *Torat kohanim* writes, "[Perhaps he is also obligated to pull out not only the stones] but also the bricks and the טורמוסין."[48] So also in the verse (Is. 58:4) "You strike wickedly with an אגרוף."[49] [So here ONE STRIKES THE OTHER WITH . . . AN אגרוף means] "with a stone[50] large enough that it could cause death[51] and damage."[52]

---

[48]There is some confusion in the wording here. Presumably the spelling טורמוסין that appears in the ms. of Rashbam is a copyist's error. Rashbam must have written something like כורמוזין or כורמוסין or קורמוזין (and presumably that is the reading that he had before him in his *Torat kohanim*), as his point is that the same Aramaic word is used there--to describe a type of brick--and here--to translate the word אגרוף. Our texts of *Torat kohanim* have other readings there--either קרומדים or קורימים or קרמודים. See Rosin here, note 17.

[49]There, also, the Targum renders אגרוף as כורמיזא, and Rashbam feels that there, also, אגרוף means some type of brick.

[50]Rashbam knows well that אגרוף in post-biblical Hebrew means "fist." See e.g. the phrase בעלי אגרופין (Sanh. 49a). He also knows that the standard rabbinic explanation of אגרוף in the Bible is that it means "fist" there, too. See e.g. BQ 90b and Mekhilta *ibid*. 6, pp. 52-53. iE, both here and in Is., explains similarly to Rashbam. However some *peshaṭ*-oriented exegetes, like Menahem (s.v. אגרוף), say that אגרוף means a fist in the Bible too. See Qimhi, who explains, in Is., אגרוף as a fist, but, in his *Sefer ha-shorashim*, s.v. גרף, distinguishes between the rabbinic and the biblical usages of the word.

Most moderns interpret אגרוף as a fist, but see NEB here: "shovel," and Ryssel, cited by Driver, "a spade or a hoe."

[51]Rashbam's language here, באבן . . . אשר ימות בה . . . , is an allusion to the language of Num. 35:17, where the issue of whether the murder weapon "could cause death" is also discussed. Rosin's emendation--ימית instead of ימות-- is, accordingly, gratuitous.

[52]In its discussion of this verse, the Mekhilta (*ibid*., p. 53) deals with the legal requirement that, if the capital penalty is to be applied, the weapon must be large enough that a reasonable person would realize that it could kill. The starting point of the discussion of the Mekhilta is that while it is to be assumed that a stone "could cause death," one might think that an "אגרוף--a fist," is not necessarily large enough to kill. Had "אגרוף--fist" alone been written in the verse, then the text would not have taught us the principle that the weapon must be one that "could cause death."

Rashbam directly opposes that assumption. Following his explanation of אגרוף, he emphasizes that an אגרוף *is* a weapon that "could cause death."

21:19-21 אם יקום והתהלך IF HE THEN GETS UP AND WALKS: But [if he does not get up and walk but rather] dies [as a result of the blow] even a long time later, then the one who struck him shall be put to death.[53] However with his slave he is not culpable unless the slave (20) DIES THERE AND THEN, but (21) IF HE SURVIVES A DAY OR TWO then the owner is not culpable.[54]

שבתו HIS IDLENESS: [Compensation for the fact] that he must be idle from work.[55]

21:20 בשבט [WHEN A MAN STRIKES HIS SLAVE] WITH A ROD: I.e. with an instrument with which a man is wont to strike his slave to discipline him. But, following the plain meaning of Scripture, if he struck him with a a sword then even if the slave were to die *after* A DAY OR TWO, the owner would be liable for the death penalty. A sword is not an instrument of discipline, but an instrument of murder.[56]

---

[53] See similarly NJPSC: "Presumably, if a fatality ensues, then the laws set forth in vss. 12-14 [e.g. 'he shall be put to death'] are operative." So also JBS and Hizq.

[54] Rashbam is explaining the juxtaposition of the law of vss. 18-19, regarding killing or injuring a fellow free man, and the law of vss. 20-21, regarding killing or injuring a slave. See somewhat similarly Mekhlita *ibid.* 7, p. 56.

[55] The standard rabbinic explanation of the text. See e.g. BQ 8:1, and Rashi, here.
There is some discussion among the medieval exegetes as to whether one should see the verb י-ש-ב or the verb ש-ב-ת as the root of שבתו here. See e.g. ibn Ezra's shorter comm., where he argues for the root י-ש-ב; however, in his longer comm. he suggests that the rabbis thought that the root was ש-ב-ת and that they were right (ונכון הוא). See also Driver, who argues that one could reasonably see either י-ש-ב or ש-ב-ת as the root of שבתו. It is possible, but by no means certain, that Rashbam is supporting the understanding that ש-ב-ת is the root of שבתו, here. See Kasher, note 368.

[56] Rashbam opposes the understanding of Rashi, who suggests (following Mekhilta *ibid.*, pp. 58-59) that the word "rod" teaches that the death penalty is applied only if the murder weapon is, like a rod, capable of causing death. Rashbam argues that, following the *peshaṭ*, the word "rod" is used not with verse 20 in mind, to tell us when "he must be avenged," (only when something as lethal as a "rod" is used), but with verse 21 in mind, to tell us when "he is not to be avenged" (only when something as relatively harmless as a "rod" is used).

Our verse is describing the law that applies to a "Canaanite slave."[57] A Hebrew slave would not be referred to as being "THE OTHER'S PROPERTY (כספו)."[58] He is rather [to be treated] (Lev. 25:40), "as

---

As Rashbam explained above (s.v. אם יקום), the *peshaṭ* meaning of the Torah text (and the standard rabbinic understanding) is that any death that is the result of a premeditated blow by an assailant is punished with the death penalty, even if the injured party lingered on his sickbed for a long time before dying. The only exception is if the victim is a slave. Then the death penalty is applied only if the victim died right away, not if he lingered.

Rashbam adds here that this exceptional rule of "a day or two" is applied to a slave only if the blow was "with a rod," i.e. the standard type of implement that a master would use when disciplining his slave.

Rashbam writes that this interpretation is "following the *peshaṭ*." He knows it is not to be found in the standard halakhic sources. In fact, as Kasher argues (note 386), a careful reading of some sources such as Mekhilta, *ibid.*, would suggest that the halakhah applies the exceptional rule of "a day or two" no matter what implement the master used when hitting his slave. Presumably, Rashbam offers his explanation as exegesis, not as a suggestion that such should be Jewish law (just as when, in his comm. to vs. 6, he interpreted לעולם as meaning "forever," and labelled that interpretation as "according to the *peshaṭ*," he clearly was offering exegesis, and not a halakhic suggestion).

However, Maimonides, in his halakhic work (*Roṣeaḥ* 2:14) offers the same suggestion as Rashbam's—that the rule of "a day or two" applies only if an implement like a rod is used—and presumably he is suggesting that such should be Jewish law. Maimonides also realizes the innovative nature of such an explanation, and he introduces it with the words "יראה לי"—it would appear to me," the formula that he regularly uses when introducing a suggestion that he knows is not to be found in the standard halakhic sources. This interpretation can also be found in Philo; see the discussion by by S. Belkin in *The Joshua Finkel Festschrift*, Heb. section, pp. 41-42.

[57]עבד כנעני, the standard rabbinic term for a slave who was not born Jewish, as opposed to the "Hebrew slave" (עבד עברי) described above in vs. 2f.

[58]Rashi and basically all Jewish exegetes offer this same interpretation—that the law here applies only to a Cannaanite slave. Many Jewish exegetes, including Rashi, offer this same prooftext, originally found in the words of R. Ishmael in the Mekhilta (*ibid.*, pp. 57-58), that the word כספו could not be seen as a reference to a Jewish slave.

I have been unable to find any classical Jewish exegete who suggests, even just on the *peshaṭ* level, that the עבד of vss. 2-11 and the עבד of vss. 20-21 is the same kind of slave. See, however, ibn Kaspi here, who pointedly refrains from offering any interpretation for this verse, and then writes: "אם היה הרשות בידינו נפרשנו ולכן נעזוב הכל—were it permitted, I would explain this verse, but since it is not, I shall just leave it [uninterpreted]."

a hired or bound laborer." All the laws that apply to all Israelites apply also to the Hebrew slave,[59] except for the fact that his master [may] wed him to a female Canaanite slave.[60]

21:21 כי כספו הוא SINCE HE IS THE OTHER'S PROPERTY: And his owner is entitled to beat him[61] for the sake of discipline.[62]

---

[59]Including the law (see comm. above, s.v. אם יקום) that if such a Hebrew slave is struck by his master and dies as a result of the blow even many days later, then the master shall be liable for the death penalty.

On the essential legal equality of the Hebrew slave to other Jews, see similarly iE, shorter comm. ad vs. 26.

[60]See Qiddushin 15a, where the assertion is made that the only extra work done by a Hebrew slave is siring children for his master. See also Tos. there, s.v. כי, where a reading of the Talmud is quoted in which the prooftext cited to show that a Hebrew slave is basically equal to a free Israelite is the phrase that Rashbam cites here, "he shall be as a hired or bound laborer" (Lev. 25:40).

[61]ודינו להכותו. Arguably Rashbam might be saying something stronger--not just that the master is entitled to beat his slave, but that the master *ought* to beat his slave. See Gersonides' commentary here, where he argues that this verse teaches that a master ought to beat his slaves, in the same way that a father should feel obligated to use his rod to discipline his child.

[62]Rashbam is completing the explanation that he offered above, ad 20:20, s.v. בשבט. There is a slight reduction in the culpability of the master, because he is doing something that he is entitled (or perhaps obligated; see previous note) to do.

When one combines the two main points that Rashbam is making about verses 20 and 21--that the "striking" described in the text is for disciplinary purposes, and that the slave described by the text is a "Canaanite" slave--one again reaches a halakhically problematic understanding. One might reasonably deduce from Rashbam's words here that it is only when dealing with a Canaanite slave, who is the owner's property, that leniency is given when death is a result of overzealous disciplinary action. However, that is not the halakhah. Mishnah Makkot 2:2 and B. Makkot 8a-8b suggest that homicide committed as a result of an overzealous attempt to discipline a child, a Torah student or even an apprentice receives a diminished punishment even when the victim was *not* a slave (and surely that leniency would apply in the case of the Hebrew slave as well). Again we must conclude that Rashbam's comments here are to be seen as being only exegesis, and not having halakhic import.

EXODUS XXI

21:22 ולא יהיה אסון AND NO HARM FOLLOWS: To the woman.[63]

בפלילים BASED ON RECKONING: I.e. based on the estimation of the judges.[64]

21:23 ונתתה נפש תחת נפש THE PENALTY SHALL BE LIFE FOR LIFE: And he is exempt from paying for the damage to the fetus.[65]

21:24 עין תחת עין EYE FOR EYE: means the monetary worth of such an eye [as was damaged].[66]

---

[63]Clearly the incident being described does involve "harm" to the fetus.
Rashbam's one word comment, "לאשה--to the woman," is the same as that of Rashi (following Mekhilta, *ibid.* 8, p. 65).

[64]So also Rashi and almost all Jewish interpreters, following Mekhilta, *ibid.*, p. 66.
Rashbam slightly changes the language of his source and uses the word "estimation" (שומת) to describe what the court does. See BQ 5:4.

[65]So also Mekhilta, *ibid.*, p. 67. The halakhic principle of receiving only the greater of two punishments (קים ליה בדרבה מיניה)--in this case death, not a fine--is operative here.
The phraseology that Rashbam uses here, ופטור מדמי ולדות, is found verbatim in BQ 8:2.

[66]Again here Rashbam does not suggest, even on the *peshat* level, that the meaning of this verse is precise physical retaliation. Rashbam rather follows the standard rabbinic reading, that the verse refers to a monetary payment. So also Rashi (following Mekhilta *ibid.* [pp. 67-69], and many other rabbinic sources.
Generally most of the classical *peshat*-oriented exegetes adopt, like Rashbam, the rabbinic understanding of this verse. See e.g the argumentation provided here by Rashbam's colleague, JBS, in support of the rabbinic understanding. But see iE's longer comm., where he finds some meaning and relevance in the literal level of meaning, and see also Maimonides, *Guide* 3:41.

21:24-5 The rabbis explained why each of these items [EYE, TOOTH, HAND, FOOT, BURN, WOUND, and BRUISE, listed in vss. 24-25] had to be mentioned.[67]

21:24-5 This [first] verse (24), EYE FOR EYE . . ., deals entirely with [injuries that involve] the loss of a limb. [In the second verse,] (25) BURN FOR BURN . . ., even though there is no loss of a limb in any of these injuries, the one who causes the injury makes payment to compensate for pain, for embarrassment and for the cost of the treatment.[68]

פצע: means a wound caused by a sword, while חבורה refers to a trivial wound, [e.g.] on the fingernails.[69]

---

[67]Again here Rashbam relies on halakhic exegesis in his *peshaṭ* commentary, this time to explain why so many examples had to be given by the text to illustrate the legal principle, and perhaps also to explain what the precise difference is between some of these terms. See Mekhilta, *ibid.*, p. 69, and BQ 84b.

[68]Generally in rabbinic law (e.g. BQ 8:1) a person who injures another person must make restitution under five different categories--the three listed here by Rashbam and also נזק, the compensation for a permanent diminution in the "value" of the person injured, and שבת, payment for the loss of income during the time that the injured party is recuperating from the injury. Rashbam says that this list of more minor injuries in verse 25 teaches us that even if the injury is such that there is no permanent damage, and there is no recuperation period for the injured party, still the assailant must make payment under the three remaining categories.

Rashbam's explanation of the distinction in types of injuries between vs. 24 and vs. 25 is essentially the same as that of Rashi, s.v. כויה. However, their explanations of the significance of the distinction--i.e. of what one "learns" from this second verse--is different. Rashi, s.v. פצע, says (following BQ 84a and 85a) that verse 25 teaches that even when the assailant *does* make restitution for the limb that was lost, the assailant must also pay for the pain of the injured party. So also JBS. Rashbam says quite differently that verse 25 teaches that there are payments made for pain even when there is *no* payment necessary for the loss of a limb.

[69]While Rashbam's interpretation of פצע is uncontroversial and generally agreed upon, his explanation of חבורה is strange. Both traditional and moderns sources see חבורה as meaning a bruise. The Mekhilta (*ibid.*, p. 69) specifically says that since bruises are covered by the word חבורה, one must interpret כויה as meaning something that does *not* produce a bruise (e.g. a wound to the fingernail). It is also the clear

21:26 תחת עינו [HE SHALL LET HIM GO FREE] ON ACCOUNT OF HIS EYE: The text refers to a "Canaanite slave."[70]

21:28 סקול יסקל השור THE OX SHALL BE STONED: According to the plain meaning of Scripture, the phrase ITS FLESH SHALL NOT BE EATEN means that after the ox is stoned its flesh may not be given to a dog or to a non-Jew for them to eat it. [This meat may not be used in any way,] even though concerning the meat of animals that died of natural causes or that were torn by beasts[71] the Torah says that one may "sell it to a non-Jew" (Deut. 14:21) or "throw it to the dogs" (Ex. 22:30), i.e. one may derive benefit from the meat of such animals [even] after they are stoned.[72] The rabbis, however, explained that [the reason

---

assumption of BQ 8:1 that a wound on the fingernail is *not* a חבורה. So also Rashi, here. And see also Rashbam's own comm. to 21:15, where he explains, following rabbinic tradition, that he who strikes his father or mother is culpable only if the assault produces a חבורה. Presumably Rashbam there was using the word חבורה in its standard sense of bruise.

It is possible that the text of Rashbam's comm. that we are dealing with here is corrupt. Rashbam may have written here the standard explanation that כויה, not חבורה, means "a trivial wound [e.g.] on the fingernails," and a copyist's error may have changed the word כויה to חבורה. It is also unlikely, but possible, that when Rashbam writes here בציפורניו he means a wound inflicted *by* fingernails, not *on* the fingernails.

[70] I.e. a slave who was not born Jewish.
Again Rashbam follows the standard halakhic interpretation (e.g. Mekhilta *ibid.* 9, p. 70, and Rashi, here), that the slave described in vss. 26-27 is not the Hebrew slave whose status is discussed in vss. 2-11. See also comm. and notes above, ad vs. 20. See also iE here, shorter comm., who mentions the Karaite interpretation that the slave here is a Hebrew slave. iE then says that there is nothing intrinsically superior about either of the two interpretations, so one should follow the traditional understanding.

[71] I.e. beasts whose meat is not kosher for Jews themselves to eat.

[72] The precise wording of Rashbam's comment here, אותם מותרים בהנאה לאחר סקילה, is difficult and perhaps corrupt. In any case Rashbam's point is understood: generally one may derive benefit from the meat of an animal that was not slaughtered properly, no matter how that animal died, even if that animal was killed by stoning. However, according to Jewish law, when any animal (not just an ox) is killed by stoning after that animal killed a human, no benefit may be derived from the meat.

that the phrase ITS FLESH SHALL NOT BE EATEN was written was to teach us that] if a legal decision has been made to kill the ox, and if the owners slaughter the ox ritually after that decision is made, then the ox's flesh may still not be eaten.[73]

ובעל השור נקי THE OWNER OF THE OX IS NOT TO BE PUNISHED: So long as he was not warned.[74]

---

[73] Rashbam contrasts his explanation with that of the rabbis. Both in the Mekhilta (*ibid.*, p. 78) and in BQ 41a the rabbis say explicitly that the phrase, "its flesh may not be eaten," is ostensibly redundant after the instruction to stone the ox. Then they explain that the phrase must have been written to cover the case of that ox which was slaughtered after the decision to stone him was made, but before that verdict could be carried out. Rashbam feels that that is not the *peshat* of the verse.

I feel that the main reason that he points that out is to oppose Rashi's commentary on this verse. Rashi (s.v. ולא יאכל) cites the midrashic explanation. Then he also cites a midrashic explanation for the phrase ובעל השור נקי. Following those two explanations, Rashi offers his own *peshat* explanation, but only of the phrase ובעל השור נקי. Presumably this would imply that Rashi is satisfied with the rabbinic explanation of the phrase, "its flesh may not be eaten," and feels no need to offer his own *peshat* understanding of that phrase. Then Rashbam offers *his peshat* explanation, which differs from the standard rabbinic understanding of *both* phrases.

Rashbam's explanation may be found also in JBS, in Maimonides, *Ma'akhalot 'asurot* 4:22 and in Mekhilta de-Rabbi Shimon bar Yohai. See Kasher, note 401.

[74] In other words, the phrase ובעל השור נקי is written here in order to emphasize more explicitly the difference between the fate of the owner of an ox who *was* warned and asked to take precautions (vss. 29-30), and the fate of the owner of an ox which has no history of goring. So also Rashi, who specifically contrasts this *peshat* interpretation with the standard rabbinic interpretation found in BQ (*ibid.*). See previous note. It should be noted that the interpretation offered here by Rashi and Rashbam is the same as one opinion found in the Mekhilta (*ibid.*, p. 80), the opinion of R. Yehudah ben Batera.

EXODUS XXI 245

21:29 וגם בעליו יומת AND ITS OWNER TOO SHALL BE PUT TO DEATH: by the hand of God.[75] And if he gives a ransom,[76] then he is exempt also from death by the hand of God.[77]

21:32 אם עבד IF THE OX GORES A Canaanite[78] SLAVE [. . . HE SHALL PAY THIRTY SHEKELS]: This rule applies only to an ox whose owner had been warned.[79] However, if the goring is done by an

---

[75] In other words, יומת does not mean that an earthly court should execute the owner of the ox. It means only that God will take care of his punishment.

So also Rashi and almost all Jewish exegetes, following Mekhilta *ibid.*, p. 85. See also Rashi's comm. ad Sanh. 15b, s.v. אימא, who labels this interpretation as one that is very distant from the *peshat*. Nevertheless, Rashbam and most Jewish exegetes simply toe the halakhic line here, perhaps because they are are uncomfortable with the implication of the *peshat*, that the capital penalty would be applied to cases of negligence. In any case, some exegetes do offer more *peshat*-oriented interpretations of this passage. See e.g. Hizquni and Luzzatto, who both say explicitly that the *peshat* indicates a capital penalty administered by a human court. Also, once again here (see notes above ad vs. 24) iE tries to find some meaning and relevance in the *peshat* level of understanding. See also JBS, who suggests that the *peshat* here implies that sometimes the owner of a goring ox *will* be put to death for the actions of his ox, particularly when the negligence can be shown to have been malicious.

See Nahm., who attempts to find exegetical grounds for the rabbinic interpretation.

[76] As outlined in vs. 30.

[77] So also LT.

It would appear that Rashbam is siding with the opinion of R. Akiva over the opinion of R. Ishmael in the Mekhilta (*ibid.*, p. 86). R. Akiva says that "the redemption of *his* life" means the life of the owner of the ox, i.e. that the ransom is paid by the owner of the ox to free himself from the greater penalty. On the other hand R. Ishmael interprets the verse as saying that the payment is described as compensation for "*his* life," i.e. for the life of the person killed by the ox. Both opinions are cited by Rashi, without expressing a preference.

[78] So also Rashi and almost all Jewish exegetes, following Mekhilta (*ibid.* 11, p. 89). See iE, shorter comm., where he mentions the Karaite interpretation that the slave described here is the Hebrew slave of vss. 2-11.

[79] I.e. the שור מועד, described in vs. 29.

ox whose owner had not been warned,[80] then the owner is exempt from payment.[81]

21:33 כי יפתח איש בור Not only WHEN A MAN OPENS A deep PIT: that is already completed and he is negligent and fails to cover it, but even IF A MAN IS in the middle of DIGGING (יכרה) a pit and he fails to cover it up each evening when he leaves his work--because he knows that the next day he will have to go back into the pit to dig some more and it would be burdensome to cover the pit every day--still he is liable [in both situations].[82]

---

[80]I.e. by a שור תם.

[81]This is the standard halakhic understanding of this verse. See e.g. Arakhin 3:3 and b. Arakhin 14b.

[82]Rashbam is opposing the explanation offered by Rashi. Both Rashi and Rashbam make the standard talmudic assumption that the second element of the verse, כי יכרה, ought to teach us something "greater" or "more novel" than what one may learn from the first element. Rashi assumes that יפתח means to uncover a pit that was already dug, and that יכרה means to dig a new pit. He then asks (following BQ 51a; and see also Mekhilta ibid., p. 91), "If one is liable for uncovering a pit that one did not even dig, is it not self-evident that one would also be liable for digging a pit ab initio oneself?" Rashi then (again following BQ) offers a midrashic solution to the problem.

Rashbam's comm. essentially says that the perceived difficulty is not a problem, because the words יפתח and יכרה mean something different from what Rashi thinks that they mean. The word יפתח, according to Rashbam, means to dig a complete pit. The word יכרה means to be in the middle of the process of digging. The text accordingly *does* proceed from the minor to the major and says that the digger is liable not only if the pit is totally finished, but also if the digging is still going on.

See notes above, ad 16:24, and below, ad 22:5, s.v. הגדיש. Note that here, in a legal passage, both Rashbam and Rashi assume that the לא זו אף זו principle of organization--of proceeding from the "less novel" to the "more novel"--ought to apply.

Rashbam's understanding of יפתח and יכרה appears to be original. Most medieval and modern commentators follow Rashi and the Talmud, but see Hizq. and Luzzatto, who are similar to Rashbam.

21:34 בעל הבור THE ONE RESPONSIBLE FOR THE PIT: I.e. the one who finished digging it (הפותח) or who was in the process of digging it (הכורה).[83]

והמת יהיה לו [HE SHALL PAY THE PRICE TO THE OWNER] BUT THE DEAD ANIMAL SHALL BELONG TO HIM: According to the plain meaning of Scripture, since the person who is responsible for the damages pays the entire price [of the dead animal], the carcass now logically belongs to him. However, the rabbis interpreted the verse to mean that any depreciation in the value of the carcass [between the time of the damages and the time when the trial took place] is to be absorbed by the person whose animal was damaged.[84]

---

[83]See comm. and notes to the previous verse.
   The phrase בעל הבור literally means the owner of the pit. Such an understanding is seen as difficult in rabbinic literature as the pit of our verse is generally seen as being on public property (see e.g. BQ 49b), and as such is not owned by the person who dug it. Rashbam's explanation here is the traditional halakhic one--that בעל הבור means the person who dug it. So also Rashi, JBS and iE (longer comm.) here, and R. Ishmael in BQ. See also Pes. 6b: "שני דברים אינן ברשותו של אדם ועשאן הכתוב כאילו ברשותו ואלו הן בור ברשות הרבים...--there are two items that do not belong to any person, but the Torah describes them as belonging to some person and these are they: a pit on public property . . . ."

[84]See BQ 10b, Mekhilta ibid., pp. 93-94, and Rashi here.
   The word לו in this verse is, at least theoretically, ambiguous. It could refer either to the one who caused the damages, the "owner" of the pit, or to the one who absorbed the damages, the owner of the animal. Rashi and JBS follow the talmudic opinion that לו refers to the animal's owner. Rashbam acknowledges the rabbinic position but notes that the most logical explanation, the peshaṭ here, is that the one who caused the damages makes restitution for the full value of the animal and then keeps the carcass. So also iE, shorter comm. (in the name of "יש אומרים--some say"), Nahm. (ad vs. 36) and Hizq.
   It is possible that Rashbam is taking issue with Rashi not only concerning the peshaṭ meaning of the text, but also concerning the way that Rashi represents the talmudic position. As Nahm. notes, the practical halakhic conclusion of the talmudic discussion is not quoted by Rashi (ולא בירר את דינו). The Talmud concludes that the implication of saying that the carcass belongs to the damaged party must be seen as related to the issue of depreciation, an issue that Rashi does not mention in his comm. So after offering his peshaṭ understanding, Rashbam then explains the rabbinic understanding and mentions the issue of depreciation, thus, to his mind, formulating the rabbinic position in a more clear and complete manner than Rashi did.

21:35 ‏וחצו את כספו‎ [THEY SHALL SELL THE LIVE OX] AND DIVIDE ITS PRICE . . .: The rabbis explained[85] the entire verse in such a way that it adds up to payment of half of the damages; they explained the value of the living ox and the value of the dead ox in such a way that the payment will work out to be half of the damages.[86]

21:37 ‏חמשה בקר‎ [HE SHALL PAY] FIVE OXEN [FOR THE OX AND FOUR SHEEP FOR THE SHEEP]: The rabbis explained[87] that [the greater penalty is applied in the case of theft of an ox, because] an ox was kept from doing work.[88]

---

[85]Mekhilta, *ibid.* 12, p. 95, and BQ 34a.

[86]So also Rashi, at much greater length, and virtually all Jewish exegetes. See also NJPSC: "one ox kills another of presumed equal worth."

[87]The opinion of R. Meir in Mekhilta *ibid.*, p. 99 and in BQ 79b.

[88]However the penalty for theft of a sheep, that has no work to do, is only fourfold payment, not fivefold.
  Rashi cites two talmudic opinions to explain the distinction between an ox and a sheep, the opinion of R. Meir and the opinion of R. Yohanan b. Zakkai. ("God has consideration for the dignity of human beings. For an ox, since it walked with its legs, the thief pays fivefold. For the lamb, since he had to carry it on its shoulders, he pays only fourfold.") Presumably Rashbam feels that R. Meir's position better represents the *peshaṭ* of the text. See also iE, who cites R. Meir's explanation (and one other interesting explanation), but not R. Yohanan b. Zakkai's.

EXODUS XXII

22:1-2 אם במחתרת IF THE THIEF IS SEIZED WHILE TUNNELING: and at night, then [we may reasonably conclude] that he is coming [willing] to kill or to be killed.[1] Accordingly, אין לו דמים--THERE IS NO BLOODGUILT, i.e. there is no punishment required to make up for his loss of life.[2] Rather, he who kills the thief is exonerated. However, (2) אם זרחה השמש IF THE SUN SHONE, i.e. if he came to steal during the day, [THERE IS BLOODGUILT IN THAT CASE].[3]

---

[1] For the assumption that a thief who comes "tunneling" is willing to kill, see Sanh. 72a. For Rashbam's phrase, להרוג או ליהרג--to kill or to be killed, see Midrash Ruth Rabba 4:1 or Rashi ad Pes. 25b, s.v. יהרג.

[2] Rashbam's explanation opposes that of Rashi (here, and ad Sanh. 72a, s.v. מאי) who suggests that אין לו דמים means that the murdered thief is legally lifeless (and accordingly he who kills that thief is not guilty of killing a living human being). Rashbam opposes Rashi's understanding in two ways. While Rashi feels that לו refers to the murdered thief, Rashbam feels that לו refers to the one who killed that thief. And while Rashi interprets דמים as "life," Rashbam understands it to mean "bloodguilt." Like Rashbam, see iE.
  Almost all moderns follow Rashbam's understanding. But see Luzzatto's impassioned defense of Rashi: "אבל רש"י היה לו חיך טועם הדיבור העברי והבין הדבר על בוריו . . . ברוך שבחר ברש"י ונתן ליראיו עין רואה ואזן שומעת --Rashi's palate, however, could distinguish the proper flavor of the Hebrew idiom, and so he understood this phrase properly. Blessed be He [God] who chose Rashi, and gave a discerning eye and an understanding ear to those who fear Him."

[3] I.e. the capital penalty would apply to the person who killed a thief who came during the day.
  Rashbam's interpretation, here, opposes the standard halakhic understanding of this verse. The Mekhilta (ibid. 13, p. 102) expressly rejects the possibility of understanding the reference to the sun shining as meaning that verse 1 speaks of a thief at night, and verse 2 of a thief during the day. See also similarly Tosefta Sanh. 11:5, and b. Sanh. 72a. Rashi and most Jewish exegetes follow the talmudic reading and interpret the reference to the sun shining as an allegory. Rashbam offers his *peshaṭ* interpretation without mentioning the rabbinic understanding and without writing

22:3 אם המצא תמצא בידו IF WHAT HE STOLE IS FOUND IN HIS HAND: i.e he did not sell it, ALIVE, i.e. he did not slaughter it, then HE SHALL PAY DOUBLE, and not fourfold or fivefold.[4]

22:4 כי יבער: means to have one's animal graze on somebody else's property.[5]

---

explicitly that his understanding is only to be considered on the *peshaṭ* level.

It is interesting to note that on this particular passage, the *peshaṭ* understanding had more popularity than usual among Jewish exegetes. See among others iE, Nahm., JBS and R. Abraham b. David (gloss of Maimonides, *Genevah* 9:8) who all interpret, similarly to Rashbam, that the text is differentiating between a thief at night and a thief during the day.

[4]Rashbam explains that the words "in his hand" and "alive" are written in this verse in order to make the contrast and the connection between this verse and 21:37 more clear. If a thief slaughters or sells a stolen animal, his punishment is fourfold or fivefold payment (21:37). But if the animal is neither slaughtered nor sold, i.e. the thief still has it "in his hand" and "alive," then the penalty is just double payment (22:3).

Rashbam's interpretation is partially in agreement with that of Rashi and partially not. Rashi says that the word "בידו--in his hand" teaches us that the animal was neither slaughtered nor sold. However, Rashi says further (following Mekhilta *ibid.*, p. 104) that the word חיים does not mean that the *stolen* animal is still alive, but rather that the *payment* should be made on the basis of living, not dead, animals: חיים שנים ישלם--he should pay double "living" animals.

Rashbam rejects Rashi's reading, which ignores the cantillation signs and the plain sense of Scripture. See JBS, who understands the *peshaṭ* in the same way that Rashbam does, but explains that that reading is in conflict with the accepted halakhah. Rashbam's reading is saying, by implication, that the payment for a stolen "ox, ass or sheep" is double, if the animal is still alive, but more if the animal was sold or slaughtered. But the Mishnah (BQ 7:1) specifically teaches that fourfold and fivefold payment penalties apply only to oxen and sheep, not to asses (or any other animal). See also iE's longer comm., where he shows that he too is aware of that problem, and similarly Qara, as cited by Gad, p. 24. Rashbam, though, simply offers his *peshaṭ* reading without apologies.

Moderns understand the text as Rashbam does. See e.g Noth and Childs.

[5]Rashi (following BQ 2b-3a) suggests that יבער is a general term for property damage caused by an animal, either through trampling or through grazing. Rashbam says that the term refers specifically to grazing. Like Rashbam, see iE shorter comm. Like Rashi, see JBS. Moderns generally understand as Rashbam does.

It should be noted that almost all Jewish exegetes avoid interpreting יבער here as a reference to a fire, an interpretation found in some few moderns. See e.g.

EXODUS XXII

מיטב שדהו [HE SHALL MAKE RESTITUTION] ACCORDING TO THE BEST OF HIS[6] FIELD: He [i.e. the owner of the animal that caused the damages] should make restitution by paying from the best[7] property that he owns, or from chattels, to the person who suffered the damages. That is how the rabbis explained the passage.[8] According to the plain meaning of Scripture, the verse means that payment should be based upon the highest quality produce found in the field or the vineyard of the person whose field was damaged,[9] for the animals that caused the damage may have consumed the best produce of the field.[10]

Hoffmann and Bäntsch, cited by Childs, pp. 474-475, and Driver. Kasher (vol. 18, appendix 6, pp. 162-164) also found a few classical Jewish proponents of that position, including Menahem (s.v. בער), some mss. of the Jerusalem Targum, here, and the opinion of a student of Rabbenu Peretz (as quoted in *Shiṭṭah Mequbbeṣet* ad BQ 22a).

[6]The Hebrew is ambiguous; "his" could refer either to the owner of the field or to the owner of the animal that caused the damages. Both opinions are mentioned in Rashbam's comment.

[7]עידית. The talmudic system assumes that there are various types of property, some more desirable than others. עידית is the technical term for choice land that is easy to sell.

[8]E.g. Mekhilta (*ibid.* 14, p. 110) and Gittin 5:1. So also Rashi, here.

[9]In other words, as opposed to the first explanation that interprets "his field" as referring to the field of the one who pays, Rashbam interprets "his field" as a reference to the field that was damaged. Furthermore, while the first explanation sees "מיטב--the best" as a reference to the type of payment that is acceptable, the second explanation sees מיטב as a description of the way that such payment should be calculated.

[10]In other words, since there is no way to judge the quality of the produce that the animal already consumed, as the evidence is no longer before us, one should assume that the quality of that damaged section was equivalent to that of the best intact section of that same field. Payment should be calculated on the basis of the assumption that what was consumed was the choicest section of the field.

This interpretation of the verse is mentioned in Gittin 48b and BQ 6b by R. Idi b. Avin, who suggests that that is how R. Ishmael understands the verse. R. Idi's suggestion is immediately dismissed by the Talmud as halakhically untenable. Like Rashbam, see JBS, who also presents both the *peshaṭ* understanding and the rabbinic position. See also Luzzatto's defense of Rashbam's interpretation against the halakhic arguments raised in the Talmud.

22:5 כי תצא אש WHEN A FIRE SPREADS: I.e. the owner of the fire did not watch over the fire properly and an ordinary wind[11] made the fire spread and cause damage.[12] [AND THE FIRE CONSUMES] גדיש, [stacked grain] that has already been harvested, OR הקמה, [grain that is still] attached to the ground, OR even [if it consumes] השדה, even if it [merely] laps and singes his neighbor's stones.[13]

---

[11] If the fire is spread by a wind of extraordinary strength, i.e. a wind that could not have been expected, then the owner of the fire is not liable.

[12] Rashbam's explanation is very similar to that of Rashi. However, Rashi says that the fire spread because of thorns, while Rashbam says that an ordinary wind spread it. The assumption that if the fire is spread by an ordinary wind then the one who set the fire is liable, is one possible understanding of the talmudic position. Alternatively it is possible that the Talmud feels that if any wind, even an ordinary one, is responsible for the fire spreading, then the one who set the fire is *not* liable. See BQ 6:4 and Tos. ad BQ 59b, s.v. לבתה, and ad BB 26a, s.v. זיקא.

Like Rashbam, see NJPSC: "the flames spread by the wind to someone else's property."

[13] The three types of damages are arranged, according to Rashbam, in descending order. It is most clear that one would be responsible for damage to a גדיש, stacked grain, and least clear that one would be liable for the trivial damages to the stones of the field.

See BQ 60a, where the Talmud attempts to explain why the Torah must list all these different items damaged by the fire. Rashbam's explanation is partially dependent on that talmudic passage: the phrase "לכחה וסכסכה אבניו--laps and singes his stones," is the explanation offered, almost verbatim, both by the Talmud and by Rashbam for what it means for the field itself to be damaged. But Rashbam's comment differs from that of the Talmud in a number of ways. First, the Talmud understands that there are *four* items listed by the Torah as having been damaged--the three that Rashbam discusses, and thorns (קוצים). (Perhaps Rashbam, like Rashi, sees the "thorns" mentioned in our verse as a vehicle for spreading the fire, not as an item whose destruction requires compensation.) Furthermore, the Talmud tries to explain why each of the four elements had to be written. It explains, for example, why it would not have been sufficient to write the least self-evident item, השדה, and then we could have figured out that one is surely liable for items like stacked grain. Rashbam does not present such arguments. For Rashbam it is sufficient to note that the text progresses from the minor to the major, i.e. from the most obvious to the least obvious.

See similarly comm. and notes ad 16:24 and ad 21:33.

כי יתן איש אל רעהו כסף או כלים 22:6-12 WHEN A MAN GIVES MONEY OR GOODS TO ANOTHER FOR SAFEKEEPING: In this [first] section (vss. 6-8), the bailee is described as *not* being liable in a case of theft or loss. In the second section (vss. 9-12), the bailee *is* described as being responsible in a case of theft or loss. The rabbis explained that the first section refers to a bailee who is *not* being remunerated,[14] while the second section refers to a bailee who *is* being remunerated.[15]

However, following the plain meaning of Scripture, the first section, "WHEN A MAN GIVES MONEY OR GOODS TO ANOTHER FOR SAFEKEEPING," refers to the guarding of removables that are commonly kept inside of one's house, and that were given to him so that he would guard them in the same way that he guards his own possessions.[16] That is why, if they were stolen from his house,[17] the bailee is not responsible, for he guarded them [in the expected manner,] as one guards one's own possessions. But in the second section (vss. 9-12), "WHEN A MAN GIVES TO HIS NEIGHBOR AN ASS, AN OX, A SHEEP OR ANY OTHER ANIMAL TO GUARD," since animals commonly graze outdoors it is to be assumed that when he entrusted them [to the bailee] he expected that the bailee would protect

---

[14]שומר חנם.

[15]שומר שכר. This distinction may be found in many places in rabbinic literature; see e.g. BM 94b and Rashi ad vs. 9, s.v. כי. Rashbam and Rashi both use the language of that talmudic passage, and refer to the two different sections as the first and the second פרשה.

[16]כשמירת חפציו. The idea that a bailee is expected to guard a pledge "in the same way that he guards his own possessions" is not the standard way that the halakhah describes a bailee's responsibility. The standard phrase is that a bailee should guard his pledge כדרך השומרים, in the manner that bailees standardly guard pledges. (See e.g. BM 3:10 and passim.) As a matter of fact, halakhists generally write that it is *not* sufficient for a bailee to guard other people's property in the same way that he guards his own property, if such guarding falls below the general standard of the way that bailees guard pledges. (See e.g. Alfasi and Rabbenu Asher ad BM 42a, and Maimonides, *She'elah ufiqqadon* 4:3.)

[17]Here, too, Rashbam's language is not entirely in consonance with halakhah. The standard halakhic position (BM 42a) is that money (as opposed to other removables) can only be properly guarded by more extreme steps, such as burying it in the ground.

them from thieves. Accordingly, if they were stolen, the bailee is responsible.[18]

---

[18]Rashbam offers a novel understanding of these verses. Mekhilta (*ibid.* 15, p. 118) mentions and then specifically rules out the possibility of saying that the Torah is making a distinction between guarding removables and guarding animals. See also the language of BM 3:1: המפקיד אצל חבירו בהמה או כלים, and the discussion there in the Talmud (b. 33b): למה ליה למתני בהמה ולמה ליה למתני כלים.

A number of commentators suggest that when the Torah speaks of "money or goods" (in vs. 6) and of animals (in vs. 9), the Torah is simply trying to give illustrative examples of the rabbinic distinction between a paid bailee and an unpaid bailee. Generally, one who guards removables is not paid, while one who guards animals is. So, these commentators would argue, distinguishing between guarding removables and guarding animals is tantamount to distinguishing between guarding for free and guarding for pay. For this explanation, see e.g. iE (shorter comm.), Nahm., Hizq. and Seforno. See also Tos. ad BM 41b, s.v. קרנא, where "Rabbenu Shemuel," i.e. Rashbam himself, suggests that some of the rabbis of the Talmud may have understood that the Torah's distinction between "money or goods," on the one hand, and animals, on the other hand, logically leads one to conclude (מסברא ידעינן) that the Torah really wishes to distinguish between paid and unpaid bailees.

Here, though, in his exegetical work, Rashbam makes no such claim. Here Rashbam depicts the two interpretations--that the distinction is "goods/animals" or that the distinction is "unpaid/paid"--as two different, unrelated interpretations. Rashbam here offers an interpretation wherein the *peshaṭ* is presented in such a way that it contradicts the accepted halakhah. (True, most bailees who guard animals are remunerated. But what happens if one such bailee is *not* remunerated, guards the animals in a responsible manner [כדרך השומרין], and still the animals are stolen from him? The halakhah would say that such a bailee is *not* responsible to pay. Rashbam's *peshaṭ* would imply that he *is* responsible.)

Rashbam could easily have presented the *peshaṭ* and the halakhah here as complementary, just as many other exegetes do and just as he himself is quoted as doing in Tos. (*ibid.*) Yet he pointedly does not. See also Luzzatto, who, following Rashbam, writes specifically that the Torah intended that a bailee who guards animals but is not paid for his services should still be responsible in the case of theft, and that the rabbis simply were more lenient than the Torah would suggest.

For a discussion of the implications of Rashbam's interpretation here, see my "Truth or *Peshaṭ*," pp. 275-278. See also the unconvincing attempts of Y. Cooperman, *Lifeshuṭo shel miqra'*," (Jerusalem, 1981), pp. 221-222, to reconcile Rashbam's position and the halakhah. And see Rashbam's comm. below, ad vs. 14, where it is clear that he does ultimately accept the halakhic idea that the distinction between bailees who pay in cases of theft and bailees who do not pay *is* a function of the question of whether or not they are remunerated.

EXODUS XXII

22:7-8 אם לא ימצא הגנב IF THE THIEF IS NOT FOUND: Our rabbis interpreted that these verses mean: אם לא ימצא, IF IT IS NOT FOUND that what the bailee says--"it was stolen from me"--is true, but rather the bailee himself stole the pledge, and if that [dishonest] bailee נקרב, HAD COME FORWARD before the judges and sworn [falsely that he was not the thief], then he himself[19] (8) ישלם, SHOULD PAY DOUBLE.[20] [In other words,] when THE JUDGES ירשיעון FIND HIM GUILTY, then ישלם שנים לרעהו, HE SHALL PAY DOUBLE TO HIS NEIGHBOR.[21]

I, however, will explain these verses according to the plain sense of Scripture. (7) IF THE THIEF IS NOT CAUGHT, THE בעל הבית, i.e. the bailee,[22] SHALL COME FORWARD [and declare][23] THAT

---

[19]I.e. that crooked bailee.

Verse 6 says that "if *the thief* is caught, he shall pay double." Now verses 7-8 add (according to this understanding) that if the thief is actually the bailee, then the bailee himself should pay double, if he had previously sworn falsely to his innocence. This comparison between vs. 6 and vs. 7 underlies the talmudic discussion in BQ 106b; see Rashi there, s.v. היקישא הוא.

[20]כפל, the standard rabbinic term. See e.g. BQ 7:1.

[21]Rashbam presents here the standard halakhic understanding of these verses, found in Rashi here, based on BQ 107b and Mekhilta (*ibid.* 15, pp. 115-120).

[22]Rashbam agrees with the standard halakhic approach of seeing the בעל הבית here as the bailee. So also Rashi.

[23]Rashbam's *peshaṭ* retelling of this verse does not differ greatly from the rabbinic understanding, except in this one point. The rabbis say that the only bailee who must pay double is the bailee who swore falsely as to his innocence and then witnesses proved that that bailee himself was the thief. In other cases, the penalty would be as outlined in Lev. 5:20-24: that he "pay back the principal amount and add a fifth part to it." See e.g. Rashi, here, Mekhilta, *ibid.*, and BQ 63b.

In his restatement of the rabbinic position above, Rashbam writes clearly that the bailee swore falsely as to his innocence (ואם נקרב ונשבע). In Rashbam's *peshaṭ* reiteration of the verse there is no mention of swearing. This aspect of Rashbam's interpretation of these verses is the most novel and halakhically daring--the suggestion that all bailees who expropriate the pledged item and protest their innocence are liable for the penalty of double payment. Such an understanding again has Rashbam offering a *peshaṭ* reading of a biblical law that reaches different legal conclusions than the accepted halakhah. See BQ 63b, where the Talmud specifically considers and rules out the possibility of reading these verses as referring to all dishonest bailees, even those

HE HAS NOT LAID HANDS ON THE OTHER'S PROPERTY, but that the pledge was stolen from him. Then the bailee will be absolved of responsibility.[24] (8) IN ALL CASES OF MISAPPROPRIATION, when the pledged item was stolen, whether that pledge was AN OX or AN ASS or A SHEEP or A GARMENT or ANY OTHER LOST ITEM about which the bailor says "כי הוא זה"--THIS IS the money that was stolen from me,"[25] then either the thief or the [dishonest] bailee[26]

---

who did not swear falsely, and see also similarly Mekhilta (*ibid.*, p. 116). Rashi, iE, JBS and almost all Jewish exegetes interpret the verses as referring to a bailee who swore falsely. Like Rashbam, see Luzzatto who argues at length *against* seeing a reference to swearing in this verse.

[24]The standard halakhic understanding is that the end of verse 7 is simply the protasis that leads into verse eight: "(7) *if* he swore that he had not laid hands . . . (8) and it was found to be a case of misappropriation by the bailee, then he shall pay double." See e.g. Rashi. Rashbam suggests that the end of verse seven is an independent statement, that an accused bailee need only swear to his innocence and then he is absolved of any further responsibility (until and unless testimony is brought to disprove his oath).

While Rashbam's exegesis of this phrase may differ from the more traditional understanding, certainly the conclusion that he draws is compatible with halakhah. Like Rashbam, see also JBS, here.

[25]Rashbam disagrees here both with the standard rabbinic understanding of this phrase and with Rashi's. As Rashi himself writes, the rabbis deduce from this phrase that swearing is generally required in cases of partial admission: if a party being sued denies part of the claim but admits part of it then he is required to take an oath. (See e.g. Mekhilta, *ibid.*, p. 119, BQ 107a and BM 3a.) According to that explanation, the words "כי הוא זה" are said by the party who is being accused.

Rashi writes that that is not the *peshaṭ* of the phrase. He says that, following the *peshaṭ*, it is the witness testifying against the bailee who says "כי הוא זה," i.e. "that that which you claim was stolen, הוא זה--that very object is still in your possession." (So also iE, longer comm.) But Rashbam argues that, at least on the *peshaṭ* level, the person who says "כי הוא זה" must be the bailor, not the witnesses (who are not even mentioned anywhere in the verse).

Rashbam, presumably is less troubled here by the traditional rabbinic exegesis than by Rashi's claim that what *he* says is the *peshaṭ* of the phrase. Rashbam begins his explanation by saying "I, however, will explain these verses according to the *peshaṭ*," and he probably means in part "I, and not Rashi." See the introduction to my Genesis volume, p. 17f., where I argue that Rashbam generally uses the term *peshaṭ* when he is arguing with his grandfather and claiming that he, and not Rashi, is the one who provides the true *peshaṭ*.

EXODUS XXII   257

SHALL PAY DOUBLE TO HIS NEIGHBOR, whichever one of them the judges[27] FIND GUILTY,[28] on the basis of the testimony of witnesses.[29]

22:9 ומת או נשבר [IF A MAN GIVES TO ANOTHER AN . . . ANIMAL TO GUARD] AND IT DIES OR נשבר [OR IS CARRIED

---

[26]It is generally understood that the phrases אשר ירשיעון האלהים and דבר שניהם ישלם שנים mean that one of two parties will be found guilty by the judges. Clearly the reference cannot be to the plaintiff and to the defendant, as there is no good reason why the plaintiff should ever have to pay double. Rashi suggests, as part of what he labels his *peshat* explanation, that the verse is describing a situation where witnesses testify against the bailee who swore to his innocence. In that situation, the judges will investigate and will force one of the two parties to pay double--either the bailee, if the witnesses are found to be believable, or the witnesses themselves, if they are found to be false witnesses (on the basis of the law of Deut. 19:19). Again (see previous note) Rashbam opposes Rashi's *peshat*, and writes more simply that the two parties who could be asked to pay double are the thief and the bailee. So also iE, shorter comm.

[27]So also Rashi and virtually all Jewish exegetes.
   Rashbam does follow standard halakhic exegesis by interpreting that האלהים in this verse means "judges." (See also Rashbam above ad 21:6 and below ad 22:26.) The Talmud (Sanh. 56b) in fact cites our verse as the *locus classicus* to prove that האלהים means "judges." Mekhilta (*ibid.*, p. 116) specifically considers and rejects the possibility of interpreting the phrase as referring to consulting an oracle.

[28]אשר ירשיעון. Above, in Rashbam's restatement of the rabbinic understanding of this verse, he paraphrases the phrase אשר ירשיעון as "כשירשיעון--*when* they find him guilty." He also adds the pronoun הוא, for emphasis, in the phrase ישלם הוא כפל--i.e. *he*, the dishonest bailee, shall pay double. Rashbam does this because, in the rabbinic understanding of the verse, it is *not* really the case that one of two possible parties could end up paying double; it is really only the dishonest bailee who could. (Of course, false witnesses could also pay double, as Rashi says, but, as noted above, witnesses are mentioned nowhere in the verse.)
   Here, though, in Rashbam's *peshat* rephrasing of the verse, he writes אשר ירשיעון, using the precise language of the Torah, and he does not add the emphatic pronoun הוא, since, in his own reading, it *is* the case that either one of two parties mentioned in the text could end up paying double.

[29]On this final point, Rashbam does agree with Rashi and with standard halakhic exegesis that the bailee had to be found guilty by the testimony of witnesses. A bailee who admits that he stole the pledge would not have to pay double. See e.g. BQ 65a-65b.

OFF]: נשבר means that the animal was torn apart by a lion or another wild animal,[30] for just as the terms מת--DIES and נשבה--IS CARRIED OFF refer to the total loss of the animal, so also נשבר means that the animal was destroyed totally when it was killed by a lion or another wild animal.[31]

One finds a similar usage [of the verb ש-ב-ר] in the story of the prophet who was killed by the lion (I Kings 13:24f.). "The lion and the ass were standing beside the corpse; the lion had not eaten the corpse nor had it destroyed (שבר) the ass" (ibid., vs. 28).[32]

---

[30]The idea that the damage referred to here was caused by a wild animal may be found in Mekhilta (ibid. 16, p. 121), LT and Ps.-Jon. See also Rashbam's comm. below ad vs. 12, s.v. ונשבר.

Cf. Nahm. (ad vs. 12), who understands נשבר to mean that the animal injured itself when walking on some precipice.

[31]Rashbam is apparently saying that the laws of bailees described here do not apply in cases of partial damage to an animal. In halakhic literature, that matter is still a question of dispute in sources from the last few centuries. See the sources collected by Kasher, here, note 234.

There is some difficulty in understanding Rashbam's approach to these verses. Vss. 9-10 suggest that in cases of מת או נשבר או נשבה, the bailee is required only to swear to his innocence and then, without any further requirements of proof, he is exonerated. However, vs. 12 suggests that a different law applies in cases where the pledged animal is "torn apart" by wild beasts: then, some proof is required ("יביאהו עד"). Now Rashbam argues here that נשבר (vs. 9) is synonymous with being "torn apart" (vs. 12). Nahm.'s approach (see previous note)--that נשבר means something different than being torn apart by a wild animal--is now more easily understood. Perhaps Rashbam is saying that vs. 12 should be read as a refinement of the law of vs. 9. In other words, in cases of "died or carried off or destroyed," generally all that is required of the bailee is an oath. However, vs. 12 adds that in the specific case of "נשבר--destroyed," since some physical evidence is available, such evidence should be brought to substantiate the bailee's oath.

Most moderns feel that נשבר refers to some injury short of total loss. Like Rashbam, see Mendelssohn.

[32]Rashbam's proof may also be dependent on the fact that, when the lion kills the prophet (in vs. 26 there), the text reads וישברהו וימיתהו.

EXODUS XXII

אין רואה WITHOUT ANYONE SEEING IT:[33]

22:10 שבועת AN OATH BEFORE THE LORD: [After the bailee swears that he did not fail in his duties,] he shall be exonerated in [such] cases of *force majeure*.[34]

ולקח בעליו THE OWNER WILL "TAKE": [I.e. "accept"] the oath.[35]

22:12 יביאהו עד [IF IT WAS TORN BY BEASTS] HE SHALL BRING IT: i.e. some of the limbs of the animal, as evidence, as it is written (Amos 3:12), "As a shepherd rescues from the lion's jaws two shank bones or the tip of an ear."[36]

---

[33]Rosin notes that these words of the Torah appear at this point in the manuscript, but the commentary on these words is missing. Rosin speculates that Rashbam may have, "as he often did," interpreted these words in the same way that Rashi did. Rashi's comment here reads: "ואין רואה' שיעיד בדבר"--WITHOUT ANYONE who could testify about the matter SEEING IT."

[34]ופטור באונסים. The word אונס is the standard term used in rabbinic literature to describe the type of losses outlined in vs. 9. See e.g. BM 94b.

Rashbam's comment means that in the cases outlined in verse 9, where there was no reasonable precaution that the bailee could have taken to prevent the loss of the pledged animal, all that the bailee must do is swear to his innocence and he is then exonerated. That is the standard halakhic interpretation of the verse. See Rashi, following Shev. 8:1.

[35]In other words, the only thing that the bailor "receives" is an oath; he gets no further compensation.

Rashbam's comment is the standard halakhic explanation. So also Rashi, here, following Onq. See also BQ 106a, and Shev. 45a and Rashi, there, s.v. ולקח בעליו. Cf. Mekhilta (*ibid*. 16, p. 124) where, according to one opinion, the meaning of "the owner shall take" is that the owner takes (and is responsible for) the carcass. So also Abravanel, Luzzatto and Cassuto. See iE (shorter comm.) for a combination of the two explanations.

[36]Rashbam's explanation opposes that of Rashi who says that יביאהו עד means "he should bring witnesses" to testify to the fact that the animal was torn to beasts. Both Rashi's opinion and Rashbam's (and even the prooftext that Rashbam uses) can be found in Mekhilta (*ibid*., p. 125). See also BQ 10b, and Nahm.'s discussion, here, of the two

22:13 וכי ישאל IF A MAN BORROWS: an animal, to do work with it.[37]

ונשבר או מת: means that the animal was torn by beasts or else died [on its own].[38]

22:13-14 בעליו אין עמו IF ITS OWNER IS NOT WITH IT: working together with the animal at the same task, [HE MUST MAKE RESTITUTION. Only if ITS OWNER IS WITH IT, working at the same task as the animal, only then HE MAKES NO RESTITUTION]. This is the plain meaning of Scripture. However, in the rabbis' midrash it is explained as meaning "even at another task," i.e. even if the lender is doing some other type of work for the borrower, then the borrower of the animal is not responsible to make repayment if the animal dies or is torn by beasts.[39]

---

explanations. JBS also offers both explanations and labels the one found in Rashbam, "the *peshat*."

[37] See similarly NJPS: "The verb ['borrows'] has no object. The theme of verses 9-12 and the phrase "it dies or is injured' make it clear that an animal, most likely a work animal, is meant."

[38] See Rashbam's comm. above, ad vs. 9, s.v. ומת.

[39] See the discussion in the Talmud, BM 95b. There, R. Himnuna suggests (as Rashbam does here) that a borrower is freed of responsibilty only if the lender is working together with his animal at the same task. R. Himnuna's position is attacked and rejected by the Talmud.

It should be noted that here, too, the *peshat* reading offered by Rashbam is not compatible with halakhah. If the lender of an animal is employed by the animal's borrower at some unrelated task, and that animal dies an accidental death, then halakhah would say that the borrower is *not* liable to pay, while Rashbam's *peshat* would suggest that the owner *is* liable to pay. The borrower either is or is not liable; both possibilities could not be true at the same time.

Rashi here offers only the talmudic understanding. So also a modern exegete with a commmitment to both *peshat* and halakhah, like Moses Mendelssohn, offers only the halakhic reading. See iE, who offers both interpretations in his shorter commentary, showing some preference for the halakhic understanding, and then, uncharacteristically, offers only the *peshat* interpretation in his longer comm. See JBS, who mentions the

EXODUS XXII

22:14 אם שכיר הוא IF HE WAS A LEASOR: I.e that he leased his neighbor's animal[40] to use it for work.[41]

בא בשכרו: In other words, he [the leasor] is paying him rent[42] [for this animal], so he is not treated like a borrower. Accordingly a leasor is not liable in cases of *force majeure*, but he is liable, just like a paid bailee, in cases of theft or loss.[43] And there is an opinion that a leasor is treated like an *unpaid* bailee and is not even liable in cases of theft or loss, but only in cases of misappropriation. The matter is disputed by R. Meir and R. Yehudah in Babba Qama.[44]

---

peshaṭ reading, but tries to find textual grounding for the rabbinic understanding, admitting that the logic behind the rabbinic position is difficult to understand.

[40]Rashbam here follows standard rabbinic exegesis in saying that the words אם שכיר הוא now introduce the rules for a fourth type of bailee, the leasor. Cf. JBS and Hizq., who say that, on the *peshaṭ* level, vs. 14b continues to discuss the rules of the previous category of bailee, the borrower. Verse 14a outlines the rule that applies if the lender of the animal comes along to work with his animal. Verse 14b discusses the rule that applies if said lender is also getting paid for his efforts. According to this understanding, there is no mention in the Torah of the rules of leasing.
    Many moderns also try to find different ways to interpret שכיר as a reference to a hired laborer, not to the hiring of an animal. See e.g. NJPSC, Childs (p. 449) and Luzzatto. Modern translations (e.g. RSV and NJPS) generally follow the understanding of Rashbam and the rabbis.

[41]Again (see vs. 13, s.v. וכי ישאל) Rashbam emphasizes that the animals described in vss. 13-14 are being borrowed or leased for the purpose of work.

[42]The phrase בא בשכרו is very difficult. It is not clear what the subject of the verb בא is. According to Rashi, it is the ox. According to iE's shorter comm., it is the damage. Cassuto says that the subject is the owner who hired out the animal. It is not certain what Rashbam thinks, but it seems that he sees the subject of the verb as the leasor: the leasor "came (בא) paying rent," and accordingly the rules of the borrower do not apply to him.

[43]This opinion is the standard halakhic opinion. See Shev. 8:1.

[44]In BQ 45b, and also in a number of other places in BT. So also Rashi.
    It is relatively rare for either Rashi or Rashbam to indicate that there are two different rabbinic interpretations of a phrase, especially when there is no doubt about which is the preferred halakhic option. (See the previous note.) Rashi, though, explains

22:15-16 אשר לא ארשה [IF A MAN SEDUCES A VIRGIN] WHO HAS NOT BEEN BETROTHED: Because if she had been betrothed, the man would be liable for the penalty of stoning, as it is written in Deuteronomy (22:23-24).[45]

The phrases כמהר הבתולות and מהר ימהרנה both refer to the payment of "fifty shekels of silver." Concerning a man who rapes a virgin, the text says that "he shall pay the girl's father fifty shekels of silver" (Deut. 22:29), and the same rule applies to the man who seduces [a virgin].[46]

22:17 מכשפה לא תחיה DO NOT LET A SORCERESS LIVE: Because sorceresses generally ply their trade in secret hiding places, like caves--as one finds concerning the eighty women [sorceresses] that Shimon ben

---

well that, according to all classical rabbinic exegesis of this verse, the verse tells us explicitly only that a leasor has less responsibility than a borrower. How much less, Rashi tells us, is not written in the verse (ולא פירש מה דינו). It could then be that Rashi and Rashbam are explaining in their comments here that it is understandable how the dispute between R. Meir and R. Yehudah arose, since the Torah did not deal with the responsibilities of the leasor in detail.

[45]There the same root is used to describe the seduced woman, "a virgin who is betrothed (מאורשה) to a man."

Rashbam may be opposing, at least on the *peshat* level, the attempts of the rabbis to learn many halakhot from this phrase, "who has not been betrothed". See Mekhilta, *ibid*. 17, p. 130, and Ket. 38a. In both those texts the argument is made explicitly that there is no halakhic "need" for the phrase, "who has not been betrothed," to have been written. Perhaps for that reason Rashbam points out that, on the *peshat* level, the phrase, "who has not been betrothed," *is* meaningful. Like Rashbam, see iE's longer comm.

[46]On this connection between the rules of the rapist and the rules of the seducer, see similarly Ket. 10a and Rashi there, s.v. כסף and s.v. כמהר, and Ket. 38a. See also iE's shorter comm., here.

Rashi here (following Mekhilta, *ibid*., p. 131) identifies מהר in this verse as the ketubbah. See Nahm.'s lengthy objection to that explanation based in part on the fact that, according to most halakhic authorities, the ketubbah was a rabbinic innovation and is not derived from the Torah. Perhaps for that very reason Rashbam shies away from Rashi's explanation here.

Shetah hanged in Ashkelon⁴⁷--that is why the Torah says "Do not let [them] live," i.e. "Do not abandon the investigation after them, do not let them stay alive because you are too lazy; rather investigate about them, so that you may put them to death."⁴⁸

22:19 זבח לָאלהים WHOEVER SACRIFICES TO THE GODS: לָאלהים is written with a *patah* vowel.⁴⁹ If לֵא-להים were written,⁵⁰ then the reference would be to the name of [the true] God. But לָאלהים means to those gods about whom I said to you (Ex. 20:3), "You shall have no other gods (אלהים)."⁵¹

---

⁴⁷Sanh. 6:4.

⁴⁸Many commentators discuss the issue of why the Torah uses this unusual phrase, "do not let [her] live--לֹא תְחַיֶּה," to describe the capital penalty for sorcery. Some, like Rashi, do not explain, but simply say that the phrase means that the capital penalty is applied. Others, like Nahm., write that because of the gravity of the crime stronger language than usual is used.

Rashbam's colleague, JBS (followed later by Hizq.), suggests that this phrase implies that a sorceress need not be brought to trial; she may be killed in any manner by anyone who encounters her. JBS then, like Rashbam, cites the story of Shimon ben Shetah from the Mishnah to prove his point. To my mind, the story of Shimon ben Shetah works slightly more smoothly as a proof for JBS's reading. Both the Mishnah, there, and the discussion in b. Sanh. 46a make it clear that Shimon ben Shetah (legitimately) did not extend due process to the sorceresses that he put to death in Ashkelon, the very point that JBS is making. It is not clear to me how Rashbam sees the story of Shimon ben Shetah as proving that investigations about sorcery should be thorough.

⁴⁹In the first syllable. So also Rashi, Nahm. and iE, shorter comm., here. The problem is that it is *not* written with a *patah* vowel in any text that has reached us. The word is always written with a *qames* vowel in the first syllable. It is very unlikely that Rashbam's comment here reflects a text where the vowel truly was a *patah*. Rosin argues (RSBM, p. 130, note 6) that Rashi and Rashbam, like a number of Jewish grammarians and exegetes, sometimes call a *qames* a *patah*.

⁵⁰With a *sere* vowel in the first syllable.

⁵¹So similarly Rashi, at much greater length.

There are, however, two differences between what Rashbam writes and what Rashi writes. Rashbam adds the verse from Ex. 20 as the text which establishes the identity of "those previously mentioned אלהים" that both Rashi and Rashbam mention

22:20 לא תונה YOU SHALL NOT WRONG [A CONVERT[52]]: Through [improper] speech. Wronging someone financially is [not] described [in *this* verse, but] in [another passage] (Lev. 25:14),[53] "[When you sell property to your neighbor . . .] you shall not wrong one another."[54]

[Our verse in Exodus speaks about not wronging a convert but actually the verse teaches that] one is not allowed to wrong *any* Jew; [converts were singled out in the verse because] the text describes the most likely occurrence,[55] as a convert [is an easy target for verbal

---

here. Rashbam also modifies Rashi's suggestion that if the form לָא-להים, with a *sere*, were written here, then the reference would be to all gods, including the true God (כל א-לוהים במשמע אפילו קדש). Rashbam, on the other hand, suggests that the form לָא-להים would be understood as a reference to the true God alone.

[52]From the continuation of Rashbam's comment, here, it is clear that he feels that the word גר in this verse means a convert, not a stranger. So also almost all Jewish exegetes. Cf. however iE.

[53]As Rosin notes here, the quotation cited by Rashbam, according to the manuscript reading, is actually a conflation of verses 14 and 17 in Lev. 25.

[54]Rashbam opposes Rashi's claim that the source for learning that wronging a convert financially is not allowed is the phrase, "nor shall you harm him," at the end of this verse. According to Rashbam, that rule is derived from Leviticus.

[55]דבר הכתוב בהוה, a common rabbinic phrase, originating with the eighteenth of the thirty-two exegetical principles of R. Eliezer the son of Rabbi Jose the Galilean. This principle has been much used in the exegesis of these chapters of Exodus. See Mekhilta *Kaspa'* 2, pp. 157-158, and Rashi above ad 21:28 and 22:17 and below ad vss. 21 and 30. Rashbam often makes use of this principle in his commentary to the next few verses (here and ad 22:21, 22:27, 23:5 and 23:19).

Rashbam explains that the most likely victims of verbal wrongs are converts. Accordingly the text writes specifically not to wrong them, although the purpose of this text is to teach us that it is in fact forbidden to wrong any Jew. Rashbam's explanation is *not* the common halakhic understanding. The Talmud (BM 59b) would imply that the rule in this verse applies only to converts. By writing this verse the Torah makes it a greater crime to wrong converts than to wrong other Jews. And there are sources other than this verse from which one can derive that it is forbidden to wrong a Jew verbally. See e.g. Rashi ad Lev. 25:17, following Sifra *Behar* 4. See BM 59b, where the Talmud applies Lev. 25:17 to the verbal wronging of both converts and other Jews.

EXODUS XXII 265

wrongs as he] can be insulted about his forefathers' deeds[56] and about his behavior while he was still a gentile.[57]

ולא תלחצנו NOR SHOULD YOU OPPRESS HIM [a convert]: By forcing him to do work for you,[58] [thinking that you can get away with mistreating him] because he has no "redeemer."[59] [The root ל-ח-צ means to force someone to do work,] as in the phrase (Ex. 3:9) "I have seen the oppression (לחץ) with which the Egyptians force them to work."[60]

This aspect of Rashbam's interpretation also opposes that of Rashi. Rashi interprets only vs. 21 using the principle, "the text describes the most likely occurrence." Rashbam interprets both vs. 20 and vs. 21 that way.

[56]See BM 4:10, where the example given of a "verbal wrong" (אונאת דברים) that one might direct toward a descendant of a convert is "Remember your forefathers' deeds."

[57]See Mekhilta *Neziqin* 18 (p. 137) and BM 58b, where the example given of a "verbal wrong" that one might direct toward a convert is reminding him of his behavior before his conversion.

[58]As noted above, Rashbam opposes Rashi's interpretation (following Mekhilta, *ibid.*) that תלחצנו means to wrong financially. BM 59b apparently interprets תלחצנו as meaning to demand the repayment of a debt. (See Rashi there, s.v. לא תהיה). See also iE's suggestion, that תלחצנו means to testify falsely concerning this גר.
Somewhat akin to Rashbam, see Noth who says that the *first* verb, תונה, refers primarily to exploitation in work.

[59]גואל. See e.g. Lev. 25:25-26 and Ruth 4:1-6 where a גואל is the closest relative that a person might have who might look out for that person's interests. A convert generally lacks Jewish family who will look out for his interests.

[60]The way that Rashbam quotes the verse here, הלחץ אשר מצרים מעבידים אותם, his proof works very well. The noun לחץ is being used to describe the way that forced labor was imposed upon the Israelites (מעבידים אותם). But that is not the way that Ex. 3:9 reads; MT reads הלחץ אשר מצרים לוחצים אותם. Arguably, Rashbam's point could also be made from the verse as it appears in MT. The לחץ is presumably connected to the forced labor of the Israelites in Egypt, even if the text does not make that connection explicitly. Furthermore, as Rosin notes, Rashbam may also have had Ex. 6:5 (אשר מצרים מעבידים אותם) in mind when he wrote his comment to this verse.

כי גרים הייתם FOR YOU WERE STRANGERS (גרים) IN THE LAND OF EGYPT: [The idea should be understood in the same way] as it is written below (23:9), "[You shall not oppress a גר, for] you know the feelings of the stranger (גר), having been strangers (גרים) yourself [in the land of Egypt]."[61]   Because the convert's pain is greater, the punishment for wronging him is also greater.[62]

22:21 לא תענון YOU SHALL NOT ILL-TREAT [ANY WIDOW OR ORPHAN]: The verb תענון is to be understood in the same way as (Ex. 1:11) "to ill-treat them (לענותו) with forced labor."[63] [The verse speaks about not ill-treating a widow or an orphan but actually one is not

---

[61]Rashbam opposes the explanation offered by Rashi as to the meaning of the clause, "For you were strangers . . .," in our verse. Rashi (following Mekhilta *ibid.*, pp. 137-8) says that that phrase implies that Jews should refrain, out of self-interest, from insulting גרים, since Jews are also susceptible to the same insult. Rashbam says that the phrase should be understood the same way as the justification offered for the similar rule in 23:9, "Do not wrong the גר, for you know the feelings of the stranger . . .." Presumably Rashi feels that the fact that the Torah phrases the justification clause differently in the two verses means that two different reasons are being offered here and there. Rashbam, on the other hand, presumably sees here an insignificant stylistic variation. The same justification is offered by the Torah in both verses, but using different language.

For other explanations of the phrase, see e.g. JBS and Nahm.

[62]עונשו מרובה; a common rabbinic phrase. As far as I can tell, the phrase עונשו מרובה in rabbinic literature invariably means that *his* punishment--i.e. that punishment that *he* shall receive--is great. See e.g. BQ 79b. Rashbam, on the other hand, uses the phrase to mean that *his* punishment--i.e. the punishment that one would get for *harming him*--is great. Cf. the phrases עונשו של שבת and עונשו של שביעית in Shab. 68a.

[63]Rashbam explains both the verb תענון, here, and the verb תלחצנו, in the previous verse, by citing verses that describe the enslavement of the Jews in Egypt. It is possible that he does so simply for the purpose of clarifying the meaning of the verbs. But it is also possible that he is drawing the readers' attention to the fact that the Torah intentionally uses language from the enslavement story in order to warn Jews not to take advantage of the underclasses of society. See similarly Cassuto and Nahm. ad vs. 20.

allowed to ill-treat anyone; widows and orphans were singled out in the verse because] the text describes the most likely occurrence.[64]

22:23 והיו נשיכם [I WILL KILL YOU WITH THE SWORD] AND YOUR WIVES SHALL BE WIDOWS: Measure for measure.[65]

22:24-5 לא תהיה לו כנשה DO NOT ACT AS A CREDITOR (נושה): When it comes time to collect the debt, do not harass the borrower by taking the pledged collateral. [The word נושה is always used in the context of seizing collateral,] as it is written (2 Kings 4:1), "A creditor (והנושה) is coming to seize [my two children as slaves]," and (Is. 50:1) "Which of My creditors (מנושי) was it to whom I sold you off." The word נושה always means the one who comes to seize the pledged collateral when the time of the debt is up.[66] [Rather] אם חבל תחבל IF YOU TAKE A PLEDGE [do so] through the court,[67] as it is written (Deut. 24:11), "You must remain outside while the man to whom you

---

[64]דבר הכתוב בהוה. See comm. and notes ad vs. 20. Rashbam is saying that the most likely victims of ill-treatment are the widow and the orphan. That is why the text writes specifically not to ill-treat *them*, although the purpose of this text is to teach us not to ill-treat anyone. Here (as opposed to ad vs. 20) Rashi also says the same thing, following Mekhilta *ibid.*, p. 141.

[65]Rashbam is dealing with the problem raised by Rashi (following Mekhilta *ibid.*, p. 144, and BM 38b): if the text writes that God will kill the offenders, why bother writing that their wives will be widows. Is that not obvious? Rashi assumes that the phrase, "Your wives will be widows," must convey some new information. It means, he says, that they will be widows, but will have no proof of their widowhood, and thus will not be able to remarry.

Rashbam, on the other hand, is willing to say that the phrase conveys no new information but serves only the rhetorical purpose of emphasizing that the appropriate punishment here, for those who oppress widows, is that their own wives will become widows. So also JBS.

On the phrase, מידה כנגד מידה, see comm. and notes ad Gen. 42:21.

[66]Rashi explains that the words חבל תחבל teach that the verses are describing seizing collateral when the time of repayment has come. Rashbam, on the other hand, says that it is the word נושה which teaches us that fact.

[67]Rashbam here follows the explanation of BM 113b. See also Mishnah BM 9:13.

made the loan will bring it out to you." But you, [the creditor,] "must not enter his home to seize his pledge." That is the meaning of the phrase, "do not act as a נושה."[68]

[69]לא תשימון עליו DO NOT IMPOSE ANY INTEREST ON HIM: in order to allow him more time[70] for repayment.[71]

עד בא השמש [IF TOU TAKE YOUR NEIGHBOR'S GARMENT IN PLEDGE YOU MUST RETURN IT TO HIM so that he will have it] all

---

[68]Rashbam opposes the interpretation of Rashi, who explains that to "act as a creditor" means to embarrass the debtor, or to demand payment when one knows that he has no money. Rashi follows in the tradition of a number of classical sources which see this law as describing the type of pose and attitude that a creditor ought to take. (See e.g. Mekhilta *Kaspa'* 1, p. 148, and BM 75b.) Rashbam, on the other hand, interprets the verse as legislating that collateral may be seized only by a court, not by the creditor acting on his own behalf. As Rashbam explains, he sees vss. 24-25 here as teaching the same law as one finds in Deut. 24:10-11: "You must not enter his house to seize his pledge. You must remain outside . . . ." According to Rashbam, being a נושה simply means transgressing the law of Deut. 24.

[69]Rosin writes (note 12) that he changed the order that one finds in the ms. and moved this comment on לא תשימון from this spot to the place where Rosin thought that it really belonged, between Rashbam's discussion of the phrase לא תהיה לו כנושה and his discussion of the phrase אם חבל תחבל. To my mind, the order of the ms. makes perfect sense for Rashbam's style. Rashbam completes his discussion of what it means to be a נושה, using parts of vss. 24 and 25 to make his point, and only then returns to explain a separate point in vs. 24, the meaning of לא תשימון עליו נשך.

[70]הרחיב את זמנו. The phrase is used by Rashi in his comm. to BM 101b, s.v. להודיע קתני. See the discussion of the phrase in *Hekhal Rashi*, vol. 1, 1201-1202.

[71]Rashbam explains "imposing interest" in a manner that is congruent with his explanation of "acting like a creditor." They both limit the actions of the creditor at the specific point in time when the debt is due and the debtor cannot pay. "Do not act like a creditor" means do not enter the house to seize collateral; "do not impose interest" means do make an extension of the time for repayment conditional on payment of interest.

EXODUS XXII   269

day long. [I explain the verse in this way] because the rabbis said that the verse describes clothing worn during the day.⁷²

22:26 ושמעתי כי חנון אני [IF HE CRIES OUT TO ME] I WILL PAY HEED FOR I AM COMPASSIONATE: "Even though the creditor has seized the collateral legally and is required to return it to the debtor only in order to do more than the letter of the law,⁷³ and [one might think] therefore that I [i.e. God] would not PAY HEED to the cries [of this debtor whose rights, from the perspective of pure justice, have not been abridged in any way,] still, because I am compassionate and merciful [I

---

⁷²See Mekhilta *ibid.* (p. 150), and BM 114b. The classical rabbinic sources explain that while Deut. 24:13 describes the way that one must behave when one seizes a poor man's *night* clothes as collateral, vs. 25, here in our chapter, describes the way to behave when one seizes a poor man's *day* clothes as collateral. Although the simple meaning of the verse is "return the article of clothing before sunset," the rabbinic sources say that the verse means "return the article of clothing at dawn, so that the owner can have it until sunset." The rabbinic sources then must say that while vs. 26 obviously describes night clothing ("In what else shall he sleep?"), vs. 25 should be seen as entirely disjointed from 26 and describing day clothing. Presumably the classical sources go to such exegetical lengths so that Deut. 24:13 and Ex. 22:25 should not be seen as saying the same thing.
  I cannot fathom why Rashbam abandons the *peshat* here and adopts the rabbinic reading. There would be no conflict between the *peshat* reading, "Return it to him before the sun sets," (NJPS) and halakhah. Even an exegetical conservative like Moses Mendelssohn, basing himself on Ps.-Jon., writes that that understanding is פשוטו של מקרא--the plain meaning of the text. Furthermore, Rashbam would hardly take pains to ensure that our verse should be saying something distinct from Deut. 24:13. Rashbam is generally not troubled by saying that two verses say the same thing, at least on the *peshat* level; see e.g. his explanation above of לא תהיה לו כנושה, or his explanation below of the phrase (28) מלאתך ודמעך לא תאחר, each of which phrases, he says, means the same as a phrase in a verse in Deuteronomy. The style of suggesting that vs. 25 here refers to day clothes, when vs. 26 so clearly refers to night clothes, seems totally foreign to Rashbam's exegetical method. I am tempted to suggest that the words of explanation, here, on the phrase עד בא השמש, were interpolated into the comm. by a hand other than Rashbam's.

⁷³לפנים משורת הדין. It is unusual for Rashbam to use that phrase, here. The requirement to return the collateral is *not* beyond the letter of the law; it is explicitly legislated in the law, here.
  Presumably Rashbam means that, using some external system of moral judgement, one might logically reach the conclusion that a collateral need not be returned on a daily basis to a debtor who defaults on his loan.

will heed his cry]." [That is why the phrase, "FOR I AM COMPASSIONATE," is written in this verse.]

However above, when the text (21-2) says "You shall not ill-treat any widow or orphan [. . . I will hear their outcry]," since there, even following an approach of pure justice, God heeds the cry [of the oppressed whose legal rights have been abridged], that is why the verse does not say there (in vs. 22) "for I am compassionate."[74]

22:27 אלהים לא תקלל ונשיא בעמך לא תאר DO NOT REVILE A JUDGE AND DO NOT CURSE A CHIEFTAIN AMONG YOUR PEOPLE: The text describes the most likely occurrence.[75] Since kings[76] and judges[77] are the ones who adjudicate monetary and capital

---

[74]See similarly JBS and the gloss on Tos. RH 17b, s.v. שלש.

[75]דבר הכתוב בהווה. In other words it is forbidden to curse anyone, but judges and chieftains are the ones most likely to be cursed, for the reasons that Rashbam enunciates, and that is why the Torah specifically outlaws cursing them. Rashbam's comment can be seen as opposing the types of explantion found in Sanh. 66a, where there is a long discussion of the halakhic ramifications of the fact that the two examples chosen in this verse are judges and chieftains. See also Rashi ad Lev. 19:14, s.v. לא, who (following Mekhilta *ibid.*, p. 152, and Sifra *Qedoshim* 2) tries to find some textual grounding to forbid the cursing of people other than judges and chieftains, and see also Tos. Sanh. 66b, s.v. מאי, where a different suggestion is made of how to derive that halakhic prohibition. Following Rashbam, there is no problem: the text here means that no one should be cursed, but there is a valid reason for singling out judges and chieftains. See similarly Nahm.'s self-declared "*peshat*" explanation, in his comm. ad Lev. 19:14.

On the phrase דבר הכתוב בהווה, see note 55 above.

[76]Rashbam understands נשיא as a reference to the king. So also iE (longer comm.) here. That understanding of נשיא is also reflected in the Mekhilta (*ibid.*): אי נשיא כאחאב וחביריו. See also the same understanding of נשיא in Horayot 3:3 (איזהו הנשיא זה המלך) when discussing Lev. 4:22.

[77]Rashbam understands the word אלהים in our verse as a reference to judges. See also comm. and notes above, ad vs. 8.

Actually, in rabbinic literature there is a dispute about whether to see the word אלהים here as "holy," i.e. as a reference to God, or as referring to human judges. See Mekhilta *ibid*. (p. 151), and Sanh. 66a-b. The conclusion of the discussion in Sanh. would suggest that the Talmud feels that one can see this phrase as referring at one and the same time both to cursing God and to cursing a judge. So also Rashi, here. Rashbam, however, explains the phrase only as a reference to cursing judges, presumably

cases,[78] it is common for people to curse them. So it is written (Eccl. 10:20) "Do not revile a king, even in your thoughts"[79] and it is written (Deut. 21:23) "a hanged man (תלוי) [leads to] קללת אלהים," i.e. when people see a person hanged, they generally curse the judges;[80] that is why the verse says (ibid.), "You must not let his corpse hang."[81]

מלאתך ודמעך DO NOT DELAY מלאתך ודמעך לא תאחר 22:28: This verse means the same as (Deut. 18:4) "[You shall give] the first fruits of your new grain and wine and oil."[82]

המלאה: refers to the *terumah* that one must give from grains; [מלאה refers to grains,] as in the phrase (Deut. 22:9), "the crop (המלאה) from the seed [you have sown]."[83]

---

because of the parallelism between אלהים and נשיא.

[78]לפי שהמלכים והדייינין דנין דיני ממונות ונפשות. The idea that kings adjudicate monetary and capital cases is somewhat strange, and would seem to go against common rabbinic law (e.g. Sanh. 2:2). A simple emendation of the word דנין to הדנין would yield the following more reasonable reading: "The text describes the most likely occurrence, since it is the kings and those judges who adjudicate monetary and capital cases whom people are most likely to curse."

[79]The prooftext shows that kings are often the ones that people think to curse.

[80]I.e. the אלהים.

[81]See Rashbam, there in Deut., at greater length, opposing the midrashic understanding of that verse found in Rashi, there (following Sanh. 46b).

[82]From the continuation of Rashbam's comm. here, it is clear that he accepts the common rabbinic understanding (see e.g. Pes. 33a) that the verse in Deut. refers to the requirement of *terumah*. So also Rashi in Deut.

[83]Rashbam opposes the explanation of Rashi, here (following Mekhilta *ibid.* [p. 153], and Temurah 4a), that מלאתך in this verse refers to *bikkurim*. Like Rashbam, see JBS. All these *peshaṭ*-oriented exegetes oppose the innovative explanation of Qara (see also iE who cites this as a Karaite interpretation), that the verse refers to the requirement that people get married at a young age.

ודמעך: refers to wine and to olive oil, ([which is also called] יצהר),[84] which are refined and clear [liquids, and are referred to as דמעה, because they are] like tears (דמעה). So Menahem also explained.[85]

לא תאחר DO NOT DELAY: [the *terumah*,] but rather give it [to the priest] first, before all the other *ma'aserot*.[86]

בכור בניך [YOU SHALL GIVE ME] THE FIRST-BORN AMONG YOUR SONS. (29) YOU SHALL DO THE SAME WITH YOUR CATTLE . . .: All of these are rules that relate to "first" things.[87]

---

[84]E.g. Num. 18:12 and passim.

[85]In his *Mahberet*, s.v. דמע.
    Actually Menahem there explains דמע as referring only to wine, not to oil. iE in his longer comm. here attributes to Saadiah the explanation that דמעך refers to oil, and not to wine. Like Rashbam, see JBS.
    Rashbam's comm. again opposes that of Rashi (still following Mekhilta, *ibid*.), who says that the word דמעך means *terumah*. Rashi admits, with his standard modesty, that he doesn't really know why the word דמעך is used to describe *terumah*. Perhaps for that reason Rashbam gives an etymological explanation for his own understanding that דמעך refers to oil and wine. Rashbam, to be sure, does agree with Rashi that the *verse* deals with *terumah*, but he does not feel that that is the meaning of the *word* דמעך.

[86]Rashbam's explanation is similar but not identical to the standard rabbinic understanding (e.g. Mekhilta, *ibid*., and Terumot 3:6) found here in Rashi. That understanding is that the verse means that *all* of the "gifts" that the Jewish farmer must give to priests and to others--*bikkurim*, *terumah*, *ma'aser rishon*, *ma'aser 'ani*, *ma'aser sheni*, etc.--should be removed from one's crops according to a set order. Rashbam, on the other hand, explains the verse simply as saying that *terumah* comes first, before the *ma'aserot*.

[87]Rashbam explains the thematic connection of the various rules in vss. 28-29. Perhaps Rashbam is opposing the explanation of Rashi (s.v. בכור בניך, following Mekhilta *ibid*., pp. 154-5), who suggests that the juxtaposition of some of the rules here has a specific halakhic purpose--to teach that the ideal time to hand over a first-born animal to the priest is when that animal is thirty days old, a rule that seems to contradict the simple understanding of vs. 29 ("on the eigth day you shall give it to Me"). Rashbam then is saying that, at least on the *peshat* level, the juxtaposition of the various rules here is for easily understandable organizational purposes.

22:30 ואנשי קדש YOU SHALL BE HOLY PEOPLE TO ME[: YOU MUST NOT EAT FLESH TORN BY BEASTS]: [You will make yourselves holy] by refraining from eating impure food,[88] such as flesh that was torn by beasts. So it also written concerning the rule (Dt. 14:21), "Do not eat anything that has died a natural death," [that the reason for that rule also is (*ibid.*),] "For you are a holy people."[89]

---

[88]דבר טמא; i.e. non-kosher food. See Rashbam's explanation of this term in his comm. ad Lev. 11:3.

[89]Rashbam again (see notes above ad. vs. 25, s.v. עד בא) cites a verse in Deuteronomy to explain a verse here in Exodus 22. Here he shows that the connection between holiness and refraining from non-kosher food is common in the Bible.

See Touitou, in *Milet* 2, 283, who discusses the possible ways that this interpretation of Rashbam may have been useful for him in polemics with Christians, who disparaged the laws of kosher food.

EXODUS XXIII

23:1 לא תשא YOU MUST NOT ACCEPT FALSE TESTIMONY: Just as witnesses are warned (20:13) "Do not bear false witness against your neighbor,"[1] so also the judges are warned not to accept false testimony.[2] Rather they should (Deut. 13:15) "investigate and inquire."[3]

[אל תשת ידך YOU SHALL NOT JOIN HANDS:][4] Even if there are [without your participation] two false witnesses, do not join them to testify [falsely] together with them, even though [you know that] the verdict will, [no matter what you do,] be given according to their [false] testimony, since there are no witnesses to contradict them.[5]

---

[1] It is possible that Rashbam is opposing the attempt of the Talmud (Pes. 118a) to establish a connection between our verse and the immediately preceeding phrase at the end of chapter 22, "cast it to the dogs." He suggests that the relevance of this verse is to be found in the greater context, in its connection to the ninth law of the Decalogue.
  On the connection between the Decalogue and the laws in chapters 21-23, see comm. and notes above ad 21:12-17.

[2] Rashbam opposes the explanations of this phrase found in Rashi (following the Mekhilta *ibid.*, p. 160), that it is a general rule addressed to all people not to listen to slander, or that it is specific rule directed to judges not to listen to one party to a legal dispute unless the other party is present. The nuance that Rashbam finds in the phrase--that it instructs judges to take steps to insure that the testimony that they are hearing is true--appears to be unique.

[3] ודרשת וחקרת. The terms דרישה and חקירה are the common terms used in rabbinic literature to describe the careful examination of witnesses by the judges. See e.g. Sanh. 4:1.

[4] As Rosin writes (note 10), although the words of the verse are not quoted, it is clear that from this point on Rashbam is no longer commenting on the phrase לא תשא שמע שוא, but rather on the phrase אל תשת ידך עם רשע.

[5] Rashbam again opposes Rashi's understanding of the phrase. According to Rashi (following Mekhilta *ibid.* [pp. 160-161]), the רשע referred to in this verse is a dishonest litigant who is trying to suborn false witnesses. Rashbam's interpretation--that this verse is a specific warning to a third witness who joins hands with two false witnesses and who

23:2 לא תהיה DO NOT SIDE WITH THE MAJORITY TO DO WRONG: [The verse is addressed to a judge and means do not support the opinion of the majority of your fellow judges] if they are, according to your understanding, ruling incorrectly, even though you know that your dissenting opinion will make no difference, because they are in the majority.[6]

ולא תענה DO NOT SIDE IN A DISPUTE WITH THE MAJORITY SO AS TO PERVERT: justice, even if they [i.e. the majority of judges who are, to your mind, ruling incorrectly] are exonerating the accused and finding him not cuplable for the death penalty.[7]

---

could theoretically argue that his testimony changes nothing--appears to be a unique understanding of *this* verse. However, Rabbi Akiva's understanding (in Makkot 1:7; see also Rashi ad Deut. 17:6) of the phrase "two or three witnesses" in Deut. 17:6--that the "third" of three witnesses is punished for false testimony although his testimony would not have been consequential in convicting the accused--is essentially the same as Rashbam's understanding of our verse. Perhaps Rashbam is attempting here to find a more *peshaṭ*-like grounding for R. Akiva's rule. See also comm. and notes to the next verse.

[6]Rashbam's explanation continues on the same theme as his comm. on the previous verse. "You shall not join hands," according to Rashbam, means that a *witness* should not join in with other witnesses that he knows are false, and now he explains the next phrase, "Do not side with the majority," as meaning that a *judge* should not do the same thing, i.e. join in with other judges who appear to him to be mistaken.

See Rashi's long excursus here about the standard rabbinic understanding of the verse and how that understanding is difficult to fit in to the words of the verse (אין לשון המקרא מיושב בהן על אפניו). Here, where one finds Rashi's perhaps most critical comment about standard rabbinic exegesis, it is interesting to note that Rashbam concurs with his grandfather. Rashbam's interpretation of the phrase, "Do not side with the majority," is essentially the same as Rashi's final explanation of this phrase, an interpretation which Rashi himself labels the *peshaṭ* understanding.

[7]Here Rashbam's explanation parts company to some degree with that of Rashi. Rashi explains the two halves of our verse as referring, respectively, to legal *rulings* offered by a judge and to legal *explanations* offered by a judge. Neither should be influenced by one's colleagues', if one judge feels that his colleagues are mistaken. Rashbam, on the other hand, inteprets both halves as referring to legal rulings, with only a slight difference of nuance between the two halves. A judge should not rule like the majority of his colleagues when he feels that they are mistaken, neither when they are ruling לרעות, i.e. to inflict some undeserved penalty on the accused, nor when they are exonerating the accused, if such exoneration constitutes "להטות," i.e. a perversion of

23:3 ודל לא תהדר DO NOT SHOW DEFERENCE TO A POOR MAN: As it is written (Lev. 19:15) "Do not[8] favor the poor or show deference to the rich." Rather (*ibid.*) "Judge your kinsman fairly."[9]

---

justice.

This difference of nuance—that the first half of the verse describes an accused who is being found guilty (לרעות) and the second half describes an accused who is being exonerated—is traditional rabbinic exegesis. See e.g. Mekhilta *ibid.*, pp. 161-162, and Sanh. 1:6 (cited by Rashi in his comm. here). There, however, the rabbis attempt to make a practical legal distinction between the two halves of the verse. A bare majority, according to the rabbis, is not followed if the ruling is לרעות, but it is followed if the ruling is to exonerate the accused. According to Rashbam, the text is not distinguishing between "guilty" and "not guilty" verdicts. On the contrary, the text is saying that the same rule applies whether the verdict is "guilty" or "not guilty." In neither case should a judge who disagrees with his colleagues simply decide to abandon his opinion and follow theirs. See JBS here, who also says that the two halves of the verse make the same legal point ("וכמו כפל מילה הוא").

It is noteworthy that a *peshat*-oriented exegete like iE accepts one aspect of the standard rabbinic explanation—that the verse implies that one does follow a simple majority when the ruling is to exonerate the accused. Presumably iE feels obliged to explain how it is that the rabbis "learned" from this verse that "the majority rules," a principle that, arguably, is the opposite of what the text really says, "Do *not* side with the majority." Rashbam, on the other hand, again has no trouble explaining the *peshat* in such a way that it is not in consonance with *halakhah*. See similarly comm. and notes ad 21:6, s.v. לעולם, and passim.

[8]Rashbam cites the phrase as ולא תשא, instead of MT's לא תשא. Esh, p. 87, notes that this reading is attested in some mss. and versions.

[9]I am not certain why Rashbam cites Lev. 19:15 to explain our verse.

In the Mekhilta (*ibid.*, pp. 162-163), there are two interpretations offered to the phrase, here, "Do not show deference to a poor man." The first interpretation suggests that extra rules can be derived from the minor stylistic variations between our verse and Lev. 19:15. Rashbam clearly takes a different approach and says that Lev. 19:15 simply reiterates more clearly what is written in our verse. Rashbam also opposes the second explanation found in the Mekhilta (and cited here by LT), that our verse is not talking about judicial rules but about showing favoritism to one poor person over other poor people when leaving sections of one's field for the poor to glean.

Rashbam might also be reacting to the question of why this verse outlaws favoritism only to the poor. Arguably, there might be more reason to be concerned about a judge showing favoritism to a rich person. Rashbam may be reacting to that problem by saying that our verse is properly understood if it is not read on its own, but together with Lev. 19:15. See also iE (both commentaries), who appears to be dealing with this question.

23:5 חמור שנאך [WHEN YOU SEE] YOUR ENEMY'S ASS: [The text] describes the most likely occurrence.[10]

עזוב תעזוב: means to help or to strengthen, as in the phrase (Neh. 3:8) "They restored (ויעזבו) Jerusalem as far as the Broad Wall," and in the phrase (Deut. 32:36), "and there is none who is saved[11] or who is aided (עזוב)."[12]

23:7 מדבר שקר תרחק KEEP FAR AWAY FROM A FALSE CHARGE: If the case appears to you [i.e. the judge] to be crooked and the witnesses appear to be dishonest but you are unable to disprove their testimony, remove yourself from that case and do not judge it at all.[13]

---

[10] דבר [הכתוב] בהוה. On the phrase, see note 55 above, ad 22:20, s.v. לא תונה.
The meaning of the phrase, here, is that while the Torah specifically commands helping out when the overburdened animal is an ass, the Torah's intention is that the law apply to all beasts of burden. The Torah specified an ass only because that is the most likely occurrence. Rashbam here follows BQ 5:7, where this precise same point--that the commandment of פריקה (easing the load of an overburdened animal) applies to all animals--is made, using the same phrase, דבר הכתוב בהוה. (The phrase occurs in the Mishnah only that one time.)

[11] עצור. It is uncertain how Rashbam understood this word in that verse. I have translated it in the way that Rashi explains it there ("נושע").

[12] Rashbam understands the phrase עזב תעזב here and the word עזוב in Deut. in the same way that Rashi does. See also Rashbam's comm., there in Deut., and Rashi's comm., both here and there. They both object to the interpretation of Onq., who says that עזב תעזב here means "to leave" with the implied object "your hatred." (משבק תשבק מה דבלבך עלוהי, i.e. "stop hating him.") See JBS who offers both interpretations.

[13] There are more than a dozen different interpretations of this phrase in classical rabbinic literature, most of them to be found collected in one talmudic passage (Shev. 30b-31a). Rashbam opts for one of the many rabbinic interpretations to be found there.
The interpretations of the phrase, "Keep far away from a false charge," can basically be divided into two large categories: those that see the words as directed to a judge, and those that see the law as a rule for all people to avoid situations that constitute or border upon dishonesty. Rashbam opts for one of the interpretations that sees the phrase as referring to a judge. This fits in to his exegesis of the greater context here: all of Rashbam's comments on vss. 1-8 of this chapter (with the clear exception of his comm. to vs. 5) explain the verses as instructions to judges or to witnesses. See notes

EXODUS XXIII

Nevertheless, if the accused is נקי וצדיק, if he is exonerated, i.e. the verdict has already been given that he is not guilty, do not kill him after that [even if new testimony or arguments as to his guilt now come to your attention], once you have heard the witnesses and reached a[n incorrect] verdict that was based on an incomplete investigation of the issue.[14] [And if you are concerned that] you are letting [an evil person like] him go free, I [God] will not let him go free,[15] for he is an evil person and he deserves to die. [I have my ways to punish him,] as it is written (Ex. 21:13) "But it came about by an act of God."[16]

23:8 יעור פקחים [FOR BRIBES] BLIND THE CLEAR-SIGHTED [AND PERVERT THE WORDS OF THE RIGHTEOUS]: When speaking of clear-sightedness the verb, "ע-ו-ר--to blind," is appropriately

---

above, ad vs. 1, where I point out that Rashi is willing (as one of two intepretations for the phrase) to interpret the words לא תשא שמע שוא as referring to a non-judicial context but Rashbam is not. And see also iE's opening words in his comment to this verse: "עם הדיין ידבר--the verse is addressed to a judge."

[14]Rashbam agrees with Rashi (following Mekhilta *ibid.* 3 [p. 171], and Sanh. 33b) that the principle of "double jeopardy" is to be derived from the phrase ונקי וצדיק אל תהרג.
  Rashbam's explanation differs slightly from that of Rashi (and the classical rabbinic texts). Rashi says that the principle of double jeopardy is derived from the second part of the phrase, from the words וצדיק אל תהרג. The Torah's instruction that one should not kill a נקי means something quite different: that a party who has been found guilty of a crime should be allowed to introduce new evidence in an attempt to exonerate himself. Rashbam does not accept that fine distinction between the נקי and the צדיק. He reads the phrase as a totality, and says that the whole phrase together teaches the principle of double jeopardy.

[15]אני לא אצדיקנו. Rashbam's comments here are actually his explanation of the words כי לא אצדיק רשע. Rashbam's explanation of that phrase is the same as that of Rashi (following Mekhilta *ibid.*, pp. 171-172).

[16]There Rashbam says, following the common rabbinic understanding, that God will sometimes make use of a case of accidental homicide to rid the world of some criminal who deserves to die. See comm. and notes, there.

used and when speaking of righteousness the verb, "ס-ל-פ--to pervert," is appropriately used.[17]

23:10-11 ואספת את תבואתה [SIX YEARS YOU SHALL SOW YOUR LAND] AND GATHER ITS GRAIN[18] CROPS: into your home.[19] Do not abandon it as ownerless. However, in the seventh year (11) YOU SHALL LET IT REST (תשמטנה), i.e. you should not sow, and YOU SHALL ABANDON IT (ונטשתה), i.e. you should not gather its grain crops.[20]

---

[17]I am not sure what Rashbam means to say in this comment. It is possible that he is reacting to the words of the Mekhilta, here (ibid., pp. 172-173). The text of the Mekhilta is also difficult to understand and there are a number of significantly different readings of that text. (See the lengthy discussion of the alternate readings in the Horovitz-Rabin edition of the Mekhilta, p. 328, note 8.) According to one such reading, the Mekhilta is saying that, since the object of the verb עור here is פקחים, but in the parallel text in Deut. (16:19) it is עיני חכמים, one must conclude that the blindness described here is not physical. Perhaps against that reading Rashbam reacts and says that the root ע-ו-ר is appropriately used about eyes (״אצל פיקוח עין״), i.e. that it is to be understood as a reference to physical eyesight even when eyes are not explicitly mentioned.

[18]From the continuation of Rashbam's comment here, s.v. לכרמך ולזיתך, it is clear that he understands תבואה as referring specifically only to grain crops.

[19]So also Rashi here.

[20]Rashbam opposes both interpretations that Rashi offers as to the difference between תשמטנה and נטשתה. Rashi's first explanation (following Mekhilta ibid., p. 175) says that תשמטנה means that one should not work the land, while נטשתה means that one should not, after a particular date, eat the produce of the land. Rashi's second explanation (following MQ 3a) is that תשמטנה refers to the more serious types of agricultural work, e.g. plowing and sowing, while נטשתה refers to less serious infractions, such as fertilizing. See also iE's suggestion that תשמטנה refers to the forgiving of debts in the sabbatical year, while נטשתה refers to the agricultural restrictions that apply then.

Rashbam explains more simply that verse 11 simply parallels verse 10. Verse 10 tells us what may be done in the first six years ("sowing" and "gathering"), and then verse 11 tells us that those same things may not be done in the seventh year. See Nahm., who dismisses the explanations of Rashi and iE, and independently arrives at the same understanding as Rashbam's, because he also feels that the two verses must be read as a unit (״הכתוב דבק בראשון״). And see Mendelssohn and Luzzatto, who both follow

לכרמך לזיתך [YOU SHOULD DO THE SAME THING] WITH YOUR VINEYARDS AND YOUR OLIVE GROVES: as what you do with your grain crops. It is common biblical style for the text to mention [specifically only] grain crops, oil and wine (דגן תירוש ויצהר). But [the intention of the text is that] the same rule applies to all foodstuffs that grow from the ground, as it is written [explictly] in the portion *Behar Sinai*.[21]

23:13 ובכל אשר אמרתי אליכם CONCERNING ALL THAT I HAVE TOLD YOU: from the day that I began giving you the commandments[22] until today, BE ON GUARD. The text again and again repeats its

---

Rashbam.

[21]Presumably Rashbam is referring to Lev. 25:7, where the phrase, כל תבואתה--*all of its yield*, is used.

Rashbam opposes the explanation of the Mekhilta, *ibid.* (see especially the alternate reading there: אין לי אלא כרמים וזיתים פירות ועשבים מנין ת"ל ונטשתה), that tries to derive from the word, ונטשתה--*you shall abandon it*," that the restrictions of the sabbatical year apply even to such things as vegetables that are not mentioned explicitly in the text. Rashbam's explanation is that grain, wine and oil are meant to be examples, i.e. that that is the Bible's way of saying "everything that grows." This kind of explanation is comparable to the דבר הכתוב בהווה explanations that he has been offering consistently in his comm. to the last two chapters. See e.g. comm. and note 55 ad 22:20.

Rashbam's assumption that דגן תירוש ויצהר is a way of describing all produce should perhaps be seen as going against common halakhic exegesis. See e.g. Ber. 36a, where the Talmud says quite clearly that separating *ma'aser* from the product of fruit trees is not required according to Torah law, and Rashi there explains (s.v. גבי מעשר) that that is because the Torah wrote (presumably in Deut. 12:17) that *ma'aser* is separated only from דגן תירוש ויצהר, which does *not* include fruit trees. However, the issue is not so clear. A number of halakhists say that the rules of *terumah* and *ma'aser* apply from the Torah to all produce, even if the Torah wrote only דגן תירוש ויצהר. See e.g. the dispute between Maimonides and Rabad in *Ma'aser* 1:9 and in *Ma'aser Sheni* 1:3, and the discussion of Kesef Mishneh, there and ad *Terumot* 2:1.

[22]הדברות, a term that refers specifically to the commandments of the Decalogue. See Touitou (*Tarbiz* 51, p. 234), who argues that Rashbam here reiterates his claim that the Israelites received no commandments from God before the revelation at Sinai, a claim which, Touitou argues, helped Rashbam in his polemics with his Christian contemporaries. See also notes above, ad 12:1 and ad 15:25-26.

warnings.[23] However, the rabbis explained (Shabbat 18a) that this [repetition] teaches that [even] vessels must not labor [on the sabbath].[24]

23:16 וחג הקציר **AND THE FEAST OF THE HARVEST**: The sacrifices written in the section *shor 'o khesev*,[25]--i.e. the "two

---

[23]Rashbam feels that, on the *peshaṭ* level, there is no need to attribute legal, referential meaning to repetitious language in the law sections of the Bible. In other words, one need not ask what new laws are to be derived from the ostensible redundancies. The repetitions serve rhetorical and didactic purposes of emphasizing the importance of certain laws.

[24]It is hard to understand why Rashbam chose to cite this particular explanation of the phrase, "Be on guard concerning all that I have told you," when there are so many rabbinic interpretations of this phrase. (See e.g. Mekhilta *ibid*. 4 [pp. 179-180], where five other interpretations of this phrase may be found. See also Rashi here.) The choice is furthermore puzzling when one considers that the Talmud in Shabbat 18a attributes this interpretation that Rashbam quotes to Bet Shamai, and sees this textual reading, then, as halakhically unauthoritative.

It is possible that Rashbam cites this one rabbinic explanation of the phrase in order to contrast more clearly his *peshaṭ* methodology with halakhic midrash. *He* sees rhetorical and didactic purposes in repetitions. However, in the rabbis' system, as Rashbam wrote above in his introduction to Ex. 21, specific "halakhot are derived from superfluities in Scriptural language."

Alternatively, Rashbam may have felt that this midrashic explanation, even if it is halakhically disputable, does have some attraction to the exegete interested in *peshaṭ*. As Hizq. notes, this midrash does fit well into the immediate context. Verse 12 legislates that the rules of the sabbath apply equally to "your ox and your ass . . . your bondman and the stranger." Then verse 13 follows immediately with the phrase, "Be on guard concerning all that I have told you," which the Talmud then says means that sabbath laws apply not only to free people and to slaves and to animals, but even to inanimate objects.

[25]The section of the Torah extending from Lev. 22:26 to Lev. 23:44. That section, which begins with the words שור או כשב, is seen as constituting one literary unit (פרשה), because that is the Torah passage that is read in the synagogue on Passover and Sukkot.

Rashbam, here, is alluding specifically to the sacrifices outlined in Lev. 23:16-20.

loaves,"²⁶ those (Lev. 23:17) which are the "offering of new grain (מנחה חדשה)" (*ibid.*, vs. 16)--constitute בכורי מעשיך, THE FIRST PRODUCE OF YOUR HANDS, in that one may not use the crops of the new year in the Temple until these sacrifices have been brought.²⁷

וחג האסיף AND THE FEAST OF INGATHERING: The holiday of Sukkot, at the time of ingathering, when "the threshing floors are filled with grain and the vats with wine and oil."²⁸ God commanded us to sit in sukkot [at that time of year] to commemorate the fact that in the wilderness they lived in tents and they had no land and no grain or wine or oil as [they had later on in the land of Canaan; they should give

---

²⁶Rosin felt that the beginning of Rashbam's comment to this verse is hard to follow and he suggested adding five Hebrew words to the text. Following Rosin's emendation, the text of Rashbam would read: "AND THE FEAST OF THE HARVEST: I.e. Shavuot, the holiday in which one offers the sacrifices written in the section *shor 'o khesev* and the 'two loaves' . . .." Rosin's emendation is possible but, to my mind, unnecessary. The text as it stands seems comprehensible, and perhaps the only emendation required is to change the words ושתי הלחם to שתי הלחם.

²⁷See Men. 10:6.
  The major problem that the halakhically-minded exegetes have with this verse is that it (and a number of other biblical verses) uses some form of the word *bikkurim* when discussing Shavuot. Halakhists know, however, that halakhah does not really connect *bikkurim* to Shavuot. (Generally, in halakhic Judaism, *bikkurim* were brought to the Temple well after Shavuot.)
  Rashbam accordingly explains that the phrase בכורי מעשיך applies to the sacrifice of the two loaves which are brought to the Temple on Shavuot. These loaves are appropriately referred to as *bikkurim*, according to Rashbam, because they are the first time in the season that the new crops are used for a *minḥah* offering in the Temple. The same explanation can be found in Rashi, here, and see also Rashi ad Men. 84b, s.v. ת"ל חג הקציר, where Rashi says that the meaning of the word *bikkurim* (in Lev. 23:17) is "the two loaves."
  Unlike Rashbam, Rashi here also provides an alternate explanation of why the words בכורי מעשיך are used in this verse: because (following Bik. 1:3) the earliest time to bring *bikkurim* to the Temple is Shavuot. Cf. Rashbam's comm. and notes below, ad vs. 19, s.v. ראשית.

²⁸An almost verbatim citation of Joel 2:24.

thanks]²⁹ to God for that. So all three holidays are connected to the agricultural produce of the land³⁰--the [times of] ripening,³¹ harvest and ingathering.

23:17 האדון ה' THE LORD, THE MASTER: The One to Whom the land belongs. [Since God is "the Master" of the land, accordingly you may rest assured that] "no one will covet your land when you go up to appear [before the LORD] (34:24)." So it is explained in the portion, *Ki tissa'*, "Three times a year all your males shall appear before האדון, *the Master*, the LORD, the God of Israel (34:23)." Immediately following that verse, the text says "I will drive out nations from your path and enlarge your territory; no one will covet your land when you go up to appear (34:24)." Similarly, a name of God is always used that is appropriate to what God does in that passage.

Our rabbis also explained concerning the verse "The Master (האדון), the LORD of Hosts, will hew off the tree-crowns," (Is. 10:33) that whenever one finds language such as this [describing God], the allusion is to the fact that God is the one who brings people in and takes people out of their dwellings.³²

---

²⁹The translation is based on the six Hebrew words, שהיה להם אחרי כן בארץ ויודו, that Rosin added conjecturally to an obviously defective Hebrew text. See Rosin, footnote 8, and see Rashbam's comm. to Lev. 23:43.

³⁰See Touitou, *Milet* 2, 286-287, who claims that in this verse Rashbam is arguing that the same type of *didactic* explanation may be found here in the Pentateuch for all three pilgrim festivals. To my mind, Rashbam is pointing out only that the same type of *agricultural* explanation may be found here in the text for all three holidays. As I see it, Rashbam offers a didactic explanation only for Sukkot.

³¹אביב. For Rashbam's understanding of the meaning of that word, see comm. and notes to 13:4.

³²Rosin writes here (footnote 10) that he does not know the source of this *derashah*. See Kasher here (footnote 237) who notes that the idea that God's epithet, "the Master," refers to the fact that God "עוקר דיורין ומכניס דיורין--brings people in and takes people out of their dwellings," can be found in Pesiqta de-rav Kahana, and in Yalqut Shimoni, part 2, sec. 14 and 391. There, however, there is no mention of the verse in Isaiah. However, as Kasher notes, one can find this *derashah* concerning the verse in Isaiah in the Zohar (2:124a). As Kasher suggests, it would seem likely that there was some further early midrashic source that has not reached our hands and that connected this

EXODUS XXIII   285

23:18 לא תזבח על חמץ YOU SHALL NOT OFFER THE BLOOD OF MY SACRIFICE WITH ANYTHING LEAVENED: I.e. the "removal of leaven"[33] should take place before the sixth hour[34] on the fourteenth [of Nisan], before the time when the paschal sacrifice may be offered,[35] which is (Ex. 12:6) בין הערביים, i.e. from the seventh hour onwards.[36]

חלב חגי THE FAT OF MY FESTAL OFFERING [SHALL NOT BE LEFT LYING UNTIL MORNING]: [I.e. the fat of] the paschal

---

derashah to the verse in Isaiah. That early source presumably was known both to Rashbam and to the author of the Zohar.

    It is possible that Rashbam's explanation of why the text here in Exodus uses the epithet, "the Master," to describe God is meant to oppose the explanation of the Talmud in Hag. 4a, according to which the reason that a slave need not "appear" before the LORD on the festivals is that he has an אדון, a master, other than God. The text, according to the Talmud, calls God here "the Master" in order to teach us that only the person who has God alone as his Master is required to "appear" before the LORD.

    Rashbam then argues that the choice of God's epithet is not for a halakhic purpose, but rather that the name and epithet chosen for God here, and in all verses, is a function of the role that God plays in each individual verse. See also the differing explantions offered by Hizq. (ad vs. 16), iE (in his shorter comm. to vs. 17) and NJPSC as to why God is referred to here as האדון.

[33] השבתת שאור; an allusion to 12:15.

[34] I.e. before noon.

[35] I.e. ביעור חמץ (the burning of all leaven products) must take place before the time when the paschal sacrifice may be offered.

    Rashbam's interpretation is the standard halakhic understanding. See e.g. Mekhilta *ibid.* 4, p. 185. His formulation of the principle differs somewhat from that of his predecessors. See Nahm.'s objection here to this formulation.

    The Talmud in Pes. 5a derives that rule not from this verse, but from the virtually identical verse, Ex. 34:25. (The text there reads לא תשחט instead of our verse's לא תזבח.) So also Rashi ad 34:25. See the discussion in Kasher here, note 239.

[36] See Pes. 5:1 and Rashi ad Ex. 12:6, s.v. בין הערביים. Apparently Rashbam accepts the standard halakhic understanding that בין הערביים, in Ex. 12:6, could refer to any time after noon. Cf. however iE's comm., there.

sacrifice, about which the text says (Ex. 12:10) "You shall not leave any of it over until morning." The same rule applies also to the *'emurim*.[37]

23:19 ראשית בכורי אדמתך THE CHOICE FIRST FRUITS OF YOUR SOIL: from the "seven species,"[38] concerning which it says in the Torah portion, *Ki tavo'* (Deut. 26:2), "You shall take some of the first fruits of the soil . . . ."[39] When you come up [to Jerusalem] for the pilgrim festivals, that is when you should bring your first fruits.[40]

---

[37] The term *'emurim* refers to those parts of sacrifices that are not eaten but are burnt on the altar.

There are two possible ways of understanding Rashbam's comment here. It is possible that Rashbam is just offering the standard halakhic understanding of this verse.

Alternatively, he might be saying that our verse applies not only to the fat of the paschal sacrifice, but to *'emurim* in general. Our verse then teaches not only about the paschal sacrifice, but about all sacrifices, that those parts that are not to be eaten should be burned before morning. This second explanation can be found in Rashi's comm. to the parallel verse, Ex. 34:25 (s.v. זבח), and appears to be the way that the Mekhilta, *ibid.*, understands our verse.

The more likely explanation appears to me to be that Rashbam sees our verse as relating only to the paschal sacrifice and as extending the rule of 12:10. There we learned that the *edible* parts of the paschal sacrifice have to be burned by morning if they were not eaten. Our verse adds that the *'emurim* of the paschal sacrifice, the parts that may not be eaten, must also be burned by morning.

The fact that Rashbam cites Ex. 12:10 in his comm. here would appear to bolster that explanation.

[38] Wheat, barley, grapes, figs, pomegranates, olives and dates. See Deut. 8:8 and Rashbam's comm. there, ad vs. 9. The rule that *bikkurim* are offered only from the "seven species" is the standard halakhic understanding. See e.g. Bik. 1:3, and Rashi's comm. here.

[39] Rashbam explains the *bikkurim* mentioned in this verse in a different manner than he explained the *bikkurim* mentioned above in verse 16. See notes there. Cf. iE who offers a more consistent explanation.

[40] Rashbam explains why the rules of *bikkurim* are juxtaposed here by the text to the rules of the pilgrim festivals. See also his next comment to this verse, s.v. לא תבשל, where he again explains the relevance of the next phrase in this particular context.

To be sure, there is no halakhic obligation that *bikkurim* be offered specifically when one comes to Jerusalem for a pilgrim festival. Still, it is likely that some (or most) Jews did avail themselves of the opportunity to bring their *bikkurim* to Jerusalem when

EXODUS XXIII

לא תבשל גדי בחלב אמו YOU SHALL NOT BOIL A KID IN ITS MOTHER'S MILK: Goats generally give birth to two kids at the same time. It was customary, then, to slaughter one of the two.[41] And since goats produce much milk,[42] as it says (Prov. 27:27) "Goats' milk will suffice for your food [and the food of your household],"[43] it was common custom to boil the kid in its mother's milk. The text describes the most likely occurrence.[44] It is disgraceful and voracious and gluttonous to consume the mother's milk together with its young.

---

they were in any case coming to Jerusalem for a pilgrim festival.

[41]Rashbam's explanation opposes that of Rashi. Rashi (following Hul. 113a-b) argues that the Hebrew word, גדי, does not mean a young goat, but means the "young" of any animal. Presumably his major purpose in arguing that way is his desire to say that the rules of not eating meat and milk together apply to the meat of all animals, not just goats.
    Rashbam explains that the word really does mean a young goat, but that the example of goats was used by the Torah even though the rule applies to all animals, based on the principle of "the text describes the most likely occurrence." (See explanation below.) So also iE.

[42]This argument can first be found in Mekhilta ibid. 5, p. 195: "מפני מה דבר הכתוב בגדי מפני שהחלב מרובה באמו--Why then does Scripture speak of 'the kid'? Because its mother is rich in milk." So also JBS in his second explanation to this verse. Curiously, cf. iE's shorter comm.: "חלב גדי אחת מעט היא--one goat has only a little bit of milk."

[43]For a somewhat similar understanding of that verse, see Hul. 84a.

[44]On this phrase, see comm. and notes above ad 22:20, s.v. לא תונה.
    Rashbam is saying that the text wishes to outlaw the boiling of any animal in its mother's milk but it chooses to use the example of a goat and its kid because that it is the most likely occurrence, since goats have so much milk and since goats generally produce multiple offspring.

This law is comparable to "it and its young"[45] and to "letting the mother go."[46] The text gave this commandment in order to teach you how to behave in a civilized manner.[47]

And since so many animals were consumed during the pilgrim holidays,[48] the Torah, in this section concerning the pilgrim holidays, warned that one should neither boil a kid in its mother's milk, nor eat[49]

---

[45] אותו ואת בנו (Lev. 22:28), i.e. the law that one may not slaughter a mother and her young on the same day.

[46] שילוח הקין, the law that prohibits taking a mother bird together with its young (Deut. 22:6-7).

The comparison of the law of "the kid in its mother's milk" with the laws of "it and its young" and "letting the mother go," may be found also in iE and in the second explanation offered by JBS here.

[47] דרך תרבות. Already in Rashbam's days, the word תרבות began to be used to mean culture, refinement or civilized behavior. Cf. a similar phrase to Rashbam's in Mahzor Vitry, 517: שהתורה מלמדתו תרבות.

Touitou correctly notes that while Rashbam does not connect his comments here explicitly to Jewish-Christian polemics, Rashbam does tell us, in his comm. to Deut. 22:6, that his explanation of that verse is to be seen in the context of Jewish-Christian polemics "כמו שפירשתי בלא תבשל גדי בחלב אמו--just as I explained concerning the verse 'You shall not boil a kid in its mother's milk'." Touitou explains that Rashbam's rationale for the prohibition on meat and milk constitutes a defense of Judaism from the attacks of Christians, in that Christians would argue that only their religion was based on compassion and mercy. Judaism, they would argue, was stricter and harsher. For that reason Rashbam feels obliged to emphasize the compassionate nature of many laws, including this one. See Touitou, *Milet* 2, pp. 278 and 286. See also Y. Heinemann (*Ta'ame ha-misvot besifrut yisra'el*, vol. 1, p. 47), who cites Rashbam's comment here as an example of how Rashbam adds humanitarian reasons to commandments that were not explained in that way before him. The second explanation offered by JBS here is quite similar to that of Rashbam.

[48] Rashbam again explains why this law is juxtaposed to the rules of the pilgrim festivals. See comm. on this verse, s.v. ראשית, and note 40, there.

[49] To be sure, the *peshat* of this verse (and of its parallel passages) outlaws only *boiling* a kid in its mother's milk, and says nothing about *eating* such a mixture. It is noteworthy that Rashbam follows the standard rabbinic reading, that midrashically expands the prohibition to include the eating of milk and meat. See e.g. the opinion of R. Ishmael in Qid. 57b.

EXODUS XXIII

such a mixture. The same rule applies to all meat and milk, as the rabbis explained in *Shehiṭat ḥullin*.[50]

23:20 שולח מלאך I AM SENDING AN ANGEL BEFORE YOU: As it is written in Joshua (5:14), "I am captain of the LORD's host. Now I have come,"[51] i.e. "[I have come] to deliver Israel."[52]

23:21 אל תמר בו: [The phrase means DO NOT REPLACE HIM, as the verb תמר is] from the same construction as הָמֵר in the phrase (Lev. 27:33), "אם המר ימירנו--If he does make substitution for it."[53] If תמר in our verse is written with a *dagesh*,[54] then the form would be

---

[50]Hul. 8:4.

Shehiṭat ḥullin is the common name of the tractate, Hullin, in the earliest sources.

[51]Rashbam explains that the angel referred to here is the one who appeared to Joshua. Rashbam follows Tanh. *Mishpaṭim* 18 and LT. See also similarly R. Hananel and Nahm.

Rashbam opposes Rashi's explanation, that connects the angel mentioned here to God's statement in Ex. 33:3, "I will not go in your midst," i.e. that God would hand over care of the people to an angel as a punishment for their disobedience. Rashi has to claim here that the text is hinting that the Jews would sin and would be punished. Rashbam, however, sees the promise as a positive development.

[52]The phrase, "to deliver Israel" (להושיע את ישראל), appears twice in the book of Judges (10:1 and 13:5). In both cases it describes the actions of a leader who helped the Israelites deal with their enemies.

Rashbam writes the words, "to deliver Israel," here in order to explain the meaning of the words, "Now I have come" (עתה באתי), in Joshua. Presumably he is opposing the explanation here of Tanh. (*ibid.*), and other midrashim, that say that the angel said, "Now I have come," because he was originally slated to come as a punishment in the days of Moses, after the episode of the golden calf. (See similarly Rashi in Joshua.) Rashbam says that the phrase implies only that he has come just in time to save the Jews during the wars that they were experiencing in Canaan.

[53]As Rashbam notes below, this interpretation is possible only if one reads תָּמֵר, without a *dagesh* in the *mem*, against MT. Still, this understanding seems to be reflected in SR 32:4.

[54]As Rosin writes (footnote 12), Rashbam's comment here shows that he was acquainted with two ms. readings of the text here: MT's תָּמֵּר, and also a different vocalization, תָּמֵר. So also Heidenheim in his *Havanat ha-miqra'*, *ad loc*. See also Esh, p. 86. And see also BH, which suggests emending the text to read תָּמֵר.

from [the prima-*nun* root, נ-מ-ר,] the same as the root of the word נָמֵר, in the phrase (Jer. 48:11), "וריחו לא נמר"--his bouquet is unspoiled,"[55] just as the word תַּפֵּל, in the phrase (Est. 6:10), "אל תפל דבר"--omit nothing," is from the [prima-*nun*] root נ-פ-ל.

But the verb ת-מ-ר here could not be [from the final-*heh* root מ-ר-ה,]--as in the phrase (Lam. 1:20), "מרה מריתי"[56]--I disobeyed"--and could not mean "to disobey." For [if it were from the final-*heh* root מ-ר-ה,] then it would have to read אל תַּמְרֶה, as in the phrase (Josh. 1:18), "Anyone who disobeys (יַמְרֶה) your commands."[57]

כי שמי בקרבו SINCE MY NAME IS IN HIM: I.e. since he commands you in My Name. But he does not have the power to pardon your offences.[58]

---

[55] See ibn Janah's *Sefer ha-shorashim*, s.v. נ-מ-ר, where he argues reasonably that neither תַּמֵּר in our verse nor נָמֵר in Jeremiah are from the root נ-מ-ר. He writes that they are both from the root מ-ר-ר. See Rosin--here (fn. 13) and in RSBM (p. 137, fn. 10)--who writes simply that Rashbam erred.

[56] Rashbam (at least as cited in Rosin's edition) quotes the phrase from Lamentations as מרה מריתי. MT, however, reads מרו מריתי. To be sure, Rashbam's inaccurate citation better proves that the root of that verb is מ-ר-ה.

[57] Rashbam directly opposes the interpretation offered by Rashi, who writes that תמר here means to disobey. See also iE who writes that the word is difficult and cites "the Spanish scholars" (חכמי ספרד) who argue, as Rashbam does, that if the root were מ-ר-ה, then the form expected here would be תַּמְרֶה, not תַּמֵּר. iE however postulates the existence of a root מ-ר-ר with the same meaning as מ-ר-ה. While Rashbam says rather directly here that the root of תמר is not מ-ר-ה, he does not spell out clearly what he thinks that the verb here actually means.

See NJPSC, which follows Rashi and sees the root of תַּמֵּר as מ-ר-ה.

[58] Like most of the commentators, Rashbam tries to explain the order of the clauses here, which make little sense when translated literally: "Pay heed to him . . . for (כי) he will not pardon your offences since (כי) My Name is in him." Rashbam explains that "for he will not pardon your offences" really means "*even though* he will not pardon your offences." Then the verse means: "Pay heed to him because, even if he does not have the power to pardon offences; still he should be obeyed as he is commanding you in My Name." In his syntactical understanding, Rashbam agrees with Rashi and with iE. However his understanding of the meaning of שמי בקרבו opposes that of Rashi who, following Sanh. 38b, explains the phrase to mean that God's Name is connected to that of His angel, Metatron (in that מטטרון and שד-י have the same value in rabbinic numerology).

EXODUS XXIII 291

23:23 כי ילך: means *FOR MY ANGEL WILL GO BEFORE YOU*.[59]

23:24 כי הרס תהרסם *YOU SHALL TEAR THEM DOWN*: Ever since my youth I, of my own accord, emended the text here to read תְּהָרְסֵם, following the paradigm of the dageshized construction,[60] and I considered the texts [here] in France corrupt[61] in their reading תַּהַרְסֵם, which is an undageshized construction,[62] on the same paradigm as תַּהַרְגֶנּוּ in the phrase (Deut. 13:10), "הָרֹג תַּהַרְגֶנּוּ--take his life." But [the text here could not read תַּהַרְסֵם in *qal*;] since the word הָרֵס is written in the dageshized construction, the following word must also be in the dageshized construction, i.e. תְּהָרְסֵם. [The infinitive absolute and

---

[59]Rashbam is again, just as in his previous comment, discussing the possible uses of the word כי. In our verse כי could be read as meaning "when," and then the clause would be connected to the following clauses. Such a reading is found in NJPS. However, Rashbam is arguing that the clause כי ילך מלאכי לפניך means "*for* My angel will go before you," and then it is to be seen as connected to the previous clauses. In other words, God is saying that the angel should be obeyed because (verse 21) he is commanding in God's name, and because (verse 23) he is the one who will help the Israelites capture Canaan.

On the uses of כי, see RSBM, p. 90, note 5, where Rosin notes that Rashbam often briefly explains the meaning of the word, כי. See e.g. Rashbam ad Gen. 49:6, and notes there, p. 353. In that passage, also, it is possible to interpret כי as either "when" or "for," and Rashbam opts for the meaning "for." See also the commentary attributed to Rashbam ad Eccl. 5:6, and Rashbam ad Gen. 18:15, and notes there, pp. 67-68.

It is noteworthy that Rashi also discusses at some length the meanings of the word כי in his commentary to this chapter. See Rashi below, ad vs. 33, and the discussion in Kamin, *Rashi*, p. 176, and footnote 71, there.)

[60]I.e. *piel*.

[61]It is a surprising to find that a medieval Jewish exegete like Rashbam is willing to offer conjectural emendations of MT's vocalization. See also his comm. ad Num. 23:7, s.v. זעמה. See also M. Ahrend's comments in *'Ale sefer*, 5, p. 44, where he argues that the anonymous "teacher" (מורה), referred to in a passage in the Lutzki ms. comm. to Job, must be Rashbam, since no one else among the Ashkenazic rabbis of that generation would have been likely to have offered the emendation of the vocalization proposed by that "teacher." See also Esh, pp. 86-87.

[62]I.e. *qal*.

the following verb must be in the same construction,] just like the phrase (further on in this same verse), "שַׁבֵּר תְּשַׁבֵּר--YOU SHALL SMASH."[63]

Later I found that the reading in all the texts in Spain and Germany[64] was [תְּהָרְסֵם], in the dageshized construction, just like the emendation [of the French texts] that I had proposed.

23:25 והסירותי AND "I WILL REMOVE FROM YOUR MIDST that SICKNESS: that comes from bad water," as I explained concerning [the waters of] Marah.[65]

23:26 לא תהיה משכלה NO WOMAN [IN YOUR LAND] SHALL MISCARRY: And people will also not die [soon] after they reach the age of majority; rather I WILL LET YOU ENJOY THE FULL COUNT OF YOUR DAYS, to come to the grave in ripe old age.[66]

---

[63]Where both the infinitive absolute and the following verb are in the *piel* construction.

The same grammatical point is made by Rashbam in his *Dayqut*, p. 47.

[64]That Rashbam, like most of the Northern French rabbis of his day, had connections with German Jewish communities and access to their ms. readings is not surprising. His assertion that he also researches the textual reading in "all the texts of Spain" is very impressive.

[65]See comm. and notes to Ex. 15:25-26, where Rashbam explains that healing is often used in contexts of making water potable, as in this verse where the previous phrase promises that God will "bless your bread and your water." In his comm. to Ex. 15, Rashbam also notes the connection between these verses in Exodus and the story of Elisha "healing" water in II Kings 2. Here Rashbam may also be alluding to that passage when he uses the phrase מים רעים, which appears in the Bible only in that story (II Kings 2:19).

Cf. Eruv. 65a, where the Talmud allegorizes the reference to water in our verse and understands it as meaning "wine." Tos. there, s.v. וקרי, asserts that on the *peshaṭ* level, the verse really refers to water. Tos. there, like Rashbam here, draws the connection between this verse and the above-mentioned passages in Ex. 15 and II Kings 2.

[66]לבא בכלח אלי קבר; a quotation from Job 5:26. Cf. the common rabbinic explanation (e.g. Qid. 38a, cited by LT here), that את מספר ימיך אמלא means that a righteous person often dies on the same day that he was born.

EXODUS XXIII

23:27 את אימתי I WILL SEND FORTH MY TERROR: A terror from God[67] on those who make war against you.[68]

והמתי I WILL CAUSE CONFUSION: והמתי should be understood as if written והממתי.[69] It means "I will cause confusion with noise,"[70] as it is written (I Sam. 7:10), "The LORD thundered mightily against the Philistines and he threw them into confusion (ויהומם)." So also [the verb ה-מ-מ refers to confusion caused by noise in the phrase (II Sam. 22:15), "He let loose . . .] lightning and threw them into confusion (ויהם)."[71]

[והמותי must be understood as being from the geminate root ה-מ-מ,] just as from the root ס-ב-ב, one says סבתי.[72] If the verb here were connected to "death,"[73] the form would be והֵמַתִּי.[74]

Rashbam explains the relationship between the two clauses of the verse. The blessing here is in logical stages, first promising successful conception and pregnancy and then promising a long life span. See similarly comm. ad Ex. 1:7.

[67] חתת א-לוהים. The phrase is from Gen. 35:5.

[68] Rashbam may be opposing the midrashic interpretations offered in the commentary of the tosaphists, Ox.-Bod. ms. 946 (cited in Gellis' *Tosafot ha-shalem*, vol. 8, p. 352) who interpret אימתי as a reference to the Messiah or to the Ten Plagues.

[69] I.e. the root is ה-מ-מ.

[70] See comm. ad Ex. 14:24, where Rashbam makes the same point about the verb ה-מ-מ, and notes there.

[71] Presumably Rashbam's proof from II Sam. 22:15 is based on the previous verse, there, "The LORD thundered forth from heaven, the Most High sent forth His voice."

[72] E.g. I Sam. 22:22. See similarly comm. ad Dt. 32:41, s.v. אם שנתי. On Rashbam's tendency to use the verb ס-ב-ב as his paradigm for all geminate verbs, see comm. above, ad 16:17-18, and note 35, there.

[73] I.e. if it were from the hollow root מ-ו-ת.

[74] So also Rashi here, at much greater length, and LT. Possibly all these commentators are arguing against a version of the Targum which connected והמתי here to the root מ-ו-ת. See Rashi: "והמתרגם והמותי ואיקטיל טועה הוא--he who renders

23:31 וְשַׁתִּי I WILL SET: וְשַׁתִּי should be understood as if written וְשַׁתֵּתִי.[75] So also the word כָּרַתִּי in the phrase (Ps. 89:4), "I have made (כָּרַתִּי) a covenant," should be understood as if written כָּרַתֵּתִי.[76]

מים סוף FROM THE SEA OF REEDS: which is in the extreme east of the land of Israel, as is proven[77] in the Torah portion, *'Elleh ha-devarim*.[78]

עד ים פלשתים TO THE SEA OF PHILISTIA,[79] which is to the west [of the land of Israel], as it is written (Is. 9:11), "Philistia from the west."

והמותי into Aramaic as ואקטיל--I shall kill' is mistaken." Alternatively, Rashbam may be opposing yet again the same ms. of the Tosaphists' comm. to the Torah, mentioned in the note to the previous phrase. In that ms., והמתי *is* seen as derived from the root מ-ו-ת.

On Rashbam's distinguishing between forms of hollow and geminate roots, see above, chapter 9 note 17, and chapter 12 note 32.

[75]I.e. the *dagesh* in the *tav* of ושתי is because the letter represents both the last letter of the root (ש-ו-ת) and the first letter of the suffix (תי). See similarly Rashi, at greater length.

[76]See also Rashbam's *Dayqut*, p. 40, where Rashbam uses precisely these two examples--ושתי and כרתי--to illustrate the pattern that final-*tav* verbs follow.

[77]The ms. reads כמו שמוכיח. Rosin here (note 8) emends to read כמו שאוכיח--i.e. "as I shall prove"--perhaps unnecessarily.

[78]See Rashbam's comm. ad Dt. 1:1, where he argues, as he does here, that the Sea of Reeds must be at the extreme *east* of the land of Israel. There Rashbam writes explicitly that the Sea of Reeds and the Dead Sea are the same body of water. He reaches that improbable conclusion because he feels that the opening line of Deuteronomy shows that when Moses addressed the Israelites in the Plains of Moab, just across the Jordan from Jericho, they were then standing מול סוף, i.e. near the Sea of Reeds.

It is difficult to fault Rashbam for his "creative" geography. It is hard to imagine that accurate maps of the Middle East were available to him. See Nahm.'s comm. to Gen. 35:16, where he, after moving to the land of Israel, corrects a geographical misunderstanding that he had had when he originally wrote his comm. in Spain.

[79]I.e. the Mediterranean Sea.

וממדבר AND FROM THE WILDERNESS, to the south, through which the Israelites wandered, עד הנהר UP TO THE RIVER, i.e. the Euphrates River,[80] which is in the north, as [it is in Babylon.] And Baylon is in the north, as it is written (Jer. 1:14), "From the north shall disaster break loose."[81]

---

[80]So also Rashi.

[81]Rashbam's lengthy geographical description is meant to prove that the Sea of Reeds really is the easternmost border of the Land of Israel. The other three geographical referents here--Philistia, the wilderness and the river--delineate the borders on the west, the south and the north sides, respectively. So, by the process of eleimination, the Sea of Reeds *must* be the easternmost border of the land. So also JBS. See also a similar, but not identical, interpretation in Rashi ad Ex. 10:19, s.v. ימה סוף.

EXODUS XXIV

24:1-5 ואל משה אמר THEN HE SAID TO MOSES: All of the preceding texts, beginning with the verses (Ex. 20:18-19), "Moses approached the thick cloud where God was. And God said to Moses: Thus shall you say to the Israelites . . .," and up to this point, all describe [teachings that were meant for the Israelites as a whole and were said by God on] the day that the Israelites heard the Decalogue.[1] [Now in our verse,] THEN HE SAID TO MOSES, Moses alone is being addressed,[2] on that same day,[3] when he was coming down the mountain, and was being told, "COME UP TO THE LORD, tomorrow, WITH AARON . . . ." Immediately following that, Moses did come down and (vs. 3) REPEATED TO THE PEOPLE ALL THE COMMANDS OF THE LORD . . . . The next day he built an altar

---

[1]This comment does not appear to be consistent with Rashbam's comm. ad 23:13, where Rashbam explains the phrase, "concerning all that I have told you," as meaning, "from the day that I began giving you the commandments," i.e. the Decalogue, "until today," implying that not all the rules of chapters 21f. were communicated on the same day as the Decalogue.

[2]See the same point in NJPSC: "The Hebrew inverts the usual syntactical order and literally reads, 'And to Moses he said,' thus emphasizing that this particular instruction pertains specifically to Moses and not to the assembled Israelites, as in previous instances." So also iE, in his longer comm.

[3]Rashbam's interpretation opposes that of Rashi, here, who claims (following Shabbat 88a) that all of the events of 24:1-11 occurred *before* the day when the Israelites heard the Decalogue. Like Rashbam, see iE and Nahm., at much greater length. Nahm. argues further that this interpretation can be found as one of two opinions in Mekhilta (*Ba-ḥodesh* 3, p. 211). Like Rashi, see JBS.

Rashbam uses the phrase בו ביום here, the same phrase that Rashi uses in his commentary to vs. 3, s.v. ויבא, to say something entirely different from what Rashi is saying.

(verse 4) and offered sacrifices (verse 5), and, on that same day,[4] he climbed up [the mountain again] (verse 9)[5] and (verse 16) THE CLOUD HID HIM[6] FOR SIX DAYS.

[The meaning of] THEN HE SAID TO MOSES is that *an angel* said to Moses, "COME UP TO THE LORD." [The speaker could not be God himself,] for the text does not read, "Come up *to me*," as it does below (vs. 12) where the text reads, "[THE LORD SAID TO MOSES,] 'COME UP TO ME'."[7]

---

[4] Again Rashbam uses the phrase בו ביום and again he is disputing Rashi's chronolgy for, as Rashi would have it, the sacrifices that Moses offered were *not* on the same day that he went up the mountain.

[5] Rashbam does not explain how he understands the three separate verses below (9, 13 and 15) that all describe Moses as going up the mountain. Presumably he sees them all as describing the same ascent that, to Rashbam's mind, took place the day following the theophany at which the Decalogue was given to the Israelites. See NJPS, verse 15, "When Moses *had ascended* the mountain" (emphasis mine) and NJPSC, vs. 12.

[6] It appears that Rashbam understands the word ויכסהו, in vs. 16, as meaning that the cloud covered Moses, not that the cloud covered the mountain. See the two explanations in Rashi, ad vs. 16 (following Yoma 4a-b).

[7] See similar arguments in Rashbam's comm. ad 19:11.

The syntactical problem here is discussed by a number of the commentators. iE and Nahm. both suggest that the construction is not so anomalous; the biblical text, they argue, will often refer to God (or to another character) by name when a pronoun would do. Curiously, Rashbam's approach here has something in common with the midrashic approach to this problem, found in Sanh. 38b. There the Talmud suggests that the anomaly in the verse can be resolved by seeing a reference here to the angel, Metatron. But it is not perfectly clear what the Talmud means by that suggestion. Nahm. (here) explains it to mean that the name of God in the phrase, "Come up to the LORD," is a reference to the angel, Metatron. Rashi (in Sanh., s.v. זהו מטטרון) says that the Talmud means that the speaker referred to by the narrator in this verse is Metatron. Rashbam's interpretation is then similar to Rashi's understanding of the Talmudic explanation.

On Rashbam's willingness (in other passages) to see the tetragrammaton as a reference to an angel, see comm. and notes above, ad 3:4, 13:21 and 19:11.

24:4 לשנים עשר שבטי ישראל [HE SET UP AN ALTAR ... WITH TWELVE PILLARS] FOR THE TWELVE TRIBES OF ISRAEL: This demonstrates that all of the tribes agreed to ratify the covenant.⁸

24:5 את נערי: [The word נערי means] the first-borns.⁹

24:7 ספר הברית THE BOOK OF THE COVENANT: That was described above (vs. 4), "Moses wrote down [all the commands of the LORD]."¹⁰

נעשה ונשמע WE WILL PERFORM AND WE WILL HEAR: That which we have already heard, WE WILL PERFORM. And the laws that He will command us in the future, WE WILL HEAR and we will observe.¹¹

---

⁸Touitou argues (*Tarbiz* 51, p. 234) that Rashbam's comment here should be seen as polemically motivated. The Christians felt that the Decalogue had some unique status as binding revelation. Rashbam then, according to Touitou, emphasizes that all of the words of the covenant were ratified by the Israelites at Sinai, for the verse here reads, "Moses then wrote down *all* the commands of the LORD," and Rashbam explained above ad vs. 1 that the laws referred to here include all the laws in chapters 21, 22 and 23.

⁹So also Rashi, following Zev. 115b. See also Rashi's comm. there, s.v. ויתיב.
The first-borns were traditionally seen as the original *kohanim*. See e.g. Rashbam's comm. ad 13:2, s.v. באדם, and notes there.

¹⁰Rashbam continues to oppose Rashi's interpretation that Moses wrote down here only those parts of the Torah that preceded the revelation at Sinai. See Rashi's comm., here and ad vs. 4, and see Rashbam's comm. and notes above, ad vs. 1 and ad vs. 4.

¹¹See Urbach's edition of *'Arugat ha-bosem*, vol 1, p. 177, where this same interpretation is attributed to "[ן]הפשטן--the *peshat*-oriented exegete," presumably a reference to Rashbam. See footnote 11, there.
Rashbam opposes the standard accepted Jewish midrashic interpretation, that this verse shows just how committed the Israelites were to Torah, for they agreed to observe (נעשה) God's commandments even though they had not yet heard them (hence the future tense, ונשמע--we *shall* hear). See e.g. Shabbat 88a.
It is intersting to note that Rashi does not comment here on the phrase, נעשה ונשמע. It is possible that Rashi feels that the rabbinic understanding of the phrase is so clearly the true meaning of the text that he does not even bother to explain the phrase here; he assumes that anyone who is able to read his comm. already knows what נעשה ונשמע means. Cf., however, Rashi's comm. ad Gen. 37:27.

24:10 ויראו את א-להי ישראל THEY SAW THE GOD OF ISRAEL: ["Seeing God" in this phrase is to be understood] in the same manner as in the phrase (33:23), "You will see My back."[12]

לבנת: means whiteness (לובן).[13]

וכעצם LIKE THE APPEARANCE: The word עצם means "appearance,"[14] as in the phrase (Lam. 4:7), "Their appearance (עצם) became redder than coral."[15]

לטהר [LIKE THE APPEARANCE OF A] CLEAR [SKY]: The word לטהר means when the sky is clear, without clouds.[16]

The standard rabbinic reading is more easily accepted if one assumes that the events described here actually took place *before* the theophany at Sinai, an assumption that Rashi makes, but that Rashbam does not. See comm. and notes above, ad vs. 1.

The interpretation found in Rashbam can also be found in LT and in iE's shorter comm. Both of those exegetes offer this interpretation as one of two or more alternatives, including the more traditional understanding. Rashbam alone does not feel required to mention the traditional understanding alongside of this new reading.

[12]Rashbam's interpretation opposes that of Rashi, who feels that the "seeing" described in this verse represents some improper activity for which the elders really deserved to die. See Rashi ad vs. 11, s.v. לא שלח ידו. That understanding can be found in many earlier sources, e.g. Ps.-Jon. and Tanh. 'Ahare 6. Rashbam, on the other hand, suggests that just as Moses legitimately "saw God's back," so also the elders here legitimately "saw the God of Israel." Similarly to Rashbam, see e.g. JBS and Nahm. Rashbam's explanation here is continued in his comm. below, ad vs. 11, s.v. ואל אצילי.

On Rashbam's conception of what it means to see God, see comm. and notes ad Gen. 48:8 and also comm. below ad 33:18 and 33:23.

[13]Rashbam's interpretation opposes the explanation of Rashi who (following Ps.-Jon. and others) connects the word לבנת to the word לבנה--brick. Rashbam's interpretation can be found also in Saadyah and in LT and in ibn Janah's *Sefer ha-shorashim*, s.v. ל-ב-נ. Like Rashi, see e.g. iE and NJPS.

[14]So also Rashi, and ibn Janah, *ibid.*, s.v. ע-צ-מ.

[15]So also Rashi, there: שהיו מראיהם אדום.

[16]So also JBS, citing Job 37:21 as a prooftext. (See NJPS there: " . . . in the heavens until the wind comes and clears [ותטהרם] them [of clouds].")

24:11 ואל אצילי YET HE, i.e. God, DID NOT RAISE HIS HANDS AGAINST אצילי, i.e. the elders, OF THE ISRAELITES: I.e. even though they "saw the God of Israel" (vs. 10). [One might reasonably be concerned that they would die after seeing God,] as it is written (Num. 4:20), "[Let them not go inside] and see the dismantling of the Tabernacle lest they die."[17]

So also it is written, concerning the men of Beth-shemesh, [that God put some of them to death] (I Sam. 6:19) "because they looked into the Ark of the LORD." Similarly it is written (Ex. 3:6) that Moses "was afraid to look [at God]."

But here [the "seeing" of God was not a reprehensible action; rather] God honored them by appearing to them because of the covenant that He was making with them. [God *generally* appears to people when He makes a covenant with them,] as I explained[18] concerning the "covenant between the pieces," [that God appeared to Abram when (Gen. 15:17) "there appeared a smoking oven and a flaming torch] which passed between those pieces,"[19] and it is written further there,[20] "On that day the LORD made a covenant with Abram . . . ." So also below,

---

[17]See Rashbam's comm. there, and see Rosin's footnote 7, there. Rosin argues against the reading of Rashbam's comment found in all the printed editions of the comm. on Num.: "כשסותרין את ההיכל נגלה ה' ואם יראו ימותו"--when they dismantle the Tabernacle, God is revealed and if they see Him they would die." Rosin suggests that the text there should be read without the word, "'ה--God"; the comm. then means that when they dismantle the Tabernacle, *the Tabernacle* is revealed, and seeing the revealed Tabernacle might lead to their death.

To my mind, the context of Rashbam's comment both here and in Numbers supports the reading that Rosin dismisses. (See also a similar understanding to Rashbam's in Nahm., there, at the end of his comm. to the verse.) Presumably Rosin dismisses that reading primarily out of a desire to save Rashbam from the ostensibly gross anthropomorphism of portraying God as becoming visible when the Tabernacle is dismantled. However, I feel that Rosin was much more concerned about such problems than Rashbam was. See comm. and notes ad Gen. 48:8.

[18]In the lost section of Rashbam's comm. to Genesis.

[19]See NJPSC there: "The principal party, here God, passes between the pieces. He is represented by the smoke and the fire, which are frequent symbols of the Divine Presence." See also Rashi ad Gen. 15:10, s.v. ויבתר.

[20]In the very next verse.

in the covenant that is made in the Torah portion, *Ki tissa'*, [God says, (Ex. 33:23)] "You will see My back," and then it is written (34:6), "the LORD passed before him," and then it is written (34:10), "[God said:] 'I hereby make a covenant'."[21]

ויאכלו וישתו [THEY BEHELD GOD] AND THEY ATE AND DRANK: They offered the burnt offerings and they ate the well-being offerings, mentioned above (verse 5), where it is written, "they sacrificed offerings of well-being."[22]

24:12 אשר כתבתי [I WILL GIVE YOU THE STONE TABLETS . . .] WHICH I HAVE INSCRIBED: I.e. the tablets written "in God's writing," (32:16) which God gave him after the forty days.[23]

---

[21]See comm. and notes above, ad vs. 10, s.v. ויראו. Rashbam continues the explanation that he began there, opposing Rashi's understanding that when the elders "saw God" they were doing something reprehensible. Rashbam explains that, as part of making a covenant, God appears to those with whom he is making the covenant.

[22]Rashbam opposes both interpretations offered here by Rashi. The first interpretation (following Tanh. *Beha'alotekha* 16) sees the eating and drinking here as an inappropriate action for people who were, at that time, "beholding God." The second understanding that Rashi suggest is that of Onq., who explained the eating and drinking described here as metaphorical: the elders "feasted" their eyes on the divine presence. Rashbam argues both that there is nothing pejorative about the phrase, and that it need not be seen as metaphorical; it simply says that the sacrifices described above, in vs. 5, were offered and consumed in the appropriate manner. So also iE.

[23]That Moses spent on Mt. Sinai. See 31:18.
Rashbam's interpretation opposes those midrashim that try to see in this verse a reference to God giving the entire Torah to the Israelites. According to those midrashim, that is why the verse says that God will give Moses לחת האבן והתורה והמצוה--the tablets *and* the Torah *and* the commandments. See e.g. Ber. 5a and LT. Rashi offers a more *peshat*-oriented version of that same explanation: God gave Moses the two tablets *in which* one can find allusions to the entire Torah.
Rashbam offers a more limited understanding of the verse. So also iE, who writes in his shorter comm.: יש אומרים "תורה" שבכתב "והמצוה" שבעל פה והנכון" כי על הלוחות לבדם ידבר--some say that 'Torah' means the written Torah, and that 'commandments' means the oral Torah; but the correct explanation is that [both terms] refer only to the tablets [i.e. the Decalogue]." So also NJPS: "the two tablets *with* the teaching and the commandments."

EXODUS XXV

RASHBAM'S INTRODUCTION

If I write in brief concerning the [next] sections of the text dealing with the Tabernacle and the breastpiece and the ephod,[1] [more] details may be found in the commentaries of Rabbi Solomon--may the memory of the righteous be a blessing!--my mother's father.[2]

COMMENTARY

25:2 תרומה: means something separated from one's wealth.[3]

---

[1] Rashbam presumably means the Torah portions of *Terumah*, which deals with the construction of the Tabernacle, and *Teṣavveh*, which opens with a description of the priests' clothing ("These are the vestments they are to make: a breastpiece, an ephod . . ." [28:4]).

[2] Rashbam's attitude here to Rashi's commentaries appears to be deferential. He says that he allows himself to be brief since he knows that the issues were covered well by his grandfather. This same attitude is reflected in Rashbam's final comment to the book of Exodus. Of course, in order to understand Rashbam's total attitude to the works of Rashi, one must look at these passages in the context of the many other references to Rashi in Rashbam's work. Most of those references are not as complimentary as this one. See the general discussion in the introduction to my Genesis volume, pp. 17-22.

I must admit that Rashbam's introductory comment here raises more questions in my mind than it solves. What precisely is the purpose of the comment at this point in the text? Did Rashbam in fact "write in brief," as he asserts here, concerning the following sections of the text? To my mind it appears that he wrote about many of these topics in an uncharacteristically *lengthy* manner. Is he simply trying to help the reader who wants to learn how the Tabernacle was constructed by suggesting to that reader to read more than Rashbam's commentary in order to understand the issues properly? Or is the major purpose of this comment to demonstrate his deference--real or feigned--to Rashi and through him to traditional exegesis? See Rashbam's explanation, in his introductory comment to chapter 21, above, of what the reader might expect to find in, respectively, his commentary and Rashi's commentary. See also notes, there.

[3] Rashbam's explanation follows that of Rashi almost verbatim. Presumably both exegetes are trying to explain why the verb, "ויקחו"--and they will take," is used; arguably it would have been more appropriate to write "ויתנו לי תרומה"--let them *give*

25:4 ותולעת שני RED YARNS: The word תולעת is the name of a yarn dyed red. The word שני is the name of the specific color (red). [One may see that תולעת means "dyed yarn,"] as it is written (Nah. 2:4) "The soldiers are מתולעים--wearing colored clothing," and as it is written (Lam. 4:5), "Those who were reared עלי תולע--on colored clothing."

Proof can also be adduced from the verse (Is. 1:18), "Be your sins כשנים they can turn white as snow; be they red as תולע, they can become like fleece (צמר)." The word שני and the word "snow" are [both used in the first stich of the quotation as they are] both names of paints used by a painter--red paint and white paint respectively. The words תולע and "fleece" are [both used in the second stich of the quotation, as they are both] names of types of wool, the distinction between them being that תולע is colored wool, while "fleece" (צמר) is white and not dyed.[4]

ושש: means linen.[5] However, all the other materials listed in this verse are types of dyed wool.[6]

ועזים GOATS: I.e. spun goats' hairs.[7]

---

me a donation or a gift." Rashi and Rashbam then explain that the Israelites are instructed to *take*, i.e. to separate the gift from their wealth.

[4]Rashbam's long comment here is presumably meant to address the issue of the possible redundancy of the phrase, תולעת שני, since both elements of the phrase appear to mean the same thing. Rashbam may also be opposing those exegetes who claim that תולעת is the name of a color (e.g. Rashi in Isaiah, and one of the opinions cited in iE, here) or those exegetes who claim that the phrase means silk (another opinion cited in iE, here). See also Rashbam's comment on the next word, ושש.

[5]So also Rashi, following Yoma 71b.

[6]Perhaps Rashbam is reiterating here that תולעת שני must be understood as a type of dyed yarn, and not as "silk." See comm. s.v. ותולעת, above, and note 4, there.

[7]So also Rashi and JBS, who both use the common rabbinic phrase נוצה של עזים for goats' hair (e.g. Shab. 28b), instead of Rashbam's more unusual phrase, שערי עזים. All these exegetes feel obliged to comment on the language here as "the Hebrew is elliptical, omitting the word 'hair,' which is left to the imagination" (NJPSC). Cf. however Rashi below, ad 35:26, where the same elliptical phrase is found and Rashi offers a midrashic explanation.

EXODUS XXV

25:6 לשמן המשחה [SPICES FOR] THE ANOINTING OIL: As the text explains below in the Torah portion *Ki tissa'*.[8]

ולקטורת הסמים: means AND FOR the preparation of THE INCENSE (ולקטורת), you should bring HERBS (סמים), as it is written in the Torah portion *Ki tissa'* (30:34), concerning the incense, "Take the herbs (סמים). . . ."[9]

25:7 מלואים FOR SETTING: [These precious stones are referred to as אבני מילואים] because each stone fills (ממלאה) the depression in the frame, just like the precious stones in a ring.[10]

25:8 מקדש A SANCTUARY: [The sanctuary is referred to with the word מקדש because] it is connected to the idea of "meeting." [God is

---

[8] See below 30:23-25, where the text explains how spices were mixed into the anointing oil.

[9] Rashbam opposes the standard understanding (e.g. Rashi) of the phrase קטורת הסמים as being a construct ("the קטורת *of* the סמים"). According to that reading, the verse says that *two* things are to be gathered: oil and spices (בשמים). The verse then explains that the spices will be used for two different purposes--for the anointing oil and for קטורת הסמים--"the aromatic incense."

According to Rashbam, the syntax is to be understood differently. The verse says that *three* separate things are to be gathered: oil, spices and herbs. The verse provides just one use for each of the three things requested: the oil will be used "for lighting," the spices will be used "for the anointing oil," and the herbs will be used "for the incense (ולקטורת)."

Like Rashbam, see also JBS and Hizq. iE, only in his longer commentary, argues at length against this interpretation which he attributes to "contemporary scholars" (חכמי הדור). Margaliot (*Sefer 'asaf*, pp. 363 and 368) cites this verse to prove that between writing his shorter and longer commentaries on Exodus, iE read Rashbam's commentary. See also Simon's arguments against Margaliot's thesis (in Simon's article, cited above in notes to 4:10).

[10] So also Rashi. See also Rashi and Rashbam below ad 28:17. Rashi and Rashbam both interpret the word differently from the Talmud (Sotah 48b), which says that the word מלואים is applied to these stones because they had to be kept whole and no cuts could be made in them. (See Rashi there in Sotah, s.v. במלואותם.) See Nahm., here, who argues at length against the explanation found in Rashi's Torah comm., and in favor of the talmudic understanding.

saying that "it is the place] wherein "I will prepare[11] and ready myself to speak to them," as it is written (29:43), "There I will meet with the Israelites."[12]

25:9 ככל EXACTLY AS I SHOW YOU: Just like the images of the vessels and the structures, images which God literally showed to Moses.[13] Just as in Babylon, God [literally] showed Ezekiel in "visions of God"[14] [the images of how to reconstruct] the Second Temple. Additionally, God "showed" Moses [how to construct the vessels and the structures of the Tabernacle] through words, by explaining to him [how to do it], as it is written.[15]

So it is proven below [that the instructions that Moses received were not just oral instructions, as it is written (25:40), "Note well and follow the patterns for them] that you are being shown *on the*

---

[11]שאתקדש. See comm. and notes ad 19:10, where Rashbam explains that the root ק-ד-ש often has connotations of "preparing."

[12]Virtually all the commentators feel obliged to explain why the term מקדש, which is generally used by the Bible and by later Judaism to describe the Temple in Jerusalem, is used here when speaking of the Tabernacle in the desert.
    Rashbam opposes the more common interpretation (e.g. Rashi and iE) that connects מקדש here to the idea of "holiness."

[13]So also LT and iE (in both his commentaries). See however JBS who writes here that there are two possibilities. The verb "show" here might imply a visual image but it might also simply refer to the oral instructions that Moses received. JBS adds that that is a standard way that people use the verb "to show". It is perhaps against JBS's position that Rashbam is going to such lengths here to prove that Moses must have seen some visual image.

[14]Ezekiel 40:2. See there and the following chapters.
    In iE's shorter comm. here, he also compares what Moses was shown to a divine vision. However, in iE's longer comm., he makes a distinction between what Ezekiel saw, in a dream, and what Moses was shown, when awake. Margaliot (*Sefer 'asaf*, pp. 363 and 368-9) posits that iE changed his mind after reading Rashbam's commentary. Simon (*Bar Ilan Annual* 3 [1965], pp. 132-133) argues at length against the logic of that position.

[15]Chapters 25 to 30 contain God's detailed oral instructions to Moses.

mountain."¹⁶ If Moses were being given only oral instructions, then the text would have read [simply "the patterns that] you are being shown." Why would the text have had to specify "*on the mountain*"?¹⁷

25:10 ועשו ארון עצי שטים THEY SHALL MAKE AN ARK OF ACACIA WOOD: The *'alef* in the word אֲרוֹן is vocalized with a *ḥataf pataḥ* because the word is in the construct: "an ark *of* acacia wood."¹⁸

Even though [it might appear from the texts that there is a discrepancy between the description of the order in which the construction actually took place and the order of the commands that Moses received, that is not the case. For] when it came to the actual construction, we find that Bezalel made the Tabernacle first and then only later made the vessels--the Ark, the table and the lampstand¹⁹--for where would one put the table and the lampstand if the Tabernacle itself had not yet been constructed? However, when the instructions are given [here,] the detailed explanations of the Ark and the table are given first,²⁰ [and only after that is the commandment about how to construct the Tabernacle explained in detail,²¹] for the Tabernacle is really made for the [purpose of housing] the Ark. The Ark is the most important

---

¹⁶See also comm. and notes below, ad 25:40.

¹⁷It is not clear to me what Rashbam feels is proven by the phrase "on the mountain." See below, ad vs. 40, where Rashbam makes the argument that Moses was literally shown the pattern of the lampstand, and Rashbam's proof there is not dependent on the words "on the mountain."

¹⁸See also iE's shorter comm. where he explains that some people claim erroneously, on the basis of II Kings 12:10, that the form אֲרוֹן in biblical Hebrew can be seen as an alternative form of the word אָרוֹן, and need not be seen as a construct form. Presumably Rashbam is also arguing here against that opinion, and saying that the *ḥataf pataḥ* here is only because the form is in the construct.

For sources that make the opposite argument, see Krinski here, *Yahel 'or*, 178.

¹⁹See the order of construction in Ex. 36:8-37:24.

²⁰In 25:10-30.

²¹In the following chapter, chapter 26.

aspect of [fulfilling the command (in vs. 8)] "Let them make me a sanctuary."[22]

25:11 זהב טהור PURE GOLD: I.e. refined gold.[23]

25:12 ויצקת לו CAST FOR IT [FOUR GOLD RINGS]: These rings should protrude from [the gold of the overlay of] the table; they should not be attached to the table.[24]

---

[22]See a similar idea in LT: "[the text] began with the Ark, since it has special holiness."

A famous midrash that appears in Berakhot 55a claims that Moses was originally instructed to build a Tabernacle, and only after that to make the vessels. Moses then, on his own initiative, switched the instructions when passing them on to Bezalel, telling him to make the vessels first and only later the Tabernacle. Bezalel, however, demurred, and asked Moses whether it was not the case that God mentioned the Tabernacle first, before the vessels. Moses then admitted that he had, inappropriately, changed the divine instructions. That midrash can be found in some versions of Rashi's comm. to 38:22.

Rashbam here is taking issue with that midrash and arguing that the original instructions to Moses logically enough mentioned the vessels before the Tabernacle as God provided details about items according to their relative importance, not according to the order of construction. On the source for the midrash's assertion that the original instructions from God placed the Tabernacle first, see Tosafot there in Berakhot, s.v. לך.

See also comm. and notes ad 36:8.

[23]See similarly iE's shorter comm.

[24]In other words, the rings should not be made separately and soldered onto the corners of the table. Rather one sufficiently large piece of gold should be taken and shaped to form the overlay and the rings that protrude from it.

Rashbam explains that the gold work that is done for the table should be done in the same manner as the gold work for the covering of the Ark and for the lampstand, i.e. hammered out from one piece of gold (מקשה). (See vss. 18 and 31 below and the commentaries of Rashi and Rashbam, there.)

I do not know why Rashbam says here that the same rule applies to the rings of the Ark. Cf. the Da'at miqra' commentary which argues that the language of this verse specifically implies that the rings of the Ark were not made מקשה, but were made separately and then attached to the Ark. See also NJPS: "Cast four rings for it, to be attached . . ." (emphasis added).

EXODUS XXV

ושתי טבעות (AND) TWO RINGS: Of the four [aforementioned] rings.[25]

על צלעו האחת ON ONE OF ITS SIDE WALLS: On the side of the width.[26] The poles then stuck out towards the direction of the hekhal. For one must assume that the length of the Ark went from north to south and that the poles went from east to west.[27]

---

[25]Our verse may, in theory, be understood to mean either that the table has four rings or that it has eight rings. If the vav at the beginning of the word ושתי is translated as meaning and, then the verse would imply that there are eight rings total. ("Cast four rings for it . . . and two rings on one of its side walls and two on the other.") That interpretation is, according to JBS, the peshat reading of the verse and it is also offered hesitatingly in Tos. Yoma 72a, s.v. כתיב ("were I not afraid of my colleagues I would suggest that the Ark had eight rings, as the verse proves--ואי לאו דמסתפינא מחברייא הוה אמינא דח' טבעות היו בארון וכן מוכיח הפסוק"). It is also the interpretation preferred by iE in his longer comm. (although in his shorter comm. iE writes that many claim that there were eight rings total, but he, iE, disagrees). For further sources that offer this interpretation, see Kasher, here, note 114.

Rashbam says that there were only four rings total. The second half of the verse, "two rings on one of its side walls . . . and two on the other," is to be understood simply as an elaboration of the first half of the verse. Rashbam's interpretation follows LT virtually verbatim. See also Rashi, at much greater length. So also NJPS: "Cast four rings for it . . . two rings on one of its side walls and two on the other." The vav of ושתי should be seen as, in the words of G.-K. (154a, note 1, b), a "wāw explicativum" ("cast four rings . . . to wit two rings on one side . . .").

[26]I.e. the shorter side, the side that was one and a half cubits long. So also Rashi, s.v. פעמותיו.

[27]The Tabernacle was divided by a curtain that ran between the north and south walls into two sections, the westernmost section or Holy of Holies, and the rest of the Tabernacle, called the hekhal, or "the Holy." The Ark was placed in the the Holy of Holies in such a way that the longer side of the Ark was parallel to the curtain, i.e. it ran from north to south. Rashbam explains that the poles were attached to the shorter sides, "the widths," and accordingly the poles ran from east to west. They were perpendicular to the curtain and thus they pointed towards the hekhal. See Illustration A.

Rashbam's explanation here is the standard rabbinic understanding. See Menahot 98a and Rashi there, s.v. ובדיו מנלן and s.v. כך היה מונח.

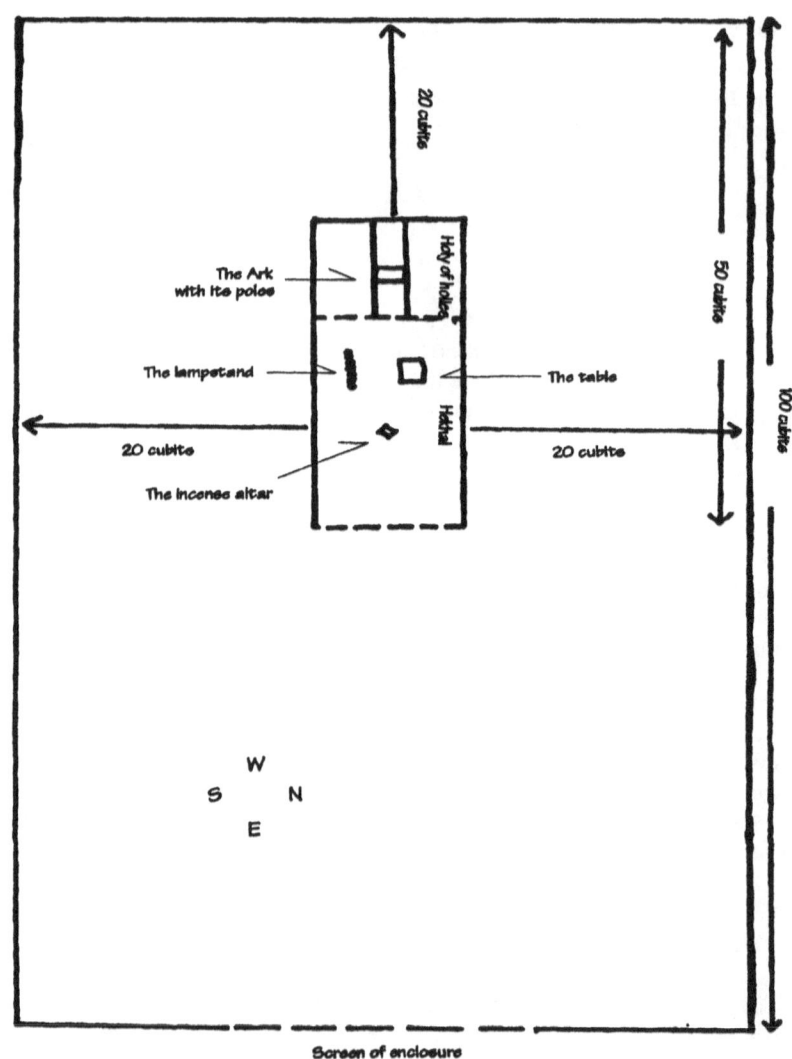

Illustration A
Layout-- Tabernacle in enclosure

EXODUS XXV

25:16 את העדות [DEPOSIT IN THE ARK] THE *'EDUT*: The tablets that were the Pact (עדות) and the Covenant (ברית)[28] between God and Israel. That is why they are called (Deut. 9:9), "the Tablets of the Covenant."[29]

25:17 כפרת: means a covering.[30]

אמתיים TWO AND A HALF CUBITS LONG [AND ONE AND A HALF WIDE] : The same as the length and the width of the Ark.[31]

25:18 כרובים CHERUBS: Birds. A cherub is a large bird with wings, as it is written (Ezek. 28:14), "I created you as a cherub with outstretched shielding wings."[32] The rabbis, however, interpreted that the cherubs had the faces of children.[33]

---

[28] On ברית and עדות as synonyms, see NJPSC, here, and see Orlinsky, *Notes*, p. 166.

[29] Rashi says that *'edut* in this verse is a reference to the Torah. So also LT. Rashbam writes more simply that it is a reference to the two tablets. So also iE who cites the prooftext, "There was nothing inside the Ark but the two tablets of stone" (I Kings 8:9). See Rashi ad 40:20, where Rashi also explains that *'edut* is a reference to the tablets. (On the apparent contradiction between Rashi here and there, see the sources cited by Kasher, here, note 123.)

[30] So also Rashi and almost all classical exegetes. See also NJPS, "cover," as opposed to many other English translations that read "mercy-seat." See the discussion in NJPSC.

[31] See vs. 10. So also Rashi, virtually verbatim.

[32] See also Rashi, there, who interprets the word כרוב in that passage in Ezekiel as meaning a bird.

[33] See Sukkah 5b and Hag. 13b. Rashi, here, and most Jewish exegetes follow the rabbinic understanding. Again one notes Rashbam's willingness to offer a non-traditional understanding of a text when he feels that it is supported by a contextual reading.

מקשה: means that the cherubs were fashioned out of the same piece of gold as the cover of the Ark was. The cherub was not [made from a separate piece of gold and later] attached [to the cover of Ark]; rather the gold [from which the cover was made] was beaten[34] with a [smith's] hammer in order to get it [i.e. the shape of the cherub] to portrude.[35]

25:19 מקצה [MAKE EACH CHERUB] AT ONE END: [Lengthwise;] widthwise the cherub was placed in the middle of the covering.[36] This was done so that the Divine Presence hovering over the cherubs would be seen from the direction of the *hekhal*.[37]

---

[34]הקישו. Rashbam is suggesting the same etymology for the word מקשה as Rashi does (ad vs. 31, explicitly, and implicitly here).

[35]So also Rashi, at much greater length. See comm. and notes above, ad vs. 12, s.v. ויצקת; and below, ad vs. 31, s.v. מקשה.
 Rashbam's understanding of מקשה is the traditional one. See e.g. Men. 28a, and Rashi there, s.v. מקשה. Cf., however, iE, who interprets מקשה as meaning "straight" or "equal."

[36]As described above, the ark, with its covering, was placed in the Holy of Holies in such a way that its length ran from north to south and its width ran from east to west. (See comm. and notes above, ad vs. 12, s.v. על צלעו.) Rashbam understands that when the text says that the cherubs were placed at the extreme end of the covering (מקצה), that means the extreme end of the *length* of the covering, i.e at the extreme north and the extreme south. (So also iE here, longer comm.) Rashbam adds that, from the *width* point of view, the cherubs were placed in the middle of the covering, half way between the extreme eastern edge and the extreme western edge of the covering. See Illustration B.

[37]The Tabernacle was divided into two parts, the Holy of Holies (in the west) and the *hekhal* in the east. The *hekhal* was twice as large as the Holy of Holies.
 The Divine Presence was understood to be hovering between the two cherubs, over their outstretched wings (see vss. 20-22). I understand Rashbam to be saying that had the cherubs been placed at the extremes of the *widths* of the covering, i.e at the easternmost and westernmost part of the covering, then the Divine Presence which hovered between them would not be seen from the direction of the *hekhal* (i.e. from the east), the place where people generally stood. The cherubs were placed at the north and south ends of the covering so as not to block the "view" of the Divine Presence from the east.
 See also Rashbam's comm. ad BB 89a, s.v. ופניהם לבית, where he explains that the cherubs constructed by King Solomon (described in I Kings 6 and in II Chron.

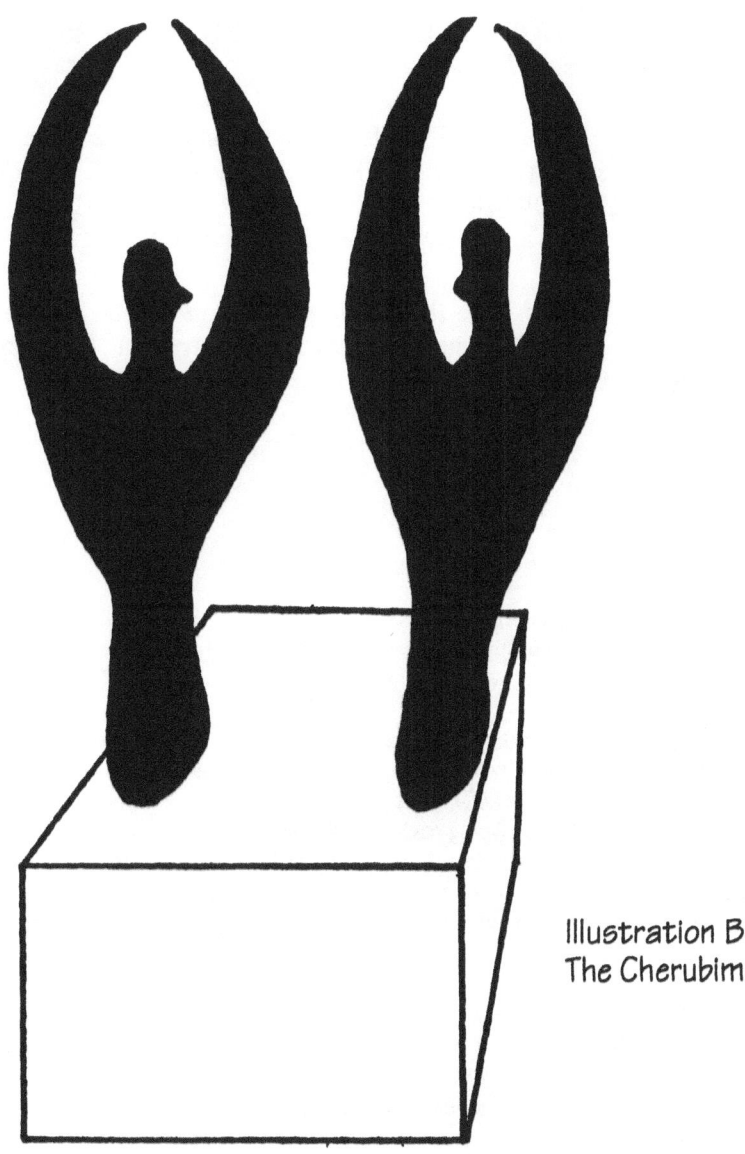

Illustration B
The Cherubim

---

3) differed in a number of ways from the cherubs of the Tabernacle, including the fact that Solomon's cherubs faced the *hekhal*.

25:20 למעלה [WINGS SPREAD OUT] ABOVE: I.e towards the direction of their heads.[38]

ופניהם FACING EACH OTHER: [This phrase means] the same as [the following phrase,] אל הכפורת, THE FACES OF THE CHERUBS BEING TURNED TOWARDS THE middle of[39] the COVERING.

25:25 מסגרת A RIM: Like the [decorative] edges[40] that are made on tabletops.[41] However, some of our rabbis say that the rim was underneath [the tabletop].[42]

---

[38]So also Rashi, at greater length. See also Sukkah 5b, where the word למעלה is seen as proving that the wings of the cherubs spread above their heads, not just parallel to their heads.

[39]The textual difficulty is that the verse implies that the cherubs faced each other *and* that the cherubs faced the covering of the Ark. Rashbam explains that "facing the covering" means "facing *the middle of* the covering." So, since the cherubs were placed on the covering at the edges, "facing each other" and "facing the middle of the covering" mean the same thing. So also Yefet (cited by iE in his longer comm). Cf., however, JBS, who says that the cherubs faced each other but that their faces were turned downwards, in a humble manner, towards the covering of the Ark. Like JBS, see also iE.

[40]לבזבזין. The word is found a number of times in rabbinic literature (e.g. Miq. 4:2), and is used by Rashi in his comm., here.

[41]So also Rashi, who specifies that this rim is like the decorative edges that one finds "on the tables of princes."

[42]See Men. 96b and Suk. 5a. Rashbam's comment to this verse is basically an abridged form of Rashi's, except that Rashbam appears to express a preference for the first of the two interpretations, while Rashi simply presents the two options. Like Rashbam, see LT and iE.

EXODUS XXV

25:27 לעומת המסגרת [THE RINGS SHALL BE] NEXT TO THE RIM: The rings are to be attached to the tabletop, below the [decorative] rim, not to the rim itself.[43]

25:29 קערותיו [YOU SHALL MAKE] ITS MOLDS: A frame[44] shaped like a container that has been broken open[45] [at the sides];[46] the bread was prepared in those molds.[47]

וכפותיו THE LADLES: The two vessels used for the frankincense [that was put onto the bread of display,] as it is written (Lev. 24:7), "With each row you shall place pure frankincense."[48]

קשותיו ומנקיותיו ITS PROPS AND ITS CLEANSERS: These items are explained in Menahot.[49] The bread of display was placed (Lev.

---

[43]Rashbam disputes Rashi's intepretation, that the rings were to be attached to the legs of the table, below the tabletop. Like Rashbam, see LT and JBS.

[44]דפוס, using the language of Men. 97a (קערותיו אלו הדפוסין). So also Rashi, here.

[45]תיבה פרוצה, using the language of Men. 94b. So also Rashi, here.
For Rashbam's understanding of the shape of the table and its vessels, see Illustration C.

[46]I.e. a frame that would be the shape of the bread. So also Rashi, here, at much greater length.

[47]Rashbam's understanding appears to differ slightly from Rashi's. Rashi (following Men. 94a) writes that more than one type of frame (דפוס) were used in the preparation of the bread of display. Rashi says that our verse's word קערותיו refers specifically only to the frames that were used to display the bread *after* it was baked. Rashbam says that it refers to the frames in which the bread was prepared. Cf. JBS, who says that קערותיו means the mixing bowls in which the dough was kneaded.

[48]So also Rashi, following Men. 87a.
The word order of Rashbam's comment (וכפותיו לצורך שני בזיכי לבונה) appears somewhat garbled to me. Perhaps the text would read better as: וכפותיו שני בזיכין לצורך לבונה.

[49]Men. 11:6 and b. 97a.

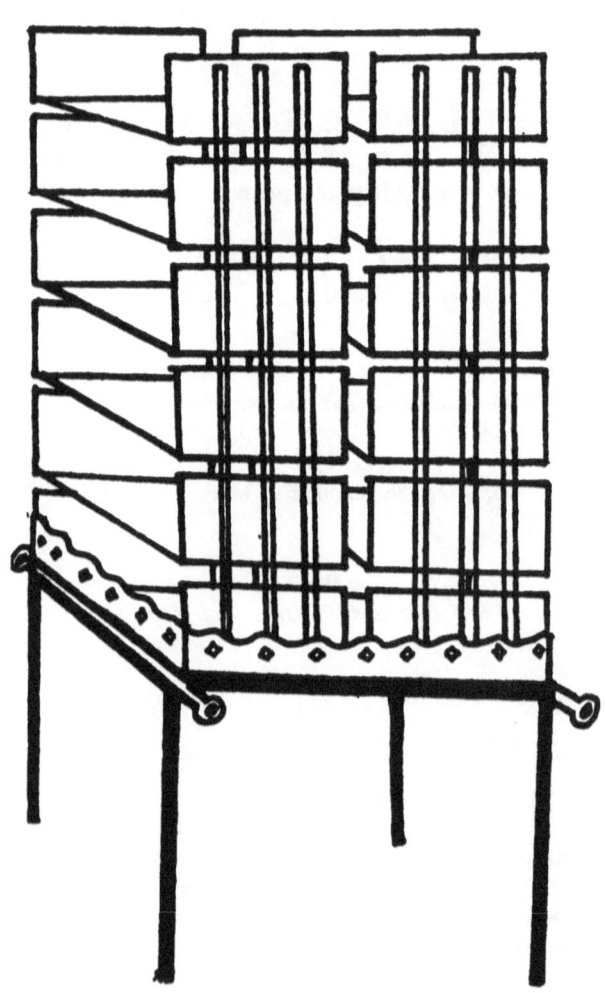

Illustration C
The Table

24:6) "in two [vertical] rows, six [loaves] to a row," one on top of the other. The table had [vertical] prongs on either side of it. The PROPS (קשוות) were shaped like halves of reeds [split lengthwise][50] and they ran [horizontally] from one prong [on one side of the table] to another prong [on the opposite side of the table]. The loaves of bread rested on these PROPS. Similarly [there were props] between each of the six loaves of bread [that were stacked] one upon the other. That is why these PROPS are referred to in another passage (Num. 4:7) as "קשות הנסך," since they serve as coverings[51] for the bread, [as they are placed] between the [vertically stacked] breads.[52]

אשר יוסך WITH WHICH IT [i.e. the bread] WAS COVERED: This refers to the PROPS (קשוות), as I explained.[53]

---

[50] חצאי קנים; the same phrase that Rashi uses here in his commentary to describe the קשוות, based on Men. 11:6.

[51] שמסככין. Rashbam (following Rashi, here, and ad Num. 4:7) connects the word, הנסך, in Numbers to the root ס-כ-כ, to shield or cover, and not to the root נ-ס-כ, to pour a libation. Similarly, both Rashbam and Rashi understand יוסך in our verse as related to the root ס-כ-כ. Cf. JBS, who connects it to the meaning, "libation," and claims that Rashi follows a midrashic reading reading while he, JBS, interprets the text as it is written ("ובע' פנים התורה נדרשת ואני פי' אחר לשון עברי")--the Torah may be interpreted in seventy ways; the way I interpreted this verse is in accordance with the meaning of the Hebrew words"). Similarly see the interpretation of Hai Gaon, cited by Kasher, vol. 22, Appendix, p. 27, and the discussion there, pp. 27-28. So also NJPS: "with which to offer libations."

[52] Rashbam's explanation of the קשוות is the same as the first explanation offered by Rashi. Rashbam curiously does not explain the meaning of the word מנקיות, in our verse. Presumably he feels, like Rashi, that the מנקיות were the vertical prongs to which the horizontal props (קשוות) were attached.

[53] In his previous comment.
    So also Rashi, following Men. 97a. Even though the relative clause אשר יוסך בהם appears to be modifying the noun מנקיותיו, Rashbam and Rashi (in his first interpretation) feel obliged to explain that it modifies קשותיו (so also iE), since they argue that the קשוות were the horizontal props, the only ones that could be seen as covering the loaves of breads.

25:30 לחם פנים THE BREAD OF DISPLAY: Following the plain meaning of Scripture, [לחם פנים means] a handsome bread, a bread that would be appropriate to serve to princes,[54] as it is written (Lev. 24:5), "Take choice flour[55] and bake of it [twelve loaves] . . .." Furthermore, [the word פנים may be seen as referring to a choice portion, as] it is written (Gen. 43:34), "Portions were served them מאת פניו,"[56] and it is written (I Sam. 1:5), "To Hannah he would give one portion, אפיים--a choice one,"[57] a portion from the plate that was placed before Elkanah, for the choicest portions are given to the paterfamilias. [The verse in I Samuel continues] "Because Hannah was his favorite"; that is why he gave her אפיים, the choice portion. "But the LORD had closed her womb"; that is why he gave her only one portion, not two portions or more, as he gave to Peninah who had sons and daughters.[58]

---

[54]As noted by NJPSC (p. 256, note 66), the word פנים is on a number of occasions in rabbinic literature connected to rich or distinguished people. See e.g. BR 79:6 and 91:5.

Rashbam's interpretation opposes that of Rashi, who says (following Men. 11:4) that the bread is called לחם הפנים because it has two sides (פנים) that are visible even when it is put on display inside of its frames. So also LT, ad vs. 29. Rashbam's interpretation appears original.

[55]Presumably Rashbam sees the proof from this verse as the fact that the verse mandates using *choice* flour (סלת).

[56]Presumably Rashbam understands that מאת פניו, in that verse, is a reference to the choice quality of the gifts that Joseph gave his brothers. Cf. NJPS: "from his table."

[57]Rashbam quotes the translation of Ps.-Jon., חולק חד בחיר ("one choice portion"), to support his interpretation. So also Rashi, there.

[58]On Rashbam's understanding of I Sam. 1:5, see also comm. and notes ad Ex. 2:6, s.v. והנה.

25:31 ועשית מנרת YOU SHALL MAKE A LAMPSTAND: to provide light for the table,[59] as it is written (26:35), "[place . . .] the lampstand opposite the table."

מקשה: means that he took a block[60] of gold and, with a [smith's] hammer, he separated the metal into branches and cups.[61]

ירכה ITS BASE: I.e. the wide "leg"[62] at the bottom, upon which the whole lampstand stands.

וקנה ITS SHAFT: I.e. the central shaft, from which three more branches branch out on each side.[63]

---

[59]Rashbam continues to explain the order in which the utensils of the Tabernacle are described here. Above, ad vs. 10, he explains why it was appropriate for the ark to be described first in this chapter. Now he says that it makes sense for the lampstand to follow the table in this chapter, since the purpose of the lampstand is to provide light for the table. See also comm. and note 78 below, ad vs. 37, s.v. והאיר, where Rashbam argues that the wicks of the lampstand were to be turned toward the table, and see also comm. ad Lev. 24:2.

Rashbam's prosaic interpretation of the purpose of the lampstand can be seen as opposed to the more spiritual explanations, such as the one offered in Tanh. B. Beha'alotekha 9 (cited by Kasher, paragraph 187)--that the lampstand's purpose was to bring the Divine Presence into the Tabernacle. The explanation that Rashbam offers can be found in Tanh. Yayyaqhel 10 ("משעשה את השלחן עשה את המנורה שתהא מאירה על השלחן--once the table was made, then the lampstand was made to provide light for the table"; cited in Tosafot ha-shalem, volume 9, page 65, paragraph ב, note 1.) See also comm. and notes below, ad vs. 37, s.v. והאיר.

[60]Or "bar." The word that Rashbam writes here, עשת, is also used in Men. 28a (citing Tosefta Men. 9:18) to describe the raw material from which the lampstand was made. So also Rashi, here.

[61]So also Rashi, at greater length. See also comm. and notes above ad vs. 12, s.v. ויצקת, and ad vs. 18, s.v. מקשה.

[62]So also Rashi. However, Rashi adds the further detail that this "leg" is supported by three smaller legs.

[63]So also Rashi (here and ad vs. 32), at greater length.

גביעיה כפתוריה ופרחיה ממנה יהיו **ITS CUPS, CALYXES AND PETALS SHALL BE FROM IT**: I.e. on the central shaft,[64] for the calyxes were the places [on the central shaft] from each of which two more branches branched out, as it is written (vs. 35), "a calyx under a pair of branches [which branch out] from it."[65]

25:33 שלשה גביעים **THREE GEVI'IM**: [The three gevi'im were three] hollow [decorations,] shaped like cups, one indentation on top of another on each branch.[66]

משוקדים **ALMOND BLOSSOMS**: There should be protrusions shaped like almonds on the sides of the gevi'im, just as [these days] silver

---

[64]Rashi, here, explains that the phrase ממנה יהיו means the same as מקשה, i.e. that the lampstand should be hammered out from one piece of metal. In other words, the last phrase of the verse simply reiterates what was written in the beginning of the verse. Rashi's understanding follows that of *Beraita' di-melekhet ha-mishkan* 9 (Kirschner's edition, pp. 190 and 235, "I might infer that its members are made [separately] and fastened to it; [therefore] Scripture says 'ממנה יהיו—shall be from it'") and Sifre *Beha'alotekha* 61 (Horovitz ed., p. 59). See also Rashbam's understanding of the word ממנו in his comm. ad 27:2.

Rashbam, here, appears to offer a novel interpretation, that ממנה יהיו, in reference to the lampstand, means that cups, calyxes and petals shall all be part of the design of its central shaft. So also iE, shorter comm., s.v. וקנה. Then Rashbam further explains (in his comm. ad vs. 33, s.v. כפתור), that vs. 33 teaches us that there should also be such decorations on the other branches of the lampstand.

Ha-torah veha-miṣvah, ad vs. 35, explains the text differently--not as saying that the cups, calyxes and petals should all be part of the central shaft, but as saying that those cups, calyxes and petals that are part of the central shaft should be made "from it," i.e. from the same piece of gold. Then another verse, vs. 35, teaches us that those additional cups, calyxes and petals that are not on the central shaft should also be made from that same piece of gold. Such an interpretation could, arguably, be read into the words of Rashbam, here, also. But to my mind the words of Rashbam sustain better the interpretation that I offered in the translation.

[65]Rashbam understands that the word ממנה, "from it," in vs. 35, means "from the central shaft," just as he says that it does in our verse. See comm. and notes below ad vs. 35, s.v. וכפתור.

[66]So also Rashi (ad vs. 31).

utensils have designs of spoons or apples on them, which are called *coloréz* in the vernacular.⁶⁷

Later I heard that in Narbonne⁶⁸ they explain the word in that manner, as connected to the word "almonds--שקדים," [and they would translate it] as *amondolez* in the vernacular.⁶⁹

כפתור ופרח CALYXES AND PETALS: For decoration,⁷⁰ on the middle of each branch⁷¹ [of the lampstand].

25:35 וכפתור A CALYX UNDER A PAIR OF BRANCHES: which branch out FROM IT. I.e. from the central shaft, which is the most important part of the lampstand.⁷²

לששת הקנים FOR ALL SIX BRANCHES: Three times [the verse writes], "A CALYX [UNDER A PAIR OF BRANCHES FROM IT,] A

---

⁶⁷The precise Old French word cited here by Rashbam is unclear. Rosin (RSBM, p. 94) and J. Greenberg (*La'aze Rashi ba-tanakh*, p. 241) both suggest that it may be the Old French equivalent of the New French, *colorés*, i.e. "colored."

⁶⁸Narbonne was a major centre of Jewish scholarship in the days of Rashbam. This is the only reference to Narbonne in Rashbam's comm.

⁶⁹I.e. "almond-shaped" or "amygdaloid."
Cf. Rashi and LT who say that משוקדים means simply "engraved" or "decorated with niello." Like Rashbam, see the opinion of Saadiah (cited by iE) and Maimonides (*Commentary on the Mishnah*, Men. 3:7; and MT, Bet ha-beḥirah 3:2).

⁷⁰Rashi (ad vs. 31) notes that the the *gevi'im* were purely for decoration. Rashbam here notes only that the calyxes and petals were purely for decoration. Perhaps Rashbam agrees with JBS, who suggests that the *gevi'im* were constructed in such a way as to collect any extra oil that might drip down.

⁷¹So also Rashi.
Rashbam's comm. here should be read together with his comm. to vs. 31, s.v. גביעה. See notes there.

⁷²It is clear from the end of this verse that the word מנורה in the phrase "six branches issuing from the מנורה," must mean "the central shaft." See similarly Rashi ad vs. 34, s.v. ובמנורה, and ad vs. 37, s.v. והאיר, and see NJPSC here: "the 'lampstand' refers to the central shaft."

CALYX . . . A CALYX . . . ." [Accordingly,] since the verse enumerated all [the calyxes and the outside branches], there was no reason for the verse to write the word SO (כן), as it did in the earlier verse.[73]

25:37 נרותיה ITS LAMPS: *Luces* in the vernacular,[74] the place where one puts the oil and the wicks.[75]

והעלה AND HE: i.e. the priest,[76] SHALL MOUNT ITS LAMPS. This refers to [all] seven lamps on the seven branches.[77]

---

[73]Rashbam attempts to explain a minor stylistic difference between the end of verse 33 ("כן לששת הקנים היוצאים מן המנורה")—thus for all six branches that issue from the [central shaft of the] lampstand") and the almost identical end of verse 35 ("לששת הקנים היוצאים מן המנורה—for the six branches that issue from the [central shaft of the] lampstand," without the word, "כן--thus"). Verse 33 reads, "Three cups shaped liked almond blossoms on one branch, three cups shaped like almond blossoms on one branch, *so* (כן) for all six branches." Rashbam explains that כן was required in verse 33 as the reader is being asked to extrapolate from the two branches that were mentioned to the four that were not. However here, in vs. 35, since all the three calyxes (from which branches branch out) and six branches are explicitly mentioned in the verse, there is no need for the word, "כן--thus".

[74]I.e. lamps. Rashi uses the same vernacular word to explain נרות in his comm. ad 30:7, s.v. הנרות, and ad Num. 4:9, s.v. נרותיה.

[75]The language that Rashi uses in Num. 4:9, virtually verbatim.

[76]Rashbam provides the missing subject of the verb והעלה. So also Ps.-Jon.
Perhaps Rashbam wishes to point out that even the first time that the lamps were mounted in place, the mounting was done by the priest, and not by Moses. See Rashbam's comm. to 40:29, s.v. ויעל, and the discussion in note 1, there.

[77]Rashbam disputes the interpretation offered by Rashi. Rashi argues that the second time that נרותיה is written in our verse, it is referring to the six lamps on all the branches *other than* the central branch. Those lamps are to be mounted and lit in such a manner that והאיר על עבר פניה—that (according to Rashi's understanding) they shed their light towards the direction of the central branch and the light thereon.
In preparation for the next pericope of his comm., where Rashbam will interpret והאיר על עבר פניה in a manner that differs with Rashi, Rashbam here lays the groundwork for that interpretation by saying that the נרות mentioned in the second half of this verse are all seven lamps, not the six outside ones.

והאיר על עבר פניה AND IT WILL GIVE LIGHT ON ITS FRONT SIDE: He should light the wicks [so that they give light] towards the עבר, i.e. opposite the front of the lampstand, towards the direction of the table,[78] opposite the lampstand. As it is written (26:35), "[place] the lampstand opposite the table," and it is written (Num. 8:2), "let the seven lights throw their light forward toward the front of the lampstand." [This means] that all seven[79] of the lamps should shine towards the front, in the direction of the table opposite.

25:38 ומלקחיה ITS TONGS: With which they take[80] the wicks and place them in the lamps.[81]

---

[78] Rashbam disputes Rashi's interpretation. Rashi (following Sifre Beha'alotekha 59) says that the phrase means that the six outside lamps should shine towards the middle one. Rashi ad Num. 8:2 (s.v. אל) writes specifically that it was crucial that the lampstand shed light on itself and not on anything else so that it would not be seen merely as a vehicle for providing light for something else.

Rashbam, to the contrary, says that the lampstand was a vehicle to provide light for something else--the table. Our verse means that the branches of the lampstand should shed their light towards the front, i.e. towards the the table.

Rashbam's interpretation--that the lampstand was meant to shed light on the table--appears to have originated in Northern France of his generation and had a certain popularity there. It is found also in JBS here and is attributed by the Tosafot (Men. 28b, s.v. גובהה), to Rabbenu Tam, Rashbam's brother.

Rashbam established the groundwork for this interpretation in his comm. above ad 25:31, s.v. ועשית. See note 59, there.

[79] Again emphasizing his opposition to Rashi's interpretation that the verse is referring to the direction of the light of the six outside branches. See comm. above, s.v. והעלה, and note 77, there. See JBS who also cites this same verse in Num. to oppose the understanding offered by Rashi. As JBS argues, following Rashi's understanding the verse in Numbers should have read "let the *six* lights throw their light . . . ."

[80] שלוקחין; explaining that tongs are called מלקחים from the root ל-ק-ח, to take. So also Rashi and iE, shorter comm.

[81] So also Rashi and iE, shorter comm. Cf. Nahm. (ad vs. 39) who disagrees, and says that the מלקחים were removable plates of gold that covered the mouths of the lamps.

ומחתתיה ITS ASH PANS: When he [i.e. the priest] would tend the lamps[82] in the morning, he would rake[83] into these pans the burnt-out parts of the lamp[84] and the leftover oil.[85]

25:40 מָרְאֶה THAT YOU ARE BEING SHOWN: [This verb is] a form that is used when a person is being acted upon by a second party.[86] In the vernacular, *es mostrez*.[87] [The phrase,] THAT YOU ARE BEING SHOWN, means that God literally showed [Moses] the pattern of the lampstand.[88]

However, the form נראה in the phrase (Gen. 12:7), "the LORD who had appeared (הנראה) to him," means that He Himself appeared; *fu veduz* in the vernacular.[89]

---

[82]בהטיבו את הנרות; a citation of Ex. 30:7.

[83]חותה; hence the name מחתות. So also Rashi, at greater length.

[84]Presumably Rashbam means the burnt-out wicks, as Rashi writes here.

[85]So also Rashi (although Rashi does not mention the oil). See also Rashi ad Num. 4:9, s.v. מחתותיה, and Rashi and Rashbam ad Ex. 27:3, s.v. ומחתותיו. Cf. Nahm. (ad vs. 39) and iE (here) who disagree, and say that the מחתות were drip pans that were placed underneath each of the seven lamps of the lampstand, into which sparks and ashes might fall.

[86]I.e. a *hofal* form.

[87]The precise form being cited here by Rashbam is unclear. Some Old French equivalent of the modern French, *on t'a montré*, is presumably meant. In the ms., the reading here, according to Rosin's testimony, is אמישטריץ ב"ל. One line later, the ms. reads אמושטריץ ב"ל. Rosin (RSBM, p. 95) attempts to distinguish between these two forms. To my mind, it would appear that there is simply a dittography here.

[88]Rashbam reiterates the point that he made in his comm. ad 25:9. See notes there.

[89]*Fut vu* in modern French. Rashbam explains the difference between the *nifal* form and the *hofal* form of the verb ר-א-ה. See also his comm. and notes ad Gen. 28:12, s.v. מוצב. Cf. Rashi, here, who points out the difference between the meanings of the *hifil* and *hofal* forms of the verb ר-א-ה. As Rosin notes (*ibid.*), Rashbam explains the distinction between the *nifal* and *hofal* forms by making use of two separate French verbs (*montrer* and *voir*, in the modern French equivalents).

EXODUS XXVI

26:1 ואת המשכן AS FOR THE TABERNACLE, [MAKE IT OF TEN STRIPS . . .]: The ten bottom strips of cloth are called "the Tabernacle (משכן)," because the Ark, where the Divine Presence (שכינה) dwells, is directly underneath them.[1]

26:3 חוברות [FIVE OF THE CLOTHS] SHALL BE JOINED: Sewn together with a needle.[2]

26:4 מקצה בחוברת ON THE OUTERMOST CLOTH OF THE ONE SET: I.e. on the edge of the fifth strip of cloth.[3]

---

[1] One might imagine that the name "Tabernacle" applies to all the different coverings of various materials (described here in vss. 1-14), to the space enclosed by those coverings and to the all the contents of that enclosure. Here Rashbam notes that the verse uses the term "Tabernacle" to describe the innermost set of those coverings. Rashbam reiterates his explanation below, in his comm. ad vs. 6, s.v. והיה. See similarly Tos. Shabbat 28a, s.v. ויפרוש, and Nahm. ad 39:33. One might also say that Rashi (ad vs. 12) uses the terminology in the same way. Rashbam's explanation of why the name is applied specifically to *this* set of coverings appears to be original.

[2] So also Rashi, virtually verbatim. See also Rashi ad Shabbat 99a, s.v. ונראין. So also NJPSC.
   Presumably Rashi and Rashbam wish to explain that even though the two sets of five strips were joined to each other with loops and clasps (as described in vs. 4f.), nevertheless each set of five strips was made up of strips that were sewn together. LT makes that point here explicitly ("'joined': with a needle, not with loops").
   See also comm. and notes below, ad vs. 6, s.v. וחברת.

[3] Rashbam's understanding of the location of the loops is the standard one and is the same as Rashi's. Yet Rashbam understands the words of the verse differently from Rashi. Rashi's understanding is that מקצה is a description of which strip of cloth gets

26:6 וחברת COUPLE [THE CLOTHS TO ONE ANOTHER]: Join together the two sets [of five strips of cloth each] with clasps, [inserted] in the loops.[4]

והיה המשכן אחד SO THAT THE TABERNACLE BECOMES ONE WHOLE: The ten strips of cloth that are called "the Tabernacle"[5] will now become one whole.

26:9-13 וכפלת FOLD OVER THE SIXTH CLOTH: In other words, half of this [sixth, extra cloth] should hang down over the front of the Tabernacle and half of the last of the cloths[6] should (vs. 12) OVERHANG THE BACK OF THE TABERNACLE, two cubits more than "the Tabernacle cloths" [i.e. the set of ten cloths described in vss. 1-6].

How does this work out? The [previously described first set of cloths, i.e. the] ten bottom strips of cloth,[7] were, after they were joined together, forty cubits long and twenty-eight cubits wide.[8] The

---

the loops--the strip that is מקצה, i.e. the one that is outermost of the five. Rashbam's reading says that מקצה teaches us where on that strip the loops should be attached--מקצה, i.e. "on the edge" of that strap.

[4]Rashbam's explanation represents the standard understanding of the verse.
  Note that the last three pericopes of Rashbam's comm. all explain words from the root ח-ב-ר (חוברות, בחוברת and וחברת). Rashbam explains that each of these words has a different meaning.

[5]See comm. and notes above, ad vs. 1.

[6]What Rashbam calls the "last" of the cloths is the cloth farthest away from the "sixth" cloth.
  In other words, after the set of six cloths and the set of five cloths are attached together to form one large set of eleven cloths, half of cloth "one" and half of cloth "eleven" (which could also be called "the sixth cloth") will be "extra."

[7]The set described in vss. 1-6.

[8]Since each of those ten strips of cloth was four cubits by twenty-eight cubits (vs. 2).

Tabernacle was thirty cubits long. [We know that] because the twenty planks that were used to construct each of the north and south sides of the Tabernacle (vss. 18 and 20) [must have] totalled thirty cubits in length [per side], since each plank is one and half cubits wide.⁹ So, when they would spread out these [ten bottom strips of cloth] over the Tabernacle, spreading the length of the strips over the thirty-cubit length of the Tabernacle,¹⁰ ten cubits of cloth would hang down over the back of the Tabernacle [in the west].¹¹ As for the north and south sides of the Tabernacle, ten of the twenty-eight cubits [of the width of the strips of cloth] cover the ten cubits of the width of the Tabernacle,¹² and, [of the remaining eighteen cubits,] nine hang down on the one side, over the north wall, and nine on the other side, over the south wall.¹³

---

⁹As it is written in vs. 16.

¹⁰ארכן לאורך המשכן. When Rashbam says the length of the strips (ארכן), he means the long side of the *set* of strips, *after* the ten strips have been joined together. It appears as if Rashi is saying the opposite when Rashi writes (ad vs. 5): "נותן היריעות ארכן לרחבו של משכן--he places the length of the strips in such a way that they cover the *width* of the Tabernacle." In fact, though, Rashi and Rashbam mean the same thing. When Rashi refers to "ארכן--the length of the strips," he means the long side of the *individual* strips of cloth, the side that is 28 cubits long, not the long side of the *set* of ten attached strips, the side that would be forty cubits long.

Rashi's way of describing how the straps were placed is the more traditional one. In fact, his words are basically a Hebrew translation of the Aramaic of the Talmud (Shab. 98b): שדי אורכייהו לפותיא דמשכן.

¹¹The strips together are forty cubits long. Thirty cubits of the set of strips cover the length of the area of the roof. And there are ten extra cubits left hanging over the back of the Tabernacle.

This calculation of Rashbam disagrees with that of Rashi. See the explanation below, note 13.

¹²Two sentences previously, Rashbam provided proof for the assertion that the Tabernacle was thirty cubits long. Here he simply writes that its width was ten cubits, without providing proof. There is, in fact, no simple textual proof for that assertion (although it is the assumption of all the classical rabbinic texts). See the discussion in Tos. Shabbat 98b, s.v. דל.

¹³In general, Rashbam's calculations here are similar, but not identical, to those of Rashi (ad vs. 5). Rashi writes that the planks used for the construction of the walls were one cubit thick. (The height and length of those planks is written explicitly in verse 16, but their thickness is not written in the Torah.) The width of the Tabernacle was 10

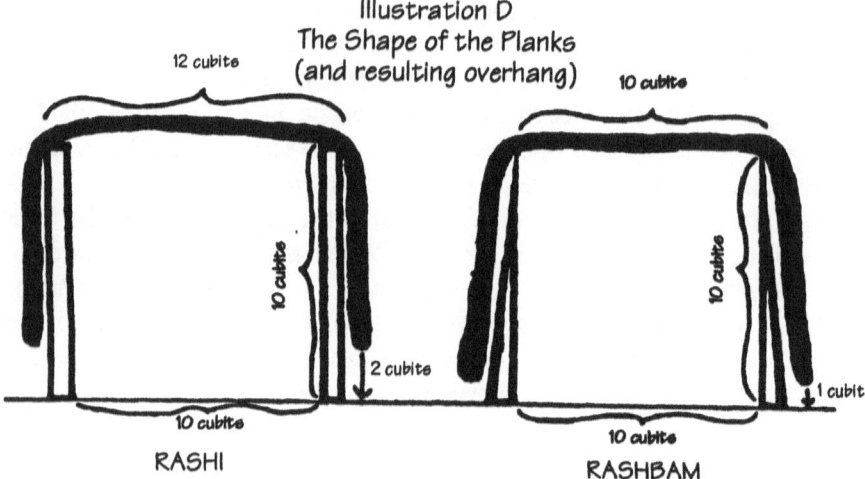

cubits, not including the thickness of the walls. So, according to Rashi, of the twenty-eight cubit-wide strips of cloth, twelve cubits were on the roof parallel to the ground--the ten cubits which covered the width of the Tabernacle, plus the two cubits which covered the thickness of the planks on the north and south side. Accordingly there were only sixteen "extra" cubits to hang down, *eight* on the north wall and *eight* on the south wall. Rashbam, though, says that there were *nine* cubits hanging down on both the north wall and the south wall.

The dispute about whether the overhang was nine or eight cubits on each side may be found already in the Babylonian Talmud, Shabbat 98b. The Talmud explains that that dispute is dependent on another difference of opinion, between Rabbi Yehudah and Rabbi Nehemiah, about the width of the planks. Both those rabbis said that the planks were a cubit wide at their bases. Rabbi Yehudah said that the planks were tapered: at the bottom they were a cubit wide, but at the top they were only a finger's breadth wide. Accordingly, of the twenty-eight cubits of the strips of cloth, none (or just two finger breadths) were required to cover the width of the tops of the planks. Ten cubits covered the width of the Tabernacle and eighteen cubits (minus two finger breadths) overhung the walls. Rabbi Nehemiah, however, said that the planks were *not* tapered; they were a cubit wide both at the bottom and at the top. Hence Rashi's explanation that, since the strips of cloth covered the thickness of the planks, there were then only sixteen "extra" cubits for an overhang, eight on the north side and eight on the south side. See Illustration D.

Like Rashbam, see LT (ad 36:34) and iE (here). It should be noted, though, that iE describes the overhang on the north and south walls as nine cubits each because he expresses doubt (in his comm. ad vs. 18) about the whole idea that the planks were a cubit wide, either at their bottoms or at their tops. Rashbam clearly accepts the idea that the planks were a cubit wide; it is implicit in his comm. ad vs. 22. (See note 36, there.) So the only explanation that is available for Rashbam's calculations here is that he implicitly follows the understanding of Rabbi Yehudah, as it is explained in Shabbat 98b.

[As for the second set of strips of cloth, the ones made of goats' hair, described in vss. 7-13,] when they would spread out on top of them[14] the strips of cloth of goats' hair which were forty-four cubits long,[15] half of [the width of] one strip--i.e. two cubits--would hang down [over the opening at the front of the Tabernacle in the east],[16] [another] thirty cubits would cover the length of [the roof of] the Tabernacle, and, as for the remaining twelve cubits, ten of them would hang down over the back wall[17] of the Tabernacle, just as [ten cubits of] the bottom set of coverings [hung down over the western wall].[18] This leaves (vs. 12) "AN EXTRA HALF-CLOTH," i.e. two cubits, more [for this set of coverings] than for the bottom set of coverings.

---

[14] I.e. on top of the first set of strips, the ones described in vss. 1-6.

[15] There were eleven strips (vs. 7) and each was four cubits wide (vs. 8). When the eleven strips were combined together (vss. 9 and 11), the goats' hair covering became forty-four cubits long.

[16] After this lengthy introduction, Rashbam now explains the phrase that he set out to explain in this pericope: "fold over the sixth cloth at the front of the tent." He says that folding over the sixth cloth means hanging it in such a way that half of its width--i.e. two cubits--hangs down over the opening, and the other half of it is part of the roof covering of the Tabernacle. So also Rashi and LT.

[17] I.e. covering the entire height of the western wall.

[18] As Rashbam just explained in the last paragraph.
    Here again Rashbam disagrees with Rashi's calculations. Rashi says (ad vs. 5) that the overhang of the first set of coverings on the western side was either eight cubits of nine cubits. In his comm. to vs. 12, Rashi says that it was eight cubits, and that the second set of coverings hung down on the western side precisely the height of the wall, i.e. two cubits more than the first set. Rashi says that that is the meaning of the reference to "the extra half-cloth" in vs. 12. According to Rashi, the half-cloth is "extra" only in comparison to the dimensions of the first set of cloths, not in comparison to the dimensions of the Tabernacle.
    Rashbam here explains differently. The first set of coverings covered the entire height of the western wall and the second set did too. The extra half-cloth--i.e. the extra two cubits more than the first set-- was larger than required to cover the Tabernacle and was, accordingly, folded over on the ground behind the Tabernacle, beyond the western wall.
    Again the source of disagreement between Rashi and Rashbam is their different understandings concerning the width of the planks.

When these goats' hair coverings were spread out after being attached together, their width was thirty cubits.[19] Ten of these cubits covered the width of the [roof of the] Tabernacle, [another] ten cubits overhung the wall on the north side, and [another] ten cubits overhung the wall on the south side. So we find that their overhang was one cubit more on each side[20] than the overhang of the bottom set of coverings. The bottom set had overhangs of *nine* cubits [on each of the north and the south sides], while this [upper] set had overhangs of *ten* cubits.[21] And that is the meaning of the phrase (vs. 13), "THE EXTRA CUBIT AT EITHER END OF EACH END OF TENT CLOTH SHALL HANG DOWN TO THE BOTTOM OF THE TWO SIDES," [hanging down to the ground and] covering [the lowermost cubit of the wall,] the cubit where the socket was. For [the plank was inserted *into* the socket and] the height of the plank was ten cubits, including the height of the socket.[22]

26:14 ומכסה [MAKE FOR THE TENT A COVERING OF TANNED RAM SKINS] AND A COVERING OF *TAḤASH*[23] SKINS ABOVE:

---

[19]Vs. 8.

[20]I.e. on both the north side and the south side.

[21]Again Rashbam's interpretation is similar but not identical to Rashi's. According to both Rashi and Rashbam, the overhangs of the second set of coverings were one cubit more on the north and south sides than the overhangs of the first set. However, Rashi says (ad vs. 8) that the first set overhung eight cubits and the second set nine cubits. Rashbam says that the first set overhung nine cubits on each side and the second set ten cubits. Again the source of disagreement between them must be their different understandings concerning the width of the planks.

[22]Rashbam is emphasizing that the bottom cubit of the north and south walls, the cubit where the planks were inserted into the sockets, was covered by the coverings. He does this presumably to take issue with Rashi, who writes (ad vs. 8) that these coverings did *not* cover the sockets on the north and south sides.

[23]NJPS: "dolphin." It is difficult to say what Rashbam thought the word תחש means. Today scholars still disagree about its meaning. See the discussion in NJPSC ad 25:5.

I.e. above the covering of ram skins.²⁴ That is what the plain meaning of Scripture implies, and that is also the way some interpret the verse in tractate Shabbat (28a).²⁵

26:15 עצי שטים עומדים OF ACACIA WOOD UPRIGHT: [עומדים means that] they placed the [lengths of the] planks vertically, not horizontally.²⁶

26:17 שתי ידות לקרש האחד EACH PLANK SHALL HAVE TWO TENONS:²⁷ The [bottoms of the] planks were grooved in the centre, so that two tenons would remain,²⁸ [one on either side of the groove].²⁹

---

²⁴In other words, verse 14 mandates making *two* more coverings for the Tabernacle, one made of ram skins and the second, the one on top, made of *taḥash* skins.
    Rashi here cites the two opinions found in the Talmud (Shabbat 28a) about the meaning of our verse. According to one opinion there, our verse describes only one covering, made in part of ram skins and in part of *taḥash* skins. The other opinion there says that there were two separate coverings, one of ram skins and one of *taḥash* skins. JBS also offers both options. Rashbam opts for the latter interpretation.

²⁵Rashbam offers the interpretation that he considers *peshaṭ*, and then cites the talmudic passage as if to say that his interpretation here is not heterodox.

²⁶So also Rashi, at greater length. They are both disputing the various midrashic interpretations of this phrase offered in Sukkah 45b, e.g. that עומדים means that the planks should be constructed in such a way that the top of the plank comes from the top of the tree, and the bottom of the plank comes from the bottom of the tree.

²⁷"'Tenon': A projecting part cut on the end of a piece of wood for insertion into a corresponding hole" (Webster's Unabridged).

²⁸I.e. enough wood was carved away so that all that remained was two tenons.
    Rashbam uses the verb להניח here to describe how all that was left after the carving was two protruding tenons. See the analysis of Rashbam's choice of wording in Kasher, here, note 64.

²⁹So also Rashi.

משולבות PARALLEL: The two tenons[30] were parallel one to the other. The [wood of the] plank was carved out all around each of the tenons, on all sides, so that the tenons of each and every plank would fit into the two sockets that were placed under each plank. And the sockets were made hollow, so that the tenons would fit into them.[31]

26:22 ולירכתי AND FOR THE REAR OF THE TABERNACLE [TO THE WEST] MAKE SIX PLANKS: [These six planks on the western side provided] nine cubits of planks going from the north to the south.[32] [However, we know that the western wall was to be *ten* cubits long.[33]] That leaves a half a cubit of open air[34] on the western wall near the northern corner, and [a half a cubit of open air on the western wall] near the southern corner. Then the two corner planks [described in vs. 23] come [to fill in the uncovered space]. These planks are each one and a half cubits wide.[35] The one on the north side [first of all] fills in the half a cubit of open air. [Then] the remaining one cubit of [the width of]

---

[30]Rashbam writes that the word משולבות should be seen as a reference to the "ידות--the tenons," which were inserted into the sockets. So also Rashi. Cf., however, Nahm., who says that משולבות is a reference to the way in which the planks were attached to each other, not to the way that the planks were inserted in the sockets.

[31]So also Rashi, at much greater length.
    Rashbam's language appears to be directed against Rashi here. Rashi writes that the tenons were to be carved out on three sides (משלשת צדיהן). Rashbam then writes pointedly that the tenons were "carved out all around, on all sides." To my mind, though, the difference is one of language only. When Rashi writes that the tenons should be carved out on three sides, he means in addition to the above-mentioned central groove. See also Rashi ad Shabbat 98b, s.v. לרבי יהודה, where it is clear that Rashi felt that the tenons would be carved out on all sides. So the tenons were hollowed out on all sides according to the understandings of both Rashi and Rashbam.

[32]Since each plank was one and a half cubits wide (vs. 16), six planks would be nine cubits wide.

[33]See comm. and notes ad 26:9-13.

[34]I.e. of area that should have been enclosed by a wall but was not enclosed by the six planks described in this verse.

[35]Like all the other planks. See vs. 16.

that plank serves to complete [the corner of] the Tabernacle and make a right angle, as [the one extra cubit of the width of this plank] sits alongside the [one cubit of the] thickness of the planks on the northern side.[36] So also the [extra] cubit[37] of the second [corner] plank sits alongside the [one cubit of the] thickness of the planks on the southern wall, [completing the right angle corner there].

So we find that the internal width of the Tabernacle, [not counting the thickness of the walls,] was ten cubits. The extra protrusion of the planks[38] was covered.[39] The walls of the Tabernacle on the outside were straight on both sides, and the angles of the Tabernacle on the outside were perfect right angles.[40]

---

[36]Rashbam must have agreed with Rashi that each plank was, at least at its base, one cubit thick. See notes above, ad vss. 9-13.

[37]"Extra" means the part that is not the half-cubit of the width of that plank that was used to provide the last missing half cubit of the western wall, at the southern end of the western wall, as described above.

[38]There were eight planks placed widthwise along the western wall, the six mentioned in vs. 22 and the two "corner" planks, mentioned in vs. 23. Each plank was one and a half cubits wide; accordingly, the eight planks had a total width of twelve cubits. So, if the internal width of the Tabernacle was ten cubits, that means that the planks protrude two cubits beyond the width of the Tabernacle, one cubit on each side. See Illustration E.

[39]By the thickness of the planks of the north and south sides, as Rashbam just explained.

[40]Rashbam's explanation is the standard rabbinic explanation found in Shabbat 98b. See also Rashi's comm. there, s.v. ואתי פותיא, where the language is very similar to the language that Rashbam uses here.

It appears to me that Rashbam knows that it would be possible to explain these verses differently, positing that the corner planks were not the same size as the side planks. Such an explanation is found in iE, here, and in a few other sources cited by Kasher, note 77. Rashbam emphasizes here that the standard rabbinic explanation is preferred, as it yields a Tabernacle with straight walls and right-angle corners.

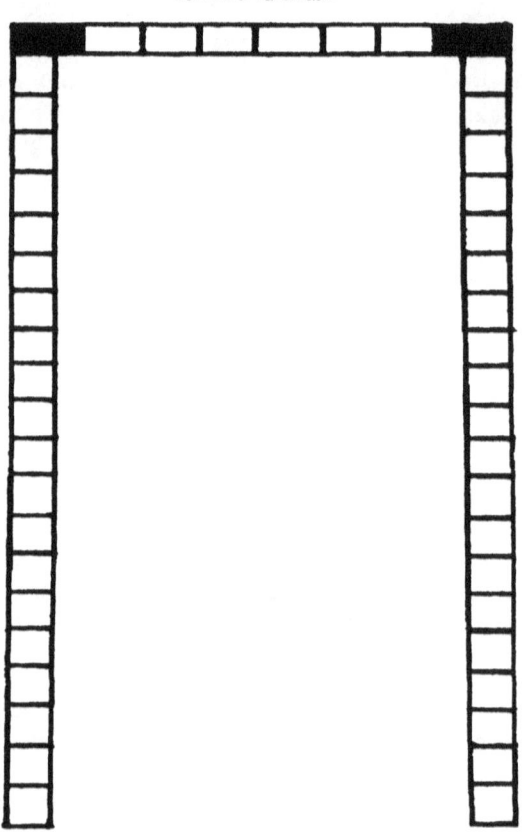

Illustration E
Planks
with special corner pieces
(flat view)

EXODUS XXVI

26:26-28 בריחים [YOU SHALL MAKE] BARS ... FIVE [FOR THE PLANKS OF ONE SIDE]: There were five rings into which bars were inserted,[41] on the outside of each plank,[42] one ring underneath the

---

[41]The bars were inserted into the rings that were on the planks. That is what held the planks together.

[42]Rashbam's explanation opposes that of Rashi. Rashi writes that there were two rings on each plank.

Rashi understands that the "five bars" per side referred to in verses 26 and 27 *include* the "central bar" of verse 28. The "central bar" does not require rings on the outside of the plank; it was inserted in holes bored through the planks. As to the four remaining bars, Rashi says that each one of those bars ran just half the length of each side. So, for example, on the north side of the Tabernacle which was thirty cubits long, two fifteen-cubit-long bars would be inserted into the rings from the east end and two fifteen-cubit-long bars would be inserted into the rings from the west end. That means that there were only two bars on the outside of any one plank, so there were only two rings for the bars to go through on the outside of each plank.

Rashbam's interpretation is that the "five bars" per side described in verses 26 and 27 were *in addition to* the "central bar" of verse 28. Furthermore, Rashbam says that all the bars ran the full length of the wall. For example, on the north wall there were five bars, each thirty cubits long, running the full length of that wall. Each one of those bars went through rings. Hence, Rashbam writes, there were five rings on each bar.

Rashi's approach is the standard classical rabbinic approach. See e.g. *Beraita' di-melekhet ha-mishkan* 1 (pp. 156-157 and 226) and other sources cited by Kasher, note 83. Rashbam's suggestion that there were five rings on the outside of each plank appears to be unique.

See Illustration F.

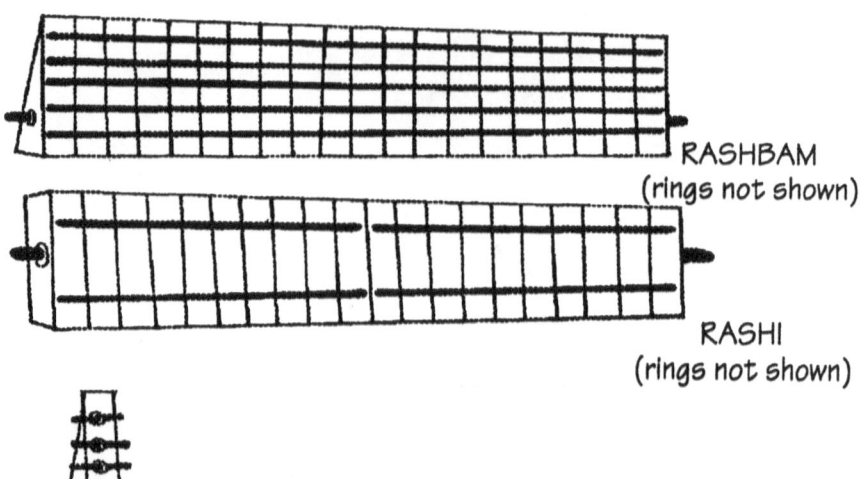

Illustration F

The Bars

other. This is in addition to[43] the "central bar" that was "inside[44] the planks." All of the planks had a hole bored through them, wherein the central bar could be inserted, inside[45] the thickness of the planks. So there were [three separate things that were meant to make the walls sturdy:] sockets below (vss. 19 and 21), the [five] external bars (vss. 26 and 27) and the central bar (vs. 28). The support provided by the central [bar], the one that ran through the thickness of the planks, was the strongest.

According to the plain meaning of Scripture,[46] there were three [separate] "central bars," one running through the north wall, one running through the south wall and one running through the west wall. [When the text says] מן הקצה אל הקצה, FROM END TO END, it means that the bar [on the northern wall] ran from one end of the northern wall to the other end of that wall. So also [the central bars] on the south side and on the west side [ran from one end of the wall to the other end]. The three walls of the Tabernacle were held together with

---

[43] As opposed to Rashi who says that the count of five *included* the "central bar." See previous note.

Most of the classical rabbinic sources explain, as Rashi does, that the "central bar" is part of the original count of five. See e.g. *Beraita' di-melekhet ha-mishkan*, *ibid.*, Zohar 3:186a ("Should you claim that that 'central bar' is an additional bar, not one of the five, that is *not* the case. The 'central bar' *was* one of those five") and other sources cited by Kasher, note 83. However, as Kasher also notes, Rashbam can find support for his reading that the "central bar" was in addition to the previous five bars in Bemidbar Rabba 6:4 ("ובריחיו'--'its bars': אלו חמישה עשר בריחים והבריח התיכון this means the fifteen bars and the 'central bar'").

[44] Rashbam clearly does not understand בתוך הקרשים as meaning "halfway up the planks," as NJPS does. Rather he feels that it means that the "central bar" ran though the middle of the planks. That is also the standard rabbinic understanding. See e.g. Rashi ad 26:26, s.v. חמשה.

[45] As opposed to the other five bars which went on the outside of the planks, through rings.

[46] As opposed to the rabbinic understanding that Rashbam cites below, according to which there was only one "central bar."

each other because of the corner planks,[47] as the bars on the north side and on the south side also ran through the corner pieces, for one cubit of [the width of each of] the corner pieces sat alongside [the one cubit of] the thickness of the side wall.[48] That means that the bars that ran through the north and the south walls also ran through the corner planks.[49]

However, the rabbis say that [there was only one] central bar [which] miraculously curved around and ran מן הקצה אל הקצה, FROM END TO END, i.e. through all three walls.[50]

---

[47]Rashbam may feel obliged to explain how the three walls stayed together because, as he writes below, his explanation differs from that of the rabbis, who claimed that there was only one central bar that miraculously ran though all through walls. A supernatural bar like that would presumably keep the three walls together very well. Rashbam then explains that even the mundane, straight bars that he thinks are being described would serve the same purpose, if placed properly.

[48]As Rashbam explains at length above; see his comm. and notes above, ad vs. 22.
The language used here is difficult (אמה מן המקצוע מכסה עובי קרש של מקצוע שני) and is not the same as the language used by Rashbam ad vs. 22. Still it is clear that he is attempting to describe the shape of the corners in the same way that he did above.

[49]Again Rashbam's explanation disagrees with that of Rashi. The measurements that Rashi provides for the length of the bars on the north and south sides make it clear that Rashi does *not* think that they included the corner pieces.
I would speculate that Rashbam also thinks that the bars on the western side included the corner pieces, for, as Rashbam described them above, ad vs. 22, the corner pieces served as part of the west wall and made a straight row with the other six planks of the west wall. Here he feels obliged to emphasize only that *even* the bars on the north and south sides (where the planks ran perpendicular to the corner planks) included the corner pieces. Rashi writes explicitly (at the end of his comm. ad vs. 26) that all the bars on the western side included the corner planks. So also LT, ad Ex. 36:8.

[50]Shabbat 98b. See Illustration G.
Rashi, here, also interprets the verse in the non-miraculous manner, as meaning that there were three separate central bars. Rashi could presumably explain better than Rashbam why, following the *peshaṭ* reading, the verse describes the central bar as running "from end to end" (מן הקצה אל הקצה). To review, the Talmud says that the phrase, "from end to end," means that the bar ran from one end of the Tabernacle's walls all the way around through three walls to the other end. Rashi says that the phrase means that while all the other bars--the external bars--of the Tabernacle were each only half a wall's length long, the central bars were the length of a full wall; that is why they

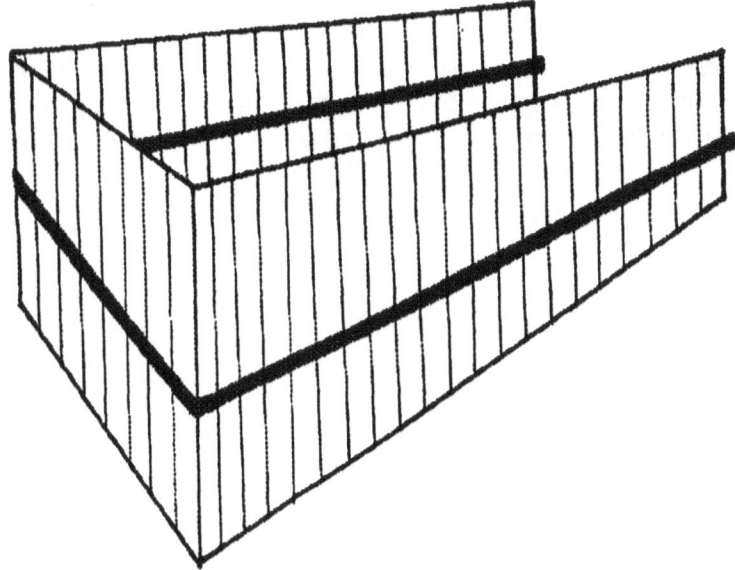

Illustration G
The One Central Bar
(according to "the Rabbis")

particularly are described as running "from end to end." Rashbam, to my mind, would have difficulty explaining why the phrase "from end to end" was applied specifically to the central bars. According to Rashbam, the lengths of the central bars were the same as the lengths of all the other bars. Accordingly, the phrase "from end to end" could describe any of the bars, so there would be no particular reason for the Torah to apply the phrase, "from end to end," only to the *central* bars.

26:31 פרכת A CURTAIN: From the context [one deduces that the word פרכת means] a partition, something that divides one room[51] from another.[52]

מעשה חשב THE WORK OF A CRAFTSMAN: חשב refers to a type of craftsman.[53] [Here it means that the curtain was embroidered,] like jackets that have designs woven into the fabric.[54] But the word רוקם [e.g. in vs. 36] means embroidered on the outside[55] with a needle.

---

[51]בית. In rabbinic Hebrew, and even in late biblical Hebrew, בית can mean a room or a part of a house. See BDB, s.v. בית.

[52]Rashbam understands the word פרכת in the same way that Rashi does. Rashi suggests that פרכת is connected to the rabbinic Hebrew word, פרגוד. Rashbam says that the context, not rabbinic Hebrew, teaches us what פרכת means. On Rashbam's attitude to the use of rabbinic Hebrew in order to understand biblical Hebrew texts, see my Genesis volume, pp. 422-424.

[53]Not to the type of craft. See similarly Rashi ad 26:36, s.v. רקם ("ולא האמן שם האמנות שם--the name of a craftsman, not of a craft").

[54]On the idea that חשב refers to embroidery, see similarly Rashi ad 26:1. Rashi adds (based on Tosefta Sheqalim 3:14) that the embroidery was done in some special manner that the design on one side appeared to have one shape, and on the other side it appeared to have another shape. Rashbam says more simply that all that it means is standard embroidery.

[55]I.e. on top of the fabric. So also Rashi, *ibid.* and ad vs. 36. However, Rashi adds that the design appeared to be the same on both sides. From what Rashbam says, it appears likely that he feels that the design known as מעשה רקם could be seen only on one side of the curtain.

EXODUS XXVI

26:32 וויהם HOOKS: That were like forks,[56] were permanently attached to the tops of the posts, so that the upper lip[57] of the curtain could be inserted into them.

26:33 ונתתה HANG THE CURTAIN UNDER THE CLASPS: The golden clasps of the roof hangings. These clasps were [on the roof,] twenty cubits from the entrance to the Tabernacle. The Tabernacle was thirty cubits long.[58] The golden clasps [of the roof hangings] could be found half way along the forty-cubit length of the ten strips of cloth.[59] So [the distance] from the curtain to the eastern entrance measured twenty cubits; this [section of the Tabernacle] is [called] the *hekhal*.[60] [The distance] from the curtain to the western wall of the Tabernacle measured ten cubits; this [section of the Tabernacle] is [called] the Holy of Holies.[61]

26:36 מסך לפתח האהל MAKE A SCREEN FOR THE ENTRANCE OF THE TENT: Since there are no strips of cloth covering [the eastern

---

[56]Rashbam says that the hooks were like forks (מזלגות). Rashi uses the rabbinic Hebrew word אונקליות to describe the shape of the hooks. Presumably there is no difference between Rashbam and Rashi on this point. Rashi (ad 37:3, s.v. ומזלגותיו) uses the word אונקליות to explain what "forks" are. Rashbam's decision to use the biblical Hebrew word may be an example of a general tendency of his to prefer biblical to rabbinic Hebrew in his comm. See e.g. comm. above ad 12:7, and note 33, there.

[57]Rashi says that the curtain was attached to a pole (כלונס) and that pole was attached to the hooks. LT writes that the curtain was attached to a rope and that rope was attached to the hooks. Rashbam, on the other hand, writes that the curtain itself was attached to the hooks.

[58]See comm. and notes ad 26:9-13.

[59]As explained above in verses 1-6.

[60]I.e. "the Holy," the part of the Tabernacle that was *not* the Holy of Holies.

[61]See Illustration A, page 310.
This same explanation can be found in Rashi and in LT here.

side of the Tabernacle], aside from the "extra half cloth," [described above,] which was "folded over."[62]

The word מָסָךְ is [not like most nouns; it is to be considered] like [a participle, as if the word] מֵסִיךְ [were written]. So also the word מָגֵן is [not like most nouns; it is] like [the participle] מֵגִין. That is why even when the words מסך and מגן are in the construct case, their first vowel does not become a *sheva*, because they are verbal forms. That is why it is written (Num. 4:25), "מָסַךְ פֶּתַח אֹהֶל מוֹעֵד--the screen *of* the entrance of the Tent of Meeting,"[63] i.e. the item protecting[64] the entrance. So also [in the word מָגֵן, the first vowel remains a *qameṣ* and does not turn into a *sheva* even in the construct case, as in the phrase,] (II Sam. 1:21) "the shield of (מָגֵן) Saul, polished with oil no more."[65] But [other words on the same paradigm as מָסָךְ, such as] דָּבָר and בָּקָר which are nouns, their first vowel becomes a *sheva* in the construct case, for example in the phrases (Num. 7:88) "herd animals of (בְּקַר)

---

[62]See vss. 9 and 12 above, and see Rashbam's comm. and notes, there.

[63]The second *qameṣ* of מָסָךְ becomes a *pataḥ* in the construct, just like the second *qameṣ* of דָּבָר or בָּקָר. However, while the first *qameṣ* of דָּבָר and בָּקָר turns into a *sheva* in the construct, the first *qameṣ* of מָסָךְ does not. So Rashbam here explains why the construct of מָסָךְ is somewhat like the construct of דָּבָר and בָּקָר, but also somewhat different. See similarly Rashbam's comm. and notes below ad 28:11, s.v. מעשה חרש.

Rashbam's explanation of the strength of the first *qameṣ* of מָסָךְ has little to recommend it. He uses this same explanation in his *Dayqut*, p. 49, where he distinguishes between, on the one hand, construct forms like צָרֵי and שָׂרֵי that "do not take a *sheva* because they are verbal forms" (לפי שלשון פועל המה לא יוכלו ליחטף), and, on the other hand, construct forms like יְדֵי and מֵי that "do take a *sheva*, because they are nouns" (לפי ששמות דבר הן יכולין ליחטף).

For another discussion of the question, see ibn Janah, *Sefer ha-shorashim*, s.v. ס-כ-ך. See also the discussion in G.-K. 27, which explains that the phenomenon of the shortening of a *qameṣ* to a *sheva* when that vowel is far from the stress has nothing to do with the part of speech involved; it occurs to the same extent in verbs, nouns, participles and adjectives.

[64]I.e. the word מסך should be seen as serving as a participle, not a noun.

[65]Again cf. ibn Janah, *ibid.*, s.v. ג-נ-ן.

sacrifices of well-being" and (Deut. 15:2) "the nature of (דְּבַר) the remission."[66]

---

[66]See also these same examples in Rashbam's discussion of the construct case in his *Dayqut*, pp. 47-48.

EXODUS XXVII

27:1 ועשית את המזבח YOU SHALL MAKE THE ALTAR: The "outer" altar, the one that was in the enclosure, [outside the Tabernacle].[1]

27:2 ממנו THE HORNS TO BE OF ONE PIECE WITH IT: Not [made separately and then later] attached.[2]

27:3 ויעיו ITS PANS: That are called *vadil* in the vernacular.[3] These pans are used to collect the ashes [from the altar] and to put them into סירותיו, ITS POTS. The pots were then used to take the ashes away, as it is written in [the Torah portion,] Ṣav 'et 'aharon.[4]

---

[1]There are two altars connected to the Tabernacle, the one described here and the one described in Exodus 30:1f. Rashbam follows the standard rabbinic understanding (e.g. Zev. 59b and Rashi's comm there, s.v. כי גמיר) and explains that the one described here is the "outer altar," not the one that was placed in the Tabernacle proper, but the one in the ḥaṣer, the enclosure or courtyard, surrounding the Tabernacle (described in vss. 9-19 below).

[2]So also Rashi here. See Rashbam's comm. and notes ad 25:31, s.v. גביעיה.

[3]The Old French word for "shovel." Rashi uses the identical vernacular word here.

[4]Lev. 6:3-4.
   Generally Rashbam's understanding of the function of the יעים and the סירות is the same as that of Rashi. Still, Rashi in his long explanation does not ever mention that the סירות were used to remove the ashes to some other location. Perhaps for that very reason Rashbam emphasizes that point, and refers to the text in Leviticus where that function of removing the ashes is outlined.

ומזרקותיו ITS BASINS: In which the animal's blood was collected so that it could be sprinkled (לזרוק) on the altar.⁵

ומזלגותיו ITS FORKS: Which were [dug into the meat in order] to pick up the sacrificial limbs and turn them over on top of the coals of the altar's wood, so that they would be consumed by the fire.⁶

ומחתותיו ITS FIRE PANS: Which were used to rake (לחתות) the coals; [ח-ת-ה means to rake a fire,] as it is written (Is. 30:14), "to rake (לחתות) coals from a brazier," and (Prov. 6:27) "Can a man rake (היחתה) embers into his bosom?"⁷

27:4 מכבר A GRATING: מכבר is to be understood like the word "כברה--a sieve," as it is written (Amos 9:9), "As one shakes [sand] in a sieve (כברה) and not a pebble falls to the ground."⁸

27:5 כרכב THE LEDGE: The recess of the altar. The top of the altar is made narrower by a recessed area [for the priests] to be able to walk around the [top of] the altar.⁹ The root כרכב is used also in rabbinic

---

⁵Again Rashbam's explanation is a variation on Rashi's. Rashi also says that the מזרקות were used to collect the sacrificial animal's blood. Rashbam adds that they were also used to sprinkle the blood, and that because of their function of sprinkling (זריקה), they are referred to as מזרקות.
 Cf. LT who says that מזרקות were used for wine libations.

⁶So also Rashi, at greater length.

⁷So also Rashi, with the precise same two prooftexts.
 Again Rashbam diverges somewhat from Rashi. Rashi describes the מחתות as serving an additional function--that of carrying coals from one location to another. Rashbam describes only the function of raking the coals.
 See also Rashbam ad Ex. 25:38, s.v. ומחתותיה.

⁸So also Rashi, at greater length (but without the prooftext from Amos).

⁹This explanation may be found in Zev. 62a.
 Rashbam's explanation disagrees with that of Rashi. Rashi writes (following Zev. 62a) that there are two different "ledges," one on the *side* walls of the altar and one

EXODUS XXVII

literature, in *Shehiṭat ḥullin*,[10] where it says עד שיכרכב.[11] The word may be applied to protrusions and to designs on vessels, and to recesses that are hollowed out of them.

עד חצי המזבח THE MIDDLE OF THE ALTAR: [The grating was placed half way up the walls of the altar, as it is important to know the location of the middle of the altar] to divide between bloods [that are to be sprinkled] on the top of the altar and bloods [that are to be sprinkled] on the bottom of the altar.[12] The mnemonic device [to remember the rules concerning the sprinkling of sacrificial blood] is: "The burnt offering of fowl--up,[13] the sin offering of fowl--down." And for

---

on the *top* of the altar. Rashi feels that the "ledge" described in this verse is the one on the side walls of the altar, one that had purely decorative purposes to it. Rashi writes that the word "ledge" can be applied to anything circular (כל דבר המקיף סביב בעיגול).

Rashbam, on the other hand, sees the word, "כרכב--ledge," as reserved for something hollowed out (or raised) and then explains that the כרכב of our verse must be the hollowed-out walkway for priests on top of the altar.

[10]On the name, *Shehiṭat ḥullin*, see comm. to 23:19, s.v. לא, and note 50, there.

[11]Rashi cites the same passage from Hul. in his comm., here.
Our texts of Hul. 25a read: כל שעתיד . . . לכרכב . In any case, the word means to hollow out. See Rashi there.

[12]So also Rashi, following Zev. 53a.

[13]I.e. if the type of sacrifice is a burnt offering and the animal being offered is a fowl, then the blood is sprinkled on the top half of the altar.

As Rosin explains, the mnemonic depends on the two possible meanings of this first phrase, עולת העוף למעלה, which could be construed as meaning "fowl go upwards," an easy phrase to remember. Then, if one remembers that phrase, and if one remembers that burnt offerings are "the opposite" of sin offerings and that mammals are "the opposite" of fowl, then all the other details of the mnemonic will be remembered too.

mammals, the opposite:[14] "burnt offering--down, and sin offering--up." All of this may be found in tractate Zevahim.[15]

27:8 נבוב לוחות [MAKE IT] HOLLOW, OF BOARDS: נבוב means hollow,[16] as it is written (Job 11:12), "A hollow (נבוב) man will get understanding."[17] Whenever they [i.e.the Israelites] would set up camp, they would fill the altar with dirt[18] and then they would sacrifice.

27:9 קלעים HANGINGS: Menahem explained[19] that קלעים here means "strips of cloth (יריעות)." He said that there is also another, separate, meaning for the root ק-ל-ע--"to carve," as in the verses (I Kings 6:32), "[doors of olive wood,] and on them he carved (ויקלע) reliefs (מקלעות) of cherubim," and (ibid., 6:18) "[the cedar . . . had] carvings (מקלעת) of gourds." I say that [it is all one meaning,] that the קלעים of the Tabernacle [were so called because they] were made through engraving and designs.[20]

---

[14]למפרע. Rashbam uses this word to mean "in the opposite order" also in his comm. to Gen. 34:9. See notes there.

[15]Zev. 65a.
Rashbam means all these rules of sacrifices may be found in Zev. The mnemonic, however, is, as far as I can determine, his own.

[16]So also Rashi. This is the standard rabbinic and modern understanding of the word.

[17]This same prooftext is cited both by iE and LT, here.

[18]Following Mekhilta Ba-hodesh 11 (Lauterbach ed., p. 284) and Zev. 61b. See Rashi here, and ad 20:21, s.v. מזבח אדמה, and see also Rashbam's comm. and notes, there. So also Ps.-Jon. here: חליל לוחין מלי עפרא.

[19]In his Mahberet, s.v. ק-ל-ע.

[20]Rashi also writes here that the קלעים were perforated with holes. See also Rashbam's comm. ad 30:10 below.
Menahem's claim that there are two separate meanings of this root--one related to engraving wood and one having to do with hangings made out of material--appears quite reasonable. (See e.g. BDB, s.v. ק-ל-ע, which makes the same distinction.)

27:10 וחשוקיהם BANDS OF SILVER: From the context, one sees that וחשוקיהם refers to [something] silver that goes around [the posts].[21]

27:12 עמודיהם עשרה [ON THE WEST SIDE FIFTY CUBITS . . .] WITH THEIR TEN POSTS: Throughout this section, you will find a post placed every five cubits.[22]

27:14 וחמש FIFTEEN CUBITS OF HANGINGS ON THE ONE FLANK: The eastern side, where the entrance to the enclosure was, was fifty cubits wide. On one flank of that wall there were fifteen cubits of hangings. So also on the other flank of that wall. And in the middle of that wall there was a screen, twenty [cubits] wide. This makes [a grand total of] fifty cubits of covering.[23]

27:18 ורוחב THE WIDTH FIFTY BY FIFTY: How did this work out? The enclosure was one hundred cubits long from east to west, for the northern and southern walls were each made of one hundred cubits of

---

Perhaps Rashbam is simply saying here that the two meanings do have some connection. Like Rashbam, see Qimhi, *Sefer ha-shorashim*, s.v. ק-ל-ע.

[21]So also Rashi. However Rashi tries to prove that meaning based on the Aramaic translation of Jud. 19:10. Rashbam may be saying, then, that he prefers to use only Hebrew parallels and, accordingly, he bases his interpretation here on context alone.

[22]Based on vss. 10-16 (and simple arithmetic). So also Rashi ad vs. 10, s.v. ועמודיו.

[23]Rashbam explains at length the simple reading of vss. 13-16. (So also Rashi ad vs. 13, s.v. חמישים.) Perhaps Rashbam goes into such detail to emphasize his disagreement with the understanding of this text in the Talmud. The simplest reading of two talmudic texts (Eruv. 2b and Zev. 59b-60a) suggests that at least one *'amora'* understood the "fifteen cubits" of our verse as a reference to the height of the hangings, not their width. See also Tos. ad Zev. 59b, s.v. ואומר, where Rashbam's brother, Rabbenu Tam, expresses amazement that anyone might interpret the "fifteen cubits" of our verse as a reference to the height, and not to the width. ("היכי מצי למימר דאגובה קאי והא מוכח קרא להדיא דברחבה מיירי--How could anyone say that [the fifteen cubits] refers to the height? The verse proves indisputably that the reference is to the width.")

hangings (vss. 9 and 11). The width of the enclosure from north to south [i.e. on the east and west walls] was fifty cubits (vss. 12 and 13).

The Tabernacle was thirty [cubits] long by ten [cubits] wide.[24] The Tabernacle was erected [lengthwise] within the hundred-cubit length [of the enclosure such that the Tabernacle's eastern wall was placed] at the edge of the fifty-cubit point.[25] This leaves an unoccupied square space of enclosure to the east of the Tabernacle that measures "fifty by fifty." On each of the [other] three sides, there are twenty cubits of enclosure;[26] since the Tabernacle's length takes up thirty of the fifty cubits that remained from the hundred-cubit length [of the enclosure, i.e. the fifty cubits that were not taken up by the eastern part of the enclosure], that leaves twenty cubits of enclosure behind the Tabernacle on the western side. The width of the Tabernacle was ten cubits. So of the fifty-cubit width of the enclosure, there were twenty cubits to the north of the Tabernacle and twenty cubits to the south.[27]

---

[24] See comm. and notes ad 26:9-13.

[25] Of the enclosure's total length. In other words, if one divides the length of the enclosure into two halves and draws an imaginary line on that demarcation point—fifty cubits from the eastern wall of the enclosure and fifty cubits from the western wall of the enclosure—then the eastern wall of the Tabernacle would be erected on that imaginary line.

[26] I.e. from the western wall of the Tabernacle to the western wall of the enclosure, and from the northern wall of the Tabernacle to the northern wall of the enclosure, and from the southern wall of the Tabernacle to the southern wall of the enclosure, all of these distances were twenty cubits.

[27] So also Rashi and LT, following *Beraita' di-melekhet ha-mishkan* 5 (pp. 173 and 231) and the interpretation labelled "פשטיה דקרא"—the plain meaning of the biblical text," in Eruv. 23b. Cf. iE, who disagrees, and also NJPSC: "the instructions do not fix the place of the Tabernacle within the larger area of the enclosure." They interpret the phrase חמישים בחמישים differently, as meaning "width fifty throughout."

EXODUS XXVII

27:19 יתידותיו ITS PEGS: Which were attached to the [bottoms of the] hangings and then stuck into the ground, so that the bottoms of the hangings would not blow back and forth in the wind.[28]

27:20 ואתה תצוה YOU SHALL FURTHER INSTRUCT: Above (25:2) the language used is "*Tell* the Israelite people to bring me a donation." [The verb, "tell" (דַּבֵּר) is used in that verse] because that command related only to one specific time period, to the construction of the Tabernacle. But here the verse says "You shall *instruct*," because the command is one that applies to all generations, for they had to contribute "oil for lighting"[29] every year. That is why the text used different phraseology here. For the verb "instruct" is used whenever the command is for [all] future generations. So it is also said in Torat Kohanim[30] and in Sifre,[31] that whenever the verb "instruct" is used the command is to be applied both immediately and in future generations.[32]

---

[28]So also Rashi.
 Rashi writes that he does not know whether these pegs were stuck into the ground or whether they were simply weights to hold down the bottom to the hangings. At the end of Rashi's comm., here, he concludes that they were stuck into the ground. However, many versions of Rashi's comm. here record that that last line was added by Joseph Qara. (See Berliner's *Peletat soferim*, p. 19, and Arend's edition of Qara's comm. on Job, Introduction, p. 20 [both cited by *Torat hayyim*, here].) In other words, Rashi's own comm. does not reach a conclusion about the issue. If we accept that ms. reading of Rashi's comm., then it may be that Rashbam emphasizes the idea that these pegs were inserted into the ground in order to resolve the question that Rashi leaves unanswered.

[29]Using the language of 25:6.

[30]*Ṣav*, 1, ad Lev. 6:2. See also Rashi's comm., there.

[31]To Numbers, *Naso'* 1 (Horovitz ed., p. 1). See also Qid. 29a.

[32]So also LT and iE here. It is interesting that two *peshaṭ*-oriented exegetes like Rashbam and iE have recourse to this midrashic principle, that צו is always used with commands that apply in all generations. (Cf. Nahm., who argues [in the introduction to his comm. to the Torah portion, *Ṣav*] that even in rabbinic literature this principle is not universally accepted.) Presumably they make use of the principle here because it helps explain the redundancy that "oil for lighting" is listed in 25:6 as an item to be collected and then reappears here in a special category. They explain then that chapter 25 listed

זך CLEAR [OIL]: Without any sediment. The olives would be pounded in a mortar; they would not be sufficiently "clear" if they were ground in a millstone.[33]

27:21 לפרוכת [OUTSIDE] THE CURTAIN [WHICH IS OVER THE ARK OF THE PACT]: I.e which is *in front of* the Ark of the Pact.[34]

---

items that were collected only once--for the construction of a Tabernacle in the wilderness--while chapter 27 adds that there is a commandment to collect such oil in future generations too (as the text itself says at the end of the next verse, "for all time, throughout the ages.")

Cf. Nahm.'s approach to the question in his comm. ad Lev. 24:2, Num 8:1 and Num. 19:2.

[33]So also Rashi (s.v. כתית), at greater length, following Men. 86a-b.

[34]The curtain did not hang *over* the Ark, only *in front of* it. Rashbam explains that the language here אשר על העדות simply means "in front of the Ark."

EXODUS XXVIII

28:4 ואלה הבגדים THESE ARE THE VESTMENTS: They are all explained below.[1]

חשן A BREASTPIECE: Following the plain meaning of Scripture, one may deduce from the context that what is meant is some type of pouch or bag, for it is described below (vs. 16) as being "doubled."[2]

ואפוד AND AN EPHOD: This word denotes a garment[3] worn by a person for decorative purposes on top of the rest of his clothes.[4]

ואבנט: means a belt.[5]

---

[1] It is possible that Rashbam writes this comment to contrast with Rashi's methodology here. Rashi ad vs. 6 writes that if he were to explain the form of the breastpiece and the ephod verse by verse, it would be difficult for the reader to put together an accurate picture. Accordingly, Rashi explains their shapes in one long pericope. Rashbam, on the other hand, says to his readers that, if we keep reading, we will get a complete picture of these articles.

See also note 6 below.

[2] See also comm. there, s.v. כפול.

See similarly NJPSC ad vs. 16: "by doubling over the piece of cloth, it became a square, taking the form of a pouch."

Rashbam's interpretation may be directed against Rashi, who writes here that the breastpiece was an ornament. However, below (ad vs. 30, s.v. את האורים) Rashi explains, like Rashbam, that the breastpiece was folded over in order to form a pocket in which items may be inserted.

[3] Rashbam may be taking issue with Rashi, who says that the primary meaning of the word ephod is "a belt."

[4] The standard understanding of the texts (here and Lev. 8:7f.) is like Rashbam's, that the ephod was worn on top of the other garments described here. See e.g. LT here: "האפוד זה בגד העליון--'the ephod' is the outer garment."

[5] Or a sash. Again Rashbam's explanation here is the standard one.

Following the plain meaning of Scripture, there is no need to mention trousers here, since the text lists only the visible garments, the ones worn for honor.[6]

28:6 ועשו את האפד THEY SHALL MAKE THE EPHOD: My grandfather [Rashi] explained the breastpiece and the ephod [at great length]. I, however, will explain aspects of them that were not explained before.[7]

28:7 שתי IT SHALL HAVE TWO SHOULDER-PIECES WHICH SHALL COME TOGETHER: In my opinion,[8] the ephod was like half

---

[6]Not garments like the trousers that were worn underneath the articles of clothing listed here. The priests' trousers *are* listed both in other texts of the Torah (e.g. vs. 42 below) and in the mishnaic lists of the garments of the priests (Yoma 7:5). Rashbam explains that our text says that it is listing here only those garments that were made "for dignity and adornment" (vs. 2). So also iE here. And see also Rashbam's comm. and notes ad vs. 40, below.

Midrash ha-gadol and a number of other midrashic sources (cited by Kasher, here, note 26) say that, from a halakhic analysis point of view, trousers *are* to be seen as included in this verse. The ostensibly redundant phrase, "These are the vestments," at the beginning of the verse, is intended to teach us to add trousers to the list that follows at the end of the verse.

Perhaps it is against such an interpretation that Rashbam is arguing here in two different ways. First he points out (s.v. ואלה הבגדים) that all that "These are the vestments" refers to is those garments that "are all explained below." And then he writes, here, that there is no need to look for hints about trousers anywhere in these verses.

See also Yoma 5b for another halakhic attempt to find a verse that hints about a commandment to make trousers for the priests.

[7]See also Rashbam's introductory comment to chapter 25, above.

Although Rashbam's comment here implies that he is not disagreeing with Rashi's explanation of the ephod and breastpiece, just adding to them, in fact, as the notes below shall explain, he *is* disagreeing.

[8]As Kasher notes (vol. 23, Appendix 8, p. 165), the "astonishing" fact that nowhere in classical rabbinic literature is there a description of the ephod led later exegetes to suggest a very wide variety of explanations. (See Kasher, there, pp. 165-169.) While most exegetes agree that the ephod covered the bottom half of the priest's body, even that idea is not beyond dispute. See e.g. Hizq. (ad vs. 27) and iE's shorter comm. (ad

a garment, that covers a man from his waist down,⁹ both in front and in back.¹⁰ This is the meaning of the verse (Lev. 8:7), "[Moses . . . put the ephod on him,] girding him with the skillfully woven band with which he tied it to him."¹¹ The skillfully woven band (חשב אפודתו) is made like a belt that is part of the ephod,¹² at the edge¹³ of the ephod.¹⁴

The two shoulder-pieces [described in this verse] literally "come together," (חוברות) entirely, in such a way that they cover the man's entire back side, from the waist up. That is why it says in our verse a second time, "they shall be attached" (וחובר), because aside from the fact that the two shoulder-pieces "come together" with each other all the

---

vs. 4) for explanations that the ephod was worn on the top half of the priest's body.
   Rashi and Rashbam are in basic agreement that the ephod was a garment that covered the bottom half of the priest's body. Yet Rashbam disagrees with Rashi about a number of issues concerning the ephod, as the notes below explain.

⁹It appears that Rashbam disagrees slightly with Rashi who says (ad vs. 6) that the ephod was tied to the priest's back slightly higher than at the waist, "opposite his heart, at the level of his elbows." (See also Zev. 18b-19a, and Rashi's comm., there.)

¹⁰Again here Rashbam disagrees with Rashi. According to Rashi, the ephod covered only the back of the priest's legs. He describes it as a type of pinafore or apron similar to those worn by French noblewomen when they went riding; in other words, as opposed to most aprons, it was open in the front, not the back. Rashbam, though, sees the garment as more similar to a skirt or a sash that covered the priest's legs both in front and in back. See Illustration H.

¹¹Rashi (ad vs. 4) also uses this verse to explain the structure of the ephod.

¹²See vs. 8.

¹³Rashbam uses language here (בתוך שפת האפוד) similar to the language used by Rashi (בשפת הסינר) ad vs. 8, s.v. אשר עליו.

¹⁴Hence the edge of the ephod reaches to the waist, the place where belts normally go. According to Rashi, though, part of this band--the part that goes in front--is not attached to the ephod, since the ephod, according to Rashi, covers the priest only in the back.

The Ephod of RASHI

The Ephod of RASHBAM

Illustration H

EXODUS XXVIII

way up to the man's shoulders,[15] the pieces should also be attached at the end to the ephod.[16]

The breastpiece is worn in front, over his heart. It is one *zeret* in length and one *zeret* in width.[17] It is attached at its top to the shoulder-pieces, and at its bottom to the ephod. So, all together, it constitutes one full garment;[18] the priest's entire body is covered by the ephod and the garments that are attached to it, the shoulder-pieces and the breastpiece.

If [one interprets that] the shoulder-pieces do not come together [to cover all of the priest's back] but rather that they are two straps[19] that go over his shoulders and attach to the chains of the breastpiece,[20] then [the construction of the garments does not make sense. For] when the priest would be busy doing the service and would bend over, the shoulder straps would separate and fall off his shoulders[21] and the breastpiece would also fall.

אל שני קצותיו [THEY SHALL BE ATTACHED AT ITS TWO ENDS: [The two shoulder pieces are to be attached to the ephod] on the priest's

---

[15] I.e. the first time that "חוברות--come together," is written in our verse it means that the two shoulder pieces "come together" on the back to cover the entire back.

[16] I.e. the second time, when it says in our verse, "וחובר--shall be attached," that means that the *bottoms* of the shoulder-pieces should be attached to the top of the ephod.

[17] See vs. 16, and see comm. and note 42 there about the meaning of *zeret*.

[18] Above (in the beginning of his comm. to this verse) Rashbam writes that the ephod is like "half a garment." Now he explains that, together with the shoulder-pieces and the breastpiece, they all form one full garment.

[19] Here it becomes clear that Rashbam's lengthy explantion is meant to disagree with Rashi who writes explicitly (ad vs. 6) that the shoulder-pieces were straps. Like Rashi, see also JBS (ad vs. 7).

[20] Described in verse 22.

[21] Rashi (ad vs. 7) argues that the straps would *not* fall down.

back side, at the two ends of the top [of the ephod], where the skillfully woven band was.[22]

28:8 ורחשב אפודתו THE SKILLFULLY WOVEN BAND: The band was used as a belt, to tie the ephod together, as it is written (Lev. 8:7), "[Moses . . . put the ephod on him,] girding him with the skillfully woven band, with which he tied it to him."[23]

28:11 מעשה חָרַשׁ אבן THE WORK OF A LAPIDARY: The noun חָרַשׁ is in the construct, and that is why the vowel following the *resh* is a *pataḥ*.[24] It means a worker *in* stone (חרש של אבן), an artist who is expert in engraving.[25] It is from a dageshized paradigm, like the noun

---

[22] Rashbam saw the ephod as a sash that surrounded the priest. According to his understanding, the "two ends" of the top of this sash met on the priest's back at his backbone, and were tied together there. The two shoulder-pieces were to be attached to those two ends of the top of the ephod.

Rashbam's explanation disagrees with that of Rashi. According to Rashi—for whom the ephod covered the back of the priest only—the reference here to the "two ends" means that the shoulder straps were attached to the ephod at the points that were farthest away from the priest's backbone.

[23] Rashbam reiterates the same point that he made in the beginning of his comm. ad vs. 7. He may be disagreeing with Rashi, here, who says that the band served decorative purposes too (מאפדו . . . ומקשטו). Rashbam describes its purpose as functional.

[24] Not a *qameṣ*.

[25] Up to this point Rashbam's grammatical explanation is identical to that offered by Rashi, here. Rashi, however, explains only the second vowel in the word חָרַשׁ, the one that, arguably, is not all that anomalous. Rashbam now proceeds to explain the first vowel of that word.

"גַּנָּב--thief."²⁶ That is why the *ḥet* is [still]²⁷ followed by a *qameṣ*, not a *ḥaṭaf*.²⁸

פתוחי חותם SEAL ENGRAVINGS: Engraved shapes, like those found on seal rings.²⁹

---

²⁶It is one of the *nomina opificum* ("names of workers or artisans") that are generally nouns formed from the intensive stem. See G.-K. 84ᵇ, b, where he also lists חָרָשׁ in the same category as גַּנָּב, points out that its construct form is חָרַשׁ, and lists some other nouns from that paradigm that follow the same pattern in the construct.

²⁷I.e. even in the construct, not just in the absolute.

²⁸I.e. not by a *ḥaṭaf pataḥ*.
 Rashbam here is discussing a grammatical issue very similar to the one that he dealt with in his comm. ad 26:36 above. (See note 63 there.) As Rashbam writes there, the standard pattern for a noun that has two *qemeṣim* (e.g. דָּבָר or בָּקָר) is that in its construct case it has a *sheva-pataḥ* pattern (e.g. דְּבַר or בְּקַר) or, if the first letter is a guttural, then the construct follows a *ḥaṭaf pataḥ-pataḥ* pattern (e.g. חֲכַם לֵב [Ex. 31:6]). However, here and in Ex. 26 we encounter words which have two *qemeṣim* for their vowels in the absolute, and have a *qameṣ* and a *pataḥ* for their vowels in the construct. Rashbam provides a different explanation for each of these "exceptions," to explain, ad 26:36, why מָסָךְ does not follow the standard pattern for nouns with two *qemeṣim*, and to explain, here, why חָרָשׁ does not follow that pattern. As noted there, the explanation offered by Rashbam for the form, מָסָךְ, is weak; there could be no reasonable argument, though, against the explanation offered here by Rashbam for the form, חָרָשׁ. Like Rashbam, see Qimḥi, *Sefer ha-shorashim*, s.v. חרשׁ, and BDB, s.v. חרשׁ.

²⁹Rashbam's explanation is similar but not identical to Rashi's. Rashi (following Onq.) understands the words the same way that Rashbam does. Neither of them explains the engraving process as being done by the *shamir* worm in the miraculous manner described in Sotah 48b. (See also comm. and notes above ad 25:7.)
 Rashi (like Onq.) assumes that that which is standardly engraved into signet rings is letters, which are generally clear and easy to read. Accordingly Rashi feels that פתוחי חותם implies that the engraving in these stones should be done in the same clear and distinct manner. Rashbam, however, assumes that shapes and designs are what is usually engraved in signet rings. So when the text says here to engrave letters into these stones "in the manner of signet ring engravings," nothing is being said about the clarity of the writing, but only about the artistic skill that would be required of the engraver.

28:12 על כתפות האפוד [ATTACH THE TWO STONES] TO THE TWO SHOULDER-PIECES OF THE EPHOD: The two shoulder-pieces of the ephod reach up [from the waistline] to the two sides of his neck, and then they bend[30] over to his front side. The two stones are placed there, at the top of the two shoulder-pieces. Chains (vs. 14) are also attached to the tops of the shoulder-pieces, and those chains reach down to the breastpiece, which is over the priest's heart. The breastpiece is attached to those chains.[31]

אבני זכרון STONES FOR REMEMBRANCE: I shall explain the meaning of this phrase below, in my commentary about the frontlet, on which "Holy to the LORD" was written.[32]

28:13 ועשית משבצות זהב THEN MAKE FRAMES OF GOLD: Each frame was like a plate of gold with an indentation[33] in it in the middle, so as to able to insert therein the chains. The end of each chain

---

[30]ונכפות. Rashbam's language here (עד צוארו מכאן ומכאן ונכפות לפניו) is almost identical to Rashi's language ad vs. 6 (אצל צוארו מכאן ומכאן ונקפלות לפניו). Perhaps the text of Rashbam should also read here ונקפלות or ונכפלות ("and then they fold over"), instead of ונכפות.

[31]Rashbam's understanding of the ways that the chains and the shoulder-pieces and the breastpiece were connected is the same as that of Rashi ad vss. 6 and 7.

[32]Virtually identical phrases are used here and in vs. 38: "ונשא אהרן את שמותם--Aaron shall carry their names" (here) and "ונשא אהרן את עון הקדשים--Aaron shall carry any sin . . ." (vs. 38). Accordingly Rashbam suggests that our verse is best understood in conjunction with verse 38. See comm. and notes below, ad vs. 36, s.v. קדש, and ad vs. 38.
    Perhaps Rashbam refers here to his comm. that will yet follow since he wishes to point out that he does not accept Rashi's understanding of "stones of remembrance" (that God will always see the names of the tribes of Israel written before Him and will remember their righteousness); he tells us that his alternate understanding will follow.

[33]From the continuation of Rashbam's comment, it seems that he means that there was a button-hole there, into which the button at the end of the chain could be inserted.

consisted of one thick piece[34] that was similar to an "end" or "border"[35]--like that which is made at the end of a silk belt and is called a *bouton*[36] in the vernacular--so that it could be inserted into the frame.

28:14 מעשה עבות [TWO CHAINS . . .] LIKE CORDED WORK: Since there also is another type of chain--[a link chain] with pieces like hooks inserted one into the other--the text had to explain that the chains of this verse are *not* that type of chain. Rather it is a chain that is braided lengthwise, like the cords that we use.[37]

ונתת FASTEN THE CORDED CHAINS TO THE FRAMES: The text as of yet has not told us where these items [the corded chains and the frames] should be placed. Below it will explain[38] that one end of each of the two chains is attached to one of the [two] rings of the breastpiece. The other [end of each of the] two chains is attached to one of the [two]

---

[34]Rashbam opposes Rashi, who says in his comm. ad vs. 25 that each chain had at the top *two* ends that were both inserted into (or perhaps tied to) the appropriate frame. Rashbam accordingly emphasizes that each one of these chains consisted at its end of *one* thick piece.

[35]גבול. Presumably Rashbam is trying to explain why these chains are called מגבלות (vs. 14) and גבלות (vs. 22). Both Rashi and Rashbam connect these terms to the Hebrew word גבול ("border"), but they disagree as to why those terms are applied to the chains. Rashi says that those terms are used because the *bottoms* of the chains are attached to the breastpiece at its edge or border (גבול). Rashbam, on the other hand, says that the chains had, on the opposite end, a "border" that could be inserted into the frames.

[36]A "button," in English.

[37]Rashi and Rashbam have the same general understanding--that the text refers to braided chains, not link chains. Rashi perhaps reads more into the phrase מעשה עבות than Rashbam does. Rashi says that the phrase teaches us that these chains were to be "not like the ones that we attach to pails used at a well, but like the ones that we attach to censers." Rashbam's comment might then be read as saying that the text is not quite so specific, and intends only to exclude link chains.

[38]Vss. 23-25.

frames. Those frames are attached to "the shoulder-pieces of the ephod, at the front."[39]

28:15 חשן משפט A BREASTPIECE OF DECISION: It is called a breastpiece "of decision," because inside the breastpiece they placed the Urim and Thummim, which provided [the answers for] the decisions required by the Israelites and [information required in order to fulfil] their needs, as it is written (Num. 27:21) "[Eleazar the priest shall . . .] seek the decision (משפט) of the Urim."[40]

28:16 כפול DOUBLED: Like a pocket. It was shaped like that because the Urim and Thummim were put into it.[41]

זרת: A ZERET [IN LENGTH AND A ZERET IN WIDTH]: A zeret is half a cubit.[42]

---

[39] Verse 25.

See Rashi's comm. here, ad both vss. 13 and 14, where Rashi also notes that the description of the chains and the frames here is incomplete and is dependent on the further details provided below in vss. 23-25. Both Rashi and Rashbam thus disagree with the interpretation that says that there were a total of four chains, the two described here and the two described below, in vss. 23-25. For that interpretation, see Maimonides, *Kele ha-miqdash* 9:8-10, and see the discussion in Kasher, note 80. Kasher also points out (vol. 23, Appendix 9, pp. 169-171) that the best texts of Maimonides show that he distinguishes between the two chains of our verse, that are called שרשרות, and the two chains of vs. 22, that are called שרשת. See Rashi and Rashbam ad vs. 22, who both write explicitly that the שרשרות and the שרשת are one and the same.

[40] Rashbam's interpretation disagrees with Rashi's first explanation (following Zev. 88b), that the term משפט is used because the breastpiece atones for judicial sins. Rashi's second explanation--that the term משפט is used because the breastpiece provided clear and truthful messages--is closer but still not identical to what Rashbam says. Rashi below, ad vs. 30, s.v. את משפט, explains משפט in a manner similar to Rashbam's interpretation here. So also LT, here.

[41] See comm. and notes above, ad vs. 4, s.v. חשן.

[42] There are a number of different opinions in rabbinic literature about what a *zeret* is. See Kasher's survey here, note 61. Rashbam offers the standard rabbinic understanding, that a *zeret* is half the length of a cubit. See e.g. Tos. Kelim, BM 6:12,

EXODUS XXVIII

28:17 ומלאת בו YOU SHALL MAKE SETTINGS IN IT: Indentations in which the stones were set.[43]

28:22 ועשית על החושן ON THE BREASTPIECE MAKE CHAINS (שרשת): These שרשת are one and the same as the chains (שרשרות), described above (vs. 14), that were attached to the frames.[44]

28:23-8 ועשית על החשן MAKE ON THE BREASTPIECE [TWO RINGS OF GOLD]: Place these rings AT THE TWO ENDS of the top OF THE BREASTPIECE, so that (vs. 24) the two chains can be inserted into them. Then (vs. 25), the two [other] ends of the chains, which are attached to frames, should be placed ON TOP OF THE SHOULDER-PIECES. As a result, the breastpiece is now attached to the ephod.[45] But it would still be possible for the bottom of the breastpiece to sway back and forth,[46] unless it too is attached to the ephod. So the text continues to explain [how to secure the bottom of the breastpiece,][47] that (vs. 26) on the bottom of the breastpiece, at its ends,

---

and Rashi ad Eruv. 21a, s.v. ושמים. See also NJPSC which writes that a "*zeret* is the maximum distance between the top of the little finger and the thumb, approximately 9 inches, or half a cubit."

[43]So also Rashi. Both Rashi and Rashbam understand the words ומלאת (here) and במלואתם (vs. 20) in a manner different from the talmudic understanding. See comm. and notes above, ad 25:7 and ad 28:11, s.v. פתוחי.

[44]In vs. 14. So also Rashi here and see note 39, above.

[45]Rashbam reiterates the explanation that he wrote above, ad vs. 14, s.v. ונתת. So also Rashi.

[46]So also Rashi, here, who describes the problem more graphically: the bottom of the breastpiece, if unsecured, would go back and forth bumping against the priest's stomach.

[47]I.e. the text has described in vss. 23-5 how the *top* of the breastpiece is secured in place (by attaching it to the chains that are attached to the frames that are placed on the shoulder-pieces of the ephod). Now the text will describe in vs. 26f. how the *bottom* of

two rings are made, one on each side, and (vs. 27) two [more] rings are made at the two ends of [the top of] the ephod, at the spot where the bottoms of the two shoulder-pieces are attached to the top of the ephod[48] and the skillfully woven band.[49] The text now has described that the rings of the breastpiece should be at its bottom (vs. 26), and the rings of the ephod should be at its top (vs. 27). Then, when (vs. 28) THE CORD OF BLUE goes FROM THE RINGS of the ephod TO THE RINGS OF THE BREASTPIECE, [it is securing] the breastpiece, above, and the ephod, below.

וירכסו: means "they shall attach."[50]

---

the breastpiece is secured in place.

[48]Generally, all of Rashbam's lengthy explanation here is the same as that of Rashi, with one exception. Rashi says that the last set of rings is actually placed *above* the priest's waist, on the shoulder-pieces (which Rashi considers shoulder-*straps*) : ואלו נתונים מעט בגובה זקיפת הכתפות. Rashbam says that the rings are placed at the *bottom* of those shoulder-pieces, at the priest's waist.

[49]The location of these last two rings (of vs. 27) is fairly clear: they are to be placed on (or near) the waist of the ephod, i.e. the top of the ephod, so that they will be close to the two rings that are at the bottom of the breastpiece, which hangs down over the priest's chest with its bottom reaching the priest's waist.

Rashbam goes to some length here to clarify how this explanation can fit into the language of verse 27. He interprets the phrase that says that the rings are to be placed על שתי כתפות האפוד מלמטה as meaning that the rings are attached to the ephod at the same place that the bottoms of the shoulder-pieces are attached to the ephod, i.e. at the waist. And he interprets the phrase ממעל לחשב האפוד as meaning that the rings are attached to the top of the skillfully woven band.

[50]There are a number of different interpretations for the verb וירכסו. LT says that it means "to lower." ibn Janah (*Sefer ha-shorashim*, s.v. ר-כ-ס) says that it means "to strengthen." Rashbam's interpretation is, I think, the same as Rashi's. Rashi uses the Hebrew root ח-ב-ר (to join or attach) to explain the word; Rashbam uses the Hebrew root ח-ג-ר, (to gird) to explain the word. I do not see any significance to this difference. (In fact, it may be that the word ויחגרו in Rashbam's comm. is simply a copyist's error, and Rashbam actually wrote the almost identical word, ויחברו.)

EXODUS XXVIII

28:30 את האורים ואת התומים THE URIM AND THUMMIM: A type of conjuring using Divine Names[51] to determine God's words. They were placed inside the breastpiece and were used to provide [answers for] the decisions required by the Israelites and [information required in order to fulfil] their needs.[52]

If the other nations have *teraphim*[53] and magic that tell them the future through the forces of impurity,[54] how much more so may it be

---

[51]So also Rashi, here, following Ps.-Jon. Cf. iE's long excursus against this interpretation, in his longer comm., ad vs. 6.

[52]Using the same language that Rashbam used above, in his comm. ad vs. 15. Cf. JBS, who claims that the Urim and Thummim had a much more limited function: they were used to divide up the land of Israel among the different tribes in an equitable manner.

There are a number of different interpretations of what the Urim and Thummim were. As NJPSC puts it: "while the fuction of the device is clear . . . [no Torah texts] carry a description of it or of the technique employed in its use." While Rashbam does not explain precisely what the Urim and Thummim were, it seems that he, like Rashi, thought of them as some item with God's name written or engraved thereon. Cf. the interpretations of LT (ad 29:15), that the Urim and Thummim and the precious stones of the breastpiece are one and the same; and of iE (longer comm. ad vs. 6), that the Urim and Thummim were made of gold and silver.

[53]See Rashbam's comm. and notes ad Gen. 31:19. There Rashbam writes that we know that *teraphim* are used for divination because, in Hosea 3:4, the word *teraphim* is juxtaposed to ephod. See also Rashbam's comm. below, ad 32:1, and ad 32:4, s.v. אלה.

[54]Rashbam clearly believes that the forces of impurity do work for divination. Jews should refrain from using those forces despite the fact that they could provide accurate information about the future. See Rashbam's comm. ad Ex. 32:4, s.v. אלה, and ad Deut. 13:3, and see my "Tradition or Context," p. 181.

done through the forces of holiness[55] (although one should hardly be comparing the forces of impurity and the forces of purity at all!).[56]

28:31 מעיל האפוד THE ROBE OF THE EPHOD: [This robe is called the robe "of the ephod," because] the ephod is worn on top of it.[57]

כליל תכלת OF PURE BLUE: כליל means entirely [blue].[58] It seems to me that the reason [that the robe was entirely blue][59] was that the robe could be seen under the ephod and the breastpiece. A function of the ephod and the breastpiece was that they served for "remembrance" (זכרון).[60] The color blue also serves for remembrance, since it is the color of the heaven. So the rabbis said[61] about the blue [thread] of the

---

[55]iE argues at length (in his longer comm. ad vs. 6) *against* the idea that the Urim and Thummim involved the use of God's Name for divination. iE says that anyone who has read Hai Gaon's responsum on the subject would not interpret in that manner. (iE's reference is presumably to the responsum found in *'Oṣar ha-ge'onim* Hag., [B. Lewin ed., Responsa section, pp. 16-27], where Hai Gaon forcefully rejects the idea of using God's Name for purposes of divination.) It is interesting that Rashbam here feels obliged to "prove" that divination through the Divine Name can work. While it is hardly posssible that Rashbam is reacting directly to iE's attack on this idea (as iE's longer comm. is generally seen as having been written *after* Rashbam's comm.), it seems likely that the type of criticism that iE records reached Rashbam's ears, and he rose to the defense of the idea that the Divine Name does work for divination.

[56]See note 66 below.

[57]So also Rashi. There is a slight difference between Rashi's language and Rashbam's. Rashi here describes the ephod as a belt (so also JBS), while Rashbam describes the ephod as a garment. See comm. ad vs. 4, s.v. ואפוד, and note 3, there.

[58]So also Rashi, following Zev. 88b (but as opposed to the explanation found in Men. 42b).

[59]Even though the other priestly garments had threads of a number of colors in them. Cf. e.g. vs. 6, where the instructions are to make the ephod out of blue thread, together with purple and red threads (and other material).

[60]Vs. 12. See comm. and note 30, there.

[61]Men. 43b and Sifre Numbers 115 (Horovitz ed., p. 126).

ṣiṣit[62]--that the blue color is similar to that of the oceans, and the color of the oceans is similar to that of the heavens, and the color of the heavens is similar to that of the Divine Throne. For that reason the robe is entirely blue, without any purple or red [threads].[63]

28:32 פי ראשו . . . פי תחרא THE OPENING FOR THE HEAD . . . LIKE THE OPENING OF A COAT OF MAIL: [פי refers to] the opening in which he inserts his head when he puts the robe on.[64]

בתוכו IN THE MIDDLE OF IT: I.e. at the top of the garment, in the middle, similar to the garments worn [these days] by [Christian] priests[65] (although one should hardly be comparing these two types of clothing!).[66]

---

[62]See Num. 15:38-9: "Attach a cord of blue to the fringe . . . look at it and recall (וזכרתם) . . .."

[63]Rashbam's explanation of why the robe was totally blue appears to be original. See LT (below ad vs. 37), who quotes this same rabbinic saying in order to explain why the cords attached to the frontlet were made of blue.

[64]So also Rashi and most other exegetes.

[65]Rashbam's comment here means that the neck opening should be closed all around, like the neck of a poncho, or like the necks of the robes worn by Christian priests in Rashbam's days.
    Rashbam's interpretation agrees with that of Rashi about one point--that the text is referring to the neck opening of the robe. But Rashi (following Onq.) says that the word בתוכו refers to the manner in which the neck opening should be made, by folding the material over upon itself, so that the fold serves as the edge of the garment. Rashbam however says that the word בתוכו simply means that the collar of the garment should be in the middle of the garment.

[66]Again (see comm. ad vs. 30) Rashbam uses comparisons to Christian practices, and again he apologizes for drawing the comparisons. He also uses a reference to Christian clothing in his comm. ad Gen. 25:25. There he does *not* apologize for drawing such a comparison, but for good reason. There he is explaining a phrase in a verse that describes Esau by referring to the type of clothing that Christians wear. To Rashbam's mind, comparing Esau with later-day Christians was something that came naturally. But to compare the high priest's clothing to that of contemporaneous Christian clergymen was not so simple. Cf. LT here, who compares the robe of the high priest to "mantles that are worn by the men of France" (כמו מנטיל הלובשים אנשי צרפת), and see Buber's

לא יקרע **IT SHOULD NOT BE TORN:** He should not make an opening for the neck at the bottom [of the material], as we do with the clothing that we wear.[67] Rather he should make it at the top; i.e. when he weaves the garment, he should leave [an empty space in the middle that will constitute] the neck opening.[68]

28:33 בתוכם [WITH BELLS OF GOLD] **BETWEEN THEM:** [The bells were placed] between the pomegranates, not inside of the pomegranates.[69]

---

introduction to LT, pp. 18-19.

[67] In clothing such as button-down shirts (or any type of clothing that has a slit at the top connected to the neck), the opening for the neck would be made at the end of the piece of material that is being fashioned into the garment.

[68] Two explanations are found in the Talmud (Yoma 72a) of what the words לא יקרע mean. According to one rabbi, the phrase means that it is *forbidden* to tear this (or any other) priestly garment. Another rabbi suggests that the phrase means that the neck of the robe should be sufficiently strong that it *cannot* be easily torn. Rashi's interpretation is essentially a combination of those two ideas.

Rashbam offers his own, new understanding: that when weaving the robe, one should not take a piece of completed material and tear an opening on the end of the piece to serve as the neck opening. Rather one should weave the material in such a way that an empty space is left in the middle of the piece, and that empty space will be the neck opening. So also JBS.

Notice that when discussing the word בתוכו in this verse, Rashi says that it tells us something about the manner in which the garment is made, while Rashbam says that it tells us something about how the finished garment should turn out. Now, when dealing with the words לא יקרע, the roles are precisely reversed. *Rashbam* says that they teach us how to weave the robe, while *Rashi* says that they describe how the robe turns out (and/or how the robe is to be treated) after it is completed.

[69] In theory, the word בתוכם could mean either "inside the pomegranates" or "between the pomegranates." In fact, both possible interpretations could be read into the talmudic paassage (Zev. 88b) that describes the pomegranates and bells. There are two readings of that talmudic text: (1) ותולה בהן, which would seem to imply that the bells were inserted "in them," i.e. inside the pomegranates; and (2) ותולה בו, which would seem to say that the bells were inserted "on it," i.e. on the robe. (See *Diqduqe soferim*, *ad loc.* in Zev.)

28:35 ונשמע קולו SO THAT THE SOUND OF IT IS HEARD: [The bells were able to make noise,] because the golden bells would bang one against the other, even though there were pomegranates protruding between them.[70]

Since God commanded that (Lev. 16:17) "When he [Aaron] goes in to make expiation in the Holy [of Holies], no man shall be in the Tent of Meeting until he comes out," accordingly God commanded [here] that

---

Rashbam opts for the second explanation. So also Rashi, here, and Rashi in Zev., *ibid.*, s.v. עינבלין. See also comm. and notes ad vs. 35.

Cf. Nahm. here, who disagrees, and explains that the pomegranates were hollow and that the bells were inserted literally inside of them (בתוכם ממש).

[70]It is possible that Rashbam's comment here should be seen as directed against LT, who says here that a great miracle occurred in the Temple that a golden bell banged against a pomegranate made of cloth and produced a sound. (See also similarly the comm. of Tosafot on Mishnah Qinim 3:6, s.v. שתי שוקיו.) Rashbam then writes that the sound was not produced by a bell banging against cloth, but by two bells banging against each other (despite the cloth pomegranate between them).

Rashbam apparently disputes the understanding of Rashi (and the simplest reading of the Talmud in Zev. 88b), who explains that the bells consisted of an outer shell of gold (זג) and a clapper (ענבל) within. If that was what a bell was made of, then there would be no need to explain how it was that these bells made noise. Rashbam feels that the bells had no clappers inside and that the only way that they could and did make noise was by one bell banging against another.

"the sound of it should be heard when he comes in,"[71] so that people should [know that they should] go far away from there.[72]

28:36 ועשית ציץ YOU SHALL MAKE A FRONTLET: In my opinion, the reason the frontlet is called a ציץ is because it is placed on the priest's forehead at a spot where people can see it. [The name ציץ is connected to the word meaning "to peer,"] as in the phrase (Song 2:9), "peering (מציץ) through the lattice." I explained the word משקוף similarly.[73]

---

[71] It is implicit in Rashbam's comm. here that the high priest must have worn this robe, with the bells attached to it, on the Day of Atonement when he entered the Holy of Holies. The standard halakhic understanding is that the priest did not; he wore other clothes (described in Lev. 16:4) when he entered the Holy of Holies. In fact, the Sifra (beginning of 'Aḥare mot 1:8) specifically writes that one might have thought, on the basis of Ex. 28:35, that the priest would be wearing his robe on the Day of Atonement, but the texts in Lev. 16 make it clear that he does not.

The same halakhically heterodox understanding as Rashbam's can be found in iE's comm. ad Lev. 16:4. See *Qarne 'or* there, where Krinski attempts to find some other rabbinic sources that might support the idea that the priest did wear his regular robe when he entered the Holy of Holies on the Day of Atonement. And see also another attempt to defend Rashbam's position in Kasher, volume 23, Appendix 17, pp. 185-6.

To be sure, a tradition exists before the days of Rashbam that the high priest had some sort of bell(s) on his person when he entered the Holy of Holies on the Day of Atonement. See e.g. Rashi ad Yoma 44b, s.v. ניאשתיק. Rashi there, like Rashbam here, connects that tradition to our verse in Exodus.

[72] A number of different explanations of the phrase ונשמע קולו may be found in rabbinic literature. iE (in his shorter comm.) quotes an intepretation that says that it means that the priest's voice will be heard by God if he fulfils all the requirements that were mentioned here. (So also Bahya here.) Another explanation suggests that the priest was to show good manners by warning God when he was about to enter God's holy place, in the same manner that a person ought to knock before entering the home of another (or even one's own home). See Vayyiqra Rabba 21:8, and see JBS here. In his comm. to Pes. (112a, s.v. ולא תכנס), Rashbam cites that second midrashic interpretation of the phrase ונשמע קולו, as part of his explanation of that talmudic text. Here, however, he explains what he considers to be the *peshaṭ* reading of the text.

[73] In his comm. to 12:7. So also Bahya, here. Cf. Hizq., who connects the word ציץ to the idea of "sparkling," (another common meaning of the root צ-ו-צ). So also BDB.

EXODUS XXVIII

קדש לה׳ HOLY TO THE LORD: The names of the sons of Israel were inscribed in the stones of the ephod (vss. 9-12) and the breastpiece (vss. 17-21) "for remembrance" (vs. 12).[74] This means that God [is being requested to] atone for עון הקדשים (vs. 38)--i.e. to accept, as compensation for sin,[75] the sacrifices of the Israelites whose names are listed beneath the frontlet on the stones of the ephod and the breastpiece. קדש לה׳ means that God is appeased about sins through sacrifices.[76]

28:37 ושמת אותו על פתיל תכלת SUSPEND IT ON A CORD OF BLUE: There was one cord inserted in each of the ends of the frontlet--which extended [across the priest's forehead and reached all the way] from one ear to the other--[and there was a third cord attached to the frontlet in its middle.[77] All these cords] tied the frontlet in its

---

[74]See the comment attributed to R. Shemaiah of Troyes (cited by Berliner in *Ketavim nivharim*, vol. 2, p. 197), that points to the doubling of the word זכרון in vs. 12 above, and says that that teaches us that both the ephod and the breastpiece serve "for remembrance." R. Shemaiah was either Rashbam's son-in-law (Berliner, *ibid.*, p. 205) or, more likely, his father-in-law (Urbach in *Ba'ale ha-tosafot*, p. 34, and I. Ta-Shma in EJ, s.v. Shemaiah of Troyes).

[75]See notes below, ad vs. 38.

[76]See also Rashbam's comm. ad 28:12 and ad 28:38.
  Both the ephod stones (vs. 12) and the frontlet (vs. 38) are described as serving fuctions for the Israelites, either "for remembrance" (vs. 12) or "for acceptance" (vs. 38). Furthermore (as noted above ad vs. 12) almost identical phrases are used to describe the frontlet and the ephod stones: "ונשא אהרן את שמותם--Aaron shall carry their names" (vs 12) and "ונשא אהרן את עון הקדשים--Aaron shall carry any sin . . . ." (vs. 38). Rashbam says that that means that the frontlet and the ephod, together, are meant to remind God to accept the Israelites' sacrifices and forgive their sins.
  Many talmudic texts (e.g. Yoma 7a-8a) describe the frontlet as appeasing God for various sins. Rashbam writes here and ad vs. 38 that appeasement is effected through sacrifices. The frontlet, together with the engraved stones below, helps the process along by reminding God about the Israelites.

[77]I have added liberally to the text of Rashbam's comm. here. The text as it stands is very difficult to understand.
  The simplest reading of the biblical text would suggest that there was only one cord running, behind the priest's head, from a hole in one end of the frontlet to a hole in the other end. That explanation may be found in LT, iE, Nahm. and Maimonides,

place. The three cords met on top on the priest's head, making a type of cap on top of the priest's headdress.[78]

אל מול פני המצנפת יהיה IT: i.e. the frontlet,[79] SHOULD BE IN FRONT OF THE HEADDRESS, on his forehead,[80] extending around from one ear to the other.[81]

Kele ha-miqdash 9:2. Rashi, though, offers a more complicated understanding. He suggests that there were three holes in the frontlet, one on each end and one in the middle. Cords were inserted in each of these holes and the three cords met behind the priest's head and were tied together there. Rashi's suggestion, as Kasher writes (vol. 23, Appendix 16, p. 184), is an innovative reading (מחודשים מסברתם) meant to solve a number of perceived textual difficulties by positing that there was more than one cord even though the Torah's text speaks of the "cord," in the singular, at all times.

Now Rashbam's text, if not emended, would be suggesting that there were, *in addition to* the cord that ran behind the priest's head from one end of the frontlet to the other, *three more* cords or threads, none of them mentioned in the text (פתיל אחד היה בשני ראשי הציץ . . . ושלשה חוטין למעלה אל הראש). I find it hard to imagine that Rashbam would outdo Rashi and suggest that attached to the frontlet there were, not one, but three cords not mentioned by the text. Accordingly I have, with some hesitation, adjusted Rashbam's text to reflect the same understanding that one finds in Rashi.

In general, it would seem that the understanding that the frontlet had three holes in it and blue cords in each of the holes was the common understanding among the Tosafists. See similarly JBS here, and see the texts assembled in *Tosafot ha-shalem*, vol. 9, pp. 201-202.

[78]כובע על המצנפת. This part of Rashbam's explanation can be found in Rashi verbatim.

[79]According to the explanation offered by Rashi and Rashbam, the subject of the *previous* phrase, והיה על המצנפת, is the blue cord: i.e the blue cord should be on the headdress. Now Rashbam notes that the subject of *this* phrase, אל מול פני המצנפת יהיה, is not the cord but the frontlet itself. See also Nahm., who clearly makes this same distinction. Cf. LT, who interprets that both phrases apply to the frontlet.

[80]Among the Tosafists, it was a matter of dispute whether the frontlet was literally on the forehead or above the forehead on the hairline. See e.g. Tos. Sukkah 5a-5b, s.v. ואל, and other sources cited here by Malbim.

[81]Using the language of Rashi (ad vs. 36), virtually verbatim.

28:38 ונשא אהרן את עון הקדשים AARON WILL TAKE AWAY ANY SIN THROUGH[82] THE SACRIFICES: Following the plain meaning of Scripture, the verse is not referring to sacrifices offered in an impure manner.[83] Rather this is the interpretation: whenever the Israelites bring sacrifices to atone for their sins--burnt offerings, sin offerings or guilt offerings--the frontlet will help the sacrifice work by bringing the memory of the Israelites before God,[84] to win acceptance for the Israelites[85] and as a remembrance for them,[86] so that they will be forgiven.[87]

28:40 לכבוד ולתפארת [AND MAKE TURBANS FOR THEM] FOR DIGNITY AND ADORNMENT: Since the turbans are worn on the head,[88] they require special efforts to make them beautiful.[89]

---

[82]From the continuation of Rashbam's comment, it is clear that he does not understand the phrase עון הקדשים as meaning "sin arising from the holy things."

[83]Rashbam is disputing the interpretation offered by Rashi, which is the common rabbinic understanding. (See Yoma 7a, Men. 25a and many other rabbinic texts.)

[84]As Rashbam explained above, ad vs. 36, s.v. קדש לה'.

[85]Explaining the words לרצון להם לפני ה', at the end of the verse.

[86]See comm. and notes ad vs. 12, above.

[87]The standard rabbinic understanding is that the frontlet served to expiate for sins that may have been done when offering sacrifices. When sacrifices are offered in such a way that the rules of ritual impurity are not fully observed, the frontlet atones for those sins and allows the sacrifices to work. However, according to Rashbam, the frontlet serves a purpose for those sacrifices that *were* offered properly. A properly offered sacrifice will be efficacious in achieving atonement for the Israelites if the frontlet is also involved in the process.
From an exegetical perspective, the crux of the issue is the meaning of the phrase עון הקדשים. Following the standard understanding it means "sins *connected with* [the offering] of sacrifices." For Rashbam it means "sins *that are expiated* through [properly offered] sacrifices." Rashbam's understanding appears to be unique.

[88]I.e. in a prominent place.

28:41 והלבשת אותם PUT THESE CLOTHES ON [YOUR BROTHER AARON AND ON HIS SONS]: When the Tabernacle is erected.[90]

---

[89]Vs. 2 above says that *all* of Aaron's clothes should be made "for dignity and adornment." Rashbam understands our verse as saying that there is a special instruction for the turbans to be made "for dignity and adornment," and he explains why. See also the final comment of Rashbam on vs. 4, above.

Arguably, our verse could easily be read differently. It could be seen as saying that, in addition to the special garments of Aaron, there are special garments for his sons--tunics, sashes and turbans. Vs. two tells us that Aaron's garments should be made "for dignity and adornment." Our verse adds that the same applies to Aaron's sons' garments. Such an understanding is reflected in the punctuation of the RSV: "And for Aaron's sons you shall make coats and girdles and caps; you shall make them for glory and beauty." The cantillation signs, however, support Rashbam's reading--that the phrase, "for dignity and adornment," applies only to the turbans, and not to the other garments mentioned in this verse.

[90]A number of commentators note that there was no intention that the instructions of our verse be implemented right away. See e.g. LT, who notes that the verse presupposes the existence of oil that will be used to anoint the priests, but the instructions about how to make that oil have not yet been given.

Rashbam emphasizes that the instruction to dress Aaron and his sons took effect on the day that the Tabernacle was erected. Such a reading is a reasonable combination of a number of biblical texts. Our verse refers to dressing Aaron and his sons as part of ordaining them (ומלאת את ידם). Chapter 29 will now continue to describe how that ordaining took place. Chapter 29 presupposes that the Tabernacle has already been built. See also Lev. 8, where the Tabernacle and Aaron and his sons are all being anointed and ordained at the same time, and see Num. 7:1: "On the day that Moses finished setting up the Tabernacle he anointed and consecrated it and all its furnishings." See also Rashi (ad 29:3), who notes that the ordaining ceremony is to take place on the day that the Tabernacle is erected.

EXODUS XXIX

29:2 ולחם מצות **UNLEAVENED BREAD:** Things that are baked in an oven are referred to as bread (לחם).[1] These unleavened breads also had oil in them[2], as they are synonymous with the, "לחם שמן--oil bread," that is listed along with "unleavened cakes" and the "unleavened wafers," in the section describing the ordaining (מלואים), in the Torah portion, Ṣav 'et 'aharon.[3]

The [way of making the other two types of bread in this verse, the] **UNLEAVENED CAKES** and the **UNLEAVENED WAFERS** is

---

[1] See also Rashbam's comm. and notes ad Ex. 12:39, s.v. עוגות.

Rashi identifies the לחם מצות of this verse as the רבוכה, a type of product that is prepared by scalding dough in hot water (see Rashi ad Lev. 6:14), not by baking it in an oven. Against that understanding Rashbam emphasizes that the term לחם is applied only to things baked in ovens.

[2] Rashbam is disputing the opinion of JBS, who says that the לחם מצות differs from the other two types of מצות listed here, in that the לחם מצות was made *without* oil. Like Rashbam, see Rashi.

[3] Lev. 8:26. There, just as in our verse, one finds three different types of bread listed: the חלת מצה of that verse is to be seen as equivalent to our verse's חלת מצות; the רקיק אחד of that verse is equivalent to the רקיקי מצות of this verse; and therefore, by the process of elimination, the לחם מצות of our verse must be described there as חלת לחם שמן, "a cake of oil bread." Hence one knows that our verse's לחם מצות must have been made with oil.

In order to show that the לחם מצות was made with oil, Rashi offers another prooftext--the phrase חלת לחם שמן here in Ex. 29:23, which, according to Rashi, means the same as our verse's לחם מצות. See iE there who disagrees with Rashi. I assume that Rashbam interprets 29:23 as iE does, not as Rashi does, and, accordingly, cites the verse in Lev. 8 as, what he considers, a superior prooftext to establish the same point that Rashi tries to prove.

described in tractate Menahot.⁴ Ten of each [type of bread] were brought.⁵

והקרבת אותם בסל 29:3 PRESENT THEM IN THE BASKET: Bring them to the enclosure [of the Tabernacle] in a basket.⁶

וחגרת אותם אבנט אהרן ובניו 29:9 GIRD BOTH AARON AND HIS SONS WITH SASHES: Concerning this verse there is a dispute in tractate Yoma,⁷ because the order in which the garments are put on in this verse is not the same as the order for putting on the garments in the Torah portion, Ṣav 'et 'aharon.⁸ Following the plain meaning of Scripture, no special significance need be attached to this distinction.⁹

---

⁴Men. 74b-75a.

⁵So also Rashi (following Men. 7:1-2 and b. Men. 77b).

⁶So also Rashi.
   Rashi and Rashbam may be pointing out that והקרבת here does not mean "to sacrifice" but rather "to present." (Later, in vss. 23-25, some of them will be sacrificed.) Also they may be noting that the phrase, "up to the entrance of the Tent of Meeting," in vs. 4, applies to all the items listed in vss. 3 and 4: the breads, the bull, the ram, Aaron and his sons are all to be brought "up to the entrance of the Tent of Meeting." See similarly iE, and the first explanation offered by Nahm., here.

⁷Yoma 5b-6a.

⁸Lev. 8:7 and 8:13. There the simple reading of the text is that Aaron was dressed in all his clothes, including his sash, and only later were his sons dressed in their clothes, including their sashes. Here in Exodus our verse can be seen to imply that all the sashes were put on Aaron and his sons at the same time.
   See also Rashbam's comm. and notes ad 39:29.

⁹אין לדקדק. A phrase commonly used by Rashbam when he wishes to say that the midrash is reading more into the text than required by *peshaṭ*-oriented exegesis. See e.g. his comm. ad Gen. 36:24, and see RSBM, p. 21, note 2.
   Some commentators did attempt to deal with the "contradiction." See e.g. LT

EXODUS XXIX 377

[29:6 נזר הקדש THE HOLY DIADEM: I.e. the frontlet.][10]

29:27 [וקדשת את חזה התנופה ואת שוק התרומה] YOU SHALL CONSECRATE THE BREAST THAT WAS OFFERED AS AN ELEVATION OFFERING AND THE THIGH THAT WAS OFFERED AS A GIFT OFFERING]:[11] Both [תנופה and תרומה] are words that refer to separating.[12] However, only the breast is referred to as being elevated, [in order to emphasize that] all that is done to it is that it is elevated and then it is eaten; on the other hand, the thigh, here, is totally burnt. However, in future generations the rule is that both the thigh and the breast are [given to the priest and] eaten [by him].[13]

---

[10]Rosin attempted to reconstruct this comment of Rashbam. The ms. reading is obviously missing the crucial word(s); it reads simply: נזר הקדש הוא. Rosin assumes that the word, "הציץ--the frontlet," should be added to the comm., and that Rashbam agrees with what Rashi writes ad vs. 6, s.v. נזר. Rosin's reconstruction is speculative but reasonable. If Rosin is right, we would also have to assume that Rashbam is explaining a phrase from verse 6 *after* explaining a phrase from vs. 9 (an unusual, but not unprecedented occurrence). See also the next note.

[11]Again here, the ms. reading is missing something. The words of Rashbam's comment are found in the ms., but not the words of the biblical text upon which Rashbam is commenting. Rosin speculates that these are the words of the biblical text that are being discussed.

Again, Rosin's speculation is reasonable. The continuation of Rashbam's comment makes it clear that he is discussing two words, one of which is applied to the breast alone and one of which is applied both to the breast and to the thigh. The term, תנופה, is applied in our verses only to the breast. The term, תרומה, is applied in vs. 27 only to the thigh, but in vs. 28 it is applied both to the breast and to the thigh. The continuation of Rashbam's comment explains this terminological switch.

[12]הפרשה, i.e. setting something apart and designating it as holy.

See also Rashbam's comm. ad Gen. 31:9, where he identifies a number of other verbs as being related to the idea of הפרשה, separation.

[13]Hence it is reasonable for the text to use the same terminology about them, when referring to the thighs and breasts of the sacrifices of future generations, and that is why vs. 28 applies the word תרומה both to the breast and to the thigh.

On the idea that the text is distinguishing between the thigh of this sacrifice and the thighs of later sacrifices, see similarly Rashi ad vs. 27, s.v. וקדשת.

On the question of the difference between תנופה and תרומה, Rashbam may be taking issue with the Sifra (Ṣav 11:11). According to the Sifra, the fact that our

29:29 למשחה בהם: means "to attain greatness in them,"[14] in the same way that anointing (משיחה) with oil [confers greatness].[15] Great ones are often called משיחים, as in the phrase (Ps. 105:15), "Do not touch my great ones (משיחי)."[16]

29:30 ילבשם הכהן THE PRIEST SHALL WEAR THEM: When he is installed to be the [new] high priest.[17]

---

verses mix together the terms תנופה and תרומה teaches us that whenever תנופה is required by the text, תרומה is also required and vice versa. (The general halakhic understanding [see e.g. Rashi here, vs. 24, s.v. תנופה] is that תנופה means "to carry back and forth," while תרומה means "to carry up and down.") See also Rashi ad Lev. 10:15: למה חלקן הכתוב תרומה בשוק ותנופה בחזה לא ידענו--we do not know why the text applies 'carrying up and down' to the thigh and 'carrying back and forth' to the breast." (This comment of Rashi is found only in some mss. and editions. It is quoted by Nahm., there, as "the words of Rashi." See also Nahm.'s own opinion, in his comm. there.) Cf. JBS, here, who says that תנופה and תרומה are synonymous, and that the text uses both terms only for purposes of stylistic variation.

[14]So also Rashi, verbatim.
    Rashi and Rashbam suggest that the verb מ-ש-ח, here and in some other passages, does not refer literally to anointing, but has a figurative meaning of imparting greatness. Cf. Nahm. here, who disagrees, and suggests that מ-ש-ח is best understood in a literal manner, here and in most other passages. The dispute can be traced back to the Sifre 117 (Horovitz ed., p. 135) where two opinions are expressed: אין משחה אלא גדולה and אין משחה אלא שמן המשחה.

[15]Rashbam adds a point to the explanation of Rashi--that the figurative meaning, "to impart greatness," is logically connected to the literal meaning of anointing.

[16]The same prooftext is also cited by Rashi. Rashi cites a further prooftext, Num. 18:8. See also Rashi and Rashbam, there.

[17]So also Rashi. Rashbam may be emphasizing this point (despite the fact that it is the obvious meaning of the text) in order to distance himself from the interpretation of LT who says that the text means that each year, before the Day of Atonement, the high priest should do a number of things to train for his priestly duties, including wearing his special clothing. In fact, Rashbam's language (בהתחנכו) may be a play on LT's language ("ומחנכין אותו בעבודה--and they train him for the service"), using a very similar word to express a very different interpretation.

EXODUS XXIX

29:35 שבעת ימים תמלא ידם YOU SHALL ORDAIN THEM THROUGH SEVEN DAYS: For the seven days preceding "*the* eighth day,"[18] which was the day on which the sacrificial service began to be performed by Aaron and his sons,[19] Moses would erect the Tabernacle every day and offer the sacrifices each day, and towards evening [each day] he took the Tabernacle apart.[20] On the eighth day--which was the first of Nisan--he erected the Tabernacle for good, as it says in the Torah portion, *'Elleh fequde*.[21] From then on, the sacrificial service was to be preformed by Aaron and his sons.

29:37 כל הנוגע WHOEVER TOUCHES: or comes close to THE ALTAR, יקדש, i.e. should purify himself before coming close to the altar.[22]

---

[18]See Lev. 9:1 and Rashbam's comm., there.

[19]Rashbam is following the standard rabbinic understanding (e.g. Vayyiqra Rabbah 11:6) that Moses served as a priest, in charge of the sacrificial service, during the seven days in which Aaron and his descendants were being ordained to become priests and to take over those duties. After those seven days, according to that understanding, Moses could no longer serve in the priestly role. Sacrifices from then on could be performed only by Aaron and his sons. The simple meaning of Lev. 8:14-9:24 supports that assumption, and see Rashi ad Lev. 9:23, s.v. ויצאו. See also Rashi and Rashbam ad 40:29, and notes there.

[20]This idea originates in Sifre Numbers 44 (Horovitz ed., p. 49), based on a midrashic understanding of Num. 7:1. It is cited by Rashi, ad Numbers 7:1. It is unusual to find Rashbam adopting such a midrashic reading. Cf. Nahm. in Numbers, who cites Rashi and then says that, while Rashi has a rabbinic source to support his explanation, the proof from the verse in Numbers is not absolute (אבל איננה ראיה גמורה).

[21]Ex. 40:2 and 40:17.

[22]Rashbam offers an intepretation that differs radically from the standard rabbinic understanding. This novel interpretation appears four separate times in Rashbam's commentary: here, ad Ex. 30:29, ad Lev. 6:11 and ad Lev. 11:8.

The standard halakhic understanding is that, in some way, "holiness is contagious" (NJPSC, here) and that something that touches a holy item יקדש, i.e. it itself will become holy. See e.g. Rashi here (following Zev. 9:1, b. Zev. 83b, Sanh. 34a-b and other sources). Rashbam intepets יקדש to mean "shall purify himself

29:43 ונקדש בכבודי IT [THE TABERNACLE] SHALL BE SANCTIFIED BY MY PRESENCE]: [I.e. God is saying] "I shall appear to the Israelites when the Tabernacle is erected," when divine fire will come and consume the sacrifices, as it is written in the Torah portion, *Ba-yom ha-shemini*,[23] [that God promised,] "For today[24] the LORD will apppear to you." And [then God did appear to them,] as it is written (Lev. 9:23-24), "The presence of the LORD appeared to all the people. Fire came forth from before the LORD and consumed the burnt offering . . . ."[25]

[beforehand]," and does not follow the standard rabbinic understanding, that יקדש means "shall [itself] become holy." David Hoffmann (in his comm. ad Lev. 6:20) pays Rashbam a left-handed compliment and calls his interpretation the one that is relatively best of all the many heterodox inteprepations that have been offered to this verse.

To be sure, while Rashbam's interpretation is non-halakhic, it is not anti-halakhic. Halakha does agree that a person should purify himself before approaching the altar. The halakhic literature, however, does not read our verse as enunciating that principle.

The interpretation offered here by Rashbam enjoyed a certain popularity among the *peshat*-oriented exegetes. Rashbam may have seen it in LT's comm. here (as an alternate understanding, listed beside the standard, halakhic reading). See also JBS and Hizq. here, and a number of other sources cited by Kasher, here, note 116. As Hoffmann (*ibid*.) notes, this interpretation is also found in the LXX and the Vulgate, here.

See the discussion by Touitou (*Milet* 2, pp. 283-284) of the possibility that Rashbam may have been attracted to this understanding for the purpose of anti-Christian polemic.

[23]Or perhaps Rashbam is saying "as it is written concerning 'the eighth day'." See comm. and notes above, ad vs. 35.

[24]I.e. on 'the eighth day,' the final day of the ordination of the priests and of the ceremony to inaugurate the Tabernacle.

[25]See also Rashbam's comm. there in Lev. where he explains that vs. 24, "Fire came forth . . .," constitutes an explanation of the manner in which "the presence of the LORD appeared . . ." (vs. 23).

Rashi offers two understandings of the phrase ונקדש בכבודי. According to his first explanation, it means that God's presence will be felt in the Tabernacle on a regular basis. According to his second, midrashic, explanation (following Zev. 115b and many other rabbinic sources), the phrase means that God exacts a higher standard of behavior from those closest to Him, and punishes them more severely than He punishes others.

29:46 הוצאתי אותם מארץ מצרים I BROUGHT THEM OUT OF THE LAND OF EGYPT: so that I MIGHT ABIDE WITH THEM.[26]

Rashi cites the classical rabbinic example of that principle--the death of Nadab and Abihu in Lev. 10:1-2.

Rashbam rejects both of Rashi's explanations. ונקדש בכבודי is, according to Rashbam, neither a general statement about God's presence being felt in the Tabernacle nor a general statement about the way that God administers justice. It is a specific statement about the events connected with the inauguration of the Tabernacle and the ordination of the priests. The phrase says that, at the end of those ceremonies, ונקדש בכבודי, i.e. God will, on a one-time basis, reveal himself through a divine fire.

Curiously Rashbam's own interpretation has something in common with Rashi's. According to Rashi's second explanation, the fire that consumed Nadab and Abihu demonstrated the general principle of ונקדש בכבודי, by punishing Nadab and Abihu more strictly than usual. According to Rashbam, the phrase means something totally different, but it still refers to that very same fire. The same fire that consumed Nadab and Abihu also consumed the sacrifices in a miraculous manner, and that is what is meant by the phrase--that the miraculous consumption of the sacrifices on that occasion glorified God. (On the identity of the fire that consumed Nadab and Abihu and the fire that consumed the sacrifices, see Rashbam's comm. and notes ad Ex. 19:8, and see comm. ad Lev. 9:23-24 and 10:1-3.)

Rashbam's interpretation of this verse appears to be unique.

[26]The phrase לשכני בתוכם is somewhat anomalous and the syntax of the verse is unclear. Rashbam's explanation is basically the same as that of Rashi and LT. Cf. a different understanding in Nahm.

EXODUS XXX

30:1 מקטר קטורת [MAKE AN ALTAR] FOR BURNING INCENSE: Not for burnt offerings or offerings of well-being or meal offerings or libations.[1]

30:6 ונתת אותו לפני הפרכת PLACE IT IN FRONT OF THE CURTAIN: In the *hekhal*.[2]

אשר על ארון העדות [THE CURTAIN] THAT IS OVER (על) THE ARK OF THE PACT: I.e the curtain that [is in front of the Ark of the Pact and that] separates the *hekhal* from the Ark of the Pact.[3]

30:10 אחת בשנה ONCE A YEAR [AARON SHALL PERFORM PURIFICATION ON ITS HORNS WITH BLOOD OF THE SIN OFFERING]: On the Day of Atonement,[4] as it is written in the Torah

---

[1]Rashbam's explantion is the simple (and undisputed) meaning of the text. See vs. 9, where the text specifies that the incense altar is not to be used for "a burnt offering or a meal offering," and verse 10 that mentions the exception to this rule. See also comm. ad vs. 10.

[2]The curtain separates the *hekhal*, "the Holy," from the Holy of Holies. Rashbam explains that the altar of incense is on the *hekhal* side of the curtain, not the Holy of Holies side. Again Rashbam's comment is uncontroversial.

[3]See comm. and notes ad 27:21. Again Rashbam emphasizes that the curtain did not hang *on* the Ark of the Pact, but *in front of* it (despite the fact that the text says על ארון העדות).

[4]So also Rashi and LT, as opposed to a number of talmudic texts (e.g. Shev. 8b) that attempt to learn more from this phrase.

portion, *'Aḥare mot* (Lev. 16:18), "He shall go out to the altar that is before the LORD . . . [he shall take some of the blood . . . and apply it to each of the horns of the altar]." But for the entire rest of the year, there was no blood on this altar, only incense.[5]

30:12 כי תשא WHEN YOU TAKE A CENSUS: When Moses gathered together the Israelite people[6] to get them to donate to the Tabernacle, he counted them.[7] The money that was collected was used for the purposes of the Tabernacle, as it is written in the Torah portion, *'Elleh fequde* (Ex. 38:25), "The silver of those of the community that were recorded came to one hundred talents . . . ."[8]

---

[5] See also Rashbam's comm. and notes above, ad vs. 1.

[6] See Ex. 35:1.

[7] See also comm. and notes ad 35:1. Chapter 35 lists all the *items* that the Israelites were asked to donate. Rashbam understands that, in addition to those voluntary donations, each person was required to donate half a silver shekel.

[8] The following verse in chapter 38 continues to explain that the silver that was listed there was acquired through donations of "a half a shekel a head, half a shekel by the sanctuary weight, for each one who was entered in the records," a precise quotation of vss. 13 and 14 here. Thus Rashbam has proved well that the verses here that describe the collection of half shekels are describing one part of the general project of collecting materials required for the Tabernacle.

Rashbam may be disputing Rashi's reading of this verse. Rashi inteprets the verse as a general injunction about counting: *whenever* the Israelites are to be counted one should not count heads, but one should collect coins and count the coins. Rashbam, however, inteprets the verse in a more specific context, as part of the project of collecting donations for the Tabernacle.

See Rashi (ad vs. 16), who writes also that God commanded Moses to count the Israelites at this point. See also Naḥm. (here), who says that our verse is properly interpreted, in the first instance, as general instructions about all instances of counting the Israelites, but that Moses realized that God must be implicitly suggesting that Moses count the Israelites now.

See also Rashbam's comm. and notes below, ad vs. 16.

30:13 עשרים גרה TWENTY GERAHS [TO THE SHEKEL]: A *gerah* is a type of coin.[9]

30:16 כסף הכפורים THE EXPIATION MONEY: The money that each person shall give as "ransom of himself."[10]

על עבודת אוהל מועד ASSIGN IT [THE MONEY] TO THE SERVICE OF THE TENT OF MEETING: As it is written (Ex. 38:27), "one hundred sockets to the one hundred talents, a talent a socket."[11]

30:23 בשמים ראש CHOICE SPICES: ראש, [some have argued,] means "choice," as in the phrase (Song 4:14) "All the choice (ראש) perfumes."
 I, however, feel[12] that the word "בשמים--spices," generally refers to something grown on trees, as it is written (Song 4:16), "Blow upon my garden that its perfume (בשמיו) may spread."[13] However, the

---

[9]A common understanding of many Jewish exegetes. See e.g. Rashi, Onq. and Bekh. 50a. Most moderns feel that a *gerah* is a weight. See e.g. NJPSC. So also LT.

[10]Vs. 12. So also LT, virtually verbatim.
 In other words, the money is called "expiation money" in our verse, for the same reason that is called "ransom" in vs. 12. Rashbam may be opposing the understanding of the Talmud (Ber. 62b; and see Rashi there, s.v. כסף כפורים ראה), that the money is called "expiation money" here because it expiated for David's later sin of counting the people (in II Sam. 24).

[11]This quotation is the continuation of the same verse (38:25) quoted by Rashbam above, in his comm. ad vs. 12, "The silver of those of the community that were recorded came to one hundred talents . . . ." That section in chapter 38 demonstrates how the half shekels were applied to the project of building the Tabernacle. So also Rashi and LT.

[12]First, Rashbam cites Rashi's intepretation of the word ראש. (So also LT.) Then Rashbam adds a possible prooftext for Rashi's position. (See that same prooftext in JBS here.) Then Rashbam proceeds to offer his own alternate understanding.

[13]Perhaps Rashbam's proof is based on the fact that "the garden," in Song 4, seems to be an orchard, as there are references to pomegranates and to luscious fruits in vs. 13, there.

term בשמים ראש refers to the resins[14] inside of a tree or to [spices] that grow in the ground.[15]

מר דרור CHOICE MYRRH: דרור means "choice."[16] So also [one may see that there are different gradations of myrrh, as myrrh is also modified by the word עובר] in the phrase (Song 5:5) "choice (עובר) myrrh," i.e. myrrh that would be accepted by merchants in all countries.[17]

מחציתו HALF: The amounts are explained in Keritot.[18]

---

[14]שרף. See Shabbat 26a, where צרי, one of the spices used to make the incense, is identified as being a שרף.

[15]Rashbam understands the word ראש, in this context, as meaning "source" or "root." Spices that have to be dug out are called בשמים ראש. See similarly Jellinek's edition of the Song of Songs comm. attributed to Rashbam (ad 4:14), where the phrase 'ראשי בשמים' is interpreted as "שרשי בשמים--spice roots."
Cf. JBS, who suggests that ראש, here, means the same thing that it meant in vs. 12, in the phrase כי תשא את ראש, and interprets our verse as meaning "Take spices *according to the following count* (ראש): myrrh, cinnamon, ..."

[16]While Rashi says that the word ראש in our verse means "choice," Rashbam says that it is the word דרור which means "choice." See similarly Onq.: דכיא--"pure" (and see Hul. 139b).

[17]See Rashbam's comm. ad Gen. 23:16, s.v. עובר, and notes there.

[18]Ker. 5a. So also Rashi here, at much greater length.
The position of the Talmud is that 500 weights of both myrrh and cinnamon are used. When the text says וקנמן בשם מחציתו חמישים ומאתים, it means that half of the cinnamon that is brought should amount to 250 weights--i.e. that the total amount should be 500 weights. Generally it is felt today that the *peshat* of the text is, as NJPS would have it, "five hundred weights of myrrh, half as much (מחציתו)--two hundred and fifty--of fragrant cinnamon . . .." See Kasher, note 137, who argues that the Jerusalem Talmud interprets our verse in that same *peshat*-like manner. See iE, here, who, like Rashbam, defers to the Babylonian Talmud's understanding, although one senses from iE's language that he does so grudgingly.

30:25 רקח מרקחת A COMPOUND OF INGREDIENTS: According to the plain meaning of Scripture,[19] רקח מרקחת means that they were chopped up and put into oil and mixed well, as in the phrase (Job 41:23), "He makes the sea like an ointment-pot (מרקחה)."[20] It means a mixture.

30:29 כל הנוגע בהם יקדש WHOEVER TOUCHES THEM יקדש: I.e he should purify himself beforehand, before touching them,[21] after they were anointed.[22]

30:32 ובמתכנתו [YOU MUST NOT MAKE ANYTHING LIKE IT] IN THE SAME PROPORTIONS: I.e. using the amounts for the spices recorded in these verses.[23]

---

[19]Rashbam presumably is opposing the interpretations offered in Ker. 5a, and quoted by Rashi, here, in his comm. to vs. 24. According to that understanding, the spices were not really mixed into the oil permanently; they were left in contact with the oil only long enough to allow the oil to absorb some of the aroma of the spices. Then the spices were removed from the oil. So also LT, here. Rashbam, however, says that the *peshaṭ* is that they were all mixed together.

[20]Rashbam understands the phrase in Job the same way that Rashi (there) does--that God mixes up the sea the same way that spices are mixed together. So also Qara, there. See also Rashbam's comm. ad vs. 35, below.

[21]I.e. the items mentioned in vss. 26-28.

[22]See comm. ad 29:37, and note 22, there.
    Again, the standard rabbinic understanding (see Rashi here, following Zev. 9:1 and b. Zev. 83b and 87a) is that holiness is contagious: whatever (or almost whatever) touches these holy things itself becomes holy (יקדש) afterwards. Rashbam again offers his own novel reading--that this verse represents an instruction to a person to prepare oneself *before* touching some holy thing.

[23]So also Rashi here, at much greater length. See also Rashi and Rashbam ad Ex. 5:8, s.v. מתכנת.

30:33 ואשר יתן ממנו [WHOEVER COMPOUNDS ITS LIKE] OR PUTS ANY OF IT: I.e. of the oil that Moses made.[24]

30:34 סמים HERBS: I explained the word סמים above.[25]

סמים ולבונה זכה HERBS, TOGETHER WITH FINE FRANKINCENSE: According to the plain meaning of Scripture,[26] first the verse writes a generalization, "TAKE סמים (HERBS)." Then it [specifies and] explains what the herbs are that it meant: "נטף ושחלת וחלבנה (STACTE ONYCHA AND GALBANUM)." [Then the verse adds,] "These are the סמים, the HERBS that I commanded that you take. In addition, take FINE FRANKINCENSE."

So, according to the plain meaning of Scripture, PURE FRANKINCENSE is not one of the HERBS.[27] The last time סמים is written in the verse it means the same thing that it meant the first time

---

[24]Theoretically, there are two possible syntactical readings of the phrase: איש אשר ירקח כמוהו ואשר יתן ממנו על זר. It could mean: "Whoever compounds some oil like that original oil of Moses, *and then* puts some of ממנו--that new, counterfeit compound--onto a layman, such a person will be cut off." Alternatively it could mean: "Whoever compounds some oil like that original oil of Moses, *or* whoever puts some of ממנו--the original oil that Moses made--onto a layman, both such infractions will be punished by the perpetrator being cut off." Rashbam's comment follows the latter explanation (which is also the standard halakhic understanding); ממנו refers to the original oil that Moses made. See e.g. Ker. 5a. So also Rashi here. Rashbam's language is virtually verbatim the language of Ker., *ibid*.

[25]As noted by Rosin, our mss. and versions of Rashbam's comm. have no previous explanation of the word סמים. Obviously something must have gotten lost from the comm.

[26]Rashbam's explanation pointedly rejects the understanding of Rashi, who follows Ker. 6b. According to Rashi's understanding, the first סמים in our verse is not an introductory generalization and the second סמים is not a summary generalization. Nor do the two words refer to the same herbs. They each come to teach us to add a certain number of herbs to the ones that are explicitly listed in the verse.

[27]As opposed to Rashi's explanation that frankincense is to be seen as the eleventh herb to be taken.

EXODUS XXX

that it is written.[28] This is common biblical style--to write a generalization and then write specific examples and then reiterate[29] and say "the above constituted an elaboration of the general statement that I made before."

Similarly in the story of Noah it says (Gen. 9:17), "God said to Noah, 'That shall be the sign of the covenant'."[30]

30:35 ממולח: means "mixed." Similarly, those who lead boats through the oceans are called "מלחים--sailors," for they mix up the waters as they travel.[31]

---

[28] Again as opposed to Rashi's understanding that the first time סמים is written in the verse, it means that we should add two more herbs to the list; and the second time סמים is written in the verse, it means that we should add five more herbs to the list.

[29] Rashbam's position appears, at first blush, to be similar to the position of R. Yishmael, quoted in Ker. 6b. According to Rabbi Yishmael, our verse is an example of כלל ופרט וכלל: of an introductory generalization, followed by specific examples, followed by a summarizing generalization. However, Rabbi Yishmael (at least in the way that the Babylonian Talmud understands his position) is not saying the same thing that Rashbam is saying. When Rabbi Yishmael identifies the pattern of כלל ופרט וכלל here, he interprets that pattern as having a hermeneutic purpose, to supply further referential meaning by teaching us something about those additional herbs that we are to add the ones listed in the verse. For Rashbam, the pattern כלל ופרט וכלל is a literary pattern that, at least on the *peshat* level, has rhetorical significance only. When Rashbam identifies this literary pattern, it is as if he is telling us not to look for any further referential meaning in the words that are repeated.

For a similar use of a literary pattern in exegesis of a legal passage, see comm. and notes ad Ex. 21:3.

[30] There vs. 12 reads: "God further said, 'This is the sign of the covenant . . .'." Vss. 13-16 then explain in detail *what* the sign of the covenant consisted of. Then, in vs. 17, God summarizes the section by repeating the generalization, "That shall be the sign of the covenant." Such an understanding is reflected in the translation of NJPS, where זאת אות הברית, in vs. 12, is rendered "*This* is the sign of the covenant," while the identical Hebrew words, in vs. 17, are rendered "*That* shall be the sign of the covenant."

[31] So also Rashi (following Onq.), at much greater length. See also Rashbam's comm. and notes above, ad vs. 25.

In the Talmud's description of the components of the incense (Ker. 6a), salt is listed. Many commentators say that the word ממולח in our verse means "salted." See

30:36 ושחקת ממנה BEAT SOME OF IT INTO A POWDER (הדק): So that on the Day of Atonement they will be able to fulfil that which is written in the Torah portion, *'Aḥare mot* (Lev. 16:12), "[he shall take . . .] finely ground (דקה) aromatic incense and bring this behind the curtain."[32]

---

e.g. iE and NJPSC. Rashi and Rashbam offer another approach. See also LT, who offers both alternatives.

[32]Cf. Rashi's comm. ad Lev. 16:12, where he asks (following Ker. 6b) why it was necessary for the book of Leviticus to instruct that the incense be דקה when the book of Exodus already said (here) that it should be הדק. Rashi answers (again following the talmudic position) that the verse in Leviticus teaches that the incense on the Day of Atonement should be ground even more finely than the regular incense that is used on a daily basis. In other words, הדק in our verse means somewhat finely ground; דקה in Leviticus adds that the incense on the Day of Atonement should be *very* finely ground (דקה מן הדקה, to use the talmudic language).

Rashbam's approach is different. Rashbam is, at least on the *peshaṭ* level, not concerned about the alleged redundancy of writing דקה in Lev. after writing הדק in Exodus. Our verse and the verse in Leviticus teach the same thing.

EXODUS XXXI

31:6 ובלב כל חכם לב I HAVE ALSO GRANTED SKILL TO ALL WHO ARE SKILLFUL: I.e. to all who [have the skill to] come do the work,[1] I *already* granted them skill. Now THEY MAY MAKE [EVERYTHING THAT I HAVE COMMANDED YOU].[2]

31:10 בגדי השרד THE SERVICE VESTMENTS: These were plaited garments used to cover the Ark and the table and the lampstand.[3] They are explained in more detail in the Torah portion, *Bemidbar Sinai* (Num. 4:6, 4:13 and 4:8): "spread a cloth of pure blue [over the Ark]" and "[spread a] purple cloth [over the Ark]" and "[They shall spread over

---

[1] I.e. the construction of the Tabernacle and its furnishings.

[2] Rashbam emphasizes that when the verse says that God grants "חכמה--skill" to "חכמי לב--the skillful," it means that these people become skillful *after* God grants them skill. Rashbam emphasizes this seemingly obvious point in order to distance himself from the talmudic homily (Ber. 55a; cited by LT and NJPSC here) that derives from our verse the idea that God gives wisdom to people who are already wise.

[3] When the Tabernacle and its furnishings were moved from one location to another.

the vessels of the table] a crimson cloth."[4] Those garments were made by plaiting.[5]

31:13 אך את שבתותי NEVERTHELESS, YOU MUST KEEP MY SABBATHS: Even the work of the Tabernacle should not be done on the Sabbath.[6]

כי אות היא FOR THIS IS A SIGN: [God says:] "When you rest as I did, it is a sign that you are My people."[7]

---

[4]So also Rashi, at much greater length.
    Rashi and Rashbam oppose the standard rabbinic usage (e.g. Yoma 72b) that sees the term בגדי שרד as a name for the priestly garments. As Rashi points out, such an understanding is difficult, for our verse clearly talks of two separate items: בגדי שרד and בגדי הקדש. Rashi realizes the innovative nature of his comm. ("אומר אני לפי פשוטו של מקרא . . . ונראין דברי --following the plain meaning of Scripture, I say . . . and my interpretation appears correct . . . "). So also iE. Cf. Nahm.'s defense of the rabbinic understanding.

[5]כעין שרד וקליעות. Again Rashbam takes the same position as that of Rashi (and writes it much more succinctly). Rashi cites the fact that שרד appears as the Aramaic translation of the word קלעים (Onq. ad Ex. 27:9), and then concludes that since קלעים means "plaited," שרד must also mean "plaited." Rashbam's language here, כעין שרד וקליעות, shows that he, too, follows the same line of thought as Rashi's.
    See also Rashbam's comm. ad 27:9.

[6]So also Rashi and iE. They all explain why the admonition about observing the Sabbath is repeated here and juxtaposed to verses that describe the construction of the Tabernacle. One may find in Mekhilta *Shabbata'* 1 (Lauterbach ed., pp. 197-199) a number of midrashic explanations of why the restriction on work on the Sabbath is repeated here. The above-mentioned exegetes prefer the contextual interpretation, here, to the midrashic ones.

[7]See similarly Rashi and Mekhilta, *ibid.*, who also interpret this phrase in terms of Israel's election.
    Rashbam provides a different understanding of the purpose of the Sabbath in his comm. ad Ex. 20:10. See Touitou, *Milet*, p. 287.

EXODUS XXXII

32:1 אשר ילכו לפנינו MAKE US GODS WHO SHALL GO BEFORE US: I.e. a type of *teraphim*,[1] made through sorcery, so that they can provide [information required in order to fulfil] their needs.[2]

32:4 ויצר אותו בחרט HE WRAPPED IT IN A CLOTH: He took the gold from each of them, gathered it all together and wrapped it up in some cloth,[3] [to keep it there] while they prepared a mold[4] made out of

---

[1] See comm. and notes above, ad 28:30, and below, ad vs. 4, s.v. אלה.

[2] שיגידו צורכיהם: the same phrase that Rashbam used above, ad 28:15 and ad 28:30, to describe the function of the Urim and Thummim.

Cf. Rashi, who suggests that אשר ילכו לפנינו means that these gods would show the Israelites the way to proceed in their travels through the wilderness.

The story of the golden calf was often a subject for Jewish-Christian polemics during the middle ages. See e.g. the story quoted in *Niṣṣaḥon yashan* (Berger's edition, p. 67), of how priests challenged Nathan Official (a thirteenth-century Jewish polemicist) by asking him, "Why did you [i.e. the Jews] make the golden calf?" And see LT below, ad vs. 25, who interprets the phrase לשמצה בקמיהם as meaning that in future generations the Jews will be belittled because of the story of the golden calf.

See Touitou (*Tarbiz* 51, pp. 236-237) who argues that Rashbam's exegesis here is to be read in that polemical context. It is meant to minimize, for polemical reasons, the severity of the Jews' infraction in this chapter. According to Touitou, Rashbam is saying that the Jews did not *really* worship idols; they were guilty only of the lesser crime of sorcery. See also comm. below, ad vs. 4, s.v. אלה, and note 11, there.

[3] Rashi writes that there are two possible explanations for the phrase ויצר אותו בחרט. The first is that it means that Aaron wrapped the gold together in a cloth. The second (the more common understanding) is that it means that Aaron made designs in the gold with a graving tool. (For yet another understanding of the phrase, see the notes below.) Rashbam adopts Rashi's first reading. See also JBS, who quotes both interpretations, and, like Rashbam, expresses a preference for the first.

There could be two possible reasons for Rashbam's choice. Perhaps he inteprets the phrase this way in order to mitigate Aaron's crime somewhat. If Aaron, in fact, fashioned the calf with a graving tool, then his statement in vs. 24 below (which Rashbam will soon discuss in this same paragraph) appears to be a bare-faced lie.

393

bitumen and wax, the way smelters do. They fashioned this mold into the shape of a calf. They poured the gold into the mold and the gold took on the shape of a calf,[5] as it is written (vs. 24), "I poured it[6] into the fire and this calf was thus completed."[7]

[ויצר אותו בחרט here means "he wrapped it in a cloth,"] as it is written (II Kings 5:23) "he wrapped (ויצר) the two talents of silver in two cloths

---

Furthermore, Rashbam wishes to claim that the calf was formed by pouring molten gold into a mold. If the mold formed the calf, presumably a graving tool would be redundant.

[4]Cf. JBS, who says that the wrapping was done to hold on to the gold until all the gold necessary was collected.
    Rashbam opposes Rashi's explanation (following a number of midrashic traditions), that Aaron did not *try* to fashion a calf, but rather that the calf was produced through sorcery. Generally many exegetes and many midrashim attempt to minimize Aaron's role in the construction of the calf. See e.g. Midrash ha-gadol here, which says, like Rashbam, that the calf was produced through a דפוס, a mold, but writes that Aaron knew nothing about the mold. Rashbam and LT (here, and especially ad vs. 24: "ויעשהו עגל מסכה כלומר הוא עשאו כמין עגל כאשר בקשו ממנו--'he made it into a molten calf' means that he himself made it into the shape of a calf, as they asked him to do") write clearly that Aaron took part (or perhaps even took a leading role?) in the fashioning of the gold into the shape of a calf.
    See also comm. below, ad vs. 24, and note 31, there.

[5]Yet another interpretation of the phrase ויצר אותו בחרט is that it means "he shaped it using a mold." See e.g. ibn Janah, *Sefer ha-shorashim*, s.v. ח-ר-ט. It appears that Rashbam is offering two separate (and presumably mutually exclusive) readings of the phrase ויצר אותו בחרט in this verse, as he writes both that the gold was wrapped in a cloth and that it was shaped using a mold.

[6]ואשליכהו. Rashbam does not understand this as meaning "I [just] hurled the gold into the fire and out came this calf." Again Rashbam is intepreting vs. 24 and our verse in such a way that Aaron's role in the fashioning of the calf is clear and significant. But, following Rashbam's understanding, Aaron's words of explanation in vs. 24 do not openly contradict the narrator's description here.

[7]For Rashbam's understanding of the phrase ויצא העגל הזה, see his comm. below, ad vs. 24, and note 31, there.

"8.(חריטים).

אלה אלהיך ישראל THIS IS YOUR GOD, O ISRAEL, WHO BROUGHT YOU OUT OF THE LAND OF EGYPT: Were they so foolish as to think that this calf, that was just made that very day, was the one that took them out of Egypt?!⁹ Rather [one must understand that] *all* idolaters know that it is our God in heaven¹⁰ who created the world. But their error¹¹ was as follows: *Teraphim* have an impure spirit in them,¹² just as prophets have a holy spirit. When the calf

---

⁸That prooftext proves well that ויצר (the identical form in II Kings and here) can mean "to wrap," and that חָרִיט in II Kings (somewhat akin to חֶרֶט in our verse) means "a cloth." This same prooftext is also found in Rashi's comm.

⁹When discussing the golden calf, Nathan Official (as quoted in *Niṣṣaḥon yashan*; see notes ad vs. 1 above) in the thirteenth century used language very similar to that of Rashbam. After noting that these Israelites had just experienced God and seen most impressive miracles, he says that clearly they could not have then become idolaters as even the greatest fools would not do something as idiotic as that (והלא כסיל שבכסילים לא יעשה איולת כזאת; Berger, Heb. section, p. 27).

¹⁰א-לוהינו שבשמים, a phrase from Ps. 115:3, a psalm that contrasts "our God in heaven" with idols that were made by human hands.

¹¹As noted above in note 2, Touitou claims that Rashbam, for polemical reasons, minimizes the sin of the Israelites by defining it as not really being idolatry, but only sorcery, or reliance on the impure forces of the world. To me it appears that Rashbam is saying that the Israelites' sin *was* idolatry; however, Rashbam says that *all* idolaters, including the Israelites in the wilderness, know full well that "our God in heaven" created the world. The sin of idolatry, in general, and the particular sin of the biblical Israelites, should be understood, according to Rashbam, in terms of reliance on the impure forces of sorcery present in this world and confusing them with the holy spirit of God.

To be sure, Touitou's anti-Christian polemic explanation is very helpful when he applies it to JBS's commentary; JBS clearly does try to describe the sin of the Israelites in such a way that it is *not* to be understood as idolatry. See esp. his comm. ad vs. 1 and ad vs. 25.

¹²Rashbam, as previously noted, believes that there are impure forces in this world and that they can and do communicate with human beings who seek them out. See comm. above, ad 28:30, and note 54, there.

spoke to them[13] using impure spirits,[14] the Israelites felt that it was speaking through the divine holy spirit. That is why they said, "These are your gods, O Israel, who brought you out of the land of Egypt." In other words, they said: "The holy spirit is in this calf, and it is as if the holy spirit is going before us." That is also why Laban, in speaking of his *teraphim*, [refers to them as gods, when he] says (Gen. 31:30), "why did you steal my gods?"[15]

God put the impure spirits of sorcery into the calf in order to test the Israelites. Similarly God put into the *'ov* and the *yide'oni*[16] impure spirits that can lessen the power of the divine agencies[17] and predict the future. [God did this] in order to determine whether they would (Deut. 18:13) "be wholehearted with the LORD," their God, and then there would (*ibid.*, vs. 10) "not be found among you . . . a soothsayer, a diviner, a sorcerer," nor anyone who believes the (Deut. 13:2) "sign or portent" of one who prophesies by using impure spirits. And [concerning those false prophets,] it is written (*ibid.*, vs. 4), "For the LORD your God is testing you to see whether you really love the LORD

---

[13] Again we see that Rashbam believes that the construction of the calf was successful in getting the impure spirits of the world to communicate with the Israelites. See previous note.

[14] The idea that the calf, because of impure spirits, succeeded in speaking or in making noises can be found in a number of midrashic sources. See e.g. PDRE 45, which claims that the calf was able to bleat because it was given that power by the evil angel, Sammael.

[15] I.e. Laban also felt that when his *teraphim* communicated with him, it was really God who was communicating with him.

[16] Methods of predicting the future outlawed in a number of passages in the Torah; see e.g. Lev. 19:31.

[17] להכחיש פמליא של מעלה. The phrase is used in Sanh. 67b to explain the ostensible derivation (on the basis of *noṭariqon*) of the Hebrew word כשפים (sorcery). Rashbam seems to be suggesting that the way in which sorcery lessens the power of God is in that the power to predict the future, that should have been God's alone, was shared by God with the forces of impurity. Cf. Rashi's explantion of the phrase in Sanh., *ibid.*, s.v. כשפים.

your God."[18]

32:11 בעמך אשר הוצאת YOUR PEOPLE WHOM YOU DELIVERED [FROM THE LAND OF EGYPT]: *YOUR* PEOPLE, not my people. WHOM *YOU* DELIVERED. I am not the one who brought them out;[19] You did.[20]

32:12 למה יאמרו LET NOT THE EGYPTIANS SAY . . .: I.e. act for the sake of Your name,[21] so that it will not be desecrated.[22]

32:16 מעשה א-לוהים המה [THE TABLETS WERE] GOD'S WORK: They were not carved by Moses. However, concerning the second set of tablets it is written (Ex. 34:1), "[The LORD said to Moses,] 'Carve

---

[18]Concerning the idea that God allows the impure spirits to share some of His powers in order to test us to see if we will refrain from availing ourselves of those spirits, see also comm. ad Deut. 13:4 and 18:13, and see my "Tradition or Context," p. 181.

At this point in the ms. of Rashbam's comm., between this comment on verse 4 and the comment on vs. 11, seven words which are a conflation of vss. 22 and 25 are written (וירא משה את העם כי ברע הוא) and no further commentary is written concerning those words. To my mind the words represent some scribal error or copyist's lapse. Cf., however, an attempted explanation of their relevance here in Rosin, note 10.

[19]Using the language of vs. 7. See the following note.

[20]In vs. 7, God, when speaking to Moses, calls the Israelites "*your* people," and tells Moses "*you* brought them out of the land of Egypt." Rashbam points out that here Moses reverses the argument and tells God that the Israelites are *His* people, and that *God* was the one who delivered them from Egypt. The same point is made in a number of midrashic sources; see e.g. Tanh. *Ki tissa'* 22. See also Rashbam's comm. above, ad 16:6.

[21]עשה למען שמך; a common phrase in biblical Hebrew (e.g. Jer. 14:7), even more common in rabbinic Hebrew and in the liturgy.

[22]Rashbam rephrases the idea of this verse in common rabbinic terminology: if the Egyptians were to come to the conclusion that God was an evil God, that would constitute חילול השם, the desecration of God's name. See similarly iE, here.

two tablets . . .'."²³

חרות INCISED: חרות means the same as "חרוט--carved," or "חרוש--plowed."²⁴

32:18 חלושה: means "victory," as in the phrase (Ex. 17:13) "Joshua was victorious (ויחלש) [over the people of Amalek]."²⁵

32:19 וישלך מידיו HE THREW THE TABLETS DOWN: When Moses saw the calf, his strength waned and he no longer had enough strength²⁶ [to hold on to the tablets]. So he threw the tablets down, a small distance away from him--in the same manner that any person would

---

²³Rashi (following Tanh. *Ki tissa'* 16) offers a figurative intepretation of the phrase, "God's work," that God is preoccupied with the study of the Torah. LT (following the idea of Avot 5:6) offers another midrashic understanding--that our phrase means that the tablets were made by God back at the time of the creation of the world. Hizq. suggests (perhaps following an earlier tosaphist tradition; see Kasher, note 163) that our verse should be read as an exclamation ("How great were those tablets! The handiwork of God Himself!") that emphasizes how great the loss of those divine tablets was to the Jewish people. Rashbam offers the simpler explanation, that the phrase is meant to make the contrast between the two sets of tablets clearer. The first was "God's work"; the second was Moses'. So also iE.

²⁴חָרוּת in the sense of "incised" or "carved" appears only here in the Bible. This anomalous form led to many midrashim, the most famous of which (Eruv. 54a) suggests understanding the word as if it were vocalized חֵרוּת, yielding the meaning that true freedom (חֵרוּת) is found only through the Torah. Rashi, here, offers the simpler suggestion that the hapax legomenon root ח-ר-ת should be understood as a variant of the root ח-ר-ט, "to carve" (whence the noun חֶרֶט, a stylus [Is. 8:1] is derived). Rashbam adds that the similar root ח-ר-ש may also express the same idea as ח-ר-ט and ח-ר-ת. See e.g. Jer. 17:1, where the word חרושה appears and stands in parallelism with the word כתובה ("written"). See ibn Janah, *Sefer ha-shorashim*, s.v. ח-ר-ת, who makes the same connection between ח-ר-ת and ח-ר-ש.

²⁵Generally the word חלושה here is interpreted as meaning "weakness" or "defeat." See e.g. Rashi, LT and NJPS, here.
    Rashbam also offers this same novel intepretatation of חלושה in his comm. ad 17:13. See also note 9, there.

²⁶תשש כחו ולא היה בו כח. The identical phrase is used in Ber. 32a to describe Moses' reaction after the sin of the golden calf. There, however, the Talmud says that Moses no longer had enough strength to *speak*.

EXODUS XXXII

throw down an item that is too heavy--so that when they fell down, they would not land on his feet and injure him.

I found this interpretation in *Pirqe de-rabbi 'eli'ezer*,[27] and it is the true plain meaning of Scripture.[28]

32:20 וַיִּזֶר: means "he scattered it." Just as one says וַיִּקֶן ("he bought"; e.g. Gen. 33:19) from the root ק-נ-ה, so also from the root ז-ר-ה one says וַיִּזֶר, and one says זוֹרֶה (as in the phrase [Ruth 3:2] "he will be winnowing [זוֹרֶה]), " and one says זָרָה (as in the phrase [Num. 17:2], "scatter [זְרֵה] the coals abroad").[29]

וישק את בני ישראל HE MADE THE ISRAELITES DRINK IT: He

---

[27] Chapter 45. There the explanation is slightly more miraculous in nature. According to PDRE, the reason that Moses was able to carry the heavy tablets was that the divine letters on the tablets helped him carry the weight. However, when the divine letters of the Decalogue saw the golden calf, they flew away, leaving Moses to carry the tablets without any supernatural assistance. This he was unable to do, so he dropped them. (A slightly variant version of this midrash may be found also in Tanh. *Ki tissa'* 26.)

Rashbam reworks his midrashic sources and in fact combines two midrashic themes--Moses' loss of strength (Ber. 32a) and the idea of the tablets being too heavy (PDRE 45)--into his own *peshaṭ* interpretation. See also Rashbam's comm. ad Deut. 9:17.

[28] Rashbam is disagreeing with the common rabbinic explanation that Moses made a conscious, independent decision to break the tablets, a decision that God accepted after the fact. See e.g. Shabbat 87a, and Rashi, here, and ad Deut. 34:12. Rashbam may also have been distancing himself from the opinion found in a number of midrashic sources (e.g. LT here) that Moses displayed great strength when he broke the tablets.

See N. Leibowitz (*'Iyyunim*, pp. 428-429) who argues at length that Rashbam's interpretation clearly could not represent the *peshaṭ* reading of this text. See also Touitou who writes (*Tarbiz* 51, p. 237) that Rashbam's interpretation is so obviously not the *peshaṭ* of this verse that it must be seen as part of his anti-Christian polemical reworking of the golden calf story. (See note 2 and note 11, above.) Cf. Rosin here, note 3, who says that Rashbam is attracted to this reading because he prefers to describe Moses in such a way that he did not destroy God's handiwork intentionally in a fit of anger.

[29] Again Rashbam comments on a *vav*-consecutive form of a final-*heh* verb. See his comm. ad 4:26, s.v. וַיִּרֶף, and note 27, there.

Like Rashbam, see Rashi, and see also LT, who, just like Rashbam, realizes that readers might have difficulty determining the root of וַיִּזֶר.

checked them the same way that adulterous women are checked.[30]

32:24 ויצא העגל הזה AND THIS CALF RESULTED: I.e the calf was thus completed. [The verb י-צ-א is often used for finishing the manufacture of some vessel,] as in the phrase (Prov. 25:4), "A vessel was completed (ויצא) by the smith," or the phrase (Is. 54:16), "to produce (ומוציא) the tools for his work."[31]

---

[30] I.e. making them drink this mixture was a type of ordeal to determine the guilt of individual Israelites, in the same way that the *soṭah*, the suspected adulteress, is "checked" by making her drink the mixture described in Num. 5:17-28.

So also Rashi (following AZ 44a) and iE. Even a modern critical exegete like Ehrlich was attracted to this explanation. Cf. Hizq. and JBS, who argue that that is *not* the *peshaṭ* interpretation of the verse. JBS argues further that the rabbis offered this midrashic interpretation for anti-Christian polemical purposes, to show the futility of "eating a god," thus mocking the Christian Eucharist ceremony.

[31] As noted already in notes 4 and 6, Rashbam understands that when Aaron says ויצא העגל הזה, the phrase does not imply surprise or a supernatural intervention ("All I did was throw the gold into the fire and, to my shock--ויצא העגל הזה, out came this calf!"). The verb י-צ-א, according to Rashbam, refers to the completion of the manufacturing process, not to something that just happens by accident.

Rashbam offers his interpretation in opposition to a common midrashic view that read the phrase ויצא העגל הזה as implying a surprising or supernatural result. See e.g. Meg. 25b, where the Talmud claims that the heretics reached erroneous conclusions (presumably about the power of idolatry) because of Aaron's words ויצא העגל הזה.

See the lengthy discussion of that text in *Tosefta' kifeshuṭah* (Megillah, p. 1219), where Liebermann argues against reading that text as meaning that the heretics *misunderstood* Aaron's words and *incorrectly* decided that the calf just happened supernaturally. (For such an understanding, see LT here.) Liebermann argues that the midrashic tradition *is* that the calf just happened to come out in a supernatural manner. The heretics, according to that midrash, were right when they interpreted Aaron's words that way. That is what Aaron said. The heretics' error was only in extrapolating from the story of the calf and concluding that idolatry, in general, is a powerful force in the world. Following Liebermann's understanding, then, Rashbam is distancing himself here not only from the erroneous viewpoint of the heretics of Meg. 25b (as Rosin, here, would have it), but, even more so, he is distancing himself from the midrashic tradition that Aaron did not fashion the calf, and that the calf just happened to come out of the fire.

Like Rashbam, see also JBS. Cf. Rashi, who says that Aaron had no expectation that a calf would result from his efforts. And see Seforno, who writes explicitly that ויצא העגל הזה means that the calf was produced without any effort by Aaron.

32:25 כי פרוע הוא [MOSES SAW THAT THE PEOPLE WERE] OUT OF CONTROL: פרוע means that they had been separated from commandments, the commandments of their Creator,[32] as in the phrase (Prov. 1:25), "You separated yourself (ותפרעו) from all my advice," and the phrase (Prov. 4:15), "Separate from it (פרעהו); do not go through it."[33]

לשמצה FOR THE DERISION: Their enemies say words of scorn and derision[34] about them. [שמצה refers to] a type of speech, as in the phrase (Job 4:12), "My ear caught a whisper (שֵׁמֶץ) of it."[35]

32:27 איש את אחיו [SLAY] EACH OF YOU HIS BROTHERS: If they

---

[32] See also Rashbam's comm. above, ad 5:4, and note 4, there.

Rashbam is disputing the interpretation of Rashi (so also JBS and LT here) who says that פרוע means uncovered in a shameful manner. Rashi cites as proof the use of the root פ-ר-ע to describe what the priest does to the hair of the suspected adulteress (Num. 5:18). That action can be interpreted as either untieing the woman's braids or uncovering her hair (or both).

On the other hand, Rashbam sees the root פ-ר-ע as non-pejorative; it simply means "separated." Only the context would determine whether the word is to be seen as having negative connotations, depending on what it is that has been separated from what.

[33] Both of these examples are cited by Rashi, above, ad 5:4. There Rashi does see a nuance of "separation" in the verb פ-ר-ע, so he cites those prooftexts. Here Rashi does not see such a nuance, but Rashbam still does; accordingly, Rashbam is the one to cite those prooftexts.

[34] לעג וקלס; Ps. 44:14.

[35] Rashbam understands the word שמצה, here, in a manner similar to Rashi and most classical Jewish exegetes. His prooftext is unusual. It is hard to understand what the verse in Job 4 proves, other than the fact that a type of speech is implied by the word שמץ or שמצה. Cf. Nahm., who offers a different interpretation of שמצה, here, and speculates about how those who offer the standard rabbinic explanation would be able to deal with the verse in Job 4.

Cf. Tos. Pes. 3b, s.v. שמץ פסול, where R. Hananel is quoted as interpreting שמצה as a reference to idolatry.

had sinned by worshipping the calf.[36]

32:29 מִלְאוּ יֶדְכֶם DEDICATE YOURSELVES: מִלְאוּ [is a *qal* imperative that] has the exact same form[37] as the [*piel*] past tense, as in the phrase (Num. 32:12), "they remained loyal (מִלְאוּ) to God."[38]

[The phrase means,] "Dedicate[39] each and every one of your

---

[36] On the simplest level, Rashbam is saying that Moses did not tell the Levites to kill their brothers indiscriminately; he told them to kill only those that were guilty.

Perhaps Rashbam is also trying to deal with the issue that troubles both Rashi and JBS here: if the people who gathered to help Moses were "all the Levites" (vs. 26), then how could one of those Levites end up killing his own brother? A Levite's brother is a Levite. If all the Levites were on Moses' side and none of them had worshipped the calf, then no Levite would have cause to kill a brother. Rashi (here and ad Deut. 33:9, following Yoma 66b) suggests that some Levites had to kill their maternal half-brothers (whose fathers were not Levites). JBS suggests that many people gathered to Moses' side from many tribes. (Verse 26 teaches us, according to JBS, that among those who gathered to Moses were the entire tribe of Levi, not that all the people who came to Moses were Levites). So when Moses says, here, that one should be ready to kill one's own brother, he was addressing those people, other than Levites, who gathered to his side.

It is possible that Rashbam rejects the common rabbinic assumption (Yoma ibid., Tanh. *Ki tissa'* 26, PDRE 45 and many other sources) that no Levites were guilty of worshipping the calf. Rashbam writes simply that the Levites were told to kill their brothers, if those brothers were guilty of worshipping the calf.

[37] The words that Rashbam writes here--כמו כי מלאו אחרי ה' לשעבר--could easily be interpreted another way. It could be that Rashbam is saying that just as מִלְאוּ, in Num. 32, is a third-person plural past tense *piel* form, so is מִלְאוּ, here. In fact, Mendelssohn in his *Be'ur* says that that is the meaning of Rashbam's comment here. Ashkenazi in *Qeren shemu'el* also interprets Rashbam's comment that way. If that is the case, then Rashbam must think that the subject of the verb מִלְאוּ is יֶדְכֶם. See the citation from Hizq. in the notes below. I have chosen to translate this difficult text in a different manner, but there can be little certainty about the issue.

[38] See comm. and notes ad Gen. 1:22, s.v. וּמִלְאוּ.

[39] Rashbam uses the word חינכו (dedicate) here, in language very similar to Rashi's (תתחנכו). Rashi is slightly more explicit than Rashbam here in saying that the role the Levites played in the story of the golden calf was the cause of their elevation to the status previously held by the first-borns of the Israelites. See also Rashi ad Num. 3:12. Rashbam does not say explicitly that the events surrounding the golden calf were the reason why that role was transferred from the first-borns to the Levites. However, the use of the word "חינכו-dedicate," here, does imply that he too accepts that explanation.

hands[40] today TO THE LORD through sacrifices,[41] for EACH OF YOU has extended his hand against HIS OWN SON AND HIS OWN BROTHER, [thus sinning] against heaven."[42]

32:32 מספרך אשר כתבת [ERASE ME] FROM THE BOOK: the book of life,[43] THAT YOU HAVE WRITTEN. [The "book" means the list

---

[40]Rashbam paraphrases the text's יֶדְכֶם as כל יד ויד שלכם, so as to explain why the text reads יֶדְכֶם, in the singular, and not יְדֵיכֶם, in the plural. See also Rashbam's comm. and notes ad Gen. 49:22 (concerning the phrase בנות צעדה עלי שור), and below, ad 35:25, s.v. בידיה.

[41]בקרבן לה׳. Ashkenazi suggests reading here כקרבן לה׳. That reading would go along better with his understanding of Rashbam's comment. See also note 42.

[42]The Hebrew phrase שלחתם ידיכם לשמים is difficult and probably corrupt. It is hard to say with certainty what Rashbam's point is, but I feel that he is saying that the Israelites who helped Moses were told now to offer sacrifices in order to do penance for the bloodshed that they perpetrated against their brothers. So also Ps.-Jon. and perhaps also Onq. (depending on what text of Onq. is used and how it is understood. See *'Ohev ger*, here, and Kasher, note 235.)

If my understanding of Rashbam is correct, then Rashbam's interpretation is diametrically opposed to that of Rashi, who says that the Levites dedicated themselves to God through their act of killing their relatives. (So also Nahm. ad Ex. 28:41 and ad Deut. 10:8.) Rashbam would be saying the opposite--that after killing their relatives the Levites had to do some action that would dedicate them (anew?) to God.

Cf., however, Hizq., who uses language very similar to that of Rashbam (and may very well be representing his own understanding and/or reworking of what Rashbam is saying here), and who interprets the ideas of this verse in the same manner as Rashi. According to Hizq., מִלְאוּ is in the past tense, and its subject is יֶדְכֶם. The verse means, "By fulfilling God's will and killing your relatives, your hands have become dedicated to God." (In Hizq.'s words: כבר נתמלאו כל יד ויד שלכם להיותכם משרתי הקב״ה שהרי איש בבנו ובאחיו שלחתם ידיכם לשם שמים.) Hizq. further adds that that is Onq.'s opinion. Ashkenazi in *Qeren shemu'el* also interprets Rashbam's comment here in that manner. If Ashkenazi is correct, then my translation above is inaccurate. A better translation would then be: "Today you have dedicated each and every one of your hands to God through a sacrifice, by extending your hands against your sons and your brothers for the sake of God."

[43]Rashbam opposes Rashi's interpretation (following a number of midrashic sources; see Kasher note 254*, here), that "the book" referred to here is a reference to the Torah. Rashbam's own interpretation, that Moses is expressing a willingness to die for the Jewish people, can be found in a number of earlier sources, including Ber. 32a. So also LT here.

of those living,] as in the phrase (Is. 4:3), "all those who are inscribed for life in Jerusalem."[44] [In other words, Moses is saying,] "Kill me, rather, I beg you."[45]

32:34 נחה [GO NOW] LEAD [THE PEOPLE WHERE I TOLD YOU]: I.e. to the land of Israel.[46]

וביום פקדי BUT ON THE DAY THAT I MAKE AN ACCOUNTING [I WILL BRING THEM TO ACCOUNT FOR THEIR SINS]: [I will punish them] little by little, when I so desire, and not all at once.[47]

---

[44] It is noteworthy that when Ḥizq. and some other tosaphists (cited by Rosin, here, note 18) offer this same interpretation, they cite *rabbinic* texts (e.g. RH 16b) to prove that "inscribing in a book" is a metaphor for being counted among the living. However, as Rosin emphasizes, Rashbam cites a *biblical* prooftext.

[45] Num. 11:15. In order to explain that Moses' words here ("Erase me . . .") mean that he would rather God killed him than wipe out the Israelites, Rashbam cites another instance when Moses challenged God, unambiguously, to kill him. See also Mekhilta *Pisḥa'* 1:1 (Lauterbach ed., p. 10), where our verse and the verse Rashbam cites from Numbers are cited as the two examples of Moses' willingness to die for the Jewish people.

[46] So also iE and many other commentators, here. Rashbam presumably makes this point explicit so that we will understand Moses' words below (33:12), "See, You tell me 'Take this people up'." See comm. and notes, there.

[47] In Sanh. 102a there are two traditions of interpretation about this verse. According to the reading of R. Hanina, God is saying here that on *one* future occasion, He will punish the Israelites for the sin of the golden calf. According to the opinion of R. Isaac, God is saying that *whenever* He punishes the Israelites for any infraction, He will add to the punishment some small amount because of the sin of the golden calf. Rashi follows that second understanding. Rashbam's explanation is also closer to that second understanding but differs from it slightly. Rashi and the talmudic Rabbi Isaac say that *all* punishments of the Israelites in the future will include some punishment for the sin of the calf. Rashbam says that whenever God wishes, He will exact punishment for the sin of the calf, but He will do so in stages (so as not to wipe the Israelites out).

EXODUS XXXIII

33:3 פֶּן אֲכֶלְךָ LEST I DEVOUR YOU: אֲכֶלְךָ should be understood as if it were written אֹכְלְךָ, i.e. "אוֹכַל אוֹתְךָ--I will devour you." Just like the phrase (Deut. 4:24), "For the LORD your God is a consuming (אוכלה) fire."[1]

33:4 עֶדְיוֹ: means types of jewelry.[2] Since they behaved like mourners, as the verse says ויתאבלו--THEY WENT INTO MOURNING, [accordingly] THEY DID NOT PUT ON THEIR JEWELRY, because God had said[3] to them (vs. 5), "Take off your jewelry."

---

[1] All exegetes and grammarians that I have seen explain אכלך as being from the root כ-ל-ה and as meaning "I will destroy you." Rashbam for some reason chooses to offer this strange explanation, that the root is actually א-כ-ל, to eat or to devour. See Melammed, p. 507, who says that this comment is simply too poor to have been authored by someone like Rashbam, and that it must be an addition to the manuscript from the pen of some lesser student or copyist.

[2] Rashbam disagrees with Rashi who (following Shab. 88a) says that the עדי here is a reference to crowns that were placed on the heads of the Israelites at Mount Sinai. There is also a midrashic explanation (Tanh. B. *Ki tissa'* 15) that identifies the עדי of this verse with weapons that the Israelites had received from God. Rashbam explains more simply that עדי here means jewelry, as it usually does.

[3] As Rosin notes, Rashbam is pointing out that vs. 5 is best understood as describing what God had said to the Israelites *before* the events of verse 4. So also iE. Rashbam is opposing the various convoluted explanations of why God would command them (in vs. 5) to remove their jewelry when they had already done so (in vs. 4). See e.g. JBS's suggestion (that they had removed their jewelry but not entirely, and now God told them to remove the jewelry completely), or Saadiah's explanation, cited by iE (that they removed their jewelry and then God told them that they should behave similarly in future instances of mourning and/or repentance).

33:7 יִקַּח: should be understood as if [the past-tense form] לָקַח ("He took [the Tent]") were written.[4]

הרחק [TOOK THE TENT AND PITCHED IT OUTSIDE THE CAMP] AT SOME DISTANCE [FROM THE CAMP]: Moses behaved towards the Israelites as if they had been excommunicated.[5] [Moses moved the Tent away] because God did not want to speak to Moses if he was inside the camp[6] of the Israelites.[7]

33:12 ראה אתה אומר אלי העל SEE, YOU SAY TO ME "TAKE THIS PEOPLE UP": As it says above (32:34), "Go, now, lead the people where I told you."[8]

---

[4]Rashbam disputes Rashi, who writes that יִקַּח should be understood as לשון הווה, i.e. a present-tense verb (meaning a verb that represents a habitual action). According to Rashi, from that point in time on Moses always took the Tent to a far-off location. According to Rashbam, though, the text describes something that Moses did once, after the sin of the calf. Like Rashbam, see iE.

[5]So also Rashi, following Tanh. *Ki tissa'* 27.

[6]Perhaps Rashbam sees this idea in God's statement in vs. 3, "I will not go in your midst."

[7]It appears that Rashbam has now offered a second, different reason why Moses moved the Tent. However, he may just be expanding and refining the theme of the "excommunication" of the Israelites. He explains that Moses moved the Tent not just as a result of a technicality--because the Israelites were under a ban. He reworks this midrashic idea in a more *peshat*-like manner. Moses wanted to be able to communicate with God. God was angry with the Israelites. So Moses moved the Tent away from the Israelites.

See iE, longer comm., who explains the idea of this verse in a similar manner without having recourse to the "excommunication" theme. Cf. JBS, who suggests that Moses moved away because he felt that the people had rebelled against *him*.

[8]Rashbam identifies the words of God to which Moses alludes here ("You say to me . . .") in a different manner from some midrashim. See LT, who says that Moses is alluding here to what God said to him in 33:1 ("Go up from here, you and the people"), and see also Shemot Rabba (32:8) where Moses is understood as alluding to what God said to him in 23:20 ("I am sending an angel before you . . .").

ואתה לא הודעתני BUT YOU HAVE NOT MADE KNOWN TO ME
[WHOM YOU WILL SEND WITH ME]: All you said was (32:34)
"See, My angel will go before you."[9] But all that I want[10] is "that
You," Yourself, "will go with us."[11]

33:13 הודיעני נא את דרכך PRAY, LET ME KNOW YOUR WAYS:
You, Yourself, should be the one to tell us the way [to go]; You will
show me the way and I will follow You.[12]

---

[9]Again, just as in the previous comment, Rashbam says that Moses here is alluding to God's words in 32:34.

From the continuation of the conversation here between Moses and God, it is clear that they are discussing whether God will lead the Israelites Himself or through an intermediary. Rashbam accordingly points out that already in 32:34 this idea was raised by God.

[10]איני חפץ כי אם, using language very similar to that of Rashi here (שאין אני חפץ).

[11]בלכתך עמנו, using the language of vs. 16 below.

Rashbam here interprets this phrase basically in the same manner as Rashi (following Tanh. B. *Ki tissa'* 15). Rashi, however, says that the reference to God's promise to send an angel to lead the Israelites is an allusion to Ex. 23:20; Rashbam connects the thought to the closer verse, 32:34.

[12]Most of the midrashim and the Jewish commentators understand Moses' request here as being that God "let Moses know" some spiritual or metaphysical truths. See e.g. Ber. 7a, where Moses' request is understood as asking God to teach him the secrets of Providence, and why it is that the righteous appear to suffer and the wicked appear to thrive. And see also NJPSC: " . . . it is clear that Moses here asks to comprehend God's essential personality . . .." See similarly other medieval exegetes (e.g. JBS, LT and iE).

Rashi offers an interpretation that he realizes deviates somewhat from the rabbinic understanding in Berakhot. According to Rashi, Moses' question is more narrow: it relates to God's relationship to Moses. Moses wishes to understand why God had chosen to reward *him*, and thus understand, more generally, who it is that God rewards and why. Rashi finishes his comment to this verse by explaining (perhaps apologetically, perhaps proudly) that his (slight) deviation from traditional exegesis is a result of his desire to interpret verses contextually (",ורבותינו דרשוהו במסכת ברכות ואני ליישב המקראות על אופניהם ועל סדרם באתי--our rabbis interpreted [this verse] midrashically in the tractate Berakhot, but my purpose is to interpret Scripture according to the context and the flow of the texts"). N. Leibowitz (*'Iyyunim*, pp. 507-8) writes that Rashi is willing to sacrifice the grandeur of the rabbinic understanding for the sake of

33:14 פני ילכו: means "I, Myself,[13] will go, as you requested," as in the phrase (II Sam. 17:11), "[I advise that . . .] you yourself march (ופניך הולכים) into battle."[14]

והנחותי לך AND I WILL BRING YOU TO A HAVEN: [God said,] "I will go with you to capture the land [and I will stay with you] until I grant you safety (שאניח לך) from all your enemies around you."

---

a contextual interpretation. See also the comments of Kamin (*Rashi*, pp. 91-95) on how and why Rashi strays from the standard talmudic understanding.

Yet Rashi's deviation from the rabbinic reading pales in comparison to that of his grandson, Rashbam. Rashbam sees no attempt on Moses' part here to learn anything, general or specific, about God's Providence. Rashbam explains more simply and (as is often his wont) more prosaically that the discussion surrounds the question of how the Israelites will be led to the land of Israel: will an angel show them the way to travel, or will God Himself? Moses is not asking God to show "His Ways," in a metaphysical sense, but to show, Himself, the way to get to the land of Israel. Rashbam accordingly expands greatly on Rashi's willingness to deviate from the older rabbinic understandings in order to offer an understanding that he considers contextually grounded.

Rashbam's interpretation is novel but, as Kasher writes (note 79), a similar understanding is found in Midrash Tehillim 90:9: "כיון שיצאו ישראל ממצרים עמד משה מתפלל ואומר איני מכיר את הדרך שנאמר הודיעני נא את דרכיך--after the Jews left Egypt, Moses arose in prayer and said, 'I do not know the way [to go],' as it is written, 'Pray, let me know the way'."

To be sure, Rashbam's interpretation can find some support in the general context of these verses. However, the word, "ואדעך--that I may know You," appears out of place if all that is being discussed is the question of travel directions.

[13]"I, Myself," constitutes Rashbam's explanation of the word, פני.
On Rashbam's understanding of פנים, see also comm. above, ad 25:30, and notes 54 and 56, there.

[14]Rashbam interprets the verse as Rashi does (following Onq.; so also JBS), virtually verbatim. The only change that Rashbam makes to Rashi's words is that he adds the words כמו שבקשת--"as you requested." Following Rashi's understanding, God's answer here appears to be somewhat of a non-sequitur after Moses' request in vs. 13 for insights into God's ways and the reasons why God has rewarded him. (See NJPSC to vs. 14: "God does not yet relate to Moses' last point . . ..") Only Rashbam can write here that God's words here are an appropriate answer to Moses' request, for only Rashbam interpreted Moses' words in the previous verse as a request that God go before the Israelites to show them the way.

[והניחותי means "I will bring you to safety in the land of Israel,"] as in the phrase (Deut. 3:20), "until the LORD has granted your kinsmen a haven (יניח) ... [in the land ... beyond the Jordan]," and in the phrase (Deut. 25:19), "when the LORD grants you safety (יניח) from all your enemies [around you in the land that the LORD your God is giving you]."[15]

He who interprets this phrase as meaning that God is promising to give Moses peace of mind (נחת רוח) by fulfilling Moses' request,[16] is offering a foolish interpretation.[17] Does God *always* say והניחותי לך whenever he accedes to some request of Moses? The words [והניחותי לך, if interpreted to mean "I will grant you peace of mind"] would then simply be superfluous language.[18]

---

[15]Consistent with his understanding that the only theme of the discussion here between Moses and God is the manner in which the Israelites will get to the land of Israel, Rashbam offers a novel understanding of the difficult phrase והניחותי לך. He correctly points out that this verb is often used in contexts that relate to the conquest of Canaan. Rashbam's interpretation is later found in Hizq., and is presented by Childs (without attribution) as a reasonable option of interpretation for our verse. ("To give rest in the Old Testament is often connected with the possession of the promised land.")

[16]It is difficult to know precisely to whom Rashbam is referring here, i.e. who it was who offered this rejected interpretation. Presumably some exegete before Rashbam used that phrase (נחת רוח) to explain the word והניחותי in our verse. The idea of this interpretation (but not the phrase, itself) can be found in Tanh. *Ki tissa'* 27, and in JBS's comm. (here and ad vss. 16 and 17). The interpretation that Rashbam rejects enjoyed a certain popularity *after* Rashbam's time. See e.g. R. Abraham the son of Maimonides (cited by Kasher, here, note 89: "טעמו הנחת רוחך--it means 'giving you peace of mind'"), and see also NEB: "I will set your mind at rest."

[17]Such strong language is not unusual for Rashbam. See also comm. below, ad 34:29.

[18]While it is clear what the point is that Rashbam is making at the end of this comment, the language of the comm. is problematic. As Rosin writes (note 9), the last words of Rashbam' comment on this verse--והלא ייתור לשון חכמה--are obviously the result of some scribal error. Rosin offers a number of interesting and speculative reconstructions of the text, and even kindly invites future generations of scholars to speculate further on the subject ("והמטיב לפרש ולהראות דרך אחרת תבא עליו" ברכה--may a blessing befall anyone who does a better job of explaining [this text] in some other manner"). I would hesitatingly suggest that the text of Rashbam's comm. should read simply: והלא ייתור לשון המה, and that speculative understanding is the one reflected in the translation above. I would also repeat Rosin's invitation to anyone who

33:15-16 אם אין פניך הולכים: I.e. if You do not come with us, (16) HOW SHALL IT BE MADE KNOWN [THAT WE HAVE GAINED YOUR FAVOR].[19]

ונפלינו אני ועמך YOUR PEOPLE AND I MAY BE DISTINGUISHED: These words represent the beginning of a new request [by Moses]. "I request from You further that I, alone, should be distinguished (שאפלא) and separated[20] from the people of Israel, that it will be known that I am a trustworthy prophet and rebuker so that the people will listen to me. And [I request] further [that] Your people--because You will go with them--be distinguished (נפלא) FROM EVERY PEOPLE ON THE FACE OF THE EARTH.[21]

---

would like to speculate further and come up with a better reading and/or a better understanding to feel free to do so.

As noted above, ad 19:23, Rashbam often feels that even on the *peshaṭ* level of reading a narrative text, superfluous language is not acceptable.

[19]Rashi and Rashbam have the same understanding of the flow of thoughts in vss. 15 and 16. Both of them feel that the beginning of verse 16 represents a completion of the thought of verse 15. However, they both feel that a new thought begins in the middle of vs. 16, with the words, "your people and I may be distinguished." Cf. JBS, who sees even the end of vs. 16 as completing the same thought begun in vs. 15.

[20]Rashbam understands the word ונפלינו in the same manner as Rashi, as opposed to those (e.g. Onq.) who connect the word to נפלאות--miracles. See also Rashbam's comm. below, ad vs. 17 and ad 34:10, where he explains that even the word נפלאות in 34:10 ought to be understood as relating to the theme of "distinguishing," not to the idea of "miracles."

[21]At first blush, it appears that Rashbam is just offering an expanded version of Rashi's explanation. (So Rosin: נלוה לפירוש רש"י והרחיבו). Both Rashi and Rashbam make the (somewhat debatable) claim that a new theme begins in the middle of verse 16 with the words ונפלינו אני ועמך. However, the similarity between Rashbam and his grandfather ends there. Rashi says (following Ber. 7a) that Moses' further request from God is related to the Israelite people. Paraphrased, Moses' request, according to Rashi, is as follows: "Just as You have agreed to accompany the Israelite people now, so I ask that You always continue to demonstrate in the future the exclusivity of Your relationship with the Israelites by never establishing a close relationship with any other people on the face of the earth."

Rashbam sees no new request here relating to the Israelites. The way in which the Israelites are to be "distinguished," according to this verse, is the same way that has

EXODUS XXXIII

33:17 גם את הדבר הזה [THE LORD SAID TO MOSES,] "I WILL ALSO DO THIS THING WHICH YOU HAVE SAID: to me, that you should be distinguished[22] [from the Israelites], and appear as their judge and leader. This is in addition to what I already[23] agreed to--that I will go along with the people." God fulfilled this promise to Moses by making Moses' face radiant.[24] Concerning that promise, God says below (Ex. 34:10), "In the sight of the whole people I shall make you distinguished"; I shall explain all this there.[25]

33:18 הראני נא את כבודך LET ME SEE YOUR GLORY: Consider--how did Moses, our rabbi, have the nerve to wish to enjoy the

---

been discussed in the previous verse--by God accompanying them to Canaan. The only new request that begins here according to Rashbam is that Moses is now asking for special treatment for *himself*--that *he* be treated differently than the Israelites. That is why the text now talks about "אני ועמך--Your people and I."

Rashbam's interpretation is novel, and, to my mind, stretched. Presumably he finds it attractive because of verse 17. There God apparently *answers* Moses by saying "I will also do this thing that you have asked, for *you* have truly gained my favor." This *answer* implies (a) that Moses has made some further request to which God must now respond, and (b) that that request had something to do with Moses himself. Just as above Rashbam offers a novel interpretation of Moses' request in vs. 13 in such a way that God's answer in vs. 14 would make sense, so also Rashbam offers a novel interpretation of Moses' request in vs. 16 in such a way that God's answer in vs. 17 would make sense. See also comm. ad vs. 17, and note 22, there.

[22]See previous note. Since Rashbam understands Moses' request in vs. 16 in a unique manner, he also understands God's reaction to that request here in a unique, and consistent, manner. Cf., e.g., Rashi, who says that God is agreeing here to Moses' request that His relationship with the Israelites be an exclusive one, or JBS, who says that God is agreeing to teach Moses God's attributes. See also Ber. 7a.

[23]See comm. ad vss. 13, 14 and 16.

[24]Ex. 34:29-35.

[25]See comm. and notes ad 34:10. Rashbam explains the phrase אעשה נפלאות there in a manner different from most other commentators. He sees it as a continuation of the theme of "distinguishing" (הפלאה), a theme which Rashbam first introduces in his comm. above, ad vs. 16.

radiance of the Divine Presence? Does not the text (Ex. 3:6) praise him that "Moses hid his face for he was afraid to look at God"?[26] God forbid![27]

[Rather one should interpret that] Moses' only intention is to ask God to confirm, through a covenant, the two things[28] that God had [already] agreed to: (1) that Moses' face would be radiant, thus fulfilling the request (vs. 16), "Your people and I may be distinguished,"[29] and (2) that (vs. 14), "'I, Myself, will go,' to grant you safety from all your enemies."[30] Moses accordingly said, "SHOW ME YOUR GLORY by

---

[26]See Rashbam's comm. and notes ad Gen. 48:8. There (pp. 338-339) I discussed the implications of this passage which, to my mind, makes it clear that Rashbam feels that God is, in theory, visible, but that righteous people do not strive to see him. In other words, Rashbam is *not* dealing here (as many exegetes do) with the question of how Moses could ask for the *impossible*--to see God. Rashbam rather is dealing with the question of how Moses could do the *inappropriate*--request to see God. Cf. Rosin's position, cited in notes to Gen. 48:8. See also my "Tradition or Context," pp. 181-182.

[27]I.e. God forbid that we interpret Moses' request here as a request to enjoy the radiance of the Divine Presence.

Rashbam opposes the exegetes, such as Rashi, who say that that is precisely what Moses is requesting here.

[28]Cf. Ber. 7a, where the Talmud says that Moses requested *three* things and God agreed to them all. See also Kamin, pp. 91-93, who shows that Rashi also saw three requests in these verses, but that his three are not identical to the Talmud's three. Rashbam, however, sees only two requests here, followed by Moses' suggestion that a covenant be made to affirm God's agreement to those two requests.

[29]See comm. ad vs. 16, where Rashbam explains that phrase to be a request by Moses that God do something to make him distinguished from the Israelites, and comm. ad vs. 17, where Rashbam explains that God agreed to that request, and that Moses' radiant face was the manifestation of the fact that God made Moses distinguished.

[30]Using the language of Deut. 25:19. The other request, according to Rashbam, was that God Himself lead the Israelites to Canaan. See comm. and notes above, ad vss. 13 and 14.

making a covenant with me concerning those things³¹ that You promised me."³²

God did the same thing in the story of Abraham. After Abraham asked God (Gen. 15:8), "How shall I know [that I am to possess the land]?" Then it is written (*ibid.*, vs. 17) that there was "a smoking oven and a flaming torch which passed between those pieces." Immediately after that, the verse (18) says "On that day the LORD made a covenant with Abram saying, 'to your offspring I give [this land]'."³³

Here also Moses asked God to make a covenant with him, and God agreed to appear to Moses as part of making a covenant, as it is written (Ex. 34:6), "The LORD passed³⁴ before him." Right after that (verse 10) it is written, "I hereby make a covenant:³⁵ in the sight of the

---

³¹Rashbam opposes a number of other interpretations of the purpose of that covenant in 34:10. According to Rashi, the covenant there was meant to reinforce the idea that the Israelites would have a closer relationship with God than the other nations would. According to RH 17b, the covenant was meant to reinforce the idea that God's thirteen attributes constitute a guaranteed efficacious prayer.

³²See also comm. and notes above, ad 24:10 and ad 24:11, s.v. ואל אצילי, where Rashbam explains at length that a theophany was a normal part of making a covenant, and that, therefore, there was nothing untoward about wanting to have God "appear" when a covenant was being ratified. Desiring to "see" God *outside* of the framework of ratifying a covenant is, according to Rashbam, the type of inappropriate behavior that a righteous man would avoid, as in the verse cited above by Rashbam (Ex. 3:6), "Moses hid his face for he was afraid to look at God." "Seeing" God, though, is a normal part of covenant ratification.

³³Rashbam's proof is that a theophany was part of the making of a covenant. See also comm. above, ad 24:11, s.v. ואל אצילי, where Rashbam offers the same interpretation of the verses in Gen. 15.

³⁴ויעבור, the same verb used in Gen. 15:17 (אשר עבר). Rashbam is opposing those midrashim that connect the word ויעבר to the rabbinic Hebrew phrase for someone who leads synagogue prayers (עובר לפני התיבה), and that say that the phrase ויעבר ה' means that God acted like the leader of prayers. See e.g. Tanh. B. *Vayyera'* 9, where that midrashic connection is made explicitly, and RH 17b and Rashi here (ad vs. 19, s.v. וקראתי), where the connection is made implicitly.

³⁵Rashbam is unique in his understanding that the events of 34:6 are part of a covenant ratification ceremony connected with the covenant mentioned in 34:10.

whole people I shall make you distinguished," just as you requested (33:16), "Your people and I may be distinguished."[36] [The text there continues with God promising that, "all the people . . . shall see] how fearful (נורא) . . .," which is a reference to [the fact that when Moses' face became radiant] (34:30), "they were afraid (וייראו) to come near him."[37]

33:19 וחנותי את אשר אחן [I WILL PROCLAIM BEFORE YOU THE NAME, LORD,] AND THE GRACE THAT I GRANT: There I will explain to you My attributes.[38]

33:23 וראית את אחורי YOU WILL SEE MY BACK: "After I pass before you[39] when I make the covenant, you will be able to see Me."[40]

---

[36]Rashbam understands that 34:10 is to be interpreted as God's agreeing to Moses' request that Moses be distinguished from all the other Israelites. See comm. ad 33:17 and 34:10.

[37]Again Rashbam has a unique interpretation of כי נורא הוא, in 34:10, as being a specific reference to the fact that God made Moses' face radiant. See comm. and notes there.

[38]Rashbam's reference here to God's attributes (מדות) establishes some connection between his interpretation and standard rabbinic exegesis of this section. According to the traditional rabbinic reading, what God is promising here--and what he reveals to Moses in 34:5-7--is knowledge of His thirteen attributes. See e.g. RH 17b, and Rashi here, s.v. וקראתי. While Rashbam also mentions God's attributes here, his understanding of the meaning (and the syntax) of this verse is not the standard one.

Rashi explains that the first half of the verse--"I will make all My goodness pass before you, and I will proclaim before you the Name LORD"--represents God's promise to teach Moses about His attribute of mercy. Then the second half of the verse qualifies and restricts the first half. God says that, despite His attributes of mercy, וחנותי את אשר אחן--nevertheless I will show grace only to some." Rashbam says that the second half of the verse is not an attempt to qualify what is written in the first half. God is promising in the first half of the verse to reveal His name to Moses (וקראתי בשם ה' לפניך), and then in the second half of the verse He is promising also to reveal His attribute of mercy to Moses (וחנותי את אשר אחן). So also Nahm. and NJPS.

[39]An allusion to the first phrase in this verse, אני אעביר כל טובי על פניך.

Just like (Jer. 34:18) "the calf which they cut in two, so as to pass between the halves."⁴¹ Covenants were made by passing through [the pieces].⁴²

---

⁴⁰Rashbam is rehearsing in short form the lengthy explanation that he offered above, ad vs. 18, that seeing God was part of the process of making a covenant.

⁴¹That verse also makes reference to a covenant. Hence Rashbam sees it as a further prooftext to show that the partners to a covenant appear to each other as they pass together through the pieces of the covenant symbol.

⁴²Like Rashbam, see Rashi ad Gen. 15:10, iE ad Gen. 15:17 and JBS ad Gen. 15:9. See also comm. above, ad 24:11, s.v. ואל אצילי.

EXODUS XXXIV

34:5 ויתיצב עמו שם HE [i.e. God] STOOD WITH HIM: i.e. with Moses, **THERE.** For Moses was already standing there, as it is written (Ex. 33:21), "[See there is a place near Me.] Stand there (ונצבת) on the rock."[1]

ויקרא בשם ה' AND THE LORD CALLED OUT HIS NAME: God called out[2] as He passed by[3] there, as the text continues to explain.[4] [One can see that God is the subject of the verb, "ויקרא--he called out," here,] for above it is written [that God Himself said (33:19)], "I will call out before you the name LORD."[5]

---

[1] Rashbam says that God is the subject of the verb "ויתיצב--he stood," as opposed to the understanding of Ps.-Jon., who sees Moses as the subject of that verb. Like Rashbam, see iE (shorter comm.) and Nahm. NJPSC suggests arguments to support both readings.

[2] Just as there is ambiguity about the subject of the verb, "he stood," (see previous note), so there are also two opinions about what the subject of the verb, "ויקרא--he called out," is--Moses or God. Rashbam says that God is the subject of "called out," just as he says above that God is the subject of "he stood." Ps.-Jon. again sees the subject as Moses. To my understanding, Rashi (following Onq.) also sees the subject as Moses. Cf. however Kasher, note 45, who disagrees. Like Rashbam, see LT and iE.

[3] Or perhaps "as He passed through there." See comm. and notes above, ad 33:18, where I explained that Rashbam sees ויעבר, in vs. 6 here, as standard covenant language, as it is used for "passing through" the pieces of the covenant object.

[4] In other words, the beginning of verse 6, "The LORD passed before him and called out, 'LORD . . .'," is an elaboration and explanation of the phrase here at the end of verse 5, "The LORD called out His name."

[5] Rashbam's reasonable prooftext was often cited by later exegetes. See e.g. *Sefer ha-zikkaron* (cited by Kasher, *ibid.*), Krinski (*Yahel 'or* 30) and NJPSC.

34:8 וימהר משה MOSES HASTENED: Moses began to bow down immediately after he saw God passing and heard His voice.[6]

34:9 כי עם קשה ערף [LET THE LORD GO IN OUR MIDST] EVEN THOUGH[7] THIS IS A STIFFNECKED PEOPLE: Still You may go in our midst, because You are forgiving and compassionate.[8]

34:10 הנה אנכי כורת ברית I HEREBY MAKE A COVENANT: About the fact that I will go with you. And [I hereby make a covenant] also[9] about "this thing that you have asked," [and that I agreed that] "I will

---

[6] So also Rashi, virtually verbatim. They both may be opposing the midrashic readings suggested in Sanh. 111a-b (and see Rashi there, 111a, s.v. אמת ראה), according to which there was something specific that God had said in the previous verses that caused Moses to pray to Him right now. Or they may be opposing the midrashic explanation that Moses was worried when God mentioned punishment to the third and fourth generation, so Moses bowed down to cut God off before He could talk about punishment to the fifth generation too. That explanation may be found in Hizq., here, and was clearly current before the days of Hizq., for iE and JBS both argue against it, here.

[7] The word כי, in this verse, is difficult. Rashi interprets it as meaning "if." iE in his shorter comm. says that it means "even though," but changes his mind when he writes his longer comm. Curiously, Rashbam does not really tell us what he thinks the word means; accordingly, my translation here is speculative.

[8] Rashbam interprets the progression of ideas here in basically the same manner as JBS and Rashi, but in language that is much more terse. As JBS writes, in 33:3 God tells the Israelites that He will not go with them "since you are a stiffnecked people." Now Moses tells God that, since God has just described Himself (34:6) as being "compassionate and gracious," that means that God can go with the Israelites even though (or "even if" or "even when") they are a stiffnecked people.

[9] Rashbam reiterates the explanation that he offers above, in his comm. ad 33:16 and 33:17, that Moses made two requests of God: that God accompany the Israelites and that God do something to distinguish Moses from the rest of the Israelites. As Rashbam explains there, God agreed to both those requests, and He fulfilled the second one by making Moses' skin radiant (34:29-35). And, as Rashbam explains ad 33:18, God's covenant here is meant to ratify His promise to do those two things.

do,"[10] that you asked that (33:16) "Your people and I may be distinguished." [I shall fulfil that request of yours when] I WILL MAKE a distinction[11] for you BEFORE ALL YOUR PEOPLE; then, ALL THE PEOPLE SHALL SEE the great deeds WHICH I AM PERFORMING FOR YOU.[12] [They will see] "how fearful (נורא) . . .," which is a reference to [the fact that,] when (34:35) "the Israelites saw how radiant the skin of Moses' face was," they (34:30) "were afraid (וייראו) to come near him."[13]

34:19 כל פטר רחם לי EVERY FIRST ISSUE OF THE WOMB IS MINE: Since it was through the plague of [killing the Egyptian] first-borns at the time of the exodus from Egypt that the [Israelite]

---

[10]Using the language of 33:17.

[11]As noted above ad 33:17, Rashbam explains the phrase אעשה נפלאות in a manner different from most exegetes. He sees the word נפלאות (generally seen as meaning "miracles" or "wonders") as meaning that God will make a distinction (הפלאה) for Moses, i.e. that God will do something that will distinguish Moses from the other Israelites. See Rashi, who also connects the word נפלאות, here, to Moses' request in 33:17, ונפלינו אני ועמך. However, since Rashi interprets Moses' request there in a manner different from Rashbam (as a request that God's relationship with the Israelite people be unique), so Rashi also interprets God's agreement here to that request consistently, and in a different manner from Rashbam.

[12]Rashbam sees the final phrase of our verse, אשר אני עושה עמך, as proof for his interpretation that Moses had made a request about some special status for himself, and God agreed to do those things *for him* (עמך). The same prooftext is cited by LT.

[13]As Rashbam wrote above, ad 33:18. The more common understanding would be that God's deeds in general, or some "wonders" that He performs on behalf of the whole people, are being described here as awesome (נורא).

See JBS, iE and LT (in the name of "ויש אומרים--some say"), who also all connect the last phrase of our verse to the fact that at the end of this chapter Moses' skin becomes radiant.

first-borns became consecrated to God,[14] that is why this verse is written here.[15]

34:21 ששת ימים תעבד SIX DAYS YOU SHALL WORK: Agricultural work. [The verb ע-ב-ד and the noun] עבודה, when not qualified, refer to agricultural work,[16] as in the phrase (Gen. 4:12), "when you work (תעבד) the land," or the phrase (Prov. 12:11), "He who works (עובד) his land shall have food in plenty."[17]

בחריש ובקציר תשבת YOU SHALL CEASE FROM LABOR AT THE TIMES OF PLOWING AND OF HARVEST: [I.e *even* at times like these, when the work] is important and people require it. How much more so at other times.[18]

---

[14]See e.g. Ex. 13:15 and Num. 3:13, where the text makes this connection explicit.

[15]The order of the verses here is unusual. Verse 18 describes Passover, and then vs. 22 describes the other two pilgrim holidays. In between there is an interruption, most of which (vss. 19-20) discusses the rules of first-borns (human and animal). Rashbam explains that the rules of first-borns are logically inserted right after a description of Passover, since it was the events surrounding Passover that originally led to the special status of Israelite first-borns. So also iE and JBS.

[16]So also Rashbam ad Gen. 26:14, and see the comm. to Job 1:3 in the Lutzki ms. Job comm. (identified by Sara Japhet as being Rashbam's comm. to Job, and cited by her in "The Nature and Distribution of Compilatory Commentaries" [Heb.], p. 203): ועבדה קרקע לעבוד ולחרוש ולזרוע.

[17]Presumably our verse constitutes one of Rashbam's major reasons for saying that ע-ב-ד, when not qualified, refers to agricultural work. Since the second half of our verse says that one must desist from "work" even during plowing and harvesting season, one may therefore infer that the "work" described in the first half of the verse is agricultural in nature.

[18]The halakhically-minded exegetes ask why it should be necessary to outlaw work at harvest and plowing time, if work is forbidden on the sabbath at *all* times. Rashi (following RH 9a) provides two alternative midrashic answers--that the verse actually teaches something about the sabbatical year (not about the sabbath), or that the verse teaches us that only personal harvest is forbidden on the sabbath (but the harvest of the 'omer is permitted). See also JBS, who writes that the rabbis learned many things from this verse because it is "an unnecessary verse" (קרא יתירא הוא). Rashbam says, much

EXODUS XXXIV

34:23 את פני האדון BEFORE THE MASTER: I already explained this in the Torah portion *Mishpaṭim*.[19]

34:26 לא תבשל YOU SHALL NOT BOIL A KID: I have already explained this verse.[20]

34:27 כתב לך את הדברים האלה WRITE DOWN THESE COMMANDMENTS: The ones written in the previous section, beginning with the words (34:11), "I will drive out before you."[21]

כי על פי הדברים האלה FOR [I MAKE A COVENANT WITH YOU] ON THE BASIS OF THESE COMMANDMENTS: That you will not follow other gods (vs. 14), and that you will not make a covenant with the inhabitants of the land (vs. 15),[22] and that you will not intermarry

---

more simply, that the verse stresses that agricultural work on the sabbath is forbidden even at those times when it is most crucial. So also iE and Nahm.

For a similar disagreement between Rashi and Rashbam, see comm. and notes below, ad 35:3.

[19]See comm. ad 23:17, where Rashbam explains why God is referred to here specifically as "the Master."

[20]In his comm. ad Ex. 23:19.

[21]I.e. the section of rules that is introduced with the phrase, "Mark well what I command you this day. I will drive out before you . . .."

Rashbam opposes the opinion of Rashi (following Git. 60b, and one opinion in Tanh. B. *Ki tissa'* 17), who feels that this verse refers in general to the writing of the (Written) Torah. Another opinion (also found in Tanh. B. *ibid.*) says that the reference is to writing the Decalogue on the second set of tablets. (That opinion can find some support in vs. 28.) Rashbam says though that the phrase, "הדברים האלה--these words or commandments," simply refers to the last words which God spoke to Moses, i.e. vss. 11-26. So also iE.

[22]See also Rashbam's comm. ad Gen. 22:1, where he sees making a covenant with the nations as a very serious crime.

with them (vs. 16), and that you will go up [to Jerusalem] for the pilgrim festivals (vss. 18 and 22-23).[23]

34:28 ויכתוב THEN HE: i.e. God, WROTE DOWN ON THE TABLETS: [It must be God who is the subject of the verb "he wrote,"] for above God said (34:1), will inscribe upon the tablets the words that were on the first tablets," and it also says (Deut. 10:4) "The LORD wrote on the tablets the same text as on the first."[24]

34:29 כי קרן [HIS FACE] WAS RADIANT: [The word קרן is] related to the idea of הוד--grandeur.[25] It is like the word קרנים in the phrase (Hab. 3:4), "which gives off rays (קרנים) on every side."[26]

---

[23]Again Rashbam's interpretation opposes the explanation in Git. 60b, according to which the second half of our verse--especially the words על פי--is an allusion to the Oral Torah. So also LT. Rashbam again interprets the phrase contextually, and says that the commandments mentioned in the previous verses are so central that our verse teaches us that the covenant is dependent on them.

[24]The simplest understanding of our verse, when taken in isolation, is that *Moses* wrote on the second set of tablets: just as Moses is the subject of all three other verbs in this verse "ויהי--he was," "אכל--he ate" and "שתה--he drank," so it makes sense to see Moses as the subject of the verb "ויכתוב--he wrote." However, many of the classical Jewish exegetes (see e.g. iE and Nahm.) insist, as Rashbam does, that God is the subject of the verb, "He wrote," in order to harmonize our verse with the two other verses cited here by Rashbam. So also NJPSC (despite the fact that the JPS translation reads, "*he* wrote," with a lower-case h). There is, however, a midrashic tradition (e.g. Tanh. B. *ibid.*) that says that our verse does mean that Moses wrote the second set himself. So also LT, ad vs. 29.

I have translated Rashbam's comm. here based on the (very reasonable) conjectural emendation suggested here by Rosin. See also Rosin's RSBM, p. 58, note 6.

[25]See also Rashi ad Num. 27:20, where Rashi explains (following Onq. there) that Moses' "הוד--grandeur," referred to in that verse, is a reference to the radiance of the skin of his face.

[26]See Tanh. B. *Ki tissa'* 20 and a number of other midrashic sources which use the words קרני הוד in their exegesis of this verse (so also Rashi) and also cite the same prooftext from Hab.

Anyone who connects קרן, in this verse, to the meaning of "horn," as in the phrase (Deut. 33:17), "He has horns like the horns of the wild ox (קרני ראם קרניו)," is a fool.[27] For many words in the Torah have [at least] two [separate, distinct] categories [of meaning]. So Menahem explained also.[28]

34:32 את כל אשר [HE INSTRUCTED THEM CONCERNING] ALL THAT THE LORD HAD IMPARTED TO HIM: [In other words, Moses now reported to the people all the commandments that he had received from God since the theophany at Mount Sinai, both the commandments that are written] before the episode of the golden calf--from the verse (25:2), "let them take for Me donations," until the verse (32:1), "Moses was so long"--and also the commandments that are written in this section[, after the story of the calf].[29]

See also Rashi, there, who compares that verse with ours and writes that when light shines through a small hole, it looks like a protruding horn (קרן).

[27]Rashi interprets קרן in our verse as meaning קרני הוד and adds that these rays of light are called קרנים because they look like horns. It is unlikely, though, that Rashbam is taking issue with that interpretation of his grandfather. It appears more likely that Rashbam here is mocking Christian contemporaries who, on the basis of the Vulgate (*quod cornuta esset*), felt that Moses literally had horns growing from his face. Concerning that understanding, see also NJPSC, here, which notes that from the eleventh century on (i.e. from Rashbam's days on) we find that a "horned Moses" is a "familiar figure in art." See also the textual notes of Childs, here.

[28]See Menahem, s.v. ק-ר-נ, who identifies two separate meanings and says (like Rashbam) that the second meaning is connected to the idea of הוד. See also Menahem's introduction to his *Mahberet*, pp. 8-9, where he provides lists of biblical Hebrew homonyms.

[29]I.e. the laws that are written in vs. 11f.the laws that Rashbam just mentioned in his comm. to vs. 27. See also iE, here, who sees a reference to the laws of verses 11 to 26 (but does not mention the laws of the Tabernacle that preceded the episode of the calf). The explanation that it is the laws of the Tabernacle that Moses is "imparting" to the Israelites here finds support from the context; see especially 35:4f., and see Rashbam's comm. ad 35:1. So also Seder Olam Rabbah 6: "את לעשות צום 'צנם' מהו המשכן--what does 'he instructed them' refer to? It refers to the instructions to build the Tabernacle."

34:33 מסוה VEIL: מסוה is the name of a type of garment. The letter vav in מסוה is part of the root, just like the vav in the word מקוה, in the phrase (Jer. 14:8), "Hope (מקוה) of Israel."

[The noun מסוה is not related to the noun סותה, "his robe" (Gen. 49:11) for] the letter tav in סותה is part of the root. מסוה and סותו come from two separate roots and describe two different garments. That is how Dunash explained these words, and he is correct.[30]

34:34 יסיר את המסוה HE WOULD TAKE THE VEIL OFF . . . AND WOULD: With his face uncovered, SPEAK to the Israelites WHAT HE HAD BEEN COMMANDED. [After he finished speaking to the Israelites,] then he would cover his face with the veil [and leave his face covered] until [the next time that] HE WENT IN TO SPEAK to God.[31] At that point he would uncover his face again.[32]

---

[30]See Dunash's *Teshuvot*, p. 26. Rashbam, like Dunash, is taking issue with Menahem, who says that both מסוה and סותה have the same root. See Menahem, s.v. ס (p. 127). Like Menahem, see iE and NJPSC, note 27.

[31]Rashbam understands the subject of "באו--he came," to be Moses: Moses came to speak to God. Cf. JBS, who understands the phrase to mean that God came to speak to Moses.

[32]So also Rashi.

EXODUS XXXV

35:1 ויקהל MOSES CONVOKED [THE WHOLE ISRAELITE COMMUNITY]: In order to take from each of them half a shekel,[1] and in order to instruct them about the construction of the Tabernacle.[2]

35:3 לא תבערו אש YOU SHALL KINDLE NO FIRE [ON THE SABBATH DAY]: Concerning holidays, it is written (Ex. 12:16), "What every person is to eat, that alone may be prepared for you." Accordingly, kindling a fire in order to bake and cook is permitted [on a holiday]. But concerning the sabbath it is written (16:23), "Bake what you would bake," before the sabbath begins, "and boil what you would boil." That is why the text tells us here that even kindling a fire for the sake of preparing food [an action which is permitted on a holiday] is not permitted on the sabbath, how much more so all the other types of "work" that are forbidden even on holidays.[3]

---

[1] See Rashbam's comm. ad 30:12.

[2] See vs. 4f., and see comm and notes ad 34:32.
   Cf. LT, who suggests that Moses gathered the people together because of (among other reasons) the importance of the sabbath legislation which follows immediately.

[3] The rabbis (Shabbat 70a) discuss the question of why the Torah would have to single out the kindling of fire when it has already outlawed all manner of work on the sabbath. Rashi here quotes both of the midrashic answers of the Talmud (that the verse teaches that "kindling" is less stringent than other types of work, or that the verse teaches that any one category of infraction of the sabbath laws is enough to make the offender culpable). See also the lengthy halakhic explanations offered by LT. Rashbam provides a more *peshaṭ*-like explanation--that since kindling a fire *is* permitted on some days when "work" is forbidden, the text has to tell us that on the sabbath that is not the case.
   Like Rashbam, see iE and Nahm. Cf. JBS, who provides another attempt to explain why one might have thought (had this verse not been written) that kindling a fire is not outlawed on the sabbath ("לפי שאינה נראית מלאכה כל כך--because it does not appear to be work at all").

35:8 ולקטורת AND FOR THE INCENSE, HERBS: In order to make incense, bring herbs.[4]

35:19 לשרת בקדש [THE SERVICE VESTMENTS] TO SERVE THE HOLY: I.e. [the coverings used] to cover the vessels of the Tabernacle whenever they travelled.[5]

35:21 למלאכת אהל מועד FOR THE WORK OF THE TENT OF MEETING: I.e. for the strips of cloth used as coverings[6] and for the curtain.[7] ולכל עבודתו AND FOR ALL ITS SERVICE: I.e. for the hangings of the enclosure[8] and for the holy vessels.[9]

Concerning the idea of Rashbam's comment here, see similarly comm. and notes ad 34:21, where Rashbam provides a logical reason why the text there specifically outlaws agricultural work on the sabbath during harvest and plowing time, instead of the rabbinic approach that attempted to learn new *halakhot* from that ostensibly redundant verse.

[4]Rashbam reiterates the explanation that he gave the first time this phrase appeared, in 25:6. See comm. and note 9, there.

[5]Rashbam reiterates the explanation that he gave the first time this phrase appeared, in 31:10. See comm. and notes 3 and 4, there.
So also Rashi, here and there.

[6]Described above, in 26:1-14.

[7]Described above, in 26:31-34.

[8]Described above, in 27:9-16.

[9]E.g. the lampstand and the table and the other contents of the Tabernacle.
In general, Rashbam's comment on this verse is meant to distinguish between the phrase מלאכת אהל מועד and the phrase כל עבודתו. The first one, according to Rashbam, refers to the *structure* of the Tabernacle; the second refers to the *contents* of the Tabernacle and to the things that surround it. The phrase מלאכת אהל מועד appears in the Bible only here. Curiously, Rashbam is, as far as I can tell, the only classical Jewish exegete to comment on it.

EXODUS XXXV

35:25 חכמת לב [ALL THE] SKILLED [WOMEN]: [חַכְמַת is to be understood as an adjective;] "a wise woman." But the word חָכְמַת[10] with a ḥaṭaf qameṣ[11] is a noun, as in the phrase (I Kings 5:10), "the wisdom (חָכְמַת) of the Egyptians."

בידיה WITH HER HANDS: [The singular ["*each woman* . . . with *her* hands"] is used, even though the verb טוו is plural, because it means that] each and every woman טוו, SPUN.[12] Similarly [one finds the use of a plural predicate following a singular subject] in the phrase (Jud. 5:26), "Her hand (ידה, singular) reached (תשלחנה; plural) for the tent pin."[13]

35:27 והנשיאים THE CHIEFTAINS [of each tribe] BROUGHT LAPIS LAZULI STONES: [They were the appropriate ones to bring those stones] because the names of the tribes were inscribed on those stones.[14]

---

[10]In verse 35, below, the same consonants--חכמת לב--appear, but with a different vocalization--חָכְמַת, instead of חַכְמַת of our verse. Rashbam explains the reason for the difference.

[11]I.e. with a *qameṣ qaṭan* following the *ḥet*.

[12]See a similar explanation in Rashbam's comm. ad 32:29, and see note 40, there.

[13]The same example of lack of agreement in number between subject and predicate is cited by Rashbam in his comm. above, ad 1:10.
  Rashbam is not saying that the same principle that explains the lack of agreement in our verse can help explain the verse in Judges. He is simply saying that the phenomenon of lack of agreement can be found often.

[14]Rashbam opposes Rashi's midrashic explanation (following Sifre *Naso'* 45), that the chieftains initially brought nothing, and in the end donated only those stones because everything else had been donated by the people.
  Like Rashbam, see JBS. Cf. iE's explanation, that the chieftains were the only ones who owned such valuable possessions.

35:28 ולשמן המשחה [OIL . . .] FOR THE ANOINTING OIL: [The] "one *hin* of olive oil" [mentioned in Ex. 30:24].[15]

35:34 ולהורות [HE HAS ENDOWED HIM WITH A DIVINE SPIRIT . . .] TO GIVE DIRECTIONS: to others.[16]

---

[15]The previous passage (25:6) that mentioned what was to be donated for the anointing oil (שמן המשחה) said that *spices* (בשמים) were what was required. Furthermore, when the recipe for the anointing oil is provided (30:23-24), again it is the spices that are highlighted. Rashbam explains here that it is still appropriate for our verse to say that spices *and oil* were donated for the purpose of the anointing oil, since the list of ingredients in 30:24 includes "one *hin* of olive oil." For Rashbam's understanding of the composition of the anointing oil, see his comm. and notes above, ad 30:25.

[16]Rashbam understands להורות to mean that Bezalel was given--in addition to all the other skills mentioned in the previous verses--the talent to teach others. So also iE and Hizq.

It is possible that Rashbam's comment here also serves a syntactical purpose. Our verse is the first time in the Bible that the verb להורות appears without an object, direct or indirect. Rashbam therefore provides the understood object, "others."

EXODUS XXXVI

36:6 אל יעשו עוד מלאכה [A PROCLAMATION WAS MADE THROUGHOUT THE CAMP] "LET NO MAN OR WOMAN DO FURTHER WORK (מלאכה) [FOR THE SANCTUARY]": [This proclamation had to be made throughout the camp] since people were doing the spinning [and other jobs] in their own homes, as it is written (Ex. 35:25), "they brought what had already been spun."[1]

36:7 דים ENOUGH: [The *mem* of the word דים is an "extra" *mem*,] just like the *mem* in the word ריקם ("emptyhanded"; Gen. 31:42), or the *mem* in the word הכנם in the phrase (Ex. 8:13), "there was lice (הכנם)."[2]

36:8 ויעשו כל חכם לב THEN ALL THE SKILLED [MADE THE TABERNACLE]: First they made the Tabernacle, and then they made its vessels, as I explained above in the Torah portion, *Veyiqḥu li terumah*.[3]

---

[1] A number of classical rabbinic texts suggest that the "work" (מלאכה) referred to here, is the carrying of items to the Tabernacle through the public domain. Our verse is then seen as the source for seeing "carrying" (הוצאה) as a forbidden activity (מלאכה) on the sabbath. (See e.g. Shabbat 96b and P.T. Shabbat 1:1.) Rashbam explains more simply that the "work" prohibited here is the preparation of Tabernacle items being done in the homes of the Israelites. For a combination of the two approaches, see JBS.

[2] See comm. and notes above, ad 8:13.
To be sure the *mem* of the word דים here could be seen as meaning "enough *for them*." See e.g. iE. Rashbam prefers to see the *mem* as "extra." Most translations follow Rashbam.

[3] Ad 25:10. See comm. and notes, there.
Rashbam reiterates his comment here, because these chapters make it most clear that the Tabernacle was constructed (36:8-37) before its vessels were (37:1-38:8).

EXODUS XXXVIII

38:21 אלה פקודי THIS IS THE INVENTORY: i.e. the tally of the silver, the gold, and the copper.[1]

38:25 וכסף פקודי העדה THE SILVER OF THOSE OF THE COMMUNITY WHO WERE RECORDED CAME TO 100 TALENTS: For 600,000 men, "one half shekel per head" (vs. 26) amounts to 300,000 shekels. One *maneh* [usually] consists of 25 skekels. A *maneh* was measured at twice its regular size--i.e. as 50 shekels--when it was used for a holy purpose. One talent consists of 60 *maneh*. So then one talent [when it relates to a holy purpose like the Tabernacle] consists of 3,000 shekels. So the count of "100 talents" [in our verse] is the equivalent of [the] 300,000 shekels [donated by 600,000 men].[2]

---

[1] See Nahm., here, who explains that there are two very different ways of reading the phrase, "This is the inventory": (1) one can see it as a summary statement of the last few chapters, meaning "the *preceding* constitutes an inventory of the Tabernacle," or (2) one can see it as an introduction to the following section (38:24-31), meaning "the *following* is the inventory of the Tabernacle." Rashbam, like Nahm., prefers the second option.

[2] And since the count of men consists of 603,550 men, there are an extra 3,550 half-shekels, i.e "the 1,775 shekels" listed at the end of our verse.
 The arithmetical calculations in this comment are the same as those of Rashi, here, and are based on the discussion in the Talmud (Bekhorot 5a).

EXODUS XXXIX

39:29 ואת האבנט AND THE SASH[ES] OF FINE TWISTED LINEN: Our rabbis disagreed about whether the reference, here, is to the sashes of all priests or only to the sash of the High Priest.[1]

39:32 ותכל [THUS ALL THE WORK OF THE TABERNACLE] WAS COMPLETED: [The form וַתֵּכֶל is to be understood as following] the same [grammatical pattern] as [the form וַתֵּרֶב, in the phrase] (Gen. 43:34), "Benjamin's portion was larger (וַתֵּרֶב)."[2]

---

[1]See Yoma 6a, and the lengthy explanation of Nahm. (in his commentary here), who points out that the source of the diasgreement is the fact that, in the original instructions to make sashes (28:39-40), the materials to be used are not spelled out.
   See also Rashbam's comm. and notes above, ad 29:9.

[2]See Rashbam's comm., there, and notes, p. 307.

EXODUS XL

40:29 ויעל עליו AND Aaron and his sons OFFERED UP ON IT every day BURNT OFFERING[S] AND MEAL OFFERING[S].[1]

---

[1] The more standard understanding of our verse would say that Moses is the subject of the verb "ויעל--he offered." Moses is generally seen as being the subject of the previous 22 third-person singular past tense verbs (in vss. 18-29). (See e.g. Nahm.'s comm. to vs. 27.) Following that understanding, one would say that our verse means that Moses erected the altar of burnt offering, and then Moses offered sacrifices there. And while Jewish law would generally say that sacrifices are to be offered only by Aaron and the priests, it is commonly accepted that during the time when the Tabernacle was being erected--until Aaron and his sons were installed as priests--Moses was the one who performed the ritual functions of the priest. Rashbam himself writes, in his comm. to 29:35, that Moses served in the role of "priest" for the seven days of dedication.

However, a number of the ritual acts described in verses 18-29 (e.g. offering the incense [verse 27]) did not have to take place during the seven days of dedication. Accordingly, some exegetes, like Rashbam here, have argued that Aaron, not Moses, is to be seen as the one who performed *those* rituals acts. See e.g. iE's shorter comm. to verse 23 ("ומשה לא עשה כן--it was not Moses who did this"). See *Ha'ameq davar*, ad vs. 23, who argues that Tosefta Menahot 7:7 implies that Aaron must be seen as the subject of many of these verbs. See also Rashbam's comm. and notes ad 25:37, s.v. והעלה.

Rashi's position on the subject is unclear. In most of our editions of Rashi, there is a comment to vs. 29 in which Rashi says that Moses continued to serve as a priest even on the eighth day, the day following the seven days of dedication. It is against such a position that Rashbam pointedly writes, ad 29:30 and ad Lev. 9:1, that, beginning with the eighth day, all ritual functions were performed only by Aaron and his sons. However, it is not clear that that pericope of commentary in our versions of Rashi should be seen as part of the text of Rashi; it is not found in the first edition of Rashi's comm. Furthermore, Nahm. writes that he saw a version of Rashi's comm. (ad vs.27) in which Rashi says explicitly that Aaron is the subject of the sentence there, "*he* burned the aromatic incense." (Our texts of Rashi do not read that way.)

Ha'ameq davar (*ibid.*) speculates that there are two recensions of Rashi's comm. to these verses. In the older recension, Rashi saw Moses as the subject of all the verbs. However, when he got older he revised his comm. and pointed out that Aaron must be the subject of some of the verbs. *Ha'ameq davar* then speculates further that Rashbam must have followed this later approach of the mature Rashi.

It is interesting to consider the possibility of another twist to these events. As I noted in my Genesis volume (p. 376, fn. 1), many people have argued that Rashi

40:35 ולא יכול MOSES COULD NOT ENTER THE TENT OF MEETING: when it was first erected, BECAUSE THE CLOUD SETTLED UPON IT, immediately [after it was erected], in order to show God's love for His people. After that, the cloud lifted off the tent and settled on top of the Ark, as it is written (25:21-22), "[. . . on top of the Ark . . ..] There I will meet with you and speak to you . . . from between the two cherubim . . .." When that happened, Moses *was* able to enter the Tent of Meeting, as it is written (Num. 7:89), "When Moses went into the Tent of Meeting to speak with Him, he would hear the Voice . . . from between the two cherubim; thus He spoke to him."[2]

One finds similarly, concerning [the construction of] the [first] Temple, that (I Kings 8:11) "the priests were not able to remain and perform the service because of the cloud, for the presence of the LORD filled the House of the LORD." At that specific time when the Temple was completed, God sanctified the Temple with a cloud [which filled the

---

incorporated into his commentary some of his grandson's insights into biblical texts or, put differently, that Rashi revised his comm. based on new interpretations offered by Rashbam. If, then, *Ha'ameq Davar*'s speculative reconstruction is correct--that it is the later recension of Rashi's comm. which sees Aaron as the subject of some of the verbs--then one might logically conclude that it is not Rashbam who followed Rashi's approach, but rather Rashi who revised his comm. following his grandson's suggestions.

[2]The problem of the apparent contradiction between our verse and Num. 7 is discussed in a number of classical sources. To be sure, our chapter implies that the cloud kept Moses from entering the Tent and it also seems to imply (verses 36-38) that that cloud cover was a more or less permanent state of affairs.

Rashi cites the answer found at the end of the *Beraita' de-Rabbi Yishmael* that appears as the introduction to Sifra. That answer does not specify when it was that the cloud was on the Tent and when it lifted. It simply says that when the cloud lifted, then Moses was able to enter. Another solution (see e.g. Tanh. *Va-yiqra'* 1) would say that the cloud cover was the permanent state of affairs at the Tent, and that when it says here that Moses could not enter the Tent, it means that he could not (or would not) go in until God called him to enter, in the first verse of Leviticus.

Rashbam's solution, while similar to Rashi's, is not identical. It appears to me that he is the first exegete to suggest that the cloud cover described here was only a temporary state of affairs that was a function of the completion of the Tabernacle.

entire Temple]. After that, God contracted His Presence and it was found only above the Ark, between its poles.³

Whoever is loyal to God's words should never depart from the commentary⁴ of my grandfather, Rabbi Solomon, and should not budge from it. For most of the laws and midrashic interpretations there are close to the plain meaning of Scripture. All of them can be derived [from the study of the superfluities of] the language [or changes in wording].⁵ "It is best that you grasp the one"--my commentary--"without letting go of the other one"⁶ (Eccl. 7:18).

---

³Rashbam's prooftext seems well chosen in that it shows that there was an extraordinary amount of cloud cover also after the completion of Solomon's Temple. In that verse, just like here, the glory of God, or His Presence, is associated with a dense cloud cover. Both verses appear immediately after the completion of houses of worship. See Noth, who also makes a similar connection between our verse and the passage in I Kings.

This same passage in I Kings is cited in the continuation of the midrashic text that Rashi cites here--the Sifra. However, there the citation serves an entirely different purpose. Rabbi Yose the Galilean quotes that verse to prove that sometimes angels are given powers to cause harm. In other words, the cloud cover that kept the priests out of the Temple was not something positive; [impish] angels were responsible for it.

Rashbam then takes this same verse, known to him in this context from Sifra, and very creatively uses it to prove his more *peshaṭ*-like interpretation.

⁴נימוקי. This somewhat unusual word--which meant "reasons" in rabbinic Hebrew and means the same thing today, in modern Hebrew--is used a number of times by the Tosafists in the sense of "commentary," and, more specifically, *Rashi's* commentary. See e.g. Tos. Pes. 118b, s.v. מן; Tos. Hag. 6b, s.v. רבי; and Tos. Hag. 16b, s.v. אב. The word was also used in the sense of "commentary" by Rashbam's uncle, Rabbi Judah bar Natan (cited by Urbach, *Ba'ale ha-tosafot*, p. 40).

⁵Rosin reports that there was a blank space on the manuscript at this point. He speculatively added some words to the text of the comm. The English words in parentheses represent a translation of Rosin's conjectural reading.

⁶I.e. Rashi's commentary.

Although much of Rashbam's exegesis here on Exodus, and on other books, is directed against Rashi's work, Rashbam closes his comm. with a respectful comment. He pays Rashi what must be seen as a very high compliment--that even if Rashi's comm. is not *peshaṭ*, it is close to *peshaṭ*.

This comment should not be seen as the sum total of Rashbam's attitude to his grandfather's commentary. It should be read together with the many specific examples of strong disagreements between Rashbam and his grandfather, and together with the other general statements that Rashbam makes about Rashi's work. See e.g. Rashbam's introductions to his comm. to Ex. 21 and to Ex. 25 and notes there.

BIBLIOGRAPHY

I. CLASSICAL JEWISH SOURCES

Abraham ben Moses Maimonides. *Perush ha-Torah*. Ed. by S. D. Sassoon. London, 1959.

Abravanel, Don Isaac. *Perush*. 4 volumes. Tel-Aviv and Jerusalem, 1954/55-1959/60.

The Apocrypha and Pseudepigrapha of the Old Testament in English. Ed. by R. H. Charles. 2 vols. Oxford, 1913.

Ashkenazi, S. Z. *Qeren Shemuel*. Frankfort, 1727.

Babylonian Talmud. Vilna, 1881.

Bet ha-midrash. Ed. by A. Jellinek. Second edition. 6 vols. Jerusalem, 1938.

Da'at zeqenim mi-ba'ale ha-tosafot. In the standard editions of the Hebrew Bible.

Dunash ibn Labrat. *Teshuvot*. Ed. by H. Filipowski. London, 1855.

Fleischer, E. *Sefer ibn Ezra lesefer shemot*. Vienna, 1926.

Friedlander, M. *Ibn Ezra on Isaiah*. London, 1873.

Gellis, J. *Tosafot ha-shalem 'al ha-Torah*. Jerusalem, 1982.

Ibn Janah, Jonah Abu'l-Walid Merwan. *The Book of Hebrew Roots*. Ed. by A. Neubauer. Oxford, 1875.

———. *Sefer ha-riqmah*. Ed. by M. Wilensky. Jerusalem, 1964.

Ibn Kaspi, Joseph. *Mishneh kesef*. Pressburg, 1904/5.

Joseph Bekhor Shor. *Perush lehamishah ḥumshe Torah*. 3 vols. Jerusalem, 1977-8.

Kasher, M. M. *Torah shelemah*. Jerusalem and New York. 1926/7- .

Kirschner, R. *Baraita de-melekhet ha-mishkan: A Critical Edition with Introduction and Translation*. Cincinnati, 1992.

Maimonides, Moses. *The Guide of the Perplexed*. Translated by S. Pines. Chicago, 1963.

———. *Mishneh Torah*. 5 vols. New York, 1947.

Mekilta derabbi Ishmael. Ed. by J. Z. Lauterbach. 3 vols. Philadelphia, 1933-5.

Menahem. *Maḥberet*. Ed. by H. Filipovski. London, 1854.

Midrash Bereschit rabba'. Ed. by J. Theodor and C. Albeck. Berlin, 1903-36.

Midrash ha-gadol. Ed. by M. Margulies. Jerusalem, 1947.

Midrash leqaḥ ṭov. Ed. by S. Buber. 2 vols. Lemberg, 1878.

Midrash rabba'. 2 vols. Vilna, 1878.

———. Ed. by M. Mirkin. Tel Aviv, 1957.

Midrash Shemuel. Ed. by S. Buber. Cracow, 1893.

Midrash sekhel ṭov. Ed. by S. Buber. 2 vols. Lemberg, 1899.

Midrash Tanḥuma. 2 vols. Jerusalem, 1971-2.

Midrash Tanḥuma ha-qadum veha-yashan. Ed. by S. Buber. Vilna, 1883.

Midrash Tehillim. Ed. by S. Buber. Facsimile edition: New York, 1947.

Mishnah. Ed. by Ch. Albeck. 7 vols. Jerusalem, 1952-9.

Moses ben Nahman. *Perush 'al ha-Torah*. Ed. by Ch. Chavel. 2 vols. 5th edition. Jerusalem, 1969.

Palestinian Talmud. Krotoshin, 1866.

Perush Avraham ibn Ezra 'al ha-Torah. Ed. by Y. Krinski. 5 vols. Reprint edition: Jerusalem, 1961/2.

_____. Ed. by A. Weiser. 3 vols. Jerusalem, 1976.

Perushe ha-Ḥizquni 'al ha-Torah. Ed. by Ch. Chavel. Jerusalem, 1981.

Perush ha-Torah lerav Shemuel ben Ḥofni Gaon. Ed. by E. Greenbaum. Jerusalem, 1979.

Pirqe derabbi 'Eli'ezer. Jerusalem, 1973.

Qara, Joseph. *Perush 'al nevi'im rishonim*. Ed. by S. Eppenstein. Jerusalem, 1972.

Qimhi, David. *Perush 'al Bereshit*. Jerusalem, 1974/5.

_____. *Perushim 'al ha-Tanakh*. In the standard editions of the Hebrew Bible.

Rashi. *Commentaries on the Talmud*. In the standard editions of the Babylonian Talmud.

———. *Perush 'al ha-Torah*. Ed. by Ch. Chavel. Jerusalem, 1982.

———. *Perushim 'al ha-Tanakh*. In the standard editions of the Hebrew Bible.

———. *Rashi 'al ha-Torah*. Ed. by A. Berliner. Jerusalem, 1962.

Rashbam. *Perush 'al ha-Torah*. Ed. by D. Rosin. Breslau, 1882.

———. *Perush 'al ha-Torah*. Ed. by A. Bromberg. Tel Aviv, 1964/5.

———. *Commentary on Qoheleth*. Ed. by S. Japhet and R. Salters. Jerusalem, 1985.

———. *Sefer Dayqut*. Ed. by L. Stein. In *Jahrbuch des Traditionstreuen Rabbinerverbandes in der Slovakei*. Trnava, 1923.

Seder 'olam. Ed. by A. Marx. Berlin, 1903.

Seforno, Ovadiah. *Perush 'al ha-Torah*. Ed. by W. Gottlieb. Jerusalem, 1980.

Sifra' de-be Rab. Ed. by I. H. Weiss. Vienna, 1862.

Siphre ad Deuteronomium. Ed. by L. Finkelstein. Berlin, 1939.

Siphre ad Numeros. Ed. by H. S. Horovitz. Leipzig, 1917.

Targum Onqelos. Ed. by A. Sperber. Leiden, 1959.

———. Ed. by A. Berliner. Berlin, 1884.

Targum Pseudo-Jonathan. Ed. by M. Ginsburger. Berlin, 1903.

Tosefta. Ed. by M. S. Zuckermandel. Jerusalem, 1938.

———. Ed. by S. Lieberman. New York, 1955.

Wertheimer, S. A. *Bate Midrashot*. 2 vols. Jerusalem, 1950-3.

Yalqut Shim'oni. New York, 1925/6.

II. SECONDARY LITERATURE ON MEDIEVAL JEWRY AND MEDIEVAL EXEGESIS

Abraham, M. "*Commentaire de R. Joseph Bekhor-Shor sur le Lévitique.*" REJ 77 (1923): 41-59.

Ahrend, M. "*Perush Rashbam le-'iyyov?*" *'Ale Sefer* 5 (1978): 25-48.

Bacher, W. *Ha-Rambam parshan ha-miqra'*. Budapest, 1896.

Baer, I. "*Rashi veha-meṣi'ut ha-hiṣtorit shel zemano.*" In *Sefer Rashi*. Ed. by Y. Maimon (Fischmann). Pages 129-164. Jerusalem, 1956.

Baron, S. W. *A Social and Religious History of the Jews*. Second edition. Philadelphia, 1952.

Berger, D. *The Jewish-Christian Debate in the High Middle Ages*. Philadelphia, 1979.

Berger, M. *The Torah Commentary of R. Samuel ben Meir*. PhD. dissertation, Harvard University, 1982.

Berliner, Abraham. *Ketavim nivḥarim*. Two volumes. Reprint edition. Jerusalem, 1969.

———. "*Letoledot perushe Rashi.*" In *Sefer Rashi*. Ed. by Y. Maimon (Fischmann). Jerusalem, 1956.

———. *Peleṭat soferim*. Breslau, 1872.

Catane, M. *Oṣar ha-le'azim*. Jerusalem, 1988.

Cohen, G. *The Book of Tradition*. Philadelphia, 1967.

Danielou, J. "La typologie d'Isaac dans la Christianisme primitif." *Biblica* 28 (1947): 363-93.

Esh, S. "Variant Readings in Medieval Hebrew Commentaries: R. Samuel ben Meir (Rashbam)." *Textus* 5 (1966): 84-92.

Friedlander, M. *Essays on the Writings of Abraham ibn Ezra*. London, 1877.

Funkenstein, Amos. "Ha-temurot bevikkuaḥ ha-dat she-ben yehudim lenoṣerim ba-me'ah ha-12." *Zion* 33 (1968): 125-144.

Geiger, A. "'Al devar ḥakhme Ṣorfat mefarshe ha-Torah." In *Qevuṣat ma'amarim*. Ed. by S. Poznanski. Warsaw, 1910. Pages 169-177.

_____. "*Toledot ha-Radaq*." Ibid. Pages 131-153.

_____. *Parschandata*. Leipzig, 1855.

Ginzberg, Louis. *Legends of the Jews*. 7 vols. Philadelphia, 1909.

Greenberg, M., ed. *Parshanut ha-miqra' ha-yehudit*. Jeruslaem, 1983.

Greenberg, J. *Foreign Words in the Bible Commentary of Rashi*. Jerusalem, undated.

Gross, H. *Gallia Judaica*. Paris, 1897.

Grossman, A. *Ḥakhme 'ashkenaz ha-rishonim*. Jerusalem, 1981.

---. *Ḥakhme ṣorfat ha-rishonim*. Jerusalem, 1995.

---. "*Mi-'genizat 'italiah': seridim mi-perush rabbi yosef qara' la-torah.*" Pe'amim 52 (1992): 16-36.

---. "The Jewish Christian Polemic and Jewish Biblical Exegesis in Twelfth Century France." *Zion* 51 (1986): 29-60.

Guedemann, M. *Ha-Torah veha-ḥayyim bime ha-benayim beṢorfat veAshkenaz*. Warsaw, 1897.

Halperin, H. *Rashi and the Christian Scholars*. Pittsburgh, 1963.

Halkin, A. S. "The Medieval Jewish Attitude Toward Hebrew." In *Studies and Texts*. Ed. by A. Altmann. Cambridge, 1963.

Halivni, D. W. *Midrash Mishnah and Gemara*. London, 1986.

---. *Peshat and Derash: Plain and Applied Meaning in Rabbinic Exegesis*. New York, 1991.

Heineman, I. *Darke ha-'aggadah*. Jerusalem, 1949.

Herzog, P. "Review of Krinski's *Meḥoqeqe Yehudah*." ZDMG 64 (1910): 219-238.

Hirschfeld, H. "Fragments of Sa'adyah's Arabic Pentateuch Commentary." JQR (N.S.) 6 (1915-1916): 359-383.

Hoenig, S. and Stiskin L. *The Joshua Finkel Festschrift*. New York, 1974.

Japhet, Sara. "Major Trends in the Study of Mediaeval Jewish Exegesis of Northern France." In her *Studies in Bible and Talmud*. Jerusalem, 1987.

———. "The Nature and Distribution of Compilatory Commentaries in the Middle Ages in the Light of R. Joseph Kara's Commentary on Job." In *Studies in Bible and Exegesis*. Volume 3. Edited by M. Bar-asher, D. Diamant, M. Garsiel and Y. Maori. Ramat Gan, 1993.

———, ed. *The Bible in the Light of its Interpreters: Sarah Kamin Memorial Volume*. Jerusalem, 1994.

Kamin, S. *Rashi: Peshuto shel miqra' umidrasho shel miqra'*. Jerusalem, 1986.

———. *Ben yehudim lenoṣerim befarshanut ha-miqra'*. Jerusalem, 1992.

Kanarfogel, E. *Jewish Education and Society in the High Middle Ages*. Detroit, 1992.

Klausner, J. "Ha-parshan ha-lohem shel yeme ha-benayim." *Leshonenu* 21 (1957): 198-205.

Kogut, S. *Ha-miqra' ben teʿamim lefarshanut*. Jerusalem, 1994.

Lasker, D. J. *Jewish Philosophical Polemics Against Christianity in the High Middle Ages*. New York, 1977.

Leibowitz, N. "*Darko shel Rashi behava'at midrashim beferusho la-Torah.*" In her *'Iyyunim ḥadashim besefer Shemot*. Jerusalem, 1970. Pages 497-524.

Lockshin, M. *Rabbi Samuel ben Meir's Commentary to Genesis: An Annotated Translation*. Lewiston, 1989.

———. "Tradition or Context: Two Exegetes Struggle with Peshat." In *From Ancient Israel to Modern Judaism*. Ed. by J. Neusner, E. Frerichs and N. Sarna. Vol. 2. Atlanta, 1989: 173-186.

_____. "Truth or *Peshaṭ*: Issues in Law and Exegesis." In *Law Politics and Society in the Ancient Mediterranean World*. Edited by B. Halpern and D. W. Hobson. Sheffield, 1993. Pages 271-279.

_____. "The Connection Between Rabbi Samuel ben Meir's Torah Commentary and Midrash Sekhel Tov" [Heb.]. In *Proceedings of the Eleventh World Congress of Jewish Studies*. Jerusalem, 1994. Division A. Hebrew Section: 135-142.

Loewe, R. "The 'Plain' Meaning of Scripture in Early Jewish Exegesis." In *Papers of the Institute of Jewish Studies*. Ed. by J. G. Weiss. Jerusalem, 1964. Pages 140-185.

Margaliot, A. "*Ha-yaḥas she-ben perush ha-Rashbam leferush ha-Ra'va' 'al ha-Torah.*" In *Sefer 'Asaf*. Ed. by U. Cassuto. Jerusalem, 1953. Pages 357-369.

Melamed, E. *Mefarshe ha-miqra'*. Jerusalem, 1975.

_____. "*Ṭa'ame ha-miqra' bedivre parshane ha-miqra'.*" In *Meḥqare ha-mercaz leḥeqer ha-folklor*. Jerusalem, 1970. Pages 185-189.

Parkes, J. *The Conflict of the Church and the Synagogue*. London, 1954.

Posnanski, A. *Schiloh*. Leipzig, 1894.

Poznanski, S. *Perush 'al Yeḥezqel utere 'asar lerabbi 'Eli'ezer mi-Beaugency*. Warsaw, 1913.

Rosenthal, E.I.J. "Anti-Christian Polemic in Medieval Bible Commentaries." JJS 11 (1960): 111-135.

Rosin, D. *R. Samuel b. Meir als Schrifterklärer*. Breslau, 1880.

Sarna, Nahum. "Hebrew and Bible Studies in Medieval Spain." In *The Sephardi Heritage*. Ed. by R. Barnett. London, 1971. Pages 323-366.

Segal, N. *Parshanut ha-miqra'*. Jerusalem, 1971.

Simon, U. "*Ledarko ha-parshanit shel ha-Ra'va' 'al pi sheloshet be'urim lefasuq 'eḥad.*" *Bar-Ilan Annual* 3 (1965): 92-138.

_____. "*Ra'va' veRadaq: Shete gishot lishe'elat mehemanut nosaḥ ha-miqra'.*" *Bar Ilan Annual* 6 (1968): 191-237.

_____. "Review of Weiser's *ibn Ezra 'al ha-Torah.*" *Qiryat Sefer* (1976): 646-658.

Smalley, B. *The Study of the Bible in the Middle Ages*. Notre Dame, 1964.

Sokolow, M. "'*Ha-peshaṭot ha-mitḥadeshim'--Qeṭa'im ḥadashim mi-perush ha-torah la-rashbam--ketav yad.*" *'Ale sefer* 11 (1984): 73-80.

Spicq, C. *Esquisse d'une histoire de l'exégèse latine au moyen age*. Paris, 1944.

Spiegel, S. *The Last Trial*. New York, 1969.

Talmage, F. *David Kimhi: The Man and the Commentaries*. Cambridge, 1975.

Thompson, Y. *The Commentary of Samuel ben Meir on the Song of Songs*. DHL dissertation, Jewish Theological Seminary, 1989.

Touitou, E. "*'Al shiṭato shel Rashbam beferusho la-Torah.*" *Tarbiz* 48 (1979): 248-273.

BIBLIOGRAPHY 449

———. "Shiṭato ha-parshanit shel Rashbam 'al reqa' ha-meṣiut ha-hisṭorit shel zemano." In *Studies in Rabbinic Literature Bible and Jewish History*. Ed. by Y. Gilat, Ch. Levine and Z. Rabinowitz. Ramat-Gan, 1982. Pages 48-74.

———. "*Peshaṭ va'apologeṭiqah beferush ha-Rashbam lesippure Moshe she-ba-Torah.*" *Tarbiz* 51 (1982): 227-238.

———. "The Method of the Rashbam in his Commentary on the Halakhic Part of the Pentateuch" [Heb.]. *Mil'et* 2: 275-288.

———. "*'Al ḥeqer parshanut ha-miqra' ha-yehudit-ṣorfatit.*" *Tarbiz* 51 (1982): 522-526.

Urbach, E. *Ba'ale ha-tosafot*. Second edition. 2 vols. Jerusalem, 1980.

———. *Sefer 'arugat ha-bosem lerabbi avraham berabbi 'azri'el*. Jerusalem, 1963.

Walfish, B. *The Frank Talmage Memorial Volume*. Haifa, 1993.

Walter, G. *Joseph Bechor Schor der letzte nordfranzösische Bibelexeget*. Breslau, 1890.

Weiss, P. R. "'*Ibn 'Ezra ha-Qara'im veha-halakhah.*" *Melillah* I-IV (1944-50).

Zucker, M. "*Lefitron ba'ayat lamed bet middot.*" PAAJR 23 (1954).

III. EARLY MODERN AND CONTEMPORARY LITERATURE ON THE BIBLE

Alter, R. *The Art of Biblical Narrative*. New York, 1981.

———. *The Art of Biblical Poetry.* New York, 1985.

———. "A Literary Approach to the Bible." *Commentary* 60 (1975): 70-77.

———. "Biblical Narrative." *Commentary* 61 (1976): 61-67.

Auerbach, E. *Mimesis.* Bern, 1959.

Buber, M. *Darko shel miqra'.* Jerusalem, 1964.

Buber, M. and Rosenzweig, F. *Die Schrift und ihre Verdeutschung.* Berlin, 1936.

Cassuto, U. *The "Quaestio" of the Book of Genesis.* Translated [from Italian into Hebrew] by M. E. Artom. Jerusalem, 1990.

Childs, B. S. *The Book of Exodus: A Critical, Theological Commentary.* Philadelphia, 1974.

Ehrlich, A. *Mikra ki-pheshuto.* New York, 1969.

Fokkelman, J. P. *Narrative Art in Genesis.* Amsterdam, 1975.

Gesenius' Hebrew Grammar. Ed. by E. Kautzch and translated by A. E. Cowley. Oxford, 1974.

Good, E. M. *Irony in the Old Testament.* Philadelphia, 1965.

Greenberg, M. *Understanding Exodus.* New York, 1969.

Gros Louis, K.R.R., ed. *Literary Interpretations of Biblical Narratives.* 2 vols. Nashville, 1974 and New York, 1981.

Hakham, A. *Sefer Shemot (Daat Mikra* series). Jerusalem, 1991.

Heidenheim, W. *Havanat ha-miqra'.* Vilna, 1888.

Jouon, P. *Grammaire de l'Hébreu biblique*. Rome, 1923.

Kugel, J. *The Idea of Biblical Poetry*. New Haven, 1981.

Levin, M. *Melekhet ha-mishkan*. Tel Aviv, 1968.

Luzzatto, S. D. *Perush Shadal 'al hamishah humshe Torah*. Philadelphia, 1964.

Noth, M. *Exodus: A Commentary*. Philadelphia, 1964.

Orlinsky, H. *Notes on the New Translation of the Torah*. Philadelphia, 1964.

Robertson, D. *The Old Testament and the Literary Critic*. Philadelphia, 1977.

Sarna, N. *Exploring Exodus*. New York, 1986.

_____. *The JPS Torah Commentary: Exodus*. Philadelphia, 1991.

_____. "The Anticipatory Use of Information as a Literary Feature of the Genesis Narrative." In *The Creation of Sacred Literature*. Ed. by R. E. Friedman. University of California, 1981. Pages 76-82.

Shapira, Y.L. *Ha-rekhasim leviq'ah*. Vilna, 1888.

Steinberg, S. *The Mishkan and the Holy Garments*. Jerusalem, 1992.

Sternberg, M. *The Poetics of Biblical Narrative: Ideological Literature and the Drama of Reading*. Bloomington, 1987.

Talmon, S. *Darke ha-sippur ba-miqra'*. Jerusalem, 1965.

———. "The Presentation of Synchroneity and Simultaneity in Biblical Narrative." *Scripta Hierosolymitana* 27 (1978): 9-26.

Weiss, M. *Ha-miqra' kidemuto*. Jerusalem, 1962.

www.ingramcontent.com/pod-product-compliance
Lightning Source LLC
Chambersburg PA
CBHW030103010526
44116CB00005B/81